*The United State
Football League,
1982–1986*

UNITED STATES FOOTBALL LEAGUE

© 1982 USFL

The United States Football League, 1982–1986

PAUL REETHS

Foreword by Steve Ehrhart

McFarland & Company, Inc., Publishers
Jefferson, North Carolina

LIBRARY OF CONGRESS CATALOGUING-IN-PUBLICATION DATA

Names: Reeths, Paul, author.
Title: The United States Football League, 1982–1986 /
Paul Reeths ; foreword by Steve Ehrhart.
Description: Jefferson, North Carolina : McFarland & Company, Inc.,
Publishers, 2017. | Includes bibliographical references and index.
Identifiers: LCCN 2017006986 | ISBN 9781476667447
(softcover : acid free paper) ∞
Subjects: LCSH: USFL (Organization)—History. | Football—
United States—History—20th century.
Classification: LCC GV955.5.U8 R44 2017 | DDC 796.332/6409048—dc23
LC record available at https://lccn.loc.gov/2017006986

BRITISH LIBRARY CATALOGUING DATA ARE AVAILABLE

ISBN (print) 978-1-4766-6744-7
ISBN (ebook) 978-1-4766-2773-1

Front cover: Houston Gamblers quarterback Jim Kelly
(photograph by Jim Turner, from the Anthony Nunez collection)

Printed in the United States of America

*McFarland & Company, Inc., Publishers
Box 611, Jefferson, North Carolina 28640
www.mcfarlandpub.com*

To my wonderful family:
Lori, Ethan and Abigail.
Thank you for allowing me the time
to chronicle a league
that captured my imagination.

Table of Contents

Foreword by Steve Ehrhart

During the second half of the 20th century, professional football captured the public interest and became the dominant sports and television institution in America. By 1980, the National Football League had vanquished all other competitors and had become the most powerful force in both the media (television, radio and print) and in the minds of American sports fans. The Super Bowl grew into the single most watched television spectacle of the year, and American industry recognized the powerful influence the NFL had on American culture. The Super Bowl became the place for corporate America to introduce advances in technology and market products on a scale never seen before.

But the NFL was an exclusive, private club that carefully and purposely controlled its very lucrative domain. The American universities and colleges, by training nearly 5,000 young men every year, provided a free farm system for the NFL. Municipalities routinely paid for opulent stadiums with taxpayer money. Thus, a huge, well-trained and well-publicized pool of labor, as well as wonderful pre-paid stadiums, were available to the NFL.

Despite a huge demand for more opportunities for the vast supply of players, coaches, fans and cities that wanted to participate in this American cultural phenomena, the member teams of the NFL collectively restricted the supply of cities that could host NFL teams. This practice of restricting the number of teams thereby created demand which in turn made the existing NFL teams more valuable. The "proof was in the pudding" as cities lusted after existing teams, forcing the cities into providing huge offers to tempt the teams into relocation. Cities such as Los Angeles, Baltimore, Oakland and Indianapolis had to compete with each other for this restricted supply of professional football teams.

On the human side, thousands of young men had trained for years in pursuit of professional football jobs, but because of the limited openings, never had the chance to follow their dreams and earn a living as pro football players. Likewise, hundreds of coaches were in turn forced off the sidelines due to the limited number of positions.

By the early 80s, with a huge number of players and coaches who simply needed an opportunity to prove themselves, with numerous cities thirsting for the chance to participate in the biggest of sports events and with millions of fans willing to watch more pro football, both in person and on television, the stage was set for one of the most intriguing and compelling episodes in the history of American sports and business.

This book for the first time accurately chronicles an amazing group of people who came together through an entrepreneurial and pioneering spirit to create the United States Football League.

It takes a special kind of adventurous risk taker to step into the arena of professional sports. It takes a lot of guts, passion and dedication, as well as blood, sweat and tears, to

1

create and build an institution from absolute scratch to take on this most powerful behemoth, the NFL, which controlled and dominated this arena of competition.

For the first time, a serious writer, Paul Reeths, the author of this book, has taken the time to scrupulously and painstakingly capture the esprit de corps and personalities of the owners, the executives, the coaches and players, as well as the millions of fans who poured their lives into the USFL.

Paul has spent more than a decade in research and has interviewed owners, executives, coaches, players and fans to weave together this chronicle of the history of the USFL.

I personally had the opportunity to witness many of the events and actions that Paul has captured here in *The United States Football League, 1982–1986.*

I had the opportunity to serve as the Legal Counsel to the Competition Committee before the league ever kicked off, then to serve as Executive Director of the League in New York, then later as the President/GM and part owner of the Memphis Showboats. During that time, I sat in on every owner's meeting and also served as Co-Chair of the USFL Executive Committee. The other Co-Chair was the owner of the New Jersey Generals, Donald Trump.

I have had the opportunity to view Paul's extensive research and he very accurately brings to life the great passion and effort that so many put into this five-year endeavor from 1982 to 1986. Paul spotlights the great players and historic games during the three football seasons of play: 1983, '84 and '85. He also sheds light on the business aspects of the USFL including a behind the scenes look at all the franchises and the struggles of a startup operation striving to carve out its own space in the world of professional football. Paul also examines one of the most noteworthy trials in the history of American jurisprudence, the infamous USFL vs. NFL antitrust trial.

You will very much enjoy reading Paul's work as he brings to life many of the great characters of the USFL:

- The outstanding coaches who prowled the sidelines, veterans such as Chuck Fairbanks, George Allen, Red Miller, Marv Levy, John Ralston, Hugh Campbell and Walt Michaels along with a brand new group who got their start in the USFL such as Steve Spurrier, June Jones, Lindy Infante and Jim Mora, not to mention colorful collegiate coaches such as Lee Corso and Pepper Rodgers, as well as many other outstanding head coaches and assistant coaches.
- The thousands of great players who created such excitement and now belong to a special fraternity who chose the "path less taken" to bring excitement and competition to American professional football. You will find your own favorite players in this book but I want to name just a few that had such great impact in the USFL: three straight Heisman trophy winners who had the strength of character to sign with the upstart new league: Herschel Walker (Heisman '82), Mike Rozier (Heisman '83) and Doug Flutie (Heisman '84); the great rookie quarterbacks who signed out of college such as Bobby Hebert, Walter Lewis, Jim Kelly, Steve Young, Rick Neuheisel, Reggie Collier, and many others; the NFL veteran stars who came over to join the new league such as Brian Sipe, Cliff Stoudt, Vince Evans, Greg Landry and Doug Williams; the more than 150 young players who had the chance to develop their skills in the USFL and then went on to great success in the NFL; and players such as Reggie White of the Memphis Showboats who became one of the great Hall of Famers in history

and Sam Mills who was cut by the NFL before Carl Peterson and Jim Mora gave the 5'9" linebacker a chance with the Philadelphia Stars, a chance he used to launch an All-Pro career in the NFL.

Paul Reeths not only captures many of the experiences of the thousands of USFL players and coaches, but he also sheds light on the trials and tribulations of the entrepreneurial owners of the USFL teams who were willing to spend not only their personal capital and reputations, but also millions of dollars in the valiant attempt to create new opportunities for their home communities.

The United States Football League, 1982–1986 analyzes in depth the remarkable and dynamic personalities of this group of maverick sportsmen. Disparate personalities such as Dr. Ted Diethrich, one of the great heart surgeons in the country and owner of the Chicago Blitz and later the Arizona Wranglers; John Bassett, the Canadian sports entrepreneur and owner of the Tampa Bay Bandits; Walter Duncan, the Oklahoma oilman who owned and then sold the New Jersey Generals to Donald Trump; real estate tycoons including Alfred Taubman (Michigan Panthers), Myles Tanenbaum (Philadelphia/Baltimore Stars), Edward DeBartolo (Pittsburgh Maulers); and others such as Billy Dunavant, the world's largest cotton merchant (Memphis Showboats), are just a few of the owners who come alive in this book.

The United States Football League, 1982–1986 also chronicles the outstanding success of such USFL executives as Carl Peterson and Bill Polian, guerrilla warriors in the USFL, who, after honing their skills in the USFL, went on to become NFL executives of the year.

The United States Football League, 1982–1986 is a terrific read that preserves and dignifies the history of the herculean efforts made by those who dared to create a new league from scratch, giving thousands of people new opportunities and challenging the dominance of the most powerful entity in the history of professional sports and television.

The USFL legacy continues even today as the NFL still utilizes instant replay with the red flag challenge, a system the USFL developed. The USFL was also the first professional football league to be telecast by a little known entity called ESPN on the fledgling distribution system of cable television. Those USFL telecasts helped ESPN survive its own early financial struggles and it is certainly ironic that while the USFL is now only a memory, ESPN is a powerhouse.

The USFL lives on today with people still clamoring for USFL historic merchandise and not a week goes by that someone does not recount their fond memories of how much they enjoyed their time in the USFL. So now, you can certainly enjoy your time by turning the pages of *The United States Football League, 1982–1986.*

As quarterback and captain of his college football team, Steve Ehrhart received an NCAA scholarship which led to a law degree. He has been executive director of the USFL, president of the Memphis Showboats, commissioner of the World Basketball League and president of the Colorado Rockies baseball team, and for 24 years executive director of the AutoZone Liberty Bowl Football Classic in Memphis, Tennessee.

Preface

I didn't know how lucky I was at the time. In the early 1980s, I was a young football fan growing up in central Wisconsin. Like so many young boys, the brutal artistry of professional football had captured my imagination: the crushing hits, the acrobatic catches and daring runs all were magnified before my wide eyes. I had learned, slowly at first, of the strategy behind the mayhem on the field, how teams studied each other's strengths and weaknesses, constantly devising new strategies to gain an advantage.

Once the football season ended, the attention of my friends turned to other sports: basketball, hockey and then to baseball through the summer. Not me, though. I occasionally enjoyed watching all of them, but football had won my loyalty. With no real free agency to keep an eye on in the 80s, I instead monitored the NFL draft, made note of retirements, pondered the ramifications of significant injuries and above all tried to figure out what key developments might transform my beloved yet struggling Green Bay Packers into title contenders. The football season couldn't arrive again soon enough.

Then in 1982 the United States Football League, a major league competitor, announced its intention to begin playing games the following year. Not only would there be more professional football to follow, but the new league would play its games during the off-season in the spring and into summer, wrapping up just before NFL training camps opened. Virtually year-round professional football became a reality! I was too young to remember other leagues such as the American Basketball Association, World Hockey Association and World Football League, all of which had tried to earn a foothold in the professional sports world, and wondered how this new USFL would stock its teams and what effect it would have on the NFL.

I felt as if I was in on the ground floor of something special as each team took on a new, unique identity. I memorized each name, color scheme and logo. I could now cheer for teams such as the Panthers, Stallions and Bandits, names considerably more exciting to me than the NFL's Browns or Cardinals. Training camps opened in 1983 after the Super Bowl, and we were lucky enough to have cable television in our home, allowing me to follow the USFL on a fledgling little network called ESPN. When play began, I could often watch three games per week, with a pair on ESPN and another on ABC. The 1983 USFL title game provided an exciting finish, much better than most Super Bowls of the era which tended to be blowouts. It was a football fan's dream come true.

Through two more seasons, one of expansion and the next of contraction, the USFL only got better on the field. It continued to sign exciting college stars and even began luring NFL players. It played in new cities such as Memphis and San Antonio, offering starkly contrasting styles of play, ranging from the tough defenses and powerful running games of the Philadelphia Stars and Birmingham Stallions to the thrill-a-minute offenses of the Houston Gamblers and Tampa Bay Bandits. Not everyone was a fan of this new league, of course, and some sports writers seemed to seize every opportunity to criticize it while ignoring any of the NFL's shortcomings. Their criticism only made me embrace the USFL all the more.

Still, cracks appeared in the facade. Swaths of empty seats were evident in Los Angeles, and the team spent the final season without an owner. Other money problems became public. Before I knew it new team owner Donald Trump began campaigning to move the USFL into the fall to compete directly with the NFL. I didn't understand why they would do so, as I loved having year-round football. But that's the course they chose, and before I knew it, spring football was just a pleasant memory. In addition, the USFL sued the NFL for more than $1 billion. To an outsider, it appeared the trial was the only hope of the league's survival.

I remember the heartbreak as Howard Cosell announced on his daily radio show that before the league could play even one game in the fall, the USFL had won its case but had been awarded just one dollar. Just as quickly as it had burst onto the scene, the USFL was suddenly gone.

Still, the league maintained a stranglehold on my imagination. I began collecting whatever USFL items I could find listed for sale in publications such as *Sports Collectors Digest*. I bought helmets, jerseys, media guides, game programs, press releases, just about anything I could find at a fair price. The rise of the Internet, and eBay in particular, meant that some previously unknown USFL treasure might be only a new search away. I quickly came to realize I wasn't the only one bidding, either. There were others who remembered the USFL with fondness, many others as it turns out.

For a college class, I assembled a small website devoted to the league, with pages for each team along with a brief history of the league. Upon graduation, I took that site and placed it on a small, local server, making it available to the world. The evolved version of that site still exists at http://www.usflsite.com. Over the years many fans and players visited and loved to share their happy memories of the league. A former San Antonio Gunslingers employee utilized the site to invite former players to a reunion in 1998 and was kind enough to invite me to attend.

A former league official penned an unfortunately-titled book, *The $1 League*, shortly after the USFL shut down, but his work left me wanting. I really desired to hear from those who had participated in the league as owners, administrators, coaches and players, rather than just rely on one person's recollection of events. To that end, I began conducting interviews and collecting whatever printed material I could find on the league to write my own book. Over the years, I assembled old copies of *The Sporting News, Sports Illustrated, Sport* and other magazines in addition to using library and online sources to comb the archives of *USA Today* and a host of local newspapers.

Early on I had the good fortune to approach Steve Ehrhart who, as the commissioner's right-hand man and then a team GM and part-owner, knew more inside information about the league than anyone else. He has been an invaluable asset in everything from fact-checking to facilitating connections with former owners, officials and coaches. I can't thank him enough for his help and his time.

Dozens of interviews with league principals form the basis of the book you hold in your hands. Special thanks are also owed to Triple Threat TV President/Owner Gary Cohen for access to the interviews his team conducted for the ESPN *30 for 30* special "Small Potatoes: Who Killed the USFL?"

In this book I have attempted to place the USFL into an historical context as the last in a line of leagues which tried to challenge established major professional sports organizations. Though the USFL drew about 25,000 fans per game, more than Major League Baseball, the NHL and NBA, NFL teams attracted more than twice as many fans per game, and received 15 times the television revenue as USFL teams, illustrating the ever-growing economic hurdle any challengers had to overcome. In the decades since the USFL's demise, no other league has attempted to challenge the NFL, NHL, NBA or Major League Baseball.

In this context, perhaps the question is not "Who or what killed the USFL?" but rather "How did the USFL survive for three years and attract some of the top football players and coaches in the nation?" My hope is that this book answers that question and shows what a fun league fans enjoyed for three seasons in the sun.

1

A New Competitor

Competition. It's the driving force behind all sports. Competing against other athletes, even against one's own limitations, spurs athletes to meet and surpass their goals. It drives them to train, to study the opposition and to develop the skills needed to gain an edge. In team sports such as football, athletes face off against each other, literally head to head, in a battle for territory and ultimately to outscore the opposition. Athletes also compete for records and accolades, and surpassing each new milestone becomes the goal of all competitors.

Competition drives business as well. It pushes men and women to risk their money and reputations in the belief that they can present a product or service better than others. They compete over resources, attention, market share, distribution channels and most importantly customers and their money. In business, one's success is often the siren call for others to enter the market to compete for a piece of the pie.

These two forces collide in professional football. Pro football brings the best athletes to the field to compete against one another with titans of business paying for their services. Business owners, in addition to competing against each other within leagues, battle other entertainment options to find new sources of revenue to help grow their teams and leagues. While baseball has long been America's past time, professional football had overtaken it in popularity in the second half of the twentieth century.

Since its modest birth in an automobile showroom in 1920, the National Football League had grown into a powerful force by 1980. It enjoyed millions of dollars of television revenue from all three networks and stadiums filled with paying fans. It had grown from a rag-tag operation with shifting membership to one of the most recognizable brands in the country in six decades. It owed much of its financial success to Commissioner Pete Rozelle who over the first 20 years of his tenure proved adept at getting NFL owners to work together for the good of the league, resulting in exploding television revenues.

Through the years, the NFL faced competition from six other professional football leagues. They ranged in success from the fourth American Football League, which saw all its teams absorbed into the NFL, to the 1970s World Football League which folded midway through its second season in a cloud of debt. With the exception of the 1950s, a competitor challenged the NFL in every decade. The competition had forced the NFL to expand its ranks. Of the 28 NFL teams in 1980, two remained from an accommodation with the All-American Football Conference in the 1940s, while ten others originated in the American Football League. In addition, the NFL launched three other franchises to combat the AFL's challenge in the 1960s. They awarded the Minnesota Vikings to steal its ownership group from the AFL, the Dallas Cowboys to battle the AFL's Dallas Texans and the Atlanta Falcons to prevent an AFL franchise from securing the stadium lease in the Georgia city. The 1980s would witness the birth of another new league: the United States Football League.

David Dixon, a New Orleans art and antique dealer, envisioned the league. He was no stranger to pro football as he had helped broker the deal between the NFL and Louisiana Congressman Hale Boggs and Senator Russell Long which brought the Saints to New Orleans in 1967 in exchange for the politicians' help in gaining Congressional approval of the NFL's merger with the American Football League. The well-connected Dixon had been instrumental in the creation of the Louisiana Superdome, the team's home field, and had helped stage several NFL preseason games throughout the 1960s.

"I always liked the name United States Steel Company," said Dixon. "I had a share of US Steel company stock when I was a young boy and I liked that name. I thought U.S. Steel … you know, that's great, so I went with USFL."

Though he maintained a friendship with NFL Commissioner Pete Rozelle, Dixon felt wronged when the NFL, at the urging of Dallas Cowboys president and general manager Tex Schramm, inserted a new minority investor from the Cowboys into the Saints ownership group without telling Dixon.

"I always held a good bit against Tex Schramm for that and a little bit against Pete, and Pete knew that," explained Dixon. "He was always very solicitous of me after that because he felt that maybe I had been screwed around a little bit."

Dixon had been toying with the idea of another professional football league since the AFL's heyday in 1965, and even considered pitching the idea to Rozelle as a type of farm league. He again met with resistance from Schramm who claimed the NFL had been studying a spring league since about 1960.

"I had the idea for a spring league ever since the days when I was a very young man, and Tulane University, my alma mater, was a college football powerhouse to a degree and certainly among the top 20 programs in the country from the middle 20s to the late 40s," Dixon explained. "They would draw 25–30,000 people for a spring practice game and so did other schools around the country. What difference does it make when football is played? If you lived in Phoenix and only played golf certain times of the year, that would be ridiculous. It's the same thing. Football is such a popular game that it can be played 12 months of the year if you want to."

Dixon gave up the notion for years, but in 1980 the entrepreneurial bug bit again and he felt that the time was right to investigate further. Since the AFL-NFL merger a decade earlier, the NFL had expanded by just two teams, leaving many potential pro football cities out in the cold. Dixon's idea had one major difference from the other attempts to begin professional leagues: his creation would play in the spring and summer, avoiding direct competition with the NFL for fan interest and media attention. He decided to tell Rozelle.

"I talked to him quite a bit because the two of us became good friends from my days of courting the NFL for New Orleans," said Dixon. "I must have visited Pete a dozen times at his office in New York. He had a very good attitude toward me. He said, 'I don't blame you. You got screwed out partly in the NFL deal. Good luck.'"

While steering clear of the ominous presence of the older league sounded like a good idea, football in the traditional off-season was an untested concept. The unmitigated failure of the WFL would certainly also create additional skepticism toward the chances for any new league.

He felt the television networks, in addition to the fans, would be interested in more football. The sport had long since become television's darling, and advertisers would, in Dixon's view, support a spring league. NFL television revenues had grown from less than $333,000 per team per season in 1962, the first year it pooled its rights as a league, to $15 million per team per season in 1982, accounting for about half of all NFL revenue. Dixon reasoned that CBS, ABC and NBC, the three major over-the-air networks at the time, would also pay for football in the traditional off-season. Its main competition on television would be early season baseball and the National Basketball Association playoffs. Dixon knew that a spring and summer league would not be able to command the same television revenue as the NFL, but even a fraction of what the older league received would be enough to give the new league a strong financial core. Plus, he could make inroads in the burgeoning cable television industry, thus far untapped by pro football.

"It hit me like a ton of bricks," he told author Alan M. Schlein. "In a front-page story about cable franchises being awarded around the country, ten names were mentioned and I knew nine of the people. I realized cable TV had finally exploded. Cable was not only an alternative to television pro football; it could break the stranglehold the NFL had on all three networks. It would change the whole complexion of pro football."

The entrepreneur began tinkering with some figures. He knew that because of the limited revenue available in the spring and summer, expenses would have to be kept in line, particularly player salaries. League franchises would sell for a mere $50,000, but owners also had to pay an irrevocable $1.5 million letter of credit to be used only in emergencies and would need to be capable of shouldering additional expenses of approximately $6 million for the first season alone. Player salaries were to account for $1.5 to $2 million of each team's expenses, while $500,000 would be directed at marketing efforts. The league office, teams and corporate sponsors would all contribute to marketing efforts. The letter of credit could be used to bail out failing teams, giving the new league a solid financial backbone, something the WFL never had. He further reasoned that investors could expect losses of about $6 million over the first two years. Dixon predicted an average attendance of 20,000 to 25,000 fans, meaning teams would not be able to rely on ticket revenue alone. He knew that it was imperative to locate franchises in major media markets to enhance the league's television appeal. The investors could certainly lose money in the short term, but if Dixon was right, their gamble would eventually pay off. In addition, several expansion franchises were planned for the second season, and each owner would receive a share of the greatly increased franchise fees from the new teams, helping to offset some of their early losses.

"Spring football was obvious because American football is easily the best television sport in the world," said Dixon. "It really can be played 12 months a year. In many parts of this country, spring football makes very good sense. Our basic idea was that we would start at a time when the weather was cold and end when the weather was at its best, unlike the NFL, which starts when the weather is wonderful but ends in the freezing cold. We felt that the market would handle such a league and that it might even be developed into a league that would be as strong or even stronger than the National Football League."

Although Dixon knew that the perceived quality of the league would be extremely important, he was also aware that the new league could not compete with NFL salaries, where average team payrolls hovered around $5 million in 1982. He wanted to see each franchise sign one or two rookies with regional appeal, preferably near their college homes. He believed that there were plenty of quality players who would round out the rosters, while the fans and media would concentrate on the stars. Besides, he reasoned the league would develop its own talent among those who never would have received a chance in the National Football League.

"I've said from the very start that the best way for us to operate is not to go after the NFL's veterans and superstars," Dixon told *Sports Illustrated*. "We will not try to sign a [Pittsburgh QB Terry] Bradshaw, a [Houston RB Earl] Campbell, a [Chicago RB Walter] Payton. The price is too high, the risk is too high. Our first-year payroll is going to be full of first-year players or their equivalent. No retreads, no rejects. We're going to create our own stars.

"We'll have troubles in the first and second round of the draft, sure. But once we get to the third, fourth, fifth rounds—there we'll be real competitive. We'll offer things the NFL wouldn't think of giving, such as three-year, no-cut contracts to the top rookies and a promise that a player will stay in the territory where he was a college star."

Dixon liked what he saw when he looked at the numbers and decided to explore his notion further. To that end, he hired Frank N. Magid Associates, Inc., of Cedar Rapids, Iowa, to do a market research study for him in October 1980. He was more than a little pleased to discover not only that those polled had little resistance to spring football, but that there actually seemed to be widespread acceptance of the idea. The study concluded that a substantial number of football fans would not only attend games but also watch them on television.

"The Magid study showed exactly what we thought it would," said Dixon. "They're a very fine survey research firm, and they showed that the American public would like football any time of the year."

That was all the encouragement he needed. Armed with his brand new 126-page study in hand to support his dream, the businessman went to work. Dixon's plan called for a 20-game season with games being played every six days in order to complete the season in about 16 weeks. The championship would be a three-game series instead of a standalone title game.

"Dixon was a visionary," said Jimmy Gould, a real estate developer who had business interests with one of the investors. "He had an absolutely positive attitude about every-thing like there's no way in the world this wasn't going to happen, come hell or high water. He was a dapper guy. He was a guy who obviously had culture, and he was a hell of a salesman."

Dixon was an entrepreneur, but football was not his primary area of expertise. He needed some way to get the attention of investors and the knowledgeable football people he needed to run the franchises that would make up his new league. He began by hir-ing John Ralston, a former coach and motivational speaker, in November 1980 as the first part-time employee of his new United States Football League. Ralston started his coaching career in 1951 and landed his first head coaching job in 1959 at Utah State. He went on to pilot Stanford University and then became the head coach of the Denver Broncos for four seasons before taking on an administrative position with the San Fran-cisco 49ers. He had spent his life in football circles and could get the attention that Dixon needed.

"I was out of work, typical of a football coach. It was an opportunity to get back into football, and I was excited about it," recalled Ralston, also noting that he believed Dixon had the ability to see the venture through. "He's very well-connected in New Orleans. He made a lot of money in antiques. He had an antique shop down there. He's a real politician who knew the governor and everybody else in the state. He was tight with everybody, including the newspaper people. He's just a wonderful guy."

"I knew John because one of my sons had been one of his team managers at Stanford when they won their great Rose Bowl victories over Ohio State and Michigan," said Dixon. "We had that little tiny bond that expanded when we got in touch with each other and were working on this project.

"John and I developed a very close friendship, and he almost certainly is the person who was most helpful to me in getting the league underway. He was a tremendous assistant who helped us find some owners, and he always was a leader and a person who maintained league-wide discipline as much as possible. John Ralston did some of virtually everything."

"I worked on everything from getting charter flights to jockstraps," Ralston told *Sports Illustrated.*

Finding Owners

If the spring league was to have any chance of success, the men had to find investors with the money to take on the incredible expenses. The two were well aware of the failure of the WFL and wanted to ensure that the same quick death would not befall this venture. Complicating their task was the fresh memory of that league and its poor performance. The WFL had been such an unqualified disaster that many investors refused to believe a rival circuit could ever survive. Dixon and Ralston knew that their league had to prove to them that the USFL would be different. He sought out men with considerably more financial clout than those who had bought into the WFL.

"The WFL had the wrong cities, the wrong stadiums, the wrong owners," Dixon told *Sports Illustrated.* "The fact that the WFL managed to last two seasons before it folded is a tremendous tribute to the popularity of pro football in the U.S."

"The two of us worked together, calling on owners for a long time before I became a full-time employee in the spring of 1981," recalled Ralston. "We just started virtually calling on the *Forbes* Top 400 richest people in order to track down some of them. I knew about a few people here on the West Coast and then we called on people all over the country. We'd just make an appointment with them. Dave was very good about talking them into talking to us at least, and then the two of us would find them.

"Dave is a very persuasive guy, and he didn't have any trouble getting their attention. Some of them said 'yes' and some of them said 'no.' It was surprising how many pluses we got. Now, they may have dropped out eventually. The one in Boston, George Matthews, stayed with us the longest, all the way to becoming an owner."

August 1981 marked a critical time for the league. The USFL had found a few investors and plenty of interest from others but needed money to continue operations. The venture was in danger of never seeing the light of day. After a meeting with potential investors in New York City, Dixon secured enough capital to continue further work. The league had conquered its first financial challenge, and the pair continued their search for owners.

"The first meeting was held in a big boardroom/conference room at the Grand Hyatt Hotel in New York City," recalled Gould. "A lot of the guys in the room were real estate guys; powerful, powerful real estate guys who clearly had connections and money and were looking for an angle and an opportunity. That meeting reminded me of the meeting in the movie *The Godfather* when they end up getting shot through the windows. It was a powerful group of people. The main guys sat in the front and one of his representatives sat behind him.

"We had tons and tons of meetings in hotels all over the United States, trying to get people to put $6 million up to get those first 12 teams going. That was a huge undertaking. You were telling people, 'take $6 million, throw it at the wall and see if it sticks.' That may not seem like a lot of money today, but it was a hell of a lot of money then. More importantly, not only was it a lot of money, but it was a bet that could create the appearance that you were a dummy. Because their egos were so strong, some of the strongest egos in the country, the last thing they wanted to say was, 'I failed.' I wondered if it would get off the ground all the time. It wasn't just once, it was several times. We delayed it a year."

"It was very tough going city by city and uncovering people. I'd have to almost dig them out of the woodwork," explained Dixon. "By word of mouth, I eventually got them all. I had some help; John Ralston was a lot of help. As I got guys, they would recommend somebody in another city, so sometimes I got them that way. We'd go into a city, nose around a little bit, and I'd find out pretty soon who had an interest. I'd go see them, and I'd sell them."

Dixon used his connections to connect with J. Walter Duncan, a wealthy Oklahoma oilman who became one of the first owners to commit to the new USFL. Duncan knew former University of Oklahoma head coach Chuck Fairbanks, also an acquaintance of Dixon.

"I knew the coach from New England who had been fired, Chuck Fairbanks," remembered Dixon. "I knew him slightly, and Chuck had a guy who I knew was a very fine man. His name was J. Walter Duncan. Walter was our first owner. He was originally slated for Chicago, because that was close to where he grew up, but he shifted to New York when we needed him there. He was a Notre Dame guy, a huge supporter. Walter was probably the biggest independent oil guy in the country at the time. He was very well-to-do."

"He was a guy who said very little, watched everybody, sat back, and when he spoke, you better shut up," Gould said of Duncan. "He was a powerful guy in an understated way. He was bright, he was quiet, and he was thoughtful. At one point in time he resisted putting up the $6 million, but he finally made up his mind to do it, and everybody just fell in line. He was a very respected man."

Coach Chuck Fairbanks joined Duncan as an owner of the USFL franchise.

"We talked to Donald Trump, of course, but he didn't pay an assessment," laughed Ralston. "I think they kicked him out of the league." In reality, the young real estate developer wasn't yet part of the league because he decided not to make the second installment payment for the franchise. He was negotiating to buy the NFL's Baltimore Colts at the time.

"We met, we talked, and after the meeting everybody went downstairs to the lobby," recalled Gould of Trump's early involvement. "We did have a drink, and I remember that he made a point of coming up to me. I had volunteered for every committee, and he came up to me and he said to me 'I'm probably not gonna do this, but if there's ever an opportunity, cheaper than what everyone has to put in for right now, why don't you call me.'"

With Chicago available, in stepped legendary coach George Allen, who was eager to land the Windy City team. He had been interested in the league from day one, even meeting with Dixon and Ralston shortly after the two began work on the USFL. Allen had coached for 12 years in the NFL, five with the Los Angeles Rams and seven with the Washington Redskins, compiling a winning percentage of .705, fourth best in league history to that point. He called Dr. Ted Diethrich of Phoenix, with whom Allen had become friends after the doctor had given a talk about heart disease to Allen's Redskins. Diethrich had founded the Arizona Heart Institute and was most famous for operating on Arizona Senator Barry Goldwater and for performing the first heart surgery on live television. The doctor had been trying to get an NFL franchise for Phoenix and had talked with former Chicago Bears owner George Halas and NFL Commissioner Pete Rozelle about the prospect. But the NFL was in no hurry to expand, and after his requests to lease Sun Devil Stadium for a USFL franchise fell on deaf ears, Allen persuaded Diethrich to grab the Chicago team, ensuring the surgeon would spend a lot of time shuttling between his Arizona home and the Windy City.

"I got a phone call from George Allen, and he said, 'They're going to start a new league in Chicago next week. Do you think you'd be interested in being involved in it?'" recalled Diethrich. "He was very excited about it, of course. We could have a lot of fun. It was really George calling me and finally we went to the meeting in Chicago. They didn't vote us in the first time around, but the fellows they voted into Chicago didn't pan out, and we did get the franchise. It was all really because of Coach Allen. I never went into this to make a lot of money. It was really for the enjoyment and the experience."

Dr. Diethrich gave Allen a piece of the club's ownership, and Allen ensured cooperation from the front office by naming his son Bruce as the franchise's general manager. The old coach disliked Halas and the Bears and looked forward to showing them up.

"Bruce and coach had a very interesting relationship," added Diethrich. "I don't think I really ever saw them sit down at a table and have a conversation except if we were all around talking football. I know he had a close relationship with his father when talking about the selection of players and football matters and so forth. It was like Bruce always had something up his sleeve. You'd look at him in the eye, and you weren't sure what was going on, but he had that little twinkle in his eye. You'd know he was up to some deal. I might not have known about it, but I knew he was talking to his father about it. You never heard him ask, 'Can we get Trumaine Johnson, dad? What do you think we ought to pay him?' I never heard that conversation; it was very much between those two. You could always tell there was something going on."

In March 1981, cable television pioneer Bill Daniels and fellow cable magnate Alan Harmon met with Dixon and other prospective owners at a Chicago airport hotel. He and Daniels were originally interested in a team for San Diego. Real estate investor Alex Spanos had expressed ongoing interest in the Los Angeles franchise, but when he bought 10 percent of the San Diego Chargers instead, that left L.A.'s USFL entry open. Because it appeared that gaining access to Jack Murphy Stadium in San Diego was going to involve lengthy legal maneuvers, the duo instead headed north to the City of Angels. Actor Lee Majors (*Big Valley*, *The Six Million Dollar Man*, *The Fall Guy*) also joined the ownership group.

On May 14, 1981, John Ralston met with Tad Taube, the chairman of Woodmont Companies, a California real estate firm. On October 23, Taube became a minority partner in a Northern California franchise, joining longtime friend Jim Joseph who had also made his money in real estate.

Taube's family escaped Poland in 1939 just months before the Nazis invaded, and he had built his real estate empire in California's Bay Area in the decades that followed. Though only a minority owner at the start, Taube quickly became a driving force in the ownership ranks.

"Joseph had been approached by both John Ralston and David Dixon and had worked with them for a while," Taube recalled. "He had attended several meetings and decided to start the Bay Area franchise. Jim had approached me initially in the context that I would invest in his franchise, and I was amenable to that possibility. We proceeded for a time with no particular agreement as to how much of the franchise I would own, what our own internal deal would be. I started attending organizing meetings for the league and became quite intimate with the early principals that were going through the process of league organization."

In July 1981, John Bassett, the former owner of the WFL's Memphis Southmen, agreed to meet with David Dixon in Toronto to discuss the rapidly evolving enterprise. Bassett's family, based in Toronto, had made its money in newspapers, television and radio and was one of the richest families in Canada. Bassett, somewhat of an anomaly in the WFL because of his ability to fulfill his financial commitments, originally intended to field his WFL team in Toronto in 1974, but when the Canadian government objected in order to protect the CFL, he moved the franchise to Memphis where they were more popularly known as the Grizzlies after their mascot. There he made a huge splash by signing away three of the Miami Dolphins' best players—running backs Larry Csonka and Jim Kiick and receiver Paul Warfield. Though they proved to be the best run team in the WFL, the Southmen went down with the ill-fated league. Bassett persisted, unsuccessfully suing the NFL in an effort to gain a 1976 expansion team when the NFL chose Tampa and Seattle instead. In addition to his involvement with the WFL, he had also been a part owner of the World Hockey Association's Toronto Toros and then Birmingham Bulls and had served on the board of the CFL's Toronto Argonauts, a team his father owned.

"I remember when I was first approached about this league, I said 'no way,'" Bassett told *Lou Sahadi's Pro Football*. "I was up in Toronto and I got a call from David Dixon from Memphis. He said I had been recommended by the Memphis people as someone who could be trusted and he'd like to talk to me about a franchise. I told him to save himself the airfare, that it was expensive to fly to Canada."

Nevertheless, Dixon made the trip. "I bought him lunch and told him he was crazy," remembered Bassett of their meeting.

"I wasn't even going to get involved," he admitted to *Sports Illustrated*. "But I remember when I first met the other owners. I looked around the table. In the WFL, I was the richest owner, but in this league, I was among the poorest. That made me feel good, confident. I thought they'd really be astute, budget-conscious guys."

The strength of the other ownership groups convinced Bassett. Rather than going back to Memphis where his WFL team had been relatively successful, he settled on Florida as a possible franchise location in November. He had several real estate investments in the area, plus his daughter Carling, an aspiring athlete in her own right, was attending the Nick Bollettieri Tennis Academy in Bradenton. In February 1982, Bassett signed on and chose Tampa as his team's home city. He had not forgotten his experience in the WFL and told those who paid $300,000 for a limited partnership in his USFL team that they had better be prepared to lose it.

Joining him as a five percent owner in the team was actor Burt Reynolds, star of dozens of movies, including *The Cannonball Run*, the *Smokey and the Bandit* series and a pair of football movies, *The Longest Yard* and *Semi-Tough*. His interest in the game had deep roots. He had been an all-state fullback in high school and had attended Florida State University on a football scholarship before knee injuries and a car accident cut his playing time short. Reynolds also recruited some famous friends who helped promote the Bandits, including country music star Jerry Reed who performed a memorable team theme song. Girlfriend Loni Anderson, then starring on TV's *WKRP in Cincinnati*, adorned posters in a skimpy Bandits cheerleader outfit, and frequent Reynolds co-star Dom DeLuise made appearances at home games.

"Now you have to remember, Burt Reynolds 25 years ago was bigger than Tom Cruise, bigger then Tom Hanks, Brad Pitt, all these guys combined," explained Bandits director of marketing Jim McVay. "Burt was bigger than all of them. The guy was unbelievable; he was number one, far and away the number one box office guy and did he have an appeal—and he was a football guy. He loved football. So here's an opportunity for Burt, who's from the state of Florida, to be involved in football, bringing his magnetism and his charm and his friends from California. Here come the chartered flights with his friends wearing cowboy hats and the Bandit jackets, and were they fun to be a part of. That was John Bassett. John Bassett really had a feel for marketing and, boy, did everybody love Burt.

"Loni was a big hit back then and of course as we were developing marketing ideas and concepts the idea was to go ahead and put Loni Anderson in kind of a Bandit cheerleader outfit and put her on the billboards. Well that made a lot of sense certainly at the time. We were scrambling to get attention. We were in an NFL city, so we got Burt Reynolds, and one of the most beautiful women in the world, Loni Anderson, is now a part of the Bandit marketing team with billboards all over town. As a matter of fact, one of the billboards disappeared, and I'm convinced that it ended up at the University of South Florida in a fraternity house or something. She was something really special."

"I don't watch anything between one football season and another football season, and during football season, I usually eat flounder because that's all they can push under the door and not disturb me," said Reynolds. "I watch everything from little league football to high school football, *love* college football, pro football whatever, and I'm very depressed when football season ends. After the Super Bowl it's a very somber feeling for me; it's like a funeral just happened. And when you say spring is a strange time to be playing football, well that's when football players learn how to be football players is the spring practice. These days there are certain colleges like University of Florida that get 30,000 people at spring games, maybe more, and it's also about the time that guys are really starting to miss it."

"We only had one true sportsman in the entire league and that was John Bassett," said Dom Camera, who became the USFL's Director of Marketing. "He understood you're not in the football business to make money, you're in it because you want to be an owner. You want to be part of the community. John Bassett believed that. I'll tell you he was a chairman of my marketing committee and I had great conversations with him. He knew what it was all about because he had been there with various leagues."

"John was special," said McVay. "John was a creative, flamboyant guy who people were drawn to; a brilliant marketing mind. This was one of those guys who was a good-hearted person, but he was a demanding, creative guy who had marketing concepts that nobody else had. This is a guy that thought at a different level. He had a way of rallying the troops, of getting people to respond to ideas and concepts that he had. So right away I was a huge John Bassett fan and he was a special talent.

"John had been a part of the World Football League, and of course his family had been involved in sports for years and years along with his daughter Carling. So John had a reputation. John was in professional hockey also with the Birmingham Bulls in the World Hockey Association, so John had a reputation. John was a charismatic guy. He was a guy who had a chance to be successful no matter what he wanted to do. I mean he was one of those guys if he put his mind to it he was going to be successful. Now John needed to stay active. He wasn't a guy that was gonna sit back. He was always doing something. I think someone described him once as a guy who would jump on a bus going the wrong way just to be going someplace because he couldn't sit still."

One owner who caught Bassett's attention was A. Alfred Taubman, a native son of Detroit who had made his vast fortune in real estate and shopping mall development. He became the principal owner of the Detroit franchise. He had been offered ownership interests in several sports teams in the past but had turned them all down. Joining him was fellow *Forbes* 400 member Max Fisher and Judge Peter B. Spivak, who became the USFL's interim president. Taubman felt that the Panthers, with their spring and summer schedule, would be a welcome addition to Detroit's rich sports scene.

"There was a judge named Peter Spivak who had been in the newspapers a little bit in Detroit, always talking about football," recalled Dixon. "Peter Spivak was close to Al Taubman. I went up to visit Peter, and then we went over to see Taubman. We had him immediately. He agreed immediately."

"I was once offered the Baltimore Orioles," recalled Taubman. "I was buying them when Max Fischer said, 'Don't buy the Baltimore Orioles. you're never going to go there to watch a game. It's not going to be fun. We'll buy the Lions.' Of course, the Fords had no idea of ever selling it. They own it, they own it right. I give them all the credit in the world for staying there and doing it.

"I was contacted by a local fellow in Detroit who I knew, Judge Peter Spivak, his name was. He was not an authority on football, but for some reason, due to the lack of anyone else, he later became chairman of the league, or something like that. He contacted me to ask me if I'd be interested. One of the members called me, and I went to a meeting and listened to everybody. It looked like a reasonable idea and quite fun.

"I really didn't know that much about football, and I still don't. I'm not an expert on football. I understand a little about marketing and how to run a business, but I'm not a football expert. None of the people were, maybe Myles Tanenbaum knew more about it, but the rest of us didn't. But we learned."

"He was an industrialist," said Mike Keller who would become Taubman's assistant general manager and directory of player personnel. "He was a giant of a guy in the Detroit area. He and Eddie DeBartolo were the two guys who actually started the shopping mall business. Al started doing it, and DeBartolo got involved in it. They were the initial guys who started the idea for shopping malls. He was in real estate; he was plugged in to all the top retail store people in the country. He was a very successful guy.

"He was the kind of guy to hire you and turn you loose. He just wanted to meet once a week or once every two weeks to get an update, find out where things were going well, where things were not going well. He'd ask me what I needed in order to make it successful. He was the perfect kind of owner to have."

Tanenbaum, interested in a Philadelphia franchise, was approached in early 1982 by Dixon. Like Taubman, he had made his money in shopping mall development and was also a practicing lawyer. While helping a client who bid on the NFL's Philadelphia Eagles, he had gained a peek into the operations of several professional football teams and liked what he saw.

"This friend of mine who lived in the Philadelphia area, whom I've known for years, had been asked about it and spent some time talking about it to whoever it was that called," Tanenbaum recalled. "Then he called me saying he wasn't going to be interested in it, so he referred it to me.

"By way of all that extensive work, I had a pretty good idea of what all the economics were, meaning the sources of revenue, revenue sharing within the NFL, the various categories of expenses to be anticipated and the level that they would be. The real issue for us was the unknowns of player salaries, the expense of the stadium plus the other operating expenses that had escalated since I did that. But we were doing research on those things."

Only after former Notre Dame Coach Ara Parseghian convinced him that the league could attract quality talent did Tanenbaum become seriously interested. "We continued to explore it further," he added. "Most of the discussions related to the structure of the league, the way we would allocate players to the teams, the playing season and the prospects for revenue from television and other sources. We became more focused on what the economics could possibly be."

When television negotiations started to heat up, he committed himself to field a team. One of his first acts was to hire Philadelphia Eagles director of player personnel Carl Peterson as his president and general manager. Tanenbaum had to give Peterson a minority stake in his new team to cement the pact, but he considered it a small price to pay for the latter's front office leadership.

"Myles had called [Eagles coach] Dick Vermeil and asked to talk to me," remembered Peterson. "Dick asked me if I had any interest. I frankly was not too interested initially until I had the opportunity to sit down with Myles and his attorneys. They were very well-to-do, well-thought-of business people in the Philadelphia community. They owned Kravco, which was the major shopping mall developer in not only Philadelphia, but also New Jersey, Maryland, and so forth. They were one of the top shopping mall developers in the country at the time, and I talked to some business people who had worked with him, and they had only glowing things to say about him: very reputable, honest, people of their word. Myles first called Leonard Tose, the owner of the Eagles, and then Leonard said that he needed to talk to Dick, since that's who I was working for and with, Dick, as the director of player personnel for all those years.

"An opportunity to be my own boss; be an equity owner was why I chose to go to the Stars. Myles and his partners, Art Powell and Harold Schaeffer, offered me 10 percent of the team as well as being president and general manager. Being able to put the whole thing together, the challenge of that is what drew me. I had been with Dick Vermeil for two years at UCLA and I think seven with the Eagles, and we had won a Rose Bowl and gotten to the Super Bowl, so I felt it was a good opportunity. Like anything, when you get an opportunity to build something yourself from scratch, it's exciting. I also had a great deal of confidence in Myles, Powell and Schaeffer. I investigated them as much as they investigated me.

"Before I made a decision to make the move from the NFL to the USFL, I wanted to feel that there was an opportunity for the league to succeed and thrive and build and grow, and I did believe that."

Prominent Washington attorney Berl Bernhard took control of the D.C. franchise after team president Gould called him. The well-connected Bernhard was a senior partner and chairman of Verner, Lipfert, Bernhard and MacPherson, a law firm he had founded in 1960. Living in Washington, D.C., also afforded him the opportunity to dabble in politics, and he had worked extensively for the Democratic National Committee, running Senator Edmund Muskie's bid for the 1972 Democratic presidential nomination. Bernhard was at first uncertain about Gould's pitch, but he bought a controlling interest in and became the managing partner of a large group of investors in the Washington team. Among them were several people who had been interested in establishing a franchise in Cleveland. They instead joined Bernhard when the Browns successfully blocked them from using Cleveland Municipal Stadium.

Marvin Warner, the United States ambassador to Switzerland from 1977 to 1979, grabbed a team for his former hometown of Birmingham. Warner served as chairman of a pair of Ohio banks and the principal owner of a financial holding company who spent most of his time overseeing his enterprises in Cincinnati. He had experience running a sports franchise, having previously owned 10 percent of the New York Yankees and 48 percent of the Tampa Bay Buccaneers. At first, he wanted the Washington franchise but jumped at the chance to own a team in his native city.

"He was tough, tough, tough, like a sergeant from the army," said Gould, who had previously worked for Warner. "He sold houses by giving away refrigerators. He owned savings and loans, he owned a bank. It was clear he didn't want to do any work. He was an older guy and had been ambassador to Switzerland under Carter and had owned part of the Yankees and part of the Tampa Bay Buccaneers.

"He believed that you manage through intimidation. He actually had a book about it that he kept on his counter. He would call me to a meeting, and he would be sitting in a Jacuzzi with a 200-degree temperature in the room, and I'd be sitting there in a suit and tie. By the time the meeting was over, I was ready to puke, but he didn't even hesitate. He would tell me to sleep in late before we got on his plane. Then he'd wake me five minutes before he was leaving for the airport to get on his plane. It was real intimidation. It was just his style."

The league continued to pursue major markets, too. The Boston franchise went to the partnership of Beantown businessman George Matthews and former NFL receiver Randy Vataha. Matthews, who had spent his life in the Boston area, headed up the Matthews Group and sat on the boards of directors of several other companies. Vataha, a California native, had been coached by John Ralston during his college days at Stanford. He later played six seasons with the New England Patriots and one with the Green Bay Packers. He and Matthews were already business partners, the two having invested in several racquetball facilities in New England.

Denver owner Ron Blanding, who had known Ralston during the coach's days with the Broncos, earned his fortune in real estate after beginning in the construction business. He had made his way from Rhode Island to Denver in 1944 as a member of the United States Air Force. He remained in Denver following his discharge and shortly thereafter bought a concrete company, which soon led to his entrance into real estate. In addition, he owned and operated two athletic clubs in the city. Perhaps the bluest collar of the USFL's owners, Blanding also knew fellow Denver denizen Bill Daniels, one of the co-owners of the Los Angeles team.

"It's a popular sport, and I thought Denver could handle a second team," stated Blanding. "We were of course going in the spring, which wasn't in direct competition with the Broncos, so all those things figured in."

Owners came and went in the early days of the league. One interested party was Herb Kohl, future U.S. Senator from Wisconsin, soon-to-be owner of the NBA's Milwaukee Bucks and past operator of a chain of grocery and department stores. Like Spanos and Trump, he decided against investing in the league, but slowly the ownership group started to come together.

"They were always an adventure," Peterson said of early owners' meetings. "You know sometimes you would come away from a meeting saying, 'Is this league going to go forward or stall and go in reverse?' It was always exciting and interesting. They were adding new franchises right up to almost, it seemed like the fall and getting ready for training camps."

"There was a little bit of a revolving door in terms of the people who had indicated an interest in forming the league," Tanenbaum confirmed. "Some people would signify their interest and then drop out, but the hardcore remained on. They seemed to be upstanding, solid, strongly economic-based individuals."

"I thought we were getting very good people everywhere," said Dixon. "Donald Trump was originally supposed to be with us in the New York area. Donald backed off for whatever reason, which hurt us because at the last minute we had to move a very strong owner, Walter Duncan, from Chicago to New York. Another person who backed away at one point, was very committed to us and is a fine man, was the owner of the San Diego Chargers, Alex Spanos. Alex was supposed to be our Los Angeles owner, so this involved some switching around. That too hurt the league a little bit. We were a very solid football league when we came into being, but we would have been tremendous with Trump in New York, Duncan in Chicago and Alex in Los Angeles."

"When Trump left, we didn't have a New York owner," furthered Gould. "He left pretty early, and that's when we asked Duncan to take over there. Now at the time, I don't think that any of us necessarily thought that he was the right owner for New York, living in Oklahoma, but we didn't have anybody else. New York was going to take deep pockets, and without New York, you weren't going to get a media contract."

All in all, Ralston and Dixon were pleased with the men they had lined up. Each of those they had convinced to join the league had already contributed $25,000 to fund league expenses. All of them had the financial resources to operate a team in the USFL. They had fulfilled their goal of landing in major markets with owners who had the resources to operate professional teams.

Though the USFL still had to fight for stadiums in cities such as Chicago, Philadelphia and Boston, the men looked proudly at the list of league cities: New York, Los Angeles, Chicago, Oakland, Detroit, Washington, Boston, Philadelphia, Denver, Phoenix, Birmingham and Tampa.

The Small Screen Is a Big Deal

Dixon knew that he also had to secure a network television contract for both revenue and exposure. To that end, he enlisted the services of TV insider Mike Trager of Robert Landau Associates who began work on securing a pact in 1981.

"I believe David Dixon originally contacted me," said Trager. "I had just finished running campaigns for Anheuser-Busch, and that's probably how he had heard of me. He called me up and said he was part of a new league and was going down the road with a group of owners. He wanted to know if I was interested in consulting with the league on its television alternatives.

"We created a presentation to show what the league was all about, the quality of the owners and things such as that. It was a really good presentation built around the concept of the league, its ownership, cities, etc. It wasn't just, 'We'll play football in the spring. Are you interested?'"

Discussion soon turned to determining the right time to reveal the league to the public. Though rumors of the USFL's organization had appeared in print since a *Football News* story in 1980, and Boston's Randy Vataha had been quoted talking about a 16-team spring league in February of 1982, the league had conducted most of its business out of the public eye. Some league officials felt that the USFL needed to finalize more details before holding a press conference, particularly firming up its ownership groups and solidifying television partners, while others such as Trager thought that a public unveiling would help attract additional investors and provide the final impetus to television negotiations.

"My point to the league was a chicken and the eggs argument," explained Trager. "Television wasn't going to drive the league. The league had to create credibility first, and announcing the USFL's formation would create credibility and drive the television deals to the finish. Things hadn't stagnated but that was the last push the contracts needed. As our own group became stronger, it became critical to announce."

"It was made clear to us that there would be no contract offer prior to our announcement," remembered Tanenbaum. "The television people were insistent that we announce the league before there was a television commitment because they did not want it to be perceived that the availability of television money was what was inducing people to form such a league."

The owners decided it was time to take another major step forward and announce the league to the public. On May 11, 1982, the USFL held a press conference at the 21 Club in New York. As acting president, Michigan's Judge Peter Spivak made the announcement to the assembled media. Spivak unveiled league plans to play a 20-game season, ending with a title contest on the fourth of July. The league revealed that 12 strong groups had stepped forward, representing Birmingham, Boston, Chicago, Denver, Detroit, Los Angeles, New York, Philadelphia, San Diego, San Francisco, Tampa and Washington. In reality, the league had closer to eight confirmed franchises at the time, some of whom were not even willing participants in the news conference.

Birmingham was the only one of the announced cities without an NFL team, though Phoenix and Oakland joined that list once the San Diego and San Francisco franchises moved to those cities. Though they announced the league would play a 20-game regular season, that number soon fell to 18 games. Much work remained including solidifying the last few ownership groups, hiring coaches, signing players, choosing nicknames and finding places to play. The men had all of ten months to accomplish those goals. Once just a rumor, the United States Football League had now gone public.

"Mr. Spivak and Dave Dixon at one particular point weren't getting along well," recalled Ralston. "Dave would call me and ask me to call Peter Spivak and he'd want something done and then Peter would say, 'No, we're not going to do it that way,' and then I'd have to tell Dave. In other words, Dave and Peter weren't speaking at that time. Right at the end it was Peter who insisted that we find 12 people and end up at the 21 Club in New York. We didn't know what would happen, but, boy, I'll tell you once we announced the league it got into full bloom very rapidly. The announcement made it much easier to find the rest of the owners, plus it got the television people in line."

Television negotiations heated up quickly, and from the beginning, ABC's Jim Spence and his boss Roone Arledge showed the most interest in the league.

"They had an agent, a guy named Mike Trager who called me in December of 1981 and told me about the plan for the league," recalled Spence. "He wanted me to meet with a bunch of owners so I could get a better sense of the league. Initially, I declined to have that meeting. I didn't want to be in the position of their using ABC Sports, if you will, to further their ambitions. I decided to let them mature a little bit before I met with them."

Though Spence initially declined to meet with the league, he eventually agreed to get together with a group of USFL owners on April 21, 1982. Among those at the meeting were Spivak, Daniels, Matthews, Duncan and Bassett. Spence now believed the USFL had the backing to survive.

"I had discussed with Roone Arledge, who was my immediate boss and president of ABC Sports, the conversation I had with Mr. Trager," Spence recalled. "Both Roone and I were intrigued by the concept. We had a programming need in the spring, and we liked the idea of football. I eventually decided to meet with a number of owners.

"Meeting with the owners convinced me they were for real. I had a number of concerns. One, were they going to have staying power? Were they going to be financially viable over a long period of time? I remember I was very candid in our meeting with the owners. I asked if they had enough financing to withstand the early storms, because there are going to be problems. Every new league has problems in the short term. They convinced me that they did have that kind of financing. They were competent, reliable people. I was impressed with them.

"One thing I remember from the meeting was John Bassett, who was probably the key owner among the group. None of the owners were more respected than John Bassett. I remember in that meeting we were talking about financing on a long-term basis. John had been involved with the World Football League that went out of business rather quickly. He told me in that meeting, 'Jim, when I was involved with the World Football League, I had more money than any of the other owners. In this league, I have less money than any of the other owners.' I was impressed by that."

"There was marginal interest from the other networks because they were carrying the NFL on weekends," Trager said. "ABC was also a bit more independent at that time. In terms of sports on cable, there was only Turner and ESPN.

"CBS and NBC had a lot more spring programming than ABC. NBC had some interest. I came from NBC, where I was the VP of sports, and they knew me so I had some credibility there. NBC and CBS were more tempered in their responses because they didn't want to jeopardize their relationships with the NFL. ABC just had the right availability. I mostly spoke with Jim Spence; he was Roone's number one."

On May 26, just over two weeks after the USFL's introductory press conference, the league revealed that it had signed a television contract with ABC. The announcement silenced those who wondered whether the new venture would ever take the field. The agreement called for ABC to televise one game each Sunday, plus the playoffs and championship game. The owners had known that the network and the league were close to reaching a deal two weeks earlier at the press conference and were certainly glad that they had heeded the advice of Spivak and Trager.

The contract served as a booster shot for the fledgling enterprise's credibility. From the start, Roone Arledge, president of ABC News and Sports, pursued the league because his network suffered from a dearth of spring sports programming. Their lineup at the time consisted of *The American Sportsmen*, *The Superstars* and *Wide World of Sports*, none of which exactly glued the sports public to their television sets in the spring. NBC, then the third-rated network, tried to wrest the contract away at the last minute with a $20 million bid for the first two years but was too late. ABC signed on for $9 million for each of the first two years and options for 1985 at $14 million and 1986 at $18 million.

"We had the first AFL contract for five years and during the course of that time we exposed them to be a viable property," Arledge told the *New York Daily News*. "If all works well, we would hope the combination of our exposure and their product would have the same result."

Veteran college football announcer Keith Jackson would handle the primary play-by-play duties while former Pittsburgh Steelers receiver Lynn Swann took color commentary responsibilities. Unlike the NFL's television deals in which virtually every game was televised in each team's home market, ABC was only obligated to televise one USFL game per week which would be seen nationally, though the network had the option to pick up additional games and feed them wherever they pleased. Another key difference in the ABC deal was the lack of a blackout provision. That meant, for instance, that ABC could show a Chicago game in the Chicago area even when the team was playing at home. The NFL, on the other hand, blacked out games that failed to sell out in the home team's market, theoretically helping keep their attendances high despite television coverage of all their games. ABC offered to cover all of the USFL's games each week, but that would have cost the USFL $3 million per year to cover production costs, a substantial part of the contract. The owners decided to take the money and worry about the television issues later.

"We had a meeting out in California a couple of weeks after our public announcement at which point two people from ABC were present and presented their proposal to provide us with television revenue," recalled Tanenbaum. "That was being matched by NBC. Both networks lobbied before the meeting with the owners with respect to which of the two networks would be most appropriate for us. We did opt for ABC. It seemed like the right move at the time, and we had no reason to think otherwise. ABC made a strong presentation, and that was subsequently backed by ESPN. The revenue was relatively modest, but I thought at the time that the most important part was to get the exposure so that our product could be advertised on television, while we were being paid for the privilege of advertising it. Most people have to pay for advertising, we got our product advertised and were paid for it.

"We were informed within a range of what to expect. It hit within the range, although at the low end of it. We had each made our calculations and realized that we were going to lose a fair amount of money, but the hope was that we would gain a following, a foothold. If we could hang in there for three or four years, we would weather it all and increase our attendance especially with the product being advertised. That was my view. Others looked at it differently. We all obviously thought that it was important that our product be seen and advertised in that sense, but I think that some felt that the financial aspect was more important."

Though content for the time being to utilize the USFL to fill a programming need on Sunday afternoons in the spring, ABC had bigger long-term plans for the league.

"My ultimate goal, my vision for the USFL, was that it would move to primetime in the spring," revealed Spence. "Starting in March, you're doing fine, but as you move into the latter part of the season and you're getting into June and later, it's really hard to generate ratings for obvious reasons. With the weather getting warmer around the country, people just aren't going to be sitting in their living rooms on a Sunday afternoon. My vision was, after x number of additional years giving the league a chance to get on really solid ground, that we would move it to primetime."

Less than a month after inking the ABC deal, the USFL ensured itself even more exposure when it signed on with fledgling cable network ESPN for two prime time telecasts each week on Saturday and Monday. Dixon had guessed correctly—cable TV was ready for pro football. The sports station beat out the USA Network and Ted Turner's Atlanta-based Superstation WTBS in negotiations. ESPN had come up with an extra $1 million to edge Ted Turner's late bid and secure the contact. Although the cable sports channel reached only about one-quarter of U.S. homes, less than WTBS, it was widely agreed that the two would make a good union. Plus, it didn't hurt that ESPN was paying the league $4 million in 1983 and $7 million the following year.

"I worked simultaneously with ESPN and Ted Turner," said Trager. "Ted was personally involved in the negotiations. Bob Wussler was also involved. Turner and ESPN were both very interested in the product. The bottom line came down to money. ESPN was also more aggressive overall, and coupled with money, that put them over the top."

In addition, ABC owned an option to buy the cable network, and USFL executives hoped the two could ultimately aid each other in covering the league. Jim Simpson took the play-by-play duties while future NBC analyst Paul Maguire provided the color commentary. The ESPN deal assured that on most weekends at least three league games would be televised, a minimum of half the schedule.

Later, ABC Radio also came on board to broadcast two games per week plus the post-season over its national network of more than 200 affiliate stations throughout the country.

Going Public

The broadcasting agreements further served to firm up the ownership groups. Those sitting on the fence now knew the venture had legs.

"By April of 1982, the league had received a tentative commitment from ABC Sports to enter into a television contract with the USFL," recalled Tad Taube. "There were also discussions ongoing with ESPN that would provide additional television revenue so, with about $30 million in prospective television revenue, we felt that we could move forward and formally announce the formation of the league and our franchise locations. Just prior to that date, days prior, after I had already made the commitment to attend the announcement, the designated owner for the Los Angeles franchise, Alex Spanos, made a deal with the owner of the San Diego Chargers to buy a minority interest in the Chargers. He felt and we felt that that represented a conflict of interest that would preclude Alex from moving forward with us.

"Here we were assembled in New York ready to attend this grand announcement with television cameras and so forth, and we had 11 owners and 12 positions at the table. The owners I knew, and at that point it was most if not all of them, induced me to take

Oakland Invaders owner Tad Taube (left) with chief operating officer Howard Friedman. Photograph courtesy Tad Taube.

a position at the table. Jim and I had a discussion at that point about whether he would become owner of the Los Angeles team and I would take over the Bay Area one or vice versa. Actually, we flipped a coin. I won the coin flip and became the designated owner of the Bay Area franchise with the tacit understanding on my part and on the part of my co-owners that my role was probably temporary and that if a permanent owner could be found that I would in effect be replaced. At that point I really hadn't put any money on the table, it was just important that I put my feet behind the table behind the sign that said 'Bay Area.'

"However, the turn of events that evolved from the formal announcement of the team and the enormous publicity that followed nationwide put me in a position where, when I got off the airplane in San Francisco, I was literally besieged by local reporters who wanted to know all about me and my plans for the franchise, who the coach was going to be, where we were going to play and all these other things. At that juncture, it made it virtually impossible for me to sidestep in favor of somebody else. It put me in a position where I would continue with the venture and participate on the same level as everybody else. That was the path that led to my involvement with the USFL."

Taube called his new team the Bay Area Invaders as he searched for a home field. He looked into Candlestick Park and Stanford Stadium before signing on with the Oakland Coliseum. The team then changed its name to the Oakland Invaders on October 19, 1982.

"An early choice was Candlestick Park, and we were refused access to Candlestick Park because of certain agreements with the NFL that stated another sports franchise would not be allowed to play there," Taube said. "That happened frequently to the league's membership. There were a lot of instances where there was a lock on the stadium put on there by an NFL team, operating pursuant to NFL rules."

Still, Taube was happy to set up shop in Oakland, recently vacated by the Raiders. The city and the NFL itself continued to fight the Raiders' move, but legal setbacks had all but ensured Oakland would be without an NFL team.

"We had an extraordinary business plan," said Taube. "We were in a market that had not even been slightly tapped. There was tremendous demand. There was an ability, had it been followed through on, to develop our own stars on a budget that was within the capability of our entire ownership group. We had a time of the year that was completely to ourselves, with no high school, no college, no pro, just the USFL. There aren't many opportunities in business that open the possibility of entering a market that you have all to yourself. We had it all to ourselves.

"The post–Super Bowl period is a horrible time for football fans who are the most addicted fans in the world with respect to sports viewing. From the Super Bowl until late August when the exhibition games in the NFL begin, the football fan has severe withdrawal symptoms, and that's why things like the draft, which is kind of a bullshit exercise, gets so much play. Everybody is looking for their football fix. If there was football going on year round, the draft would be another administrative procedure. That's one reason. We were playing at a time of the year when there was huge demand for this type of activity that was completely unsatisfied."

Joseph took over as head of the L.A. franchise before finally winding up in Phoenix in August of 1982, seven months before the league was due to kickoff. He knew Los Angeles was a tough sports town already with two NFL teams and felt that the burgeoning Arizona city would be a far more receptive community. Daniels and Harmon, rebuffed in stadium negotiations in San Diego, ended up taking the Los Angeles market. If Joseph was disappointed with his move to Phoenix, he hid it well. A member of his ownership group, an Arizona State alum, had been able to secure a lease for Sun Devil Stadium even after local Dr. Diethrich had failed and been forced to Chicago, much to the doctor's chagrin.

Nearly a year before the USFL was to play its first game, Joseph had already been on a whirlwind tour of the league that took him from California's Bay Area to Los Angeles to Phoenix.

"We used to joke that Jim was the only man to own three franchises in the USFL in the span of less than six months," laughed Taube. "Jim was convinced that the L.A. market was a very tough market and that Arizona offered an opportunity to bring professional football to a market that had long been hungry for pro football. Keep in mind at that time that Los Angeles was supporting the Rams and the Raiders and not necessarily with great enthusiasm. It's a very difficult sports town. Harmon and Daniels, on the other hand, had come from the world of cable television. In fact, Daniels was referred to as 'the father of cable television.' They perceived that the opportunity was there. That was more their background."

With ownership in place, Dixon began to take a backseat in league matters. Their money now on the line, the team owners began voting on important league issues. As his fee for organizing the USFL, Dixon gained the rights to a league franchise, but he would not field a team in its inaugural season. Instead, he sought to sell the franchise rights once the USFL had proven its viability.

"They had taken control of the league away from me, and I don't mean that in a formal or adversarial way, but they decided that they knew everything," said Dixon.

"Dave did not play an active role in the operation of the league," said Colorado attorney and former coach Steve Ehrhart who had been doing work for the league for several months. "He did a terrific job of bringing in ownership and helping put the foundation in place prior to the summer of '82, but by that summer because he had chosen not to operate a team, he was not an active participant in the operation of the league. His main mission was to sell his franchise.

"He didn't come to league meetings and didn't participate, but he was certainly very, very active in following the progress and being tuned in to which cites were interested in expansion franchises and who were the candidates. It was not an easy situation. He had a singleness of purpose which was to get the money for his team from someone."

Finding a Commissioner

Detroit co-owner Spivak had been conducting league meetings in the early days as Dixon and the owners searched for the USFL's first commissioner. They sought someone not only capable of fulfilling the duties of the position, but also a person with a recognizable name in football circles who could promote and lend credibility to the league. First, they tried to pry Pete Rozelle from his post with the NFL. He quickly turned down a lucrative offer. They also considered Chicago Bears General Manager Jim Finks who nearly landed the NFL's top job after Rozelle retired several years later. Though Dixon pushed for Finks, the owners decided against him.

ESPN president and chief executive officer Chet Simmons rose to the top of their list. He had all the broadcasting experience the league sought, having served as the first president of NBC Sports from 1977 to 1779 before signing on with the fledgling ESPN. He was no stranger to NFL challengers, either. He had started at ABC in 1957, and had helped craft the American Football League's first television package. Upon moving to NBC in 1964, his relationship with that young league helped his new network land the circuit's next television contract, a deal which all but assured the AFL's survival and brought the NFL to the bargaining table to work out a merger agreement. Simmons had also worked to acquire the rights to televise Major League Baseball, NCAA football and the 1980 Summer Olympics before jumping over to the brand new ESPN in 1979 as that network's first president. At ESPN he had pioneered coverage of the early rounds of the NCAA basketball tournament and the NFL draft as well as being instrumental in the creation of the network's staple daily news program, *SportsCenter*.

"Chet and I go back to my very first day at ABC Sports," recalled Spence. "Actually, the organization was not yet ABC Sports. This was 1960 and it was called Sports Programs Incorporated which was the predecessor organization to ABC Sports. Sports Programs Incorporated was under contract to ABC to provide the sports programming. ABC didn't even have a sports department in 1960. The guy who ran Sports Programs was Ed Scherick, who was Chet's boss. Scherick hired me, and my initial duties were to work as a production assistant, a gopher if you will, on a college football scoreboard show we did, an American Football League scoreboard show and a filler program after boxing on Saturday nights, a bowling show called 'Make That Spare.' I was hired for those three shows. Scherick shook my hand, welcomed me aboard and said, 'Please go out and see Chet Simmons. He'll get you squared away.' I went to see Chet Simmons, walked into his office, and he congratulated me and asked me when I wanted to start. I said, 'Well, right now is fine.' He said, 'Why don't you go out and have lunch and come back.' I went out to lunch, came back and stayed for 25 years. That was the first time I ever met Chet Simmons, the day I was hired.

"We had an excellent relationship. He was a very nice person, maybe a little too soft, if you will, but a very nice, honest, decent human being. I liked Chet a lot then and still do today."

"I was at ESPN at the time, and kept hearing about this new football league by David Dixon and I said, 'Who the hell's David Dixon?'" Simmons recalled. "I didn't know, and they started to throw some potential owners names and I didn't know any of those either nor did I care. I had enough problems and challenges at ESPN to worry about a new football league, but like everything else in sports I think that if somebody had an idea, and something was new, I'll keep watching; keep my eye on it."

"I was co-chair of the commissioner's select committee, and the thing that drove us to him more than anything else was the fact that he was at ESPN," Gould said. "He had the television background and was a key guy at ESPN. Clearly we saw ESPN as a force; they weren't there yet, but they were moving in that direction. I think the biggest influencer was that we knew how important media was. We knew that without television we would never make it. I wouldn't say he was the most knowledgeable about football, but we wanted a television guy. That's why we went after him, and we were very lucky to get him. Mike Trager was one of our consultants, and I think he knew Chet. Mike at the time was a consultant to the media committee."

"Every time there was an owners' meeting I was there during the league's formative stage," added Trager. "I was responsible for recruiting Chet Simmons when they were looking for a commissioner. I helped them contact Chet because we had worked together at NBC."

Though he had never been involved with a professional sports organization outside of television matters, Simmons knew what it took to survive in the age of TV, and his recent time at ESPN had kept him on the cutting edge of sports broadcasting. On June 14, 1982, the USFL announced at a press conference in Los Angles that it had found its first commissioner in Simmons.

"It was something new, something extremely different," said Simmons. "It was a challenge. I like startups as ESPN had been. It was something that was intriguing because I had never done anything like that before. It had always been television. This was quite interesting because I thought there was some pretty good money available from the prospective owners at the time to give it a reasonable chance."

Broadcasting executive Chet Simmons joined the USFL as its first commissioner after overseeing the startup of ESPN. Photograph by Jim Turner, from author's collection.

"Chet was the consummate respected pioneer in television," Ehrhart recalled. "Here was a guy who had grown NBC. To have the vision of not only building NBC Sports, but then ESPN is incredible. Many of the people who are still at ESPN pay tribute to Chet, that he was able to create a whole new concept of television sports. He carved out a brand new style of in-depth coverage. He presided over the very beginning of the new network, and he was also able to hold this grand enterprise together during the early years of financial challenge. When it was losing huge amounts of money, he was able to build the enterprise, hire the right people and continue to keep Getty Oil funding the losses. Getty was a totally different company, an oil company, and it was a different endeavor for them to invest in the network and keep it going. He was masterful in doing that. Even today, a guy like Chris Berman will say that from '78 to '82 it was a huge challenge to build a new concept that nobody understood: a 24-hour sports-only network. Chet built the idea of a one-hour sports news show called *SportsCenter* into one of cable's mainstays, and today one of the most recognizable sports shows in history. This was at a time when television sports news was still three minutes at the end of the local newscast.

"He understood the technical aspects of TV as well as the economic aspects. Many others had an unrealistic expectation as to what television could accomplish. Some members of the league expected television had a bottomless barrel of money, which was certainly not true. Chet did a marvelous job tempering those expectations, keeping everybody going and building from ground zero. In fact, the USFL became a great success as a television entity."

"I can remember the morning that I got off the train from Greenwich, Connecticut where we lived," Simmons said of his arrival in New York. "Vanderbilt Avenue runs alongside Grand Central Station, and I stood there in the middle of the street, taxis honking at me, and I said, 'You know I am the only employee of the USFL. I'm the commissioner; I gotta go buy their pencils. I gotta go do all of this. How the hell am I going to do all of this?' That was a very frightening morning."

Simmons quickly went about assembling the league office. To that end, he tabbed Ehrhart as his director of administration and legal counsel. Ehrhart's firm had specialized in sports law and had represented over 100 NFL players and coaches. He was familiar with the world of pro football and immediately became Simmons' right-hand man. Peter Hadhazy, a former general manager of the Cleveland Browns and New England Patriots, signed on as director of operations. The new commissioner hired Dom Camera who had previously run an NBC station when Simmons was president of NBC Sports, to spearhead the league's marketing efforts. Camera had been working with the North American Soccer League's television efforts.

"I actually was on with the competition committee even before Chet was hired," recalled Ehrhart. "My initial contact was through the coaches. I had represented players and coaches in the NFL. My law firm was initially retained by the competition committee, and I was originally contracted by the competition committee back in the springtime. I remember my law office tracking down and borrowing World Football League contracts from 1974, Canadian Football League contracts, NFL contracts and other league contracts, trying to come up with a really good, workable standard player contract.

"I think I was Chet's first formal employee, besides maybe his secretary. There were the two or three of us in borrowed offices up there in Rockefeller Center. I was sitting up there late every night staying in of all things, the Hyatt, which Trump owned on 42nd

Street. I would walk over to this borrowed set of offices at Rockefeller Center. Chet and I were thinking there was no possible way we could pull this all together.

"Initially, it was a 24/7 scramble. Chet was such an expert in television that he did a lot of work in the television area. He was well known as the former president of NBC Sports and then president of ESPN. So I was kind of doing the nuts and bolts; putting together the drafts and player administrative and legal issues, getting the office staffed up, bringing on people. I was proud to be Chet's right hand man. He taught me an awful lot. He's certainly one of the good guys in sports."

"Peter Hadhazy, who had come from the NFL, was a football guy," said Simmons. "He understood the game, he understood the business. Steve Ehrhart obviously was my number one guy. He had come out of a football background as being an agent and being a player in college, so he knew a lot of people in the industry. We had some guys a step below. Peter hired a very good guy to run the officials. We had a good guy to run statistics and all that, run the operation of a league office and drafting and moving players and all that. These were two very good young men."

"We had to set up a schedule," recalled Camera. "Originally we had the teams all set up, so that was Peter's job. He set up a sensational schedule so that there were developing rivalries before we even kicked off. We knew that New York and L.A. would be a natural rivalry. We knew that Philadelphia and Boston would be a natural rivalry, so we started to establish that. We tried to make Chicago and Washington a rivalry because you had George Allen in Chicago, and he was the former head coach of the Washington Redskins. We started to build it that way, and we worked it out so that each team would get exposure on ABC."

"When Chet and I got back to New York and got some offices open, then it became apparent we needed to get a seasoned football operations guy," added Ehrhart. "I can remember Chet and I meeting with Peter [Hadhazy] for dinner at Sparks Restaurant. We met with Peter and sealed the deal. Here was a guy who had been the general manager of the Cleveland Browns. He joined with us that fall when we were just getting moved into the offices there at 52 Vanderbilt. Peter had started a real good football operations department. It was terrific because he had great experience and he had the ability and diplomatic talent to be able to talk to everyone from coaches and general managers in the NFL to college people. He was a good evaluator of talent, not only in the office but on the field and in coaching, helping set up training camps and rules and waivers and trades. In those days we had TWX and Telex machines; there was no Internet. You had the waiver wire, the click-clacking of the waiver machine. Peter got all that started in the office.

"He was a very talented guy with good experience from the NFL. He loved the NFL. It was tricky getting him hired because he was close with Pete Rozelle. I think he had talked with Rozelle before he made the move to come over and join the USFL. At that time and place, there was still a benign relationship. The powerful NFL smiled at this new group of guys trying to start a league. Peter told me he got Rozelle's blessing to come join us."

"I was lucky with timing because Chet called me up and said that he had just signed on as commissioner of the United States Football League, and he wanted to talk to me and a very close friend of mine since high school, Peter Hadhazy, who had also been a former head of the Browns," said Camera. "So I said, 'sure, Chet, I'd love to talk with you.' He asked if I'd talk to Peter and see if he might be interested, too. Who knows if I was the beard or what. Peter was the reason why the league even knew how to kick the ball off. We had no clue otherwise. Chet signed both Peter and I. I started in July of '82, and Peter started later that month, and a guy named Steve Ehrhart, who was the league counsel, started right about that same time. So there were four of us who took over offices at 52 Vanderbilt, and we just created the league. We had David Dixon's study and his philosophy that you build your own stars, hire the best coaches, play in stadiums that were known: that was all credited to David. We started to implement that plan, and we were going to play in the springtime.

"Chet was impossible to squeeze money out of because he was concerned about ownership, 'Oh, we can't do this, we can't do that,' he'd say. I said, 'Chet, I can't run around and cut television deals, get radio contracts and set up licensing and marketing without getting some staff.' So we started to hire people."

With the commitments from broadcasters came major sponsors such as Anheuser-Busch, General Motors, the Miller Brewing Company, Pan American Airways and the Chrysler Corporation. The USFL relied on these sponsors to handle much of its marketing.

"Dom was a very aggressive guy who knew his way around New York City and the ad agencies," said Ehrhart. "Dom helped bring in some of the additional deals such as Pan-Am, which became our official airline, and Chrysler as our official vehicle. I remember Lee Iacocca coming into the offices. Dom built a staff in marketing and sales just like Peter brought in some people there in the operations department."

"All I wanted, which was unique at the time, was for everybody who wanted to be involved with the USFL to put us in their advertising," explained Camera. "So if Dodge, which was the official car of the USFL—we gave away a car at every home game of every team—was running national advertising, they always tagged, even in other sports-type advertising, 'the Official Car of the United States Football League.' We did the same thing with Pan-Am. We cut deals with Pan-Am when they provided teams with charter service. The teams paid to a degree, but they got an extremely great discount, and in turn in their national advertising they would always tag, 'the Official Airline of the United States Football League.' Also in their in-flight video every month we'd run a new one-hour special about the USFL, which was really a highlight film or a blooper film. We were really the first league that poked fun at ourselves. If a guy made a mistake, we showed it. Now everybody does it, but back then it was sacrosanct. The NFL had John Facenda and the great NFL Films. But with us if a guy did something funny, we showed it. We also showed the great catches, the great players and so forth. It was a matter of building a league as a people's league. That really was the philosophy. It was a people's league, and football was the national pastime. You could play it anytime of the year. We used to tell people, 'You can have coffee at a fall football game, and you can have iced coffee at our games.'

"We had an official cheese of the USFL. We sold sponsorships to everything, myself and my people. We sponsored everything. If it moved, we sponsored it because that's what we had to do. We needed other people's advertising to promote the league because I never had an advertising budget. If you're going to rely on ABC or ESPN to promote you, forget it. they're putting you into a rotation, and maybe they'll talk about their upcoming game, but I needed campaigns going locally, regionally, nationally that would show that logo, talk about it."

The Teams Take Shape

With the league office ramping up, the USFL's franchises started coming together. One by one, the names and logos that would make each team a reality were unveiled. George Matthews, a sailor in his spare time, took the advice of his secretary and christened his Boston entry the Breakers. Bassett named his franchise Bandits not after partner Burt Reynolds' movie character in *Smokey and the Bandit*, but after his daughter's German Shepherd. Former U.N. delegate Marvin Warner, also famous as a breeder of thoroughbreds, went with Stallions. Berl Bernhard's fascination with politics made Federals a natural for Washington. Denver chose Gold in part because of the gold rush's importance in Colorado history. Also going with a historical theme was New Jersey's Generals, named so because of the number of actual generals stationed in the Garden State during the Revolutionary War. Many of the other nicknames were the result of name-the-team contests publicized in local papers. Wranglers narrowly beat out Rattlers in Arizona. Blitz portrayed the tough image that Allen wanted for the Chicago team, while Bay Area Invaders conveyed the same meaning for Taube's team, plus it rhymed with the recently departed Raiders. Philadelphia wanted Stallions after the city's beloved Rocky [the "Italian Stallion"] but after Birmingham beat them to it, settled on Stars instead. Los Angeles chose to ignore its crowded highways when picking Express as its nickname. Finally, the Michigan Panthers fit right in the Motor City, joining the city's Lions and Tigers.

"Michigan got a late start," recalled Ehrhart. "Alfred Taubman was a towering figure, and certainly he was so well respected in Detroit, but they were much slower in getting people hired and assembling their organization. They were the very last team to get in their colors, the very last team to get in their logo, the very last team in a lot of areas. I can remember other owners saying, 'You gotta get on Michigan.' We had all 11 other team colors and logos into the league office and ready for production, and we couldn't have the full set until they got their stuff in. The irony of all this is that though they were the last in getting their organization together, once Taubman and his people concentrated on the team, they certainly surpassed some of the early starters."

Dixon had long before determined that the USFL needed to play in top level stadiums. To this end, the league's members began to hunt down their playing fields.

"At the outset finding ownership was the key," said Ralston, describing their early work. "Then as we were going along, it was organizing meetings, setting up the hotels and starting on the stadium leases. That was very important to ensure that we could get all the top stadiums no matter where they were."

"I talked to Pete Rozelle about it," Dixon said of the NFL interfering in USFL stadium negotiations. "I said, 'Pete, look I'm not out to cause any fistfights or anything, but all these stadiums are available to us under antitrust law. If you want us to sue you, I've got some guys who'll do it, but I don't want to sue anybody.' Pete passed the word quickly around the league. We were thinking about a team in Dallas initially, and I went into see Tex Schramm, and he said, 'Be my guest.' He said they knew the law and there would be no problem. The availability of those stadiums was a huge breakthrough for the USFL. I knew they were available the first time I talked to my lawyer."

Despite promises to the contrary, the NFL appeared to be making it tough for the USFL to get the facilities it wanted.

"I was told many times by certain people, 'You will not get into this stadium. It won't happen," added Gould. "That was the line that Edward Bennett Williams used on me in

Washington, DC. 'You will not get into RFK Stadium,' but I did. When we went after RFK Stadium, I got to know the authority and spent time with them. I told them, 'We're going to play here. We'll do whatever it takes.' Remember football did not have antitrust protection like baseball did. There was no way they were going to keep us out. They were bluffing. The stadium was the big thing. If you can get into the stadiums, you actually have legitimacy. Once we were able to knock those down, that gave us a lot of opportunity to believe in ourselves."

The Generals struck first by inking a deal in July of 1982 for Giants Stadium in the Meadowlands, New Jersey, home of the Giants and Jets. As part of their agreement, the team would be known by the New Jersey label rather than New York.

"Walter Duncan had to go through a lot of political issues to get into Giants Stadium," said Ehrhart. "Remember the Giants controlled the stadium, and the Jets were on their way over. That created a huge roadblock. Duncan hired a big New York City law firm that was politically connected to make sure they could get into the stadium. At the time we had to utilize the precedent that a municipality cannot deny another entity the right to lease a public stadium. The NFL in some cities was trying to block anyone else from playing in the stadiums. There was some important precedent-setting case law which was what most of our people had to rely on to get into the NFL-shared stadiums. New York was one of the most difficult stadiums for us to get into."

After investigating Candlestick Park in San Francisco and Stanford Stadium, the Invaders locked up the Oakland Coliseum, recently vacated with the Raiders' departure for Los Angeles. In L.A., the Express settled down at the Raiders' new home, the cavernous Los Angeles Coliseum, while in Washington the Federals landed at RFK Stadium, home of the NFL's Redskins. The Stallions worked out an agreement to play at Legion Field, and, after much legal wrangling, the Chicago Park District opened Soldier Field to the Blitz despite threats by the Bears to sue the district. The Stars also had to put up a fight, this time with baseball's Phillies, before winning the use of Veterans Stadium. Michigan chose the Silverdome in Pontiac, Michigan, and the Wranglers were allowed the use of Sun Devil Stadium, thanks to a friend of Jim Joseph. In nearly every case in which a USFL franchise would share a facility with a National Football League team, the NFL squad complained that they had not been treated fairly and that the USFL had been given a sweet deal. Several NFL teams even threatened to sue the stadium commissions or USFL teams to keep them out. That strategy worked in San Diego, where the older league kicked up enough fuss to keep the USFL out. Much of the NFL's efforts went into subtler pressure away from the public eye.

"In those years the NFL did everything they could to submarine us," said Ralston. "Not right out in front of everybody, but they certainly did it behind the scenes." Fortunately, he, Dixon and a team of lawyers had been working with several stadiums for months and were able to fight though most of the roadblocks.

Outside of San Diego, the Breakers suffered through perhaps the toughest stadium situation of any team in the league. The only suitable pro field in the Boston area was Schaefer Stadium in Foxboro, but it was controlled by the owners of the New England Patriots. Even if they could work out an agreement for its lease, Matthews and Vataha did not want an NFL franchise as its landlord. The team then faced the same dilemma that the Pats had confronted in the 1960s: Boston just does not have many football stadiums suitable for a professional team. The franchise next tried 37,000-seat Harvard Stadium, but was turned away. Finally, the Breakers settled on tiny Nickerson Field on the campus of Boston University. The Patriots had also come to the same decision 23 years before. Before the start of the USFL season, seating capacity was boosted to just over 21,000, but it remained by far the league's smallest venue. It did not help the team's credibility much to be playing on a tiny college field, and the Boston press never let them forget it.

"They ended up in a place they weren't that happy at, the old Nickerson Field," Ehrhart explained. "That was BU's field, and it was small and antiquated. They were never very pleased because they couldn't get into where they wanted to be. It was something they never felt was a long-term solution."

In other stadium developments, groups seeking expansion franchises in Minneapolis and Pittsburgh were already initiating legal maneuvers to win the rights to the Metrodome and Three Rivers Stadium, respectively. They did not want to go through the same delays found in San Diego, Chicago and Philadelphia. Even before its inaugural training camps opened, the league had announced plans to expand by four teams for the 1984 campaign, part of Dixon's strategy to pump money back to the original owners as well as sell his own franchise. Among the cities being considered were Pittsburgh; Atlanta; Minneapolis; San Diego; Seattle; Tulsa, Oklahoma; Charlotte; Anaheim and either Dallas or Houston. Pittsburgh had the best chances, while Houston was also a strong possibility due to Dixon's interest and his remaining franchise option. The league first interviewed expansion applicants at its meeting in Tampa on December 13, three months prior to the inaugural season.

The Coaches

While the quality of the players the league would attract was still open to debate, the credentials of its coaches were not. The USFL quickly compiled a stable of extremely capable men to man the sidelines. The first to sign on was Chuck Fairbanks in New Jersey, who was given the responsibility of presiding over the league's largest market. Few doubted that Fairbanks was the right man for the job. He compiled a 52–15–1 mark with three bowl wins in six years with the Oklahoma Sooners and went 46–41 with the Patriots, including a playoff appearance in 1977. His time with Colorado had not been nearly as successful, but most felt that had more to do with the Buffaloes lack of talent than Fairbanks' coaching abilities. Cementing his status was the fact that he helped recruit the Duncan as an owner. Fairbanks would hold a minority stake in the team.

Robert "Red" Miller was a popular choice to be the first head man of the Denver Gold. Miller had directed the Denver Broncos from 1977 to 1980 and led them to an appearance in Super Bowl XII. The Broncos were widely criticized for firing the well-liked coach who had gone 42–25 in his tenure there, and the Mile High fans welcomed him back with open arms. He had begun his coaching career in the AFL with the Boston Patriots during that league's inaugural season and later worked as an assistant at Buffalo, Denver, St. Louis and Baltimore. Fairbanks hired him in 1973 as the Patriots' offensive coordinator.

"Ron Blanding in Denver did a superior job of marketing and brought Red Miller on board," Ehrhart said. "Red went to every single service organization and club meeting and sold the most season tickets. The Denver Gold had the highest season ticket base of any team in the league in those early days. Red Miller was so respected and had been to the Super Bowl with the Broncos in 1977, so in 1982 he wasn't that far away from when he had been a Super Bowl coach."

Widely heralded as one of the game's greats, George Allen, who had led the Los Angeles Rams and Washington Redskins, joined as Chicago's coach. After beginning his career as an assistant with George Halas's Bears, he had compiled a 116–47–5 record in 12 years as a head man with Los Angeles and Washington, never finishing a season with a record worse than 8–6.

Among other innovations, he was the first head coach to make special teams play a priority by hiring a coordinator for that phase of the game. He also employed the NFL's first security officer to prevent his practices from being spied upon. Allen, renowned as a workaholic who expected the same of his players, was one of the first coaches to institute a 16-hour work day during the season, often sleeping at team headquarters to maximize his productivity. Though he kept in excellent shape, he often ate ice cream or peanut butter for meals because they were easy and quick. "I have told my team that God, family and football are the three most important things in their lives," said Allen. "During the season, football comes first. And we all should have some leisure. Leisure time is the five or six hours you sleep each night."

One of the NFL's legendary coaches, George Allen guided the fortunes of the Chicago Blitz. Spurned by the NFL since 1977, despite never suffering a losing record in 12 seasons as a head coach, the free-spending Allen jumped at the chance to take on the NFL. Photograph by Jim Turner, from author's collection.

A master motivator, Allen disdained young players and stocked his clubs with aging veterans, earning him the nickname "Trader George" for his tendency to trade draft picks for proven talent. The Rams had struggled through seven consecutive losing seasons before Allen took over in 1966 and won for five straight years. He was let go following the 1970 season after the Rams were unable to capture an NFL title, and moribund Washington immediately snapped him up. The Redskins had jumped above the .500 mark just once in the 15 years before Allen joined the franchise. His Washington teams won for seven straight years, and his time with the Redskins and the "Over the Hill Gang," had earned him national attention. In particular, Allen began his tenure in the Capitol by pulling off a 15-player/draft pick trade with his old employer, the Rams, in which he sent seven draft picks and one player to Los Angeles in exchange for six vets and one draft choice. The coach then traded that one pick to Green Bay for a veteran receiver. Those were just two of the 19 trades Allen would orchestrate that offseason to remake the Washington roster.

"When challenged for his decisions

and asked by, I recall, Warner Wolf, about the future prospects of a more senior lineup, my father replied, 'The future? This team hasn't been to the playoffs in over two decades and you're worried about the future? The Future is now!'" recalled Allen's son George during his father's Hall of Fame enshrinement ceremony in 2002. "And, indeed, it was, and they consistently won and made the playoffs."

Sensing ownership wanted to take back some control to keep spending in check Allen balked at a contract extension with Washington following the 1977 season and was subsequently fired. Instead he rejoined the Rams in 1978. The reunion did not go well, as Allen chafed under the authority of GM Don Klosterman and veteran players resented the coach's grueling work schedule. Rams owner Carroll Rosenbloom replaced him after just two preseason games.

"My experience with George Allen began in 1966 when he was hired to lead the Los Angeles Rams out of the depths of despair," said NFL great Deacon Jones at Allen's Hall of Fame induction ceremony. "I remember walking into the locker room that first morning and seeing little signs plastered all over the place. Little sayings that you might find pasted on a grammar school wall: one-liners that seemed ridiculous. The Rams had not had a winning season since 1958, and we needed a miracle worker not a schoolteacher. We all looked at each other and shrugged. But, then we met Coach Allen. And that was exactly what we got—a miracle worker of the utmost degree.

"He drove us to make the most of ourselves and he made us winners, finishing the season with an 8–6 record. And we learned to love those little sayings of George Allen. How did he do it? Teamwork, hard work, pride, determination, and competitive spirit. Every stop he made, every level of football he coached he had a winning season using these five points that I believe makes a champion."

"In sports, the only measure of success is victory," Allen said. "We must sacrifice everything to this end. The man who can accept defeat and take his salary without feeling guilty is a thief. I cannot think of a thing that this money can buy that a loser can enjoy—fancy cars, clothes, parties, and pretty women are only window dressing. Winning is the true goal. Only the winner's alive, the loser's dead whether he knows it or not."

"He was very friendly, an affable guy," said Diethrich. "He was a tremendously driven person, driven in the care of his own health, running every day. He was driven in his profession and always thinking about what he was doing in football. He was very intense, particularly at game time and leading up to game time. If it wasn't a good game, you could tell he was very concerned about it, but he was always a gentleman."

Allen had been out of coaching since his firing in Los Angeles and felt that he would not receive another shot in the National Football League, mostly because he had a bad habit of overspending and then burning bridges upon his departure. As a result, he was enthusiastic about the possibility of a new league from the start and had met with Raiders' owner Al Davis several times to get advice on how to make it a success. Allen, who joined fellow coach Fairbanks as a team minority owner, would fill another of the league's major markets as the field general of the Chicago Blitz.

The Oakland Invaders rewarded John Ralston for his contribution to the league's formation with their top job. Ralston had been a coach for more than two decades, beginning head coaching duties in 1959 with Utah State. He stayed there for four years before moving on to Stanford for nine years, where he led the school to two consecutive first place finishes in the Pacific Eight Conference in 1970 and 1971 and Rose Bowl victories after each of those campaigns. His success there led to an NFL job in 1972 with Denver, which had never finished a season with a winning record. Ralston's Broncos went 34–33–3 in five years with three winning seasons before he was replaced by Red Miller. Ralston had taken an assistant position with Philadelphia in 1978 before joining the front office of San Francisco for two years.

Dick Coury, who began his career as an assistant at Southern California in 1965, left an assistant job with the Philadelphia Eagles for the Boston Breakers. He was no stranger to the challenge of beginning from scratch, having started the football program at Fullerton State College in 1968 and 1969. He coached the new team the following two seasons, and then took a job with the Broncos for two years. Coury first cut his head coaching teeth in the WFL with the Portland Storm, where his team finished with a 7–12–1 mark. He left for Philadelphia in 1976 and worked there until the USFL called after the 1981 season. He was known as one of the nicest men in the game.

"I've been with every league that they've had, other than the World League [of American Football]," said the coach. "I've always wanted to be a head coach and felt like it was an opportunity for me to prove that I could be one. That was the main reason I did it. Coach Vermeil also encouraged me and had recommended me for several NFL jobs. On a couple of those, I came in a close second, if second is close. I thought it was a good opportunity for me, which it certainly turned out to be."

Likable NFL assistant coach Dick Coury guided the fortunes of the Boston Breakers, taking the no-name team to within a whisker of a playoff berth in 1983. Photograph by Jim Turner, from author's collection.

Two coaches from the Canadian Football League joined the fold. Ray Jauch left a successful stint with the Winnipeg Blue Bombers for the Washington Federals. He started out as an assistant at Iowa before landing a job north of the border with the Edmonton Eskimos in 1966. After four years as an assistant, he took over the reins of the Eskimos and led them to a Grey Cup title in 1975. Hugh Campbell replaced him in 1977, and after a year as the club's director of football operations, Jauch departed in 1978 for the top job in Winnipeg. Even though he was unable to win a title in five seasons with the Blue Bombers, he still exited the league as the circuit's fourth most successful coach ever.

"I knew John Ralston, and he contacted me about the league, wanting to know if I was interested," recalled Jauch. "I said, 'Yes, I would be.' The biggest problem I had up in Canada was that there was no retirement plan for the coaches. One thing I was looking forward to is seeing if they did enough for the coaches in the USFL, to where you could do your own retirement plan. That's the reason I went."

Campbell, who joined the Los Angeles Express, had dominated the Canadian league while with Edmonton. His squads had captured the CFL's last five Grey Cups, and he went 70–21–5 with the Eskimos, including a 12–1 mark in post-season action. Campbell played in the CFL from 1963–68 with the Saskatchewan Roughriders as a receiver before he started his sideline career in 1970 with Washington State. The next year, he took his first head job at Whitworth College, an NAIA school that had won just one game the prior two seasons. Over the next five years, Campbell's Whitworth team won two NAIA titles. He then took assistant positions with Saskatchewan and Winnipeg before taking over for Jauch at Edmonton.

Rollie Dotsch, the highly respected defensive coordinator of the Pittsburgh Steelers, grabbed the head job in Birmingham. At the collegiate level, Dotsch started his apprenticeship in 1958 at Northern Michigan University. He moved onto Colorado and Missouri and then landed his first NFL job with Green Bay for the 1971 season. He stayed with the Packers for four years before heading to New England and then Detroit. In 1978, he landed in Pittsburgh, where he took over one of the league's toughest defenses.

Former Oklahoma State boss and Atlanta Falcons assistant Jim Stanley joined the newly renamed Michigan Panthers. In 1973, following several college stints and one with Winnipeg of the CFL, he took over the top spot at Oklahoma State, where he compiled a 35–31–2 record in six seasons. After his tenure with the Cowboys, Stanley landed a job with the New York Giants for a year and then moved to the Atlanta Falcons, where he spent the 1980 to 1982 campaigns.

Rookie professional football head coach Steve Spurrier grabbed the reins of the Tampa Bay Bandits in 1983. The former University of Florida Heisman Trophy winner crafted a dangerous, unpredictable offensive scheme which gave league defenses nightmares. Photograph by Jim Turner, from author's collection.

No one took more flak from his fellow owners during the coaching search than Tampa Bay's John Bassett. After a long search, his Tampa Bay Bandits tabbed Duke offensive coordinator and 1966 Heisman Trophy winner Steve Spurrier as its first leader. "I walked into the guy's house. He's laid back. A TV set was on flickering because the tube was going out. On top of the TV set was the Heisman Trophy, and in front of it was a poodle named Bandit. There was no way out," Bassett explained at the press conference announcing Spurrier's hiring.

Spurrier won the 1966 Heisman as the University of Florida's quarterback so he would be no stranger to Tampa fans. He spent nine years on the playing field with the San Francisco 49ers, where he put together unremarkable numbers as a passer and occasional punter. San Francisco traded him to Tampa Bay, where he failed to win a game during the Buccaneers' first year of play. The experience was enough to convince him to give up playing and head for the sidelines. He served as an assistant at Florida and Georgia Tech prior to revitalizing Duke's fortunes.

Known for his innovative offensive strategies and wild play-calling, the 37-year-old Spurrier led the Duke offense from 1980 to 1982, helping the Blue Devils rank as high as 12th in the nation in offense, fifth in passing, at one point during his final year at the school. He felt the competitive imbalance of college football hurt the Duke program against larger schools, and welcomed the opportunity of a new league in which all teams were starting from square one. He also relished the chance to continue to refine his offensive play calling in an environment that not only allowed innovation but encouraged it.

"Word was out that there was a new pro league being started," recalled Spurrier. "I was the offensive coordinator at Duke in 1982, and Bugsy Engelberg, who was kind of a director of player personnel for the Bandits, only not called that, called me up. We were doing well at Duke, ranked high in the nation in offense. 'Bubba,' he said—he called everybody 'Bubba'—'Bubba, we want you to be our offensive coordinator.'

"I told him I was already an offensive coordinator. The next place I go, I want to be the head coach.

"John Bassett and some of his minority partners flew up to Durham, and I took them all out to a famous local steakhouse to talk. Mr. Bassett had a good time. After dinner I took them to meet my family and then drove them to the airport. He said on the way to the airport, 'We want you to be our head coach.' I agreed, and I flew down, not knowing what I would make, but we had the press conference and I was announced as the head coach.

"He offered me $50,000 for my first year. I told him I was thinking more like $75,000. Wouldn't $75,000 look better to others in the league than $50,000? I got him to move from $50,000 to $60,000. The next year he said, 'I'm going to take you up to $125,000.' I said, 'That'll be all right.'"

"Tampa's John Bassett was maybe the craftiest owner, and he had the experience of the WFL," added Ehrhart. "John always had a plan. He was one of the last guys to hire his coach. Once the summer of '82 came, David Dixon was not involved, not a participant in the league's activities. One of David's early mantras was that you had to hire big-time, name coaches, specifically coaches with NFL experience. He would get mad at John, and John would say, 'I've got this covered, I've got this covered.' Other owners would say, 'You have to force Bassett to hire a head coach.' That was sort of my role in interacting with all these people: calling and getting ready for league meetings, and we met quite often. John said, 'I know what I'm doing here. Tell them to go screw themselves. I've got a coach in mind, and he's going to be as good as anybody you've got.'

"Later he clued me in on it—he couldn't let anybody else know—but he'd already picked out Steve Spurrier who was still coaching at Duke, and he wanted to finish the year at Duke. So all through the fall of '82, while all these other guys were hustling putting teams together, thinking they're getting way ahead and that Tampa's going to be a big failure, John had quietly put together crafty veterans and young guys. John of course was holding the line dollar-wise. John was doing it very budget conscious, just as Ron Blanding was in Denver. Save our money for future battles. All along he had Spurrier, and as soon as the college season was over he announced his coach. But before that there was a lot of anxiety and a lot of people excited about if Bassett was ever going to hire a head coach."

"John Bassett was a sensational owner because he was a working owner," recalled Camera. "He worked his team; that was his major thrust. He put his other things aside, and he made the Tampa Bay Bandits the best run operation. And he ran it on the skinny.

He didn't have an enormous budget. He did marketing with gutsy ideas. He would review different things, and he came up with some great ideas. John Bassett worked it. He hired a coach nobody knew, Steve Spurrier. They knew who he was, but nobody knew he was a genius. He was 38 years old, I think, when he hired him. The quarterback John Reaves was probably 37, so he got guys that could play the game and were well-coached. He was an outstanding owner."

"Bassett was great," Trager added. "He understood sports and television. He was a very savvy guy who had learned a lot from when he was an owner in the World Football League. He was also a good mediator between the owners who didn't understand the issues as much. He was always able to explain the issues well."

Finally, the Arizona Wranglers grabbed ex–Atlanta assistant Doug Shively after negotiations failed with San Jose State's Jack Elway, BYU's LaVell Edwards, UCLA's Terry Donahue and Illinois' Mike White. He joined Michigan's Stanley in his flight from the Falcons. Stops at Virginia Tech, Kentucky, Clemson and North Carolina preceded his first pro assistant job with New Orleans under Hank Stram. Following two seasons there, in 1977 he went to Atlanta, where he coached under Leeman Bennett, a former college teammate at Kentucky.

"Jim Joseph was behind on getting a coach hired," remembered Ehrhart. "I remember trying to recommend some people. In fact, I remember flying down with Lou Saban, the former head coach of the Boston Patriots, Buffalo Bills and Denver Broncos, who at the time was president of the Yankees under George Steinbrenner. Lou and I flew out to California together so Joseph could interview him, but Joseph decided not to hire him."

The Philadelphia Stars had yet to play a game but already found themselves looking for their second head coach. George Perles had originally accepted the Stars' job in July 1982 but suddenly left for Michigan State in December when he was offered the opportunity to coach the Spartans. Offensive coordinator Joe Pendry was the only one of Perles' assistants who did not follow the coach. That left Peterson scrambling for a head coach a scant six weeks before training camp was to open.

"In late November or early December he called me in the middle of the night, and he was very upset, very emotional, and he said, 'Carl, I hate to do this to you and Myles, but I just got the offer that I always wanted for my whole life from my alma mater Michigan State,'" recalled Peterson of Perles' departure. "The athletic director there, Doug Weaver, had secretly gotten a hold of George after they fired Muddy Waters. George had interviewed for that job, but Muddy Waters had got it three or four years before. It's George's alma mater, and they told him, 'If you still want the job, it's yours.' George told them, 'I want it; I just have to call Carl and Myles.' He called me, and we met in the morning. He was very emotional, and he said, 'I hate to walk out and leave you less than a month before training camp and just a few short months before the inaugural season, but this is what I want.' I said, 'George, I've always believed you have to follow your heart. I'm obviously sorry to lose you, especially at this late date, but we'll make do. Go follow your dream.' We've always been friends since then, and I was always welcomed on his campus when he was the head coach there. He's a really delightful, great guy. He walked, and I had to begin the search for a new head coach."

Stars ownership was upset that the university neglected to ask the team's permission to talk with Perles, but they realized they couldn't stop the coach from taking his dream job. "I just wish this had been handled in a more gentlemanly fashion," team owner Tanenbaum said in *The Sporting News*. "There's confusion because of backdoor maneuvering." The Stars threatened MSU with legal action before the two parties settled out of court for $175,000.

"There was a meeting of team owners in July 1982 at which time we were each supposed to be there with a general manager, a head coach and a strong indication that we would be able to play in the top stadium in our respective cities," said Stars managing owner Myles Tanenbaum. "We went there with a general manager and a head coach, and we were the only team that had both of those. We also were well along in negotiations to play at Veterans Stadium in Philadelphia. No one else was anywhere near where we were. We were doing a lot of work over that summer and into the fall signing players.

"George, who was a very fine man, left because it was his life's ambition to coach at Michigan State, where he and his wife had met and went to school. He had one son at Michigan State and another at Kent State that they transferred as part of the inducement to get him to come. He had told us that he was going to tell the AD where to shove it because he had passed over George to get a different coach the previous time. But they really reached out to him, and George, notwithstanding the contract, succumbed, and he then told us that he was leaving. We urged him not to and to at least give us more time for public relations purposes, if nothing more. Here we hadn't even pumped up a ball, and we were losing our head coach so all the instant credibility went right out the window."

"The ownership came to me and asked, 'Who are you going to hire? What can we do? It's late in the game,'" remembered Peterson. "They threw out some names that I smiled at: Joe Paterno at Penn State, Sid Gillman who had coached for Dick Vermeil and was coaching for Dick when I left the Eagles. I said, 'I can certainly research those guys, but I think we need a younger guy who can accommodate a startup league. It's not all going to be perfect. He's got to be a teacher, a coach the players respect, and he's got to know the game.' I knew who I wanted. I interviewed a couple people, but the guy I wanted was Jim Mora."

"Jim was coaching at that time as the defensive coordinator of the New England Patriots, and they were in the playoffs. I guess it can be known now, but I called Jim and asked if he had an interest. He said, 'Well, I don't know. We're right in the middle of the playoffs. I probably want to wait until we get through.' I said, 'We need to talk about it now because we don't have a lot of time.' I clandestinely jumped on a plane and flew up to Boston and quietly met him late one night for dinner in the midst of him preparing for the playoffs. He had done a great job for New England. I think they had two shutouts that year under Ron Meyer, the head coach. The only thing I could get him to promise was that when they were finished with the playoffs, he would quickly fly down to Philadelphia and take a look at it, meet the ownership and that kind of thing.

"We were building offices down at Veterans Stadium at the time and until then we were in temporary offices down at the Kravco offices in King of Prussia. He said he would visit, and I had to wait another week when their season concluded. He did come down, and this was a guy I knew very well. We coached together for Dick Vermeil as assistant coaches at UCLA. I knew him before that when he was coaching at Colorado. When you're in college coaching, you run across other coaches all the time because you're competing for players. I had run across Jim many times when I was at UCLA and he was at Colorado. Then Dick hired him when Dick came in, so I knew Jim, knew his abilities. He left us after one year to take the defensive coordinator position with Don James at

Washington and then moved on to Seattle and then New England. I was very hopeful he would take the job.

"He came down, but he did not bring his wife Connie with him which was not a good sign. I thought, 'This is not good.' He looked around and I showed him everything in one day, where we were going. We were not even in our offices yet at Veterans Stadium, but they were being built. I took him through that; we put on our hard hats. I explained what we had and where we were. I put him on the plane, and he asked, 'How long do I have to make up my mind?' I said, 'Jim, we've got to go to the Senior Bowl in less than ten days, and then we've got to get ready to sign players to come to the USFL. You have to hire a new staff, and then we're going to training camp in Deland, Florida, at Stetson University the first week of February. You have about 24 hours.'

"He took off, and went home. I really thought he was going to call back and say no. But he called back and said, 'I'd like to do it. Let's do it.' I said, 'Terrific.' I knew Jim had other opportunities, certainly in the college profession. He had been recruited to be a head coach at Oregon, Hawaii and some other places, but his only head coaching experience was at his alma mater Occidental. I saw what kind of coach he was coaching our linebackers at UCLA and then after that. He had a great command of players and coaches, disciplinarian, but a guy who was a fine teacher, and that's what I needed because this was a new startup league."

"Carl was able to bring to me a slew of potential coaches whom we met with and interviewed," added Tanenbaum. "Each time, I would leave the interview scratching my head, saying, 'This guy sounds great. Why are we interviewing more?' Each time it would be the same thing until finally I said to Carl, 'Listen, don't ask me about any of these people because I can't help but think in terms of who would be most likely to help us sell tickets. Just get the best coach you can find, who you feel the most comfortable with.' He called me up about a week after that and said, 'Well, I have a coach for us.' I said, 'Gee, I'm so happy, I'm thrilled, I'm glad. We can really get to work now.' I was intentionally saying a lot of words without saying 'Who is he?' Carl finally asked, 'Don't you want to know who he is?' I replied that sooner or later I figured he was going to tell me. Carl said, 'Jim Mora.' Well, Jim was the only coach that I had not met in advance.

"Jim was a marvelous man with a great family and we had three incredibly great years together. He had a burden of putting together a coaching staff before heading down to Florida for our preseason training, and he just about got them all signed up in time for camp. He really put together a great staff."

"He was the glue that kept everything together," said running back David Riley. "He was no nonsense. He was sometimes hard to read, but you always knew where he was coming from. Time management: you knew if you were supposed to be out there for practice at 3:00, and you get there at 3:00, you're already late. His thing was that you need to be out there before. If practice started at 3:00, you need to be out there at 2:50 or 2:55. You don't get out there at 3:00.

"As far as strategy, Coach Mora worked our tails off. We hit almost every day all the way up to that Friday when we would get a little reprieve before we played on Saturday or Sunday. We were constantly taking it to each other every day."

The new head coach had just a couple of weeks to assemble a staff and compile a playbook before the start of training camp. Mora began coaching at his alma mater Occidental College in California from 1960 to 1963 and took over the head coaching duties for the following two seasons. He then joined up with Stanford, where he worked with the linebackers under John Ralston for three years. Mora next moved to Colorado for six seasons before joining Dick Vermeil at UCLA. It was there that the coach first met Peterson. Mora took over the defense at Washington in 1975, a stop which lasted three years. He jumped to the pros with Seattle in 1979 before serving with New England for one year.

"Carl and I had coached together at UCLA in 1974 and we had remained friends through the years," explained Mora. "I was a defensive coordinator for the New England Patriots during the 1982 season, and Carl contacted me late in the season to ask me if I would have an interest. I said, 'I might, I don't know.' After our season I went down there and spent a day or two with Carl, he offered me the job and I took it.

"In fact, when I went down there I probably was not leaning toward taking the job. But when I saw what they were doing and spent time with Carl, who I have a lot of respect for, and had a chance to see the situation, see the organization, what I considered to be being run in the first-class way, I felt it was something I wanted to get involved in."

"We went to the Senior Bowl, and I don't think we had the chance to look at one player," added Peterson. "We were in attached rooms, and he was in one room interviewing potential assistant coaches. I was in the other room interviewing potential players we would draft, college players playing in that game. Then we would switch places because he at least wanted to see the players, and I wanted to meet the potential coaches. He did a great job there, got almost all of his staff selected, and we zeroed in on some guys in the draft: Kelvin Bryant, Irv Eatman and Bart Oates."

Philadelphia enjoyed one advantage over several USFL teams in that Peterson not only had a good relationship with Eagles coach Dick Vermeil but had also spent the past five seasons as the director of player personnel in Philadelphia. He knew where to find talent, or as he put it, "I knew where the bodies were buried." The NFL team even directed some of its cuts over to Peterson, helping Philadelphia make up for the time it spent searching for a coach.

"Frankly, I had an inside source, Lynn Stiles, who replaced me as the director of player personnel with the Eagles," admitted Peterson. "Lynn and I kind of had an agreement that when he was getting ready to release a player, he'd let me know first so we'd kind of be standing in the parking lot waiting for that player as he was released to say, 'Hey, you didn't make it here in the NFL, but you have a great chance to start playing right away.' That really helped us, and we ended up with Chuck Commiskey and some other guys that way."

"We had the very best from the Canadian League with Ray Jauch and Hugh Campbell," Ehrhart said of the league's coaches. "You had some of the very best—George Allen, Chuck Fairbanks, Red Miller, John Ralston and Rollie Dotsch—out of the NFL. Then you had a young star who nobody knew at the time, Steve Spurrier. It was an amazing collection of quality people. You had the best talent in the coaching ranks as well as people who knew how to get players. Carl was a good example there. When George left, he didn't miss a beat."

The NFL was beginning to take notice. The new league had stripped them of several of their top assistant coaches, and with George Allen writing the checks for one of its teams, the USFL might take some players, too, even if the old coach's philosophy collided with some of the USFL's more fiscally-conservative members.

"I think it was a little bit of shock and a little bit of anger," said Dixon of the NFL's initial reaction. "Nobody likes competition, and we weren't direct competition, so I don't

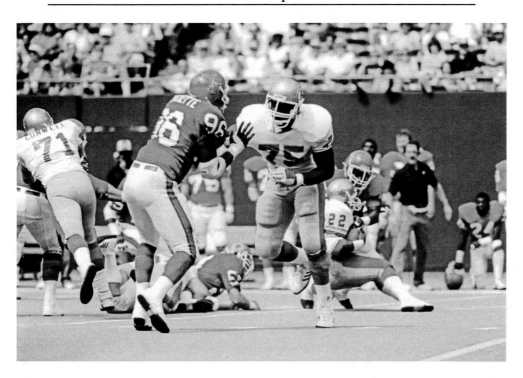

Offensive tackle Irv Eatman (75) became a key cog of a tough Stars team which frequently rolled over opponents with its running game. An eighth-round selection in the 1983 NFL Draft, Eatman would later play 11 NFL seasons after three years in the USFL. Photograph by Jim Turner, from author's collection.

think they took us that seriously or badly at first. Also I had very excellent relations with Pete Rozelle."

While most NFL league and team officials were reluctant to go on the record about their new competitor, several owners were already realizing the USFL's potential to cause them headaches. A Washington restaurateur hung a 6-foot-by-8-foot Federals logo in his restaurant as a favor to team owner Berl Bernhard, a regular customer. Unfortunately, Redskins' owner Jack Kent Cooke was another frequent customer, and he threatened to take away the restaurateur's RFK parking pass and stop eating at the establishment if it was not taken down. The owner relented and removed the bird.

As with other challengers before it, the USFL tinkered with pro football's rules for its games. The league would make the two-point conversion after a touchdown an option just as the AFL had in the 1960s. The USFL also adopted the college rule of stopping the clock on first downs to allow the chains to be reset but restricted its use to the final two minutes of each half. Officials further split defensive pass interference into two categories. Unintentional interference carried a 15-yard penalty while an intentional foul was brought to the spot of the infraction. The NFL had a spot of the foul penalty regardless of intent, while a maximum of 15 yards was awarded in college football. As in college ball, receivers would need just one foot in bounds to make a catch, not the two the NFL required. In addition, the USFL allowed kickers to use a one-inch tee on field goal and extra point attempts.

The Players

Slowly the players began to trickle in. Commissioner Simmons had no intention of engaging the established league in an expensive battle for star players. He reiterated the USFL's pledge to honor NFL contracts: "We will not go into a bidding war with the NFL for players," Simmons told the *Daily News*. The league would, however, go after a select number of free agents. "But if a player has a contract, it will be honored," added Simmons. "We will not be raiding. As we learned from the WFL, it would be disastrous."

That isn't to say that the USFL was uninterested in NFL players or vice versa. A bitter player's strike called after the second game of the 1982 campaign forced the cancellation of nearly half the regular season and had left many players eager to find an alternative to the established league, both for more jobs as well as leverage when negotiating contracts. Outside of a few skirmishes, football had avoided the ugly labor trouble that haunted baseball throughout its history, but that all changed with the 1982 strike. Angry players went back to work after 57 days, in time to finish out the season and play a hastily reworked playoff round but only after the season had been practically destroyed. Without another league to provide leverage, players had no alternative but to go back to work. Union leader Ed Garvey and future head of the NFLPA Gene Upshaw, who had taken a larger role in negotiations, along with the players welcomed an alternative with open arms.

"Coming out of that '82 strike, a lot of the NFL players were anxious to get bigger salaries and come play in a newer, more exciting league," said Ehrhart. "We were right in the middle of that strike. I was shuttling between some of the NFL Players' Association meetings when Rozelle and his guys were in huge fights with Gene, who was young then and a firebrand. It was really a knock-down, drag-out. I can remember running back and forth from our office, across Lexington Avenue to the players association hotel in the middle of the night, talking with some of the player reps whom I had known and represented. They were certainly very encouraging.

"The players and coaches realized that the creation of a new league would be great for the sport. It would give more opportunities and more positions, and give players who might not have received the opportunity, a shot. It would also, and this is a lot of what Garvey and his people were thinking, it would also create what they couldn't get through their own leverage: higher salaries. There was no question that there was a cooperative effort coming from the players and the coaches. The coaches and the players were all rooting for us to succeed and were helpful.

"Part of some of our early success was engendered by the players who wanted more jobs. They knew the value of a new league, that it would be helpful to them to put some pressure on salaries and create new opportunities. In my earlier life, I had represented a lot of players in the NFL as an attorney, so three or four or five of the player reps just happened to be old clients of mine. I can remember in the fall of '82 when we were just basically trying to get set up, hadn't even kicked off yet, we were meeting with a number of the NFL player reps and even having some talks about whether some players should even come over and join our league. Of course later a whole bunch of them did. We were creating another opportunity."

"We had a cap, a very important cap, on what you could spend on players," said Taubman. "And there were lots of players around who had been disappointed, but they were very competent, very capable players. There were lots of people interested in playing football. It wasn't a question of getting a team together. That wasn't a problem.

"Football is unique in the fact that it has all its teaching and training facilities without paying a dime for it. College football is the training ground, and that's a huge investment opportunity. And there's all kinds of players, thousands of players. Consequently, it's not a question of getting players. In any sport, that's the first thing."

"There are a lot of football players," agreed Peterson. "Our mantra was that there were probably 4,000 senior college football players each year in all divisions from the major universities to small colleges. There's a lot of talent out there that knows how to play the game of football. There's room for them and for two leagues."

"Our colleges and universities are producing so many quality players, but it's kind of a crapshoot of who gets to play in the NFL," added Keller. "The difference between a player who makes it and one who doesn't is a coach's opinion, and the difference between being scouted and not scouted is a scout's opinion. He has a bad day or he has a hangover and goes out to watch practice, and he doesn't like anybody, doesn't even like himself, then he goes back and reports, 'There are no prospects at Arkansas' or 'There are no prospects at Michigan State.' Teams don't have time to go back and figure out if he's right or not; they take his word for it. His word becomes a self-fulfilling prophecy because then a guy doesn't get scouted, never gets a chance unless some other team really likes him."

"Peter Hadhazy set up an operation at the league level that was phenomenal," furthered Camera. "Every procedure, everything ever done, we got total respect. The Canadian Football League worked with us on wires and transfers on contracts, and even the NFL did the same thing. If a player was released from the NFL, we first had to get that release from the NFL before we signed him. It was really a very good cooperation that came about because of Peter's professionalism.

"Remember, the NFL had its strike. They had run into a real collective bargaining problem. So we had players showing up at our 52 Vanderbilt office, saying 'If I don't play, I want to sign with you guys. Will you allow me to have a half-season contract?' That was all played out in the media, but we would never do that because that's not the way leagues coexist."

On August 5, 1982, UCLA All-American tight end Tim Wrightman became the first player to sign with the USFL, inking a contract with the Blitz. His rights had been held by Jim Joseph's Phoenix franchise, but Allen signed him to spite the Bears, who had drafted the player. Just a week later, Chicago landed former Baltimore Colts and Detroit Lions quarterback Greg Landry. Boston held the passer's rights, but Allen made him a better offer. The coach later worked out a trade with the Boston front office for the rights to four players on the Chicago negotiating list.

"I told George I'd like to be able to talk with my players before he does," Boston's Dick Coury cracked to the *Washington Post*. "Rozelle couldn't control George for 14 years. If we can somehow do it, we'll already be one step up on the NFL."

"There were a few dustups," laughed Ehrhart. "I remember getting a few calls saying, 'George Allen is tampering with our players.' I got some angry phone calls at night saying the Chicago Blitz talked to people they weren't supposed to. We had that territorial allocation which was very smart, but Chicago was the team that people were most after because they had 'talked to' their players.

"George was smart. I don't think people have given him enough credit for how smart he was. He had an amazing memory and could recall players and coaches from any generation of football: past, present and future. He was always a step out front of everybody, both in a positive way and maybe in pushing the envelope, too. He was way ahead of everybody. He was signing the first players. We never knew whether he was signing them and giving them extra money, but his son Bruce was also there with him. George and Bruce were probably most out front signing players. Their NFL experience made them a powerhouse right off the bat. Together George and his son Bruce were a force.

"Our suspicion was that there was a lot of contact between the Allens and other teams' protected players, where if we'd been in a more established situation, there would have been penalties. But these players were not under contract to anybody. There was no question that there were an awful lot of people blurring the lines, saying, 'I know somebody that knows this guy. We're new. Let's just get him into the league,' rather than worrying about if his rights belonged to somebody else. We were in a fast-track getting ready for camp that first year, starting from zero, trying to get rosters built. It smoothed out in years two and three. By then you had established rosters and teams were not looking to stock from zero to 50. They already had established rosters, so it wasn't the kind of problem it was the first year. Agents were part of that whole process. An agent would be trying to get a player signed whose rights belonged to Birmingham, for example, and he'd go to George Allen to promote his player and try to get a salary out of one team and then force the other to try to trade the territorial rights.

"I tell you there was a lot of gray lines versus fudging when someone would come in and say, 'This guy is going to go to the NFL unless he can sign with our team.' Another team would say, 'How would you know that? You've been tampering with my team.' Then it would get to, 'Bullshit, screw you.' There were a lot of these supposed friendly kinds of communications that led to some very heated confrontations regarding tampering. Of course, we were going so fast in so little time we didn't have the ability to have investigators dig into it. I can remember trying to keep the peace and try to figure out a way to make things work and maintain a competitive balance."

Allen, Diethrich and the Blitz were quickly making football people aware of the USFL's potential to shake things up, even if sometimes it was the league's own teams. Some were beginning to remember the words of Washington Redskins owner and former Allen employer Edward Bennett Williams: "George was given an unlimited budget—and he exceeded it." The old coach left no stone unturned in his search for players and personnel and Diethrich had opened his pocketbook to make it happen.

"I so much admired Dr. Diethrich, a famed heart surgeon," said Ehrhart. "He was very proactive, and almost on a daily basis he'd call me in New York and touch base as to what was going on. I'd always be very nervous when he'd call me because he would be in the operating room. I'd say, 'Ted, I can't be talking to you now; you've got open heart surgery going on.' He'd say, 'No, no, Steve, you have to understand, heart surgery is like a football game. There's a lot of time when I have to go to the bench and some of the other doctors are in there. I've got my mask on and my gloves, but I've got a microphone here. It's just like a football game. In a four- or five-hour operation, there's a lot of time going back to the huddle and time in between plays, so I have time to talk in between surgical procedures.' I still was so nervous. It got to the point that when my secretary would tell me, 'Dr. Diethrich's on the phone,' the first thing I'd ask is, 'Are you in the operating room?' He'd say, 'Yes, but I'll tell you when I have to get back into the heart.' I'd say, 'Then I'm not talking to you.' It scared the crap out of me."

"Teddy was a great guy. He was wonderful, but he was more a fan than he was an owner," added Camera. "He would rather be the doctor on the sidelines or the guy assistant coaching with George Allen. He was in love with George Allen, and rightfully so. George was easy and knew his way around. But George got what he wanted, and they figured out every way to not circumvent the rules but to run on a line. Bruce Allen was sensational. If there was something he could find a way to do, he would do it. Hadhazy and Bruce would fight every day, and then they'd be at the bar together the next time everybody came into town for a meeting. The good doctor was a good man who was very supportive of the league, but his whole point of reference came from George."

"He was a good football man from the standpoint of X's and O's and calling the plays, but not a good businessman," Diethrich said of Allen. "He was the only coach in football who could out-spend an unlimited budget. He had no concept about the economics. The person who was responsible for the economics was his son Bruce.

"I found out a lot of it after the fact. Bruce didn't come to me and say, 'Well, doc, we're going to get Trumaine Johnson, and we're going to pay this for him. We're going to get Stan White, and going to pay too much for him.' He didn't do that.

"Coach would say, 'Doctor, I really think that if we can get this guy, he would make a big difference for us. If we could get this end from UCLA, take him from the Bears, it will help us.' Half the time I thought that he wanted to get him from the Bears just to show off Papa Bear. Most of the time, I heard about it afterwards."

"I was considered one of the hotshots in personnel development in the United States Football League, so I was always dealing with Bruce and with George," recalled Michigan Panthers personnel man Mike Keller. "They wanted a player we had, a fellow named Tom Piette. Tom was a Michigan State guy; I think he was a center. He made our team that first year as a backup. We liked him; he was a good team player. The guys on the team liked him and he fit his role; never complained and did what was asked of him. George and Bruce, a lot of the time they would do it in tandem; they would both be on the line with me. They wanted to trade for Tom Piette. For some reason they thought he was going to be the greatest center who had ever played. I talked with them and said, 'Let me think about it. Let me talk to the coach.' I pitched it to Jim Stanley, and he thought the same thing I did: Tom was a good team guy, and we thought, 'Tom's not going to help them. He's better off playing his role, staying with us, and down the road, he might get a chance to play.' We didn't think he was as good as George and Bruce thought. They had offered like a third round pick, and I said, 'No, no.'

"We ended up trading Tom Piette to the Chicago Blitz for eight 1984 draft choices and a couple of active players! All for this guy who was never going to play. I finally said to Stanley, 'As much as we like Tom Piette … all these draft choices, we can't turn it down.' It was an unbelievable trade. I've never seen anything like it before or since. The more we said, 'No,' the more they wanted him. That was George Allen. George was so paranoid. He figured the reason we wanted this backup guy was because he was so good he had to have him. We finally said, 'Okay, you can have him, and we'll take your draft picks and players.' It was the most unbelievable trade in the history of pro football."

"I was actually the first case of tampering in the USFL," explained Jim Foster, who worked in the Arizona Wranglers' front office at the time. "It wasn't with a player, it was with me. While I was still in the NFL with NFL Properties, I had interviewed with the Chicago Blitz, Arizona Wranglers and Birmingham Stallions. All three of those teams made offers to me. I liked Chicago a lot, but the deal didn't look as good to me at the time because I knew it was going to be a real tough marketing situation. I knew [Stallions president and general manager] Jerry Sklar in Birmingham, and I thought I'd go to work down there. At the last minute, I asked my wife, 'Which way do you want to go?' and she said, 'Frankly if I had my druthers, we'd go to Arizona.' So I said, 'Okay, fine.'

"I took the job with Arizona, and I'd been there about two weeks. I remember the call distinctly because my wife was at home unpacking some boxes in the bedroom. The call came from Bruce Allen, saying that they really wanted me to come to Chicago, and I said, 'That's just not possible, guys, because I took the job in Arizona.' He said, 'Yeah, we know. We're calling you at your house there. We need a really good marketing guy in here, and you're the guy. We really want you to reconsider staying in Phoenix because we want you to come to Chicago.' I said that I just got to Phoenix, and I couldn't do that. And Bruce Allen goes, 'Everybody has their price. What's your price?' I said I made a commitment to the Arizona Wranglers, and he goes, 'We can deal with that. We can take care of that. We'll just sit down and talk to them because it's very important that Chicago have a strong franchise. If we can take care of that, what would it cost to get you to come here?' Well, I threw out an outrageous number which was quite a bit more than I was getting paid by Arizona. And Allen said, 'We can do it. We'll pay you that. If we can make the arrangements with the Wranglers, will you come to Chicago?' I said that I had to think about it. I got off the phone and told my wife and she dropped the box she was holding on the floor. They called me back a couple hours later, and I said that if something could be worked out with Arizona I'd go.

"The next day the owner of Arizona called, just steamed, and asked me why I was going to Chicago. After he asked me what the hell was going on, I explained the whole situation, and he told me, 'They already announced that you're going to Chicago.' I said that that wasn't fair. To make a long story short, the league office fined Chicago for tampering with me as an employee and I didn't move there. What ended up happening was that Arizona matched the salary to keep me in Phoenix even though they didn't have to."

Foster notwithstanding, one thing was for sure: George Allen was living up to his reputation as a great recruiter. The Blitz's opening day roster would be laden with seasoned NFL veterans mixed in with high-priced rookies.

Other experienced pros who jumped to the new league included quarterback Mike Livingston from Kansas City (Boston), tight end Raymond Chester from Oakland (Oakland) and defensive end Cedrick Hardman from San Francisco (Oakland) who would also become an assistant coach with the Invaders.

Kicker Tim Mazzetti, otherwise known as the "kicking bartender," had been working at an ABC affiliate since being cut by the Atlanta Falcons. He was most famous for connecting on five field goals in a 15–7 Atlanta win over the Rams on *Monday Night Football*. Mazzetti had retired after turning down an opportunity with the Cleveland Browns but jumped at the chance to sign on with the Breakers.

"The only reason I semi-retired is that I refused to play in Cleveland," he explained. "I got traded to Cleveland at the end of the '81 season, and I really did not want to move my roots. I had been in Atlanta for a while, I owned a nightclub, and I was doing sports casting and all that good stuff. The trade kind of pulled the rug out from underneath my feet, and I was too young and naïve to know any better. I remember meeting with Cleveland's Art Modell and Sam Rutigliano, who was the head coach at the time. I said, 'Really, my heart's not in it.' They said, 'Son, this is the NFL. You don't play for us, you don't play.' That was the wrong thing to say to a 26-year-old, so I said, 'Well, then I guess I'm not going to play.' I went back to Atlanta and went to work for WSB, the ABC affiliate, fulltime.

"Then in '82 was when the announcement of this startup USFL came along. I was enjoying and making a living doing television, but I knew it wasn't something I was going to do for the rest of my life. I just didn't have the passion for being a reporter or a news guy for sports. I love sports, but I liked playing them; I didn't know if I wanted to cover them. I was actually looking at what I was going to do next. One option was to go back to school and get my MBA. Another option was to maybe swallow my pride and come out of retirement. At the time I was at the peak of my career. Instead, this league came out. I was literally sitting around the newsroom one afternoon with about 30 minutes to kill when I picked up the phone and called the league office in New York, told them I was a reporter for the ABC affiliate in Atlanta, said I was doing a story on the USFL and asked when I could get some information. Back then there was no email, so they faxed me the information including the names of the football teams, coaches and directors of player personnel along with phone numbers. So over the ensuing couple of weeks, I made some phone calls.

"I decided I didn't want to go anywhere on the west coast, I wanted to stay in the East. I basically went down five or six east coast teams and started dialing for dollars. It was pretty funny. I called one of the teams, I think it was the Birmingham Stallions, and the director of player personnel came on the phone. Because I had played in Atlanta, I had a very highly recognized name in that area, including Alabama. The guy got on the phone, and I said, 'This is Tim Mazzetti,' and he said, 'Look, I don't appreciate these kinds of prank calls,' and hung up on me. Before I could get a word out and tell him I was thinking about coming out of retirement, he hung up on me.

"I ended up calling Boston, and at the time my brother worked for the Bank of Boston and was living there. I was close to my older brother, and I thought Boston wouldn't be a bad place to play. So I called them up and talked to the director of player personnel, Tom Marino, a good old Italian boy. He recognized my name, most people did because I led the league and was All-Pro the year before, and a lot of people had questioned why I hadn't gone back and played. And because I was doing some television work, I was still pretty visible. He gets on the phone and says, 'Is this Mazzetti?' I answered, 'Yes,' and he said, 'I can't believe it. I have to get somebody on the phone that you'll know.' It was Dick Coury. He was one of the assistant coaches under Dick Vermeil back when I had first tried out for the NFL in 1978 for the Philadelphia Eagles before I landed with Atlanta. I always took a liking to Dick. He was a very likable guy, and he gets on the phone. I said, 'Hey, Dick, I didn't know you were the head coach there.' He said, 'Yeah, I hear you're thinking about coming out of retirement.' I said, 'Yes, I'm thinking about it,' and he said, 'Well, you have to come play for us.' I didn't make any more phone calls after that."

Not a fan of the Falcons' penny-pinching ways, Mazzetti found Boston's management easy to deal with.

"One of the issues I'd always had with Atlanta from the first day I got there was they were one of the stingiest teams in the NFL," he said. "They just ran a very, very poor football operation, which explains why they basically had a losing organization for much of their franchise history, other than literally the three or four years I happened to play there. They ended up firing or trading a bunch of us because they wanted to cut payroll. We had lost to Dallas in the second round of the playoffs and were this close to going to the Super Bowl, and they fired half the people to cut payroll by half a million, and they just didn't care. The way they ran that business was very, very poor, and I had always had problems. The two times I'd negotiated a contract with them, I had issues with them, once when I had an agent and once on my own. It would always go down to the last minute, and they were always haggling over everything. It was very painful, and there was no loyalty. There was no desire to want to be a part of that team because of the way the front office was managed.

"Fast forward to the Breakers, and the three owners were Randy Vataha, Bob Caporale, who was a sports agent and very well-respected attorney for a major law firm in Boston, and their primary investor who probably put up five or ten million bucks, George Matthews. I actually went to training camp with the New England Patriots in 1977, six years earlier and because I had played, I obviously knew Randy. I had also played racquetball with him in an NFL racquetball tournament, so Randy and I knew each other. Bob was a sweetheart. The negotiation of our contract lasted all of 30 minutes."

"The initial player contracts were for relatively low salaries, signing guys who were good, quality players but nobody had signed the hugely expensive players," recalled Ehrhart of the initial player contracts. "Chicago had the most expensive player when they had signed Tim Wrightman, the very first contract that had come in. Most of the contracts were pretty rational, pretty reasonable, and we were getting some pretty good rosters built. At that time there was some very good cooperation from the NFL to encourage these people like Carl and Hadhazy, George, John and Red, all of these guys who had great relationships and core groups in the NFL. They were relying on them and calling them to see who could play."

"At that time during the year there was nothing going on in sports," furthered player agent Jerry Argovitz. "People who are football fans are football fans. I thought it was a new league and had a new beginning and an opportunity to do things that maybe the other league wasn't doing. And I felt really, really good that there was enough players to go around that could fill a league. Every player is not six foot five and runs a 40 in 4.44 seconds. I mean there were a lot of players who just missed the cut because they didn't match the stamp that the NFL put on a player prior to even drafting him. So there was a need for job opportunities for the players and this league furnished that. Not just players, personnel as far as coaches, assistant coaches, general managers; I just thought it was a great opportunity for the fans, too."

On January 4 and 5, the USFL held its first draft in New York's Grand Hyatt Hotel, a facility owned by Donald Trump, who was still keeping a close eye on the circuit. The early date gave the league a jump on the NFL, whose draft was not held until April. In response, the older league had tried to move its draft to February, but the NFL Players' Association kept them from doing so. A total of 600 players, 50 per team, were drafted in the USFL territorial and open drafts, the highest one-year total ever for a professional football league. The selection meeting took 15 hours and 41 minutes over two days to complete. The L.A. Express made Pittsburgh quarterback Dan Marino a worthy first selection and New Mexico tackle Don Elliott an equally worthy last pick. Elliott was cut before the season began.

Simmons had pioneered NFL draft coverage on ESPN, so he knew how to present the proceedings to the media. In addition, his former colleagues at ESPN carried highlights on *SportsCenter*, ensuring the USFL draft received national attention.

The other 312 choices were taken in the territorial draft, the USFL's way of ensuring that local stars would stay where they had the greatest drawing power. Each team was allowed to make 26 picks from an assigned group of schools. For instance, Oakland was allotted choices from the University of California, Stanford, San Jose State, Fresno State and Cal Poly San Luis Obispo. The system had its share of irregularities as well. Because of weak local schools, for instance, Boston had Nebraska included in its reserved universities, and New Jersey saw Tennessee and Oklahoma included on its list.

"In our situation, we had Boston College, Boston University and Harvard," remembered Breakers coach Dick Coury. "Most teams had two or three big-name football colleges, and we didn't have any that first year. What they did to make up for that was they gave us Nebraska, which helped, thank God. We were able to get some good players from Nebraska, guys who didn't make it in the NFL or just wanted to play in the USFL, and that helped us a lot. In those days, Boston College was playing pretty good, but not great. Boston University was average, and Yale and Harvard were good programs but Ivy League football."

"I was on the competition committee, and it was not my idea, but we had a territorial draft which allowed you to draft players from the colleges and universities closest to you," Peterson recalled. "We had Pittsburgh, Penn State, Temple University and Lehigh plus one kind of at large school with North Carolina, which was a great stroke for us with Kelvin Bryant and William Fuller. Then we had an open draft. Then the other part of it was that we had NFL teams from which we could take players who had been released, obviously starting with the Eagles and Steelers. I had a lot of knowledge about those players."

"I was a senior at Alabama," recalled receiver Joey Jones, a Birmingham draftee. "I had been told I might get drafted in the second or third round of the NFL draft. I was a smaller player, and the Stallions just seemed like a good fit. I was able to stay in Alabama, and if I went to the NFL, I didn't know where I'd go."

"By and large it worked fairly well, especially with an Anthony Carter going to Michigan and Bassett maybe the best at getting Florida-based people," Ehrhart added. "He had that with his coach, a former Florida Heisman Trophy winner, bringing together Florida people. It didn't work perfectly because New York, for instance, didn't have the kind of high-powered college teams in the area that other teams did. Kent Hull was a former Mississippi State center, but he ended up being a protected player by the Generals. Back in the spring when I was still a lawyer for the competition committee when we were having the meetings and deciding which universities would be associated with which teams, we knew we had to make some stretches to help distribute talent evenly. It's a natural for Denver: there's Colorado and Colorado State and schools like that. It was not a natural for places like New York where you didn't have the kind of college atmosphere around there. When Mississippi State was assigned to them, there was a hue and cry asking how Mississippi State was assigned to the Generals. There was always a suspicion that the Generals had a line on Kent Hull. Smart football people knew if you had a great center; that went a long way to building your team. Generally, it worked well, though there was a blurring. George Allen was one of the guys who always said, 'Let's get people in the league. Let's not worry if they're in our territory or not.'"

Pro football rookies embraced the hundreds of new opportunities provided by the USFL, just as their veteran counterparts did.

"I was quarterback at LSU, and I finished in the fall of '82," said Alan Risher, an Arizona draftee. "I was an all-SEC quarterback and actually played in the Senior Bowl in Mobile for the South. The USFL draft happened about a week after the Senior Bowl, and I got drafted by the Wranglers in the 15th round, which doesn't sound all that great, but I don't know what the criteria was to draft anybody. The first year there were 12 teams and they had about a 30-round draft to help the teams put together a roster. I got caught off guard because I didn't know what the USFL was, to be quite frank about it. I didn't have an agent so I had to hunt me down somebody to represent me. When I got back from the Senior Bowl the pro scouts in the NFL were telling me I was going to be an eighth to thirteenth round pick if I was picked at all. I wasn't considered a tremendous NFL prospect at the time, so I opted obviously to check this USFL situation out."

"There was talk in the fall of '82, which was my senior year in college, that they were going to start a new spring league, so all of us that had aspirations of being pro football players were happy because that would be another outlet," added Sean Landeta, who had been chosen by Philadelphia. "You had Canada, you had the NFL, now maybe here was another league so my thoughts were to play in the NFL, that's what I was shooting for. The first week of January the USFL has their draft and I was drafted, and I knew this was a league that was going to play at least two or three years. We worked out a contract with them and I decided to play there because I thought if I went to that league and I punted well, the NFL might look at me a little bit better than a kid coming from a Division II school who punted well, who maybe they thought could play or couldn't. I felt if I went to a pro league and performed well I wouldn't be Sean Landeta from Towson State, I'd be Sean Landeta from the USFL, another pro league, so that was my thinking at the time."

Signing those who were either going to be low draft picks or who might go undrafted altogether was one thing, signing big names was quite another. Many observers, considering the USFL's high draft picks nothing but a publicity stunt, openly questioned the league's ability to sign the talent it had drafted, especially in light of the World Football League's failure to ink top college names not even a decade earlier. Not since 1966, the last year in which the AFL and NFL drafted independently of one another, did a rival league compete with the NFL for talent to any great degree.

"We had the ongoing strong position that we were going to have this salary cap," explained Ehrhart. "Then there was pressure beginning to say we had to have a couple of stars. There was a lot of discussion through that fall, all very positive with camaraderie about it, as to whether we would have a 'wild card,' so that you would have a salary cap but then you would have one or two player exemptions to the salary cap for purposes of marketing star power, so to speak. We made the considered decision that in order to separate ourselves from being minor league, we had to get some great players out of the NFL or out of college."

"You couldn't tell each team they could only spend this and that, so it really came down to the fact that New York City was New York City and in order to get a media contract and to get bigger dollars from ESPN and ABC you needed to have some big names," agreed Gould. "We needed marquee names that were going to drive the ratings. It was all about television ratings. you're going to get enough fans in the stadiums on the days that you had your game, but it was all about the ratings."

"I had spoken to Dave Dixon who was the one who gave birth to the league," said Argovitz. "I believe he had called me and initiated a phone call; and we talked. I set up a meeting with the other owners to explain to them how essential the young college players were to the league, and that they needed to have some marquee players. All we were looking for was some competitive bidding.

"I convinced the owners of the USFL that in order to have a successful league they needed to sign some marquee players in the skill positions. And they needed to take advantage of signing undergraduates; giving them an opportunity to get a payday in professional football, eliminating the risk of injury if you will. They also had an advantage because they drafted three months before the NFL drafted so if they acted swiftly they could go out and get a few marquee players and a lot of the other players would not be drafted highly in the NFL, and you could get those players signed. And you had to have a budget beyond the set budget for a couple players."

The USFL quickly answered the doubters with a rash of big signings. Chicago again led the way by inking bruising running back Tim Spencer from Ohio State just two days after the draft. Spencer, who was the second overall selection right after Marino, finished his career as Ohio State's second all-time leading rusher after compiling 1,371 yards his senior season. Less than a week later the Washington Federals came to terms with the fourth pick, running back Craig James out of Southern Methodist. James and Eric Dickerson had formed the Mustangs' overpowering "Pony Express" backfield, and Dick-

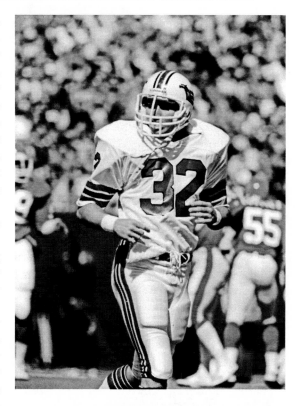

Running back Craig James joined the Washington Federals in 1983 as a rookie out of SMU. Injuries hampered two seasons in Washington, and he joined the New England Patriots in 1984. Photograph by Jim Turner, from author's collection.

erson was also a first-round selection, by the Arizona Wranglers. James had been named an all-Southwest Conference player three consecutive years and had set a Holiday Bowl record from 225 yards rushing in 1980.

"It was half a million dollars a year guaranteed," said James. "I knew I was slotted in the first round, and that was probably twice what I was gonna make as a first rounder in the NFL, and it was guaranteed money. I think I entered pro football as at that time, the highest paid player ever, you know Herschel came along a few weeks later and he trumped my deal, but you know I can just remember hearing from a lot of the NFL guys, 'Boy this guy has done nothing and he's getting all this money,' so what the heck."

With the ink not yet dry on James's deal, quarterback Reggie Collier from Southern Mississippi joined the Birmingham Stallions fold. Collier was the first quarterback in NCAA Division I history to run and pass for 1,000 yards in the same season, but was most well-known to Birmingham fans for leading his team to a 38–29 upset of Alabama the year before. Dangerous Grambling wide receiver Trumaine Johnson, a two-time Southwest Athletic Conference Most Valuable Player, became the second first-rounder to enlist with the Blitz, and the Panthers captured the tenth overall selection in Wisconsin defensive back David Greenwood. The Stars signed top pick, offensive tackle Irv Eatman from UCLA, who had played on both sides of the ball in his college days. All told, USFL clubs eventually signed seven of their top 12 choices. Johnson, Collier, Spencer and James were all projected as sure first-rounders in the upcoming NFL draft, while Greenwood and Eatman were thought to be solid second-round selections. Other high picks such as Marino, Dickerson and Arkansas defensive lineman Billy Ray Smith seriously considered USFL offers before choosing to wait for the NFL draft.

The Stars added to their offensive line with second round pick Bart Oates, a center from Brigham Young. Chicago continued to sign its picks, getting defensive back Frank Minnifield out of Louisville in the third round. That same round, the Panthers secured the services of quarterback Bobby Hebert of Northwest Louisiana. After narrowly missing out on Marino, the Express tabbed their triggerman in round five with Tom Ramsey from UCLA. With their very next pick, the Express took Ramsey's college teammate, receiver JoJo Townsell.

"What we did is we went out and we had the sign-ability factor," explained Michigan's Keller. "I put together a whole bunch of criteria for our coaches and scouts to consider in signing a player. It was not the usual criteria; it was a whole new batch of criteria because we were a rival league. We had to have a whole list of compelling reasons for a guy to sign with us.

"The key part of it was that we had to convince him that it was in his best interest not to wait for the NFL draft. We did our draft in February, because we were going to training camp in March. We told him he couldn't dilly-dally around until April for the NFL draft and still be in our league.

"Bobby Hebert became a very, very good player, but he was one of those guys who was projected to be down the road a little bit. He was not projected to be a high draft pick. We went in and told him this was his opportunity to get his foot into pro football, and down the road there probably would be opportunities for him to move on to the National Football League. We tried to use that. We think you're a good player, and we think that what you have to do is to continue to play and continue to develop and you will be an NFL player at some point, but right now you're not. That's kind of the way we went with Bobby Hebert who went to Northwest Louisiana State. He was not ready for the NFL probably at that time. He was a big, strong kid, but he had his weaknesses."

Hebert was an interesting case from the beginning. No one argued that he had athletic potential, but he had been injured for several games during his junior and senior seasons. One of the reasons he signed with the USFL rather than waiting for the NFL draft was that he had been married in college and needed the cash.

"I was on food stamps for like four months," remembered Hebert. "Northwestern Louisiana wasn't like going to a big university where they slip money under the table to help you."

"I looked at Michigan when they took me in the draft. I was like, 'What are the guarantees?' Here is the Michigan Panthers, they're guaranteeing me $250,000. Now the country boy that I was, you know it's the old saying that a bird in the hand is better than two in the bush. And here I had a daughter my senior year in college so I had a wife and kid to support, so you know I basically tell [Cowboys VP] Gil Brandt, 'Well, what can you guarantee me?' 'We don't do that.' I told my wife Teresa, 'We're going up to Michigan. I don't know if there are any Cajuns up there, but that's where we are heading.'"

The territorial part of the draft included some important agreements as well. Philadelphia got running back Kelvin Bryant out of North Carolina, considered one of the best backs in the country to run behind Eatman and Oates.

"We got to training camp, and there was like 12 running backs and two fullbacks," remembered Stars running back David Riley. "I was one of the tailbacks, and I was competing for the position along with Allen Harvin, who played at Cincinnati. They drafted Kelvin, and when he came in we all watched him work out. The next day at practice there were like four tailbacks and 12 fullbacks. He could flat out do it. After the practice, I told our running backs coach Jim Skipper, 'I want to try my luck at fullback.' Everybody knew that Kelvin was going to start."

"The territorial draft gave us exclusive rights to him, so no one else in our league could bid on him," Peterson said of Bryant. "But now we're talking about if they want to wait until the NFL draft in late April or do they want to come to this new league, the USFL, and play real games right now and get your pro career started early. Obviously money talks also. We had to be competitive. We actually had a salary cap which George Allen and some guys immediately went right past. It was a salesman's job, and Jim did a great job and everybody in the organization did a great job trying to convince them that this is the best place to start their pro football careers."

Michigan gave the Cajun Hebert an athletic target and kept wide receiver Anthony Carter close to home, inking the explosive Wolverine just before the season began. The elusive Carter had been named the Big Ten's MVP his senior season, came in fourth in the Heisman voting and finished his college career as Michigan's all-time leading receiver. He had been projected to be an NFL first round selection.

"Each team in the USFL had reserved five colleges or universities, and they had first shot at all those players," added Keller. "For instance, we had Michigan, Michigan State, Eastern, Western and Central Michigan. We scouted those territorial schools very hard because you had to have at least two players from each school, but you were able to reserve over 20 players. Obviously we got most of our players from Michigan and Michigan State, but had we had to have some Central, Western and Eastern Michigan players."

The Wranglers tabbed Arizona tight end Mark Keel, the Panthers picked up Albanian-born Central Michigan kicker Novo Bojovic, the Invaders chose California linebacker Gary Plummer, and the Bandits got Florida A&M tackle Nate Newton as other territorial selections.

If the NFL had been dubious of its newest challenge, it now knew the USFL meant business. Several front office people lamented the talent that their new competitor had sucked out of their upcoming draft. "We were asleep as a league," Dick Steinberg, the director of player personnel for the New England Patriots, told the *Boston Globe*'s Will McDonough. "We should never have let this happen."

"Our hands are tied," Washington Redskins General Manager Bobby Beathard told *Lou Sahadi's Pro Football*. "It's frustrating. If we'd have gone head-to-head with them this year, I'm sure we would've won our share of players because we have more ammunition.

"We would've found out a lot of things about the new league. But this way [with the NFL's late April draft], we're handcuffed. We can only sit around and wait for the draft and there's no telling how many more will be gone by then."

"This was going to be the strongest draft since I was in the business," New York Giants personnel boss Tom Boisture told McDonough. "But now the USFL knocked off some pretty good people on us. This draft will still be good, but not as great as it was going to be." Furthermore, many players were waiting to see offers from the NFL before deciding on the new league. The USFL was not done yet.

Player agents were ecstatic over their new bargaining chip.

"We were very aware from the inception, and I should say excited because the state of the NFL at that point was there was absolutely no freedom for players," agent Leigh Steinberg said. "From leaving campus, a team would have exclusive draft rights, and a player would have no choice but to sign with the team that drafted him until the end of his contract. Then he'd have no choice but to re-sign with the team for a 10 percent raise with an option clause or to retire. Teams had total and complete power, and players had no options. There had been an alternative league in 1974–75 when I began my career, the World Football League, and I knew what the competition from another league would mean to the players, which is more jobs and an aggressive acceleration in player salaries because of competition so there was a fair degree of excitement and anticipation of the start of this league."

"Once the USFL came to life, the player's salaries went up drastically because now for the first time the sports agent had an opportunity to negotiate with another team," recalled Argovitz. "Players had options. The seasoned players, the veteran players had options. The young players had options. Prior to the USFL coming into being there were no options in the NFL. The NFL was a total and complete monopoly. If you didn't want to take the contract they offered you, like [Detroit Lions GM] Russ Thomas told me one time, 'Go north; go to Canada.' So you had no options. You either took the contract they offered you or you didn't play, sat out."

"We always had discussions about salary caps," recalled Simmons. "We always had those who wanted one and those who didn't want one. Those who didn't want one said, 'We're in legal jeopardy if we have a salary cap.' It would simply come down to who has the most money. If I'm sitting with a team with limited resources, I'd want a salary cap. If I'm Alfred Taubman and have all the money in the world, I don't care, just go get me the best players you can and let me win. Those were our salary cap discussions. Was it legal? Was it illegal? The guys who felt that it was illegal, they were very comfortable because they could cite various legal precedents that would make salary caps illegal because it would be a restraint of this or that. I'm not a lawyer, and I couldn't tell you, but we had lawyers and they weren't sure. The only way to do it was to test it, and I don't think they had the guts to do that."

"I would say that 50 percent of the teams adhered to the salary guidelines and the other 50 percent did not," estimated Camera. "There were six teams: Tampa Bay adhered to it, Denver adhered to it. Arizona did, too. Michigan was off the target. Philadelphia was close. Boston adhered to it. New Jersey had adhered to it, so I'd say 50 percent of the teams did. Then we established a rule where you could have one or two superstars that you wanted to sign, and we started to see guys sign players that could give real marketing assistance. We allowed that. Then something like 80 percent were within the cap. It was a problem. It was free enterprise. It's America. Maybe it's changing nowadays, but it was just a guideline. Owners were going to do their best. They thought, 'I don't want parity, I want to win!' Don't forget, it was written that all teams should be equal: the best thing was to have every team being .500. The NFL was doing that way ahead, but guys wanted to win. The greatest thing for an owner is to go into a restaurant and for them to say, 'Mr. Tanenbaum, we have your table here,' because he's the owner of a team."

Not every player enjoyed an immediate windfall. "I was actually making more money at Xerox then I was with the Bandits my first year," said Tampa Bay receiver Eric Truvillion. "So I took a pay cut to go play pro football. That's crazy nowadays but that's what was happening."

The Best College Football Player in the Country

By far the biggest name to sign with the new league would have to wait until just a couple of weeks before the season started. It was then that the USFL shocked the pro football world by announcing that running back Herschel Walker of Georgia, the reigning Heisman Trophy winner, had joined the New Jersey Generals. His contract, rumored to be for three years and a then astounding $3.9 million, made the runner the highest paid player in the nation. Before the USFL had played a game, it had captured the best player in all of college football and would feature him in the country's largest media market. The deal immediately drew comparisons to the signing of Joe Namath by the American Football League's New York Jets nearly two decades earlier.

A three-time All-American at Georgia, Walker ran up an incredible 5,259 yards, the third highest total in NCAA history, and he had compiled those numbers in only three seasons. In his 33 games at the university, he averaged 159 yards per game on 5.3 yards per carry, and scored 52 touchdowns. He finished his collegiate career with ten NCAA records, at times looking like a man among boys, and had led Georgia to a national title in his freshman year. Despite nursing a broken thumb early in his final college campaign, Walker ran for 1,752 yards and 17 touchdowns with 55 runs of ten yards or more. The star runner's fame had taken another leap forward just a few weeks earlier when he had pulled a 67-year-old woman out of an overturned wrecked car while on a jog.

Walker's contract caused a stir for another reason. He was still a junior in college and thus ineligible for the NFL draft for another year. According to NFL rules, league teams could not sign underclassmen who had not exhausted their eligibility. The restriction was one of the NFL's earliest rules, instituted to prevent its teams from raiding college rosters and earning the wrath of sports writers and fans alike at a time when college football was much more popular than the pro game. The restriction also gave college coaches a sense of security in that their players had to wait until they exhausted their college eligibility. Essentially, players had to play collegiate football for free for four years before they could think about earning a living with their skills.

"I looked into challenging the system after my junior year," SMU tailback Eric Dickerson told *Sports Illustrated.* "The lawyers tell you court settlements could take three years, and by that time you're out of college anyway."

Unbeknownst to USFL brass, Argovitz had visited Walker on more than one occasion in an effort to woo him to the league. While the agent denied his ulterior motive was to sign the runner as a client, Walker's contract opened the possibility of other underclassmen joining the USFL.

"Jerry Argovitz called me from Houston and said, 'There's a real opportunity to get Herschel Walker into the league,' and I asked, 'How would we ever do that?'" remembered Blitz owner Ted Diethrich who owned Walker's USFL rights. "I was in Aspen at Christmas time, right before Georgia's Sugar Bowl appearance in New Orleans. A Lear jet picked me up and we went to Athens, Georgia, and met with Herschel and then we made arrangements a couple days before the Sugar Bowl to meet with him and his family. I remember driving outside New Orleans to some hotel he was staying in with his parents. We wanted to get him in the league, and Jerry was intent on that. He said, 'We get him in the league, and we're really going to catapult this thing.'

"I had really mixed feelings about it. I didn't appreciate the impact of it when we were doing it. I didn't think this was going to open the floodgates and change the whole

New Jersey Generals running back Herschel Walker lines up in the backfield. Photograph by Jim Turner, from author's collection.

atmosphere. I'll admit I was a little naïve about it, but I liked Herschel. He was a gentleman."

Though the NFL's prohibition against underclassmen had not seen a real court test, other leagues had seen similar rules challenged. The NBA, for instance, had required that all players wait four years after their high school class graduated before entering the league. After leaving college as a sophomore, Spencer Haywood joined the rival American Basketball Association for a season before attempting to join the NBA's Seattle SuperSonics in 1970, a year before he was eligible by NBA rules. He and Sonics owner Sam Schulman battled the league all the way to the Supreme Court, which sided with Haywood. A settlement opened the door for underclassmen to play in the NBA.

Neither hockey nor baseball required players to complete any time in college. It was routine for Major League Baseball teams to draft players right out of high school.

Walker's deal caused a major uproar in the football world, though, and several college coaches threatened to bar USFL personnel from their campuses in retaliation. The NFL, already reeling after losing several of college football's top stars to the upstart league, seized the opportunity to lambaste the USFL at every opportunity for stealing a player from college.

"With him being an underclassman, it had never happened before," recalled Generals public relations director Kevin MacConnell. "There were no such rules as far as I could remember to get out early. So for the USFL, it was kind of a catch 22. At the one side we did need someone like Herschel to help boost the league and get the league the exposure that it probably needed at that point. It was getting good exposure, but nothing like once Herschel got there, so I think it was a catch 22, because were we doing the right thing?

I remember the night it happened going with Chet Simmons to be interviewed for *Nightline*, and that was the whole controversy. What you did the NFL never dreamed of doing. It wasn't the right thing to do by some people's thought but at the same time for our league, and to get done what we needed to get done, it was probably the best thing that could happen for us for that time."

"In fact, we were told to stay off the Georgia campus," remembered Gould. "I was ordered off. I never went on the campus, but it was such a brazen move to take an underclassman in those days that you were hung in effigy. I mean this guy was the greatest walking college football player and we took him out of school before his senior year, which of course became the trend."

"There was no set law that said he couldn't sign to play with us; it was just the NFL philosophy," explained Camera. "The colleges are a minor league for the NFL, and that's how they treated it. You got into college, you were drafted by a team in pecking order, and you negotiated with that team and couldn't sign with anybody else. That's illegal; it's restraint of trade, but they got away with it for years. We just said, 'Why not? If a kid wants to come out and play, we'll pay.'"

"There was nothing that said you couldn't sign him," furthered Argovitz. "We didn't have league bylaws that we made up that we couldn't sign undergraduate players. The NFL had that because they had a minor league system and their minor league system was collegiate football. So in order to not disrupt the system, they made a rule that you couldn't sign a player until his class graduated. So even though some of these kids were financially disabled and didn't have the means to go out and buy shoes or clothes themselves but were great college football players, they had to continue playing college football or wait until their class graduated to have an opportunity to ever get paid. And that was totally unfair. It was a deal set up by the NFL and their relationship with collegiate football. It worked for each of them but certainly didn't work for the young players."

"There was only one Herschel Walker. Herschel was a freak of nature. He was big, he was handsome, he was chiseled. He was intelligent, he was smart, he was caring. He came from a great family, and he wanted an opportunity. He proved himself in college, he proved it his freshman year and sophomore year, he's everything in college football. He was a walking endorsement for college football. And the opportunity for this league to sign a Herschel Walker, it was just a marketing coup."

Though college coaches and the NFL decried the signing as evidence the USFL was preying on college football players, the reality was quite different. Concerned that another injury might end his pro career before it even began, Herschel Walker approached the USFL almost immediately after his final college game, a loss in the 1983 Sugar Bowl.

"They came to us, we didn't go to them," said Simmons. "His lawyer came and told us they wanted Herschel to sign with the USFL. The NFL would not touch him because he hadn't graduated, and if we didn't sign him they would sue us, just that was it, sue us. Here's little old us, we've got more money than God up there with all of our owners, but nobody wants to be sued, so we sent Steve Ehrhart who was in the league office to go get Herschel and find out what's going on."

"Herschel definitely approached us. We didn't go seek him," confirmed Ehrhart who became the point man in Walker's negotiations with the league. "In addition to the people around him, his family and his advisors, he very much personally felt that because of a running back's longevity issues, because he'd had an injury, because he'd already won the Heisman, that it was time for him to earn a living, much like the decisions that are made today. I remember getting the call shortly after our draft from Jack Manton who said he was his agent. I said, 'College players aren't even supposed to have agents.' He said, 'Herschel is ready to sign. He's gonna play. He's won the Heisman and had an injury. Basketball allows underclassmen to sign, and he wants to sign in your league.' Manton may have said he was a friend of the family at the time, but that's one reason I didn't want to talk to him, I wanted to make sure. From a legal point of view I was certainly well aware of the Spencer Haywood case in the NBA.

"Herschel then called me himself and said that very same thing. He told me outright their plan. They wanted to go to New York, because of the analogy of Joe Namath in New York as the star of the AFL 20 years earlier. It was always geared toward the Generals. Our plan initially was not to sign undergraduates, but when Herschel made the legal case and the personal case, we didn't have much of a choice.

"After Herschel approached us and said he wanted to sign, we debated it internally and looked at the legal issues, talked to ABC, and then made the decision that we could not turn our back on him and just say, 'No, we're not going to do anything.' Walter Duncan and I flew down and met with Herschel in Georgia. We then spent a lot of time with him, his future wife Cindy and Jack Manton, and then worked out the contract over a period of several weeks. It did include an interest in an oil well. It was with the New Jersey Generals, so Walter Duncan had the final say-so. It was Walter's money. Herschel was personally involved along with his agent and his family."

At times, Walker appeared reluctant to finalize the deal, though he was anxious to start earning a living. The Heisman Trophy winner met with Generals owner Duncan on February 17, less than three weeks before New Jersey's opener, for nearly the entire day before signing a contract that night. The Generals owner told Walker that he had until 7 a.m. the next morning to change his mind. The running back returned just two hours later, saying he had indeed changed his mind. At a news conference the following day, Walker denied doing anything to jeopardize his eligibility. His coach, Vince Dooley, also denied the existence of any contract with the USFL.

According to NCAA President Dr. John Toner, Walker would have certainly been ineligible to return to Georgia as soon as he signed the contract even if it contained a clause allowing him to back out. Further, Manton's initial overtures to the USFL on behalf of the runner may have been enough to end Walker's eligibility even before the contract was signed. While the Georgia faculty appeared eager to turn a blind eye to any facts that would make Walker ineligible, the NCAA may not have followed suit.

"Dooley knew all about it," Camera said. "Dooley knew Herschel was getting out. He knew that Herschel had just won the Heisman, and he didn't want to stay for the next year. Dooley knew totally about it. The money was good."

"It was the Georgia people who then pressured Herschel not to sign it," added Ehrhart. "I don't think it was that Herschel got cold feet. I think there was enormous pressure on Herschel by everybody at Georgia to stay and play that senior year. Over that period of time, Herschel had called and said that he felt that he wasn't ready to make the move. I said, 'Herschel, it's whatever you want to do. You came to us.'

"I remember the press conference when Dooley said that there had never been a contract signed, but that was not true. There were several hundred media there; people from all over the country were there because it had been leaking out that Herschel may have signed. Had he signed? Had he not signed? Was he coming back?

"Herschel had signed the contract, and the Georgia administration was aware of that. It was a huge national story. The Georgia people denied that he had ever signed a contract, but I had a copy of the contract. I didn't say anything to anybody. We were just going back about our business because we had a lot to do. We were getting ready for training camps to open; this was January of '83, leaking into February. I went back to New York, and then one of the Georgia assistant coaches called and said, 'Herschel really does want to sign. It's just that he's being pressured so much.' He then asked if I would fly down to meet some of the Georgia boosters in Palm Beach, Florida. I asked what it was all about, and he said I just need to go down there.

"I went down there to meet with them, and these Georgia boosters took the position that they were trying to get us to back off, and they offered a bribe to have us pull back the offer so Herschel would have to stay at Georgia. They said, 'Well, if you do this we'll pay you money and then we'll also buy the Jacksonville franchise.' We were already into expansion mode, so there was already publicity about us expanding into Jacksonville. I refused any of that stuff, saying, 'This is a decision for Herschel, not for people like yourselves: wealthy Georgia alumni.' I remember calling Walter Duncan and saying, 'I've never been offered a bribe before, but I think this is happening now.'

"We took the position that we had an agreement with Herschel, but this was not something that we were trying to push, so if Herschel didn't want to come play, that's fine, but we felt that Herschel did want to come. It was the Georgia interests from the administration to the football coach to the alumni that wanted to keep him there. He was the hottest property in football."

The USFL also faced unexpected, last minute competition for Walker's services.

"Then the Dallas Cowboys got into the act," added Ehrhart. "Even though the NFL claimed they were not meeting with him, the Dallas people had an intermediary that offered him more money to sign with the Cowboys because Dallas always coveted him. They were very careful to have cutouts in between, because Rozelle would never have allowed it. Everybody knew that the NFL rule at this time which prohibited signing players with remaining eligibility was kind of an artificial thing. Without having the players association involved, the opinions were all the same: unless you have a collective bargaining unit that gives you protection by bargaining as a unit, an individual had a right to earn a living and you can't just bar him from earning his living. It's illegal restraint of the right to work to bar a young man from playing. Despite the NFL rule, the Cowboys made an offer to Jack Manton. The Cowboys got into it, and I give credit to Herschel because Herschel later said he had made a commitment to the USFL, and he finally decided after all this back-and-forth stuff that he was going to honor the original deal. So the same terms and conditions he had signed earlier were the terms under which he eventually ended up reporting to the Generals training camp."

Though the USFL knew that getting Walker into its stable was a coup of previously unimaginable proportions, it had also found itself in a precarious legal position, making the decision to sign him even easier.

"There was another case that came up almost the same time," recalled Ehrhart. "There was a punter from Arizona, Bob Boris. His lawyer was also rattling the sabers, saying, 'You can't deny a guy the right to play.' He was much lower profile, but we looked at it and we did have owners' meetings about the fact. Most of the owners realized that there was no legal authority to say that we could deny any young player the right to earn a living. That was the accurate legal position. I remember talking to David Stern from the NBA, and we compared notes about the NBA's policy. The NBA had worked out a program with their players association after they had lost the Spencer Haywood case. We knew and I think most of the owners got their own independent counsel, too, and they knew you run the risk of turning down a player who obviously has the ability to play by barring him from his right to earn a living. Then there was talk that there would be a class action suit filed. The insulation that other more-established leagues had was that they had player associations that collectively bargained their rights away, but we were in an especially vulnerable legal position because we did not have a players collective bargaining agreement in place because there was no players association.

"We did look at it legally, and we determined that we were not in a position to turn down a player. It was such a special circumstance that we weren't in a position to say no. It was certainly debated among the ownership. In the final analysis everybody agreed on both fronts: number one, from a legal point of view it was the right thing to bring him into the league, and number two, it made sense to have a Walker wild card exception to the salary cap. Then everybody kept talking about the Namath-Jets analogy; if we just had lower-paid players that did not have name recognition, then we needed to spur not only the recognition of the league but also television ratings and ticket buyers."

"Walter Duncan, who was the owner of the New Jersey Generals, said to me at a luncheon, 'I want to bounce something off you. We're thinking about signing Herschel Walker. What do you think?'" recalled ABC's Jim Spence. "I counseled him against it. I said, 'Walter, I think it's a big mistake. you're going to have the colleges up in arms in terms of future former college players coming to the USFL. Colleges are just going to be furious.' He listened carefully, 'I understand what you're saying.' Then, as we know, he went ahead and signed Herschel. Later on he told me, 'I remember that conversation we had. I just wanted to let you know we felt we were subject to major litigation if we did not sign him.'"

Unknown at the time, Walker had nixed a three-year, $1.5 million deal from the Canadian Football League a couple of years earlier, showing that he had his eyes on an early professional career before the USFL was even an option.

"I talked to Herschel before his collegiate career was over, not as his agent," said Argovitz. "Through an attorney I learned he was thinking about going to Canada after his sophomore year, and I urged Herschel to stay in college another year because a new league was coming and at that point, in my opinion, the new league would be interested in signing Herschel. I said to go ahead and finish his junior year and see what the opportunity was. I met with his mother and father and encouraged them because they were concerned if Herschel got hurt, it could end his career and all his financial opportunities would be dissipated. I convinced Herschel to stay in college another year and sure enough the USFL was born."

The NFL claimed it would not follow suit and sign underclassmen. Dallas Cowboys coach Tom Landry, among others, chided the USFL for interfering in the education of college players. He may not have realized that just 29 percent of NFL players held degrees.

"That was probably the end of the benign relationship with the NFL," Ehrhart said of the Walker signing. "Because the Cowboys, although it was never publicly reported and they would probably deny it to this day, were smart enough to recognize that he was getting away and thought, 'Hey, we better be there.' I'm sure Jack Manton if he was under a polygraph would say that he got an offer from the Cowboys for more money than we signed him for in the USFL. I think the Cowboys and Tex Schramm had probably been in contact with Rozelle, and they were worried about letting a great player like that get out of the league. Then the NFL all of a sudden said, 'Holy shit, we have a competitor here now.' Instead of sending over the players who got cut and being happy with the league because we were signing players they had to cut, that started the competition."

The USFL promised that it would keep its hands off other underclassmen, and the college coaches grudgingly withdrew their threats to bar USFL scouts from their campuses. Even though the league maintained that Walker was an exception, they continued to claim that if an underclassman was to sue the league over the rule, the USFL would surely lose the case. Many believed that disgruntled Oklahoma star running back Marcus Dupree would be the player to bring such a challenge. The league sought the NCAA's help in defending the rule but never received any assistance.

With Walker now in the USFL fold, the league had its first true superstar, and media and fans alike both took notice. Following the Walker announcement, New Jersey sold more than 15,000 season tickets, more than 10,000 of them of them in the first couple of weeks after he was signed.

"The Herschel Walker signing was just incredible," recalled MacConnell. "I'm 24 years old, and there had been a rumor he was going to sign with the Generals. Then it kind of all went away. We practiced one morning at the University of Central Florida, and I came back to do some interviews and get some work done before going back in the afternoon. The secretary said, 'Hey, somebody called … there's something about Herschel Walker coming to play for us….' She wasn't a football fan, so she didn't know how big this was. One thing led to another and the phone started ringing off the hook. I was young, and I did the worst thing a PR director could do: I literally took the phone off the hook. I just could not keep up with all the calls. On top of that, there was a sports editors convention in Orlando that week. We're at a hotel where there's a big pool and courtyard in a U-shape with the pool and patio in the middle. I walk in, and all of a sudden there's like 30 guys walking toward me, and the phone is still ringing off the hook. Two SIDs from Central Florida who were great guys and wanted to help me, they can't get to me. This is 1983, there's no cellphones.

"Before I knew it, the thing was just like a wildfire, just unbelievable. Eventually we did confirm it. Chet Simmons came in and we set it up for him to be on *Nightline*. The next day Howard Cosell wanted to get Chuck Fairbanks and Herschel Walker on *Sports-Beat*. At one point I'm on the phone, and I have Howard Cosell on hold, Bryant Gumbel on hold, because he wanted him on *The Today Show*, and David Hartman from ABC. I'm a 24-year-old kid, and I had all three of these guys who wanted to get him first. Then we go to the press conference, and its 250 people, just a zoo.

"Chuck Fairbanks was a great guy, good to me both personally and professionally, but he was not one for a lot of words. He just wanted to get him on the field and get going. From a league standpoint, it was the biggest hit for us as we were trying to sell tickets so we had to do a press conference. We do it, and it's just a zoo. I had never seen anything like it. The league even sent in their PR guy, George McFadden, who had been a PR director for the Broncos and 49ers, and he said the same thing, 'I've never seen anything like this.'

"Then Herschel goes on the field and practices. In the Citrus Bowl, they had set up for Keith Jackson to interview Herschel, and ABC was sending a helicopter for him. Irv Cross from CBS's *NFL Today* is there, and he wants to get him first. He's standing right next to me, and I said, 'Look, Irv, I want to help you, but I can't. ABC is doing our games, and they get him first. You can't get him.' He said, 'Well, I'm going to get him as he's going to the helicopter.' There was a producer for ABC Sports there, and he said, 'Don't you dare let that man get to him.' Practice ends, and Chuck talks to the team. I'm hovering right by Herschel, and I grab him, and I mean shoulder pads and all, and say, 'We gotta go.' He starts jogging out to the helicopter, and so does Irv Cross. I'm like, 'Herschel, take off! Irv Cross can't do this.' Herschel being the polite guy that he is, wants to talk to this man who he's seen on TV. He doesn't know. I'm like, 'Herschel, you can't.' So now the four of us, including the ABC producer, are sprinting to the helicopter, and I don't have to tell you who came in last. Herschel gets in, and the ABC producer pushes me in after him. I end up laying on Walter Duncan's lap, the owner of the Generals, and Herschel's lap. All that just to get him out of there. Irv Cross never got him.

"From that point on it got better, but every place we went we'd have a separate press conference for Herschel. So whether we were in Michigan or Los Angeles, we'd have a special one for him. It got so crazy, so many people wanted him, at camps we set aside an hour twice a week that if you wanted to talk to Herschel, you could. Once we went on the road, every town we went into we'd have a press conference at the hotel when we first got there."

"The day Herschel arrived with the Generals in Orlando where they were training for the first season, I'll never forget that," said team radio announcer Charley Steiner. "He arrives in a helicopter with the owner of the Generals in the first year who was an oil billionaire named J. Walter Duncan, and he paid a bushel full of money for Herschel, and this was the arrival of a star. At that point he was the best college football player in the country who was leaving school a year early to seek fame and fortune in the USFL, and doesn't every kid want to aspire to that? Herschel did! And there was this sense … of something was happening. And again Herschel was one of those guys that was big enough, even at 20, to go around life with one name. So here was Herschel Walker and his arrival immediately made the Generals the Yankees of the USFL. We were the big kids on the block. Hey, this was gonna be fun."

"That was great," exclaimed Spence, eager to utilize the star's popularity on ABC telecasts. "We had confidence in the league obviously. We needed programming in the spring so we were bullish on it, though not without concerns. We also thought that because it was football, the ownership group was solid and we were going to do our best to promote it and produce the telecasts as effectively as we could, it had a good chance even before the Walker signing. That certainly was a nice shot in the arm at the beginning."

"Out of the whole thing, Herschel handled himself with a lot of class," added Ehrhart. "He was in a very difficult position. It turned out to be the right decision."

Others feared what the signing might do to the already compromised salary structure. USFL owners had previously decided to allow one or two "wild card" players per team who wouldn't count against the suggested budget for player salaries. With Walker in the fold, the temptation for others to keep up with the Generals would be great.

"They went out and signed Herschel Walker. There went your salary cap," Simmons said. "I could have all the gentlemen's agreements in the world, but if I see a player I want and I have the money to buy him, I'm going out and getting him and screw the rest of you. It's not an easy business, and it wasn't and it won't be.

"It was an owners decision. Generally, I was in favor of signing one very big name, and this was the big name that came along that the NFL wouldn't touch under their laws. We were threatened by his representatives that he would challenge us if we didn't take him. What right did you have not to give this talented young man the opportunity to make a living? Go fight that in Congress. It's very difficult. So we went ahead, and they decided what team he should go to, which was obvious he should go to the biggest media market in the country and that was New York. And away we went."

"There was some opposition," remembered Oakland owner Taube. "I think I was opposed to it because I felt we weren't being true to our operating plan which was to develop our own stars, and we weren't really giving it a chance to happen. I was also concerned about the break in the compensation agreements that came about as the result of paying Herschel Walker a lot more money than any of our other players would be getting. There are a lot of reasons from my standpoint why I did not think that was a good thing. I was in the minority, and the majority of owners decided it was a good thing and we went forward with it."

"The words 'instant credibility' were used in a variety of circumstances," said Philadelphia owner Myles Tanenbaum. "Getting a TV contract will give us instant credibility. Getting Herschel Walker signed will give us instant credibility. Getting a lot of other things will give us instant credibility. We had more instant credibility than you can shake a stick at.

"Herschel Walker was a two-time all–American, and I think that it really meant more to the NFL perhaps than it did to the public at large. Obviously, his was a name that was very visible, highly recognized because he received the Heisman Trophy. Plus, he's a fine young man. Getting him to opt to play in the USFL was a significant factor in providing us with exposure and some kind of credibility."

"I think John Bassett, of course, was raising hell, saying, 'This is totally terrible. We've exceeded the salary cap. This is the worst thing to happen,'" said Ehrhart. "John later told me he was glad Herschel was in the league, and he was just stirring everything up so that when the Generals came to Tampa, there would be an extra 10,000 people there. I think that's the way most people felt. It was such a coup that Herschel Walker, the best player in college football, would choose the USFL before we even kicked off. The credibility, the ticket sales, the television ratings, and with him a class guy, it was an unbeatable situation, though there was a lot of consternation about what would be the impact on salaries."

Even those within the USFL's ranks initially opposed to the signing came to see it as a positive for the league, particularly when they saw the amount of media attention it generated for their teams. Concerns about salary escalation were somewhat allayed by the fact that the league had made a collective decision.

"The Herschel Walker signing was really not a break in the agreement," explained Taube, one of the league's most fiscally conservative owners. "What happened there was the league was getting a lot of flak from the media about so-called no-name players. The media, for a lot of reasons, did not want the USFL to succeed, I think partly because they were being influenced by the relationships they had with the NFL and they didn't want to see those relationships negatively impacted in any way by being good soldiers with respect to the USFL. They used almost any opportunity they could to criticize the league, and the most obvious and easiest criticism was that we had all these players that nobody ever heard of. So the league as a matter of league policy decided to go after the most visible football player in American at that time and that was Herschel Walker. That was a collective act. The signing was not outside our agreements, but it was essentially an expansion of the agreement."

"Now if I'm another owner I say, 'Okay, I've got to go do something. I've got to put somebody up, maybe not as high up as Herschel Walker, but I have to get somebody that people will recognize. I also have to get players who will defend against this caliber of player,'" added Simmons. "So it started, the battle for who's going to win what, how much you're going to buy, who you're going to buy and how much you're going to spend."

The burden for actually paying Walker fell on Generals owner J. Walter Duncan, who along with his head coach Chuck Fairbanks had been two of the leading opponents of signing underclassmen. Realizing that its television partners would benefit from the signing as much as the league, USFL officials made a push to get help with Walker's contract.

"We contacted ABC, and ABC was very much in favor, saying, 'Absolutely, Herschel Walker is the number one football name in America,'" recalled Ehrhart. "Remember, he had saved an accident victim by lifting a car off the trapped person. He was the quintessential football player, NFL or college football, so they were excited. They said, 'Yes, we need you to sign him.' Everybody looked back to 20 years ago when Joe Namath signed with the New York Jets. That was just going to be an unbelievable kind of thing that nobody could count on. A league that a lot of people in the country hadn't even heard of by that time would all of a sudden get the biggest name in football, pro or college. It was never debated where he would go.

"During that period after that, I had contacted Walter Duncan, and we talked about it. I was with Chet when he called ABC, and they said, 'Absolutely, you need to do that.' We did talk about whether ABC would help contribute to that, and they said, 'No, but you need to sign him.' We asked ABC because there was talk back in the Namath era that's what had happened with NBC, so we asked ABC, but I can remember Jim Spence saying that it would be great and very much encouraged us to do it but said there would be no extra money coming from ABC. There was some suggestion that ABC should put some money into the pot to do that, and there was some debate on if it should be a league-funded deal. Somebody might have raised a quick question about that, but there was no long debate about that. In the final analysis Walter Duncan covered 100 percent of it, no contribution by any other owner."

"Walter signed Herschel which he didn't want to do," explained Camera. "He didn't believe in signing kids out of school, but he was talked into it for the sake of the league and he did it. We needed New York to have an image, and Duncan stepped up. A lot of the other owners didn't want to step up, and Duncan didn't agree with signing a kid out of school, but he put his money where his mouth was."

"Duncan was a sweet, nice guy," said Simmons. "I think he'd do most anything for the league, and I think he recognized the importance of having a Herschel Walker play in New York, or the stadium across the river."

"He was very analytical, a very smart and wonderful guy," added Ehrhart. "He recognized that in the New York media market, you had to grab their attention, and by signing him it would energize the marketplace. In retrospect, with the huge rush of season tickets he did pay for himself."

In one other note surrounding the deal that seemed to be of minor importance, Walker's agreement made the rights to the Generals' first pick, running back/receiver Gary Anderson of Arkansas, expendable so they were later traded to Tampa Bay. The Bandits began negotiations with him and his agent Jerry Argovitz.

Walker's signing and the USFL's deals with other high draft choices not only thinned out the NFL draft, they also created a ripple effect across all NFL salaries. "The rookies this year will be the highest paid group as a whole, in history," said agent Tony Agnone in *Lou Sahadi's Pro Football* magazine. "That's usually the case anyway, but this year, the increase is going to be dramatic, perhaps as much as 20 percent.

"I think things are going to get a little bit crazy next year. Players will no longer have that unknown out there. They'll have a choice.

"I think the USFL went in with expectations that they were going to have to compete with the NFL, no matter what anyone tells you. It's a similar product at a different time and they're trying to get the best possible player, just like the NFL is trying to get the best possible player."

"We could calculate what the NFL had paid in draftee salaries in 1982," agreed agent Leigh Steinberg who represented tackle Irv Eatman. "1983 was the first year of feeling the effect of the leverage. It manifested in two ways. First, with the players who signed there. I knew what a first round offensive lineman was being offered in 1983, and Irv Eatman signed for a large premium. It manifested also in leverage. For instance, Tony Eason was drafted in the 1983 draft by the New England Patriots but he was also sought after by the Boston Breakers. He signed with New England for a major premium over what players had received in 1982."

While the smoke from the Walker affair cleared, players with pro experience continued to sign on with the USFL. Former Buccaneers backup quarterback Chuck Fusina caught on with Philadelphia as did San Diego receiver Scott Fitzkee. Quarterback Johnnie Walton, who had last played for the Eagles in 1979, became the first signal caller for the Boston Breakers, joining former coach Dick Coury. He had led the WFL in passing in that circuit's shortened 1975 season when he was with the San Antonio Wings. Linebacker Stan White became the first player to leave an NFL team for the new league when he bolted the Detroit Lions for the Blitz after his contract in Detroit ran out. Former Minnesota Vikings' running back Chuck Foreman had a brief stint with the Express before being cut. Center Tom Banks, an All-Pro with the St. Louis Cardinals, moved over to the Birmingham Stallions, and receiver Frank Lockett, cut from three NFL teams, enlisted with the Breakers. Former Redskins defensive end Coy Bacon stayed in Washington with the Federals, and Houston linebacker John Corker took his skills to Michigan.

George Allen, for one, combed the entire country for players, and the Blitz boss went so far as to visit a prison to recruit former player and then inmate Michael Sifford. The team also recognized an excellent opportunity for free press coverage when it gave *Sports Illustrated* writer Rick Telander a tryout. Of course, the writer's return to the gridiron turned out to be a story for the magazine. Neither man made the team.

"Some teams got offended when we had tryout camps in Phoenix, and Los Angeles," recalled Bruce Allen. "But we signed over 300 players and we processed those contracts; then gave a lot of those contracts to other teams in the league through the waiver wire."

After unsuccessful negotiations with Stanford's John Elway, the Invaders landed their quarterback in Fred Besana, who had enjoyed brief stints with the Bills and Giants before retiring from pro football five years earlier. He had been running a beer distributorship and serving as an insurance executive since leaving the NFL in the late 1970s but had kept his skills sharp by playing semi-pro ball for the Twin City Cougars in Marysville, California.

The Breakers threw another twist at the NFL when they inked Cincinnati Bengals tight end Dan Ross to a "futures" contract to take effect in 1984. Though Ross was under contract to play for the Bengals during the upcoming 1983 NFL campaign, his new pact with Boston would take effect after the season, making him a member of the Breakers.

In effect, the player became a lame duck for Cincinnati, a fact not lost on their management, who questioned how hard he would play. It was the first such contract a league team had made with a big-name NFL player and reminded many of the contracts that NFL stars such as Ken Stabler had signed with the WFL. Many of those players never played a down in the WFL due to its chronic financial problems, but the agreements served to put even more upward pressure on salaries. While this type of deal technically didn't violate league policy against signing NFL players under contract, it was a definite gray area. Many feared that the NFL would retaliate with some futures contracts of their own with USFL players who showed promise. In the meantime, NFL teams moved quickly to lock up free agents such as Washington running back John Riggins and Detroit quarterback Gary Danielson before the new league could sign them.

"The term was called future contract where you would sign a player to the USFL at the end of his contract and in the meantime he would work for you as a marketing person," explained Gould who would later become a player agent. "It was a brilliant concept in those days because the player wasn't going to play for you for three years or two years, whatever it was, but they would help you sell tickets and market the thing. And it wasn't a violation of the NFL contract because at that time their contract didn't run a full year, which it does now."

"That began a run on players in the NFL leveraging their own position, trying to get people to come into the league," Ehrhart said of the Ross signing. "There was a big debate as to whether that was appropriate or not. The NFL was of course fighting mad because they didn't want to have any of their players playing out contracts and then leaving after their contract was over. Player salaries had been so restricted by the NFL because they had no competition and players had no real ability to move, no true free agency. That was their one bit of leverage, the ability to sign a futures contract."

The NFL quickly expanded its roster size by four, allowing the league to lock up an additional 112 players.

Teams also looked north to Canada for talent, as several CFL players joined coaches Ray Jauch and Hugh Campbell. Jauch brought talented Saskatchewan receiver Joey Walters to Washington. Quarterback Ken Johnson left the Toronto Argonauts to join the Denver Gold, and Panthers general manager Jim Spavital also made his way from Saskatchewan.

Going Camping

USFL teams gave their new players a chance to show their talents, breaking camps in Florida and Arizona on January 31, the day after the Washington Redskins topped the Miami Dolphins in Super Bowl XVII. Birmingham, Boston, Michigan, New Jersey, Philadelphia, Tampa Bay and Washington all trained in Florida. The Stars camped in Deland, the Stallions chose Daytona Beach, the Federals tabbed Jacksonville, the Panthers picked Ocala, the Bandits stayed home in Tampa and the Generals and Breakers settled down in Orlando, even sharing the same hotel. Arizona, Chicago, Denver and Oakland set up shop in Arizona. The Blitz, Gold and Invaders trained in Phoenix, and the Wranglers put on the pads in Casa Grande. The Express held its camp in the L.A. suburb of Manhattan Beach.

"The whole experience came on quick," laughed Philadelphia Coach Mora. "I got hired just a few short weeks prior to training camp, and I had to hire a staff during that time and then get ready for training camp. It was pretty hectic there for a few weeks. I was hiring guys, and some of the guys I hadn't even met ever before, but I talked to them on the phone or brought them in for an interview. Some of the guys I knew, others I hired over the phone on somebody else's recommendation. We hopped on a plane and flew down to Deland, Florida, and at that time we hadn't had a chance to have a complete staff meeting. In fact, our running backs coach, Jim Skipper, we didn't even hire him until we were in training camp. He was at the University of Oregon at the time. We had our first staff meeting the night before our first practice in Deland.

"I remember going out there, and we had something like 120 players. I didn't know any of them. I had a roster that I carried around with me, and we had their names taped to the front of their helmets. I was just trying to get to know my staff, get a plan put together for our offense and defense and kicking game and get to know our players so I could make good decisions on who to keep and who not to keep. It was pretty hectic because we had really just gotten together a day or two before that."

The competition in most camps was fierce. To be sure, the top draft choices and some of the seasoned pros were almost certain to make the rosters, but precious few players were guaranteed spots. Several of the teams took well over 100 players into camp despite a one-week deadline to cut down to 70. For example, the Express took 177 players to camp and had to cut 107 of them within a week. At one point, the Blitz had a whopping 340 players under contract but ended up taking relatively few, 85, into camp. The squads eventually had to cut down to 40 players on the active roster and could also dress a third quarterback. Developmental squads were set at ten players per team.

"We were one of the youngest teams going into that training camp in Florida," recalled Michigan Panthers receiver Derek Holloway. "There were all these new people coming in and sometimes we didn't have enough helmets and uniforms for some people when we first started."

"The first training camp, the players were coming in on this huge shuttle bus," added Philadelphia Stars tight end Ken Dunek. "There were some were very recognizable names such as Lydell Mitchell; one of the most talented players in professional or college history shows up on our shuttle bus. There were a lot of great players who tried out and didn't make the team including a couple of former teammates of mine from the Philadelphia Eagles. I have memories of that shuttle bus going in and out with some of these recognizable names plus players you've never heard of."

"There are some players out here that you know can't play, that I know can't play," Arizona coach Shively told *The Sporting News* early in camp. "But I think they deserve the courtesy to get their chance to work out in pads." Richard Brose was one of those players in Shively's camp. A former "Mr. Arizona," he once earned his living as a gigolo in Los Angeles. Apparently the occupation didn't keep him in football shape. He was an early cut.

Others were just trying to survive.

"In '82 I tried out for the Cincinnati Bengals," said running back Harry Sydney, who found himself in Denver's camp. "I tried out for Seattle my first year out of college, got cut. Tried out for Cincinnati, got cut. I believe it was Red Miller who gave me a call, and I went out for tryouts. Training camp was in Casa Grande, Arizona, so I went out there and for $10 a day, we beat each other up. It was the most violent football ever played by mankind. You didn't have to be a great athlete. Everybody who thought they were a tough guy tried out."

"In those days, it was a lot more physical," agreed Hebert. "Today because of the collective bargaining agreement, you can't have three straight days of two-a-days, for instance. We'd have *ten* straight days of two-a-days and hitting every day. I'm not saying it was live on the quarterbacks every day, but you would get hit every now and again, generally because guys were out of control and just being really aggressive."

"We went to camp with what seems like 200 football players," recalled Washington's Craig James. "We were in shorts, shoulder pads and head gear and so you would think it wouldn't be full contact. We got guys out there blowing each other up. And we got nobody taping it! We didn't even have a crew videotaping the practice, and we'd cut some-one the next day. I'd say, 'Where is that number 83? That guy was a pretty good player.' 'He got cut.' How the heck did they know if the guy was good or not? There is no video to support it."

"We were at Casa Grande Resort, a resort about 45 miles southeast of Phoenix, kind of a hotel-resort type place," remembered Wranglers rookie quarterback Alan Risher. "We just pulled up cold turkey and tried to figure it out. We had about seven quarterbacks in camp, and everybody was pulling together trying to figure out what the hell we were doing. I got there about a week late, finally got into camp and got after it, trying to figure it all out."

The league had decided against preseason games, opting instead for a handful of scrimmages. This ensured that the first weekend of games on ABC would be the league's openers, preseason or regular season, a fact the network could use to market the opening week broadcasts. Not that any USFL team shied away from the public. A Bandits' intrasquad scrimmage on February 5 drew more than 1,000 spectators. The teams made sure that they saw the competition in training camp, though, so they could gauge where they stood. The franchises training in Arizona squared off in a four-way scrimmage on February 19 and 20, for example. The scrimmages were often so competitive that the players referred to them as games.

Chicago's training camp uniforms looked awfully familiar to Stan White. He found out that they were the same ones worn by himself and the other NFL "all-stars" in the two players' union games held during the 1982 strike.

"This is like an NFL camp before all the veterans get in," the former NFL player rep told *Sports Illustrated*. "So, the only thing we're missing is the buildup of veterans. We may be comparable to one or two of the NFL teams already, and I know we're as good as most NFL teams at the skill positions. I've been fighting against the NFL so long. Now I can really compete against them.

"The problem in the NFL is that the owners look at their success as a tribute to their management. They consider players interchangeable. Here they realize how important the players are. There's more of a symbiotic relationship than in the NFL. There are a lot of players who will come to this league, where relationships are better."

A minor stir came out of a Tampa Bay Bandits practice when reports placed former Miami Dolphins place-kicker Garo Yepremian in the camp. It turned out that it was an error that a would-be player never corrected. Yepremian was philosophical about the case of mistaken identity. "All I can say is that maybe somebody who was bald-headed, very virile and masculine showed up and said he was me," he explained to *The Sporting News*. "I can understand why somebody would want to do that."

The Breakers and Generals proximity in the same Orlando hotel provided an amus-ing moment for players on both clubs. When Boston traded defensive back Steve Raefort to New Jersey, he moved to another room just ten feet away from his first one. The trade meant that Raefort would no longer be able to enjoy the beer breaks that Coury occasionally let the Breakers take during practice sessions. Tim Mazzetti was also proving to be a fun addition to the Breakers camp.

"As one of the conditions of me coming out of retirement, I finagled a right to bring a television camera and shoot a five-part series for my television station in Atlanta that ended up winning a local Emmy," said Mazzetti. "It was called 'The Diary of a Returning Pro.' I brought my favorite cameraman down to our first week of training camp, and this was all approved by the league and by Dick Coury and the Breakers, too. It felt a little bit weird, and I caught a lot of shit from the players because I was walking around with my own camera crew and shooting a series while trying out for the team.

"I was in pretty good shape and even though they brought in a couple of other kickers, I knew right from the start I pretty much had the job, not because I was the veteran or had the name recognition, but just because I knew I was better. That was fun and interesting, and I still have the tape from that. It was actually a pretty good series.

"Our training camp was down at the University of Central Florida, which is somewhere between Tampa and Orlando, I think. We were living in the dorms with the college kids. I remember playing around with a soccer ball with the womens soccer team, and apparently UCF had one of the best teams in the nation. It was stuff like that that was so much more casual. That was part of my series; it certainly wasn't like the NFL. And I interviewed some of the players, where they were coming from, and I did some bios of some of the players who were trying out. They were playing semi-pro or working in a bakery or butcher shop or working in construction. It was pretty neat. It's what you would expect of a start-up league which had, I wouldn't say a shoestring budget, but certainly not a multi-billion dollar NFL budget. It was just a blast."

Many of the players were not well known, and a few of the coaches weren't either. According to *The Sporting News*, while Arizona's Doug Shively introduced his assistants to the Wranglers, one player said, "I don't want to offend you, sir, but what is your name?"

A lot of the men enjoyed the new atmosphere, one that was much less structured than that of an NFL team. "It was a lot of fun in the strict sense of the word," said Oakland Coach Ralston. "Finding a practice facility, getting an auditorium-type setup for team meetings, setting up breakdown meeting rooms and offices for the coaches—there's a lot involved in that. We had excellent cooperation from a lot of people. Tad Taube set up a limited partnership and involved a lot of business people in the greater Bay Area and they were all very helpful."

Other than the rules, the USFL also adopted some other programs to differentiate itself from the National Football League. First, the owners formed a committee to investigate drug abuse in pro football. At the same time, the NFL was dragging its feet on similar measures, something that had drawn increasing criticism. The new league also set up a program to help its players finish their college educations. This was particularly important since many of the players that the league would draft would have to leave school a semester early to participate in the upcoming season. Of the 187 drafted players who signed with the USFL in 1983, 87 of them would take advantage of the program during the off-season. Bobby Hebert of Northwestern Louisiana was one of the players to do so.

"The college education scholarship plan was really a terrific program," explained Ehrhart. "We incorporated this plan early on when we were drafting the players contract. It said that any player would get his college education paid for. That was partially because we were a spring league, and one of the arguments the NFL was using was, 'We're not going to take a player until he finishes his college degree.' That was mostly hypocrisy because players, once they finished their eligibility and were true NFL prospects, were working out and getting ready for the draft. We instituted that plan for two reasons. One, it was for the players themselves. In the fall of '82, they finished their eligibility, so in the spring of '83 they'd be playing for us, so we said, 'Look, we know you have to withdraw from college, so if you're concerned about the university taking your scholarship away, we built it into the player contract that you will receive a scholarship to finish whatever school you have left.' A lot of players did take advantage of that. We also did it to combat the position of the NFL trying to tell a player we were taking him out of school. From a media point of view, too, people were attacking the league, saying, 'They're taking people out of college.' So I think it worked very well. There were a number of players who would come and make sure they got their stipend, their tuition paid. I think it was a terrific program. The money in the NFL now is so huge that people hardly worry about it, but especially for a fringe player at the time, he had a chance to go back and get his education.

"It was a lot more important for the NFL to make sure the colleges built their stars and trained their players to get them NFL ready, than it was for them to finish their college careers. I think in that case the USFL was on a higher road than the NFL. We were acknowledging it and actually providing an incentive for the player to go back and get their degree. The incentive was built into the contract, and the only way to get it was to go back to school. It was well intentioned, rather than being hypocritical."

Slowly, the teams began to take shape. Many observers thought that the Chicago Blitz had the potential to be runaway champs, and some members of the media were comparing them to the Cleveland Browns whose dominance in the old All-American Football Conference helped bring a premature end to that circuit. The Browns won all four AAFC championships from 1946 to 1949 before the league partially merged into the NFL.

On paper, Chicago put together a terrific offense featuring the experienced Greg Landry at the helm with rookie Tim Spencer and former New York Jet Kevin Long in the backfield. Explosive rookie Trumaine Johnson and Wamon Buggs lined up as two of the circuit's best receivers, and former Detroit Lion Stan White anchored what appeared to be the USFL's top defense. The Blitz had a great mixture of rookies and veterans playing under legendary coach George Allen and were odds-on favorites to end the season hoisting the championship trophy. They were also the favorites to have the highest payroll in the young league. The talent haul had come at a price far in excess of original league guidelines, and Allen had not let a thing like negotiating rights get in his way when he saw someone he wanted. Though the league had no salary cap, there was a parameter for player salaries that Dixon had made known since day one.

"We were advised by our lawyers that to come to an agreement on a salary cap could be a violation of antitrust laws," explained Tad Taube. "So instead we had a gentleman's agreement. Of course, that's only okay as long as you have gentlemen agreeing."

Allen's tendency to ignore that agreement concerned a number of owners. "There are 12 partners in this league, and we all agreed on a figure," explained Denver owner Ron Blanding in *The Sporting News*. "Let's just do the agreement, that's all. If you want to change it and make the figure higher, fine. We'll all sit down in a room and vote on it. But the way it is now, you've got one team spending $5 million and the others spending $2 million."

Never one to shy away from a fight, Allen struck back. "You ought to ask Ron Blanding when he's going to sign some players from his draft," he answered. "He's sold more season tickets than anybody else in the league, and the draft is the way to go. He owes that to his fans, instead of being concerned about someone else."

The rest of the league was not so quick to throw in the towel. Despite a late start, the Stars had put together a great offensive line with Irv Eatman and the brother tandem of Brad and Bart Oates. North Carolina's Kelvin Bryant led the running game, and Fusina provided veteran leadership at quarterback. Mora and his hastily assembled staff had done an admirable job, but they were concerned about their defense.

"In fact, we were down in Deland, and there were some other teams down in Florida, too: the Tampa Bay Bandits and I think the Birmingham team might have been training down there," recalled Mora. "We would go practice against some of these other teams, and we didn't fare too well. We didn't look like we could stack up against some of these teams, and I had some real concerns. Our defense especially got some criticism in these scrimmages, and I know some of our players named our defense the 'Doghouse Defense' because it was in the doghouse because it didn't do very well."

"We really struggled in training camp," added Dunek. "We only had two preseason games, and the last one we played Tampa Bay, and their offense took it to our defense pretty well. We weren't exactly sure what to expect. As a matter of fact, because of that poor performance, our defense got nicknamed the Doghouse Defense because they were in the doghouse."

Still, they were somewhat buoyed because Peterson had found a gem of a linebacker, an unknown named Sam Mills. At five feet nine inches tall, other teams considered Mills too small to play the position, and he had been cut by the Cleveland Browns and Canadian Football League's Toronto Argonauts twice. He had been teaching at a New Jersey high school when he found out about the USFL. Though Cleveland coach Sam Rutigliano admired Mills' work ethic, he couldn't envision playing a linebacker that small.

"I got a call from Sam Rutigliano before I hired Jim in the fall of 1982," recalled Carl Peterson. "He said, 'Carl, we're cutting a guy, and I believe the only reason we're cutting him is because he's five foot nine. This is one terrific football player. He's an inside linebacker named Sam Mills, and he's from that great football factory Montclair State University in New Jersey. He's had a run in Canada, and we got him as a free agent. He just gave us a great camp. I think you should sign him for your new league, and whatever you do, don't cut him before you see him hit.' I took that knowledge, and we signed Sam Mills for a $500 signing bonus and two-years at, I think, $20,000 and $22,000.

"We had our first three-day mini-camp under George Perles, no pads, just shorts and that. At the end of mini-camp, George said, 'Carl, Sam Mills is a great kid; he's got a big heart, but we can't play professional football with a five-foot-nine middle linebacker. I really think we ought to let him go.' I said, 'George, I'm going to follow Sam Rutigliano's advice, we're not going to cut him until we see him hit.' George leaves and we got Jim. We had a mini-camp in Philadelphia before we went to training camp in Florida. Same thing. After the mini-camp, Jim comes to me and says, 'Carl, he's a great kid, but we can't play professional football with a five-foot-nine middle linebacker.' I said, 'Jim, we're going to take him to camp, and we're not going to cut him until we see him hit.' We went to camp, and one of the things I'd always done as a personnel director was that I always had all the coaches, assistant coaches, coordinators and the head coach, rank and rate every player every day after two-a-days. Every single night without question the best defensive player at practice was Sam Mills. Vince Tobin loved him and so did Jim. We called him the 'Field Mouse' because he would slay the elephants, and he was just five-foot-nine, but Lord, what a football player."

The Generals appeared to have the best running back in the league and maybe all of football in Walker, but New Jersey was tough to figure out after that. Running back Maurice Carthon from Arkansas State would provide some needed blocking for his back-field mate. Almost by default, Bobby Scott, a 12-year veteran from the New Orleans Saints, landed the quarterbacking duties. The defense looked better, with the linebackers particularly strong. Generals' supporters were also glad to have coach Fairbanks' years of experience on their side.

Birmingham featured the elusive Collier at quarterback and a strong defensive coach in Dotsch but had claimed 13 players off waivers after the final cutdown, leading many to wonder how much talent they had. Michigan was sure to keep things interesting with the Hebert-to-Carter combination but was also the youngest team in an infant league. They would need some time to work together, especially their offensive line. Hebert, the rookie quarterback out of Northwestern Louisiana, had proved to be one of the team's most pleasant surprises, climbing from third on the Panthers' training camp depth chart to the starting signal caller spot. Tampa Bay looked to be an explosive offensive team. With unpredictable Director of Football Operations Lewis "Bugsy" Engelberg searching the country for talent and coach Spurrier calling the shots, they would be fun to watch.

"They'd already signed several players by the time I signed on," said Spurrier. "We also had a draft, 16 or 17 rounds or something like that, and I ended up taking about four guys from Duke. I leaned on Bugsy to do a lot of the personnel stuff. I hired John Rauch, who was kind of a mentor, to let me know if we were on the right track."

Their 32-year-old quarterback John Reaves, who had last played for Houston in 1981, was a particularly interesting case. Sitting on the bench with Minnesota in 1979, he felt crestfallen that his career was nearing an end. He admitted that he dealt with his depression by turning to drugs, and was arrested for driving while intoxicated twice in eight days. The quarterback tried to quit his habits, but slipped back into substance abuse. He soon separated from his wife and children. In July of 1980, he fought with the manager of a bar, who pressed charges to have him committed. Reaves fled from the police, and while he was hiding out, took stock of what had become of his life. At that time, he became a born again Christian. He turned himself in to the police and set about getting his life in order. He then rejoined his family, paid off his debts and had avoided further problems. For him, the USFL meant the second chance for his career that he felt he had already received in his personal life.

"I know a lot of people cringe when they read the bad stuff about me continually," the passer told *Sports Illustrated*. "Like my mother. She hates to see it brought up. But I just ask her to try and understand that it's inevitable. It does hurt somewhat. But, then again, I made the mistakes, albeit they were three years ago. I think people realize that changes have come over me." The Bandits were banking on it.

Oakland and Los Angeles both signed several NFL vets and would not lack for leadership. Talent, though, might be a whole different story. Invaders quarterback Fred Besana looked sharp in several scrimmages. On the other end of the spectrum, the Gold, Breakers, Wranglers and Federals were unknown quantities. Despite strong ticket sales, Denver had drawn fire from others in the league, particularly George Allen, for its thrifty ways.

Arizona had started late with the post-draft hiring of Shively and had been playing catch-up for much of training camp. Neither sported any name players of note. Outside of Craig James and QB Mike Hohensee from Minnesota, Washington looked weak. Boston, though, stood out as the league's poor sister. It had failed to sign any name players, and its small stadium ensured that few Bostonians would notice. Johnnie Walton emerged from training camp as the starting QB over the injured Mike Livingston. Many observers felt that coach Dick Coury was going to have to work miracles just to keep the team competitive.

Season ticket sales also showed a mixed picture around the league. League franchises averaged about 17,000 season tickets sold prior to the inaugural campaign. Bolstered by Walker's presence, New Jersey had totaled more than 35,000 with nearly half of those coming in the week after the runner's signing. The Denver Gold, yet to ink anyone of note, came in a close second with more than 34,000 season passes sold. The popularity of coach Red Miller and the difficulty of finding Broncos tickets made the Gold an appealing alternative. Oakland, at 23,000 tickets, and Tampa Bay, at 22,000, were also doing very well. The recent loss of the Raiders had helped the Invaders' marketing, and the Buccaneers' inept play had bolstered the Bandits' efforts. Similarly, the Express flirted with sales around the 20,000 plateau despite having to contend with a pair of NFL teams in town. With demand driven in part by the scarcity of Redskins tickets, Washington had sold nearly 19,000 season tickets. Birmingham stood at about 14,000, while Arizona's late hiring of a head coach and agreement with Sun Devil Stadium kept ticket sales around the 15,000 mark. Chicago, despite its rash of signings and a legendary coach, was around 14,000 as was Philadelphia and Michigan. Boston, on the other hand, had sold just over 3,500 season tickets, leading to speculation the team had just one year to turn things around.

A Difference of Opinion

While teams such as Boston, Denver and Washington abided by the original plan of limited spending, others such as Chicago had quickly tossed it out the window. This fact did not escape the notice of reporters watching the league. The Blitz appeared far ahead of much of the rest of the league in signing top draft picks and NFL veterans, and their payroll reflected it. Trumaine Johnson, Tim Spencer, Greg Landry and Stan White had not come cheap. George Allen maintained that Chicago was a tough market and that in order to survive, the Blitz had to sign high-quality players whom the fans would recognize. Denver countered by reminding the coach that all the owners had agreed to a spending limit and for one club to ignore it put the rest in jeopardy of being noncompetitive. The war of words between Chicago and the Gold escalated publicly. Commissioner Simmons stepped in to tell the clubs to save their battles for the playing field. Unfortunately, the commissioner was unable to clear up the issue, and many in the league felt that it was impossible to mandate any kind of salary cap. One thing was certain, though, Denver's trip to Soldier Field in week three, the first meeting between the clubs, was going to be interesting.

"I was one of the low salary believers," recalled Blanding. "I thought it was important to keep our costs down and give the league a chance to get going. That's what I think became one of the main problems in the league.

"Allen and I got along great. I mean we had our arguments, but once the arguments were over, he was a pleasure to be around. It was just his philosophy of life. It had always been that way even when he was with Washington. He'd pay anybody anything to get whatever he wanted. He didn't care about what the costs were. He didn't care whether there was a profit or a loss. All he wanted to do was win. Well, you can't consider just one part of a business. You have to take it all into account. In my mind, he was a nice guy with the wrong philosophy."

"Bringing together that many economically and philosophically diverse and strong-minded people from different places and backgrounds creates a challenge to get them all moving in the same direction even in Major League Baseball, and it's hard to keep people focused on the same agenda. It's always difficult to bring so many strong-minded people together, but we had very good cooperation during that fall period," said Ehrhart. "People were asking why Tampa didn't have a coach, but John Bassett in his crafty way had already picked one out but couldn't reveal who it was. People were down on Michigan because they were late getting going with colors and so on. Then there was some criticism of Chicago, and should we do an investigation of their player contracts. The player contracts were rolling in on a daily basis during the fall as we got ready for kickoff. I called it, 'the golden six months of full cooperation.' It was a pre-competitive golden half a year.

"I've sat in Major League Baseball meetings and a lot of other meetings, but for those first six months there was as good a quality of singleness of purpose and cooperation using all the strengths of the owners as I've ever seen. Of course, there had been no games played, so people weren't angry with each other yet. It was amazing how up until the first kickoff, there was really a good *esprit de corps*."

Some bickering aside, the teams had taken shape. As the dawn of the season approached, the teams shifted from their Arizona and Florida training camps to the cities they'd call home for at least the next 18 weeks.

After years of planning and preparation, the United States Football League was at last ready to kick off its first season. Once just a concept, the USFL had a dozen teams, hundreds of players and a growing number of fans. What had started out as a gleam in David Dixon's eye was finally ready to take the field as the first new football league in nearly a decade. Would the public accept football in the spring? After all, a rival football league had never peacefully coexisted with the mighty National Football League and none had ever tried it in the spring.

Perhaps Simmons best summed up the USFL's challenge. "The American public thinks of football in fall and winter because it is used to it," he explained to *The Sporting News*. "That's a habit. We have to go about changing that habit, that's all. We just have to reach the person who has his mind set on hot chocolate and get him to switch to cold lemonade."

2

Football's Spring Debut

The USFL divided its franchises into three divisions of four teams each for its opening season. The Atlantic contained the Boston Breakers, Philadelphia Stars, New Jersey Generals and Washington Federals. The Birmingham Stallions, Chicago Blitz, Michigan Panthers and Tampa Bay Bandits called the Central home, while the Arizona Wranglers, Denver Gold, Los Angeles Express and Oakland Invaders filled out the Pacific. The Atlantic and Pacific divisions were both geographic naturals, while the Central featured two southern teams and two from the Midwest. The three division winners and the team with the next best record would advance to the playoffs. The wild card team would meet the team with the best record in one playoff matchup, while the other two division titlists would square off in the other postseason game.

On March 6 of 1983, the day of the USFL's inaugural games, the playoffs were a distant goal for its teams. Most players concentrated instead on just learning their play books and getting to know their teammates in anticipation of the opening games. The league's inaugural weekend opened just 35 days after the Washington Redskins defeated the Miami Dolphins in Super Bowl XVII and featured two intriguing contests, both of which would be spotlighted on ABC. The first featured George Allen's homecoming in the nation's capital, this time as the coach of the Chicago Blitz to face the hometown Federals. Allen would return to RFK Stadium, where he had compiled a 41–10–1 record, for the first time since December 17, 1977, his last game as the Redskins' coach. He had led Washington from 1971 to 1977, guiding them to the Super Bowl in his second season. Despite his success, he was fired after contract negotiations broke down with Redskins president Edward Bennett Williams. When the USFL called offering him another chance to take the field, Allen didn't hesitate.

"Wherever you were with Coach Allen, people recognized him," recalled Don Kojich, who worked with Chicago's public relations. "The first game we played for the Blitz, we played on the road in RFK in D.C., George's return to Washington, where he was the coach of the Redskins and the Over the Hill Gang and everything. We got a tremendous amount of publicity out of it. I remember the electricity in the atmosphere surrounding that game and Coach Allen's return to D.C."

On the other hand, Coach Ray Jauch's Washington team may have been relieved that so much of the attention had fallen on Allen and the Blitz. In their first displays of the bad luck that would come to characterize the franchise, the Federals found themselves locked out of their practice field on their first day in Washington.

"There was a picture in the paper that first year when we came back from training camp and tried to get into the old Redskin practice field," remembered Jauch. "The fence was all covered in overgrown vines. We couldn't even get into the practice field. They took a picture of me tearing these vines away. Our practice field was situated in a place where all the surrounding area was covered in concrete. It used to rain all the time and all that water would run down to our practice field. We'd end up practicing in mud the whole time. It got so bad that one time I took the team to the stadium and we practiced on the ramps where the people walked in."

The truck hauling all the team's equipment from their Jacksonville training camp site broke down en route to the city the same day. To worsen matters, their locker room was burglarized later in the week. Thunderstorms and an antique show had also interrupted practices, and running back Buddy Hardeman had been arrested for attacking a policeman. The Feds had not had a good week leading up to their opener.

The worst was yet to come when Allen's Blitz dismantled the Federals in the Washington rain. Wamon Buggs recovered Trumaine Johnson's fumble in the end zone for the first points in Chicago history, Kevin Long added a four-yard run and Trumaine Johnson caught a 23-yard scoring toss from Landry before halftime to give the Blitz a 21–0 lead. After a scoreless third period, Paul Ricker latched on to a 10-yard Landry aerial for another score. Quarterback Mike Hohensee came off the Washington bench to replace the ineffective Kim McQuilken and, after throwing a pair of interceptions in the end zone, finally hit Walker Lee with a 19-yard touchdown pass to give Washington its first and only points deep in the fourth period. Allen had come out of Washington a winner again, this time by a 28–7 margin. The crushing loss hurt the spirit of the Feds fans, but 38,010 Washingtonians turned out for the game. Many stayed until the end in spite of the blowout and the rain and loudly cheered the home team's late score that averted the shutout. Grounds keepers had to dye the grass green so that it would look decent on television.

New Jersey's opener at Los Angeles drew the lion's share of attention on opening day. The contest featured the league's top two markets in a perfect ABC television matchup. More importantly, however, was the debut of Herschel Walker. Generals coach Chuck Fairbanks claimed that Walker would see only a few plays, but the Express believed differently. New Jersey hadn't paid millions of dollars to have Walker seen sitting on the bench in a nationally televised contest.

The Los Angeles crowd of 34,002 gave the star runner an extended cheer in the pregame introductions, and he looked sharp at the start, ripping off a nine-yard run on the second play of the game. The Express struck first on the scoreboard, though, on Vince Abbott's 23-yard kick. Walker then responded with a five-yard scoring jaunt minutes later. Dave Jacobs missed the extra point but made up for it with a 38-yard field goal to give New Jersey a 9–3 advantage after one quarter. Los Angeles took control of the contest over the next two periods, grabbing a 20–9 advantage on two Tom Ramsey scoring tosses.

The double digit deficit effectively took Walker out of the Generals' conservative game plan in the fourth. New Jersey managed to close within 20–15 on a Bobby Scott to Tom McConnaughey touchdown pass, but their two-point conversion was unsuccessful. Still, the Generals had one last chance. After an unsuccessful fourth-down gamble by coach Hugh Campbell, the Express gave New Jersey the ball at the Los Angeles' 31-yard line in the final minutes. Scott drove his team to the five where it faced a third and three. Scott was then sacked for a nine-yard loss, and his fourth down throw to Larry Brodsky came up inches short of the first down. Replays appeared to show that Brodsky had gained enough yardage to move the chains, but the officials ruled otherwise. Los Angeles held on for a 20–15 win. The Generals offense struggled throughout the game as Walker gained

New Jersey Generals running back Herschel Walker looks for yardage against the Los Angeles Express in the inaugural game for both teams at the Los Angeles Coliseum on Sunday, March 6, 1983. Los Angeles won 20–15, while Walker gained 65 yards on 16 carries. Photograph by Jim Turner, from author's collection.

a disappointing 65 rushing yards, and Scott ended the day with three interceptions. He was also picked off on their two-point conversion attempt.

With the attention of most observers on those games, the first kickoff in USFL history occurred earlier in the day in Tampa in the hometown Bandits' contest against the Boston Breakers. Owner John Bassett had the game ball delivered into Tampa Stadium by a parachutist and arranged to give fans scarves to wear to support their new hometown team. Boston's Tim Mazzetti tallied the first points in league history with a 30-yard field goal late in the first quarter. The Bandits' Ricky Williams answered the kick when he scored the first-ever touchdown on a five-yard pass from John Reaves midway through the second period. The first game, in fact, turned out to be one of the best of the weekend with five lead changes. The third quarter featured a 102-yard interception return that was not brought back for a touchdown. Boston's Terry Love picked off a deflected Reaves' pass in the end zone and ran all the way back to the Bandits' three-yard line before Tampa Bay receiver Eric Truvillion hauled him down from behind. Boston eventually scored on a short run by Tony Davis. Reaves atoned for the interception with touchdown passes of six and 33 yards to Truvillion and Willie Gillespie, respectively, to grab a 21–17 advantage. Behind Walton, the Breakers drove to the Bandits' 13 in the final minutes, but Ken Taylor picked off the quarterback's last ditch pass at the five and Tampa Bay ran out the clock. Williams galloped for a game-high 97 yards and caught six passes for 49 additional yards. Most importantly, 42,437 enthusiastic Tampa Bay fans had attended the contest.

Another Sunday game saw the Invaders whip the Wranglers, 24–0, in front of 45,167 at Phoenix's Sun Devil Stadium. Arizona treated the crowd to a Beach Boys concert before kickoff, helping to make up for the lackluster performance of their team. Oakland's Wyatt Henderson pulled in three passes for 92 yards including scores of 53 and 19 yards. Arthur Whittington added a scoring run and Kevin Shea kicked a 45-yard field goal. Besana completed 15 of 22 throws for 239 yards with two scores and no interceptions. On the other side of the ball, veteran lefty Todd Krueger struggled to move the Wranglers and rookie Alan Risher took over in relief. In a strange side note, the league fired the entire statistics crew after the game because of numerous problems.

"We did the first major professional level football game with a concert prior to the game," recalled Arizona assistant general manager Jim Foster who had joined the franchise after serving as promotion manager of NFL Properties. "I brought the Beach Boys in and we had a major promotion around that. It had been done with professional baseball as a post-game thing, but I decided to do it as a pre-game event. My whole philosophy was we have to get them out here so they can see it, and I'm going to spend some money to do that. We put on a great show that day. People loved the concert. The fans were worked up into a pretty good frenzy waiting for their first taste of professional football in the Valley of the Sun and out came the Wranglers for the first time to the last drumbeat of 'Good Vibrations.' It was all downhill from there. It wasn't just a shutout; it was a boring football game."

In other action Sunday, the Stars traveled to Denver and came out a 13–7 winner in a fierce defensive battle. Philadelphia built up a 13–0 advantage on a short Chuck Fusina touchdown run and a pair of David Trout field goals, one of them a 50-yarder. Although it took more than three quarters, Ken Johnson finally got the Gold offense moving. He replaced Jeff Knapple who had tossed four interceptions. Johnson capped one drive with a one-yard scoring run and brought his team all the way to the Stars' two in the waning seconds. His fourth and goal pass to Larry Canada came up short, however, and the Stars hung on for the win in front of 45,102 fans at Mile High Stadium.

"I remember our opening game in Denver, Colorado, at Mile High Stadium," said Stars GM Peterson. "There was a snow storm the night before, and we were the last plane in with our football team. They came out and dusted off the seats and 45,000 walked in to watch the Denver Gold play the Philadelphia Stars of the USFL, and I think we were all taken aback. Stories like that were happening all around the league."

"When I first got there after training camp, I decided I was going to go for a jog," said Gold running back Harry Sydney of Denver. "I didn't realize the air was so thin. I went about two laps and thought I was going to die. I thought something was wrong with me. I didn't understand the effects of the altitude at a mile high. I was going to go see a doctor, but I just had to get used to the altitude.

"What was great about Denver was the fans. Everybody talks about football country, but back in those days in Denver, it was incredible. We had so many people at the games, and they loved football at that time of the year."

In the lone Monday night tilt, Michigan kicker Novo Bojovic hit first half field goals of 49, 49 and 48 yards for all the points the Panthers needed in a 9–7 victory. The kicker, one of the most superstitious players in the league, always played with garlic in his right sock and a white glove on his left hand for good luck. They apparently had paid immediate dividends. Rookie quarterback Reggie Collier provided the Stallions' only points of the night on a three-yard run. He finished the night with 76 yards rushing in 13 attempts but suffered three interceptions. Hebert and company held on to the ball for more than eight minutes near the end of the game to seal the win. A reported crowd of 30,305 looked on under the lights at Legion Field in the debut of ESPN's live game coverage.

The first weekend in USFL history was in the books and league officials could hardly have been more pleased. Attendance averaged 39,171 per game, well above projections, and four of those crowds, excepting Washington and Arizona, saw close, exciting games. In addition, ABC had garnered a terrific 14.3 rating for the first weekend, buoyed by Walker's debut. Typical NFL games averaged 16.5 ratings the year before.

Arizona's Jim Asmus was one of the goats of opening weekend. His punts had averaged a measly 30.4 yards each and he missed two short field goal attempts in the Wranglers' shutout loss. Coach Doug Shively brought in additional kickers to compete for the job, owner Joseph called in a sports psychologist to talk to Asmus, and the kicker changed his uniform number from 13 to 16 just in case that was throwing him off.

"Doug brought in 15 kickers, and I had to compete against every single one of them," laughed Asmus. "I met so many different personalities. Kickers have a reputation for being odd, and I'm not saying I'm totally normal, but there were some real oddballs there. I spent two hours after practice competing against these people.

"Everyone was down after the first game because everyone showed quite poorly. They hired a psychologist, a hypnotist really, but they called him a 'mind psychologist,' and they were going around using him on a lot of players. They wanted to do it with me, thinking maybe they could help me focus a little bit more. After he did my evaluation, I remember the comment he made. He said, 'You know what? You're actually pretty solid. I'll be honest with you; the coaches wanted me specifically to work with you. But after working with some of them, they need it a little more than you.' I said, 'That's good to know.'"

After the results of the opening weekend, Arizona stood as an overwhelming underdog in its week two Saturday night clash with the mighty Chicago Blitz. Coming off their dismantling of Washington, the Blitz looked ready to run their record to 2–0 at Sun Devil Stadium. The Wranglers desperately turned to rookie Alan Risher behind center, making his first pro start against Allen's veteran defense.

"Todd Krueger who had spent a year on injured reserve in Buffalo with the Bills and had then signed [with the Wranglers], in the eyes of the coaching staff won the job in training camp," recalled Risher. "I don't think they thought I was quite ready yet. I had come off a pretty full Orange Bowl senior season, and I think they were going to try to work me in. But we got beat 24–0 by Oakland in the opener in Sun Devil Stadium, so it didn't take them long. After I got in the game in the fourth quarter I moved the team pretty well, threw some nice balls, and they said, 'Hell, we're going to start him.'"

Though Asmus made good on a pair of first half field goal attempts, the Blitz countered with a 15-yard Landry to Lenny Willis scoring toss and a field goal of their own to take a 10–6 halftime lead. Chicago extended its advantage in the third period on a Paul Ricker reception, a short burst by Kevin Long, and another Ricker touchdown early in the final frame. The only things that went wrong for the dominating Blitz were a pair of missed extra-point kicks by Frank Corral who had injured his hamstring in practice the prior week. The Wranglers countered with a Risher to Mike Smith touchdown pass, but after Asmus' point after was blocked, they trailed 29–12 with 11:23 left in the game.

Risher gradually and surprisingly led Arizona back into the game. First, he completed an 85-yard drive by hitting Jackie Flowers with a 10-yard scoring pass. He capped the march with a miraculous two-point conversion throw to Mark Keel. Trying to escape the Chicago pursuit on the conversion attempt, Risher drifted back nearly 35 yards and somehow completed an accurate toss to Keel as he was falling forward to the ground.

"I called the play and lined us up in the wrong formation," Risher admitted. "When I got to the line of scrimmage, I knew I had lined us up opposite of what we should have been based upon what I had called. So I started the improvisation process immediately because I knew I had already screwed up the deal. I started running around back there and found Mark Keel in the endzone."

The Wranglers defense held, and Arizona's young quarterback moved his team again, ending that march with a nine-yard toss to the leaping Neil Balholm. Asmus' extra point brought the Wranglers to within 29–27. Another Blitz drive fizzled, and Risher and company took over 58 yards from pay dirt with one timeout and just over a minute remaining. The passer used four completions and a clutch first down scramble on third and ten to lead the Wranglers down to the Blitz 17 in the waning moments. The beleaguered Asmus trotted onto the field and lined up to try the game-winning kick with four ticks left on the clock. Before a national audience on ESPN and 28,434 fans at Sun Devil Stadium, he redeemed himself from the previous week's failures by splitting the uprights and giving the Wranglers an improbable 30–29 win as the Arizona crowd went into a frenzy. The comeback looked great on television and showed that the USFL might be more competitive than many had thought. Maybe Allen's Blitz weren't going to crush the rest of the league after all.

"I felt really good," said Asmus. "I didn't really feel all that nervous, and I felt pretty confident about it. I remembered the emotion. I had been fortunate in that in my career in high school and college that I had never missed a game-winning field goal. I couldn't imagine it going the other way. I remember just after the kick was gone, you could see the whole sidelines go bananas. Alan Risher was a great asset in that game. He made so many remarkable plays, hitting Jackie Flowers and Neil Balholm for scores. It was really great to contribute on that part. It was a really good feeling to be on the other end."

"The players went bananas," laughed Risher. "The thing I remember most is that we had about 30,000 people that night at the game, and everybody stayed until the very end. As far as being in the ballgame, they were standing up and cheering the entire fourth quarter. When we came back, it was an experience I'll never forget. I went on to play two years in the NFL, but it was the highlight of my five-year professional career because it was such a big upset that we beat George Allen and the Chicago Blitz."

In other second-week action, Tampa Bay remained unbeaten by tipping Michigan, 19–7, at Tampa Stadium. Greg Boone, subbing for the injured Ricky Williams, ran for 157 yards on 31 carries and tallied a seven-yard touchdown for the Bandits. The visiting Breakers collected their first win at Denver by a 21–7 margin. Walton completed 20 out of 28 throws for 234 yards and a pair of scores. The Stars' 25–0 crushing of the Generals featured the second consecutive subpar performance for Herschel Walker as Philadelphia's defense limited him to 60 yards on 13 carries, while Philly's Kelvin Bryant ran for 114 yards on 24 tries with a two-yard touchdown. New Jersey quarterback Scott gave up three more interceptions to a Stars defense that had allowed just one score in two games.

Quarterback Bob Lane's touchdown sneak in overtime propelled the Stallions to a 20–14 win over the Invaders. Lane started the game because Reggie Collier had sustained a hip pointer against Michigan the previous week, but when Lane was ineffective, Collier replaced him and guided Birmingham to two touchdowns. Lane had to come back for the overtime session when Collier re-aggravated his injury. In the Monday night affair,

Los Angeles beat Washington, 20–3. Mike Rae, now splitting quarterback duties with Tom Ramsey in Hugh Campbell's offensive scheme, threw for a pair of scores in the second quarter.

Attendance had fallen slightly to 36,192 per game but remained solid. ABC's ratings began to level off, falling to 7.2, still well above preseason expectations and its direct competition.

Week three brought the much anticipated clash between Chicago and Denver. Front office personnel from the two teams had publicly argued about player spending. Frugal Denver owner Ron Blanding and free-spending Chicago coach George Allen had been particularly vocal. On the field, the low-salaried Gold had scored only 14 points in two games, both home losses, and hadn't shown much spark at all. The Blitz, on the other hand, had whipped Washington in the first week but fell to a great Wranglers' comeback the following game. They were seething over the loss to Arizona and anxious to prove that it was a fluke.

While league observers expected a spirited game, neither team was prepared for what greeted them on their March 20 game day. Thanks to 20-mile-per-hour winds, the wind chill factor stood at a mere four degrees and eight inches of snow fell throughout the game. It was not what players expected when they signed on with the new spring league.

Predictably, Chicago's defense dominated Denver in the wintry conditions on the way to a 10–0 Blitz advantage. John Roveto, subbing for the injured Frank Corral, converted a short field goal before Landry hit Willis for a 42-yard touchdown strike. Running back Harry Sydney kept the Gold in the game with a 36-yard run that set up a Brian Speelman field goal and then added a 30-yard scoring jaunt following a fumbled snap by the Blitz punter. A Roveto kick early in the fourth gave Chicago the lead once more at 13–10.

Finally, Denver mounted its only sustained drive of the ballgame, scratching and clawing its way to the Chicago one with 22 seconds left. Facing fourth down, the Gold could have kicked the field goal for a tie or tried for the touchdown and the win. With the bad blood between the teams and the less than ideal kicking conditions, Coach Red Miller chose the latter. Quarterback Ken Johnson ran the option, shuffling out to the left before bouncing into the end zone with the winning score. Denver managed just ten yards passing and had tossed three interceptions but somehow won the game. No one was smiling at the 16–13 victory more than Ron Blanding. It must have eaten at Allen and Diethrich to lose to the owner and his bargain bunch.

"We went up there and playing against a legend in George Allen, we were playing for something," said Sydney. "It was fun. Once we punted the ball, and the wind was blowing so hard, we lost 15 yards."

In other games, New Jersey fell to 0–3 after being whipped 32–9 by 3–0 Tampa Bay. A league record crowd of 53,370 at the Meadowlands saw Herschel Walker manage only 39 yards on 19 carries. While the USFL welcomed the large crowd, league officials were not nearly as happy over the performance of the offensively-challenged Generals. It was quickly becoming clear that they had very little to offer outside of Walker. The Bandits' John Reaves connected on 19 of 29 throws for 255 yards and three touchdowns.

A tiny crowd of 12,850 in Birmingham saw the Stallions fall, 17–10, to the Stars in uncharacteristic 20-degree temperatures. Kelvin Bryant continued his great play with 176 yards rushing, and Allen Harvin also contributed with a two-yard touchdown scamper and a 67-yard kickoff return to set up another score. Reggie Collier tallied the only Birmingham touchdown before he left the game due to his hip pointer. Despite the loss of the rookie quarterback, the Stallions drove to the Stars 12 in the final minute before giving the ball up on downs. For the third straight week, the Stars' defense had proven to be the difference.

The resurgent Wranglers made it two in a row at home with a 21–14 decision over Los Angeles. Asmus nailed kicks from 57 and 41 yards out in the win. The Invaders' Fred Besana connected on 24 of 30 passes for 338 yards and touchdowns of 45, 22 and 32 yards in Oakland's 33–27 triumph over the Panthers at the Silverdome. Washington joined New Jersey as the circuit's two winless teams after a 19–16 setback at Boston. The Breakers scored ten points in the final four and a half minutes thanks to two bad snaps by the Federals' Dave Pacella. The first mistake occurred on a punt and set the Breakers up for a one-yard touchdown run to tie the game. The Feds drove to the Boston 25 and lined up to try a field goal, but Pacella's next snap sailed over the holder and Walton needed just two passes to get Mazzetti in range for his fourth field goal of the game with 27 seconds left on the clock.

Washington Federals

The loss was Washington's third straight to begin the season, but its first close one. From the start of the year, it appeared obvious the team wasn't going to be much of a factor in the Atlantic Division race. The Federals finally cracked the win column the next weekend when they hosted Michigan but made it exciting by missing an extra point kick and blowing a nine-point cushion before rallying in overtime, 22–16.

It was all downhill from there as Washington seemed to find a new way to lose every week. They suffered a 34–3 Easter Sunday blowout at Philadelphia, allowed a game-winning 98-yard touchdown pass in a 22–21 loss to Arizona, missed a short kick in the waning seconds against New Jersey and allowed a player who had been in school a week earlier to run for the winning score late in their battle with Tampa Bay. Back-to-back blowouts against Birmingham and Chicago preceded a narrow loss at Oakland. Quarterback Mike Hohensee's last-second scramble came up one foot short of the endzone and tying the Invaders. The Generals came calling again and won on a 50-yard kick in the mud that cleared its mark by inches. A week later, Denver downed them 24–12 to send the Federals' record to a league-worst 1–13.

"I was 21 or 22 years old so I asked Coy Bacon, 'Is this really pro football?' laughed star rookie running back Craig James. "'Kid, you gettin' paid, ain't ya?' 'Yeah, I guess so, but it sure doesn't feel like it around here.'"

"I didn't really have a feel for where we were compared to the other teams," admitted head coach Ray Jauch. "I have to be honest; when we started the season it seemed as if a lot of teams were in the same boat we were in. We just had a run of a lot of bad luck. If anything could go wrong, it went wrong for the Federals."

They broke their losing string with an 18–11 triumph at Arizona, a team in the midst of its own losing streak. The following week, Washington again played the Michigan Panthers tough but left with a 27–25 loss on a late field goal. They closed out the season on a high note with wins over Los Angeles and Philadelphia, leaving them with a 4–14 mark, tied with Arizona for worst in the league. Though they played several close games, the Federals seemed to find new ways to lose almost every week.

"The funniest one that happened was in Boston at Nickerson Field," added Jauch. "It boiled down to the end of the game, and we were lining up to kick a field goal to win it. Our regular snapper had gotten hurt and we had our second team snapper in there. He snapped the ball over the head of our holder, it bounced around and went all the way back to the other end of the field. Boston fell on it, kicked a field goal and beat us. You talk about snatching defeat from the jaws of victory, that's what we did right there."

Washington lost eight games by seven or fewer points and five games by a total of ten points thanks in large part to a kicking game that hit just 17 field goals in 34 attempts. First-round draft pick Craig James finished the season with 823 yards on the ground despite missing several games with a back problem. He ran for 744 yards in the final 11 contests after returning from the injured list. Three Feds quarterbacks—McQuilken, Hohensee and veteran Joe Gilliam—managed only 21 touchdowns to 33 interceptions. Billy Taylor caught 64 balls for 523 yards, and Joey Walters grabbed 63 for 959 yards. Safety Doug Greene finished second in the league with nine interceptions for 121 yards, and Eric Robinson led the league with a 29.0-yard kickoff return average. He had many opportunities as Washington tied Arizona by giving up the most points in the league (442). Due to injuries and ineffectiveness, just 26 players lasted the entire season and 79 players called themselves Federals at one time during the year. Only one opening-day starter on the defensive line lasted the season. A total of 23 players, including 14 starters missed at least one game due to injury.

An exasperated Jauch grasped for any way to spark the team.

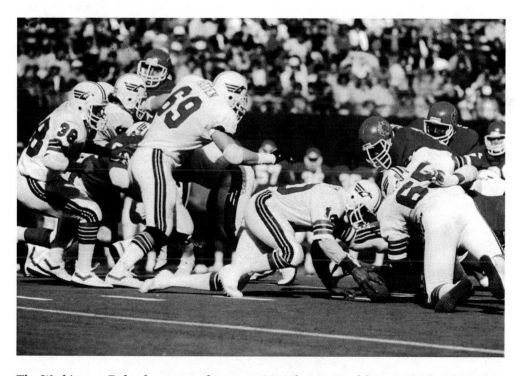

The Washington Federals attempted to resuscitate the career of former Pittsburgh Steelers quarterback Joe Gilliam who had not played professionally since 1975 and had battled drug and alcohol dependency for much of a decade. Photograph by Jim Turner, from author's collection.

"We were having a tough time, and we were playing New Jersey," he said. "We kicked off to the Generals, and boy, we pinned them back there on the ten-yard line. I'm on the sidelines thinking, 'We're getting off to a good start here. Maybe things are going to change.' I'm standing there looking over at the play, and I see them pitch the ball to Herschel Walker. I said to myself, 'If he makes the corner, we're in trouble.' Sure enough, he made the corner and comes running down the field toward us, right along our sideline. So I thought to myself, 'We've been having such a hard time, I'm just going to run out onto the field and tackle Walker. Somebody's got to do something to get our guys fired up.' Walker's about 6'3" 235 at the time, and I'm zeroing in on him. He didn't see me at all, even though he was running right at me. As he came at me, he got bigger and bigger and bigger, and I figured there was no way I was going to hit this guy. I just stepped back onto the sideline and let him go. Probably the smartest thing I ever did."

The season proved an utter disaster off the field as well. No-shows regularly outnumbered spectators after the first game, and Washington averaged just 13,850 fans per contest. After the opening day crowd of 38,010, the next largest turned out to be 13,936. The Feds pathetic play and numerous injuries kept attendance to a minimum. To complicate matters further, the team played five of its first six home games in driving rains. Reports placed Jauch's job in jeopardy for the last half of the season before the squad's late showing earned him another year.

"It was hard; it was very difficult," added Jauch. "We were having such a hard time, things just weren't going right, and it was raining all the time. I was driving into work one day, and I thought, 'If I had a gun, I'd shoot somebody.' Then I got to thinking about how to loosen our guys up. I got to the park and talked to our equipment guy. I asked, 'Can you get me a starters pistol?' He said, 'Sure,' and he got me one.

"The day before, we had two guys get into a fight at practice; things were getting tense. One of the guys was a kid I knew pretty well from Canada. I got both of them into my office, and I told them, 'I want both of you guys to get into a fight today. Pretend to fight. I'm going to break it up three times. The first two times I break it up, you guys start it up again and the third time, just follow my lead.' I didn't even tell them what I was going to do. My coaches didn't even know it. I had this gun in my pocket, and the two started to fight. Coaches were getting mad at me, saying, 'C'mon, do something about it. You can't let this go on!' It built and built. There was a TV guy there, and I told him to stick around practice for a little while. I told him what was going to happen and to keep his camera running for the third time. It happens a second time, and then the third time I whip my gun out and shouted, 'I've had enough of this!' I shot at the one guy, and his eyes got really big, and he just fell over backwards. Coy Bacon actually thought I had lost it. He ran to the parking lot and wouldn't come back to practice. He thought I had gone crazy. The irony of the whole thing is that several years later Coy Bason ended up getting shot in D.C.!

"They were a really good bunch of guys. They took a lot of criticism, and they never said anything. They never bitched about anything or complained about anything. They didn't say, 'We don't have this or we don't have that.' They just did it; they just went out and tried."

For the Feds, even the routine became an adventure.

"We were going over to Georgetown University because it was raining, and so we all had to dress up at RFK and drive over on a bus to practice at Georgetown," recalled James. "We practice in the rain, and when we're coming back, our bus makes the wrong turn and is going in front of the Jefferson Memorial and it high centers. The bus is stuck. It's raining, so we all have to get off and thumb a ride or get a cab to get back to RFK stadium. Now you're looking at pro football players thumbing a ride or getting in a cab. I got in a cab with two or three different guys, buddies, teammates. We're in there with shoulder pads and we're sitting in the cab and I say, 'Hey does anyone got any money?' The cabbie was running the risk of getting shafted on that deal."

From the beginning, unfavorable comparisons to the Super Bowl champion Redskins were unavoidable. Team president Jim Gould resigned in late May, reportedly under pressure from Bernhard, and soon found his way to the Tampa Bay Bandits. After one season, the Washington Federals appeared to be in serious trouble.

"I got a call from the commissioner, and I put together a team in Washington, DC, called the Washington Federals, in literally like 60 days with Berl Bernhard and a number of other people," recalled Gould, who had moved over from Birmingham prior to the season. "We ended up losing ten games in a row. We became kind of the bookies dream because they always knew they could count on us. It was kind of sad actually.

"Early on Berl and I had a great relationship. Unfortunately, at that point in my life I worked hard and played hard, so I probably was my own worst enemy. I worked morning, noon and night, and I would say that I also was a product of the 60s so I think that basically my style and Berl Bernhard's style did not jibe with each other. He hired a guy to be general manager of the team who was completely the wrong guy. Nice guy, but totally in over his head. I was very dissatisfied with the club, the team that we put on the field, and I took the blame for it."

"Washington had no real ownership," said Camera. "It was a bunch of lawyers. That was a problem. We had to spend time with them, and we knew we had a problem with them early on."

New Jersey Generals

Expectations were higher for the New Jersey Generals, owing to the presence of Herschel Walker. Los Angeles, Philadelphia, Tampa Bay and Boston dispatched New Jersey in quick fashion, though, sending them to 0–4 to begin the year. Their celebrated runner, in particular, struggled, while revealing an alarming tendency to put the ball on the ground.

"He's running tentatively," complained New Jersey Coach Chuck Fairbanks in the *Herald-Journal*. "He's doing too much footwork—maybe he wants to make the big play, but the big play has to happen. When it's right, it'll happen. When it's not there, you can't make it happen."

Fortunately for Fairbanks, Walker got on track with 177 yards as New Jersey took out Arizona, 35–21, in game five. He would run for more than 100 yards in his next four outings, but New Jersey could only split them to hit the season's midpoint at 3–6. They entered the second half of the campaign with three more losses to slide out of playoff contention completely before Herschel chalked up 194 yards in a narrow victory at Washington. Wins against L.A. and Arizona followed defeats to Oakland and Philadelphia. A 34–10 loss at Boston closed their disappointing 6–12 campaign.

Walker earned a measure of redemption, though, when he cemented the league rushing title with a total of 1,812 yards for the season. He had shown that he did indeed have the talent to star in the league after his slow start. In addition to his league-leading rushing total and 17 touchdowns on the ground, he also topped the Generals' weak receiving corps with 53 catches for 489 yards and became the leading scorer among non-kickers with 110 points. He did all this despite the presence of four rookies on the offensive line.

"I would suspect that, even if we made no changes from this team next year, and there will be changes, Herschel is going to be a better back," Fairbanks told the *Patriot Ledger*. "He'll have an opportunity to get himself ready for the entire pre-season camp and he won't just have come off a vigorous college season.

"People talk about the pressure put on Herschel, but it wasn't pressure that affected him. He can deal with pressure. What I think got to him, if anything, was the expectations people placed on him. I have never seen a young athlete who walked into a situation where he was supposed to be the whole team, and where he alone was supposed to make us a winner."

An unsettled passing game headlined first by Bobby Scott and then by Jeff Knapple produced a paltry 12 touchdowns, least in the USFL, and coughed up 27 interceptions. As bad as it was, the defense was even worse. They finished eleventh against the rush and dead last against the pass. The line was unable to provide consistent pressure on opposing quarterbacks, and the unit finished third from the bottom in scoring defense, giving up 437 points during the season, an average of 25 points per game.

The hype over the Heisman-winning back helped the Generals average 35,004 fans per home game in their inaugural season. His signing had boosted the numbers considerably. New Jersey failed to beat a team with a winning record during the season with their half dozen wins coming against Arizona and Washington (twice apiece), Denver and Los Angeles. The franchise's poor record had been a bitter disappointment to the league which had hoped to showcase its most marketable superstar. Fairbanks had not been much of a help either, holding Walker out of games at crucial junctures, including late in the nationally televised opener. An absentee owner further exacerbated the franchise's trouble procuring media attention.

"J. Walter Duncan was an outstanding person, a gentleman," said Camera. "First time I flew in a private plane was in Duncan's plane. He would fly in from Tulsa. He bled that he couldn't give New York a winner in his first year. He loved Chuck. He thought Chuck would do a great job, and Chuck made a terrible mistake. He figured his offense, and his experience, combined with the fact that he had beaten most of the other coaches before, he figured he would be able to put together an offense that resembled a college offense, and it really wasn't very good. He had Bobby Scott at quarterback, and he couldn't throw the ball 15 yards! Bobby Scott was a good player in his day, but his arm was shot. When they put him in there, the other teams figured it out early on. We used to practice in Florida, and we'd have two or three teams practice at the same site. We used to scrimmage the opposing teams to save costs, and everybody knew everything about every player. They had all been analyzed by one combine scouting program, and everyone knew Bobby Scott had a problem with his arm, but Chuck thought it would work out, no problem."

Michigan Panthers

The Michigan Panthers also started their inaugural campaign very slowly. They followed up their opening night win over Birmingham with four straight losses, including one to the Federals who would not win another in their first 14 tries. With his team at 1–4, owner Alfred Taubman stepped in and hired a new offensive line, hoping to salvage the season. He signed guards Thom Dornbrook and Tyrone McGriff and tackle Ray Pinney, all former Pittsburgh Steelers, in the hope of giving young Bobby Hebert some time to throw the ball. His move proved effective, and the Panthers bolted, knocking off New Jersey, Chicago, Los Angeles, Boston, Arizona and New Jersey again. Both offense and defense had come around, and the rest of the league paid the price. Hebert and receiver Anthony Carter proved to be a deadly combination, while John Corker and the defense took advantage of nearly every opportunity.

"When I look back at that we were still coming together as a team," recalled Hebert. "Everyone was new. The addition of those three Steeler linemen made an unbelievable difference. That's what turned our team around."

"We started the season 1–4, and then we went out and got some of the guys from the Pittsburgh Steelers offensive line: Thom Dornbrook, Ray Pinney and Tyrone McGriff," recalled receiver Derek Holloway. "When we got those guys it was like a different team. We started running the ball well, and that opened up the passing game."

"We thought some of our young guys were going to come along quicker," Panthers director of player personnel Mike Keller said of the offensive line. "That was my mistake. We drafted some young guys who eventually turned into pretty good players, but they weren't ready for primetime. All this talent that we had, without an offensive line, the quarterback didn't have enough time to throw, the running backs didn't have anywhere to go. I went to Al Taubman, and he said, 'Mike, what is it that you need?' I said, 'We've got to go out and get some experienced offensive linemen.' He said, 'Go out and get whoever you need.' Basically, he gave me a blank check, although what we ended up getting the guys for was almost nothing.

"When we were signing guys out of the National Football League, it wasn't for as much as some guys were saying because their contracts were so low at the time. The best offensive line in football at the time belonged to the Pittsburgh Steelers. We signed three guys off that Pittsburgh Steeler team. Ray Pinney was the main guy, and then we signed Tyrone McGriff and Thom Dornbrook. That went together with Wayne Radloff, a Georgia rookie we had who turned into a helluva player. Now we had the best offensive line in the United States Football League. When you have the best offensive line, you're able to run the ball and protect Bobby Hebert, so now our passing game started to gel and our running game started to gel, and it made our defense better because they weren't under pressure every game."

They sandwiched a 43–7 pummeling of Tampa Bay between disappointing losses to Birmingham and Philadelphia. They pounded Los Angeles and survived a scare against Washington before heading into Soldier Field for a showdown with the Chicago Blitz. Rookie Hebert showed his rapid maturation with five touchdown throws in a crucial 34–19 win against George Allen's veterans in 100-plus degree heat.

Needing a victory to clinch the division, they walloped visiting Arizona, 33–7, to capture the division title and a postseason berth. Eleven wins in their final 13 games made the 12–6 Panthers the hottest team in the USFL.

"I was so happy for the team and the coaches and how far they came from the early part of the season," Keller said. "There was so much uncertainty; so many trials, coming from 1–4 and clawing our way back into the championship race and starting to gel at the end of the season. We were a very good football team. At the end of that first season, I thought at the time that we could have beaten half of the National Football League—the lower half, not the upper half. We would have been a very representative team, with the potential to be a playoff team in the NFL by the end of the season."

Michigan entered the season with 24 rookies, more than half its roster. Most of their resurgence could be credited to their offensive development. Behind his new line, Hebert had the time to grow into the circuit's highest rated passer. The Panthers allowed just 20 sacks over the course of the season, enabling him to connect on 257 of 451 throws for 3,568 yards and a league-high 27 touchdowns, 11 in the final four games. He also topped the USFL in yards per pass.

"Bobby had that Cajun accent," remembered receiver Derek Holloway. "We had put in a blitz package. When the strong safety was going to blitz, Bobby was supposed to say 'Snake.' But Bobby couldn't say 'Snake'; he would say 'Nake.' We kept saying, 'Bobby, you have to say 'Snake.'' Every time we went up to the line, he would say 'Nake, nake!' We ended up changing it because Bobby couldn't say the word, 'Snake.' He just couldn't get it out.

"Bobby was a good guy, and we worked well together."

Tight end Mike Cobb led Michigan with 61 catches for 746 yards, while Carter came on strong after a slow start and made 60 grabs for 1,181 yards, an impressive average of 19.7 yards per catch. Ken Lacy finished third in the league with 1,180 yards on the ground.

The offensive unit finished second in the USFL in scoring with 451 points, just five points behind top-ranked Chicago. It tallied 199 of those points in the last six weeks. Defensively, linebacker Corker terrorized opposing quarterbacks with 28 sacks, almost double the number of his closest competitor in the league. Dave Tipton added 12 and all told, the team dumped opposing quarterbacks 74 times, second most in the circuit.

"I think we did a real good job of finding players, not just to spend money on, but spending on guys like Derek Holloway who were real competitive but the NFL was never going to look very hard at him because he was so short," added Keller. "But he had speed, desire and toughness. He was a strong guy, and he could block. We found guys like Derek Holloway, guys like Ray Bentley from Central Michigan. He had such an instinct for playing the middle linebacker position, but he was never even going to be drafted by the NFL because he didn't run a 4.8 40 as a linebacker. He was probably a 5.2, 5.3 guy, but he never took a wrong step."

An immigrant from Yugoslavia and one of the more colorful characters in the USFL, Michigan Panthers kicker Novo Bojovic played with a single white glove on his left hand and a clove of garlic stuffed inside his kicking shoe. Photograph by Jim Turner, from author's collection.

The franchise averaged just 22,250 fans per game, but drew more than average over its final three home contests as the fans, wary of the Lions' losing ways, responded to the team's turnaround. A May game against New Jersey attracted 32,862 when tickets were offered on a two-for-one basis. More importantly, though, the Panthers had captured quite a bit of attention in championship-starved Detroit with their late-season run. The Lions, on the other hand, hadn't hosted a playoff game since the 1957 NFL championship game.

"Detroit was curious initially, but we were so bad initially, we had a lot of fans disguised as empty seats for the early part of the season," explained Keller. "When we started to win, they started coming back."

"We were more popular than the Detroit Lions, and you know all the fans really wanted to see a game, the Panthers against the Lions," recalled Hebert. "I think if you looked at the 28 teams at that time and how good we were, I'm not saying we would have been in the top ten but we would have been in the top 14. I think truly that we could have beaten the Lions, but what would the Lions have to gain if they beat us? Well you beat an up and coming team, but then if we beat them, the Lions, they could never live that down."

Tampa Bay Bandits

Following wins over Boston, Michigan and New Jersey, Tampa Bay found itself one of two undefeated teams through week three. Spurning expensive, big-name players, coach Steve Spurrier had instead installed a daring offense, dubbed "Banditball," to make up for any lack of big-name talent. Their plan continued to work in week four when they knocked Philadelphia from the ranks of the unbeaten, 27–22, thanks to a strong first half from quarterback John Reaves.

"That's Banditball," Spurrier told *USA Today* after the Philadelphia win. "It's wide-open, no-huddle offense, and throwing it all over the lot."

They dropped two of their next three and also lost Reaves with a broken wrist. Fortunately, they had a competent backup to call on in Jimmy Jordan who would lead them to wins over Washington and Oakland with a loss to Philly in between. Jordan, though, bruised his shoulder and

The elusive Gary Anderson joined the Tampa Bay Bandits' backfield midway through the 1983 season and quickly became one of the league's most dangerous players in Steve Spurrier's unpredictable offensive scheme. Photograph by Jim Turner, from author's collection.

would miss a couple of weeks himself. Into the breach stepped running back Gary Anderson, freshly signed after Tampa Bay acquired his rights from the Generals in the Herschel Walker deal. He and new quarterback Mike Kelley led the squad to victories over Arizona and Oakland to move them to 9–3 on the season. Following a blowout loss at Michigan, they celebrated the return of Jordan with a 45–17 crushing of Birmingham. Big losses to Chicago and Boston, though, left them tied for second in the division with but two games left. The Bandits managed to knock off Denver in a thriller but dropped the finale to Birmingham, leaving Spurrier's troops on the outside of the playoff picture.

"Spurrier was a great offensive mind and great motivator," said defensive tackle Fred Nordgren. I really enjoyed playing for him. It was really fun to play for him, and he really fit in well with the Tampa Bay area. People really supported him as a coach, and of course being a Florida Heisman Trophy winner, it really played well with Bassett's marketing genius."

"Before the season started, these NFL guys had picked us dead last in the USFL," recalled Spurrier. "They said Tampa has a college coach who knows nothing about pro football and a lot of players no one's ever heard of. We won our first four in a row, but it didn't last. One thing that was helpful for the Bandits was that the Buccaneers were pretty sorry at that time."

Led by the triumvirate of Reaves, Jordan and Kelley, Tampa Bay topped the league in passing offense with 4,580 yards. They also led the USFL in first downs, passes attempted and completed and finished second to Michigan in net yards gained. Danny Buggs spearheaded the Bandits' receiving corps with 76 grabs for 1,146 yards, while Eric Truvillion, once a quarterback at Florida A&M, caught 66 passes for 1,080 yards. "E.T." also grabbed a league-high 15 touchdowns. Although Boone topped the squad in rushing with 694 yards, Anderson became the featured back the second half of the year and ran up 516 yards. The addition of offensive lineman Fred Dean of the Redskins further helped the Bandits. After keeping the team in games for several weeks, the defense faltered down the stretch and gave up the fourth most points in the league. Still, they ended the season as the USFL's second toughest unit against the pass. Defensive tackle Ken Times paced the defense with 11 sacks.

Despite the late-season struggles, Tampa Bay finished as one of the inaugural season success stories. The Bandits averaged just shy of 40,000 fans per game, the second best number in the league behind Denver. Spurrier's daring style had made the team competitive without having to pay for expensive players. If it hadn't been for startup costs, the Bandits would have turned a profit for John Bassett in just their first season. Once reluctant to join the USFL, owner John Bassett had worked wonders in an NFL market and become perhaps the USFL's biggest cheerleader. He led the league's expansion efforts and could proudly point to his own team as a prime example of how to conduct business in the USFL.

"You could tell that he was, I don't want to say heads and tails beyond everybody else, but he definitely had marketing savvy," New Jersey's Kevin MacConnell said of the Bandits owner. "He knew exactly what he wanted to do. He had another owner obviously, Burt Reynolds, who gave them name recognition and if you went down for a Tampa Bay football game there was something exciting about it. They drew well, they marketed the team very well, you could sense that there was something about Tampa Bay that was different than all the other teams in the league. Especially the first year, the second year I think some teams caught up. But the first year I just sensed, when we went and played there, there was something about them that was totally different than there was from the other teams in the league."

The Bandits had to deal with an increasing number of problems caused by the NFL's Buccaneers. After Maas Brothers, a department store, began sponsoring the USFL team, the Bucs' cheerleaders ended an agreement with the store and signed with another chain. The NFL team also tried to prohibit its statistics crew from working games for the rival league. The crew quit its NFL responsibilities and then kept statistics exclusively for the Bandits. Hugh Culverhouse's franchise further challenged its new rival on use of the Tampa Stadium message board, souvenir sales at the stadium and even use of the 30-second clocks.

John Bassett had put together an organization that was second to none in the USFL, and he had done so in an NFL market. The Bandits countered the Bucs' moves with more promotions and doing whatever they could to get attention in the Tampa Bay area.

"We had all kinds of stuff," remembered Jim Gould, who briefly joined the franchise's front office after leaving Washington. "When I was with him, John Bassett in Tampa had a burn the mortgage night. He invited all the fans to bring their mortgages, and he picked somebody out of the stands, and he literally burned it, so that they no longer had a mortgage. We were very creative. We drew some large crowds."

"John Bassett did a marvelous job in Tampa Bay," added the Stars' Carl Peterson. "He truly captured that city and its excitement for professional football and away from the Tampa Bay Buccaneers of the NFL. I think there was actually a point there when they were outdrawing them attendance wise, certainly in merchandise sales. He had an idea a minute. I mean everything from burning the mortgage at half time, to the people he brought into the organization as part owners: Burt Reynolds, and his wife [Loni Anderson]. It was fun and exciting, and he made it that way and I think he had the right idea in the head coach, Steve Spurrier who I have known forever. Steve understands sports entertainment and likes to do some fun things."

"We used to have women up in the stands with bikinis on and dudes with their shirts off," laughed Bandits offensive lineman Nate Newton. "I mean they do that in Pittsburgh, but it's cold. Who's enjoying it? They're just doing it because they want to be on TV. Our girls and guys were doing it because it was hot. There was beer everywhere, just fun. We would go places and just be with the fans."

Above all, the Bandits managed to have fun, thanks in large part to Spurrier's style and the relationship he had with his players.

"Steve was definitely innovative, ahead of his time," said receiver Eric Truvillion. "All the things that he was doing, the formations, the offense, what you saw later on at the UF where he went on a stretch for ten years winning about ten games a year—that was the end product of what you saw in Banditball in the earlier years. Steve was not afraid to put the ball up, try trick plays, do whatever needed to be done to win a game. So he came in with a young perspective, and just kind of lit it up."

"Banditball was unpredictable, it was totally spontaneous and wonderful," Burt Reynolds recalled. "It was colorful. It was all those things that we make movies about; we make movies about dreams. I'm in the business of making dreams, and it was a team made up of guys that dreamed of playing someday for money and being in pro football, and some didn't have anything but guts, and everything it takes to be a football player except natural ability, and then we had some brilliant athletes, wonderful athletes. It was a conglomeration of all those things and those guys that are right on the cusp of making it in the National Football League, and they hang around and they hang around and eventually sometimes make it three years down the line, but I'm talking about the last guys to get the cut. The league was full of them, and the 'Bandits' was a perfect name because they were outlaws and fun."

"We had Nate Newton at Tampa Bay, who would go on to a great career with the Dallas Cowboys," remembered Spurrier. "Nate came to us from Florida A&M at 295 pounds, and he was the best offensive lineman I've ever been around. He could run like you wouldn't believe for such a big guy. I think the NFL overlooked him.

"Well the first year he was with us, he weighed in the 295 to 300 range, the second year probably 310 to 320 and by the third year he got up to 340 or 350. I used to fine him for his weight, every pound over a certain weight, and he accumulated $1700 in fines. At the end of the year, I called him into my office and said, 'Nate, you don't make enough for me to fine you like this. I can't take your money, but you need to work on losing this weight. It isn't healthy for you to be this big.' I had an envelope with 17 $100 bills in it, and I handed it over to him. His eyes got real wide and he said, 'Thank you, thank you, coach, you're a great guy!'

"I later learned that he went straight from my office over to Popeye's Chicken, where we got a discount, and ordered two buckets of chicken."

"When you look back and you see the elements, the components that were available for the Tampa Bay Bandits: Jerry Reed and Banditball; Burt Reynolds and his gang; Steve Spurrier, young, good-looking, former Heisman Trophy–winning quarterback from the University of Florida, and the Tampa Bay area, which is a hotbed for football, I mean we really had a lot of elements that lined up," said McVay. "That's why many people considered the Tampa bay Bandits the model franchise in the USFL. And I tell you what; we had a lot of fun. That was a ball.

"'All the fun the law allows,' and you know we had a lot of good people and everybody pushing at the right time. The football team came together. Steve Spurrier did a wonderful job coaching the team. The product, the promotion, the pricing: all these elements had to come together, and they really did. The Tampa Bay Bandits in the early 80s was the number one supported professional football team in the Tampa Bay area. Everybody loved the Bandits. We were more popular than the Tampa Bay Buccaneers back then."

Birmingham Stallions

Unlike the Bandits, the Birmingham Stallions didn't have to worry about NFL competition. The Alabama city's only previous brush with pro football ended with the collapse of the WFL in 1975. Starting 1–2 and with only occasional services from oft-injured rookie quarterback Reggie Collier, they managed to tip Arizona before falling to Boston, Chicago and Denver in quick succession. Struggling offensively, the 2–5 club brought in Pittsburgh Steelers receiver Jim Smith to steady the passing game. The move, coupled with a defensive surge, seemed to help the Stallions turn their season around. They rattled off five straight wins even after losing Collier for the remainder of the year. Included in their streak was a 35–3 pounding of Washington and an overtime decision over Michigan, one of the hottest teams in the league.

Just as quickly as they had jumped back into the race for the league title, they fell right back out. Birmingham lost four of its next five to drop to 8–9 before a victory over

Tampa Bay ended their season with a .500 record. Owner Marvin Warner further showed his commitment to making the Stallions a winner by announcing that three-time Pro Bowl running back Joe Cribbs of the Buffalo Bills would join the team the following season. Cribbs had already notched a pair of 1,000-yard seasons in his brief NFL career and would add another during the 1983 campaign.

"Marvin was the quintessential politician," Ehrhart recalled. "Most of the people called him 'Ambassador.' He had been an ambassador and was very erudite, very articulate. He had the experience in politics, and he was one of the owners who counseled against over-spending in the first year. There were some who said, 'Hey, we've got this great opportunity so we have to invest now.' The guys who were on one side said, 'We're investing in this,' and the guys that were on the other side were accusing them of over-spending. Marvin was on the side of the anti-spenders.

"You read today about Washington saying, 'We're going to spend our way out of this situation. Let's go spend some more money.' Marvin's quote he'd usually bring up in the league meetings was, 'You can't solve every problem by throwing money at it. Washington has been doing that forever and it never works.' He was on one side of the fence; he ran a more economical franchise, but he did step up when we made the decision to bring on two wild card players. He was one of the first guys to step up, and he signed Reggie Collier, the great quarterback from Southern Miss who had beaten Alabama, a wonderful athlete. Then the second year he brought on Joe Cribbs. He had done exactly what we debated at length in ownership meetings about whether to have these wild card players."

"I loved the ambassador," Camera added. "Old Marvin was delightful. Marvin was a political guy, he knew his way around. Birmingham was a great city, a tough market to penetrate. Football is king there, but its college football. College football is king. They wanted to get on the map, and Marvin did a wonderful job. He was from Cincinnati, but he had good people around him. He worked very hard to make sure that Birmingham got good press, and he was very big with the political types so they were always giving him support. The problem with Marvin was that he'd fly in for the games and fly out. Marvin was tight. He didn't like to spend money, especially his own. I enjoyed Marvin. He made me laugh.

"They were competitive. He hired Rollie Dotsch who was one of the best coaches around. He would have been a superstar head coach in the NFL. He was smart, he was an offensive line coach who became a head coach, built a very powerful team, and they just beat the hell out of you on the field."

The Stallions lived up to their early reputation as a tough team to figure out. Their one recognizable star, Collier, sat on the injured list when the team experienced its greatest success. Lane led the club to a 7–4 record down the stretch, but the running game really moved the ball. They finished first in the league with 3,017 yards rushing despite the absence of a 1,000-yard back. Ken Talton topped the Birmingham runners with 907 yards. Stallions quarterbacks combined to throw 15 touchdowns with 27 interceptions and gained just 2,998 yards through the air, the second-worst total for any USFL team. The defense finished around the middle of the pack.

Birmingham was one of just three USFL cities the first year without an NFL tenant. The Birmingham Americans had won the only World Football League championship in 1974, but their successors, the Vulcans, had closed up shop suddenly the following year along with the rest of the league. The city had been burned once, and the attendance picture told a mixed story. The franchise averaged 22,046 fans per game with a low of 5,000 in terrible, rainy conditions early in the year and a high of 42,212 for the Los Angeles game in the middle of their winning streak. In addition to the franchise's 2–5 start, team president Jerry Sklar pointed to several early-season cable telecasts and poor weather as further contributors to the attendance. In addition, local "blue" laws which prohibited alcohol sales on Sundays also did not help. Although crowd support for the season had fallen below projections, the late-season improvement showed that the jury remained out in Birmingham.

"I thought we had one of the best organizations in the league with Rollie Dotsch as our head coach," said receiver Joey Jones. "He was a great coach and had four Super Bowl rings from his time with the Steelers. All the management, from Jerry Sklar on down, ran the team first class. I know we didn't have as much money as some other teams, but I was very impressed with the organization."

Arizona Wranglers

Because of a late start, the Arizona Wranglers looked to be the Pacific Division's weak sister from the opening gun. The Wranglers followed a 1–2 start with losses to Birmingham and New Jersey to put themselves in a quick hole. A 98-yard Alan Risher to Jackie Flowers scoring toss gave Arizona a narrow win over Washington, but they followed with a listless defeat to the Boston Breakers before topping Denver in their next game. At 4–4, they held a share of the division lead. It all quickly fell apart, though, as they lost their final ten games, not many of which were close. They had to contend with their own poor play in their final home game against Washington, and the Arizona heat also took its toll.

"It was hotter than blazes," laughed assistant general manager Jim Foster, who was in charge of the Wranglers' marketing effort. "We had the two worst teams in the league, vying for the worst record, and I had to do something to prop it up. I came up with something called the World's Largest Tailgate Party, which we actually pulled off. I got all these sponsors and vendors to provide food and basically if you had a ticket to the game, you could get in free to this huge bazaar of food and entertainment across the street from the stadium." Some of the entertainment included several bands and an attempt at the world free-fall record, set when the daredevil plunged 15 stories off a mining crane into a foam rubber pad. More than 16,000 fans took him up on the offer. "Considering how bad we were at that point, I'm amazed that thing came off as well as it did," added Foster.

A total of 35 rookies made Coach Doug Shively's roster, accounting for a good many of the team's mistakes. Inexplicably, 14 players cut from the team caught on with other USFL clubs, and five became starters. Director of player personnel Bill Baker resigned during the year.

"Doug was a nice guy off the field, and I'm sure he's a great assistant coach," said kicker Jim Asmus, who was cut in midseason. "As a head coach though, I'm not so sure. For example, there were a lot of assistant coaches he recruited, and they were all from Florida and Alabama. I'm sure they were credible coaches in college, but it just wasn't a very cohesive unit. The coaches didn't really create a great atmosphere, which quite honestly showed with the final record. It's too bad because there were some really talented players who were there. They got rid of some more talented players and opted instead for some of their college players that they knew better. That happens; it's the politics of sports.

"My teammates were great: Alan [Risher] and Mark Krueger, Cal Murray. We had such a close knit group. I used to hang out with the linemen, and everyone was somewhat complaining about the coaches, but it was a job and we had to realize that. We were young at that time, for sure, and I think there was a lot of team cohesiveness, but as far as the coaches, I didn't really care too much for a lot of their antics.

"I kicked a 58-yard field goal, which they marked as 57, but before I went out there Doug told me, 'You make this one or you're gone.' I thought, 'Boy, way to send me out on that one.'"

Guard Frank Kalil, after having several holding penalties called against him over the first few games, believed that he had been targeted by the officials. To combat the problem, he changed his number from 67 to 75 before a game in the hope that the subterfuge would help his cause. The officials did not flag him the entire game, and one even asked him what happened to number 67. "I told 'em he was waived," Kalil told *The Sporting News*.

Tricks could not help their defense which finished last in the USFL and was particularly ineffective against the run. A look at the offense, however, showed that they were not solely to blame for their collapse in the second half of the schedule. The Wranglers scored just 261 points, last in the entire USFL. Their running game lagged as third worst in the circuit and averaged just 3.7 yards per run. They nearly had to abandon it altogether late in the year. Calvin Murray topped the squad with 699 yards, and Alan Risher performed admirably at quarterback, throwing for 2,672 yards with 20 touchdowns and 16 interceptions before bowing to injuries. Mark Keel caught 65 passes for 802 yards while Jackie Flowers and Neil Balholm each grabbed 63 balls for 869 and 703 yards, respectively. Flowers also hauled in 11 touchdowns, including scores in seven consecutive games. The franchise's late start had hindered its search for players, and Doug Shively's staff, largely composed of former colleagues from Clemson University, failed to inspire the players. Joseph fired the coach in September.

"We started off 4–4 and went on to lose ten straight games," said Risher. "With all due respect to our coaching staff, we had a college coaching staff that didn't know much about the pro game, especially offensively. We got pretty stagnant in our offense, and people finally caught on to what I was doing, running around and throwing the ball. We didn't play very good defense, either. We were in the bottom one or two in defense. We were always behind. It was a tough last ten games, I can tell you that.

"I think we were put together so late that we were kind of winning with smoke and mirrors early on, even winning four ballgames against some of the other competition. I don't know how much Coach Shively had personnel-wise to actually coach there. We had some decent players in spots, but overall we were probably in the bottom half of the league in talent. I thought he did a pretty good job with what he did. He assembled, however, a staff that didn't have any real experience. Some of the people on staff had only coached at the college level and read college offenses and things like that, and I think he probably made a couple mistakes there. I don't really know who he had the opportunity to go out and hire and who wanted to take a chance on the league from a coaching perspective."

Despite the problems, Arizona drew an average crowd of 25,776 fans per game. That number fell when they didn't bring in more than 22,000 over their final five home contests with a low of 16,656 in their final home appearance against Washington.

Fortunately, the ball club spent much of their losing streak on the road to avoid the summer heat in Arizona. Joseph estimated first year losses at around $2 million, or half a million more than they had projected.

"You just knew Arizona was going to be a problem, mainly because of the fact that there was no leadership out there," said Camera. "The climate was perfect. Arizona was supposed to be where the good doctor wanted to be, but Joseph had more money and he got the market. Diethrich had his heart institute out there, so the bottom line is that Jim got the team and did nothing with it."

Denver Gold

Likewise, the Denver Gold appeared destined for the USFL's lower echelon. They had stuck to the league's original spending constraints and refused to budge on the matter, even eschewing the chance to hire wild card marquee players. After falling to Philadelphia and Boston to begin the year, Denver surprised Chicago, stopped Oakland and then beat the Michigan Panthers to inch above the .500 mark and stake their claim as one of the USFL's early surprises. Another tough performance ended in an overtime defeat to Tampa Bay before they tipped Birmingham the next week on a long Brian Speelman field goal.

Like their Pacific mates the Arizona Wranglers, they saw their hopes for the season tumble around them on the heels of a five-game losing streak. The skid, combined with a personal feud with team owner Ron Blanding, cost popular coach Red Miller his job.

"The one thing I remember about Red Miller besides the fact he was an NFL legend, is that year when people got cut, the owner at that time wanted to send them home on a bus, and Red wouldn't let that happen," said running back Harry Sydney. "He was a football guy. He tried to make it as much like the NFL as he could.

"Ron Blanding was a guy they thought was a shrewd businessman, and he was one of the most down to earth guys there were. He might have been tight, but you knew where you stood with the guy, which was cool."

"Red was chafing under the budgetary constraints of the Gold," recalled Ehrhart. "The media picked up on it, reporting the team had rented cars from Rent-A-Wreck instead of from Hertz, or something like that. Some of it was pretty humorous. There came a showdown between Red, who like many of our coaches, was used to NFL budgets, and Ron. Ron and Red actually had a physical confrontation. There was an accusation that Red had pinned Ron up against the wall. Both of these guys contributed mightily to the success of the Denver Gold, but it was ultimately going to come to a showdown. There was a physical confrontation and then Ron fired Red.

"Under the standard coaches' contract, Red brought an arbitration claim, so I appointed an arbitrator in Denver to hear their case, Dan Hoffman, who was a noted attorney in Denver who later became the Dean of the University of Denver Law School, one of the highest profile lawyers in Denver. There was some new law that brought up whether there was more damage to an employee who was fired than just having to pay his salary. I think it was very groundbreaking because Red's point was that it's one thing to just pay off someone's salary, but is that also denying his opportunity to do what he wants to do and have a platform for other opportunities? It's one thing to just sit at home and get your paycheck, it's another thing to take away your opportunity to coach. Some of the issues that face us every day were brought into that case. Was it a termination for cause by the physical altercation? Red's point was that he was trying to do what was best for the team. Ron's point of view was that he was facing up to the George Allen 'exceed the budget' style.

"Red Miller did a great job coaching a team that probably had lesser talent than a lot of the other teams, and Ron Blanding built a great entity, so I have great respect for both of them, but when they were put under the same microscope, the same pressure, trying to win and succeed in business, it kind of blew up between the two of them.

"NFL Commissioner Rozelle and the Cullen Bryant case were in the back of my mind. The NFL commissioner's office was supposed to be all-powerful and make all decisions. Our mission that Chet and I had talked about at length was that we wanted to be fair to all parties and not have the commissioner just be the owners' tool, which was the criticism of Rozelle. They had the Rozelle Rule and he could just send a player to another team until Cullen challenged it. We had a situation with an owner-coach dispute, so instead of having Chet hear it and make a decision, we picked a totally independent arbitrator who was hugely respected in Denver.

"I think it was a big contribution to fairness in sports that no one from the league tried to be there to control it, monitor it or influence it. I think he ruled that Blanding had just cause to terminate Miller. Once I appointed the arbitrator, we let him conduct the hearing and write the ruling. We got a copy of it later. We made a contribution by showing that there was a way for the league to run and have fair relationships with its players, owners and coaches. I was an owner in baseball for a couple of years, and I could see how that worked. They fired Fay Vincent because Fay stood up to them, and they put in one of their own, Bud Selig. What we did was somewhat groundbreaking, and I think that other sports could benefit by using the model we used there. The USFL was very progressive in this difficult area of fairly governing employees in a sports league."

The Gold tottered to 4–8 behind an offense ranked worst in the circuit. The firing of the former Broncos coach did not set well with the fans or the local media who pinned the blame for the team's poor record on Blanding's thrifty ways. Charley Armey took the head coaching reins on an interim basis before they turned to former Broncos quarterback Craig Morton for the remainder of the season. Ironically, Morton had played under Miller in Denver, helping the Broncos to their only Super Bowl appearance up to that time. His arrival helped to mollify the fans' discontent with Miller's dismissal and provided the spark for consecutive victories over Birmingham and Washington, leaving them at 6–8 and just a game out of the Pacific lead. Unfortunately, a late fumble near the Oakland goal line left them on the short end of a 16–10 decision, all but ending their playoff hopes. They closed out the season by whipping Arizona and then losing to Tampa Bay and Los Angeles.

The pair of defeats closed out an up and down year for the Gold that saw seven wins, 11 losses and three head coaches. Only Arizona (261) scored fewer points than Denver (284), and not even the third-ranked scoring defense could save the day. Despite the defense's ability to keep them in the game, it managed a league worst 28 sacks. Harry Sydney, who had been cut by Seattle and Cincinnati in the NFL, gained 801 yards rushing with a 4.6 yards per carry average and scored nine touchdowns. Not surprisingly, Denver finished on the bottom of the league in passing offense. They gained a paltry 2,541 yards in the air, more than 450 fewer than any other team. Gold quarterbacks were picked off 36 times compared to 19 touchdowns. On a bright note, Denver topped the league in attendance at 41,736 per game, and Blanding became the only owner in the USFL to turn a profit in his first season.

"We concentrated more on finding good players at the right price," said Blanding, explaining the financial success of his club. "We were willing to take players who didn't have the big name but had the ability rather than some of the others who wanted the name players and were willing to sacrifice the money. That was one of the things that helped us.

"We also paid a lot of attention to our franchise. Some of the teams were a sideline for their owners and they assigned the problems to some people who didn't have the interest that an owner would have. We were very hands on. Maybe we didn't have the football experience, but we had business experience. We got help finding the players, but then we'd make the decisions on which ones were right for the team. We wanted a lot of camaraderie."

On the downside, the Denver press interpreted many of the owner's efforts toward remaining within the original fiscal guidelines as cheapness. His rift with Miller exacerbated Blanding's problems with the media.

"I think the media played that up," said the owner. "I'll always remember John Ralston and I talking about that. We were discussing renting cars down in Arizona, and he said, 'Don't pay a lot of money for the cars. You can rent these from a company called Rent-A-Wreck.' The media grabbed that. Red Miller and I didn't get along very well, and

Running back Harry Sydney, cut in training camp by two NFL teams, spent his first two years of professional football with the Denver Gold. After a year with the Memphis Showboats, he played five years for the San Francisco 49ers, where he won a pair of Super Bowls, and one for the Green Bay Packers before becoming a coach. Photograph by Jim Turner, from author's collection.

he could take advantage of some of the things that were done. And I remember they talked about how we did that. That is one of the things that can be used in a negative way, when in fact there was nothing wrong with it. There's only something wrong with it if somebody wants to put it in the paper and say it's wrong."

That criticism came to a head following the firing of Miller. Although David Dixon had to have been proud, Blanding began to think about selling the franchise following the season.

"To start with we had some good fan reaction, but we started getting a lot of negative press there," he said. "That could have been myself causing that. I don't want to underplay that. But we were determined to run our club the way that we wanted to run it and not let anybody tell us what to do. Sometimes that irritates some people who want to be involved who we don't want to be involved. That's why I think we started getting that kind of reaction. We certainly drew well the first year despite all the problems we had."

Los Angeles Express

The Los Angeles Express opened promisingly with victories over New Jersey and Washington before losing at Arizona and Chicago. A home win over Oakland preceded three losses in four games as they won only at Tampa Bay during the stretch that saw them fall to 4–5 at the midway point.

Victories over Boston, Denver and Arizona offset losses to Birmingham and Oakland, but three straight defeats ruined their postseason plans. They topped Denver in their final game of the year to close at 8–10, only a game out of the division's modest penthouse.

One thing can be said for the 1983 season of the Los Angeles Express: it was exciting. Seven of the franchise's eight wins came by seven points or less. The main problem for the 8–10 team was an anemic offense which pushed across only 296 points, third fewest in the league. The running attack finished dead last in the USFL with 1,739 yards and a measly 3.6 yards per carry average. Rookie Tom Ramsey and veteran Mike Rae split the quarterbacking duties in Coach Hugh Campbell's system and combined for 3,939 yards, 24 touchdowns and 24 interceptions with neither having much of an edge. Ricky Ellis came in third in the league with 69 catches for 716 yards. Linebacker Eric Scoggins paced the defense with 12½ sacks, end Greg Fields added ten and tackle Eddie "Meat Cleaver" Weaver contributed 8½.

"My lasting impression of the first season, even though they went 8–10, not a great year, was that this was the model that would have worked," said *Los Angeles Times* writer Chris Dufresne. "I thought what they tried to do that year had a chance. Modest expectations, modest payrolls, get some local stars. I liked their idea of territorial picks. They had a lot of local talent. College stars from USC and UCLA were on that team, and that made a lot of sense to me. At quarterback, L.A. had Tom Ramsey from UCLA and Mike Rae, a USC quarterback who shared time, so you had a former UCLA and a USC quarterback sharing the quarterback spot for the inaugural spring season. I thought that kind of measured, slow growth was the way to go.

"The head coach was Hugh Campbell, a very respected coach coming down from Canada after winning several Grey Cups. He was kind of a fish out of water in L.A., in that his personality was very low key, very measured. He didn't have the pizzazz you might expect of a coach in L.A. I thought he symbolized really what the league should have been. You look at the first Express media guide with Hugh Campbell on the cover, and he looked like American Gothic if he would have had a pitchfork in his hand and a cow behind him. I thought it made sense. They knew their place. Had they kept on that slow train of growth and built some credibility up slowly, this is what the original founders had in mind for what a franchise should be."

The final attendance picture gave owners Alan Harmon and Bill Daniels reason to pause. Playing in the country's second-largest market, they averaged just 19,002 fans per game and failed to draw more than 17,000 in any of the final four home contests. Even worse, the cavernous Coliseum looked practically empty with the modest crowds. In addition, poor television ratings in the city dragged down the national average for the league's games. They knew that L.A. was a tough market to crack but hadn't expected such an uphill battle. Harmon blamed much of the attendance problem on poor marketing and estimated a $2.5 million loss for the season.

Oakland Invaders

Unlike L.A., the city of Oakland received the Invaders with open arms. With the Raiders' recent departure, Bay Area football fans turned to the new USFL team, though not to the same degree they had supported the Raiders. A shutout win over Arizona in the opener and a narrow victory over Michigan alternated with an overtime defeat to Birmingham and a disappointing loss to Denver. After falling at Los Angeles, they beat up on Boston, but their see-saw campaign continued when they dropped a 17–7 decision to visiting Philadelphia and suffered a 21–9 blow at Birmingham.

Sitting at 3–5 but only a game out of the Pacific lead, they battered Arizona before losing to Tampa Bay. They repeated their pattern with a win over Washington before falling to the Bandits again. The Invaders finally put together consecutive wins when they downed the L.A. Express, New Jersey Generals and Denver Gold to stake sole claim of the division lead. A defeat to Philadelphia only delayed their division championship for one week until they could dispatch of Boston. A blowout loss at Chicago dropped them to 9–9, but they would breathe again in the playoffs.

Oakland's .500 record didn't turn many heads, but it was good enough to win the Pacific Division and earn one of the USFL's four post-season berths. The Invaders longest winning streak lasted three games while it didn't drop more than two consecutive decisions.

Predictably enough for a .500 team, Oakland outscored its opposition by just two points, 319–317, over the course of the season. Running back Arthur "The King" Whittington broke the 1,000-yard mark on the ground with 1,043 yards despite playing the entire season with a hernia and then cracked ribs late in the year. Chester topped the squad with 68 receptions for 951 yards; Whittington caught 66 balls for 584 yards, while Gordon Banks grabbed 61 passes for 855 yards. Stan Talley finished the campaign as the USFL's best punter with a 44.00-yard average, including one 75-yard kick. Cedrick Hardman paced the defense with eight sacks. Quarterback Fred Besana proved to be one of the league's biggest surprises as the durable former semi-pro player finished second in the league in passer rating with 3,980 yards and 21 touchdowns in spite of being sacked 71 times, a pro football record, for 560 yards in losses.

"I saw him playing semi-pro football with a team up in Marysville [California], and that's when I got excited about Fred," said Coach John Ralston. "When I was with the Broncos in 1976, we were easing Charlie Johnson out of professional football. We made him a quarterback scout and we told him to go out and watch the top 15 quarterbacks in the country. That was his job and he was paid a fairly good salary for that. When he came back, I asked him who was the best quarterback he saw, and he said a backup quarterback at the University of California at Berkeley. And I said, 'Heaven's sakes, who's that?' He said 'Fred Besana is backing up Joe Roth, another outstanding player.' Charlie Johnson was that enthralled with him after watching several outstanding quarterbacks all over the country. So that lodged in the back of my head all the way to setting up the Oakland Invaders. I got after Fred Besana in a hurry, especially when I knew he was playing for $50 a week for a semi-pro team. I figured I could pay him a few bucks more to play for the Invaders."

Oakland managed well at the gate, averaging over 31,000 fans per game, but still lost an estimated $1 million according to Ralston. Still, many of the other franchises had fared worse, and Oakland's warm reception provided plenty of hope for the future.

"The first season was a very euphoric season," recalled owner Tad Taube. "You can't really understand unless you've lived it, what goes into putting a team on the field, what goes into putting fans in the seats. You can't imagine the euphoria associated with having done all that and having gotten good fan support and having a season that ends up in the playoffs. Getting into the playoffs, sharing with the coaching staff, players and my other owners what, in my opinion, was an enormous accomplishment, was the high point, especially given the fact that we played it straight. We didn't cheat on player compensation."

Boston Breakers

The Boston Breakers had been saddled with the worst stadium in the league in Nickerson Field. The front office had stuck by the USFL's salary guidelines, ensuring few big names would dot the sidelines, and the team had sold the fewest tickets in the league. To the surprise of many in the league, Coach Dick Coury would mold a surprisingly competitive team out of his bunch of castoffs. After narrowly losing to Tampa Bay in the opener, they downed Denver, Washington, New Jersey and Birmingham in succession and proved themselves an opportunistic bunch in the process. After splitting games with Oakland (7–26) and Arizona (44–23), they faced the 6–1 Philadelphia Stars in a crucial Atlantic Division matchup. It was the Stars, however, who shot out to a 20–0 in the third quarter and then withstood a Breakers' flurry that saw them trim the final to 23–16, narrowly missing a last second chance to tie. The emboldened Breakers looked forward to the rematch.

A gutty effort fell short the following weekend against Michigan, and the Los Angeles Express extended their losing string to three games with a 23–20 decision. Boston began its climb back into the race with wins over Denver and Washington before the rematch with Philadelphia in week thirteen. The contest began much as the first one, with the Stars grabbing a 10–0 halftime advantage while stifling the Breakers offense. Boston stormed back on two Tim Mazzetti field goals and a Johnnie Walton touchdown pass, but Philadelphia answered with a touchdown of its own to make it 17–13. That's where the score stood when Walton and the Breakers took possession on their own 35 with less than two minutes left. Walton expertly led his team down the field until the offense stalled at the Philly 14. On fourth down, with time left for but one more throw, Walton fired a pass to Charlie Smith in the end zone. The throw glanced off Smith but to the delight of Coury and company, fellow receiver Frank Lockett snatched the deflection out of the air for the winning score, touching off a wild celebration.

Boston rallied again its next time out for a 21–15 victory over Chicago, their fourth win in a row, but a 31–19 defeat at Birmingham surrendered the Atlantic title to Philadelphia and dropped the Breakers a game behind the Blitz in the wild card hunt. Following a victory over Tampa Bay, they lost a big game at Oakland, and not even a 34–10 whipping of New Jersey could get them into the playoffs when Chicago also proved victorious in its finale.

The 11–7 finish after nearly unanimous predictions of gloom did much to offset their disappointment toward missing out on the postseason. Coury had molded a tough, tightly-knit squad that never quit.

The coach's efforts were not lost on his players. "He's an incredible person in that he's one of the few coaches anywhere who knows how to treat a player like a man and like a person rather than a piece of meat," kicker Tim Mazzetti told *The Sporting News*.

"Dick's so positive it's disgusting. When I was in the NFL, when a player would mess up, the coach would look away. He'd play this stupid game of, 'I don't like you.' Then, when you do well, he's all over you, hugging and slapping you.

"It should be the opposite, which is the way it is with Dick. When you miss is when you need someone's support. You don't have to slap me on the back when I make one. I know I made it. Thank you. That's my job. It's when I miss that I need support.

"Earlier in the year, I missed a field goal. It was a damn good kick and it was windy. But I missed it. I hit the upright and it bounced back. Well, Coury, so damn positive, runs out onto the field and slaps me on the back and says, 'Damn it, great kick. Could've been good from 60.' I said, 'Coach, I missed.' But that's the kind of guy he is."

Out of football since the conclusion of the 1979 NFL season, 35-year-old quarterback Johnnie Walton helmed the Boston Breakers in 1983, becoming one of the league's biggest surprises in the inaugural season. Photograph by Jim Turner, from author's collection.

The coach had a simple explanation for the way he dealt with his team. "The thing I have always tried to do since I was a coach, all the way back to high school," said Coury in the *Boston Globe*, "is to remember to treat people the way I wanted to be treated. I don't see any reason to act differently now that I'm a head coach in the pros."

The team received an additional unexpected boost from the quarterback position. After coming out of retirement, John Walton's surprisingly strong season ended with 3,772 yards and 20 touchdowns as he led the third best offense in the league and the second best passing unit.

"Johnnie Walton was very sharp," Coury recalled. "He actually didn't want to continue playing in the NFL because he was a backup with the Eagles to Ron Jaworski, who was a good player and the number one guy on the team. Johnnie was offered a head coaching job down where he's from at Elizabeth City State University, and he decided to go into coaching. Johnnie and I used to kid each other when I was coaching quarterbacks with the Eagles. Every now and then, Johnnie would come up to me after he'd completed a pass and say, 'When you get your head coaching job, you have to take me with you.' When I got the job, and he had left the Eagles maybe a year or two before that, I called him right away and said, 'Remember that deal we had where whoever got a head coaching job first, the other guy was going to come with him?' He said, 'I'll be right there.'"

The offensive line did its part by allowing just eight sacks the entire year. In addition, Richard Crump ran for 990 yards with 12 touchdowns (eight running and four receiving) for the league's second worst running attack, while Nolan Franz gathered in 62 passes for 848 yards, and Charlie Smith caught 54 balls for 1,009 yards. Offensive coordinator Roman Gabriel had done a marvelous job with the unheralded unit. Linebacker Marcus Marek from Ohio State headed up a defense that kept the Breakers in most games. Mazzetti finished second in the league in scoring with 119 points.

"The year in Boston was a great year for us," recalled Coury. "We came from nowhere and played right up to the last game for an opportunity to get into the playoffs. We just had a group of guys who played real hard and worked hard."

"It was a blast," said Mazzetti. "I'll be honest with you, my memories of the NFL are good, and I had a tremendous amount of success with Atlanta, but the memories of the USFL are even better. It was so much fun. It certainly became a major, first-class operation, but to begin with we were kind of fly-by-night. Everyone was still getting their stuff together. We didn't have any long-term contracts. We ended up playing in the small BU, 15,000-seat college stadium. It was a completely different environment after having played in places like the SuperDome, Texas Stadium and Atlanta-Fulton County Stadium, with 70,000 screaming fans. It was a lot of fun and a lot more relaxed.

"Playing in BU's stadium, Nickerson Field, which was really just a glorified Division II or III college stadium, with 15 or 20,000 people showing up and with people looking out of their dorm rooms, is something I'll remember. College kids were hanging out dorm windows because Nickerson Field is bounded on one end, just like Franklin Field in Philadelphia where I went to school at Penn. One end of the stadium had offices and dorm rooms, so people were hanging out watching our practices and games. It was just a blast, especially for somebody who had been at the height of his career. We had gone to the playoffs two out of three years for Atlanta and played some really big, pressure-packed games, and got a tremendous amount of publicity including Monday night games and things like that, to all of a sudden be playing in this league, and I hate using the term 'rinky-dink' because there was no part of it that was 'rinky-dink,' but it was smaller.

Everything was very well managed, but because they didn't have the facilities, contracts and exposure, it was a lot more casual."

The Breakers faced an uphill battle to draw fans to Nickerson Field, and the final numbers reflected their struggle. The team averaged just 12,817 fans per home game but drew more than 15,000 for its final four contests at Nickerson. Assured of losing money from day one, majority owner George Matthews and his partners made it a priority to find a better stadium before they hit the field again.

"The guy in Boston, Matthews, and his partner Randy Vataha were two people who thought that they were right all the time," Camera said. "Not that they were being negative, they just didn't get it. I'm a Yankee fan, and they had a typical Red Sox mentality. It doesn't matter, we'll suffer through it, but we know we're right. That was a problem. They forgot to market the team and sell tickets. They were so caught up in trying to be the best team on the field, which they weren't, that they never did enough marketing. They never had a good marketing person, and they never wanted to take any direction. They didn't want the league office to give them structure, so they were a problem."

Chicago Blitz

Chicago faced the opposite expectations of Boston entering the season. They boasted some of the best young talent and veteran leadership in all of football, not to mention one of its top coaches. The Blitz screened hundreds of players before setting their opening day roster. But after they thumped the Feds in week one, they dropped two squeakers to Arizona and Denver, sending Allen searching for answers. In two weeks, his club had been beaten twice in the final seconds by two teams without nearly the talent the Blitz put out on the field. In fact, Allen was just beginning the roller coaster ride that was the 1983 season for the Chicago Blitz.

Chicago atoned for its poor early start by besting Los Angeles and then whipping the undefeated Bandits, thanks in large part to six interceptions by safety Luther Bradley. Their third win in a row, over Birmingham, was countered by a narrow loss to Michigan. They struggled to an overtime decision over New Jersey before again toppling L.A. and Washington to push their record to 7–3, good enough for a share of the Central Division lead.

After collapsing against Philadelphia in week 11, they again beat New Jersey in overtime in a game that cost them the services of quarterback Greg Landry with a broken ankle. They toppled Arizona the next time out but fell to Boston a week later. Another blasting of Tampa Bay helped to lift their spirits and regain a share of the division lead, and a win over Birmingham moved them into sole possession of first place at 11–5. The Michigan Panthers spoiled their hopes by handing them a 34–19 setback and tying them for first place. A win over Oakland was not enough to offset their two losses to Michigan. With both teams tied with 12–6 records, the Blitz had to content themselves with a wild card trip to the playoffs

A wild card spot was not what the Chicago brass had in mind when shelling out the huge money to build the team, but at least they were still alive in the race for the USFL's first championship. The Blitz ended the regular season as the league's top scoring outfit and boasted the USFL's fourth-best ground game. Tim Spencer, with 1,157 rushing yards, and Kevin Long, with 1,022 yards, both cracked the 1,000-yard mark. Despite missing the last third of the season, Landry finished third in the league in passing, completing 188 out of 334 throws for 2,383 yards with 16 touchdowns and nine interceptions. Trumaine Johnson, who topped the league in receiving with 81 catches for 1,322 yards and ten scores, lived up to his billing as one of the most dangerous and athletic talents in the league.

As good as the offense was, the defense proved to be even better. They allowed fewer yards than any other squad, finishing first against the pass and second against the rush. The circuit's second stingiest scoring defense was led by a dominating front including Joe Ehrmann (13½ sacks), Junior Ah You (11½ sacks), Kit Lathrop (8 sacks) and Karl Lorch (6 sacks). Luther Bradley intercepted a league high 12 passes, including eight in two games against the Bandits. He had picked off a total of nine in his 56-game NFL career with the Lions. The Blitz also topped the league in scoring thanks to several defensive touchdowns. It was clear that if it hadn't been for a couple of injuries and late collapses, Chicago would have dominated the regular season.

The always intense Allen pushed for the USFL to attain parity with the NFL within five years.

"We had played the Boston Breakers the first year, and Boston had a quarterback named Johnnie Walton who was in his mid-to-late 30s," Blitz front office man Don Kojich recalled. "We had a very good defense, and we held Boston to under 200 yards total offense, but we ended up losing the game. Greg Landry was injured at the time, and we found out our second team quarterback played with a concussion. On the flight back I was in back of the coaching staff and front office but in front of the players. A couple of players in the back, including our third team quarterback were laughing and cutting it up a little bit in the back of the plane, and all of a sudden George gets up, storms to the back of the plane and reads the kid the riot act. And I swear, I thought he was going to throw the kid out at 40,000 feet over the United States."

The team averaged just 18,090 fans per game or about half of what Allen predicted before the season began. Five times, the team drew fewer than 14,000 to Soldier Field. It topped 32,000 to see Herschel Walker and the Generals, bad weather helped to cut into the total, and the team further blamed several television appearances. In spite of the star appeal evident on the team, it had fallen 7,000 fans per game below Dixon's initial projections.

Philadelphia Stars

The Stars had great talent and terrific direction from general manager Carl Peterson, but when George Perles resigned as head coach, they had been forced into a late start that left new coach Jim Mora and his hastily assembled staff scrambling two weeks before training camp. Contrary to expectations, they exploded out of the gate by beating Denver, New Jersey and Birmingham. After tripping over Tampa Bay for their first defeat, they ran off eight consecutive wins that left them on the verge of a division title before the season was two-thirds old. The defense showed its dominance over the stretch, three times holding opponents under ten points. It was a far cry from the unit's showing in training camp.

A narrow loss to Boston, on a deflected pass caught for a score, ended their winning streak, but they bounced back quickly with victories over Michigan and New Jersey to clinch the division title. Oakland and Birmingham became their fourteenth and fifteenth victims, but, with talented running back Kelvin Bryant sitting out, Washington knocked them off in the final week.

Though one of the last teams to tab their head coach, the Stars still appeared a step ahead of the rest of the league from day one. Peterson, a great judge of football talent, had pulled seven of his 22 starters away from other USFL clubs. Contrary to their pre-season showing, the strength of the Philadelphia Stars proved to be their defense. Coordinator Vince Tobin oversaw the unit that gave up the fewest points in the league, an average of 11.3 per game, and often kept the squad in games when the offense struggled. They finished first against the rush, allowing just 104 yards per game, but curiously they managed only 35 sacks, third least in the league. The defense collected 34 interceptions and 28 fumble recoveries as the Stars ended the season with a whopping plus-35 turnover differential.

Linebacker "Slammin'" Sam Mills, cut by NFL and CFL teams because his 5'9" frame had been judged too small for the pro game, led the way with 195 tackles, 141 of them unassisted. Mills, called "Field Mouse" by his teammates, developed a reputation as a fierce tackler. "That little guy sure can hit," fellow Stars linebacker John Bunting, a former Eagle, told *The Sporting News*. "He should be licensed."

"Sam Mills was the best player in the USFL," opined Fusina. "He was also the best person I knew in the USFL. He was cut by a Canadian football team because of his height. They didn't see what was inside. This just illustrates what kind of a guy he was. One day Sam and I went to do a promo cooking show on public television because Myles asked us to do it. The guy asked Sam to grate some cheese for the recipe we were making. He hands Sam this big hunk of cheese, not telling him how much was needed. This guy and I get to talking while we're chopping things up for the dish, and I think he forgot about Sam. Ten minutes later, we looked back, and Sam is just sweating with this mountain of grated cheese in front of him. He had grated the entire hunk. Sam would do anything for anyone, and he would do it the best he could until the job was complete. He was as humble and nice as could be."

"Sam Mills, from start to finish, he would go full speed," agreed backfield mate David Riley. "We would have to tell him to calm down. Every once in a while, Coach Mora would tell us we could just put on our helmets and shorts for a bit more laid back practice, but all the running backs would want to put on full gear because they knew Sam was on the defensive side of the ball, and he had one speed and one speed only."

Mills also took more than his fair share of ribbing from his close-knit Philadelphia Stars teammates.

"We were playing in the Los Angeles Coliseum, and we were in the visiting locker room," recalled tight end Ken Dunek. "We had nicknamed Sam Mills 'Field Mouse' because of his size. David Riley, our fullback, went into the men's room and there was a junior urinal. He put a footstool next to it and placed Sam Mills' name and number on the junior urinal as a practical joke."

Despite getting a later start than anyone else in the league, Mora had pulled the Stars together and molded them into a tough unit.

"We had a terrific team, 15–3, our record was just unbelievable," recalled Landeta. "Even after we were winning he would still be on us, still be on us, and collectively we would think, 'God, we're 12-1, 12-2, he's all over us. What's going to happen when we lose?' When we lose we think he's going to kill us, and he'd do the exact opposite, say,

'You know what, you guys played hard, we didn't get that one. We're doing well,' and that's when I said to myself, boy, this guy is a good coach. You know, lifts you when you feel you need a lift, but when things are going good you can't just think that everything is okay cause that can change in a second."

Offensively, Bryant came in second to Walker in the rushing race with 1,442 yards and 16 scores for the USFL's second-best running team. Chuck Fusina completed 238 of 421 passes for 2,718 yards with 15 touchdowns and just ten interceptions. Fusina was 29–3 as a starter at Penn State and brought that success with him to Philadelphia.

"I remember when I talked to Joe Paterno about him before we signed him," Peterson told the *Philadelphia Daily News*. "He said, 'Chuck doesn't look good throwing the ball, doesn't look good running the ball, doesn't even look good in his uniform. But he does one thing that you and I want the most from any player. He wins.'"

"Carl Peterson did a great job finding talent," stated Fusina. "We had the best two players in the league. On offense, we had Kelvin Bryant, and on defense we had Sam Mills. They were the best, most consistent players in the league."

Unfortunately, the on-the-field dominance failed to translate into paying fans. Attendance averaged just 18,650 on the season, even though the Stars won eight of their nine games at Veterans Stadium. After an initial home crowd of 38,205 for the New Jersey contest, the next largest attendance came in at 20,931 against Chicago. Two April games drew less than 11,000 paying customers. Bad weather hurt, and it didn't help that Philadelphia had been the center of an attendance scandal in the World Football League, either. In 1974, the hometown Bell had claimed crowds of 55,534 and 64,719 for its first two home games, but tax records revealed just 13,855 and 6,200, respectively, had actually paid to attend the games. Huge blocks of tickets had been handed out to corporate sponsors, while other tickets had been handed to passersby. The scandal destroyed much of the WFL's circumspect credibility. The Stars were not going to make the same mistake.

"I think the best way to describe it is a guy said to me one day, 'I'm not sure I quite understand the philosophy of your league. You televise your home games, but not your away games,'" recalled team owner Myles Tanenbaum. "I told him that wasn't by design. We played 18 games in the season, nine of which were at home. Seven of our nine home games were televised, and they were not blacked out in Philadelphia. We were really advertising our product, but it was not necessary to go to the stadium to see the team. We had a very young crowd.

Elusive running back Kelvin Bryant quickly became the focus of a Philadelphia Stars offense that put a high priority on maintaining possession and grinding down opponents. Photograph by Jim Turner, from Richie Franklin's collection.

People who either couldn't afford to or weren't able to get tickets for the Eagles were coming to see the Stars play."

Postseason

Commissioner Simmons and the rest of the league office had to be pleased with the playoff pairings. George Allen and his high-profile Blitz would take on the Stars, owners of the league's top regular-season record. The surprising Michigan Panthers would try to continue their winning ways before a large home crowd against the Oakland Invaders who had come out of a dogfight in the Pacific Division.

In the USFL's first ever playoff tilt the wild card Chicago Blitz traveled to Veterans Stadium in Philadelphia to face the Stars where a disappointing crowd of 15,684 was on hand for the contest on Saturday, July 9. Looking to avenge their 31–24 loss to Philadelphia earlier in the season, the Blitz jumped on top early. They grabbed a 14–0 advantage on a first quarter Kevin Long touchdown plunge and a three-yard scamper by quarterback Bobby Scott in the second period. Interceptions by Virgil Livers and Luther Bradley on Chuck Fusina's first two passes set up the scores. Kelvin Bryant's 10-yard jaunt got the Stars on the board, but Scott countered with a 10-yard scoring toss to Trumaine Johnson following a Chuck Fusina fumble. With nothing going his way, the Philadelphia quarterback let his fullback do some passing and Fusina closed out the first half scoring when he caught a 12-yard TD pass from Allen Harvin with just 39 seconds left in the opening half. The Blitz nearly caught Harvin before his throw, but Fusina grabbed the underthrown ball while on his knees, scrambled to his feet and dove into the end zone. The score brought the home team to within 21–14 as the squads headed into their locker rooms.

Three Stars turnovers, all by Fusina, had set up the Chicago scores.

Things did not get much better after the intermission as the Blitz dominated the third quarter as well. Mack Boatner caught a 12-yard scoring pass and Frank Corral kicked a 32-yard field goal for the only points of the period to make it 31–14. David Trout split the uprights on a 42-yard kick to start the final period, but Tim Spencer gave Chicago a seemingly insurmountable 38–17 advantage with a one-yard scoring run with 12:04 left on the clock.

That's when the USFL's best regular season team finally got on track. A suddenly hot Fusina briskly led his squad down the field, covering 80 yards in seven plays before he hit Scott Fitzkee with a 17-yard touchdown toss with nine and a half minutes left. A 37-yard pass to Fitzkee provided the key play of the drive. "I felt the game change right then," Fusina recalled in *Sports Illustrated*. The Stars' Jonathan Sutton picked off a Scott throw along the sidelines, and Philadelphia used another seven plays to cover 68 yards, the last two on a Fusina to Jeff Rodenberger scoring pass. That brought the home team within 38–31 with just under five minutes remaining. Again the Blitz faltered, and the Stars took over at their own 30-yard line. Fusina steadily brought Philadelphia closer, until with 50 seconds left, he spotted Tom Donovan alone in front of the goal line. Eleven yards later, Donovan was in for the tying score, a play he celebrated by doing his trademark somersault in the end zone. The Stars had overcome a 21-point deficit and sent the game into extra time.

Philly won the overtime coin toss and started with the ball at its own 27-yard line after the kick return. They continued their offensive dominance and 13 plays and seven minutes later, they found themselves at the Chicago one. Fusina handed to Bryant who dove over the top of the pile for the winning touchdown in the league's first ever playoff game. The top two scoring defenses in the league had combined on a 44–38 overtime thriller.

"By halftime, we could feel their weariness," Irv Eatman stated in *SI*. "We said, 'They're tired.' We knew we had to pound them, make them feel their age."

"Even if we were down, we were going to go after it," added Fusina. "Everything went wrong in the first half, but then everything went right in the second half. When you went up against a George Allen team, he was such a great defensive coach, you really had to play your best."

"We must have had George Allen's number that day," furthered David Riley. "I know Sam got up and he spoke to everybody, and Coach Mora and the other coaches said what they needed to say. We always felt like we were never out of a game. If you believe as a team, and you believe in the guys right beside you, you can overcome anything. We just kept plugging away and started making plays. It became a snowball effect. No matter what they did, they couldn't stop it. When somebody gets momentum going, you have to do everything you can to kill it. They just couldn't stop the momentum, and we carried it over into overtime and wound up winning the game."

Fusina completed 22 of 34 passes for 254 yards with three touchdown throws and four interceptions. He made up for his mistakes by catching a touchdown toss, contributing several key scrambles and by hitting on ten passes in a row and 13 of 15 throws for 150 yards in the final 12 minutes. Fitzkee caught six throws for 102 yards and the score that got them rolling. The running game more than did its part by rolling up 306 yards. Teamed together in the backfield for the first time all season, Bryant rambled for 142 yards on 24 carries with a pair of scores, while Harvin ran for 87 yards and threw a touchdown. They overcame seven turnovers to pull out the wild ballgame, thanks mostly to Fusina's inspired play late in the contest.

"You could make an argument to this day, you just show that game to 20 football fans, gray out the helmets and everything and say, 'Just watch this game,' that could be arguably maybe the greatest game ever," said Stars punter Sean Landeta. "I know it was the only game in the three years I played for the Stars that I didn't punt once. It was the only one, and I never got in. But just the amount of points, the comeback, a playoff game, it was just an unbelievable game to watch. Terrific, I remember that."

"It was unbelievable because we were behind by such a large margin and came back to beat them," Mora said. "We just kept battling. We had a good team. I think we were the better team, but we just got behind. It was just a matter of us not quitting, not giving up, and that was very much a characteristic of those Stars teams. Even when we got behind or were in close games, we found a way to win. If you look at a lot of our scores that first year, even during the course of the three years, there were a lot of games where the statistics weren't necessarily overwhelming in our favor, but we found a way to score more points than the other team. And we always played *good defense*, and when you play good defense you always have a chance. That doesn't mean we didn't have a good offense because we did, but our defense kept us in a lot of games."

"It was just a terribly exciting game," remembered Stars owner Myles Tanenbaum. "On the way home from it, I got a call from the man who had founded NFL Films, Ed Sabol. He told me that it was one of the three most exciting games he had ever seen. He rated it number three and then went on to tell me what the other two were."

Meanwhile, the Blitz players and coaches were kicking themselves. One of the USFL's top defenses had surrendered 21 points in less than 12 minutes of game time and had allowed more than 300 rushing yards in the game. They had also caused seven turnovers and scored 38 points with just 218 yards of offense. Long topped the team with 76 yards on the ground with a score, while Spencer managed just 34 yards. Scott threw only 14 passes, connecting on eight for 96 yards with two touchdown tosses and a scoring run.

"We always went to a chapel Sunday morning before the games," recalled Blitz owner Dr. Ted Diethrich. "The ritual was training breakfast, then chapel, then getting ready for the game. I remember this day. When we walked out of chapel, I was looking at the expressions of the players, and I had a really bad feeling in the pit of my stomach that we weren't up for this game, so when we got beat I wasn't surprised. I knew the players well, not as well as coach and Bruce, but I talked to them and was around them a lot, and I just really had a very bad sense about that game. I remember coming out of chapel and thinking to myself, 'I just don't feel good about this.'"

The next day, Michigan hosted Oakland for the second berth in the championship game. In an unusual move and one contrary to league mandates, Panthers owner A. Alfred Taubman cut ticket prices for the contest and offered free parking in order to coax a large crowd for the nationally televised game. Normal prices of $14, $12.50 and $11 were slashed to $8.50 and $5 for the postseason game. The team sold 30,000 tickets shortly after the owner's announcement, and a USFL-record crowd of 60,237 fans took him up on the offer. In addition, a gathering of more than 6,000 fans attended a rally for the Central Division champions the Saturday night before the game. Their enthusiasm was understandable. No Detroit team had captured a championship since the Tigers' World Series win in 1968. The Panthers were also looking to avenge a narrow 33–27 loss to Oakland in week three.

"The biggest thing we did there was to bring 60,000 people into the stands, which was amazing in the first year," remembered Taubman. "It got a lot of people very enthusiastic. Unfortunately, the Lions weren't doing well. They still aren't. They haven't changed their position in the league. At the time, they were spending the most money and getting the least number of wins in the whole league."

The teams started slowly before Fred Besana finally got the Invaders offense moving. He led his team 78 yards in 14 plays before sneaking in from the one on fourth down late in the first quarter. Bobby Hebert immediately led the Panthers back on their next possession. Michigan drove 80 yards in six plays, capped by John Williams' five-yard scoring run to tie it up. Minutes later, Novo Bojovic connected on a 38-yard kick to give the home team a 10–7 lead. Michigan held the Oakland offense once again and took over near midfield late in the first half. Hebert used eight plays to get the Panthers down to the three-yard-line where they faced a fourth and one. Coach Jim Stanley nixed any notion of a field goal attempt, and Hebert instead hit Carter for a touchdown and a 17–7 advantage heading into halftime.

Michigan began the second half with the ball, but Invaders linebacker David Shaw picked off Hebert's attempted screen pass and returned it 19 yards for a touchdown to put Oakland right back in it at 17–14. But the Panthers had come too far to be caught now. Ignoring the mistake, the young Michigan quarterback used 11 plays to cover 80 yards, culminating with his one-yard scoring run. The key play of the drive was also one of the most exciting and unconventional of the game. Hebert hit Ken Lacy with a short pass and the runner broke a pair of tackles to get a first down before Invaders safety Marcus Quinn caught him and started to drag him to the turf. Suddenly, the running back pitched back to Williams who carried it for an additional 31 yards, sending the crowd into a frenzy in the process. On their next possession, Hebert connected with Anthony Carter for a 56-yard gain, and Lacy capped the drive with an 18-yard jaunt into the end zone late in the third period for a 31–14 Michigan lead. Following a 79-yard drive, Cleo Miller ran three yards for Michigan's final score with under two minutes left. Besana hit Marc Lewis with a six-yard scoring toss, and after Kevin Shea connected on the extra point to make the final score 37–21, the Michigan fans could hold back no more. They stormed the field, causing a premature end to the game after they tore down both goal posts with 25 seconds remaining.

"I remember them tearing down the goalposts," laughed Holloway. "The fans rushed onto the field to tear down the goal posts, and I was trying to rush off the field before that happened!"

"The thing I remember about that game was that we had 65,000 fans, the largest crowd in the league that first year, and they were loud and they loved us," added Keller. "After we won, we were the darlings of Michigan. The Lions hadn't won anything since the Bobby Layne days."

Hebert connected on 18 of 27 passes for 295 yards and a touchdown, while Lacy led the way on the ground with 73 yards. Carter caught three passes for 78 yards and a score to lead the winners.

Besana clicked on 23 of 35 throws for 258 yards with scores via the pass and the run. Gordon Banks grabbed seven passes for 96 yards, but the ground game managed just 60 yards, and the Invaders also lost two fumbles.

"I thought we would play exciting football, which we did," said Michigan owner Taubman. "The first year I had more people in the stadium for the playoff than the Lions did all year. That's a matter of record, we had 60-some thousand people in the stands, and they were very enthusiastic about it."

Next up was the league's first championship game, dubbed 'The Game with No Name' by some of the press, at Denver's Mile High Stadium. The USFL awarded the contest to the city after it became clear that they would lead the league in attendance. A crowd of 50,906 fans and a national television audience on ABC was on hand for the Sunday night showdown between the Philadelphia Stars and the Michigan Panthers.

"It was a great atmosphere, a Super Bowl–like atmosphere," remembered Stars tight end Ken Dunek. "Alabama sung the national anthem; the stadium was sold out; the place was rocking. There were jets flying overhead. It was a nationally-televised night game. It had a Super Bowl–type of atmosphere."

It took a while for both teams to get going, but Hebert led the Panthers down the field, and Novo Bojovic hit a 33-yard field goal just before the first quarter expired. The Cajun highlighted the drive with a 20-yard scramble on a third and 15 play. Philadelphia responded quickly and matched the kick with a 30-yarder from David Trout midway through the second period. The three-pointer capped a 13-play, 64-yard drive. Not to be outdone, Michigan set off on another long drive, this one covering 80 yards in ten plays. Hebert hit Derek Holloway with a 12-yard touchdown pass with just over two minutes remaining in the half. The Panthers defense held, and they took the 10–3 advantage into the break.

Another 80-yard drive, this one in 15 plays, resulted in Hebert's second scoring toss to Holloway, a 14-yarder. In danger of falling out of the game, Fusina led the Stars back into field goal range where Trout connected on a 28-yard effort early in the fourth. Then a Hebert mistake cost Michigan dearly. His throw to Holloway sailed high, and Mike Lush picked it off. The safety lateraled the ball to Scott Woerner who returned it to the Stars' 41-yard line. Fusina marched the Stars downfield and hit Willie Collier with a 21-yard scoring pass. Collier made an incredible diving catch on the play and also hauled in the two-point conversion pass to bring Philadelphia within 17–14 with 8:49 remaining in the game.

Michigan gained one first down on its next possession but soon bogged down. Greenwood punted and Woerner made a major mistake, letting it hit at the 20. The ball rolled dead at the five, and the Stars had to play conservatively. They ran three plays before Sean Landeta boomed a 52-yard punt. From there, Michigan crept to the Philadelphia 48 where it faced a second and 10. Stanley called for an out pattern to Holloway, but Hebert recognized a blitz at the line of scrimmage and audibled to a deep out to Carter. The shifty receiver pulled up at the 36 in front of corner back Antonio Gibson, made the grab and slipped past both Gibson and Woerner on his way to the end zone for a 48-yard touchdown. Carter whipped the ball high into the stands in celebration and slapped high fives with fans along the end zone wall. The Panthers led 24–14, and they only had to slow the Stars the rest of the way. They did just that, and the Stars final drive ended when Fusina hit Rodney Parker with a short scoring pass as time ran out. The two-point conversion throw to Scott Fitzkee made the final score 24–22 as fans once again stormed the field.

"We had played Philadelphia earlier that year and they had beat us, so we knew the

Nicknamed the "Cajun Cannon," Bobby Hebert led the Michigan Panthers to the USFL's first title. The Louisiana native played in the USFL for three seasons before embarking on a 12-year NFL career. Photograph by Jim Turner, from author's collection.

Stars were going to be a tough team," recalled Holloway. "In game-planning, we knew they used a lot of blitzes and we had to break off our routes a lot. We practiced a lot of strong safety and free safety blitzes and breaking off our routes. The pass that Anthony caught was on a blitz. I've seen it a thousand times; I cut across the field and got a block that freed him into the end zone."

"The Stars, they had Scott Woerner at safety, Mike Lush was their defensive back, and they were blitzing," explained Hebert. "I remember we had a long count to make sure they weren't trying to disguise it, so I knew that I was probably gonna get hit. But I said, 'If I'm not worried about getting hit and I'm standing there tough, Anthony Carter is gonna beat whoever's guarding him.' And so normally if you bump and run, you might run a fade or a quick slant, or normally if the guy's off you run a quick slant. Well we decided when he was off the corner back, I think it was Antonio Gibson if I'm right, he runs like a square out. So I already hit my fifth step, I mean I threw it, got hit. And Anthony Carter's gonna make people miss and I knew right then, that when he went and scored that, y'know what, we're gonna win this game. We gonna win the championship."

President Ronald Reagan called from aboard Air Force One to offer his congratulations to Coach Stanley and the USFL's first champs. "I just wanted to congratulate you and all the members of the Michigan Panthers," said the President. "You showed great determination and I'm sure it's doubly sweet since it came after a slow start. Having played football myself and having broadcast it for a number of years it's great to see your finish. My best wishes to the Panthers, the Stars and all of the USFL."

By jumping out early, Michigan took the Stars out of their run-heavy game plan. Fusina threw 47 times, completing 25 for 192 yards and two scores, while Bryant carried 13 times for 89 yards. Fitzkee added five catches for 58 yards.

"I don't think we were wide-eyed," said Mora. "I think I might have screwed it up a little bit. I might have overworked our guys. I've always probably worked teams too hard, and I think maybe we went into that championship game a little bit tired. We had the game the week before with the Blitz when we came from behind and won the game in overtime, and that might have taken a little bit out of us. We just didn't seem as sharp that night against Michigan. I don't think we played up to our potential, but don't take anything away from Michigan. They were a pretty good football team, but I don't think we played our best football."

"I'm not sure if we had anything much left in the tank after the previous week and the comeback over Chicago," added Dunek. "We played hard and ended up losing that game by two points to a very talented Michigan team with Bobby Hebert, Anthony Carter and Ray Bentley."

"We didn't really play like we did during the regular season," furthered Fusina. "It was not as close as the final score. They outplayed us, especially on offense. Our defense did okay, but Bobby played really well and made a lot of big plays. We weren't able to do that. I think in a way the loss helped us in the future because we used it to play even better."

With John Williams on the sideline with a bruised toe, Cleo Miller contributed 80 yards to the Panthers' ground game, while Ken Lacy added 56 to help keep the Philadelphia defense honest. Corker capped an incredible season with a pair of sacks, Carter finished the day with 179 receiving yards on nine catches, but Hebert, who completed 20 of 39 throws for 314 yards and three scores, was tabbed the game's Most Valuable Player.

"It was a true joy, because it was professional football but it was still almost like in between college and the NFL, where you really truly love to play for the joy of the game," recalled Hebert. "I was rewarded handsomely at that time, but most of the guys, they were just glad to be there. This is their dream: they wanted an opportunity to play pro ball, had never had a shot in the NFL, but they got to be part of a championship."

The win struck a chord in championship-starved Detroit which was also suffering from a high unemployment rate.

"At a neutral site game, we had fans storming the field," recalled Ehrhart. "There was so much excitement. A young Magic Johnson was at the game along with renowned boxer Sugar Ray Leonard. In the melee, Magic Johnson grabbed my nine-year-old son and put him up on his shoulders to spirit him away from the onrushing crowd. To this day, Magic is still my son's hero."

"I remember them storming the field in Denver," remembered Hebert. "After we won the championship game in Denver in '83, we stayed up all night. The next day I was on *Good Morning America* and CNN, which had just started, talking about the game. We landed in Pontiac when we flew back, and there was 12,000 or 15,000 people who met us at the airport."

"It was like a fairy tale. I wasn't even 23 years of age, and here we were winning the championship. In a matter of six months, it was truly a rags to riches story. I got this MVP trophy, and on the trophy it says 'Atari.' Atari was one of the sponsors. I can remember by winning MVP and Most Outstanding Offensive Player, I ended up getting two first class airline tickets to anywhere in the world from Pan-Am, which isn't even around anymore, with hotel and all that. I told my wife, 'We gotta go as far as we can go.' So we ended up going to Hong Kong and Singapore and staying at the Hong Kong Hilton and the Intercontinental in Singapore. That was part of Pan-Am's sponsorship of the MVP award. That was unique, and part of why I think of it as a rags to riches story."

3

Success at a Price

The USFL's showing in its first postseason thrilled league executives. One playoff game had featured an unforgettable comeback that culminated in an overtime victory for the home team and the other had drawn a raucous league-record crowd who left equally jubilant. In contrast to the Super Bowl, which had earned a reputation as a yearly yawner thanks to several blowouts, the league's first title game had gone down to the final few minutes, when two of the USFL's young stars combined on a big play to win it.

First season attendance had met projections at over 25,000 per game. Just as importantly, the television ratings also pleased USFL leadership. The championship game drew an 11.9 rating and 23 share nationally in prime time and was even better in Philadelphia and Detroit. The City of Brotherly Love gave the game a 25.6 rating while Detroit garnered a 38.1 rating and whopping 61 share. The Detroit numbers were higher than those for any Lions game in more than ten years. The Sunday night telecast finished second overall in its time period. The previous week's playoff games had also fared well with the Saturday contest pulling a six rating and the Sunday game getting an eight. Both telecasts beat out their competition on CBS and NBC.

Jerry Solomon, whose employer D'Arcy McManus handled the Anheuser Busch advertising, was one of those thrilled with the exposure the beer company received all season long, saying they had more than received their money's worth from advertising on USFL broadcasts.

ABC's Jim Spence stated the network made a $12.3 million profit over the course of the season on their USFL telecasts, making it ABC's second most profitable sports property of the year after the World Series. The network had expected a 5.0 rating going into the season, but buoyed by the 14.3 rating and 33 share for the first weekend of games, had instead pulled a 6.0, 20 percent above their expectations. All told, 30 percent more people had tuned into the network for USFL games than the year before the league launched. That number was typically much higher in league cities, proving that the USFL was getting some of the important exposure it needed. Unfortunately, Los Angeles, the country's second-largest market, averaged a 5.3 over the season, still above ABC's estimates but lower than other league cities. The network had helped its own cause by providing regional coverage on 12 weekends instead of the four it had originally planned.

"Everybody said, 'They have a game of the week on ABC Television,'" said Camera. "Well, what does that mean? We had to work it all out, and we had to make certain we had enough exposure with each team. We tried to get them to carry a secondary game, which was a problem. They were doing a game of the week with six cameras, and that was it. ABC was run by Jim Spence, and they weren't going to pour a lot of money into it. They just wanted to have programming on a Sunday afternoon. We had to massage that, so maybe we were able to get two feeds, so if one game was a blowout they could maybe go to the other game."

Ratings had dipped in the middle of the year because of strong competition from the National Basketball Association playoffs and summer weather that tended to keep football fans outside and away from their TVs, but viewership remained surprisingly strong overall. Buoyed by the numbers, ABC increased the cost of a 30-second commercial during league games from $25,000 to $35,000 for the next season, and the network generated $34 million in ad sales, much better than they could have done on Sunday afternoons without the USFL. Roone Arledge's gamble had paid off handsomely for his network. NBC, whose late bid for the original broadcasting rights had come up just short, noticed its counterpart's success and began negotiations with the league for the next contract. Unfortunately, all of the numbers were lost on many sportswriters who foolishly insisted on comparing them to the NFL's ratings, which typically topped 16.0 in the fall. Neither ABC nor the league ever deceived themselves into believing that they could match that number, especially considering that the USFL was breaking ground in a different season, not to mention that far fewer people stayed in front of their televisions in the spring and summer than in the fall and winter.

"We proved at the very beginning, to some degree, that people will watch professional football whenever it's played," added Simmons. "The first week was a testing week, and we did extraordinarily well in ratings. The next week it went down a bit and stayed pretty good during the first year, although it did drop to the level it should have been. It gave me the opinion that there were enough people out there to watch, that if we gave them product that looked good, sounded good, reported good and played good, people would follow it to some level. We found that there was an audience there. There is an element out there of people who will follow football at all levels, and professional football to a greater degree because they can follow the players for a much longer time than they could in college. It was a sport that you knew you had an opportunity to start with, and you just had to embellish the product to a point where people would get hooked by it."

ESPN was just as happy with its ratings as league games began with a 5.0 mark and drew an average score of 3.28 in 1983. Those were great numbers in the early days of cable, and league games quickly became the fledgling network's most popular fare. At the time a 2.0 rating on a cable network was considered very good. The USFL ratings amounted to an increase of 50 percent over those realized by the station in the fourth quarter of 1982. The numbers were particularly impressive since the channel showed 34 games over the course of the season without many of the marquee match-ups given to ABC. The cable network's coverage also provided additional exposure for the league two nights a week.

"We had the ESPN deal, and they really had no live professional sports at that time," Camera added. "They had nothing, just tractor pulls and things like that. They were terrific to work with, and they assisted us. They did a great job and were willing to do as much as they could. At that time, they weren't owned by ABC, so we had to keep those separate."

"Year one of the USFL was *almost* what we had wished for," added Simmons. "The ratings started high, then they plateaued but that's okay. That happens, now we got to figure out why and we gotta figure out how to fix it. We got to put our finger on the name players that we want to go after, it can't be a lot, just a few, a handful, at least from our perspective. We didn't need every team loaded up with big name players. We needed a couple of really good players who would speak positively about the league, and pay them the money. If I were to wrap up year one, I'd say reasonably successful."

The Double-Edged Sword of Television

Still, some within the league thought the widespread coverage also came with a down side. Attendance in cities in which the home team's games were often televised, particularly Philadelphia and Chicago, suffered. Both the Stars and the Blitz made a number of television appearances when they were playing at home, and with a lack of regionalization, blackouts and cross feeding, their attendance had suffered. Birmingham faced the same situation in the early going, having its first three home games aired on ESPN, and many of the franchises felt that television hindered the live gate. USFL owners pointed to the NFL's TV contracts which televised all games. All away games were sent back to a team's local market, generating additional fan interest. Home games that were not sold out were not televised in the home area which theoretically helped to generate ticket sales.

"The blackout just killed us," said Oakland's John Ralston. "You've got to black out the game if we don't sell 20,000 tickets or something like that. We didn't do that. In Philadelphia, for instance, with lousy weather, people just wouldn't go to the games. It looks awful, too."

Dixon agreed. "We should have insisted on blackouts, although maybe not with a sellout such as the NFL has. The league averaged nearly 26,000 attendance in its first year which was remarkable considering that there were no blackouts. Pete Rozelle told me once that if the NFL had no blackouts that their average attendance would drop from around 60,000 down to around 35,000 within two to three years. I think he may have been right, even today. Televised football is so good that you almost want to say, 'Why go to the game?'"

Other owners pointed out more perceived deficiencies in the television deals. Denver's Ron Blanding hated being unable to televise Sunday games in Denver when the Gold were on the road, thus reaching more fans, unless either ABC or ESPN picked up the contest. "It was a very important part of the league," he recalled about the television deals. "I know there were negotiations going on all the time because we were going to die unless we got that contract changed. What we had with ABC and ESPN was not going to be adequate to make the league viable."

"It certainly was the wrong contract if only for the reason that you couldn't feed your games back into your home city. You couldn't even have them on television if ABC was doing a game. Even if you were at home and you wanted to do it. If ABC was on, you couldn't do it. That's really important when you're trying to build fan loyalty."

"The television contracts that we had were very ill-advised," offered Taube. "The failure of the league to negotiate carry-backs which would have given the teams some measure of continuity when they were on the road was a serious issue that hurt attendance. There wasn't the right kind of continuity, particularly in the major markets."

"We left some money on the table during the television negotiations, no question about that," furthered David Dixon. "We got $9 million from ABC league-wide and the story has always been that they made $30 million on us that first year. We had a professional negotiator who was a good, capable person. That was Mike Trager, and it was his first time doing that sort of thing. He did a good job and I'm not being critical of him. We could have had better television money, though. All of us were very pleased to get the $9 million and with the ESPN deal thrown in there, we had pretty close to $1 million per team which was a lot of money in those days."

Trager disagreed with the criticisms.

"It was a fallacious argument," he countered. "Baseball teams were blacking out their games locally, too, until they figured out that the exposure is what's important. That's the argument I made to the USFL owners. More exposure results in more tickets sold. ABC would not have done the deal with a blackout provision. Are you going to televise a Generals game and black out eight million New Yorkers? It would have been crazy to black it out because we were in all major markets.

"There was always understanding on television. The ownership that talks about not understanding it now, understood the contracts. Sometimes ownership can be naive about how television operates. They were getting more than $1 million per team. Several owners led by Warner claimed they didn't understand the lack of blackouts. Not true. All of them were briefed and all had copies of the contracts.

"I think they understood the contracts until they didn't want to understand the contracts. They were getting almost $20 million in rights fees for a league that hadn't played any games."

"There was a debate about whether they should black out the local markets in order to increase ticket sales," confirmed Ehrhart. "In the end, it was my recollection that we needed the exposure more than we needed the blackouts."

"These guys were essentially real estate people; they had made their money in real estate around the country," Simmons said about the USFL team owners. "None of them had any kind of real experience in television, except for maybe John Bassett who had been involved in other football leagues and other startups in sports, not only through himself but his daughter Carling who was a ranked tennis player at that point. John was really the most involved owner from all aspects of owning a professional sports team. Bill Daniels had a knowledge of cable in general, but I don't know if it came down to sports in particular, but knowing Bill he had enough people who could give him the kind of advice he needed to go forward. Bill was a very cooperative owner and a really good guy. They all *thought* they knew what it was, but they didn't necessarily know."

Not all of the USFL owners looked upon the situation as a problem. They felt the exposure was invaluable and would pay off with ticket sales down the road.

"Because we were in a large market and because we were a very good football team, we were on quite a bit," Peterson said. "I got to know a lot of guys including Chris Berman and some other guys who were starting up in the business at that time. They enjoyed televising it. Even though the stands weren't filled, it was important to get our product out to the public and what better way than television. People started watching it in the spring as an alternative to other spring televised sports. The ratings were exceptional for the springtime when, yes, you see baseball periodically but you see golf and tennis. But people love football and they love football all year round. We didn't get a great deal of money, but we did get money from both the network and cable. That really was a key, and it was essential that we be exposed, that we get the product out there. That was huge. That really helped generate a demographic that wanted to follow the USFL. A younger demographic, yes, but I still run into people who grew up watching the USFL and still rave about it, whether I'm in Philadelphia or even Kansas City."

Whether or not some owners believed television lured fans out of the stadiums, a reported 2,807,788 people walked through USFL turnstiles in 1983, an average of just over 25,000 people per game. The opening weekend brought out an average of 39,171 spectators per venue, a figure which dwindled to about half that number toward the latter part of the season. Poor weather in many locations had also done its share to keep people at home. Even so, the USFL had hit Dixon's projections squarely on the head, a fact again lost on those who stubbornly insisted on comparing the fledgling league's popularity to the 60-plus-year-old NFL.

"Attendance surpassed estimates," Trager said. "I thought the bulk of the franchises were well run. Sure, there were some weaker run teams, but that's the case in every league. The first year was very solid. The only issue was could they control spending."

"It was a great time of the year," added the Generals' Kevin MacConnell. "We're in training camp when the Super Bowl is being played, so for those who loved football, there was no gap. You just went right into more football, and it was really good football."

The solid ratings and perception that the league was losing some ticket buyers to television led several owners to believe that ABC was getting a sweetheart deal. Higher than anticipated expenses became the catalyst for calls to renegotiate the contract. Led by Birmingham's Marvin Warner, several owners insisted that Simmons try to get a better deal out of the network.

"Marvin could be very difficult," Ehrhart recalled. "When the NFL pressured Roone Arledge about supporting a competitor, and Arledge offhandedly commented, 'Well, they're a property like bowling,' Marvin was incensed. Roone later tried to justify his statement and clarified that bowling was a very valuable product in its place. It was successful and made money for ABC. Marvin and some of the others were livid because they felt it was a knee-jerk response to cater to the NFL and not allow the USFL to become a major competitor, which we had made the decision by that time to do. We had the ability to get stars, we had the ability to capture the American public, so I remember Marvin was very angry about Arledge's comment, saying 'Is that the way our partner's going to be? We're trying to make this as good as it can be, and they have a lot of pressure coming from the NFL. They'll serve that master, and they're going to put us in our place and we'll be a 'bowling league.'"

"ABC entered in good faith with us back in the spring of '82," said Tanenbaum. "They were advertising our product and hired on Lynn Swann and Keith Jackson, their top college football guy. I thought they did a reasonably good job, but they were catching a lot of heat from the NFL. Roone Arledge then made an unfortunate comment which was for the consumption of the NFL. He said the USFL was like bowling, it fit a sports entertainment bill, but don't get too excited about it. That got a lot of people upset. He couldn't take it back after he said it."

"We knew attendance could never carry us," said Camera. "I'm not making excuses because that's not my nature, but we knew attendance couldn't carry it because we had to keep the ticket prices reasonable. I wrote many position papers on this. And we were playing at an off time of the year. We knew that early on, the first six games or so, we'd be okay, but after that you had baseball and a lot of other conflicts. We just couldn't raise ticket prices to the point it would help make up the difference for when attendance would start falling. It was going to be a problem. We determined, and I agreed, that we had to get more out of television. We were providing a product, and we were doing six and seven ratings. People would kill for that now, and with terrific demographics. The bottom line was that we could only get additional revenues out of the broadcast partners."

"They expressed an interest for more regional telecasts," recalled Spence "They had expressed some concerns about the ratings dropping, and they thought that if we regionalized games, creating pockets of interest around the country as opposed to one national telecast around the country, that the league would be better served and ABC Sports better served. So we added regionals in 1984 at a considerable production cost, but that was the main request that we had the first year, that we add regional telecasts to help increase the ratings."

By most accounts, particularly the television numbers, viewers enjoyed USFL games. The league had eschewed exhibition games due to its ABC contract, and with a large number of rookies in the league and all players adjusting to each other and new systems, some ragged play resulted in the first few weeks. Execution steadily improved as the season wore on, and blowouts became less frequent. Seven points or less decided half of the first season's games, 54 out of 108, as compared to 47.3 percent for the NFL in 1983 and a shade above 40 percent in 1982. Even league doormats Washington and Arizona lost several close games.

Young Stars Abound

The USFL announced its first All-League teams, selected by sportswriters and broadcasters who covered the circuit. All told, ten members of the champion Panthers landed a place on the first and second teams. Seven members of the Blitz, six Stars and six Bandits also made the cut. From the beginning, the league wanted to develop its own stars rather than steal them from the NFL. They were successful in that mission with 13 players, one-fourth of the All-League selections, having just completed their rookie season of professional football.

Michigan quarterback Bobby Hebert headlined the first team with fellow rookies Herschel Walker and Philadelphia's Kelvin Bryant named as the top running backs. Chicago's Trumaine Johnson and Tampa Bay's surprising Eric Truvillion grabbed the receiver spots, while cagy veteran Raymond Chester of Oakland made it at tight end. All of the specialists were rookies with the exception of Chester. Tackles Irv Eatman of Philadelphia and Ray Pinney of Michigan, guards Buddy Aydelette of Birmingham and Thom Dornbrook of Michigan and center Bobby Van Duyne of Tampa Bay made up the top offensive line.

On the defensive line, Birmingham's Mike Raines and Chicago's Kit Lathrop were chosen at end and Tampa Bay's Fred Nordgren was tabbed as the top nose tackle. Michigan's John Corker and Chicago's Stan White took the top two outside linebacker spots while Philly's Sam Mills and Boston's Marcus Marek grabbed the inside spots. Corner backs Jeff George of Tampa Bay and David Martin of Denver along with safeties Luther Bradley of Chicago and Scott Woerner of Philadelphia made up the first team secondary. Martin also made the list as the USFL's best punt returner while Washington's Eric Robinson, the lone Fed to make the list, picked up honors as the top kick return man. Kicker Tim Mazzetti of Boston and punter Stan Talley of Oakland rounded out the first team selections.

In addition, the league selected Bryant as its Most Valuable Player and Chester as its Man of the Year. Hebert took Outstanding Quarterback honors, Herschel Walker grabbed the Outstanding Running Back nod and Trumaine Johnson landed Receiver of the Year. Rookies claimed all four spots. On the other side of the ball, John Corker earned Defensive Player of the Year honors, and Kit Lathrop claimed Outstanding Lineman honors. Talley landed Special Teams Player of the Year and Philadelphia's David Trout won the Leading Scorer award. Dick Coury captured Coach of the Year honors for his efforts in molding a nameless Breakers squad into a playoff contender.

"The original talent of the original 12 teams from the front offices to the coaches to the general managers was terrific," said Ehrhart. "It was phenomenal the kinds of people we had involved. That's part of the reason we were able to get so many great players, too."

"We came out of the box strong," said Tampa Bay's Jim McVay. "The TV ratings were off the charts early on with ABC and ESPN, the crowds were spectacular, and people had an appetite for football. You know, that first year there were a lot of good signals, there were a lot of good signs. I mean this had a chance to take traction. We really felt that if we continued to market properly, if all the decisions, the right decisions, were made top to bottom, we had a chance. We needed to be careful with the salary cap, we needed to continue with the marketing emphasis, we needed to make sure we had players. Each team had a number of players for marquee purposes: the glamour guys, the quarterbacks, the running backs that people were attracted to. So, we knew that there were a lot of elements, a lot of issues that needed to be addressed, but we did feel early on that there really was a potential for spring football. That appetite for professional football is really strong in the American culture."

Seeking Improvement

The league sought to build on its strong start in year two while firming up the foundation it had built in its inaugural campaign, placing additional pressure on Commissioner Simmons.

"When people ask me what's wrong with the league, I say, 'Well, it's not *My Fair Lady* but it's not 'The Ugly Duckling' either,'" explained Simmons to *Sports Illustrated* in 1983. "Look, it's barely a year since formation of the league was even announced. Then ABC said it would cover us, then ESPN, then we hired name coaches, then we held the draft, then we signed Herschel—the timing was terrific. We were building up to the start of the season with incredible momentum. But the problem was that things were going *too* well. People expected the child to be born a full-grown adult. It didn't happen. This operation is in its infancy. People simply have been expecting too much."

Some of the people who expected more from the USFL included the league's owners, but they did not have the league's on the field accomplishments in mind. Instead, Simmons' performance had come under fire, particularly because he had been unable to renegotiate the television deals and because some felt that league meetings would sometimes get out of control. The commissioner struggled to lead the sessions of headstrong businessmen and occasionally became the target of the owners' wrath. To ease the situation, Chicago Blitz owner Dr. Ted Diethrich suggested the owners establish an executive committee, and his compatriots agreed. The new group would be made up of three owners who would help guide the league, taking away some of the commissioner's power.

"A lot of the owners in short order started to bully Chet," Camera said. "That was their mentality because Chet was a television executive, and having come from that, these guys liked to have coffee with China, and Chet was a thinker, had great ideas and could run an operation, but these owners figured he was an indentured slave. That was part of the problem we had. They were so used to saying to guys, 'You do this, and you do that. We're paying you a million dollars a year, or whatever they were paying him, you do what we tell you.' So that was a problem Chet had to deal with.

"Don't forget that he was being compared to Pete Rozelle. It's awfully tough to be compared to the greatest commissioner ever. Pete Rozelle was a great PR guy, but he'd cut your nuts off if he had to. Pete was smart, so Chet was caught in that comparison.

"If you're going to be a commissioner, you have to be decisive. I'd go into see Chet, and I'd say, 'Chet, you're going to get a call from an owner. I just told him to go fuck himself, and I hung up the phone. He's wrong, he's out of line, etc.' And he'd say, 'Well, what are you doing that for?' And I'd reply, 'What am I going to do? He's driving me nuts. He's got his marketing guy running around like a lunatic, not knowing what he's doing. We have to sell tickets.' Chet would get nervous waiting for the phone call from the owner. By the time the owner called him, he'd say, 'No, Dom's got a good point. He was right.'"

"The Executive Committee arose because there was a general consensus that Chet Simmons just didn't have the strength of personality to control all these owners," said Tad Taube. "For a while, they had a good influence on some of the policies that were followed by the USFL, particularly in 1984, when there was an inclination to break ranks.

"I wrote a lot of letters, and I tried to be a calming influence. I think I had a lot of respect and following from the owners because they elected me as chairman of the Executive Committee, but I was really not in a position to take on that kind of responsibility given my other business activities. I yielded that position to John Bassett. In hindsight, maybe if I had been able to do that job, I think I might have been able to avoid some of the very bad decisions that were made.

"John was probably the best informed and the most creative of our owners. He had been one of the founders of the World Football League, and I think for a while he did a good job as head of the Executive Committee. With support from both Al Taubman and myself, he was able to keep things from getting away from us in terms of our control over compensation and other issues."

To help the league office with the increasing workload, the USFL brought on outside counsel Bill McSherry whose role with the league would quickly grow over the next 18 months. McSherry boasted considerable experience in sports, helping craft the American Basketball Association's merger with the NBA in 1976 as well as working with the NHL's New York Islanders and the NBA's New York Nets. Like Ehrhart, he had also represented athletes including tennis' Jimmy Connors and Evonne Goolagong.

"A mutual friend of mine and Steve's [Ehrhart] named Daniel Hoffman who was a lawyer in Denver had worked with me on the merger of the four ABA teams into the NBA in 1976, one of which was the Denver Nuggets," recalled McSherry. "Dan represented the Nuggets, and I represented all four of the teams. Dan gave Steve my name when Steve came to New York to become the executive director but they had already hired Paul Weis as the counsel. I guess it was in late 1984 I was on a trial in California, and I got a phone call from Steve in New York. One of my partners took the call, and they asked if I could do some work for them, probably on the Chicago team. When I got back to New York,

I figured out what the problem was and went out to Chicago. After that it was just one deal after the other."

Meanwhile, the NFL had changed its stance toward the league considerably. Once content to ignore the newcomer and wait for it to die of its own volition, the NFL owners and coaches now saw it as a threat. They quickly began to make things tougher for the USFL. For one, most teams barred the new league's scouts from training camps and press boxes.

"Now we were a known quantity," explained Keller about the league having a year under its belt. "What it did was that it alerted the NFL that now it had a competitor on its hands. It made it much harder for us to surprise the NFL on guys. The price of doing business went up because the NFL started paying everybody more in the NFL."

"The NFL was counter-punching because they knew we were trying to get more money out of the television networks, so the NFL was putting more pressure on them, saying, 'Bullshit, don't you give them anymore. They're our competitor.'" Ehrhart said. "At first everybody was singing in a circle, everybody from the players to the agents to the NFL was happy. As soon as we became a strong competitor for fans, TV dollars, players and public attention, it was no more of the 'damn you with faint praise.' It was 'Katie, bar the door,' as far as the reaction back from NFL teams. Salary escalation just jumped hugely in '83 and '84 because of competition for players. As a result, the NFL said you're not welcome in our camps anymore."

"It didn't take long before somewhat of an adversarial position developed between the two leagues," agreed Stars GM Carl Peterson. "Certainly, Dick [Vermeil] was very cooperative in regards to players who were not going to make the Eagles roster, and we played at a different time of the year. When they would get through their training camp in August and players were being released, I would talk to Dick and ask him, 'Do you think that this guy could help our young league or is this a guy who could benefit from our league?' and he would say 'yes' or 'no.'

"Specific to Vermeil and perhaps in some other isolated instances, my association with the NFL helped me to build the Stars, but it didn't take long before the National Football League's office came out pretty strong that they should be aware or somewhat concerned about our league. I remember some great statements by my good friend [Dallas Cowboys president] Tex Schramm, stating that this would be a flame-out league, and that we wouldn't have any players or coaches of any ability, and that they shouldn't even pay much attention to us. He was wrong in some of those aspects, that's for sure."

From even before the opening gun, the league faced an uphill battle with some of the media. To be sure, the USFL drew more than its fair share of coverage. Unfortunately, some of it had a negative slant. Art Spander, a Bay Area columnist who also wrote for *The Sporting News*, was a prime example of some of the media's bias against the league. He entitled one of his even-handed articles, "Football is Not the Spring Game," as if God Himself ordained otherwise. Likewise, *Sports Illustrated* joined the chorus with a five-page spread entitled, "Football: A Rite or Wrong of Spring?" At least they appeared to be keeping an open mind. While some reporters realized there was simply no way they could compare a one-year-old league to an entity with the tradition and history of the NFL, others insisted on forcing the comparison and loudly declaring the USFL as the hands-down loser.

"The newspaper guys were all convinced we should be playing in the fall," explained Camera. "Most of the newspaper guys were NFL guys; they were shills for the NFL. They would always see the glass as half-empty. They were going to write it with a slant. You couldn't get a legitimate story out of the *Times*, but we had big support at *USA Today* because they started when we did. *USA Today* gave us great coverage."

Another media ally was ABC's Monday Night Football broadcaster Howard Cosell.

"Howard was a big supporter in many, many ways," Simmons said. "He would talk positively about it, not all the time, he'd give us a rap once or twice. Howard was a good friend I knew for many years, and he would walk into the office without an invitation. It was one of the things about Howard. You'd be sitting at your desk and the next thing you know there he is. He'd be looking at you saying, 'Where's that vodka bottle? Can I smoke in your room?' Howard, whatever you want as long as you say nice things about us."

The Financial Fallout

To be sure, the new league had its share of challenges. While none of the owners expected to turn a profit right away, many had to shudder when they looked at their bottom lines following the first season. On top of the heap, Denver made a slight profit while Tampa Bay came close to breaking even. The rest of the group was not nearly as lucky. The other franchises lost an average of $3.3 million apiece, $1.3 million in excess of Dixon's original estimate of $2 million per team per year for the first three years. While revenues followed fairly closely to the founders' approximations, expenses, particularly those for player salaries, were way out of whack. While the addition of wild card players helped the league's marketability, they played havoc with the bottom line. Michigan also suffered from a huge payroll and posted a league-high $6 million deficit, ironically making the champion the leading money loser. Fortunately, Alfred Taubman, one of *Forbes* 400 richest men in America, could shoulder that kind of loss better than most NFL owners. It was too much for Judge Peter Spivak, Taubman's minority partner who had helped lead the USFL before Simmons' hiring. His role had been reduced before the season began, and he had faded largely into the background with Taubman in control of the team. He now departed the franchise, leaving the USFL without one of its early voices. He wasn't the only one concerned.

"I would say the first breach of the gentlemen's agreement happened shortly after the league commenced play," said Taube of the salary guidelines. "We had a team in Michigan, the Michigan Panthers, which was owned by my friend Al Taubman, and Taubman was a guy who is not used to losing at any level. He lost, I think, three out of the first four games, and thereupon decided he was going to bolster the ranks of his team in order to make them more competitive. He did that basically, as I recall, by recruiting and hiring three or four very visible linemen from the world champion Pittsburgh Steelers and paid them significantly more than would have been possible to pay under our salary cap agreement. That was the first break in the ranks, I would say."

"The second week in the season, Tampa Bay beat Michigan at Tampa, and I was sitting with Taubman, and he said, 'We're not going to have this anymore. We've got to go out and get some players, too,'" added Ehrhart. "He decided the Michigan Panthers were going to become competitive, and that's when, as John Bassett used to say, he went out and signed the Pittsburgh Steelers offensive line. By that time, he already had Anthony Carter and Bobby Hebert under the wild card exemption, but that exemption was already

Michigan Panthers majority owner A. Alfred Taubman (second from left) celebrates his team's title with minority owner Max Fisher (second from right), USFL Commissioner Chet Simmons (far left) and Panthers coach Jim Stanley on July 17, 1983, at Denver, Colorado. Photograph courtesy family of A. Alfred Taubman.

blown up. It wasn't just one or two players that would be the stars when Michigan signed the linemen. Now we're having teams go over the budget with players that are more than a wild card exemption of a star quarterback or a star running back. The signing of those key linemen was a key reason the Panthers ended up winning the title."

"We didn't break the rules on the budget," responded Taubman. "We were way under on the budget. We were hiring with a very, very businesslike eye. We wanted to win, but that wasn't the main aim. We wanted to have some fun; that was all."

Not having much fun was Dr. Ted Diethrich who estimated Blitz losses at $3 million for the year, while Birmingham dropped a modest $2 million, in line with Dixon's estimates.

"We certainly paid some high prices for some players, probably more than we should have," admitted Chicago's Diethrich. "We probably paid too much for Trumaine Johnson, for instance, but Bruce was so sure we had to do that. I'm sure our player budget was higher than, maybe not the Generals, but certainly the Denver group. If you look at that and if it continued like that from a financial standpoint; that would have been pretty bad for us."

"Once they started playing on the field, teams got beat and coaches started saying, 'I can't win with these guys,' and then it started," Ehrhart said of the burgeoning USFL payrolls. "It was unbelievable. It was like the doors were knocked down by the flood. Coaches would press the owners, who would ask, 'How come we lost that game?' Coaches would reply, 'These guys can't play. I have to get better players.' Agents for all the players were banging on the doors of the USFL teams, saying, 'Hey, I've got Ray Pinney of the Pittsburgh Steelers. They're being hard-asses in contract negotiations; the Steelers won't pay what he deserves, but Ray will come play for you for this amount of money.' It was like a deluge. We were able to close the door on the undergraduates, at least for a year, but the players coming out of the NFL were a different story. Remember, the NFL had been able to restrain salaries for so long because they didn't have any competition, and after the bitterness of the strike, players were willing to talk and we were in a position to compete for them. Here they are first string mainstays on the offensive line of a championship team, and we were able to sign guys like Ray Pinney for $150,000. It wasn't even that dramatic a salary. You look at now a starting tackle in the NFL is making several million dollars. It was a storm, which once it occurred; it was difficult to fight back.

"There was debate amongst ourselves as to the sustainability of these salaries. There was no question that the $1.5 million target had been exceeded. That period of time came to a crashing halt. The relationship with the NFL was much different now. Every good player from the NFL wanted to come negotiate with the USFL. Coaches' jobs are on the line if they don't win. They go in to see their owners or general managers and say, 'If we could just sign this guy, we can win.' There's pressure to sell tickets if you win. Michigan proved that. They were the furthest team behind in putting their organization together, their players together, but because they reacted quickly after they got beat by Tampa, they won the title. This same process occurs in every single league, and it was no different in the USFL. The owners who want to win spend the money to do so."

"They depended upon the people they hired, and the people they hired whispered in their ear, 'We used to do it this way,'" Simmons said of the owners. "What am I going to tell you? Tough business. You better be ready for a really large dose of stomach churning if you're going to get into this business."

"It was the owners," agreed Blanding. "We were digging our own graves. The competition caused it. Everybody wants to win so the general feeling is that you pay a little more for players, you get better players. That's what caused costs to go up."

Several of the owners voiced concern over the numbers and the lack of spending restraint among their compatriots. In a letter to the other owners that would come back to haunt them all, Oakland's Tad Taube wrote, "If we are not successful in establishing player [salary] caps, I can guarantee you that there will not be a USFL within three years, irrespective of improved revenue [from] television…. We have sighted the enemy and they are us!"

Expansion

Overall though, optimism pervaded the league. Just a year before it had been little more than a figment of David Dixon's imagination, but after its first season, it had exceeded even the owners' own expectations. The achievements had come at a higher than projected cost, but they were eager to keep pushing forward.

"There was some great talent on the field," said Ehrhart. "All in all, if anybody could have imagined a year earlier that we'd achieve what we had achieved, to be in a position to expand, to develop the fan base and develop the infrastructure, it was a huge success."

"I thought we were okay. I thought we had an opportunity if we could just go slowly," agreed Simmons. "I was in favor of a star here and there. I thought it was necessary for the public. I thought it was necessary for the team and for the writers, broadcasters and telecasters who covered the games. Building slow was going to be better than fast. We had a very small, for the most part semi-experienced, league office. We had some guys who came out of the NFL that I knew. I tried to hire people I knew or had some knowledge of who they were or what their reputations were. But we were a very small, inexperienced league office, and we were battling with very, very wealthy men whose egos were well beyond their ability to stay up with what professional football was. It was a fight every day."

"There was a battle and a pressure to get more money out of television," added Ehrhart. "Then there was a push back from television, and it was fueled by the NFL pressuring everybody not to give us anymore. In the local markets, the Tampa Bay Buccaneers pushed back on the Bandits. Anybody who was a Bandit person was now *non grata* with the Buccaneers. There was that kind of a push back. That was one of the things that pushed us into the expansion."

Expansion became a hot topic even before the inaugural season. Dixon had planned on quick growth from the very beginning, realizing that the money it brought the USFL would help offset some of its early losses and placate the original owners. The USFL founder already held his own USFL expansion franchise, his fee for organizing the league, and he was eager to sell it, virtually ensuring expansion by at least one team. After flirting with the possibilities of adding between four and ten new teams, the USFL eventually grew by six franchises.

"We actually looked at it in the fall of '82 because we had applications from a lot of people, people of substance in good cities," Ehrhart said. "We had an expansion committee and John Bassett and I were pretty much the guys who traversed the country interviewing expansion candidates.

"It was a way to get more revenue into the league. We certainly did want quality cities and quality people. I remember having a conversation with Al Davis at a meeting in Los Angeles about the time of the expansion. Based on his experiences when he built the AFL, Al advised me, 'Be careful of expanding too fast.' His advice was certainly good and proper, but as I told him we had such a voracious appetite for revenues because the owners were spending so much money. They then had this opportunity to expand after a successful first season.

"I was explaining to Al how we had been caught in this cycle. We had become so competitive so quickly. We had smart general managers, smart coaches, and players were working with us. It was an exciting league. The brand of football was appealing to the players and to the public. So that put the engine of revenue and expenses into overdrive, trying to find more revenue for fast increasing expenses.

"The USFL team owners had invested millions of dollars in operating their teams in 1983, but that was nothing compared to the purchase price of an NFL franchise, for instance, which would have been in the $100 million range. There was a difference of opinion among the owners of where the tipping point was where the dollars that had been spent were investments into assets, rather than saying we had to go out and sell the future to cover the costs. Several owners were all over us, demanding, 'You've got to get more money! You've got to get more money!' Al's advice to me was very thoughtful and solid, and we discussed the whole issue of expansion and whether it was wise or unwise. We were caught in this cycle that we needed to raise revenue to cover the higher operating costs. The owners saw that they had started this a year earlier and now they saw that people were paying $6.25 million for the same thing for which they hadn't paid an upfront franchise fee. They saw that they had added value by covering the costs of their operation in the first year."

"Expansion was done because that's where John Bassett and a lot of guys said, 'Hey, we can make some of our money back,'" added Camera. "It was money that they had never put up but they had run up in operating costs. They thought, 'We can get it all back. We're the hottest thing around.'"

"The reason we expanded was that we wanted the franchise fees," confirmed McVay. "It's good to expand if the market is such that it merits expansion. You can take the franchise fees and grow your product, grow your brand. It made sense to do all those things. But what you don't want to do is expand prematurely until you get the original group settled in a nice, functional format unless you have to. The league needed to do it to bring in more revenue, expansion fees. All of a sudden guys are losing money, and they say, 'Hey, let's expand. That'll give us more money and time to grow it.'"

Pittsburgh captured the USFL's first expansion franchise in late April in a move that greatly strengthened the USFL ownership ranks and fired a shot across the NFL's bow at the same time. Edward DeBartolo Sr., bought the team which would begin play in 1984. He was the world's largest developer of shopping malls and also had considerable experience in sports ownership. At one time or another, he had owned pieces of the NHL's Penguins, the Major Indoor Soccer League's Spirit, the Pittsburgh Civic Arena and a trio of horse racing tracks. DeBartolo's involvement drew interest from the media and the NFL because his son, Edward DeBartolo, Jr., owned the San Francisco 49ers. Paul Martha, a former NFL player, lawyer and high-ranking DeBartolo employee spearheaded the team's purchase.

"Paul Martha was a former NFL legend and also DeBartolo's *consigliore*, as we referred to him," said Ehrhart. "He was also president of the Penguins at that time, another DeBartolo franchise, and he was Eddie Jr.'s right-hand guy in helping build the 49ers. He was the guy who came in, and may have been *the* key guy in helping bring the '82 strike to a conclusion. At the time Ed Garvey was still leading the charge there, and it was a pretty bitter strike. Paul was very much in the middle of helping resolve the '82 strike as a mediator. A year later Paul and the DeBartolo family were in the middle of acquiring a USFL team and that somewhat led to the huge animosity that occurred between Rozelle and DeBartolo. At the very same time, Paul understood the dynamics of pro football. It was Paul and the DeBartolos who basically signed up for the first expansion franchise in the USFL."

The elder DeBartolo's new venture flew in the face of NFL Commissioner Rozelle's cross-ownership policy which prohibited football owners from owning a team in another sport. But months earlier, the North American Soccer League won an antitrust case against the NFL over the policy. Rozelle didn't have a legal leg to stand on to prohibit an NFL owner's father from owning a USFL team. The older league threatened to force the family to divest itself of one of the teams, namely the 49ers, but after its threats to the DeBartolos were ignored, the NFL instead asked the 49ers owner to leave the room when NFL owners discussed the USFL.

"Rozelle threatened DeBartolo saying they couldn't own teams in both leagues, and Paul and Eddie Jr. were hauled out on the carpet," Ehrhart added. "Rozelle was very mad at Eddie Jr., and that's why the Pittsburgh Maulers was not in Eddie Jr.'s name; it was in

Edward DeBartolo Sr.'s name. They were being very careful. They kept it out of Eddie Jr.'s name to keep it separate. Paul was such a key figure in all of it, as both a former NFL star and a well-respected lawyer. Paul was handling negotiations, and I had flown to Youngstown to try to finish the contract for expansion. This is probably early '83, so by that time the strike had been settled in the fall of '82, and Paul had been instrumental in doing that. In a subsequent meeting, Paul and Eddie Jr., met me at the hotel in New York City after they had their meeting where Rozelle was calling them on the carpet and telling them that they couldn't own the team in the USFL if they wanted to continue as members of the NFL. That's when the DeBartolo family said, 'We're not going to bow to the pressure of Rozelle. We're going to do this because we think the USFL is a terrific opportunity.' That's when they put it in the dad's name. They were two technically separate entities. Paul was in the middle of that whole business, and that inter-relates with the league.

"We had a big battle amongst ourselves, inside our league, over do we admit DeBartolo. Some of our owners thought it would be a negative to allow basically an NFL owner to come into the league. There was this supposed Chinese wall between father and son, but everybody knew they did everything together. We had an NFL ownership group that saw the value of having a spring league and wanted to own teams in both leagues. The first USFL expansion team was purchased by one of the paragons of NFL ownership!"

The newest USFL owner immediately launched a counterattack. Pittsburgh management began discussions with quarterback Dan Marino, drafted in the first round by the Miami Dolphins but still unsigned. In November, the team announced a four-year agreement to play at Three Rivers Stadium, which promptly sent the Steelers screaming bloody murder, claiming that the stadium had given the upstarts a better deal than they had. The USFL franchise took the name Maulers in honor of the men who formed the steel that made the city famous.

"We had applications from all over the country: Seattle, Minneapolis, Pittsburgh, Jacksonville, Orlando, Memphis, Houston and more," recalled Ehrhart. "Even as early as 1982, we probably had applications from ten solid groups in different cities, so we tried to sort through those. The one that took the greatest precedence was Pittsburgh because Paul Martha had had exposure to what we were doing and Chet had a long relationship with Mr. DeBartolo Sr. We went over to visit and meet with Ed Sr. at his place in Tampa, and Paul and I worked on the actual documentation. They were the first expansion team signed and in the league despite their ordeal with Rozelle chastising Eddie, Jr. saying that he couldn't own a team in both leagues. That didn't come to finality until 1983, though we started in '82. We started the conversations with Paul and the DeBartolos in '82 and finalized the deal in '83 for play in '84, so we're talking about six to ten months of negotiations and planning there."

Houston stood next in line and officially joined the league on May 11. A group headed up by Bernard Lerner, Alvin Lubetkin and player agent Jerry Argovitz bought the rights to the city from league founder David Dixon for a discounted rate paid up front.

"Another reason we were forced into expansion is because David Dixon was out there," Ehrhart explained. "His fee for creating the league was that he technically was supposed to own a franchise. Some of the owners were concerned that David had the right to a franchise, but he chose not to put the money into it. The owners were putting all this money into a startup, so to speak, and David, once there was value in the franchises, was going to sell his franchise. He had the right to a franchise under the original agreement. He was out and about the country with a '13th franchise' in his hands. He was going to make that deal, and obviously you couldn't expand with just one team, so we eventually ended up with a six-team expansion but one of the teams was done by David. He sold and kept the money from the Houston guys. Had David not been out there, maybe we would have delayed expansion for a year. Maybe it would have been better, but there was no choice because he was going to do it. He had the legal right to do it. He saw there was value in the franchises, the $6.25 million value that had been put on expansion franchises by the ownership.

"Dixon made it clear that this was the deal they made, and it would be approved. Argovitz was out front of the operation, but there was a group of investors including Lerner and Lubetkin, two other guys who were more business oriented. Lerner was very financially sound; they had a sound financial group and a sound plan to play at the Astrodome. We needed to be in Texas at the time because we did not have a team in the state. Football in Texas made good sense for everybody. Dixon got his money and we got a franchise in a large city in the state of Texas."

"David was following the expansion candidates very closely, and wanted the information from John Bassett and myself, about who they were," Ehrhart added. "He ended up focusing in on the Houston situation because he was looking to sell his franchise rights in this way. Some people talked to him and said, 'Why don't you hold off,' but the league was going great guns, so he wanted to sell then. The league office was in a difficult spot because on one hand David Dixon would say, 'I've got the right to sell this. I don't have to answer to anyone else. I own this franchise.' He just was looking to sell for the cash.

"Of all the franchises, we had the least information and least knowledge about the inner operations of Houston. Jerry Argovitz, Lubetkin and Lerner all at various times came to league meetings. The three were all visible at one time or another. We had met them, and I remember going to Houston, but we did not do the same level of due diligence and involvement with them. There were some tense moments with David saying that it was his franchise, and he could sell it as he saw fit. This was the guy who was the initial founder of the league, but he was not at that time expending money, although I'm sure he spent some money during the organizational period."

"He used to call me sometimes three or four times a day when we were in the league," remembered Diethrich of Argovitz. "He was very excited. He was always trying to think of things that could make us all more successful. He was probably a bit of a loose cannon, but a friendly, jovial guy. I never knew exactly what he was going to come up with. I always had to think twice before I said, 'Yes.' Jerry is a character."

Argovitz represented such NFL stars as Detroit's Billy Sims, Tampa Bay's Hugh Green, Baltimore's Curtis Dickey and Buffalo's Joe Cribbs. Cribbs followed his agent to the new league when he signed on with Birmingham. To avoid an obvious conflict of interest, Argovitz agreed to give up his agent business in order to purchase the team but only after completing contracts for a handful of remaining players, Sims included. Singer Kenny Rogers would join on as a minority investor and the team would be called the "Gamblers" after Rogers' popular tune, "The Gambler."

"There was a big debate about the name of the team, and we talked to ESPN and ABC about the word 'Gamblers,'" Ehrhart recalled. "I can remember there was some consternation. Should the name 'Gamblers' be utilized? On one side of the ledger it connoted gambling on everything from games to other things, but the winning argument was made by the three guys who pointed out that Houston was a city that had been founded on people gambling on oil. Then there was the old Western gambler and the Kenny Rogers song, 'The Gambler,' so that was their theme song and that had been made into a movie. Their whole theme was based on the 1800s and the Wild West, Houston, cowboys and gambling, in that sense."

"We became owners of the Houston franchise which we named the Houston Gamblers," recalled Argovitz. "That brought up quite a stir, and a few days later I get a telegram from Roone Arledge who was at the time the president of ABC, one of the most major people in all of sports and all of TV. His telegram said that, 'I don't think it's appropriate to have gambling associated with professional football. And if you wanna name your team the Houston Gamblers, we will not televise your games on TV. We're not going to televise any of your games.' I thought about it for a little bit, and I wrote him a telegram back and said, 'Roone, you got Jimmy the Greek making lines on television every week. I think you're being a bit hypocritical and think if you took gambling out of football, you would probably end up having more people watching ice skating on Sundays.' So I said, tongue in cheek, gambling had nothing to do with the name 'Gamblers' at all. The Houston Gamblers, you know, are in the state of Texas. A lot of oil production there, a lot of risk taking. Houston was literally the hottest part of the country as far as people moving there. Jobs, opportunities, Houston was in a tremendous growth period. People from all over the country were moving to Houston, picking up their belongings wherever they were and coming to Houston for better opportunities, to gamble. To me, putting all my money in the USFL was certainly a gamble. So I thought the name was very appropriate, and that's the kind of football that I wanted to play. You know fourth down was an offensive down. In fact, we even stated one time that we might not in fact hire a punter."

"He was a pretty good guy," Dixon said of Argovitz. "Jerry was a tough negotiator. He tried to trick me by leaving a listening device in a private room at his headquarters where I was talking with my wife. I got my wife's attention and pushed my finger to my lips while pointing at the thing. Jerry was trying to get me to get the price down, but that's okay. I wanted $4 million, and I got the $4 million from him."

The Houston ownership trio began seeking additional investors. After almost being forced to play at Rice Stadium, Houston inked a deal to make the Astrodome their home field. Dixon, the man who had dreamed up the concept of a spring professional football league, was now out of the USFL, albeit with a significant profit.

"I was out of the league from the middle part of the 1983 season on," he recalled. "I had seen the signs of what the owners were doing in the way of signing players and I felt that they were making mistakes. I decided to sell my rights to Houston while the selling was good."

On May 16, San Diego won the next USFL franchise, awarded to principal owners Bill Tatham, Sr., and Jr., who had made their fortune in banking and real estate, and minority owner Kenneth Rietz. The elder Tatham had been involved with the Portland team in the World Football League, and counted Bassett as a friend. The league loved San Diego and the city's weather which was not frequented by the rains that had plagued other USFL cities. The new owners acknowledged they faced an uphill battle to gain access to Jack Murphy Stadium even though they already had commitments for several thousand season tickets. The NFL's Chargers, baseball's Padres and North American Soccer League's Sockers all claimed that they were worried about turf damage, but USFL officials believed that it had more to do with possible financial damage to the teams.

Chargers' owner Gene Klein not only didn't want to share the market, but three players his club drafted–Gary Anderson, Tim Spencer and Trumaine Johnson—had already opted for the USFL.

"We were fighting for a lease, and the NFL was doing absolutely anything it could at every juncture to keep us from doing business, even in San Diego" said Billy Tatham, Jr. "They were claiming that one more football team was going to put too much stress on the grass. I called James Watson of The Toro Company, who was their number one agronomist who did the U.S. Opens and all that stuff. He flew out to San Diego, went to Jack Murphy Stadium, pulled out a pocket knife and got down on his hands and knees and dug out some of the turf. He said, 'I can tell there are turf problems—it's completely faulty—but it's got nothing to do with having too many tenants.' We killed that whole argument, and Watson even testified for us at the city council meeting. He took a big piece of mud and put it right in front of every city councilman. In other words, he called them on their bullshit."

Still, the San Diego Stadium Authority voted 5–3 to bar the new team from using the stadium. A subsequent appeal to the city council fell on deaf ears even after the Tathams increased their rent guarantee by $100,000 per game. The Tathams had also become sick of Klein's constant criticism and meddling and vowed to take Chargers players with them if they had to move the club. The stadium authority refused to reconsider its vote, and the owners were forced to begin negotiations with Skelly Stadium in Tulsa, Oklahoma. The new Oklahoma Outlaws were born on July 6.

"The one that had the most difficulty was the one in San Diego," recalled Ehrhart. "By the time the Tathams were trying to get into San Diego, the golden days of cooperation with the NFL were gone, and we were the enemy. That would have been in the period of time getting ready for the '84 season, spring-summer of '83. That's why they ended up in Oklahoma. They originally bought the franchise as an expansion team to be in San Diego. That was the most egregious of the stadium issues."

Jacksonville came on board on June 10 behind chief investor Fred "Bubba" Bullard, and the league publicly announced the franchise four days later. A Jacksonville native, Bullard made his money as a Florida land developer. In addition to the expansion fee, he would pay John Bassett, who held the rights to all of Florida as an original owner, $2.75 million dollars for the right to join the Bandits in the state. Three weeks after the franchise announcement, former Miami Dolphins star Larry Csonka joined the team's front office. The team, to be called the Bulls, announced it would play in the 70,000-plus seat Gator Bowl.

"When he was made general manager, Larry gave us instant credibility because of his stature in the National Football League and with all of the things he had done with his football career," Bulls coach Lindy Infante explained. "It immediately gave us a lot of credibility in that there was a name attached to the team that everybody could relate to."

Bullard's interest in the USFL had grown as he watched the league throughout the first season, and he originally wanted to buy the Breakers and move the team to Jacksonville. He did not want to keep Dick Coury and the rest of his coaching staff on board, but instead planned to have Florida State coach Bobby Bowden take over the coaching duties. Boston owner George Matthews who had developed a close relationship with his head coach rejected the deal when he heard of Bullard's plans.

After two months of rumors, the league officially awarded the fifth expansion team to San Antonio on July 11 in front of 1,200 football fans, a mariachi group and a marching band. Characterizing the confusion that would become the ownership group's trademark, the investors announced the deal in May even though it had not yet been finalized by the USFL. Although league officials liked the city, they weren't so high on principal investor Clinton Manges or Alamo Stadium, a relatively tiny Depression-era facility used principally for high school football.

Manges, a Texas rancher who had made much of his money in the oil market, was involved in a lawsuit with Seattle-First National Bank over a defaulted $40 million loan. The bank was suing him for $100 million in damages, while Manges was countersuing the bank for $1.5 billion and the *San Antonio Light* for $100,000 for allegedly jeopardizing Manges' bid for the team with unfair reporting. Beyond that, he was known as a mover and shaker in Texas politics, a good friend and campaign contributor of equally contro-versial Texas Attorney General Jim Mattox and several other Texas state officials. In 1982 alone, Manges had run up more than $1 million in political contributions. Many observers and some of the local media felt that state officials were paying him back with various favors. Thanks to Mattox's intervention, Manges had successfully fought Mobil Oil for mineral rights on 64,000 of the 150,000 acres Manges owned in South Texas. He was also a convicted felon, having been found guilty of lying on a loan application two decades earlier. In his book, *Once Upon a Time in Texas*, noted civil rights lawyer David Richards called Manges "probably the most controversial private figure in the state."

"Clinton was working right out of school pumping gas at a service station south of San Antonio," recalled Greg Singleton who would join the team's front office. "One day, he's at the station and sees Lloyd Bentsen, Sr., the father of the Texas senator who would later be a vice-presidential candidate, come into the station. Clinton knew Bentsen Sr. was a big oil man. Well Bentsen asks him where this Mr. Green lives. Clinton went inside, got right on the phone and negotiated to represent this Mr. Green. He went out to Bentsen and said, 'You don't have to go up there anymore. You can talk to me. I'm his represen-tative.' Bentsen liked Clinton's style and took him under his wing, got him established."

"Clinton looked like one of the Flintstones," Camera said. "He was a classic good old boy from Texas. While everybody had private jets, Clinton had a private propeller plane. He offered to fly us somewhere and I told him that was okay, but I'd find a different way. I had flown in these different jets with some owners, and the last time I flew with Taubman, he got a spider crack on the window at about 20,000 feet, and I thought I was dead. Chet and I were looking at each other thinking we were dead, so I wasn't flying any more private planes."

"The guy who was kind of our receptionist for the Gunslingers was also Manges' helicopter pilot," explained assistant coach Tim Marcum. "The road from the highway up to Manges' big mansion in south Texas was paved by the county, and he had landing lights along the driveway so he could also use it as an airstrip. He could fly his plane in and out of there and fly a helicopter in there. He had a great collection of guns, a bowling alley in his basement and a great big pool. His helicopter pilot told me that when the Seattle SeaFirst people came down, they were surveying the land and wanted to do an inventory of the cattle. Those big ranches, you don't know how many cattle you got. You have momma cows and they have calves and then they have calves, so it's hard to keep a count of them. The pilot took the SeaFirst guys up in the air so they could count the cows. He'd fly over in one area, and they'd count the cows. They'd fly over another area, and they'd count the cows. But all that area looks the same. They counted a few heads of cows like five times."

San Antonio Gunslingers owner Clinton Manges surveys newly-renovated Alamo Stadium in 1984. Photograph by Tim McGrath.

In order to join the USFL, Manges agreed to upgrade Alamo Stadium, an aging high school field, to the tune of $2 million, increasing seating capacity from 22,300 to 30,000 for 1984 and to 50,000 for the 1985 campaign. Unfortunately, the Gunslingers still had to fight the local school board to gain access to the field. They faced another battle with a neighborhood coalition that fought the team's plans to use the facility. Even in a city without an NFL or baseball team, a USFL franchise faced stadium challenges.

"At the time when Clinton contacted us he was listed in the *Forbes* 400," Ehrhart said. "He was one of the key guys down there, sort of a rough and ready guy who wanted to do something for his home area in South Texas. I went down to his ranch, and I remember him making me airsick in his helicopter flying over his big hunting preserve. We checked him out, and certainly at the time he had the resources. *Forbes* and our due diligence people, our staff of lawyers, who were checking him out, all gave him high marks. We knew he was kind of a maverick, but he paid his expansion fee and believed he could get a new stadium built in San Antonio. San Antonio was the kind of city that would be a good long-term city."

One of the reasons the USFL eventually accepted his application may have been the announced formation of the International Football League, which threatened spring and summer competition with the USFL beginning in 1984. The IFL was the creation of Dennis Murphy, who had worked with WFL founder Gary Davidson to create the American Basketball Association and World Hockey Association. Members of the Houston group were also apparently interested in the IFL before reaching an agreement with Dixon. If Manges was not allowed to join the USFL, he could have moved his money to the IFL.

"There was a group that was attempting to get going, and that was another factor in the Tulsa situation," said Ehrhart. "There was always somebody out there. We talked to a group that didn't file an expansion application with us, and they were the guys trying to start the league. I remember them saying that if they couldn't get an expansion franchise in the USFL, then they were going to start their own league."

As it turned out the USFL had nothing to worry about from the IFL. The loop planned teams in Canton, Ohio; Charlotte, North Carolina; Houston; Los Angeles; Memphis or Nashville, Tennessee; Miami; Milwaukee; Lincoln, Nebraska; New York and San Jose, California. The erstwhile league designated Australia, Japan and Europe as future expansion areas. Dallas and New England were further targeted for league membership. Faced with the loss of Houston and Memphis, not to mention the elimination of San Antonio as a possibility and the lack of a television contract, the league withered away without playing a single game.

A late run by Memphis earned the USFL's sixth and final expansion franchise. Logan Young, Jr., a food company executive who served on the executive committee of Mid-South Pro Football, Inc., was awarded the new team on July 17, the day of the league's first championship game. His organization had been trying to secure an NFL franchise for the city for several years but when the older league decided against expansion, Young set his sights on the USFL. His group finally won a team on July 17, but he soon found himself in over his head. In stepped William B. Dunavant, Jr., a local cotton magnate also involved in Mid-South, who bought a controlling interest in the new team.

"Logan Young, who was great friends with Bear Bryant, bought the team and after Coach Bryant passed away, he asked Coach Bryant's friend Charlie Thornton who he should hire and he said he should hire me," recalled head coach Pepper Rodgers. "That's how I got involved. I don't know whether Logan at the end had enough money. It certainly was an expensive proposition, and Billy Dunavant, one of the biggest cotton dealers in the world and a sportsman himself, bought the team from Logan.

"He was very motivated, very competitive. He was a wonderful owner who would do what it took to win. He would spend money. Nobody would be more competitive at anything than Billy. He was a wonderful tennis player, competed at a very high level. You couldn't ask for a better owner."

Each of the expansion clubs agreed to pay $6.25 million spread out over three years for the honor of joining the league, with the exception of Houston which bought the rights from Dixon for a discounted rate paid up front. Dixon received an additional $61,000 from the league to help cover his costs in the deal, ending his direct involvement with the USFL. Logan Young provided an insight into the true price of launching a team when he estimated that it cost him an additional $2.5 million in other expenses to start the Memphis franchise. The income from the USFL's television contracts would have to be split 18 ways instead of 12 starting in 1984, but the money from the expansion fees more than offset the loss in television revenue for the original teams.

San Antonio, Jacksonville, Tulsa and Memphis were not the large markets that the league would have hoped for, but none of them faced NFL competition. Houston and Pittsburgh, on the other hand, fit in very nicely with the league's strategy of filling major markets in part to increase television ratings. Fortunately, Jacksonville and Memphis both appeared to have strong local backing. The league did not want to lose Manges' money to a rival, and the Tathams had no choice but to forget San Diego and concentrate on Tulsa. With six new markets ready for the USFL's second season, the league put further expansion on hold despite interest from several other markets.

"Seattle was very serious," recalled Ehrhart. "They had their money together and they were going to play in the Kingdome, but we couldn't add them. That was simply because we were already pushing the envelope to go to six. There were good solid applicants in Minneapolis and Atlanta. John Bassett and I actually had interviews with Seattle and Minneapolis. I'm not sure we got past written communications with the other two, but I remember the Minneapolis people coming to see us. There was a group in Tulsa who made an application. When the Tathams ran into stadium problems in San Diego, we suggested they get together with the folks in Tulsa. There were probably a total of 15–20 applications, some of them didn't have everything buttoned up with stadium leases, credible financial money and that kind of thing. I recall several of them were solid, for sure Minneapolis, Seattle and Atlanta stuck out. It wasn't that they were rejected; it was that the timing didn't work out.

"I still have a picture of John and me from a visit to Charlotte, North Carolina, with the caption, 'Would you buy a franchise from these guys?' That was from George Shinn, who later went on to own the Charlotte, then New Orleans Hornets of the NBA. We got him into sports." Shinn would host USFL pre-season games in Charlotte the next two years.

While USFL owners welcomed the influx of expansion money into the league, some wondered if they had mortgaged their future by adding so many teams after just one season.

"John Bassett was the head of our expansion committee, and I loved John," Peterson said. "He was an international guy. John was a marketing guy, and he saw this not only nationally but internationally. I remember the first couple of meetings he was throwing up pictures of not only expansion cities in the US, but Toronto, Mexico City, London, it was worldwide, and we were just finishing our first year as a fledgling league trying to survive. But John was a big thinker, and he was able to push it hard and fast. Steve Ehrhart understood what was going on. He like all of us was a little concerned at how fast we should grow and should we try to do it at this rate. Hindsight is 20/20, but it was too fast and too much."

"The driving force was the expansion fees," stated Simmons. "Why would you expand if you had a league that was running on fumes at that point, even in the second year? What kind of teams would you bring in? Who would you bring in? In all as you look at it in retrospect, it was nonsense. The expansion was nonsense, but at the time it made sense. It brought money to the league, the teams.

"Two more teams would have made some sense. You needed a lot more to give these guys sufficient additional money to go out and run their teams. Some of these guys had very little income. Their attendance was hurting, and the television revenue didn't change, so they were fighting for additional forms of revenue, and that way was through expansion."

"Certainly in hindsight, expanding was a mistake because it impacted several teams that were already in operation, creating a competition that made it more difficult for them to draw fans because they weren't keeping up with the other teams, particularly the newer ones as well as several of us that had some really good teams right from the start," Tanenbaum said. "If we had stayed at 12 for a couple more years, we may very well have found ourselves in a better position because the strength of the teams would be better because the talent would have been spread over a smaller group. I think in hindsight having expanded as fast as we did was a mistake. At the time, personally I thought we were going a little too fast on that, and I didn't see the reason necessarily to do it immediately. Had we held off for another year then we may have had more interested people coming in after that after seeing two years of USFL football. It would have given us time to gear up for it appropriately."

"The ownership that came in the second season was where most of our mistakes were made," added Dixon "Two or three of our owners needed expansion money to stay afloat and that's why we expanded by six teams. There were some cities that came in that didn't create a major league image. Good cities, but you put a team in Tulsa or in San Antonio in a little high school stadium and that sort of thing really detracts from the image of the league."

"We all felt really good about the expansion," countered Ehrhart. "When people blame the expansion, I'm not sure it was really the expansion that contributed to the downfall. If anything, it brought some cash to the current owners, helping solidify them. Plus, it established some value that a year earlier did not exist. Now they had asset value.

"We all thought, 'Here we can bring in the fabled DeBartolo family which had won a Super Bowl championship in San Francisco.' To have quality owners with football experience like that in the league, it made sense. David did the deal with the guys in Houston. Tulsa was originally sold as a San Diego expansion franchise. We thought another west coast team would be good for the West Division. Houston and San Antonio went well with Birmingham and the Central Division. Jacksonville was a football hotbed, and in some ways we were looking at what had worked the first year. Was it in the non–NFL cities and was there demand? What kind of stadium could you get? Tatham was a guy who had experience in sports, and Fred Bullard was a quality guy. Billy Dunavant solidified the Memphis deal. He was the guy who started the National Indoor Tennis Tournament in Memphis and was the world's largest cotton merchant. When you step back away from it we really didn't have control of the Houston deal, we had DeBartolo in his home town of Pittsburgh, Jacksonville was a hotbed and Memphis which had the best team in the World Football League."

"The decision to expand after the first season: that was all John Bassett," McSherry added. "Now you can question that decision, but the reality was that most of the original teams wouldn't have been able to play a second season if they hadn't had the revenue from expansion."

"One or two of the owners confided in me, 'Well, this is keeping us going,'" Dixon admitted.

"When the money started coming in, there was no one there saying, 'Don't take the money,'" furthered Gould. "There were obviously operational issues coming from the commissioner's office and there were people who wished we'd never done it."

"The expansion decision was a difficult decision because I think in the minds of most of us that were part of the so called original 12, expansion was essentially a good thing," said Taube. "It was a validation that other people wanted to climb aboard. It was a good thing because we were then able to charge reasonably high franchise fees to get the new owners on board. We certainly needed the money. It was a good thing because we thought that the imprint of the USFL would cover a broader market and help us negotiate better TV agreements than we already had.

"I was [in favor of expansion] and I really believed that it was pretty much consensus that the owners felt that this was a good thing for the league and it was something that we should pursue in a controlled basis. I mean we didn't want to just hand out franchises to just anybody. We felt that we wanted to have people that were financially solid, that could handle the costs associated with the next season and thereafter. We wanted people that were compatible with the original group."

"On the one hand, when you add markets, in theory at least, you're going to have higher ratings in those markets which have teams," said ABC's Spence. "On the other hand, we were somewhat concerned they were expanding too quickly. Maybe they ought to have stayed smaller longer and made sure their product was solid and sound. We had mixed feelings. We thought they expanded too quickly, but we also thought that it would probably help us to a certain degree because the television rating should increase."

"I was in a difficult position at that point," Simmons said. "I knew why they wanted to expand because they needed the money in order to keep going. An expansion needs a lot of thought: who, what, where, when: where should we go, who could the owner be, how much should we charge, where are we going to get the players from. Just to go and say 50 percent made no sense, at least it didn't make any sense to me. If you want to expand a couple at a time, but find the right ones, and they went around digging like looking for potatoes and found these owners and God knows what they were. Steve and John Bassett would go and talk to these guys. We tried to look at their wealth, and I use the word 'wealth' because everyone knows what it costs to run a football team, or at least they have a perspective that it's expensive."

While the Getting's Good

The new owners were not the only ones busy during the USFL's first off-season. Arizona Wranglers owner Jim Joseph had originally wanted a team in the San Francisco Bay area. He leapt at the opportunity to place a team in Los Angeles instead, but was forced out by Bill Daniels' and Alan Harmon's prior claim to the mecca. He moved on to Phoenix where he ran into stadium difficulties, an exhausting search for a head coach and a team that performed pitifully for much of the year. He had been criticized for not spending on marquee players, and he wanted out. With expansion teams selling for $6 million, he knew the time was right to make a move.

Joseph found an interested buyer in the most unlikely place: the USFL ownership ranks. Chicago Blitz owner Dr. Ted Diethrich, another absentee owner, had spent too much time shuttling between his Phoenix home and Chicago. The doctor still believed in the league but wanted to move operations back closer to home and his heart practice. He had originally wanted the Phoenix team, anyway, but hadn't been able to complete a stadium deal. He had played the good soldier when he took over ownership of the Chicago franchise when J. Walter Duncan shifted to New Jersey. Now, he was ready to grab the Phoenix market, but he had one major stipulation before making any kind of deal. He planned on taking the Blitz roster with him, including Coach George Allen and his entire roster. Diethrich knew he had a great group of players and was not about to start from scratch. As part of the bargain, he wanted to send the former Wranglers to Chicago under new ownership, thus keeping both rosters largely intact. It would all look extremely strange, but the deal had the advantage of keeping Diethrich and George Allen in the league without destroying their marquee roster. It had the distinct disadvantage of moving one of the USFL's strongest franchises out of Chicago and one of the weakest into the Windy City.

"It was terrible because I was very busy here in Phoenix," explained Diethrich. "It was taking a toll on my ability to do research and education and all the things I do in addition to taking care of patients. I could see that was not really going to work out long-term. Of course, I wanted to go back to see the games. I would work usually through Thursday night or Friday morning, and then I'd fly out to be there for Saturday and Sunday before flying back Sunday night. Or if we were out of town, I'd fly to wherever we were. That was hard because I was so busy. That was the reason I decided that if I was going to stay in this at all, I really needed to have the franchise here in Phoenix. It had nothing to do with Chicago. I loved Chicago, the fans were great and the press was good to us up there. It was just very difficult for me to be part of it like I wanted to and be so far away.

"I flew to San Francisco and met Joseph at his office and said, 'I'd really like to get the team down in Arizona, and I think it would be better for me.' If I recall, Jim said, 'Can we do a deal where I'd stay part in?' I don't remember why that didn't work out because that probably would have been a pretty good idea, but in the end we came to an agreement where we became the Wranglers."

With Joseph and Diethrich willing, the only other thing needed to make the plan a reality was to locate a buyer for the Blitz. To that end, Diethrich found fellow heart surgeon Dr. James F. Hoffman of Milwaukee. On September 30, 1983, Hoffman took control of the Blitz for a reported $7.2 million price tag.

"Diethrich was very adamant that he was going to do this deal," Ehrhart recalled. "He was not going to stay in Chicago, period. Therefore, it was very difficult for the other owners to say they were going to somehow vote no and tell him he couldn't move. He bought the Arizona team, so what are the legal ramifications to saying, 'No, you can't do that?' And Hoffman had put up his $1.5 million letter of credit, though he certainly didn't have the wherewithal of the Taubmans and DeBartolos. It was a situation in which there weren't any other choices in such a short time frame. Although there was considerable teeth-gnashing, Diethrich had been in since day one, and he had gone to Chicago really against his desire in order to help get the league going."

Hoffman and Diethrich then completed one of the largest and strangest trades in sports history. Diethrich took nearly the entire Blitz roster with him to Arizona and gladly sent Hoffman the Wranglers. A few players remained with their original teams, largely due to contractual issues. Quarterback Alan Risher, who had beaten Allen's Blitz with an incredible comeback in week two, and tackle Jeff Kiewel stayed in Phoenix, while receiver Marcus Anderson, corner back Virgil Livers and quarterback Tim Koegel remained in Chicago. Against Diethrich's objections, the league ruled the "Blitz" nickname had to remain with the Chicago club.

"In a perfect world, you would have said no," Ehrhart said of the franchise trade. "In an established league of 30 years, you could have said no, but there was not a legal ability for us to say, 'Ted Diethrich, you can't do that.' There was a lot of discussion about what was practical. In the whole discussion about getting people where they wanted to be, the pride in their community was important. We had six fresh ownership groups coming in. In retrospect, it's easy to say we never should have let Diethrich move, but that was not going to happen. He was going to move no matter what. I remember him telling me flat out, 'I'm not going to do this again in Chicago. I have my business, my family, my career, my life is in Arizona. I'm going to move or not do it anymore.' When six groups are in flux, you can't vote that down."

Veteran linebacker Stan White lined up with the Arizona Wranglers defense in 1984 after a year with the Chicago Blitz. Prior to inking with the USFL, White enjoyed a successful 11-year NFL career with the Baltimore Colts and Detroit Lions. Photograph by Jim Turner, from author's collection.

"I don't think a lot of the owners accosted me personally, but I know the commissioner really hated it, and I suppose that Ehrhart didn't like it either, and with good reason," allowed Diethrich. "I don't blame them for the feelings because I think the Blitz had a good start up there, and Chicago was a big network market. George Allen was a big, well-known, long-tenured coach, so I really couldn't blame them. I guess finally they voted and I don't know how we got it, but we did. I wouldn't be negative of any of the owners or administrative staff who would say, 'I wish Ted hadn't done that. That wasn't a wise thing for the league.' In retrospect, it was selfish. It was a decision that if I was going to stay in and be part of it, I'd have to have it closer to home because the way it was working was not going to work with my profession."

Strange as it was, the franchise swap was not the first in professional football. In 1971, Baltimore Colts' owner Carroll Rosenbloom had tired of the city and the criticism that he received whenever the team failed to win a championship. He still wanted to own a team, just not the Colts. Selling the franchise and buying another one would have cost him more than $4 million in taxes alone in addition to lawyers' fees and other costs. When Los Angeles Rams' owner Dan Reeves passed away, Rosenbloom arranged for Robert Irsay, a Chicago heating contractor, to buy the team. The two then traded franchises even up. The one difference between that transaction and the Diethrich deal was that both NFL teams remained intact with no players switching hands. In a move similar to the Wranglers-Blitz deal, the Philadelphia Eagles and Pittsburgh Steelers had swapped franchises following the 1940 season, with players moving from one city to the other.

"Anybody who was a heart surgeon and could run a football team, my hat's off to them," said Simmons. "I thought he was generally somebody who was interested in the league. Moving from Chicago to Arizona made sense from a personal point of view because that's where he was from and where he had his clinic."

Far from being disappointed to land the talent-thin Wranglers roster, Hoffman sounded glad to be rid of the former Blitz players and their huge contracts. "If I had the opportunity to buy the Blitz as it were, I would not have even considered it," he told *The Sporting News.* "The front office was terrible. Player contracts were heading for absolute disaster." He put most of the blame for the burgeoning payroll on George Allen and his son Bruce, the general manager, both of whom were headed to Arizona. Unfortunately, he may not have realized that he had lost a considerable amount of talent in the exchange.

Hoffman was not nearly as happy when he found out that the Allens departed with $100,000 worth of equipment belonging to the Blitz, including footballs, game jerseys, weights, film projectors, filing cabinets and socks, none of which were supposed to be a part of the deal. Diethrich stepped in to say that he had originally intended to take the Blitz name with him but since the league nixed that idea, he would see that all the equipment was returned to Hoffman's team.

Jim Joseph, on the other hand, had to be ecstatic over the turn of events. Unable to field a team in California where he originally wanted it, he had to sit through a year of inept play and sizable financial losses. His sale to Diethrich, though, brought him a reported $7.2 million, more than double what he had laid out. Joseph had made a profit on the USFL, and after a year flying back and forth to Chicago, Diethrich finally owned a team in his hometown.

Meanwhile, Harvard University once again turned down the Boston Breakers' request to use its stadium for the team's second season. The school cited its spring sports commitments and turf conditions for upcoming Olympic soccer games in its decision. Rumors surfaced that the franchise would move to Indianapolis where the Hoosier Dome was then under construction. There they would have had to play in a smaller stadium for at least one season until the dome could be completed. They soon ruled out Indianapolis, though, and the Breakers looked West at Seattle, Hawaii and Portland, Oregon. Jacksonville real estate developer Fred Bullard also wanted to buy the Breakers before he opted for an expansion team. Finally, on October 18, George Matthews decided instead to move the team to New Orleans where they would play in the Superdome, a vast improvement on Nickerson Field to put the case mildly. David Dixon's home city would gain a USFL franchise after all, allowing him to keep an eye on the league, albeit from the outside now. Matthews later revealed that he had hashed out an agreement to use Sullivan Stadium in Foxboro, Massachusetts which would have kept the team in the Boston area, but he did not want to be at the mercy of the NFL Patriots, whose owners controlled the stadium. Before the end of the year, real estate developer Joseph Canizaro and a partnership completed a deal to buy the Breakers. At first, Canizaro opted for 31 percent of the franchise but ended up buying 82 percent of the team's stock. With Matthews out of the picture, former co-owner Randy Vataha remained as president of the club.

"They were very good the first year," Coury said of Breakers ownership. "They were like everybody else, trying to get things organized. We started from nothing. You have to get a place to practice, you have to get a place to play, get your team together, and all those things were difficult for them. Financially I'm sure it must have cost them some money because they sold it after the season ended. Even several weeks before the season ended there had been some talk about us moving to New Orleans."

"The guy who bought the team was Joe Canizaro, who was a heavy duty developer in New Orleans," Breakers kicker Tim Mazzetti added. "When I went to play down there I ended up meeting Joe, and he found out I went to the Wharton School of Business and that I had an Ivy League education. He came to me at one point in the season and said, 'Screw this football stuff. You want to make some real money, come work with me in real estate development.' I knew I had to grow up sooner or later, so I started working for him in the offseason of 1984, and I've been in real estate ever since.

"He's an amazing man in the sense that he's a completely self-made multi-millionaire, not just once but twice around. Joe actually was a millionaire in his own right in the stock market before he lost everything back in the '70s. He then started up again and got into the real estate development side of the business and is really probably one of the key people responsible for the skyline of downtown New Orleans as it looks today. If you're familiar with New Orleans, there's a major avenue that comes right off the highway and is anchored on that side, the inland side, by the SuperDome, with the Mississippi River on the other side. And this main six-lane avenue called Poydras Street now has about a dozen A-class office buildings, towers, all up and down that avenue as well as numerous hotels. That avenue is just a few blocks off the beginning of Bourbon Street in the French Quarter. Joe was responsible for developing five major projects along that avenue, so he was a pioneer really, a major contributor to the city. Even as recently as Hurricane Katrina and the terrible aftermath a few years ago, and Joe is a major supporter of the Republican Party, he was picked to lead a businessman's group to work closely with Mayor Nagin to redevelop New Orleans, and Joe came in as chairman of that. He's also former chairman of the Urban Land Institute, he owns a bank now, and he's just been highly successful."

Bill Daniels and Alan Harmon also opted to sell their team, relinquishing the L.A. Express to J. William Oldenburg, a San Francisco mortgage banker, for between $6 and $7 million in December 1984. Like Joseph and Diethrich, the duo had grown weary of constantly flying to see their team while struggling to gain a foothold in the market. They also grew concerned with mounting player expenses.

"I remember talking to Bill Daniels, and he said, 'This is not what I signed up for. I'm getting out while I can. I didn't get into this to get into bidding wars with other teams.'" recalled *Los Angeles Times* writer Chris Dufresne. "The model that everyone bought into, the John Bassetts and the Bill Daniels, the model of a formidable but different league from the NFL that would be in the spring, that would have modest salaries and provide pretty high quality entertainment, that model was blown up."

"Harmon was great; he was terrific. Bill Daniels was, too," explained Camera. "But they were Denver guys. They were trying to run the L.A. franchise, and that hurt. Had they had Denver, it would have been terrific. Harmon was a good guy, and Bill was wonderful, a professional. He knew what had to be done, and he was very much a big supporter of Chet."

"They were both from Denver originally, and their offices were in Denver," added Ehrhart. "During the foundation of the league in '82, I had known Bill Daniels in Denver prior to starting the league. It was never a perfect fit. It's just that the agreement with ABC required a team to be in Los Angeles. Bill and Alan took that team, so I'm not sure it was ever a long-term plan that they had because they both had their businesses and residences in Denver."

The 5'6" Oldenburg promised to breathe more energy into the Express. He owned Investment Mortgage International Inc. in San Francisco as well as a savings and loan in Utah. His accounting firm stated that the bombastic Oldenburg's net worth stood at $100 million, easily qualifying him for USFL team ownership, but far shy of the billionaire status his company's biographical sketches claimed. He was just a decade removed from a failed real estate project in Seattle, though IMI, which arranged loans for risky construction projects in exchange for large fees, appeared to be growing rapidly. The new owner immediately set about imprinting his own stamp on the franchise. He named Don Klosterman, former general manager of the Rams, to the same post with the Express and let him know that his pocketbook was wide open. Singer Wayne Newton also bought a minority interest in the team.

Klosterman, known as the "Duke," brought a wealth of experience to the team along with a keen eye for young talent. He had performed as general manager for the AFL's Dallas Texans, the forerunner of the Kansas City Chiefs, and Houston Oilers before later taking the same position with the NFL's Baltimore Colts and Rams. He had been forced out of professional football by Rams owner Georgia Frontierre when she took over the team following her husband's death. Klosterman was glad to be back in the game and eager to show that his banishment had been a mistake.

"Don Klosterman, who they called 'The Duke of Dining Out' or the 'Duke of Del Rey,' had been a former athlete," said player agent Leigh Steinberg. "He had panache, style, elegance; he dressed with elegance. He had a knack for knowing every significant person in Los Angeles and seemingly the United States after he had been the GM of the Rams.

"Just to show you who Don Klosterman was, later that year the Olympics came to Los Angeles, and he asked me if I'd like to go to the opening ceremonies. I said, 'Yes,' so he showed up at my house that night, and he's got Jane Fonda and [politician] Tom Hayden in tow along with Ethel Kennedy and Frank Gifford."

"He hired a dear friend of mine and a great football executive in Don Klosterman who for many years was running the LA Rams," recalled Carl Peterson of Oldenburg. "I remember him coming into the meeting, one of his first meetings, might have been the very first one, talking as fast as I've heard anyone speak, and he was elated about hiring Don and the future for the LA Express to the point where he took his shirt off and was waving it in the room in the meeting, I'm not sure why, maybe he was still enjoying the previous night and had imbibed in a little wine ... what an extraordinary guy. Someone, I think who was quite filled with himself, but he was an interesting person in the USFL."

"With his bulbous nose, he reminded me a little bit of like a W.C. Fields with a Napoleon complex, short man's syndrome," Dufresne said of Oldenburg. "He obviously had a flair about him and a magnetism that could captivate."

"Chet and I went out in 1983 to visit Oldenburg who had his offices up in the Bay Area," Ehrhart remembered. "I had never seen sound-activated walls. He would say something and the wall would roll back. We were stunned. I had never seen that. I had never seen clap-on, clap-off. He was living large and rolling in the fast lane. He had his whole office suite set up to where the entire office wall would swivel around when he would give some kind of voice command. I remember he put on a heck of a show."

Los Angeles became the fourth of the original 12 teams sold before the second season kicked off, three of which had been held by out-of-town owners.

Ron Blanding expressed his desire to sell the Gold but stipulated that the team had to remain in Denver. One major issue complicating the deal was his asking price of $12 million, nearly twice what the expansion teams had just paid. Blanding defended the price by pointing out that his was the only team in the league to turn a profit, while topping the USFL in attendance, all with a bargain basement payroll. He had been vilified in Denver for his refusal to spend money and for the firing of popular coach Red Miller. Like Dixon and Daniels, he feared that his fellow owners would only increase their spending on player salaries, and he wanted to get out while he could.

"Costs started to expand and it didn't look like they were going to get any better," Blanding explained. "I thought that would lead to an unsuccessful league. The costs of operations were going to expand, and our revenues weren't going to expand. That isn't a very good situation."

"To some degrees it was indicative of some of the problems we were facing," Ehrhart recalled of Denver's position. "We had basically become an NFL in so many ways, yet we didn't have the cash flows to sustain that. Ron did not sign the wild card players. I can remember some other owners being critical, saying that Denver's getting the value of Detroit signing Bobby Hebert and Anthony Carter and New Jersey signing Herschel Walker, and they're not signing those kinds of star players. Ron would say, 'I drew more people than you did,' and they'd reply, 'That's because you got the benefit of all the national attention to the USFL and the visiting teams.'

"It happens an awful lot. It's still there today in sports, the struggles you have in baseball between the big city teams and the small markets. Does Steinbrenner carry more than his weight? Yet he earns more revenue. We were a small major experiencing some of these pressures.

"It's been interesting to see over the past 30 years how other pro leagues have dealt with that. Like the NBA with its salary penalty clause where teams that go above the cap have to pay a penalty. Or Major League Baseball, if you exceed the pool, some goes to the lesser markets. We debated that and had that going on at length. Did teams such as Denver and Oakland that first year sign the marquee players because their payrolls weren't as high? That led into all these divisions about who was spending and who was not. Then there was the pressure from the NFL, the issues of some of the owners wanting to sell out and did we or did we not use up some of our future by the expansion by six teams? Those kinds of things became exacerbated."

Enter "The Donald"

With four 1983 franchises already sold and another for sale, the New Jersey Generals would become the biggest team to change hands. In a familiar story, the Oklahoma-based Walter Duncan had spent a lot of time traveling back and forth between his home and that of the team. He began seeking a buyer for the club.

A September story in the *New York Times* claimed that he had sold the Generals to Lonn Berney, a New York attorney who planned to move the team to Brooklyn within two years. In fact, the two parties had held some preliminary meetings, but that was the extent of it. Also rumored to be interested in purchasing the Generals was Houston Astros and New Jersey Devils owner John McMullen. The reports served a much greater purpose, though, in spurring the interest of Donald Trump, the 37-year-old real estate magnate who nearly bought the Generals when the league was forming more than a year earlier.

The brash Trump was never at a loss for words, especially when detailing his own many successes. The builder of the famous Trump Tower in New York City was as bold as he was rich, a difficult level to reach for any man. *Forbes* estimated Trump's net worth at $200 million.

"I initially talked to Donald about a New York team or a New Jersey team, and he was very interested and attended a lot of early meetings," recalled Dixon. "Rumor has it that the NFL cornered him just enough to make him pull away from the USFL so that's when we got Walter Duncan to switch from Chicago to New York."

"Walter never was comfortable in the big city," added Ehrhart. "He was an oil man through and through, a wonderful gentleman, and when he and I were down in Georgia, signing Herschel Walker, I could tell this wasn't his baby so after the first year he put the team up for sale and Donald Trump bought the team from Walter."

"Walter would have loved to have been a winner," explained Camera. "He put his money up to sign Herschel, and once he saw it was going to get out of hand and you had to do a helluva lot more in New York than fly in for the games, he got out, and that's when Donald came in."

"He was just a quiet, reserved guy, just the opposite of Donald," MacConnell said of Duncan. "He was very unassuming. He was a nice gentleman. If I had said pick out the owner of the Generals, I'm not sure many people would have picked him out. He looked like he could have been your grandfather, could have been your neighbor, just a quiet, unassuming guy who was always in the background."

"I think that losing Walter Duncan was a blow to the league," said Dixon. "Not that Donald Trump was not a good owner, but we lost a good owner with Walter Duncan. He might have been our best owner. I liked Walter a lot and he was a very, very smart guy and a quality guy."

"Walter was a wonderful gentleman and a guy who you were proud to be associated with in every way," added Ehrhart. "He treated everybody around him with respect. You had great respect for Walter. He and I had become fairly close because we had spent that time together during the Walker signing traveling to Wrightsville and Athens, Georgia, one time under assumed names, and then going to a number of Generals games because we were right there with the league office in New York. He had known of Trump before, when Dixon had talked with him. Walter had visited with Trump and when he told me about him he said, 'This guy is going to be much better than I. He's young and public relations oriented. He and his family are well known in New York City. He's got the kind of capability as a New York developer that I don't have being an Oklahoma oil man. He knows how to make it happen in New York.' Walter truly believed it would be a terrific move for the league to have Donald take the team in New York."

"I got a phone call from Walter Duncan, the oil man who owned the New Jersey Generals," remembered Gould, who had moved over from Washington and joined John Bassett's management team with Tampa Bay. "He could have called anybody, but he called me because I think he saw that I had the connections to do this, I was passionate about it, and I needed the money. I got the call, and he said, 'Jimmy, I've watched you, and I'm tired of going to 18 games from Oklahoma. My father just passed away, and I have property in over 30 states.' He was worth over $1 billion. He said, 'Why don't you go sell the team for me, and I'll pay you $300,000. Write down all the guys you know who are worth $100 million or more who might want to buy the club for $8.5 million.' The only guy who I had ever met who fit those criteria was Donald Trump who I met briefly at the first meeting at Trump Tower. At that time Donald Trump was clearly becoming one of the most powerful men in New York.

"I tried my hardest to get through to Trump. I dialed his number repeatedly, and he wouldn't take my call. I got creative and called a buddy of mine who lived in Cincinnati where I was from. We had the most incredible high-butter fat, high-sugar ice cream you've ever eaten in your life called Graeter's Ice Cream. I got ten pints of that Graeter's Ice Cream, because I heard that one of Trump's secretaries, Lisa was her name, went out for an ice cream cone every noon. Most of his people never went out for lunch, but she did. So I had ten pints of ice cream flown to New York and had a limousine—again I'm working off very little money, but I figured what the heck—and I had it taken to Trump Tower. She got it, opened it up and went crazy over it. I sent every flavor you could imagine from Black Raspberry Chip to Double Chocolate Chip to Toffee to Mocha, etc.; it's phenomenal ice cream. She started eating it, and the limo driver called me, and said, 'She's got it.' I tried the number again, and you would have thought I parted the waters. She got on the phone and said, 'This is the best ice cream in the world. Everybody in the office is eating it. Let me get Mr. Trump for you.' He actually walks out of a board meeting and gets on the phone and says, 'What do you want? You've completely disrupted my office.' I said, 'I don't really want to bother you, but I have a football team, and I thought you might want it.' He asked, 'Where?' I said, 'New York.' 'How much?' I told him eight and half million. He said, 'Get to New York.'"

Later in September, Trump reached a deal with Duncan for a reported $10 million, a number that Trump would later regularly dispute. He claimed that since the money would be paid over a number of years, the actual value stood between $4 and $5 million. Of course, that did not sit too well with the six new owners who had just committed themselves to pay $6 million for each expansion franchise. Trump wanted everyone to know what a good deal he had arranged. Regardless of the price, Trump became the new owner of the New Jersey Generals and would soon place his own unmistakable stamp on the team and on the league as a whole.

"It took me two months to sell the team," Gould remembered. "I sat in a hotel for six weeks on my credit card while he screwed around. Finally, I said somebody else kind of wanted the team, and then he jumped on it. He bought it. I ended up becoming president of the New Jersey Generals. He clearly wanted to bring the price down that I had quoted him, and he didn't move on it until he felt that somebody else wanted it. I had released that John McMullen was going to buy the team after so many months of Trump screwing around. The minute I did that, he moved. He wanted what others wanted. He didn't want what nobody else wanted. He had very much a movie studio mentality. If those around you want it, get it and get it for a better price; take it away from them. That was just what drove him.

"I went to John [Bassett] and told him, and he was not opposed to it but he was worried because all he knew about Trump was that he was a 'big game hunter.'"

Trump soon released Coach Chuck Fairbanks and revamped the front office. He made it clear that he would improve the team, no matter what the cost. Trump would give the Generals a much larger media presence than it had enjoyed in its inaugural season.

"This is the Trump of 1985 who was a whole different animal than the Trump of today," said McSherry. "The Donald of 1985 was a very brash, know-it-all, aggressive greenmailer. He was known for holding companies up with the threat that he would take them over and drive out their management, which is not a way to become popular. He just really was not a likable person. The Trump of today has become famous on television for being a comedian, the 'You're Fired' guy.

"First of all in 1985 he didn't have any real money. It was all borrowed money. He borrowed billions of dollars to build his casinos and Trump Tower. It wasn't until the year 2000 that he started to realize that he could let his name be on a building, let his management company manage the property, get a licensing fee for letting them use his name, and let somebody else put up the money to build the building, which he's done very successfully. He's got all these golf courses, mansions and hotels all over the country. Now he's probably acceptable to the NFL."

"I had heard of him, but I didn't know a lot about him," MacConnell said. "I had never been to the Trump Tower. I remember seeing something on a TV show in New York a couple months earlier about him; they just did a little feature on him. Then three weeks later I'm standing in his Trump Tower at the press conference, and it was just going to be night and day. Everything was cranked up to another level. The publicity that we were getting! The media just followed after him. We didn't lack for any exposure during the season or after the season. Everything had a different feel to it. We're on the back page of the *Post*, the *Daily News*, the *Times* every day with Brian Sipe, or we're going to sign Lawrence Taylor or Don Shula, etc. It was just night and day."

"They were really exciting times, and the USFL was a very small thing for me," said Trump. "At that time I was doing a lot of big buildings. I was doing the Grand Hyatt Hotel and lots of others. Trump Tower was starting in terms of what I was doing and that became a tremendous success. Many of the things I did were very successful. This was a little bit of a diversion, and it was very interesting to me. I really thought that there was a point in time where you could successfully take on the NFL in their own season and do very well."

Trump had grand plans for the future, one that involved changing the skyline of New York City. He planned to eventually move his new team into New York City's Shea Stadium which was being vacated by the Jets after owner Leon Hess announced that his team intended to join the Giants at the Meadowlands in New Jersey. If all worked the way he planned, Trump would own the only professional football team that actually staged its games in the country's largest city. He could use that fact as leverage to push a deal for a new facility. He planned to build his own domed stadium in New York, dubbed the Trumpdome, which would house the Generals and other sporting events. But he knew to gain approval from the city and state, his franchise would have to play in the fall in order to create enough revenue to make the project viable. Trump planned to force an accommodation with the National Football League with his Generals and maybe a couple of other USFL teams joining the NFL. He hoped that his investment of a few million dollars in the Generals would turn into a $70 million NFL team through a merger. He saw even greater potential in the Trumpdome. He believed he could draw another NFL team to occupy it with him, probably the Jets, as well as filling it with everything from concerts to Olympic trials. The payoff would be enormous.

"It's just a scenario," *Football Digest* quoted Trump at his first press conference after buying the team. "I think we can build up parity and then perhaps go directly against the NFL in a fall-winter schedule."

"I did have a quote, and it was a very well copied quote, 'If god wanted football to be played in the spring, he or she, wouldn't have created baseball,'" recalled Trump. "It was pretty well circulated, but I felt that way. I mean I went into this to make it a first class league, not a spring league, and I think there was a couple of owners that were very strong that agreed with me, but there were some that didn't and they were very happy playing in the very deep shadow of the NFL."

At his first owner's meeting in October of 1983, he struck a similar chord. "When my turn came to address my fellow owners, I stood up and explained that I hadn't bought into the USFL to be a minor league owner playing in the off-season of spring," he wrote in *Trump: The Art of the Deal*. "I pointed out that the greatest number of fans, and by far the biggest pool of network television dollars, were concentrated in the fall. I reminded my fellow owners that because the NFL had just gone through a long, bitter players' strike the past fall, many fans were feeling restless and alienated. And finally, I argued that we had a chance to put the NFL even further on the defensive by moving aggressively to sign top NFL players whose contracts were coming up, as well as the best graduating college players."

"I remember his first league meeting vividly," Peterson said. "He was in the back of the room pacing back and forth; he couldn't stay in his seat. And finally Chet Simmons, our commissioner, stopped the meeting and said, 'Donald, we would like to take the opportunity on congratulating you and welcoming you into our league. Would you like to say anything?' And he jumped up and said, 'Would I like to say anything? I wanna show you this,' and he held up two papers, I think it was the *New York Post* and the *Daily*. He said, 'Look at the back page here, the sports page,' and of course it was filled with 'Trump buys Generals.' He said, 'Do you know how much this advertising would have cost me if I had to pay for it myself?' He was a real estate developer, I mean the guy knew what he was doing and knew that it was a great entree for him to build his name and his image."

"By purchasing the glamour team of the young, upstart USFL, he bought himself the back page of the tabloids, the gossip pages, and then ultimately the front page," added Steiner. "I've always felt that the USFL, in Trump's mind, was all about Donald. And I saw very little indication of it any other way."

"Donald felt that he knew everything about football when he walked into the first meeting," recalled Keller. "He said, 'I know a lot about football, and I'm gonna do great. You guys just listen to what I have to say because I think it's really gonna help you.' This guy didn't know whether a football was pumped or stuffed. With all the guys we had in the league, George Allen and everyone else, here's Donald Trump who's going to tell everyone how it should be done. I remember at one of the meetings when Donald was pontificating about something, I was sitting next to Al Taubman and I nudged him and said, 'Geez, Al, what about this guy?' Al knew him well because they were both in real estate. He said, 'Don't worry, Mike, I can control him.' Famous last words. Nobody can control Donald Trump."

"All the meetings with Donald all merge into one big blob of ego and everything else to do with Donald's way of business, to push and shove to get to the front of the line so he could say, 'Everybody join me because I know what I'm doing,'" said Simmons. "There was no question in my mind why Donald wanted in. He had always professed that he wanted to own a football team in New York City, and he wanted to own a team in the National Football League. I think that his main objective was to get a team, and if he could get one in the USFL, then by whatever hook or crook he could try to force the situation into a combination between the National Football League and the United

States Football League. He thought the NFL would say, 'Let's take a couple of their teams or cities, and we'll be rid of them, done with these expansion leagues in the future.' I think that's the way his head went."

"There was no question that Donald was on a strong campaign to move us to the fall, and Chet was on the other side of that debate," Ehrhart recalled. "Chet certainly had the expertise in television, but Donald was strong-minded, so there were some problems. I had great admiration for Chet, but Donald had drawn many owners into his realm of having to move to the fall and going head-to-head with the NFL. I think Chet's position was that might not be the right path to take. It's hard to govern strong-minded business guys who were used to running their own businesses. Governance of strong-minded, powerful egos who are on different agendas is not easy. There were certainly some issues in the air."

"We hosted a lunch for him in the executive dining room at ABC, and Charlie Lavery who was our program planning vice president and I represented ABC Sports," remembered Spence. "At the luncheon was Chet Simmons and 'The Donald.' At that lunch Trump espoused the merits of moving to the fall, but he also started off by saying, 'By the way, you guys don't really have a contract. It's just a memorandum.' I said, 'Excuse me?' He said, 'You really don't have a contract.' He wanted to start from scratch in terms of the television deal, and he started talking about going to the fall. I said, 'Time out. We're not going to talk about anything unless there's a clear recognition that we've got a firm, binding agreement.' This was January of '84, so we were beginning the second year, and we had options for '85 and '86 and a continuing negotiating position for '87, signed. Chet Simmons had signed the agreement. Trump was doing his thing and Chet, to his credit, said, 'Donald, we have a signed agreement with ABC,' so that ended that. He had taken a position that what the league had signed was really not binding, but quickly backed off that based on my statements and Chet's statement that the agreement was in fact firm.

"I remember walking out of the meeting with Lavery, saying, 'Oh boy, I don't like what I just heard.' It just seemed as if there was nobody strong enough there to say, 'Time-out, Donald,' and that he was hell-bent to go to the fall. When he mentioned, 'You guys don't have a contract. You just have a memo,' I think he said that primarily because he wanted to get out of the spring. Our contract was for spring football. I think from the moment he decided to get involved, the ultimate goal was to move to the fall and into the NFL.

"In that meeting he also made it sound as if he had evidence, which he didn't because it wasn't true, that Pete Rozelle and the NFL were putting pressure on ABC Sports, specifically Roone Arledge, my boss, for the league not to move to the fall. That was totally untrue."

Trump relished the attention given to him as the owner of a professional sports franchise. While he could build skyscrapers that changed the New York City skyline, he might earn only four inches of space in the *New York Times* for the project. When he just mentioned that the Generals were interested in an NFL player, he could receive a sizable article in the *Times* and other major newspapers throughout the country. He began to show up on halftime shows during the NFL season, much to the chagrin of Pete Rozelle and company. Trump talked openly of moving the USFL to the fall and reaching parity with the NFL.

"He was very active from day one," Ehrhart said. "His personality would not allow him to be quiet and sit back. I think early on everybody was very excited about his enthusiasm. We knew how important the New York market was, and Walter presented how he felt bad about leaving, but in a sense, he was doing this to help the league by bringing in a young vibrant owner with unlimited resources to help build the New York franchise. Through the fall of '83, it was seen as a positive. As I recall, he didn't immediately say we've got to move, but he did say, 'We have to build the league and become competitive with the NFL. We can play football at the highest levels. We have the kind of coaches and we're getting the kind of players.' Of course, we had the stadiums. He had a different situation as he was in the same stadium as the Giants and the Jets. From day one, he said we had to be competitive with the NFL. As we went through that period of time, he started talking about moving to the fall to be truly competitive with the NFL."

All the offseason franchise sales had the net effect of undoing the franchise shuffling necessitated when Trump had originally pulled out of the running to be the Generals first owner. Six USFL teams had been held by out-of-town owners in the inaugural season. Just two of them remained one year later: John Bassett with Tampa Bay and Marvin Warner with Birmingham. Both had other ties to their USFL communities beyond their teams. Bassett had real estate interests in Florida, while Warner, an Ohio resident, was a Birmingham native.

"We had some people who had to move around to make it work with Daniels and Harmon going to L.A., a San Francisco guy Joseph going to Arizona, Oklahoman Duncan to New York and Diethrich to Chicago," explained Ehrhart. "There were some unnatural fits, so the adjustment took place after the first year. It was not an easy task for a league that had only been in business for a year."

Signing Triggermen

With Trump leading the charge, a half dozen new teams and several additional new owners meant increased competition for players. As promised, the USFL targeted the quarterback position in the offseason. The first to join on for the second year was University of Miami signal caller Jim Kelly. Even though he was coming off an injury shortened senior year, he was chosen fourteenth overall by the Buffalo Bills in the 1983 NFL draft. A separated right shoulder had required surgery and had kept him out of all but three games during his final year at Miami. Everyone knew that he was tough. He had even been recruited out of high school to play linebacker by Penn State's Joe Paterno before he chose Miami, but many wondered if his arm would regain its strength.

"I blew my shoulder out during my senior year in college, and they told me I would never play football again," Kelly said. "For me, I was a lot different from everybody else coming out that year because I had a major shoulder surgery, and the big question was, 'Could I still throw the football?' Could I take a hit again? You have all the confidence in the world that you can play with anyone, and then something like that happens, and they have to insert three metal rods in your right arm and tell you you'll never have your range of motion back, you start to have your doubts."

"He's a guy that I really thought could make this league special with his swagger and his talents," furthered Chicago Blitz GM Bruce Allen who knew Kelly's brothers from when they all attended the University of Richmond. At the time Kelly was negotiating with the Bills. "The negotiations were not going well, but then I got a phone call that said he was going to sign the next day, and I called to the Buffalo offices and they put me through to his agent. I told him to get out of there. He told me what the deal was and there was a press conference the next day. I said 'That's a bad deal. We will give him more than that.'

"I'm in Chicago and they are in the Buffalo offices. I told the agent to get out of the offices and we will talk that night. I said, 'There's no way they won't pay you more if you walk out of there.' Somehow they got out of there. Obviously we don't have the cell phones we have today. We had to go through Buffalo secretaries."

"Bruce Allen was the gentleman that called when I was in my negotiations with the Buffalo Bills and about ready to sign that contract," recalled Kelly. "He said, 'Do not sign anything. We've got an offer he cannot refuse.' That offer was 'Who do you want to play for?' That's when I went to Tampa Bay, Chicago, Houston and wound up signing with the USFL.

"I knew when the time came for me to play, I had to seriously consider playing there. Of course, we also thought we could use them, use the new league, to see what we can get from the NFL. Then it turned out to be a better situation than we thought it would be."

Though he had concerns about Kelly's arm following the shoulder surgery, Gamblers part-owner Jerry Argovitz made a push to sign the passer. Houston planned to operate a pass-happy run and shoot offense, necessitating a first-rate thrower.

"Once we filled our coaching roles and positions and we made a commitment to a run and shoot offense, we now needed to make a commitment to personnel, and obviously you need a trigger man," explained Argovitz. "And the trigger man I was interested in was Jim Kelly, who was injured his senior season in Miami. There were a lot of questions about his healing, and his ability to continue to play football."

"The offer was, I can play for any team I want to in the USFL, and that automatically perked my mind," remembered Kelly. "Then we went and talked to Tampa Bay, Chicago, and then when I went to Houston. I met with a guy by the name of Jerry Argovitz, who was our owner. He said we are going to bring this person in, we are going to do this, we are going to do that, and I thought Houston, Texas? Astrodome: perfect weather for a QB. This is a no brainer. I think the Buffalo Bills didn't think I would sign the contract, and then I signed and the rest is history."

"They came to Houston and the next day I was out in the park," added Argovitz who wanted to test the quarterback's arm. "I was running routes, and Kelly was throwing me the ball. I was about 50 yards down the field. He hit me with the blazer, and it broke my ring finger on my left hand. So at that point, I realized his arm strength was fine."

"I remember him pulling me aside and he took me into a park in the city of Houston, Texas and wanted to play catch," added Kelly. "Come on now, I know why you're doing this, you want to see if I can throw. I broke his finger because I wanted to show him that I could still throw the football. I think it was about the third or fourth pass, but he kept on playing catch with me, not for very much longer because I think it swelled up pretty bad, but I remember he treated me like I was one of his sons. He really did. I got along with him great. He knew exactly how to handle players."

Kelly's contract contained a unique clause that required he be among the three highest paid quarterbacks in the league at all times.

"When I was drafted by the Bills, I cried to be honest with you," Kelly recalled. "I'm saying, 'You've got to be kidding me,' because I saw the reputation prior to that. They weren't bringing in the top players, they were letting other players go, and the attendance wasn't very good. Then the USFL was there, and I already knew about the year before. Here we are with Herschel Walker, and you start looking at all the names that played in the USFL, and add myself and Steve Young and a few others to the equation. Prior to that, it was really more leverage to get the NFL to step up and pay a little more. Of course, you're not going to be stupid about it."

"When I negotiated with Jim, we did several things," explained Argovitz. "Number one, he was paid very well, as good or better than the NFL would have paid him. He realized this was a new league, his agents realized it was a new league, but I told Jim this was a chance to be Joe Namath. He could be the picture, the showcase of the USFL, and I said the offense that we're gonna put on the field, that we're committed to, the run and shoot offense, you'll be the most prolific passer in football history, because that's what this offense can do. And if you'll pay attention and follow the coaches, this is at your fingertips. Besides, it's cold as hell in Buffalo."

Kelly's University of Miami teammate and Vikings fourth-round pick Mark Rush, a running back, and Kiki DeAyala, a defensive end from Texas, also signed on with the Gamblers. Before Kelly inked his deal, the team was said to be making a strong push for San Diego Chargers quarterback Dan Fouts. Rumor had it that former Argovitz client Billy Sims, a star running back with the Detroit Lions, was also close to joining the team. Another rumor had the Gamblers stockpiling players in an effort to challenge the league champ at the end of the USFL's first season.

With six entire rosters to fill and everyone looking to improve, the other teams were equally busy. After discussions with Fouts, the Oklahoma Outlaws agreed to a deal with quarterback Doug Williams, a five-year starter for the Tampa Bay Buccaneers. He wasn't a Charger, but the Tathams were overjoyed to land the passer. Williams was the NFL's only black starting quarterback at the time and openly wondered if his negotiations with the Buccaneers would have gone differently had he been white. He had thrown for more than 12,000 yards with the team and was the only quarterback to ever take the Buccaneers to the playoffs. As an added bonus, the USFL had dealt the Buccaneers another blow in the battle for Tampa Bay.

As a starting quarterback in the NFL, Doug Williams led the Tampa Bay Buccaneers to an NFC title game appearance in just the team's fourth year. In 1984, he spurned the Bucs to sign with the USFL's expansion Oklahoma Outlaws. Photograph by Wilf Thorne.

"I was talking to Jerry Argovitz who had just signed Jim Kelly," recalled Billy Tatham. "Argovitz was an agent down in Houston. Jerry said there were two or three guys available, one of which was Doug Williams. I don't care what anyone says, there was a lot of racism going on and probably still is to an extent. Williams was an absolute stud, a great guy and a smart guy; probably the best young quarterback in the NFL. He was a free agent. Doug had just tragically lost his wife, and he just wanted out. He hadn't been treated very well by [Buccaneers owner Hugh] Culverhouse. Doug was represented by Jimmy Walsh, and I met him and Doug under assumed names at the Oral Roberts Hotel. Doug and I just happened to be the same age, and we just hit it off. I kept dad out of this deal. We all shook hands, and I handed Doug a $1 million check."

Cliff Stoudt jumped at the chance to leave the Pittsburgh Steelers' bench and took the starting job in Birmingham. He had languished behind Terry Bradshaw for years and relished the opportunity to join former Steeler receiver Jim Smith and coach Rollie Dotsch down South, this time as a starter. With Bradshaw hurt during the 1983 season, Stoudt ran for 497 yards for Pittsburgh, tops for NFL quarterbacks that year. He threw for 2,553 yards and 12 touchdowns but also tossed 21 interceptions while working without the Steelers' top three receivers, Lynn Swann, John Stallworth and Smith, on the field. Even a 10–6 record and division title were not good enough for Pittsburgh fans who expected a Super Bowl win every year. They booed Stoudt lustily almost every time he took the field. The quarterback admitted that the jeering got to him and was happy to find a new home. "I tried to commit suicide," he joked to *Sports Illustrated* about his bad days in Pittsburgh. "But the bullet got intercepted."

With Stoudt prepared to take over, the Stallions traded Reggie Collier to Washington, also in need of help behind center after part-time 1983 starter Kim McQuilken unexpectedly retired. McQuilken would instead work on radio broadcasts of Feds games. Collier would split time with the other 1983 starter Mike Hohensee.

In other quarterback signings, Glenn Carano, who had not thrown a pass in an NFL game in three years, bolted his six-year backup role with the Dallas Cowboys for the number one job with the Pittsburgh Maulers. Chicago Bears quarterback Vince Evans left the NFL team but did not move far, joining the cross-town Blitz.

But the biggest mover and shaker during the offseason was Donald Trump. He began phase two of his grand strategy by improving his team on the field and spending a lot of money to do it. He solidified the Generals passing game by inking quarterback Brian Sipe of the Cleveland Browns to an $800,000 a year contract, thus firming up one of New Jersey's weakest positions. Sipe, the NFL's Most Valuable Player in 1980 as the leader of Cleveland's "Kardiac Kids," had thrown for more than 20,000 yards in his career, including 4,132, the third best season total in league history, in his MVP season. He was coming off his best year since the MVP campaign, having thrown for 3,566 yards and 26 touchdowns in 1983. Trump acknowledged that in addition to improving what had been a troublesome position for the Generals, he also relished the chance to hurt the NFL in the process.

"For us, it was a great signing," recalled MacConnell. "Donald was going after the best he could get. It gave us great exposure, great credibility. Here was an NFL quarterback, All-Pro, and the year before we had struggled at quarterback with Bobby Scott. It gave us a backfield of Maurice Carthon, who ended up having a great NFL career, Herschel Walker and Brian Sipe. It didn't get much better than that."

The league had added no less than five big name passers for the coming season. The owners had realized the importance of the quarterback position not only in the public's perception of the quality of the league but also for the excitement of the action on the field.

"We had to change the marketing plan," said Camera. "We had to strengthen ourselves at the skill positions. Once you have to do that, it means money. Each team had to have a very solid quarterback; therefore, you had to sign him. You didn't have to worry about wide receivers and running backs. The NFL has running backs you've never heard of who all of a sudden are gaining 1,500 yards. We built the line, it was never a problem. The wide receivers were good. Our defenses were never as good as the NFL. That's where the weakness of our league was, but the consumer couldn't tell. Who can tell if a linebacker is running a 4.9 instead of a 4.6 like in the NFL? You could still close on a runner. We knew we had to build on skill."

"I give Al Davis full credit for his strategy of targeting quality quarterbacks as he had done with the American Football League," added Ehrhart. "The AFL had been able to grab several of the best

New Jersey Generals owner Donald Trump lured former NFL MVP Brian Sipe away from the Cleveland Browns in 1984. Photograph by Jim Turner, from author's collection.

passers of the day 20 years earlier. I borrowed his philosophy of 'Let's get the quarterbacks.'" That's why we made the effort to sign Jim Kelly, Steve Young, Doug Williams and Brian Sipe. We not only were able to get the terrific young quarterbacks coming out of college, we were able to get the NFL Player of the Year in Brian Sipe. That was the strategy, and I certainly give credit to Al Davis."

The Floodgates Open

Other players continued to sign on with the league. Cincinnati Bengals wide receiver Chris Collinsworth agreed to a futures deal with Bassett's Bandits to take effect in 1986. His contract was much like the one that teammate Bengals teammate Dan Ross had signed with the Breakers the year before. Chicago added Green Bay tight end Gary Lewis, and Houston used family ties to capture Buccaneers linebacker Andy Hawkins and Oilers receiver Ken Burrough. Hawkins' brother Mike was also with Houston, while Burrough's brother Gene served as the franchise's general manager. Arizona inked offensive lineman Dave Huffman from the Minnesota Vikings, while nose tackle Pete Kugler of San Francisco took his talents to the Stars. Tampa Bay grabbed Green Bay defensive end Mike Butler, and Washington tabbed Bears' linebacker Bruce Herron. Defensive end Dave

Stalls moved from the Raiders to the Denver Gold, and safety Mike Fuller, another Bengals veteran, opted for the Birmingham Stallions.

The New York Jets lost corner back Jerry Holmes and linebacker Ron Crosby to the Pittsburgh Maulers and defensive back Johnny Lynn to the Los Angeles Express. The departures and potential loss of star defensive end Mark Gastineau infuriated Jets owner Leon Hess, particularly since four of the team's draft picks also signed with the USFL. Lynn later bought his way out of his Los Angeles contract so he could re-sign with New York with the Jets reportedly footing at least part of the bill. The NFL found it much more difficult to hang on to its players now that they had a lucrative alternative.

Though run by former offensive coordinator Lindy Infante, Jacksonville concentrated on defense with its NFL signings, coming to terms with linebacker Tom Dinkel of Cincinnati, defensive end Don Latimer of Denver and safety Don Bessillieu of the Raiders. A five-year NFL veteran, Bessillieu was best known for saving an unconscious woman after her car had plunged into a lake at a golf course. After sprinting across the course to get to the victim, he had pulled her free just before the car disappeared under the water.

The Generals, not surprisingly, captured the most headlines and made the biggest haul of NFL players with eight. In the process, they addressed several of the team's weakest areas and cost several NFL general managers some sleepless nights. Not coincidentally, Trump's courting of NFL players and coaches made a lot of noise in the press. Simmons was right about Trump: he knew how to get attention. First and foremost, though, the signings almost completely rebuilt New Jersey's defense. The Generals began with the secondary, agreeing to terms with corner back Kerry Justin and safety Greggory Johnson, both from the Seattle Seahawks, and Kansas City Chiefs' safety Gary Barbaro, a three-time Pro Bowler. Barbaro had picked off 39 passes in seven seasons with the Chiefs. Three new linebackers joined the fold in Cincinnati's Jim LeClair and San Francisco's Willie Harper and Bobby Leopold. Rookie defensive end Freddie Gilbert of Georgia would take over a defensive end spot.

"I remember when Gary Barbaro came over from the Kansas City Chiefs," said Steiner. "This was an All-Pro safety, and it was not a glamorous running back/quarterback kind of signing but it was a legitimate signing to add to the legitimacy of the franchise."

Trump did not forget about the offense either. After starting with Sipe at quarterback, he improved the passer's protection by grabbing Cincinnati guard Dave Lapham. Trump had quickly assembled a team stocked with expensive NFL-caliber players, much to the chagrin of many in the league who believed the flamboyant New Yorker was upping the ante much too quickly. Some of the owners wondered if Trump had wasted much of his money. They argued that better players were available and that all Trump had done was to anger the NFL. Trump argued that he was also paying for the publicity generated by stealing those NFL players. Plus, he was applying a lot of pressure to the other league. He had made it much more expensive to do business in the world of professional football.

"The one thing I do remember is he always wanted to come into the booth, he always wanted to talk after the game," said Steiner. "What am I gonna do, say 'Get the hell out,' although I thought about it!"

One of the biggest names to sign with the USFL before its second season was one who ended up not playing a down in the league. Not surprisingly, Trump again stood in the middle of the mix. New York Giants linebacker Lawrence Taylor inked a personal

 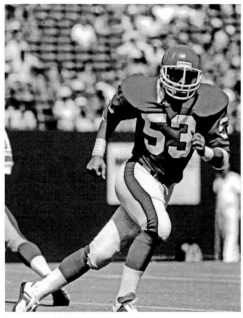

Top, left: Seven-year NFL veteran, and three-time Pro Bowler, safety Gary Barbaro joined the New Jersey Generals in 1984 after sitting out the 1983 NFL season in a contract dispute. Injuries spelled the end of his career after his lone season with New Jersey. *Top, right:* Linebacker Bob Leopold joined the New Jersey Generals in 1984 after four seasons with the San Francisco 49ers. He played another year in the NFL after two seasons in New Jersey. *Bottom, left:* A 12-year veteran of the Cincinnati Bengals, linebacker Jim LeClair joined the New Jersey Generals in 1984 and helped turn the defense from one of the league's worst units into one of its best. *Bottom, right:* After ten years with the Cincinnati Bengals, offensive lineman Dave Lapham joined the New Jersey Generals revamped roster in 1984. All photographs by Jim Turner, from author's collection.

services deal with the Generals' owner to take effect after the 1988 NFL campaign. Trump didn't let the fact he infringed on the territorial rights of the Philadelphia Stars, who owned player rights to the University of North Carolina, get in his way. The colossal contract called for the linebacker to make $3.25 million over four years.

"One day I read in the paper that Lawrence Taylor was unhappy with what the New York Giants were paying him," said Gould. "He was making about $250,000, and he had been defensive player of the year two years in a row. So I called him, and I got a hold of him, and I invited him to Trump Tower and told him that if he came to Trump Tower sometime in the next couple of hours to meet with myself and Mr. Trump that we would give him a million dollar signing bonus. He was there within an hour and a half, and he had a suit and tie on with a button popping off the middle of it. He kept holding on to it, and we cut a deal with him right on the spot without his agent or anything, and we signed him to a contract with the New Jersey Generals for the future. Then we just sat back, put the contract in the vault, and paid him his money, wired him his money into his account. Then the phone just started ringing, somehow Mike Trope, his agent, called [Giants GM] George Young and was flipping out at the time, and then you know we went after Mark Gastineau of the Jets. We figured if we were gonna build America's team then we were just gonna wreak havoc. I probably should have had bodyguards around me."

Less than three weeks later, the Giants ended the deal when they bought Taylor's way out of the pact for a $750,000, according to Trump. The Giants also ended up paying Taylor an extra $3 million for his services. Not only had Trump forced the Giants to increase Taylor's salary significantly, but they ended up paying him for the pleasure, money that Trump could use to lure others. The Jets, meanwhile, more than doubled Gastineau's salary in order to avoid a similar situation.

"The deal I did best was signing up Lawrence Taylor," Trump said. "I signed up Lawrence Taylor, and I actually sold him back for a profit."

"We got on the phone with George Young through Mike Trope and we sold him back the contract," recalled Gould. "Trump and I effectively took a two-week option and made a $750,000 profit. And it had never been done before. Taylor was happy because he got a new contract from the Giants for an enormous amount of money, and Trump's attitude was, 'Look, I never wanted Lawrence Taylor to not play for the Giants. I never wanted him to be unhappy. I'm Mr. New York.' So he really was shrewd beyond what I had ever seen before. He was the greatest self-promoter I had ever witnessed in my life, and clearly he, by putting his name on everything he has, that's what drives him. That's what his thing was. He was doing a favor for New York. In his mind, he was actually keeping the best player, arguably the best player, the best defensive player in the league in New York and happy."

"I remember all the exposure it was getting," Kevin MacConnell, New Jersey's public relations director, said. "Here are the Generals going head to head with the Giants, who … maybe they weren't America's Team, but to me the Giants, Packers and Bears were what the NFL was all about. The Maras were class, and here we were trying to grab one of the greatest players in the NFL at that time. Even the downside, the exposure we were getting for the Generals, was terrific. Our fans saw that we got Brian Sipe and now we're going after Lawrence Taylor, so I think there was no downside. Even if he didn't come, just the exposure we got and the fact people saw that Donald Trump wanted the best possible team he could put on the field was worth it. Every day was the saga of Donald and Lawrence, back-and-forth, back-and-forth. Then if it wasn't Lawrence Taylor, it was

Gary Barbaro, it was Brian Sipe, guys from the Oakland Raiders, Don Shula, Walt Michaels, it was always somebody. We were in the paper all the time. There was always something that we were in the paper for."

"He was General Trump, and I was known as his secretary of war," laughed Gould. "Effectively, I became his first apprentice, but I had a higher stature to a degree because I was president and making a lot of money. I had really declared war on the NFL. I guess we all had, but I was taking it pretty seriously. I was driving their prices up. I went after Lawrence Taylor who was very unhappy. He had been the most valuable player in the league for two years. I knew he was unhappy, so I brought him to Trump Tower and signed him, then sold him back to the Giants two weeks later. My job was to drive prices up, declare war and figure out a way for us to get into the NFL."

Trump's spending spree caused headaches for the NFL who saw several of its players leaving to join the young league or using it as leverage to gain much larger salaries. Even more irritating for the NFL was that many of the New Jersey owner's deals were being announced on its own pregame and halftime shows.

"I went to two meetings with him," said agent Leigh Steinberg. "The first with Mark Gastineau who was playing for the Jets and prospectively might have signed with Trump. The meetings would be at Trump Towers. Before meeting with him, they said Mark and I needed to sit and watch 'The Trump Story,' which was a promotional film before we were granted entry. I came back later with Warren Moon to talk about him in the league, and I had to watch the film again. I'm a quick study, so I could have written a paper on the film."

"What motivated Trump was getting America's team, the best ballplayers he could possibly get and making sure the NFL's network, Brent Musburger and those people we got the news to every week, announced a new signing," added Gould. "We put on a war strategy that was second to none. And that strategy was very simple: every Sunday announce a new signing, and we did. We worked with a lot of different people to make sure that the world knew that the USFL was not going away. Remember, we didn't play during the football season, so if we had a new signing every week, that was pretty critical. We had people we were going after who went back to the NFL, and we had people we signed. It was clearly a war."

In addition to grabbing NFL talent, Trump also assured that the USFL's first superstar would remain in his fold when he signed Herschel Walker to a four-year, $6 million contract extension.

"I know the one goal of Donald's was to lock up Herschel forever," MacConnell said. "And I remember being in Florida and actually his goal was to come down and lock Herschel up for as long as he could; that was his goal. He wanted Herschel to be a General forever. Be it in the USFL or eventually the NFL."

"Quite frankly we had an unlimited bank account so we could actually pull this off," stated Gould. "The rest of the league wasn't real happy with us, because this unspoken 'two marketing guys per team' was certainly not gonna be. I felt what we were doing was really driving home the theme that we were here to stay. We had a media contract, we had the ABC deal, we had the ESPN deal, we had Chet Simmons that came from ESPN as our commissioner–I mean we were serious. We were not gonna mess around anymore."

Trump's spending also pressured his fellow USFL owners into an expensive battle to keep up with him. Trump was turning the thumbscrews on everyone concerned, and many in his league did not appreciate the sudden change.

"When I read that they'd signed Lawrence Taylor, for example, I said 'Oh my God,'" exclaimed Dixon. "Lawrence Taylor is the best defensive player in the history of the game maybe, but they just made a mistake. They should develop their own talent. And there's plenty of talent to develop."

"On the field, there were some great ballgames, great TV ratings and great enthusiasm looking forward," said Ehrhart. "But we knew there were also some business problems with teams moving, and owners getting ready to sell. Though we had a successful year on the field, there were still some situations that required round-the-clock monitoring. We had to assimilate the expansion teams, deal with relocations and some sales, and we were only a year old. There was a lot to be done. The governance was certainly a very challenging thing when you had so many fluid situations.

"When Trump came in it became pretty obvious that Donald was going to be a pretty powerful force within the league; the young lion, so to speak. Certainly he was a persuasive guy who had super-strong opinions. He used to say, 'I looked at this league before it started, and I almost decided to come in. Now that it's achieved so much, I want it to achieve more until it is on a par with the NFL and we should be in the NFL in time. I'm going to build the Generals to be just as good as the Giants and the Jets.'"

In a letter to a handful of owners, Oakland's Tad Taube warned, "It may be in Don Trump's best interests to pursue a strategy which gains him leverage, politically or otherwise, to move to Shea Stadium and become the NFL franchise that the City of New York is apparently ready to underwrite at any price. But Don's best strategy for the Generals could be devastating for the USFL as a whole."

"Trump was threatening to move to Shea Stadium, which he never would have been able to do, but he didn't tell anybody he couldn't," said McSherry. "My understanding was that after the Jets moved to New Jersey, the Mets weren't going to let any football team play there."

"Donald Trump made a major change in the USFL," Diethrich recalled. "The original owner of the Generals, Mr. Duncan, he was a great gentleman, really a fine guy, and I think he gave integrity to the board. When he sold and Donald came in, it was a different atmosphere. I've seen Donald Trump on TV and that series he has, and he really is like that. That's not somebody's imagination. He's a domineering kind of personality. I'm not saying that's bad as he's obviously a millionaire and very successful, but in terms of dealing with his colleagues and partners, it wasn't nearly as pleasant and friendly in the atmosphere, attitudes, decision-making and so forth as it was before he came on board."

"There became some divisions very quickly in the league," Ehrhart remembered. "Certainly, Trump and Bassett were on different sides of the fence. Bassett was a very strong personality, and John had been through other leagues. I'm not sure that Donald appreciated that. There were 17 others that had to thrive and succeed as well. There was now much more acrimony in the various agendas than existed prior to the kickoff of the first season even though we had as many differences and debates about things such as wild card players. There was a huge rivalry between New York and Philadelphia. Myles and Donald did not see eye-to-eye. Philadelphia felt that their best strategy was to play in the springtime and coexist in the same city with the Eagles, the Stars being the champion team in the spring and the summer and then the Eagles taking over in the fall. Carl had done a masterful job of doing that because he had been an executive with the Eagles so he had kept a good rapport with the Eagles. But Donald believed in full scale battle stations, so he followed up."

As a result, the player signings continued unabated. The other USFL owners faced a simple choice: keep up with Trump or fall behind and suffer the consequences.

The new reality of the USFL included signing players for more than just marquee value. It was an expensive game that increased costs even for owners who didn't want to play it. According to the original plan, the USFL needed a sprinkling of stars to heighten interest in the league, but its teams were now regularly targeting NFL players at all positions. NFL salaries jumped 25 percent over 1983 levels, following an increase of 24 percent the year before as the older league sought to head off the exodus to the USFL and agents artfully used their new-found leverage. Dixon argued it should have avoided overpriced linebackers and corner backs which threw the entire salary structure out of whack.

"I thought the USFL could have created their own talent instead of raiding the NFL," said Dixon. "That was the expensive way to do it and not the correct way, not the best way for the owners in the long run."

"Everyone knew that these were premium deals," said Leigh Steinberg who represented BYU passer Steve Young, Memphis' Walter Lewis and Jacksonville's Ed Luther. "I understood that the player and I were getting the benefit of a league that needed to pay for opportunity cost. It wasn't as if I felt as if I was somehow bamboozling somebody. Those negotiations for Ed Luther and Walter Lewis were essentially fast, easy and totally refreshing. There was no free agency in the NFL, and there was no alternative. There was no free agency for veterans. This was a really exciting time for players and for agents. It was the first taste of contractual freedom and choice."

"Our ownership was made up of a bunch of self-made men from all different walks of life, and we had a lot of different personalities, a lot of adventuresome souls and sometimes we'd agree and sometimes we disagreed," Argovitz opined. "In my opinion, a lot of the owners didn't know if a football was stuffed or pumped at the beginning because it was a new venture for them and everybody wanted to have their voice heard. Everybody had their own opinions. And we had to work thorough a lot of solutions. Some guys wanted to go out and spend a fortune on having an offensive line. They didn't realize, you know, that you needed to be able to have the marquee players. No one really heard about a center until he was off sides."

"One of the things that happens in professional sports and I think that it's probably the reason that the owners have made such a mess of the whole industry and makes us, those of us who are involved in that business, if you can call it a business, behave like a bunch of blithering idiots is that sooner or later we all become intoxicated with the idea of winning, and you start making some very bad decisions," added Tad Taube. "In our case, it was more than the team; we were talking about the viability of the league.

"A lot of the owners in our league did not have the financial resources. It was a dichotomy. On the one hand, you had owners who were not necessarily very affluent making competitive decisions about players and salaries that they couldn't afford to make. On the other hand, you had owners who really could have taken any level of financial hit that were more concerned and more conservative. Donald Trump was a good example. All the weaker owners, the people who kind of idolized Donald, would try to emulate him, except that he was so much smarter that he could do it without spending money and they couldn't. The Lawrence Taylor thing was a perfect example."

"I was the guy who was against what they wanted to do for the most part, but I was like a soft wind in a forest," sighed Simmons of the owners. "I could yell and scream and carry on; I could do that pretty good. They couldn't care less."

Almost as many players signed on with the new league as were rumored to be nego-tiating with it at one point or another. San Antonio showed interest in Oilers running back Earl Campbell, although the man negotiating for the runner had never met Campbell and had no authority to make any deal. Generals president Jim Gould indicated an interest in Broncos' quarterback Steve DeBerg before the team signed Sipe. New Jersey also pur-sued Raiders QB Marc Wilson before Al Davis signed him to a bigger contract. The Express continued to pursue rookie Steve Young, BYU's brilliant young passer.

Detroit running back and Jerry Argovitz client Billy Sims finally signed a contract with the Houston Gamblers but a problem developed when he later re-signed with the Lions. Sims was a bona fide NFL superstar who had made three straight Pro Bowls and had won the Heisman Trophy in 1978 at the University of Oklahoma. Sims inked the Gamblers contract when Argovitz represented him, a situation that appeared to be a conflict of interest and contrary to the Houston owner's agreement to give up his agent business. Shortly after agreeing to the Houston deal, Sims replaced Argovitz as his agent and claimed that his former agent failed to accurately describe Detroit's offer. Sims and the Lions filed suit to have the Gamblers contract voided, and Houston countersued. A federal judge sided with the player, and Sims returned to Detroit. Sims contradicted himself 13 times when he was cross-examined and failed to remember several points of fact, causing Argovitz to exclaim, "Billy couldn't remember who his mama was." All in all, it was an ugly affair that made everyone, but particularly Argovitz, look bad. The suit also cost Houston more than $200,000 not to mention a good deal of public embarrass-ment.

Another Argovitz client, Joe Cribbs, faced a similar situation after he signed with the Birmingham Stallions. The Buffalo Bills had included a right of first refusal clause in Cribbs' last contract. In the event that he became a free agent, the Bills would then be able to match the offer of any other NFL team. Buffalo contended that the clause should also apply to teams in the new league. This time, though, the USFL hung onto its star when a court upheld his contract with Birmingham. It helped that Cribbs, unlike Sims, contracted with a team that his agent did not own, thereby avoiding many of the conflict of interest questions that reared their ugly heads in the first trial.

"There was a lot of stuff starting with these futures deals with Chris Collinsworth and Ross and Brian Sipe," recalled Ehrhart. "Sims signed but never did play in the USFL. Cribbs very much wanted to play in Birmingham and did play and played well. Of course, most every player agent was trying to create leverage between the two leagues, so basically there was something flying around every day."

Far from content to just pursue NFL talent, the USFL also continued its chase of the best rookie players available. One deal in particular generated a good deal of positive press. The Pittsburgh Maulers made it two Heisman winners in a row for the league when they signed Nebraska running back Mike Rozier the day after his Cornhuskers lost to Miami in the Orange Bowl. He was one of just two runners to gain 2,000 yards in a college season with 2,148 in 1983 with 29 touchdowns. The only other back to eclipse the 2,000-yard mark was Southern California's Marcus Allen. Rozier ran for 4,780 yards and 49 touchdowns in his playing days at Nebraska and held the NCAA career record with an incredible average of 7.86 yards per carry. The Maulers won the first pick that they used on the running back in a lottery among the other expansion teams. No one outside the league office actually saw the drawing, leading to speculation that the league awarded Pittsburgh the pick because they knew Edward DeBartolo's team could sign him. Whatever the case, Rozier agreed to a three year, $3.1 million deal, and the USFL had its second consecutive Heisman Trophy winner in the fold.

"I know Herschel real well, and he decided to come out early for the USFL," Rozier explained. "I figured if Herschel would do it, then why not play in the USFL instead of the NFL. And I knew that if the USFL folded, we'd wind up in the NFL anyway because teams would have our rights. So I wasn't really worried about it being a new league. It was still football, 11 guys on both ends, offense and defense. It was still the same thing, but we were younger guys trying to prove something to the NFL and to the fans."

With the infusion of Dunavant's money, Memphis tabbed Tennessee defensive end Reggie White, a sure NFL first-rounder, and Alabama quarterback Walter Lewis. White, known as the "Minister of Defense" because he was also an ordained Baptist minister, was a consensus All-American at Tennessee who set a school record with 32 quarterback sacks in his collegiate career. The Showboats settled on the athletic Lewis after Ken Stabler of the New Orleans Saints turned down the club's one-year, $1 million offer.

With most of their roster spots wide open, the expansion teams became especially busy. Rick Neuheisel, the Rose Bowl MVP passer from UCLA, caught on with San Antonio, and Jacksonville inked receiver Gary Clark out of James Madison and linebacker Vaughan Johnson of North Carolina State. Johnson was a *Sporting News* All-America as a senior and had the distinction of being the nephew of league MVP Kelvin Bryant.

Sports Illustrated writer Paul Zimmerman estimated the USFL eventually signed at least 32 of the top 100 1984 NFL draft prospects, including the likely top four picks in Steve Young, Mike Rozier, Reggie White and Herschel Walker, who finally would have been eligible for the NFL draft.

Taking a page from Trump's book, J. William Oldenburg had also proven that he was serious about improving the L.A. Express and would spare no expense to do so. Los Angeles added Kansas quarterback Frank Seurer and Brigham Young tight end Gordon Hudson. The interesting part about Hudson's signing was that Oldenburg knew he would have to sit out the year with a knee injury. It did not escape the attention of the press that Hudson also happened to be the best friend and teammate of a young quarterback named Steve Young, the sure number one pick in the NFL draft. To further entice Young, the Express completely rebuilt their offensive line with Oregon's versatile Gary Zimmerman, Baylor tackle Mark Adickes and Texas center Mike Ruether, the three top-rated offensive linemen coming out of college. They also nabbed veteran lineman Jeff Hart from the Baltimore Colts. The running game had been abysmal the year before, so they signed Kevin Nelson from UCLA and Clemson's Kevin Mack to join with returnee Mel Gray. While his spending mirrored or perhaps outpaced Trump's, Oldenburg built Los Angeles in stark contrast to the way Trump retooled the Generals. While New Jersey pursued NFL veterans, the Express assembled one of the finest crops of rookie talent ever. Both spent an incredible amount of money in their competition to design the best team in the league.

"There was an offensive lineman named Mark Adickes, and he was negotiating with Klosterman and Oldenburg over a lunch somewhere," recalled *Los Angeles Times* writer Chris Dufresne. "Klosterman told me this story, that he had Oldenburg sitting next to him, and they're in negotiations. They're trying to come to a compromise or a deal and Oldenburg blurts out at the table, 'Don, I like this kid! Give him anything he wants.' So Klosterman asks Mark Adickes to write down what he thought he deserved on a napkin and Mark Adickes writes down $700,000, handed it to Klosterman, and that's what he got. Adickes said they called him 'Limo' because he was literally delivered to the practice field in a limousine."

"With or without Steve Young, the L.A. Express will be *the* professional football team," Oldenburg stated in *Sports Illustrated*. "Not just in the USFL, but in the USFL and the NFL. I'm used to winning, to nothing less than becoming the best. Donald Trump can get all the press he wants, but when it comes to business he can't carry my socks."

"He hires Don Klosterman, very reputable, long-time general manager of the Los Angeles Rams, great personnel guy," added Dufresne. "He told Klosterman, 'Build me the 1978 Pittsburgh Steelers.' He was like, I mean, come on, this is the second year of a spring league. And so Klosterman's going 'Okay.' He was like a kid in a candy store. Give a personnel guy a blank check, which is what he got, and go find me the best players. So Klosterman knew what he was doing, he went out and he signed 31 players I think that year, and I think *Sporting News* called it like one of the greatest recruiting hauls in the history of professional sports. And they spent $12 million on players."

The Stakes Are Raised

"We got much more publicity, much more of a true feel that the league was getting serious," said Breakers kicker Tim Mazzetti. "Trump came in with the New York franchise, the New Jersey Generals. There was some real serious money that was going into it. A lot more players like myself were defecting from the NFL and coming over. That changed it from this little, kind of fly by night, and I hate using that term because there was nothing unprofessional about it, but just playing in a smaller stadium versus now we started getting mainstream. It had much more of an NFL-type feel to it. We were starting to get a lot of publicity, the level and quality of the players had improved, they were spending some real money, both on players and infrastructure."

All of the excitement surrounding the batch of new players had come at a heavy price. Salaries, already inching upward, skyrocketed with six new owners trying to catch up with their counterparts and several more trying to keep pace with Trump. The soaring expenses gave several of the original owners reason to pause, John Bassett among them.

"He was very knowledgeable because he was the only owner out of our original 12 that really had hands on experience running a football team," Taube said of Bassett. "He was one of the owners in the World Football League, and he brought that experience to use and he talked about it frequently. We learned a lot from John. He was also a very good promoter, which he proved with the performance of the Tampa Bay Bandits. He was a moderate in terms of trying to stay within our budgetary agreements. So I would say that he was one of the good guys who was trying to preserve the concept that we all agreed to and which he, by the way, articulated on a number of occasions, we had to agree to because he didn't think that the league could survive if we didn't."

"There was huge positive excitement around the entire country about the league at that point," said Ehrhart. "We had expanded to 18 teams and brought guys like Trump into the league. Every player in the NFL and their agents along with the college guys were talking with us. Now the college season was on and people were still talking about the league. It wasn't just, 'Hey, let's go to the old, established NFL' anymore. It was basically an even playing field for college players. We had signed so many good players and now we were getting those great young quarterbacks. In October there was high enthusiasm, not only inside the league but outside the league, although there were some, such as Tad Taube and John Bassett warning about spending. Donald was saying, 'We can take on the Giants and the Jets.' There was great enthusiasm, yet the storm clouds were gathering."

"I was very concerned about the whole process of following through on our original concept of controlling expenses, particularly player salaries, until we could demonstrate that there were television revenues that were capable of supporting a more expansive approach to hiring players," explained Taube. "I also bought in totally, and do to this day, to the concept that there were literally thousands of very competent football players, a relatively small percentage of whom had the opportunity to play in the National Football League. The rest with talent levels either just below or in some cases equal to NFL players, were available to our league at low salaries. I totally supported the original concept and became very distressed by the temptation that was out there constantly for owners to attempt to sign this one player or these two players or three players that were going to make a competitive difference for their franchise. We actually kept the lid on player budgets in place relatively effectively during the first season, even with the signing of Herschel Walker.

"The agreed on salary guideline was $1.5 million per team the first year. There were a number of franchises who were able to come in at 1.2 or 1.3, and in that context, George Allen was not playing by the rules because he was probably operating at something north of a million eight. It was not like the discrepancy that developed during 1984, though. People came in who we didn't know all that well. People came in who had other ideas about the league. They weren't part of the process of, in effect, developing the original concept. By 1984, it became difficult to maintain any discipline as far as salaries were concerned."

"The original plan to me was let's crawl before we walk, walk before we run," agreed Peterson. "Let's see where we are in five years. Let's stay with a reasonable salary cap. Build this league, show the National Football League what we can do and that people will come and support pro football in the spring. Sometimes people get a little over-anxious and perhaps too excited about some initial success. They get away from the game plan, and then things start to unwind."

"The entire concept of discipline on budgets and player salaries and so forth went completely to hell in a hand basket," summarized Taube. "There was no end in appetite to sign big names. We were off to the races. We were quickly reaching parity with the NFL on player compensation, because it wasn't just at the star level. You have to understand, once you lose your discipline in terms of player compensation, it permeates through the whole organization."

"Even though they were solid on a long-term financial point of view, when we saw the kinds of monies they were spending, yes, we were concerned," added Spence. "Like the expansion of the league into new cities, we had mixed feelings. On the one hand, you sign stars and in theory at least it should help the television ratings. On the other hand, we recognized that they were spending a ton of money. They spent a ton of money on Steve Young. He was a well-known quantity, and we were delighted to see the Steve Youngs and Jim Kellys signed, but we knew the league was probably reaching beyond where they should financially. We had mixed feelings again."

"The awareness going into the second year was terrific, but the NFL was leveling the guns and the agents and players were driving up the price enormously," Ehrhart said.

"Once you open up the door to wanting the best players, it became difficult to back up. Your fans demanded quality, so it was certainly not the nice little puppy it had been a year earlier. The dog was big and escaping from the backyard."

"Having been in the NFL for almost eight years, I knew how they thought and worked and I knew the people involved would be competitive," remembered Peterson. "There wasn't anybody more competitive than Tex Schramm. We competed against him when I was with the Eagles starting in 1976 and it took us until 1980 to beat them and win not only our division but the NFC championship to get to Super Bowl XV. Tex was not going to lie down, and neither were a lot of other guys there."

The NFL, once dismissive of its new competitor, had changed its tune considerably in one year. While Rozelle publicly took a diplomatic tone, others such as Dallas Cowboys president Tex Schramm and a few NFL team owners seemed eager to lambast the USFL at every opportunity.

"Their ratings are horrible. It's a non-event," growled San Diego Chargers owner Gene Klein in *USA Today*. "I've tried to watch a few games. Frankly, they're so boring, so dull. Everyone I talk to, they have no interest in watching football at this time of year. It's out of sync."

"I wouldn't categorize this as war—I'd downgrade it to a skirmish," NFL Commissioner Pete Rozelle told *Sports Illustrated*. "We have had four of those since I came into pro football. The old All-America Football Conference, the original American Football League, the World Football League and now this. I can't predict what will happen in 1984 and beyond. There are only two certainties in all of this: one, an escalation of player salaries and, two, litigation. If the USFL has enough money and is willing to spend it, I think they might make a go of it."

With the swift rise of player salaries, Rozelle established a committee of NFL owners with the nebulous task of studying the effects of the USFL.

"It's not a go-to-war committee," Rozelle stressed in the *New York Times*. "We just want to take an overall look at our future. So many things are changing today. The committee will look at everything—the U.S.F.L., the courts, the colleges, all the problems in sports that have manifested themselves and affect our league."

New Coaches

New teams, new owners and new players meant that the league needed more men to mold its squads. A total of nine new coaches joined the USFL ranks, meaning that half the teams would be headed by a league rookie. After dumping Chuck Fairbanks, Trump quickly went about his search for a head coach, attempting to lure big names such as the Washington Redskins' duo of coach Joe Gibbs and general manager Bobby Beathard. After that bid failed, he made overtures to Miami Dolphins' head man Don Shula. Trump claimed that he nixed the deal when Shula asked for an apartment in Trump Tower as part of any agreement, a great bit of promotion if nothing else. Trump then found his man in Walt Michaels. The coach began his career with the Raiders before catching on with the Jets. He was with New York for their stunning Super Bowl III upset of the Baltimore Colts and later became the defensive coordinator of the Philadelphia Eagles. He rejoined the Jets in that capacity under Lou Holtz in 1976, and after Holtz suddenly resigned toward the end of the season, Michaels took over the team the following year. He led the Jets to a playoff berth in 1981 and the AFC championship game in 1982 before he was forced to resign, a move that New York fans widely criticized. Trump found a solid coach and a way to stick it to the Jets all in one swift move.

"He was different than Chuck," recalled MacConnell of Michaels. "The thing about Walt is that he had a great relationship with the media. The media loved him. Just the way things ended with the Jets, he was a fan favorite and a media favorite. He loved the media. He had no problem doing any interview, any time. He was open with them. There was also a sense he got a raw deal with the Jets. His hiring helped get us exposure. He was very good with the media."

John Hadl, a quarterback for 16 years in the National Football League, took over as the new field general of the Los Angeles Express after Hugh Campbell jumped ship to take over the Houston Oilers top job. Not coincidentally, the Oilers were extremely interested in Campbell's former Edmonton quarterback Warren Moon who had led the Eskimos to five Grey Cup wins. Before Campbell departed L.A., the Express courted the CFL passer. Hadl left a stint with the Denver Broncos tutoring John Elway, the number one choice in the 1983 NFL draft.

Hadl's hiring enabled Express general manager Don Klosterman to continue a long relationship with the former passer. He had signed Hadl to quarterback the AFL's San Diego Chargers in 1961, and 12 years later, the G.M., then with the Rams, acquired the passer from the Chargers. He then traded him to Green Bay the following year. After his retirement from the playing ranks, Hadl later became an assistant coach with the Rams before he took a job as the quarterback and receivers coach of the Broncos.

The Pittsburgh Maulers looked within the league for their first coach, Philadelphia offensive coordinator Joe Pendry. The 36-year-old had served under Bobby Bowden at West Virginia University before becoming an offensive coordinator at Kansas State, West Virginia and then alongside Jackie Sherrill at Pittsburgh prior to joining the Stars. Pendry was the longest-serving member of the Stars coaching staff and the only member of George Perles' staff to remain in Philadelphia.

After Bobby Bowden turned down the job, Fred Bullard tabbed Cincinnati Bengals offensive coordinator Lindy Infante as the right man for the Bulls. Following a stint with the WFL's Charlotte Hornets, the coach received his first offensive coordinator position when the New York Giants fired Bob Gibson following the "Miracle at the Meadowlands," a play on which Giants quarterback Joe Pisarcik fumbled away an apparent victory. Giants' management canned the entire staff after the season, and Infante took a job with Tulane for a year before catching on with the Bengals in 1980. The offense struggled for one season, but hit on all cylinders the following year as Cincinnati climbed all the way to the Super Bowl before succumbing to San Francisco. Bengals owner Paul Brown fired the coach and sued him for breach of contract after he heard about Infante's pact with Jacksonville but eventually dropped the lawsuit. Several days after his release, Infante dressed up in a beard, mustache, hat and sunglasses and waited outside a Bengals' practice session to get autographs. Several players, including quarterback Ken Anderson and receiver Chris Collinsworth, signed before they realized who he was. He later joined his former pupils for a few beers.

"I went back up to Cincinnati and decided to make the transition, but it was late in the offseason for Cincinnati," remembered Infante. "I made an agreement with Jacksonville that I would take the job with them as long as they would let me coach out the season in Cincinnati so I didn't leave them short-handed that late in the offseason. The people here in Jacksonville agreed to do that, and I went up to Cincinnati and told them I decided to take the job in Jacksonville with the new league but I was not going to go until after the football season was over, however long that lasted. Paul Brown's opinion was that it wouldn't be good for a team in the NFL to have somebody on staff who was getting ready to be a coach in the USFL, which I guess was a competitor, so he said they were going to let me go. That's the way it's gotta be. I said that's what I want to do, so they said, 'Okay, we'll see you later.'"

San Antonio landed Gil Steinke who had run the show for 23 years at Texas A&I, an NAIA school. There he compiled a 182–61–4 record, earned six national championships and captured the association's coach of the year honor four times. Steinke was unique in that he actually coached from the stands for most of his tenure, using runners to send instructions to the sidelines. He finished his career at Texas A&I with 39 consecutive wins and three championships in a row but had been out of coaching for seven years. The numbers were very impressive, but NAIA coaches rarely took a path directly to the pros.

Memphis hired Pepper Rodgers, a former head man at Kansas, UCLA and Georgia Tech. The Georgia Tech job brought him back to the school which he had quarterbacked for three seasons. Rodgers was noted for his wry Southern humor and one-liners, known to his friends as "Pepperisms."

NFL veteran Marv Levy earned the unenviable task of rebuilding the Chicago Blitz. He began his head coaching career at California where he tutored Craig Morton, the head coach of the Denver Gold. After a job at William and Mary, Levy jumped to the pros, taking an assistant position with the Eagles. Soon he moved over to the Rams and worked under another USFL boss, George Allen. He followed Allen to the Redskins before landing the top spot with the CFL's Montreal Alouettes in 1973. There his squad won the Grey Cup in 1974 and 1977 which led to an NFL job with the Kansas City Chiefs from 1978 to 1982.

"I had been with Kansas City and been let go after the '82 season," recalled Levy. "Then I did some broadcasting of the USFL games the next year. In '84, I got a call from a man I didn't know at all from Chicago, his name was Ron Potocnik, and he was going to be the general manager of the Blitz. I was living in California, and he asked me if I might have an interest. I knew George Allen was coaching the Chicago team, but that was one of the weirder things that happened—the owner of the Chicago Blitz bought the Arizona team and unbeknownst to me, they switched rosters, too.

"The Blitz had been a pretty strong team the year before, and the Arizona team had been a weak one. I learned about the roster swap after I got here. Not until I got here did I understand that there was actually a roster swap of a team that had been pretty strong with one that hadn't been."

After interviewing Levy, the Houston Gamblers also chose to go with a former NFL coach in Jack Pardee, who had narrowly lost the Tampa Bay Bandits coaching job to Steve Spurrier the year before. In his first head coaching position, Pardee faced more adversity in one year than most coaches see in an entire career. He headed up the WFL's Florida Blazers whose players and coaches weren't paid the final 12 weeks of the season. With the league crumbling around them, Pardee somehow convinced his men to play on. They played well, earning a berth in the title game before falling to the Birmingham Americans by one point. The performance proved good enough for the Chicago Bears who hired him for his first NFL head coaching job. He led Chicago to the playoffs for the first time in 14 years in 1976 and earned National Football Conference Coach of the Year honors. He later jumped to the Redskins where he earned Associated Press Coach of the Year accolades in 1979. He had been contacted by several USFL teams in 1983 but was wary of the new league after his WFL experiences. He liked what he saw in the USFL's inaugural campaign enough to change his mind.

A defensive coach by nature, Pardee left the offense in the hands of Darrell "Mouse" Davis, former head man at Portland State. Davis pioneered the pass-happy run and shoot offense which featured four wide receivers and no tight ends. His Portland State team led the NCAA with 49.2 points per game in 1980 topped by a 105-point effort against Delaware State. The run and shoot looked like the perfect style of play for a team known as the Gamblers.

"When I interviewed Jack Pardee who was out of professional football at that time, Jack was working in the oil business in Midland, Texas," Argovitz remembered. "So when I brought Jack down to interview him, to talk to him, when we offered him the contract, he made a commitment to come with us. Before he signed, I told him that I'd already hired the offensive coordinator. And Jack said, 'That's a little bit unorthodox.' And I said, 'I've never done this before, but this is how I wanna do it.' He said, 'Well, who's the offensive coordinator?' I said, 'Mouse Davis,' and he asked, 'Who's that?' I said, 'He's the one that runs the run and shoot offense.' He said, 'What's that?' I said, 'Well, you'll never lose

Two of the USFL's new coaches in 1984: Chicago Blitz coach Marv Levy (left) greets Houston Gamblers coach Jack Pardee on June 10, 1984, at the Astrodome. Photograph by Wilf Thorne.

your job, Jack, if we don't score enough points. Your job is just like McDonald's is: quality control. You lead the team; you're the head coach, but the fourth down is the offensive play.'"

"Jack was no question about it, a defensive man," said Davis. "He just let us take it and run with it. The first meeting or two he was sitting in the meetings, and then after that he took care of the defense. We had a very good relationship. Everything worked out well."

Unsuccessful negotiations with Redskins' assistant Jerry Rhome preceded the hiring of Steelers defensive coordinator Woody Widenhofer as the first head man of the Oklahoma Outlaws. Widenhofer, an 11-year member of a Pittsburgh staff that won four Super Bowls, became the third Steelers assistant to leave Pittsburgh for a job in the USFL after Rollie Dotsch and George Perles.

Leaving Early

With its coaching vacancies filling up, the USFL's attention turned back to the players. In spite of the USFL's attempts to mollify college coaches following the Herschel Walker signing, underclassman continued to take a look at the USFL. Contending that rules prohibiting players with remaining eligibility from turning pro were unconstitutional, the league proposed a system by which such players would have to go through a review process before turning pro. At least that way, the league reasoned, it would make it more difficult for the underclassmen to leave school. Many college coaches continued to resist any changes but failed to offer any other solutions.

The issue finally came to a head when University of Arizona punter Bob Boris sued the league over its eligibility requirements and won. Instead of an overall ban on underclassmen, the USFL would review each player on a case-by-case basis. Boris won a $200,000 judgment and signed on with the Outlaws. The two sides later reached a settlement that included $75,000 in legal fees and $25,000 compensation.

"We had several lawsuits against the league, basically because of the college eligibility rule," recalled McSherry. "We lost a case in Phoenix where the USFL was found to have violated the antitrust laws for trying to create a college eligibility rule, which was bullshit because we had already signed undergraduates.

"Up until that time, I think it was the NBA that fought most of the legal fights over the college eligibility rule. Football, being the national treasure that it is, I don't think there was much litigation between college students and the NFL."

Several league and team officials were particularly upset with the NCAA for failing to support the league's efforts to find a compromise before the suit. "The NCAA tells us to fight it to the end, but it hasn't contributed dime one," Arizona general manager Bruce Allen told *The Sporting News*.

Not surprisingly, the first case reviewed following the Boris decision was that of talented running back Marcus Dupree, and the league quickly threw open its doors for the runner. Nearly every major college program wanted the runner when he finished high school, and the battle for him had inspired the book *The Courting of Marcus Dupree*. He starred at Oklahoma as a freshman in 1982, but left the Sooners in the middle of his sophomore season after lingering disagreements with coach Barry Switzer. Dupree transferred to Southern Mississippi during the season but soon found out from the NCAA that he could not play again until 1985. In addition, the runner's mother had been working three jobs to support him and his younger brother who had cerebral palsy and needed an operation. Clearly, this was the special case the league was looking for. After the Boris case, Dupree quickly signed a deal with the New Orleans Breakers. The Express also pursued him, but he wanted to stay close to his family and their Philadelphia, Mississippi home. The Breakers presented Dupree to the fans of New Orleans in a horse-drawn carriage surrounded by cheerleaders and a Dixieland band. Still wanting to keep an eye on his creation, David Dixon showed up to check out the hoopla.

Breakers owner Joe Canizaro cited the runner's hard-luck family situation and a raw deal from the NCAA as reasons for signing the 19-year-old. This time, there would be no furor over signing a player with remaining college eligibility. The contract called for a $300,000 signing bonus with the first year of the $300,000 salary guaranteed.

Stars owner Tanenbaum cited the antitrust consequences when explaining why the league fought Boris and not Dupree. "We got the news from our counsel that we don't have a defense," Tanenbaum told *The Sporting News*. "It's one thing when you're turning down a guy like Bob Boris who's playing for $40,000, where treble damages are $120,000. But it's another with a guy like Dupree, where we've already priced his services. Triple his contract and he'll own the damn television contract. The damages are just too great. We can't risk it."

The Push for the Fall ... and a Push Back

Meanwhile, Trump continued to make headlines nearly every time he opened his mouth. He was most vociferous in his advocacy of switching to a fall schedule. Had there been any doubt before, the other owners now realized how serious he was. Trump reiterated his claim that he had not joined the USFL to be an owner in a minor league. This time, though, he went a step further, suggesting the league immediately buy out the four weakest teams and reduce itself to 14 franchises. Considering that a half-dozen teams had yet to play their first games, the proposal did not find much support. He wanted to force the move to the fall as soon as he could. Trump even tried to get league games off of ESPN for the coming season.

This did not sit too well with ESPN commentator Paul Maguire. "He has to learn that this league can't be built individually," Maguire told *The Sporting News*. "It's going to take a joint effort. He should sit down and think before he says something or have somebody write it out for him." ESPN televised 36 games that year.

"To be very clear, he was one of the greatest self-promoters of all times, maybe the best in certain respects," said Gould. "He was smart, very organized, very detailed, and he read everything. He always asked everybody, 'What's up?' That's the first thing he would say is, 'What's new?' or 'What's up?' He would immediately get to see how you would answer. If one got on the telephone and said, 'What's new, what's up?' you've got a hundred different ways you can go with that answer, but it defines you. If you say, 'Well, the sky is blue,' you've got about a 30-second chance with him. If you said, 'I'm buying a company for about one-tenth the price of what it's worth,' you got a longer time with him. He's all about making money."

The New Jersey owner sent letters to his fellow owners urging the move to the fall and then followed his written comments with a speech at a January owner's meeting in

New Orleans, much to the chagrin of Bassett and several other owners. In order to placate Trump, Simmons established a long-range planning committee to look into the issue of switching seasons. Trump met considerable resistance at the meeting and in the days following it, and Tanenbaum in particular warned everyone that Trump would have no problem simply paying them to go away if he could get the Generals into the NFL. Still, Trump managed to wrest control over television negotiations away from Simmons.

"We clearly did not want to go to the fall," explained Spence. "We had Monday Night Football and we had a college package, so we already had two football packages that our sales department was selling. We did not want to have a third football package in the fall to add to our sales inventory. In addition, there was some concern that if we went to the fall, we'd be competing against the NFL on CBS and NBC. There was a question of how well we would do. We really wanted the USFL in the spring. We needed the programming on Sunday afternoons in the spring. That's where we wanted the USFL. We were concerned about the talk of moving to the fall, especially concerning Trump. Being the kind of person he was and is, we knew that he could probably take control of that league pretty readily."

"Even though there was great optimism and a lot of positives, it was a very wearing offseason with all the franchise sales and trying to get everything together and digest expansion," Ehrhart remembered. "When Donald came in everybody was excited initially, but there came a time when it became Donald trying to exercise his will. There was some angst between Chet and Donald. I don't think it was when he first got into the league, but in that first year because Donald kept wanting more of everything. That was just Donald's style, his personality."

The division within the league became particularly pronounced between Trump and Bassett, who was convinced not only that the USFL was working in the spring but that it needed to remain there for the foreseeable future. Though the two maintained a cordial relationship, they frequently butted heads on the league's direction.

"John Bassett was a great guy, he did a very good job, but it was a very limited job, and his Tampa team while good, it was peanuts," opined Trump. "It was never going to crack the big league. But the Tampa team was one team. You had other teams that weren't going to make it. My team was very successful as an individual team, but if I'm good and somebody else is unsuccessful, that doesn't help me very much."

"I don't think Trump saw Bassett as a smart businessman," Gould said. "I don't think that he disliked him; he just thought his idea was just small potatoes, lettuce and tomatoes. I can tell you, having worked with both of them, they're both diametrically opposed on almost every level of life. Yet together, they probably could have done wonderful things."

"From my recollection there was a couple times where they viciously disagreed," added Peterson. "I would agree with the thought that there was enough respect. There was great respect for Bassett by Donald Trump and vice versa. They both wanted success for their franchises first, hopefully for the USFL. They were both very bright guys in how to promote a team, a league, a sport, and of course Bassett had done this with tennis in Canada. It was a healthy respect but they did differ in their thoughts without question."

"I would think that the two combatants that happened most were Trump and John Bassett," furthered Simmons. "And they would go after each other in the meetings. John couldn't sit still in the meetings. He'd be up and walking and so forth, and they would battle between the two of them. There would be no screaming or anything, but they were trying to make their own point about what should happen to the league and both were intractable. John was always logical, because of his background, and Trump is illogical. 'Let's go to the fall; we'll be great in the fall; we're gonna get teams in the fall. We're going to take the league to the fall; doesn't anybody understand what I'm saying? I can get this done. Just let me go do it.' I don't think he could have walked across the street."

"Donald always sat down next to John Bassett," furthered Camera. "And John Bassett, and I'm sure if you ask Donald he will deny it, controlled him. Because he could say to Trump, 'No you're wrong, you're full of it. That's great, yeah, you wanna build something that's great, but this is a football league. No, no, no we're gonna play in the spring.' It was amazing to see. He wouldn't take on Bassett because down deep he really respected him. He respected the fact that he had a successful family. It was a big thing for Donald. He really was a family guy and he would always ask about John's daughter Carling. He'd say, 'Hey how'd Carling do last week?' And Bassett would use his standard line, 'Well, she did well in the tunnel but the biggest problem she had was getting out of the ladies' locker room.' You know there was always a little one liner from John with that little sensitive laugh, and Trump loved it."

"It was like standup comedy sometimes, back and forth," remembered Argovitz of the Bassett-Trump battles. "I think Donald said something like, 'John was born with a silver spoon in his mouth' or vice versa, but they were always at each other because they were diametrically opposed to what we should do and what the outcome was going to be. But they both loved football and they both wanted to see the best for the league. They just had a different view on how to do it."

"I put Donald on my marketing committee, and I put Bassett on the committee," laughed Camera. "Every problem owner we put on the marketing committee, because if you put them in one group, you're better off. Sometimes I'd say to Chet, 'You know we're going to lose this vote. We have Bassett *and* Trump agreeing, so we're done. We're going to have to go in that direction.'"

Looking Ahead

It seemed that no amount of news, good, bad or indifferent, could help some franchises. Washington's season ticket sales had fallen under 11,000, a full 7,000 fewer than the year before. Their front office knew they faced an uphill battle and did what they could with limited funds to turn the situation around. The Federals invited fans to RFK Stadium in November to watch the 1983 highlight film, such as it was, in an effort to bolster season ticket sales. They also let fans get their ankles taped and try on Federals uniforms. Over 1,000 fans attended and the franchise sold 225 season passes. Just 87 people were taped including two women in their 50s and a one-and-a-half-year-old girl who had her wrist taped.

The other franchises showed a mixed picture on the eve of the USFL's second season. Generals' fans responded to Trump's efforts with season ticket sales of 32,000, 4,000 less than the year before. The Bandits also stood at about 32,000, a figure which represented a gain of some 10,000 people. Denver slipped to 26,000, down nearly 10,000 from the inaugural campaign, and Oakland stayed steady at 23,000. Michigan's championship increased their total to 22,000, up about 50 percent from the previous season. Thanks to the new blood provided by Diethrich, Arizona came in at nearly 19,000, about 4,000 more than in 1983, and Birmingham drew close behind with 18,000 or about 4,000 more than in 1983. Los Angeles' rash of rookie signings had failed to generate much interest in the City of Angels and the Express sold just 13,000 season passes, a drop of one third from their first year. The Stars' appearance in the championship game and the league's best regular season record did not help early sales in Philadelphia as fans purchased only 13,500 season passes. New Orleans' total of 11,000 was far from great but represented a vast improvement over the 3,500 the club had sold in Boston the prior year. Of the returning teams, the Blitz plummeted to the bottom of the list, generating just 8,800 sales. The Chicago fans had not taken kindly to the franchise swap.

Among the expansion teams, Jacksonville led the way with more than 22,000 season tickets sold. Memphis, nearing 18,000, was also strong. Pittsburgh sold 2,200 tickets in the three days after Rozier's signing and shot up to 15,000 by the time the season began. Oklahoma stood at 13,500, while Houston struggled at around 10,000. San Antonio sold just 5,000, due in large part to bad press and the problems with Alamo Stadium. Thanks to legal squabbles with neighbors around Alamo Stadium, Gunslingers management had to fight for the use of the facility until February 8, less than three weeks before the season opener. Those fighting the team feared traffic problems on game days. The protracted battle ensured that they would not be overwhelmed.

A Disaster in the Making

With the season openers approaching faster every day, the league came face to face with its first full blown emergency in Chicago. Dr. James Hoffman looked to be in trouble with the Blitz since the day he took over the franchise. While he had created headlines with a three-year, $6 million offer to Chicago Bears star running back Walter Payton, employees in the franchise's front office soon found out he had been late in paying several bills. Hoffman had severely underestimated the expenses involved in running the franchise and greatly overestimated his own net worth. He was trying to line up Chicago investors to reduce his stake in the club but had committed to hold at least 51 percent of the team. Other league owners soon learned that Hoffman had paid just $500,000 up front for the franchise and $200,000 in initial operating expenses, with the rest of the $7.2 million purchase price due in installments. Rumors spread that Diethrich had even posted Hoffman's $1.5 million letter of credit to push the sale through.

Drowning in red ink, Hoffman began looking for a scapegoat. Team president Ron Potocnik made an easy target thanks in large part to a bungled trade involving future New Orleans and current Cincinnati Bengals tight end Dan Ross. Of course, many of Potocnik's shortcomings on the job could be traced to Hoffman's cash flow problems. The owner was unable to pay nearly $450,000 in signing bonuses owed to several players before the league took the amount out of his line of credit, which may have really been Diethrich's money. Faced with the failure of its team in the nation's third largest market, league personnel director Carl Marasco flew in to oversee the Blitz in hopes of lending some stability. The club named Bill Polian, an astute judge of talent who had been with Coach Marv Levy in Montreal and Kansas City, as its director of player personnel, but it was clear that Chicago was a mess.

"During our training camp, as I understand this, Hoffman quit," explained Levy. "He didn't have the funds to take care of what he needed. He couldn't sell it to anybody, and he just quit. All of a sudden the team was up for grabs, and the league had to run the Chicago Blitz that year."

"We had absolutely a major league problem," Camera said. "We had the league running it. Jimmy Foster was the marketing guy out there, brilliant guy. The problem with Jimmy Foster is that he thought that he could turn it around. He came up with a campaign, 'Puttin' on the Blitz,' and spent a million dollars in advertising on television and radio with Vince Evans. It was a delightful campaign, but he didn't have any money! He thought that tickets would be sold, and I kept saying to him, 'Jimmy, what are you, crazy? Where are you getting all this money?' And he'd say, 'Well, Dr. Hoffman said make it happen.' Make it happen!? How do you do it with no money?"

"The league office had to basically take over the Chicago team," recalled Ehrhart. "We sent Carl Marasco out there to run the team, and this is where I knew Bill Polian was going to be a future star in the NFL because of what he did there. I remember calling Bill when he was a young personnel guy and saying, 'Bill, you need to help hold this together.' Marv was still the head coach. Obviously you could tell that these two guys did unbelievable quality work holding together a situation where the ownership was cracking. The guys kept their cool, and Marv Levy was unflappable. Bill Polian took the bull by the horns and later went on to become one of the great executives of the NFL with three different teams that he's built: Buffalo, Carolina and the Colts. One reason I think he's great is that he was truly a guerrilla warrior out there, making due without having a big machine like the NFL behind him. It is really remarkable that these two guys were able to operate in such a difficult situation with no money. They foreshadowed their future great working relationship with the Buffalo Bills that would lead them each to be inducted into the Pro Football Hall of Fame."

"Diethrich was an excellent owner, but his heart was really in Phoenix," said David Dixon. "He moved his team to Phoenix after the first year and that left us with a Chicago team that had to be operated by the league. That's where Walter Duncan would have been there forever. That hurt us."

Instead of getting better, the situation worsened, and there was little the USFL could do about it. Unsurprisingly, investors were not lining up at the Blitz's door. Soon, the league began paying Chicago's bills to keep the franchise afloat. With the club teetering on the brink of collapse, the league stepped in and took complete control of the franchise. They tried to cut costs wherever possible and on a February day, dubbed "Bloody Friday" by the staff, Marasco called nearly the entire front office into a room and fired them all, Potocnik included. Marasco took over as president of the team.

"Hoffman wanted out," Potocnik told *Inside Sports*. "I don't know if he couldn't afford to pay our operating expenses and signing bonuses, or that he just wouldn't pay them, but the fact is he didn't. He needed a scapegoat so he could get out, and that was me."

"I was let go from the Blitz before the end of the season," remembered Blitz PR man Don Kojich, who survived the initial cut. "I vividly remember it. We were playing in San Antonio, and I advanced the game. As a PR person, when you advance a game you go out there a few days ahead of time, meet with the local media, pitch some story ideas and work on making the travel arrangements, making sure all the hotel rooms are set and they have all the keys lined up so you can check in properly, making sure the buses were at the airport. This is pre-9–11, and the buses actually came out to the tarmac and picked the players up right off the tarmac. So you're making all these preparations. I went out to San Antonio to advance the game, and we played at some old stadium there and we lost the game. I came back and went into the office on Monday morning. I was told, 'We're cutting back, and you're relieved of your duties. You did a hell of a job. Turn in your keys.'"

Among the other casualties was executive vice-president Jim Foster, who had finally moved over from the Arizona Wranglers. The club blamed his dismissal on spending too much money. Evidence soon surfaced publicly that he had operated within the guidelines he was given and his "Puttin' on the Blitz" campaign had resulted in the sale of nearly 9,000 season tickets despite the franchise's obvious troubles. He later sued the league, and settled for payment for the time he was out of a job and for team expenses he had paid out of his own pocket.

Hoffman had run out of money and soon drifted out of the picture completely, refusing to pay any Blitz bills. With the season rapidly approaching, Chicago became a rather expensive ward of the league. Worse yet, the television contract with ABC stipulated the USFL had to have teams in the top three television markets–New York, Los Angeles and Chicago—or the network would be entitled to a substantial rebate on its rights fees.

"It was screwed from the get-go," said Foster of Hoffman's ownership stint. "We had an owner who you could write a book on what he was and wasn't. I was reading the media guide which was already on its way to press, and his bio said that he had played quarterback for the Denver Broncos. I got upset with my media relations guy and said, 'Are you sure he played for Denver?' He said, 'Well, he told me he did.' So I called the Hall of Fame in Canton, Ohio, because I knew some people there and found out the guy had never played for the Broncos. As near as we could figure out, he went to a free agent open tryout camp, threw a few passes and said he was on the team. Jim Hoffman—we used to call him Tim Conway because he looked just like him. He could have been his twin brother.

"Hoffman didn't have anywhere near the money that he represented. We spent a lot of money in advertising and marketing. I told him before I took the job, 'If you hire me, you'd better be prepared to open up your wallet in Chicago. You're not going to get by on the sly here.' Then, a month before the season was supposed to start, kaboom, the whole thing falls apart."

"There was a big debate," Ehrhart remembered. "Do we let Chicago go down? Some of the owners said, 'Screw 'em, if they can't pay their bills, let it go.' But there was so much good going on, and everybody felt we couldn't allow a team to fail. There was a lot of debate and initially pain to make sure it stayed alive."

Preparing for the Season

In Denver, owner Ron Blanding's penny-pinching ways caused player personnel director Tom Marino to step down from his post. "I don't see the point in having a player personnel director on this team," Marino told *The Sporting News*. "I don't see how anyone—and I know I couldn't—could function in this job." In large part because of continued media criticism, Blanding stepped up his efforts to sell the club. He continued to be one of the decreasing number of owners who strongly believed in sticking to the original financial model of limited player salaries.

"You could see that things weren't moving in the right direction," Blanding said of the league as a whole. "Maybe some of them were status quo and some others were going backwards a little bit, but it wasn't making the progress that it had to make to be successful. We thought it was time to move on."

Fortunately, the USFL's players were hitting the field in preparation for the season, drawing some attention away from the financial issues. Training camps again produced some strange situations. The Panthers had $2,000 worth of equipment stolen from one of their trucks. Included in the theft were 42 footballs, 40 jerseys and 16 pairs of shoes.

Chicago and Memphis pulled off the league's largest trades to date when the Blitz sent 21 players whom they were about to cut to the Showboats for one late round draft choice. Five days later, Memphis released 20 of the players with offensive lineman Clint Davenport the only survivor. Chicago's housecleaning left just 20 former Wranglers on the roster after the cutdown to 58 players.

The phones were removed from all the players' rooms at the Oklahoma Outlaws camp as a disciplinary measure but were later returned when the team realized it had no way to give wake-up calls. Oklahoma's trainer made up for the mistake when he filled the squad's water tanks with beer on the last day of camp.

The New Orleans Breakers attracted nearly 2,000 would-be players to a tryout camp, causing coach Coury to quip to *The Sporting News*, "If we'd had this many people just come and watch in Boston, I'd have been happy."

More than 42,000 people, including 31,000 season ticket holders who got in free, turned out at Tampa to watch the Bandits battle former Bucs quarterback Doug Williams and the Oklahoma Outlaws in an exhibition game. Williams played for three quarters, but much to the home crowd's delight, the visitors fell, 15–6.

Meanwhile on Florida's east coast, the Jacksonville Bulls were overwhelmed by the response they received. More than 8,000 fans turned out for the team's first scrimmage, and not long after that, 25,000 people attended a preseason game against the Houston Gamblers. Even better, the team had already sold more than 43,000 tickets for its first regular season game. The league had found more open arms for its second Florida franchise.

"I had a brainstorm of having an open tryout in the Gator Bowl one afternoon for anybody who thought they were good enough to make our team, as much for public relations purposes as for finding players," laughed Bulls Coach Lindy Infante. "I remember going over to the stadium, and I didn't even have a coaching staff yet. I had some guys who came in and helped evaluate players. My thought was that we'd have 100 or 200 players come out who thought they were good enough to play. I remember a guard coming to me before we opened the gates, and he said, 'Coach, you better come out here. We have a problem.' I asked what it was, and he said, 'We've got so many people out here, we cannot even control them at this point. They're all getting antsy, and we have close to a riot going on out there.' So I went out and got on the bullhorn and asked them to be patient. When we opened the gates up we gave everybody a number to pin on their shirt or jersey. We had so many players out there it was virtually impossible to get anything done well. We spent hours out there just trying to get everybody to run a 40-yard dash. One of my coaching friends said he had coached more people that day than he did the rest of his coaching career.

"We had so many players show up … or people who thought they were players. Literally, one guy was a bus driver, and he came out to run the 40-yard dash in some leather shoes. It was that kind of a thing. When it was all said and done, we sat down and looked everything over the best we could, and if somebody caught one of the coaches' eyes, maybe because he ran a fast 40, we put his name on the list. We probably had at least 500–600 people out there. One guy, a receiver, came up to us afterward and said, 'I don't think this is fair. I drove all the way down here from North Carolina, and I ran one pass route.' We had so many people we couldn't give everyone ten or 15 pass patterns to take a look at them, but we did the best we could. I think we invited six, seven or eight players to our main camp from that whole mess, and none of them made the roster even after the first or second cut. It was not productive athletically, but it was a public relations move that was chaotic at best."

New Express coach John Hadl received a less than warm welcome near the end of camp when recently released defensive end Greg Fields punched him, leaving a cut above the coach's left eye. Two years earlier, the Atlanta Falcons had to have police remove Fields from camp after they released him. He clearly believed in going out with a bang, not a whimper. He joined the San Antonio Gunslingers who decided to hang onto him.

The Houston Gamblers found a ton of trouble the only night their coaches waived curfew. One player was arrested for drunken driving, another for public intoxication and yet another for beating up two policemen. The Houston coaches decided to enforce the curfew for the rest of camp. Fortunately for Argovitz's team, Jim Kelly was not among the guilty parties.

Several players remembered the relatively laid-back atmosphere of the camps. "What were they going to do—cut us?" asked Tampa Bay's Nate Newton. "All of us had already been cut two or three times. We were supposed to be the bottom of the barrel. The pressure was off. We could relax, play ball and have some fun."

Breakers kicker Tim Mazzetti enjoyed training camp for an entirely different reason. Co-owner Bob Caporale had helped Mazzetti land the sports anchor position for the CBS affiliate in Boston, WNEV, a position he would no longer hold with the team's relocation to New Orleans.

"I got paid more from the television station than I got playing," laughed Mazzetti. "I actually had a great financial year that year, though I worked my ass off because when you're doing sports casting in Boston, especially in the fall, you had the Bruins, Red Sox, Patriots, Celtics, all the colleges and high school, its non-stop. I was putting in 70 and 80 hour weeks, working seven days week, 12 hour days. I busted my ass more than any other job I've had, but I made a lot of money. Ironically, when I heard they were moving the team to New Orleans, which was probably around October or November, there was part of me that was saying, 'You know what, I'm so burned out from this damn job, I'm actually looking forward to going back to football!' The idea of two-a-days was actually quite attractive."

With hundreds of new players in the fold, team owners were keeping a close eye on their investments, including the latest Heisman Trophy winner.

"Mr. DeBartolo was a class act," said Camera of the Pittsburgh Maulers owner. "He came in, got Pittsburgh, signed Rozier, and we kept up the streak of Heisman guys. He did everything that had to be done. I'll never forget it. We were scrimmaging down in Florida before the season, and DeBartolo drove up in his old black Cadillac. He drove himself. He came on the field, and they put in Rozier so he could score a touchdown from about two yards out. DeBartolo got back in his car and drove away."

Bigger and arguably better, the USFL was ready for its second campaign. With larger payrolls all over the league, everyone involved realized the importance of the season for the future of the USFL. If the first year had been a mixed success, the second would have to be an unqualified one if the spring experiment was to continue much longer.

"On the outside everything looked terrific," said Ehrhart. "We had 18 teams and were coming off a very successful season. We had new exciting players such as Jim Kelly in Houston. We had the freshness and excitement of Memphis and Jacksonville with huge crowds. It looked terrific, but I certainly felt as if we were keeping our fingers in the dyke in some places."

4

Bigger and Better

The addition of six expansion teams and the Breakers' move to New Orleans meant that the USFL had to realign for its second season. Instead of the three-division alignment of the year before, the league split its 18 teams into Eastern and Western conferences, each with two divisions. In the East, Pittsburgh replaced Boston in the Atlantic Division, joining holdovers Philadelphia, New Jersey and Washington. Newcomers Jacksonville and Memphis plus Birmingham, Tampa Bay and the relocated Breakers made up the Southern Division. The Western Conference's Central Division featured expansion franchises Houston, Oklahoma and San Antonio in addition to the "new" Chicago Blitz and the defending champion Michigan Panthers. The Pacific Division remained unchanged with Arizona, Denver, Los Angeles and Oakland.

Washington Federals

To everyone's surprise, the Federals had largely stood pat with no major acquisitions even though they were coming off a 4–14 season. Reggie Collier, traded from Birmingham, figured to share time at the quarterback position with Mike Hohensee. Ugly preseason losses to Tampa Bay and Pittsburgh did little to fuel any optimism for the franchise's second year.

"We traded for Reggie Collier in the offseason, and I thought he was going to be pretty good," said Federals Coach Ray Jauch. "He didn't really pan out, and Hohensee didn't do as well as I thought he would. That's about the only thing we did. We really didn't do all that much. I don't think our general manager had the resources to improve our team. We were never given the leeway to do that. He would have liked to have done more, but his hands were tied."

As impossible as it might sound, the 1984 edition of the Federals proved to be even worse than the 1983 version. Their very first game of the season provided a gloomy preview when the expansion Jacksonville Bulls waxed them by a 53–14 margin, costing Jauch his job. Owner Berl Bernhard went so far as to unfavorably compare their play with that of "a bunch of untrained gerbils" in a *Sports Illustrated* article.

"I remember him saying that," said Jauch. "It's like you're General Motors and you call your cars a bunch of lemons. That's how smart that was.

"We didn't really have a big-money guy. We were owned by kind of a limited partnership, made up of different investors. We didn't have any Donald Trump, so we didn't have the wherewithal to do what they did. It was a struggle.

"What are you going to do? We couldn't bring anyone in. I was out beating the bushes trying to find a training camp site in Florida. We were in Jacksonville the first year, then we went to a little wholesale place that was a little cheaper. Everything went on the cheap. We stayed in a Quality Inn, or something like that, and trained at a small college. We had to bus our guys back and forth all the time.

"The league got started, and they had a formula that they were going to follow. They were only going to compete with the NFL for like fifth-round draft choices on down. Everybody would have one player that was known, and then everyone would try to get more local talent to build their teams. After the first year, that all went out the window. There just weren't any rules for some teams.

"I think the Washington Federals always stuck to the original plan. We had a lot of good guys, I really liked the character of our players, but we didn't have many really great football players."

The beleaguered Bernhard handed the coaching reins to offensive coordinator Dick Bielski. The move proved to be of no avail, though, as Washington lost its first eight games of the year, several by embarrassingly large margins. Neither the oft-injured Mike Hohensee nor newcomer Collier could get much going from behind center. While the 1983 edition lost several close ballgames, only two of the Federals first eight losses came by seven points or less.

Looking to trim the budget, Bernhard granted star running back Craig James' request to be released from his contract. James, who had missed four games due to injury in 1983, suffered a new injury in the Feds' week two game against the Stars. He healed up enough to join the New England Patriots in time for the NFL season.

Victories over Oakland, New Jersey and New Orleans helped to ease the pain a bit, but a 3–15 record again left the Federals looking up at the rest of the league. During the season, Bernhard reached an agreement to sell the franchise to Sherwood Weiser, who would move it to Miami for the 1985 season. Weiser soon hired former University of Miami coach Howard Schnellenberger for the 1985 season. "Schnellenberger is a great coach, and he's looking for a challenge," Feds tackle Dave Pacella told *The Sporting News*. "We're certainly going to give him one."

Bielski's squad finished with the fourth-worst scoring offense, while his defense gave up 492 points, tops in the league. Runner Curtis Bledsoe, one of the few bright spots, gained 1,080 yards on the ground in place of the departed James. Hohensee, who saw most of the action after week five, threw for 2,766 yards with 17 scores and 20 interceptions, while Collier added 969 yards in the air but threw just six touchdowns compared with 12 interceptions. Joey Walters turned in a spectacular year on the receiving end with 98 catches for 1,410 yards and 13 touchdowns despite the unsettled quarterback situation. The Feds turned the ball over 53 times, nearly three times per game and second most in the USFL. Washington ended the year with the circuit's worst defense, finishing dead last against the pass and second from the bottom against the run. One of the few bright spots was Mike Guess who intercepted 11 balls, the second best total in the league. The defensive line proved to be a particular problem as linebacker Joe Hines led the weak charge with eight sacks.

The franchise's incredibly poor performance, even considering the low standards established in its inaugural year, and the impending sale to Weiser kept the Federals' attendance at a bare minimum. The team drew a paltry 69,243 for the nine-game home season, an average of just 7,694 per game. By comparison, expansion Jacksonville twice drew more in one game than the Federals did all season. After 12,067 showed up for the first game against Philadelphia, it was all downhill from there. Just 4,432 came out for a midseason tilt with Memphis. In their two years of play, the Feds escaped last place in their division just once in 36 weeks and tied for the worst record both seasons.

Oakland Invaders

The defending Pacific Division champs faced a much different USFL in their second go around. The infusion of talent throughout the league had not touched the Invaders, who were determined to stick by the league's original salary structure. Oakland hoped to claim its second playoff berth with nearly the same roster it used the year before minus tight end Raymond Chester who retired to become the franchise's director of community relations. As it turned out, Bay Area fans would get to see two seasons for the price of one. The first, spanning the opening nine games, was utterly forgettable. Nine straight losses led to the firing of head coach John Ralston, the league's first employee, who was replaced by vice president of administration Chuck Hutchison.

"I regrettably had to terminate him, and I still regret it to this day because John is such a wonderful man, and I should have just said the hell with it, we'll ride it out and spare the person," said Taube. "I think I inflicted a bit of harm on John for which I've been eternally sorry. I lost nine straight games, and a lot of that was attributable to John's inability to recognize a reality that we went into training camp without an offensive line coach. He believed in his heart of hearts that we had a guy, and finally when I talked to the guy who was a Denver Broncos coach, it turned out that was not his understanding at all. He had a conversation with John, and said, 'Let me think about it.' So John, being the eternal optimist that he is, translated that in the affirmative and we went into training camp without an offensive line coach. Nothing happens in the offense if the offensive line isn't working. So basically I had good reason to do what I did, but I still regret it and I've regretted it ever since."

Taube later announced that Los Angeles Raiders defensive coach Charlie Sumner would lead the team the following year but would work in the front office for the remainder of the season.

"The closest I've come to play-calling is when I got a computer football game when I was about 15 years old," said new coach Hutchison in *The Sporting News*. "And, as I remember, my sister took care of me pretty good."

A futile offense, which at one point went 12 consecutive quarters without a score, punctuated the Invaders' struggles. With quarterback Fred Besana being sacked at a record pace and the running attack grinding to a halt, the club was not only winless but boring.

Everyone felt the effects of the losing streak. "When I was walking into the stadium, I doubled or tripled my escort because I was afraid I was going to be assassinated," Taube recalled. "I was being subjected to terrible media reporting about what a terrible owner I was and what a cheapskate I was."

It got so bad that Taube sent a letter of apology to season ticket holders, an unusual step in any league. It said in part, "I take full responsibility for the problems we've had on the field and commit to you that ownership will take whatever financial, management, coaching or player personnel steps necessary to develop a winning football program with a total commitment to excellence on the field and a special commitment to the community we serve."

It was no accident that Taube used the term "commitment to excellence," a phrase often used by Raiders boss Al Davis.

And then came the Invaders' second season. Rookie running back Eric Jordan ran wild in a 17–13 decision over Chicago in week ten, Oakland's first win of the year. With Jordan paving the way, Denver and Arizona became their second and third victims, while Besana found his groove against Memphis, Oklahoma and then Jacksonville. Suddenly, the Invaders looked like a different ball club, a good ball club in fact. Six consecutive victories landed them just two games out of the divisional race. They topped Michigan for their seventh in a row, but a narrow loss to L.A. and a blowout at Denver finished their season at 7–9.

The Oakland Invaders' split personality made for a year that was hard to dissect. The opening act proved awful, with Oakland outscored 218 to 82 over the first half of the year on their way to a 0–9 record. The second turned into one of the league's hottest squads with a 7–2 mark down the stretch. They outscored their opponents 160 to 130 and won all but one of the close ones. The defense played consistently throughout the season but frequently had to carry far too much of the load. All told, the team finished on the bottom of the league in scoring. But considering their poor start, the Invaders had made things exciting over the last nine weeks.

Running back Eric Jordan's emergence keyed the recovery, and he ended the season with 744 yards rushing with a 5.5 yard-per-carry average. The passing attack was simply awful for nearly the entire season, with 2,444 net yards. Behind a porous offensive line, Besana completed 257 of 446 attempts for 2,792 with 14 touchdowns and 12 interceptions. Gordon Banks led the receiving brigade with 64 catches for 937 yards. Defensively, Marcus Quinn's 12 interceptions, best in the USFL, topped the ball-hawking "Bruise Brothers" defense that produced 46 turnovers, the high water mark in the league. Defensive end Dave Browning finished with 14 sacks, while punter Stan Talley received a good workout, kicking a USFL-high 110 times for a 41.5-yard average, including an 81-yard boomer.

The franchise's on-the-field struggles directly influenced the team's attendance. They started with a season-high 41,200 for their first home game but dropped over the next three contests to a low of 14,828 against Washington. As the team began its ascent, so did its attendance, eventually reaching 29,687 against Jacksonville. They ended up averaging 23,644 per game or nearly 8,000 less than the year before. Invaders management had their misgivings about the rampant spending throughout the league that they believed had led to their decline.

"We got off to a terrible start because we hadn't added enough in the way of personnel and we lost some coaches," remembered Ralston. "I was kind of surprised a little bit [at his dismissal). I continued to spend time working with the Invaders in scouting because we wanted to continue to build the league.

"Right from the start, we wanted to try to control the salaries and didn't want that to get out of hand. We preached that all the way along, that we had to control that. We would have looked like hypocrites had we gone the other way."

"The 1984 season was a very difficult time for me because three things were happening that were really bad," recounted Taube. "One is that I was put in a position where I had to make a decision on a coaching change that involved an individual that I had and have a great deal of affection for, namely John Ralston. Second was the impact leading to that decision as well as the aftermath, which is when we lost nine games in a row, and

I became a virtual pariah on the sports page in the Bay Area. Thirdly, and that was something that added to my frustration, I saw things happening that caused me to believe that the league might be beginning to unravel."

Pittsburgh Maulers

The signings of Mike Rozier and Glenn Carano gave hope to new USFL fans in Pittsburgh before the season began and boosted season ticket sales to the point of respectability. Rozier found himself under the microscope in the Steel City, just as Herschel Walker had in New York the year before. Unfortunately, an ankle injury sustained by the runner in the Orange Bowl would hamper him the entire season and reduce his effectiveness.

Both the team and the running back started slowly with losses to Oklahoma, Michigan and Birmingham. The defeat to the Stallions in their first home game, in front of the USFL's first sellout crowd, was particularly galling since it came against former Steelers quarterback Cliff Stoudt, long a favorite whipping boy in the Steel City.

In fact, the campaign would not get much better for the Maulers. Two wins over the Federals and one over the Invaders marked the only times Pittsburgh cracked the win column. Several close losses made it a bit more exciting, but the season still was a disappointment considering the presence of Rozier. A 31–21 setback to Denver, in which the Maulers led 21–0 in the second half, typified the campaign.

During the year, team owner Edward DeBartolo dropped the axe on head coach Joe Pendry, who refused to meet with the owner after a loss, and replaced him with offensive line coach Ellis Rainsberger. Rainsberger had previously coached the offensive backfield for the Gold in 1983 and before that was the offensive coordinator for the CFL's Winnipeg Blue Bombers for five years. Former NFL assistant Hank Bullough would later be announced as the next head coach, but the team would wait until 1985 for him to take the helm.

Rozier topped a surprisingly poor running game with 792 yards despite missing nearly six games, while Carano threw for 2,368 yards with 13 scores and 19 interceptions. Greg Anderson led the squad with 63 catches for 994 yards and a half dozen scores, while Jackie Flowers finished with 51 receptions for 904 yards and eight touchdowns, with all but four of those catches for 16 yards coming after his acquisition from Chicago. Tony Lee and Eric Shubert combined to hit just 12 of 23 field goal attempts and miss four extra points, while Larry Swider ended the year as the circuit's second-best punter with a 42.0-yard average. Defensive end Sam Clancy starred with 16 sacks, but injuries kept many of the squad's top performers out for several games during the team's first season.

"When I came out of college I had a bad ankle sprain from the Orange Bowl, and I wasn't 100 percent," Rozier admitted. "I still tried to play on it, but I wasn't 100 percent."

After a sellout crowd of 53,771 turned out for the Maulers first home contest in March, the next highest total numbered 24,880 for a blowout loss to Houston. The franchise failed to draw more than 18,000 for its final three games. Still, they averaged 22,858 at the gate for a 3–15 USFL team.

New Jersey Generals

The minute Donald Trump bought the New Jersey Generals one thing became clear: they were not going to remain in the Big Apple's sports shadows for long. His offseason haul of NFL talent made the franchise one of the favorites to vie for the league's second title. His signing spree had drastically improved his football team, while drawing criticism from some of his fellow owners. Just 20 players remained form the 1983 squad, and seven new players would start on the defensive side and four new ones toed the line on offense.

Ten-year NFL veteran Brian Sipe joined the New Jersey Generals in 1984, just four years removed from an NFL Most Valuable Player campaign. He joined the Jacksonville Bulls in 1985 before injuries hastened his retirement. Photograph by Jim Turner, from author's collection.

The addition of veteran quarterback Brian Sipe would give the Generals another option besides Herschel Walker left, Herschel Walker right, Herschel Walker up the middle. It had taken the team five weeks to capture its first win in 1983, but few in the USFL expected that forgettable performance to be duplicated.

The revamped defense provided most of the muscle in wins versus Birmingham, Jacksonville and mighty Philadelphia before Jim Kelly and the run and shoot derailed them at Houston. They responded by whipping Washington, Los Angeles and Memphis to move their record to an impressive 6–1, a far cry from the 2–5 mark they held at the same time the year before. Following a loss to Arizona and a narrow victory at Pittsburgh, they took care of Michigan and Oklahoma. Unfortunately for them, the Stars had shot out to a 10–1 mark, leaving New Jersey a game behind in the Atlantic Division.

They somehow managed to follow that three-game winning streak with an embarrassing loss at Washington and then struggled to pull out games against weak sisters Pittsburgh and Chicago. They suffered a 40–14 defeat at Tampa Bay, but clinched a wild card spot in the playoffs when they downed New Orleans the following week. They tuned up for the postseason by knocking off both Denver and Philadelphia, handing the dominant Stars their only two defeats of the season.

A look back at the 1984 New Jersey Generals shows drastic improvement from the 1983 squad all around. In particular, the defense shone as only two teams allowed fewer points, while offensively just five scored more than the rejuvenated squad. Thanks to a pair of 1,000-yard backs and the additions of former Bandits tackle Doug Mackie and

While helping rip open holes for Herschel Walker, bruising fullback Maurice Carthon came into his own in 1984 when he ran for 1,042 yards. After three seasons with the Generals, Carthon played eight more in the NFL, seven with the New York Giants before embarking on a lengthy coaching career. Photograph by Jim Turner, from author's collection.

Cincinnati Bengals guard Dave Lapham, the Generals finished second in the league in rushing. Walker topped the team with 1,339 yards and 16 touchdowns while Carthon added 1,042 yards and 11 scores. Despite playing with a bad shoulder for much of the season, Walker's 128 total points earned him second place in the league scoring race.

"He matured so much the first year," MacConnell remembered. "He was quiet. He didn't say a lot. Here's this 20-year-old kid who had all this stuff thrust upon him. I was amazed at the way he handled it [in 1983]. The next year he came back even better. Not that he was immature the first year, I wouldn't say that. But he was so much more comfortable. He was just one of the guys. He was like a college kid. There was nothing about him being Herschel Walker, no ego. Myself and my assistant would go out and have dinner with him on nights they weren't eating together as a team. He would do anything for you, never turned down an interview. Anything you need. It was amazing as a 20-year-old what he went through, what he had to handle. Then he turns around and the next year he's even better.

"I was always so impressed that he was able to accomplish what he accomplished. Nothing fazed him. He never lost his cool. There was one time in Oakland when a reporter wanted to do a column, and the Oakland Invader media guy said, 'He's a good guy, let him do it.' Well, they got off on this tangent about something, I don't know what it was, but I'm thinking, 'My God, if I'm Herschel, I'd deck this guy.' I can't remember what it was, might have had to do with religion or something. I remember the guy was really trying to nail him. This is unbelievable. Maurice Carthon, Herschel's roommate, looks at me almost like, 'Holy shit, where's this going?' I'm thinking this interview's over, and I'm about to step in and say, 'This is not what we had set up for you to do.' Herschel kind of went back to him, and they had a big conversation for an hour. The interview ended up going great, and the column turned out great."

Sipe stabilized what had been a terrible passing game with 2,540 yards, 17 scores and 15 interceptions in spite of a lack of top quality receivers. Tight end Jeff Spek and Walker led the way with 40 catches each, tying them for fortieth in the USFL. The defense finished the year with 27 interceptions, six more than the year before. The unit improved to the USFL's fourth best and became especially tough against the run. Rookie Jim Byrne topped the team with six and a half sacks. Rookie Roger Ruzek improved the kicking game with 17 field goals in 23 attempts and 102 points.

Trump's offseason additions took the Generals from a 6–12 record in 1983 to a 14–4 mark in the team's second season. The club averaged 37,716 fans for each of its nine home dates, a very respectable number in and of itself, but less than 3,000 per game above the 1983 figure. More than 50,000 showed up for the April 29 matchup with Michigan, the highest total since the inaugural home game. But when the franchise was fighting for a playoff berth, it drew 23,114 against New Orleans and followed with just 28,915 against Denver to close the home slate. Trump had invested quite a bit of money and gaining an additional few thousand tickets didn't come close to making it up for him.

The flamboyant owner continued to make headlines with his mouth. He challenged the New York Giants to an exhibition game with a $1 million purse to go to charity. He also remained a vociferous advocate of moving the league into the fall.

"You have to look at what the guy did for the league," MacConnell said. "He did so much for the league in just the exposure. You want that type of owner, a guy who's going to spend money and try to get the best players he possibly can. I think he did a lot of good for the league. Our franchise was one of the best, if not the best. Tampa had a great franchise, Colorado, Michigan, they were all good. The Generals were a good franchise when Walter and Chuck started it, but Donald took it to another level. Say what you want, but the guy brought a ton of exposure to the USFL that I'm not sure anybody else could have gotten, and he did it in the biggest market in the country."

Oklahoma Outlaws

Led by former Buccaneers quarterback Doug Williams, the expansion Oklahoma Outlaws bolted from the gate and became one of the USFL's early surprises. They began by topping Pittsburgh in the rain, losing to Denver in overtime and then squeaking by San Antonio and Chicago. At 3–1, their largest margin of victory stood at seven points, and they had prevailed by three and four points in their other two wins. After Arizona clobbered them in week five, they took on Jim Kelly and the Houston Gamblers, somehow pulling out an incredible 31–28 victory. Doug Williams hit Al Williams with a Hail Mary touchdown pass to tie the game on the final play of regulation, and the pair combined on a flea-flicker to set up the winning score in overtime. They welcomed defending champion and 6–0 Michigan the following week with a stunning 20–17 upset and followed that one by beating Washington to move their record to 6–2 and forge a tie at the top of the Central Division standings. After playing in the rain and snow for most of the early season, they forged a reputation as a team that played its best in inclement weather.

"We hired Woody Widenhofer, the defensive coordinator of the Pittsburgh Steelers, as our coach," said Billy Tatham. "Woody comes in the first day and asks, 'What kind of a deal do you have with Doug Williams?' I said, 'Woody, let me put it this way. His contract is longer than yours and it's more expensive, so Doug is going to be here for sure.' We go into training camp, and Doug is a great human being, great with people, brilliant on offense. Not 60 days later, Widenhofer is quoted in the newspaper as saying, 'If I have to go to war, I want three guys: Jack Lambert, Jack Ham, both Steelers he had coached, and Doug Williams.' That's how fast Doug rose in Woody's perceptions."

As the weather warmed, it was all downhill from there, though, as the Outlaws dropped their final ten games of the year. Injuries caught up with the over-achieving squad as did a tough schedule. The pass defense played horribly in five straight blowouts that crippled their playoff hopes, and then the struggling offense failed to score twice in the final five games.

Oklahoma registered just 251 points in 18 weeks, second worst in the league, while giving up 459, third worst in the circuit. They had a tough time keeping defensive ends healthy and at one time had four of them out with injuries, another ailing and but one healthy player at the position. They were using a couple of nose tackles to shore up the spot.

On offense, the running game, or more accurately the lack thereof, proved to be a problem the entire year. They finished dead last in the USFL with 1,556 yards and a negligible 3.7 yards per carry average with just ten touchdowns on the ground. Doug Williams completed 261 of 528 throws for 3,084 yards with 15 touchdowns and 21 interceptions, while his late-season fill-in Rick Johnson threw for 602 yards and one touchdown with 12 interceptions. Turnovers proved to be a killer after their fast start. The Outlaws gave up the ball a whopping 61 times, eight more than any other team, and finished minus 20 in turnover differential. One bright spot was receiver Al Williams who shone with 50 catches for 1,087 yards, a sparkling average of 21.7 yards per catch, with seven scores. Unlike the rest of the offense, he finished the year with two of his best games.

The franchise averaged 21,038 fans per home appearance, not bad considering the collapse down the stretch and the chronically bad game-day weather they faced in Tulsa. In fact, their first contest in the cold and rain against Pittsburgh drew a season-low 15,937 fans. Their biggest turnout numbered 29,324 for the Michigan game, but after a month of losing on the road, the club fell to 16,378 and 17,195 for its next two contests, its second and third lowest turnouts of the year. The Tathams wanted to avoid the weather altogether by getting the city to build a domed stadium. They acknowledged that they faced an uphill battle with local officials to get the project off the ground and began looking at other locations as a home for the Outlaws.

"At that time the only stadium was Skelly Stadium in the older section of town, meaning there's no parking," remembered Bill Tatham. "I literally looked at it and wondered where everybody was going to park. The university said, 'Don't worry about it. We draw over 30,000 per game paid.' So we figured no problem; people here know where to park. We finally open up operations, spend millions of dollars, and I will never forget this: the very first opening game, we're playing the Pittsburgh Maulers. They come in with the DeBartolos and the Heisman Trophy winner Rozier, and we announced an attendance of something like 17,000 in the pouring rain. The editor of the *Tulsa World* walks over and asked, 'Why did you intentionally under-announce the crowd? I've been coming to these games for 25 years, and you have 30,000-plus. I know you had over 30,000.' It's probably the first time in history anybody's been accused of under-reporting attendance. We had hired the assistant athletic director Bill Wall, to be our business manager and he overheard the conversation. He said, 'I'm working for you guys now, so I've got to tell you, the university for years has been over-announcing its crowds to stay in Division I.' So I said, 'They don't draw 35,000?' 'Oh no, closer to 15–20,000.' So there was no place to park after all."

"Bill, Jr. was a smart guy, a lawyer," Camera recalled. "He was another guy who could sell venom to a snake. He would smile at you and tell you what you wanted to hear. He was a good owner. His father was delightful. He had big sideburns, cowboy boots, the whole nine yards. I'm probably in the minority, but I thought they were good people and I liked Billy. I think they had a big plan in their own mind of what they wanted to be and where they wanted to be. They did a good job. Tulsa was tough because we had two cyclones, or whatever they were, hit there during games. It was unbelievable. What could go wrong there did, but they did a good job. Billy Junior did a good job, and the father was a class guy."

Michigan Panthers

Unlike their slow start the first season, the defending champion Panthers bolted to the league's best record in the early going. Close wins over Chicago and Pittsburgh preceded a shutout of Denver. A late defensive stand provided a victory over tough Arizona, before the offense took center stage the next week in a 52–34 demolition of Houston. Their sixth win in a row, though, came at a tremendous cost, and sapped much of their momentum when star receiver Anthony Carter broke his arm against San Antonio, knocking him out for the rest of the year.

Losses to Oklahoma, Birmingham, Tampa Bay and New Jersey had the team reeling before they held off Houston to break the losing string. The Panthers then dropped games at New Orleans and Los Angeles, and Philadelphia toppled them in the Silverdome to push them back down to the .500 mark. They rallied to sweep San Antonio, lost to Oakland, and closed out the regular season with a pair of victories that allowed them to squeak into the playoffs as a wild card entry.

"We won the first six and then Anthony Carter broke his arm," said Keller. "Anthony had become a big-time playmaker. I don't know if there was anyone who could cover him in our league. Bobby Hebert and he were just on the same page. I remember the game against San Antonio and seeing it along the sideline. He went up and came down and broke his arm.

"We had Derek Holloway, and Derek was great, but we didn't have that guy they had to double cover. Derek was a helluva little player; he's only about 5'6"; he was a smurf. Anthony, who wasn't a big guy, had this great speed and leaping ability. With the two of them, it was tough for defenses to double. But without Anthony, we didn't have any other receivers who were as good. Losing one player like Anthony really changed the dynamic of the team. We weren't a bad team, but we weren't a team that could strike quickly. Once we didn't have a passing game that could strike fear into anybody, then they were able to shut down our running game. We found ways to win, but we weren't the same team after we lost Anthony."

"It was against San Antonio, he went up and his arm got caught behind him," recalled Holloway of Carter's injury. "When he fell down on the ground, he landed on his arm and broke it. We ended up winning that game, but after that we lost like five out of six or six out of seven. We had some other injuries that hurt, too. John Corker got hurt at some time. David Greenwood got hurt somewhere along the line, so we had some other injuries besides Anthony. We had key injuries to key members of the team."

Season-long contract squabbles with several players, particularly Hebert, took their toll on a club that also dearly missed Carter for the final two-thirds of the season. Ken Lacy signed a futures contract with the Kansas City Chiefs and Hebert's agent publicly dangled his client in front of several NFL teams, even after signing an extension with Michigan. In addition, several other injuries kept key players such as Tyrone McGriff, Lacy, Williams, David Greenwood and Thom Dornbrook out of the lineup for long stretches.

Hebert, under constant pressure and playing on a bad knee, threw 500 times, completing 272 for 3,758 yards, 24 touchdowns and 22 interceptions. Holloway had a great year filling in as the number one receiver in Carter's stead with 62 catches for 1,219 yards and nine touchdowns. John Williams paced the ground attack with 984 yards and eight touchdowns and a 5.0 yards per carry average, while the addition of fullback Albert Bentley aided the running game later in the season. Novo Bojovic finished third in the loop in scoring with 112 points and connected on 22 of 29 field goal attempts. Larry Bethea led the defensive charge with 11 sacks while John Corker dropped to just eight after leading the USFL the year before.

Still, the campaign proved to be a success in a more important way. The franchise took advantage of its 1983 championship by increasing its average attendance by more than 10,000 per game, to an average crowd of 32,457 fans. After an opening night crowd of 22,428 with a snowstorm raging outside the dome, the Panthers drew more than 40,000 for their next four home contests. Once the losing set in, the fans shied away, dropping steadily from 42,655 on April 15 to just 15,838 on June 18 against Oklahoma.

Jacksonville Bulls

Immediately after the USFL established a team in Jacksonville, it became readily apparent that they had found another great Florida market to complement Tampa Bay. The Bulls exceeded all expectations with a 53–14 whipping of Washington in their opener in front of nearly 50,000 spectators but came back to earth for the rest of the season.

"We played Washington and we beat them rather badly, 53–14, at home, and we had a huge crowd there," Jacksonville coach Lindy Infante remembered. "We had a huge crowd in the Gator Bowl, got off to a big start and were just on a roll. And I thought, wow, this is quite a group of guys. It was an exciting ballgame, not because it was close and tight, but it was exciting for us because we were hitting on all eight cylinders in our first game after putting the team together. It was gratifying."

More than 70,000 fans turned out to watch their next battle, a controversial narrow loss to New Jersey.

"The highlight or lowlight, whatever you want to call it, was that we had gotten ourselves in a position right at the end of the game, maybe the last play, to kick a field goal to win it," Infante recalled. "The official who was underneath the upright slipped and when he got up he waved it off. Had that gone through we would have won that second ballgame as well."

Plucked from the Cincinnati Bengals, Gelindo "Lindy" Infante brought his innovative offensive scheme to the Jacksonville Bulls as the popular Florida franchise's head coach. He would go on to coach the Green Bay Packers and Indianapolis Colts, winning NFL Coach of the Year honors at Green Bay in 1989. Photograph by Jim Turner, from author's collection.

After dropping three consecutive games they bounced back at L.A. before losing to Memphis, Birmingham and San Antonio to drop to two wins and six losses. They took out Memphis, 12–10, on the strength of a late safety, and then made it two in a row by crushing Oklahoma. A six-game losing streak killed their postseason aspirations, before they finished with two victories, an overtime decision over New Orleans and the last in a driving rain against visiting Pittsburgh to end a 6–12 season. Owner Fred Bullard became so frustrated at one point that he stormed the field during a game to chew out the officials.

"That was against Houston late in the year, and we were struggling a little bit," Infante remembered of Bullard's trip on the field. "They waxed us; just beat us up and down the field. You're emotionally attached to a team, especially after all we'd been through, and the officials in a lot of people's eyes weren't making some correct calls, with a lot of them going against us, and that compounded the problem of us not playing well and them playing very well. Late in the game Fred actually challenged the officials right on the field. He was the owner; he could do anything he wanted to. If he wanted to go over and hit one of them, he could do it as far as we were concerned. We had no control over it. It was embarrassing to everybody concerned, but what was more embarrassing was that we just weren't playing very well that day."

"'Bubba' Bullard was the best," said Camera. "He was a former running back, a great guy, a builder. He was so fired up on everything. He ran on the field one time and argued with the official. They threw a flag on him. They couldn't believe this guy, built like a brick shit-house, running across the field. They were like, 'Who's that?' And it was Bubba Bullard. He had a great wife, and every time you went down there they would invite you to the home. Fred was a terrific guy. He hired Larry Csonka, who knew what he was doing, and they were an exciting team, they were good. Jacksonville we knew would be a great market, and it is. It turned out to be a great market."

The Bulls' anemic running game, topped by Larry Mason's 495 yards, came in second worst in the USFL, while Robbie Mahfouz headlined the passers with 2,174 yards, 11 touchdowns and 13 interceptions. Gary Clark spearheaded a solid receiving corps with 56 catches for 760 yards, and Perry Kemp and tight end Paul Bergmann also consistently contributed throughout the year. Don Bessillieu, the team's MVP, paced the secondary with seven interceptions and led the squad with 157 total tackles and 118 solo stops. The defensive unit recorded the fewest sacks in the league.

A 6–12 season was not normally much to smile about but a 6–12 season coupled with an average attendance of 46,730 was. The Bulls led the USFL in per-game attendance and set league records with two crowds in excess of 70,000 people. They averaged more fans than seven NFL teams did that year. The numbers had dipped a bit after Jacksonville lost a few games but were still well above Bullard's and the league's wildest expectations. Many in the USFL also recognized it as one of the better marketed franchises in the circuit.

"I'm from Florida, played at the University of Florida and ended up being a young assistant there for seven years," Infante said. "We played Georgia once a year in the Gator Bowl, and I knew what the fan support there was. I knew how much Jacksonville really craved and wanted a National Football League team. They had tried on several occasions to get owners to move their teams there. Then there had been some other leagues that had come through there such as the old World League. It's a football area. The whole southeast, I think is very football oriented, not that the rest of the country isn't, but football was *the* sport. There was always enough interest that if somebody would put a good product out on the field, they would show up in numbers. I never for a minute doubted that, and it was one of the reasons I decided to take the job. Surely knowing people in this area and how much they love their football and how much they back their teams, especially with us playing in a different time of the year, there would be no doubt that we'd have big crowds. I did not envision some of them as big as we had, but I thought we'd be one of the attendance leaders."

Los Angeles Express

Much as Donald Trump had transformed the New Jersey Generals into an instant contender, owner J. William Oldenburg and general manager Don Klosterman had done the same for the Express, albeit with youth over veteran experience. Oldenburg tore open his wallet to ink 31 players in a two-month stretch including 20 of the top collegians in the country. "He wanted me to design a car to go 180 miles per hour," Klosterman told *Sport* magazine. "I told him what it would cost. He never backed off." By midseason, just 15 players remained from the 1983 team, including only nine starters on a roster that featured an astounding 31 rookies. They restocked the offensive line with four new players and added Kevin Nelson to give some punch to the running game. The Express threw new coach and former NFL quarterback John Hadl and special assistant Sid Gillman, an offensive guru, into the mix.

Much to Oldenburg's dismay, L.A. stumbled into its second season, compiling a 2–4 mark six weeks into the campaign. In spite of the new blood, the Express looked inept offensively, scoring no more than 14 points in a game, prompting Oldenburg to make one more big rookie signing that promised to improve their fortunes. Following often contentious negotiations, Los Angeles agreed to terms with quarterback Steve Young of BYU on what was reported as an astounding $40 million deal.

"The chances going into it that they would sign Steve Young were virtually nil," said Young's agent Leigh Steinberg. "Steve grew up very traditionally, wanting to play in the NFL with a picture of Roger Staubach hung up over his bed."

The task to get Young's attention fell to Klosterman.

"He concocted a very clever strategy to sign Steve," explained Steinberg. "He knew how traditional Steve was, and he made a football argument. Klosterman had hired John Hadl who in 1983 had coached John Elway, who had been the top pick in the 1983 NFL draft. He had just had the job of tutoring the top quarterback and integrating him into pro football. He had also hired Sid Gillman who was a top offensive mind and known as the architect of the modern passing game. On the line they had Gary Zimmerman who they had signed as a college player and who went on the make the Hall of Fame. They had Mike Ruether, another excellent lineman. They signed Gordon Hudson, Steve's tight end from BYU. They had Kevin Mack, the running back. They had JoJo Townsell, a good receiver from UCLA. They wanted to make a football argument that Steve would get great tutelage and teaching and make a better transition. They knew that was the only way to potentially get him."

"The truth about it was that it was an annuity, funded by a million dollars, that was going to be paid out over 40 years," explained Young. "So if you took a million dollars and had an annuity and held it by somebody in Bill Oldenburg's name, it was going to pay out in 2022. It was going to start building up, so over 40 years it was going to pay $40 million. That was the contract. No one would think that's a contract, but that is the way they promoted it and it was a disservice to me, I think, if I looked back on it. I was young and I just didn't need the pressure. It was a good contract for that time, it was good money, there is no question about it, don't get me wrong, but it wasn't $40 million."

Young, the great-great-great grandson of Mormon leader Brigham Young, finished as the runner-up in the 1983 Heisman Trophy balloting behind Mike Rozier and would have been the first choice in the upcoming NFL draft by the Cincinnati Bengals, a notoriously cheap team which had already lost several players to the USFL along with offensive coordinator Lindy Infante. That had helped Los Angeles get the attention of Young and Steinberg. The astounding contract called for his salary to be paid out in escalating amounts over 43 years, making the actual value of the deal around $12 million. He reportedly received a signing bonus of $2.5 million and starting yearly salary of $1.5 million with deferred money coming his way until the year 2027. Nevertheless, the $40 million figure was an extraordinary number for the time and found its way into dozens of head-lines.

If anyone was worth that kind of money coming out of college, most football observers agreed that the first team All-American Young was the man. In his senior year, he threw for 3,902 yards with 33 scores and ran for an additional 544 yards. Showing his athleticism, Young scored the winning touchdown in the 1983 Holiday Bowl on a flea-flicker, running the final 20 yards through the Missouri defense to pay dirt with just 23 seconds left. Among the 13 NCAA records the passer set, he broke marks for completion percentage (71.3 percent) and total offense in a season with 395.1 combined rushing and passing yards per game.

"The USFL had actually been built in a very clever way," said Steinberg. "In 1983 they signed Herschel Walker, giving them a powerful, major star in the nation's biggest city. They also signed Jim Kelly. Essential to their strategy was knocking down Los Ange-les, the nation's second largest city. We have always been a city of stars. Los Angeles for years was the city of Wilt Chamberlain, Jerry West, Elgin Baylor, Kareem Abdul-Jabbar, Magic Johnson, etc. Having a good-looking quarterback was always a hallmark of the Rams. The USFL went through the 1984 draft and essentially picked it clean. They signed Mike Rozier, the Heisman Trophy winner. They signed Reggie White, the defensive player of forever. What they needed was that All-American quarterback to lock down Los Ange-les, and that's where Steve Young came in."

"At the time, I was living in Greenwich, Connecticut, and I read in the local Green-wich paper that Steve Young, the great Brigham Young quarterback was going to be home with his parents for the holidays at Christmas time," Ehrhart recalled. "So I looked in the phone book in Greenwich and called him up and said, 'Steve, I'd like to visit with you about this new league, the USFL.' So he popped in his car and drove over to the house and we started talking and then got him in touch with the LA Express because we already had Herschel in the New York market. Here was Steve Young, a wonderful talent. We thought that maybe going to LA would be the best situation. So I enlisted Howard Cosell to help out on this one, and I can remember Howard getting on the phone with Steve's father and saying this was a great opportunity, and he talked about the Joe Willie Namath story of Joe signing with that other new team in a league 20 years earlier and then how he became a star. Howard was very helpful in getting Steve Young to make that step to sign with the USFL."

"Sam Wyche comes out from the Cincinnati Bengals and says, 'We are going to draft you, first choice,'" recalled Young. "And I think, 'Well, you know Kenny Anderson is there, could be great. I don't know.' Don Klosterman comes up and says, 'We want you to come to LA.' At first you're thinking, 'I'm the number one pick in the draft, I'm not going to go to the USFL. I'm just not gonna do it.' And then he starts selling: LA, his Rams history. 'Sid Gillman is down here. You want to play QB, you want to learn to play the position–Sid is going to teach you it. John Hadl is going to coach you. This is the team and these are the guys: Mark Adickes, Mike Ruether, these are big-time, young offensive linemen. I got JoJo Townsell. I got Gordon Hudson, your buddy from BYU, playing tight end.' I thought the way the league was set, either I would play in the league forever, or I would play a couple of years and then come out a free agent and still get coached by great coaches. So I got sold pretty quickly."

The negotiations had not gone without a hitch. Following a marathon bargaining session March 3 that stretched well into the night to iron out the details of the pact,

Young and Steinberg flew to the San Francisco offices of volatile owner J. William Oldenburg the next day to finalize the pact.

"They thought they had the deal done pretty much, so I flew in Bill's jet to San Francisco," recalled Young of his trip to Oldenburg's office with agent Steinberg. "I'd never been to San Francisco. I think that was my first trip, though I've made many since. He's in the Trans America building, it's his birthday, so he's got his Bentley pick us up at the private airport and taking us over to the Trans America building. Up we go and he's got this sign, 'Steve Young, welcome, Steve,' and Leigh said, 'I promised your dad I would give him a call.' I wanted to finish the contract with him. My dad, who is a lawyer, wanted to hear about it and to make sure everything was copacetic. Leigh gets on the phone and starts telling my dad, 'Here is the clause 14' and dadadada. So my dad says, 'Wait a second,' and I'm sitting waiting and an hour goes by."

"The problem is that we get up there in the late afternoon, and we have a lot of contractual stuff to get finished," recalled Steinberg. "No one had told Bill Oldenburg this. Now it's basically dinner time, and he expects we're just going through the formality of signing when we've got a day, many hours at least, to go. He's stuck up in his penthouse up on the 30th-whatever floor, and I'm sitting with the lawyers going through what's probably going to be hours of paperwork. Unbeknownst to us, he's waiting to go out for a birthday dinner with his family. He's sitting, waiting for the signing, and no one's done any kind of job preparing him for this.

"At one point the lawyers are sitting there, now it's like 7:30 or 8:00 at night, and he bursts into the room, 'What's the holdup?' Someone said, 'We're working on guarantees.' He takes a big wad of hundreds out of his pocket and says, 'Here's all the f-ing guarantees you'll ever need,' and throws these hundreds all across the room."

"Bill Oldenburg comes in and says, 'What's the problem? I'm going to my birthday party. I want to announce this thing; what's the problem?'" added Young. "Leigh says, 'Hold on, hold on,' and another hour goes by and I'm sitting there waiting. Bill comes in and starts getting kind of irritated, and he says, 'What is it; what is it, more money?' And he points at me, 'What is it, more money you want, money is the problem?' He takes a wad of hundreds out of his pocket and throws them at me. 'Is that what you want, more money?' Well, it doesn't hurt, I have nothing right now. So I'm kind of quietly picking them up. Are these my hundreds? I've never seen so much money in my whole life. I don't have 20 bucks to put together from college."

"He comes back later, now it's about 9:30, 10:00, and he says, 'Now what's the problem!?'" continued Steinberg. "We're just steadily going through work, and I had LeGrande Young on the phone. Oldenburg said, 'Tell him to stick the f-ing Mormon Temple' and I'm trying to hold the phone as close as I can to my chest. It gets to be like 11, 12, and I'm like, 'Guys, why don't you tell him this is not getting done tonight?' His minions are sort of afraid to do that. I said, 'You should have prepared him from the start.'"

"Now he's getting pretty upset, and Leigh is like, 'Hold on,' cause my dad doesn't want to sign it until it's right," said Young. "Oldenburg comes in, and he's just flying off the handle, and he says, 'You guys, you think it's about money,' and he's screaming at me, poking me in the chest. 'You think you could take me?' I told Leigh later, 'He doesn't poke me again because he is gonna get it. You know, I'm not gonna put up with that.'"

"Now it gets to be about two in the morning, and Oldenburg breaks in and says, 'Get Steve and Leigh into my penthouse!'" recalled Steinberg. "Both of us get up there, and by this point he had been drinking steadily all night. He started poking Steve in the chest: bam, bam, bam. 'You're not good enough to play on my team! I've offered you the biggest contract ever, and you're balking. I need someone with decisiveness!' Bam, bam, bam, his finger's poking at Steve's chest. Steve looks at him and says, 'Mr. Oldenburg, with all due respect, if you hit me again in the chest, I'm going to deck you.'

"At that point, Oldenburg turns and there are a whole bunch of drinking glasses on his bar area in his office, and he sweeps the glasses off and they go crashing into the ground, and there's glasses breaking and shards everywhere. It was a very bizarre scene. He's still angry and frustrated. We'd been sitting in there, and he's lecturing and now it's about 3:00. He grabs a chair and he's about to throw it out the window! Steve, who's pale-faced, grabs his arm to keep him from throwing it. The next thing you know Oldenburg's called security, and Steve and I are unceremoniously marched out by security guards and we end up on California Street in San Francisco on an early Saturday morning with nowhere to go."

"So it's just this chaotic thing. Finally, he throws us out, 'You're out; get out of my building!'" said Young. "Late at night I'm thrown out of the building. We get onto the streets of San Francisco and I go, 'So, Leigh, now what?' He goes, 'Well, you got a couple of hundred bucks. That's probably okay, isn't it?'"

"Don Klosterman meets us out there," Steinberg said. "He's hyperventilating, and I'm afraid he's going to have a heart attack."

It was not the first time that Oldenburg had lost his temper during his brief tenure as owner of the team. When informed of the likely attendance for the team's first game, he tossed four chairs in a Beverly Hills restaurant.

Young, Klosterman and Steinberg convened at Steinberg's home. "While we're at my house we started getting calls from Pete Rozelle, telling Steve to wait for the NFL," added the agent. "Then Howard Cosell calls to push the USFL. Then Roger Staubach called to push the NFL. Then Joe Namath called to push the USFL. The lobbying was getting hot and heavy because word had leaked out."

Steinberg gave the Bengals a chance to match Young's deal. "I called up Mike Brown who had the first pick in the NFL draft," Steinberg explained. "He could have signed Steve at any time because once they're done with the Super Bowl, the team with the first pick can pick at any time. I asked him if he was interested in matching something along that order. Mike Brown said, 'Oh yeah, if I found oil under Spinney Field,' their training field in Cincinnati." Cooler heads prevailed, and Young and the Express soon finalized the pact.

"The press conference was at the Beverly Wilshire Hotel, the biggest press conference I'd ever seen, partly because that's what the USFL was looking for: this impact. Steve's having second thoughts, not about playing for the league, but he's having a visceral reaction to being held up as sports economics run amok. It takes another half hour for me to coax him out of the green room. It's a huge press conference. The press conference leads the Dan Rather evening news. It's front page headlines across the country; it's the front page headline in the *L.A. Herald-Express* and the *L.A. Times*."

Young debuted at home in a 26–10 loss to New Jersey, though he finally put some spark into their anemic offense. Another loss at Denver followed, but Young led the Express to 27 points, by far their best effort early in the season. He notched his first win, 23–17 over Memphis, but they quickly lost a shootout at Chicago to fall to 3–6, four games off the pace in the Pacific with half the year gone.

To no one's surprise, Oldenburg was running out of patience. Earlier in the year, he had explained his unhappiness with the progress of the club to his rookie head coach to which Hadl responded by reminding him of the number of rookies on the team. The volatile owner then threw a plate of food at the head coach. The old quarterback tossed some of the food back at his boss before someone broke up the fracas. After the game in Denver, Oldenburg appeared on the verge of firing Hadl and shoved an Express employee who tried to calm him down. He finally backed off and decided not to attend all of his team's road games anymore.

"He was all glitz and all show and came off that way," said Argovitz. "I remember an incident with him and Don Klosterman in the owner's box one time. They got into a food fight."

Then the young squad began to put all the pieces together. As their quarterback settled into his role, the Express nipped Houston in overtime, took care of Pittsburgh, lost a close one to powerful Philadelphia, defeated Michigan and pulled out a narrow victory against Arizona to reach the .500 mark at 7–7. All of a sudden, the playoffs were within their reach.

Unfortunately, the denizens of Los Angeles didn't seem to notice. Just 11,702 came out to witness the win over Arizona which gave the team sole possession of second place in the division and tied them for the top wild card berth.

They continued their hot play by pummeling Washington, taking care of Oklahoma and holding off Oakland to clinch the division crown. Young sat out their season finale, a loss in the rematch to Arizona, in order to rest up for the franchise's first postseason clash.

Young, who completed 179 of 310 passes for 2,361 yards with ten touchdowns and nine interceptions, sparked the team's turnaround. The southpaw also ran for 515 yards on 79 tries with seven scores; all that with a late start while having to learn the offense and adjust to his new teammates in less than four weeks.

Not only one of the top passing prospects in the nation, Young was also known as a genuinely humble and likable guy. Although he could have afforded much better, he drove a 1965 Buick that police in Provo, Utah, once tried to tow because they thought it was abandoned. He was as uncomfortable being known as the $40 million man as he was with his new-found wealth.

"We were playing in Washington, and my folks came down to watch the game," Young laughed. "The BYU games weren't necessarily the same kind of crowds. This was the first time they had seen kind of a pro crowd. I go back to pass and it's pouring rain, and I haven't had this happen before or since, I go back to throw and the ball falls out of my hand, lands on my shoulder and rolls down my back. The defender runs it in for a touchdown. And you hear in the corner of the stands, '40 million down the drain!' and so it starts to get a chant up in the stands.

"I don't know this is happening. My folks are sitting, just quietly watching the game, hoping that nothing horrible happens. So my mother who can't stand these kinds of things, she hears them, '40 million down the drain!' and she stands up and yells at them, 'It's an annuity! Don't you know, it's an annuity? He's a good boy. He's a good player, you know.' These guys turn and look at her, and my dad is quietly kind of moving away. And they yell at her, 'No wonder he can't play, look at yourself!' They just attack her. She's like, 'What, me?' So, welcome the $40 million man, she's like being the $40 million mother didn't go well for her."

Rookie Kevin Nelson topped a much-improved running attack with 828 yards and seven scores of his own while JoJo Townsell led the receivers with 58 catches for 889 yards and another seven touchdowns. Tackle Lee Williams paced the defensive charge with 13 sacks, Eddie "Meat Cleaver" Weaver added 10½ and safety Troy West intercepted six passes. The Express, outscored by 35 points despite their 10–8 mark, did not have a dominating defense or an overpowering offense, but they did have a lot of good young ballplayers who gelled into one of USFL's better teams by the end of the year. Their roster still featured 30 rookies at the end of the season, including 15 who had been projected by scouts to go in the first four rounds of the NFL draft. Klosterman referred to his haul as "the greatest assemblage of talent ever."

Unfortunately, the football fans of Los Angeles failed to recognize the franchise's efforts. They averaged just 15,361 per game, hitting a low of 8,000 on March 25 against Jacksonville. Their high of an alleged 32,082 came in the season opener against Denver, but they gave more than half those tickets away and failed to even draw 20,000 to a game the remainder of the season. Even Young's signing resulted in just 100 new season ticket sales in the two days after it was announced. On the other hand, Herschel Walker's agreement with New Jersey in 1983 and Rozier's deal with Pittsburgh earlier in the year had resulted in the quick sale of thousands of tickets for their respective clubs. Oldenburg, Klosterman and Hadl had assembled one of the best young teams in football and very few people in L.A. cared. One problem was the competition for the entertainment dollar in the city. On the day Young made his pro debut, other events in the area included a Dodgers-Angels exhibition baseball game, the Long Beach Grand Prix, San Luis Rey Stakes at the Santa Anita Racetrack, the NCAA Women's Basketball Finals at UCLA and a Lakers home game.

The attendance problems were only the tip of the iceberg. The Securities and Exchange Commission was investigating Oldenburg for a real estate transaction in which he bought a piece of property for $800,000 and sold it to a savings and loan he controlled for $55 million. He had also been named in 17 fraud lawsuits stemming from a land deal in Seattle. He settled those complaints without admitting guilt after running afoul of the SEC which had continued to monitor his deals. In addition, his company, Investment Mortgage International, had far less equity capital than the bombastic owner claimed when he purchased the franchise, having lost money for four straight years before turning a modest profit in 1983. Following the season, a California bank charged him with fraud for diverting a $17.5 million letter of credit to the team and other enterprises.

"I heard the checks stopped coming to the team office in Manhattan Beach from San Francisco where IMI, Oldenburg's company, was based," said Dufresne. "That's when I first starting getting whiffs that something was wrong. They were making player payroll, but checks were being delayed and other people in the office weren't being paid. They weren't paying their landscapers and things like that; things were going awry. This was May of '84, right in the middle of their playoff run. "

The Express, one of the youngest and most talented teams in pro football, was dangerously close to becoming another expensive ward of the league.

Philadelphia Stars

The Philadelphia Stars had just one thing on their minds coming into the 1984 campaign: a championship. They had come up short against Michigan the year before and were eager for another chance at the trophy. They had little to prove following their 15–3 season and knew they would contend again, even in the new and improved USFL. What no one could have predicted was their thorough domination of the league in 1984. After two sluggish wins, they lost their first game of the year to New Jersey in week three. The defeat seemed to wake them up, and they began to play even better than they had the year before. The Stars won their next 14 games to pull well ahead of the rest of the Atlantic Division, and the league for that matter. Only the Generals, who upended them again in the season finale, were able to beat the powerful Stars.

The team had a knack for winning, much as the Washington Federals had an aptitude for losing. Instead of dropping all the close ones, Philadelphia won nearly all of them. When the defense, which always kept them in the game, had a rare off day, Chuck Fusina or Kelvin Bryant simply took charge. Just three wins away from their ultimate goal, no one wanted to face the hungry Stars in the playoffs.

As he did the first year, Bryant finished second in the USFL in rushing with 1,406 yards and 13 touchdowns despite missing three games with knee and ankle injuries.

"He was an excellent running back and an outstanding young man in character, dedication and leadership," said Philly owner Myles Tanenbaum. "It meant a lot to me personally to have him as one of our players because I really feel very strongly that he was a fine individual, representative of a number of fine individuals we had on our team."

Fusina took much of the pressure off the running back by topping the circuit in passing, connecting on 302 of 465 throws for 3,837 yards with 31 touchdowns and just nine interceptions. He spread the ball around as Willie Collier caught 56 of them for 757 yards and Scott Fitzkee made 55 catches for 895 yards. The defense was just as good as it had been the year before, if not better. They ended the season ranked first against the rush and second against the pass. Safety Mike Lush led the secondary with seven interceptions, and the addition of rookie corner back Garcia Lane steadied the unit, a questionable area before his emergence. Philadelphia finished the year tied for first in turnover differential at an impressive plus 19, with a league-high 46 takeaways.

"The defense just gelled under defensive coordinator Vince Tobin," explained Dunek. "It was led by Sam Mills and some other great defensive players: Antonio Gibson, Scotty Woerner, Mike Lush, Donny Fielder, John

The runner-up for the 1978 Heisman Trophy, quarterback Chuck Fusina joined the Philadelphia Stars following a career as an NFL backup. Photograph by Jim Turner, from Richie Franklin's collection.

Bunting, who was an anchor on the Eagles defense for years. The defense really played incredibly well."

Peterson remembered when he had built the Stars the prior year and he had to scramble to find a head coach just weeks before training camp. "As always in this position, I have a short list of who I feel are the most talented assistant coaches and coordinators in the National Football League, and I immediately went after a good friend and a guy I coached with–Jim Mora," said the general manager. "I knew about his abilities, and I also admired his coaching with the New England Patriots as the defensive coordinator. Jim put together a staff very quickly. He had coaches in mind like Dom Capers, Vince Tobin, Vic Fangio and a lot of other guys who became excellent coaches in our league.

"The key is knowing where to go for players and coaches. Perhaps we had a little better idea in that regard. Jim did a great job. I knew I wanted someone who would be a teacher on the field as well as a coach, someone who would be able to develop young players because we were a young league, and also be receptive to the fact that this wasn't going to be on the same level as the NFL. I was going to do everything possible to make it as close to that as we could in regards to training camp, travel, accommodations, facilities, and whatever else you need to win. Having coached myself, I think I have a pretty good understanding of what it takes to be successful on the field as a coach and a player. The first time around, everything we did was for the first time. We needed a guy who would be flexible enough to handle that, and Jim was able to do that exceedingly well. We put together a pretty good organization and team and started to have some terrific success."

"Our owner Myles Tanenbaum, I don't think any of us as players have any idea of the things he did back then to make sure our situation was run beautifully," related punter Sean Landeta. "He shared things with me through the years that we as players never knew that he did, but we were run first class. I remember when I went to the NFL right after the USFL, except for the 70,000 people in the stands as opposed to 25,000, and the notoriety, everything was parallel."

The notoriously tough Philadelphia sports fans who had been slow to notice the team the previous year turned out in much greater numbers during year two. The franchise averaged 28,668 at home, an improvement of more than 10,000 per game over the previous year. Michigan, their opponent in the 1983 title tilt, saw similar results. The Stars had not only turned the box office corner but also invited favorable comparisons to the NFL's Eagles in the local and national media. Their advertising invited fans to, "See football the way it ought to be played" and a private plane flying over Veterans Stadium during a game carried a banner that read, "Losing is for the Birds."

"Our very first series on offense, three straight incompletions," Peterson told *The Sporting News* after an early season game. "I heard boos then, and I smiled. I know in Philadelphia that means you've been accepted. The crowd showed that they cared."

New Orleans Breakers

The New Orleans Breakers added running back Buford Jordan and tight end Dan Ross to Coach of the Year Dick Coury's group of over-achievers. Now in the more spacious confines of the New Orleans Superdome and under new ownership, Coury and his men started their second season with a bang. Defense led the way in their first two games, both victories, and the offense received a boost when the franchise signed talented but troubled Marcus Dupree, an underclassman who had last played at Oklahoma. New owner Joe Canizaro had opened his purse strings to build a winner in his hometown.

Their potent running game and tough defense paved the way for blowouts over Memphis and Jacksonville, and Johnnie Walton combined with Frank Lockett on a scoring bomb in overtime to topple Chicago, 41–35, and push the Breakers record to 5–0. Birmingham handed them their first defeat of the year a week later, but New Orleans then took a close one over Pittsburgh to forge a tie for the Southern Division lead. After being swamped by Tampa Bay, they rebounded with a narrow win over Denver.

"We started out with a bang, and Joe spent some big money in drafting Marcus Dupree which was a huge headline," said Mazzetti. "He was a horse, he was amazing. That was starting to approach NFL quality. We were playing in the Superdome. We probably only averaged 30 or 35,000, about half capacity, but we were starting to draw some good crowds."

The rest of the schedule would not produce nearly as many victories. They won only one more game the entire season, against Michigan, as turnovers and poor offensive play took their toll. Even in their 10–3 win over the Panthers, they coughed up the ball four times. Jordan and Dupree provided a nice one-two punch, but the aging Walton had a tough time finding his targets.

The Breakers' offensive strength lay in their running game, spearheaded by Jordan's 1,276 yards and outstanding 6.0 yards per carry average. The versatile runner also caught 45 passes for another 427 yards. Dupree, hampered the entire year by minor injuries much as he had been in his brief college career, totaled 681 yards and nine touchdowns in limited action. Walton threw for 3,554 yards on 280 of 512 passing with 17 touchdowns and 19 interceptions. As expected, Ross improved the tight end position, catching 65 balls for 833 yards, while Lockett made 56 grabs for 1,199 yards for an ample 21.4-yard average and eight touchdowns. Marcus Marek led the defensive charge with six fumble recoveries, and Junior Ah You, obtained in the offseason from Arizona, added nine sacks. Tim Mazzetti continued to be one of the USFL's top kickers, hitting 21 of 27 field goals and all 35 of his extra point attempts for a total of 98 points.

The move from Boston turned out to be an unqualified success off the field as an average of 30,557 fans came out to see the Breakers games in New Orleans with a high of 45,269 for the home opener against Memphis. Once the team started losing the attendance fell off, not reaching 24,000 over the final five home dates, but even the low mark of 21,053 against Michigan was better than any crowd they had seen in Boston.

"The fan support was excellent," said Coury. "We won five games in a row, and we were averaging about 45–50,000 down there. Then we got to 7–2, and we couldn't win another game for the longest time. For a while, we had a chance to outdraw the Saints because they were struggling.

"We had the fans send in plays through one of the banks that advertised on my TV show. We encouraged fans to submit plays, and we would pick out one of those plays to run during the game. If your play was picked out, then you came on my TV show the next week to explain it. We had a lot of fun with that. We didn't go for the conventional plays, either. We always wanted something like a flea-flicker or reverse or some crazy spread, something that wasn't a normal play. We had a lot of fun with that all three years we did it, and there was a lot of talk about it. Once in New Orleans, a prisoner sent a play in. We would get maybe 100 plays a week sent to us. We'd pick one out and use it in the game, and we always used it. We'd let the people who sent them in know that we planned to use it and in what part of the game. The fans really enjoyed it. I'd do it if I were an NFL coach. One play out of 65 or 66 you get isn't going to make much of a difference. Sometimes they work better than the ones you have, anyway."

Houston Gamblers

One thing about the Houston Gamblers seemed certain: they would be exciting. Gamblers owner Jerry Argovitz never hesitated to cause a controversy whether it be with the name of his team or the attempted wooing of former client Billy Sims of the Detroit Lions. His acquisition of some great football talent, most notably quarterback Jim Kelly, showed he was serious about placing a high-quality, exciting team on Houston's AstroTurf. His squad would be the first American pro team to feature the run and shoot offense, a wide-open passing attack that featured four wide receivers, one running back and no tight ends on most plays. The main question surrounding his plans was if Kelly, who had suffered a shoulder injury at Miami that wiped out most of his senior year, could pull the trigger well enough. Argovitz made it clear he intended his team to dominate the USFL, even if his quarterback wasn't so sure about the unconventional offense at first.

"I said, 'Jim, let's go have lunch, I wanna talk to you,'" Argovitz remembered about his team's first training camp. "So him and I are having lunch and I said to him, 'You know, you and I are gonna look like the two biggest buffoons in all of professional football. We're gonna be the laughing stock.' He said, 'What do you mean?' I said, 'Number one, it looks like you're gonna wind up playing second string, and I'm the stupid one that signed you for all this money. The other quarterback is looking much better than you, and if he's much better than you, then you will be second string and I'll be looked on as not a very good businessman.' Once Jim got his competitive juices flowing, realized that that was the offense, he proved everything else in the records he wrote in all of football."

"At the beginning I didn't think it was suited for me because I wasn't a running quarterback; I was more of a pocket passer," Kelly said of the run and shoot. "Mouse Davis probably helped me make it in the NFL because I worked on my foot quickness more than I ever had. I learned how to throw on the run, and I became a better all-around quarterback."

Glenn Ellison, a high school coach in Ohio was the first to use a version of the explosive offense in 1958. Seven years later while an assistant coach under Woody Hayes at Ohio State, he wrote the book *Run and Shoot: The Offense of the Future*. Mouse Davis, Houston's offensive coordinator, incorporated Ellison's ideas as a high school coach in Oregon and took them with him to Portland State in 1975. There he took over a losing, underfunded program and turned it into an offensive juggernaut under future NFL quarterback Neil Lomax. During his senior year, Lomax led the Vikings to victories by scores of 93–7, 105–0 and 75–0. The team broke 20 Division I-AA offensive records in Davis' six-year tenure. The run and shoot required the quarterback, receivers and running backs to read the defense simultaneously with the receivers adjusting their routes on the fly. Helping guide Kelly and his receivers was coach June Jones, a former run and shoot quarterback who had played under Davis.

"Great guy to be around; a great coach and a great individual," Kelly said of Davis. "I love the guy. He was no nice, so easy to talk to. He told it the way it was. If he thought it would make you better, he told you. Sometimes as a young kid you think you know it all to a certain extent but there comes a point in your life when you really have to open up your mind and open up your ears and listen. I was able to do that with him."

"We had this drill, we'd run five guys out," remembered Davis. "You'd run four receivers out in the pattern and just bring a single back underneath, and Todd Fowler was a hell of a kid, a tough kid. He comes out, and he just flat-ass ran right over me. He didn't even see me. It scared him because he thought I was really going to be pissed. I said, 'Todd, you pretty near killed me.' Kelly thought that was the funniest thing he'd ever seen, and he couldn't stop laughing. I said, 'You no-good sucker, what are you laughing at?' He ran right over me, just flattened me. It was a pretty good lick, coming from Todd. He ran right over to me, 'Oh gosh, I'm sorry coach.' And then when Kelly started laughing then he thought it had to be okay because Kelly's laughing. Frickin' Kelly, he thought that was the funniest thing he'd ever seen."

Houston played Tampa Bay tough in their opener but dropped a 20–17 decision before smacking San Antonio the following week. Impressive offensive performances against Chicago and New Jersey spelled two more victories, but Michigan came calling with their potent passing attack and scored a 52–34 decision before Oklahoma eked out a win in overtime to knock the Gamblers to 3–3, three games behind the Panthers in the Central Division.

"Jim Kelly is a special guy," said Jones "He's one of those winners and competitors. He was struggling with it early, the first four or five games, but historically it takes four or five games, sometimes a whole season, to really get a grasp on what we were doing because it was so different than anything that was done before. Even Warren Moon, when I was with the Oilers, in the playoffs he said, 'You know, coach. I think I'm finally getting this.' He was having a Pro Bowl year, and he was just getting it. The next three or four years he shot the lights out of the National Football League. Jim Kelly was kind of the same way; it took him four or five games, but once he got it, he got it."

Kelly and company stormed right back into the race by pulling away from Washington, Oakland and Arizona, and not even consecutive overtime losses could quiet the emerging offense which proceeded to throttle Pittsburgh, Oklahoma, Jacksonville, Denver, Chicago and Memphis, with a close triumph over San Antonio in the mix. Their seven game victory streak, with an average winning margin of more than 23 points, earned them the division title and a trip to the playoffs.

"We had just installed it a year and a half earlier in Canada and took Toronto from a 2–14 record to an appearance in the Grey Cup the following year," Jones said of the run and shoot. "They lost that Grey Cup, but the next year they won it. So we had been through the transition before. The USFL, I thought, really changed the game of football. I can remember watching our guys play and get it, and see the confidence grow. That year we broke every professional record. From that standpoint I felt that we impacted the game. Not many people have the chance to change the game of professional football. I thought Mouse Davis's offense and the way we played did change the game.

"It's unbelievable how the production of quarterbacks and receivers has changed over the years just because of the impact Mouse had on the game of football itself, the schematics of how the game is played. It impacted the game itself, not just the USFL. It impacted the NFL; it impacted colleges; it impacted high schools."

Pegged early as an explosive offensive team, the Gamblers did not disappoint. They scored an incredible 618 points, a pro football record, and 79 more than the next highest

Houston Gamblers quarterback Jim Kelly drops back to pass against the San Antonio Gunslingers. A first-round draft choice of the Buffalo Bills, the former University of Miami quarterback spurned Buffalo for the USFL. Photograph by Wilf Thorne.

total in the league. Predictably, they topped the USFL in passing and total offense as well. Kelly completed 370 of 587 throws for a pro football record 5,219 yards and 44 touchdowns with 26 interceptions. He tossed at least one touchdown in every game.

"The run and shoot offense was the most explosive, exciting offense at that time in professional football," Argovitz said. "It was an offense that mainly put up points. The red zone could be on your own 20-yard line. I think Jim Kelly and our own personnel proved that. It was made up of speed. If the defender covered the inside, our receiver went outside. If they covered outside, they would go inside. There were no called, diagrammed plays, it was a read offense. The key was that you had to have the football in the quarter back's hands, by the count of 1, 1, 2, 2, 3, 3, the ball had to go. We put together this offense, and it was hard for the other teams to go against it because they hadn't seen it before. It was exciting, and fans today still talk about the Houston Gamblers and the most exciting, entertaining football that they've ever seen."

"They drove you nuts!" exclaimed Stars Coach Jim Mora. "The Houston Gamblers, all those little receivers, and Kelly at quarterback—it was a hard team to defend and stop. They had talent there and an excellent quarterback. They were gonna make yards and score touchdowns. It was just a different type of offense that you had to prepare for. It was tough."

Kelly became the first passer in American football to eclipse the 5,000-yard mark in passing (Warren Moon had done it twice in the CFL) and his 44 touchdown passes were the most ever in a single season until Dan Marino threw for 48 a few months later during the 1984 NFL campaign. His yardage and touchdown numbers still stand as rookie records. He totaled nine 300-yard games and added 493 yards on the ground with five touchdowns. He was one of just eight Gamblers to start every game, and he did that despite being sacked 75 times, a far less desired league record. Kelly credited Davis for his quick mastery of the run and shoot.

"All I knew about Mouse before he came in was: Portland State, Neil Lomax and how much he threw the football, how much he loved to throw the ball, and then automatically for me, I automatically thought touchdowns, yardage, winning, and playing in a dome," said Kelly "If you're going to throw the football, you want to play somewhere where the elements are in your favor and I had it all. And then he brought in these little guys, that we called the Mouseketeers: Ricky Sanders who played in the Super Bowl with the Washington Redskins when they won, I think he broke a record, Gerald McNeil, wound up being called the 'Ice Cube,' played with the Cleveland Browns. Richard Johnson caught close to 100 passes in the NFL with I think the Detroit Lions, and it was fun; unbelievable fun."

"We had some really good receivers," added Argovitz. "They were unknown players, most of them, but they had speed. They were little guys, but Gerald 'Ice Cube' McNeil weighed in at about 135 pounds soaking wet. We had a guy named 'Duce' [Richard] Johnson, who was our S back. He was a slot back basically, and he had great hands, fast. We had tremendous speed. We had four guys on our team that could run a 40-yard dash under 4.4, which is world-class speed. They could have been in the Olympics as a relay team."

"Jim is a great kid," said Davis. "He had a great relationship with his receivers, and he had almost a linebacker's personality. You'd knock the shit out of him, and he'd get right back up, ready to go. He was a tough kid with a great arm, great touch. He did have that relationship with his receivers that made him the quarterback he was. No question about it. He came from a family where his brothers were all linebackers, and he easily could have been a linebacker. But his daddy had made him throw from the time he was a little kid. He just threw the ball and threw the ball. He said sometimes he'd go home, and he knew his dad was going to make him throw, and he'd almost want to cry. I asked him, 'How do you feel about it now?' 'Pretty good.' He was a great guy. If you don't like Kelly, you're probably a bad guy."

That fleet group benefited most of all from the rookie passer's stellar season. Richard Johnson set a pro football record with 115 receptions for 1,455 yards and 15 touchdowns. Ricky Sanders joined him with 100 catches for 1,378 yards and 11 scores, and Todd Fowler ran for 1,003 yards on 170 tries, a 5.9-yard average and 11 touchdowns. Though limited by injury for nearly half the season, Sam Harrell gained 697 yards and 14 scores.

"Get them the football and let them run with it," laughed Kelly. "That's pretty much what the run and shoot was all about: quick passes almost like the K-Gun that we ran, like what Tom Brady runs, get these little guys who can run with the football and let them do their magic."

"The biggest challenge was always the perception that you couldn't win with it," said Jones of the run and shoot. "We changed that by proving that you could win with it. We always talked about the passing game and throwing the ball with four wideouts. Everybody said, 'You gotta be able to run the ball to win championships.' Well, we always kept that part of the offense quiet, but when you look at that part of the offense, Todd Fowler ran for over 1,000 yards and Sam Harrell had a bunch, too. They can say what they want, but we ran the ball well and we got it in the end zone. Even though we talk about the pass, running the football was a big part of the run and shoot."

On special teams, Toni Fritsch led all scorers with 130 points, hitting 21 of 26 field goal attempts, while McNeil and Clarence Verdin proved to be a deadly duo on punt and kickoff returns, respectively. Corner back Will Lewis paced the team with eight interceptions and Pete Catan tied for second in the league with 16 sacks. Nose tackle Tony Fitzpatrick added 13 and end Cleveland Crosby contributed 11 and a half.

"We set every pro record that had ever been made with the precision we had," Mouse Davis said. "Of course, Kelly was great, and we had a bevy of receivers. At that time, it was kind of new that we were running four wides in the spread. The things that we were doing weren't common at that time, so we had great success. And it was a fun group. We had some talented players and a talented quarterback who lit it up pretty well."

"Argovitz in Houston put that team together," recalled Camera. "It was sensational because he knew as an agent where all the bodies were buried. He put Mouse Davis in who was nuts but it was a great team to watch. Jimmy Kelly was just a great guy for the league."

The Gamblers averaged 28,152 fans at home with a high mark of 38,754 on March 26 against Michigan. They followed that one with just 16,710 against Washington, their season low, but did not fall below the 20,000 mark the rest of the year. Of more concern was the growing animosity among Houston's three principal owners: Jerry Argovitz, Alvin Lubetkin and Bernard Lerner. The three argued on the best way to run the team, and Argovitz's penchant for publicity caused further problems. The rock group ZZ Top had reportedly negotiated for Lerner's 29.25 percent share before Jay Roulier, a Denver real estate developer, decided to buy it.

Chicago Blitz

The Chicago Blitz should have been one of the favorites to win the 1984 USFL title. They should have returned 1,000-yard backs Tim Spencer and Kevin Long, spectacular wideout Trumaine Johnson and seasoned veteran quarterback Greg Landry. They should have brought back the USFL's top-rated defense and legendary coach George Allen. But former owner Ted Diethrich took the coach and most of the players and headed for the deserts of Arizona where they became the new Arizona Wranglers. Meanwhile, the Blitz had been replaced by a core of former Wranglers, a few ex–Chicago Bears, and a host of unknowns who would be playing under new head coach Marv Levy, an NFL and CFL veteran. In fact, the team considered itself an expansion squad as just 16 members of the Wranglers and four members of the Blitz remained to start the season. Their new owner, Dr. James Hoffman, had been forced to abandon the ship in January and the franchise had been taken over by the league. Nearly the entire front office had been fired, assuring a limited marketing presence in the city. One thing was for sure, this group, dubbed the "Blanglers," was no favorite to win the 1984 championship.

"We drafted the same big-name guys who were being drafted in the NFL, but we couldn't compete at all to sign them," Levy said. "When the doctor dropped out, the league took over and it was just being supported by the league to keep the team there, so they weren't putting any more into it than it took just to get by. We had to do what we had to do the best we could."

"We were playing the Chicago Blitz, and it was Memorial Day, and it was the coldest, nastiest Memorial Day," recalled Generals head of public relations Kevin MacConnell. "We had snow, rain, it was nasty. I remember we played and there was nobody there. After the game, Brian Sipe, and it was probably a line he stole from somebody, said, 'I was going to put my hands up to quiet the crowd, but there was nobody there.' One of the other guys said, 'We should have just introduced ourselves to the fans. It would have saved time.' They announced the attendance at like 4,108, and our reporters all moaned, 'No, no way.' There was an injured player on the Blitz in the press box, and he turned to our guys and said, 'In Chicago, the four is silent.' It really looked like there were 108 people there."

The team's troubles kept the league office occupied especially early in the year. Concerned that money woes would keep the Blitz from playing their first game, the league dispatched Steve Ehrhart to head off any trouble.

"Chicago opened the season at Michigan, and Michigan was coming off a great championship year," he recalled. "They had a very nice crowd at the Silverdome, and I remember going to the game. There was a terrible snowstorm, but the reason I went was that I had a backpack full of cash because we were concerned that there would be some kind of a crisis with the Chicago team. I had maybe $20,000-$25,000 or so. We were cognizant of ten years before with the World Football League with the sheriff trying to grab uniforms or something like that. The Chicago team was, from a financial standpoint, imploding. I remember trying to get from the airport to the Pontiac Silverdome, I was in a cab and the roads were blocked. It took like four or five hours to get there because of the snow and ice. Fortunately, there was no crisis.

"By that time we knew we were going to operate the Chicago team from the league office through the year. I had the money as an emergency reserve in case there would have been a problem, but there never was. It was never publicly acknowledged. We had so many great things happening, we didn't want to have some crisis such as somebody not pay the bus driver or something like that."

Disagreements in managing the ward of the league became heated at times. At one point, Levy got into a shouting match with Carl Marasco, who was overseeing the team's finances for the league. Levy felt that Marasco was butting into personnel matters that had nothing to do with the club's bottom line. Unbeknownst to Levy and personnel director Bill Polian, Marasco traded wide receiver Jackie Flowers, one of the Blitz's best performers, to Pittsburgh, leading to a standoff that nearly resulted in Levy's dismissal. After an appeal to Chet Simmons, the two men patched up their differences.

"Carl Marasco was supposedly only going to handle the financial aspects of it, but boy, he jumped in and started trading players and everything else," said Levy. "I called the commissioner's office and asked what was going on. The commissioner told him to back off and just handle the finances."

"Basically we were operating the team," Ehrhart said of the league office. "Carl Marasco actually moved to Chicago during the year, but having consummate professionals like Marv Levy and Bill Polian there certainly helped. I give Bill and Marv great credit. I could tell Bill was going to be a super executive. When you don't have any money, and you're trying to operate on a very limited 'have-to-have' budget, he was able to put together a representative team and make it work as if there wasn't any lava underneath the volcano when it could have spilled over at any time.

"Carl was there tasked with trying to get through with the least amount of expenditure and of course, there was always going to be pressure to be first class, have a winning operation and be competitive with teams like the New Jersey Generals or Michigan Panthers, teams that had plenty of resources. There certainly were clashes there, but overall the three of them did a terrific job under very difficult circumstances."

"Basically, we got through it by laughing our way through," Levy recalled. "They couldn't even buy toilet paper, so at Christmas Bill and I gift-wrapped toilet paper and distributed it to everybody in the organization. There was a good group of guys playing for us, too. They understood it pretty well and were cooperative and played hard. We were competitive. It was a good group, and I see some of them now and then on the street. We stayed pretty well-focused. Despite the difficulties, internally we worked well with each other—Bill, John [Butler) and I and the rest of the coaching staff.

"You were so aware of things like turning out the lights to avoid running up the electric bill. Fortunately, we were able to laugh about it because we weren't poverty stricken. We weren't starving."

"Once the league made the commitment to keep it going, and that's why we sent Carl out there, it ran fairly well, but it was hard," added Ehrhart. "The guys, Marv, Bill and the players, too, get great credit. It was a situation that not only had training tape around the ankles but around the whole franchise."

"When I arrived here with Ron Potocnik, who I liked very much, he asked me for a recommendation on a director of player personnel," recalled Levy. "I mentioned some guy who was up in Canada named Bill Polian. We hired Bill as our director of player personnel. I had coached in the mid–1970s with Montreal in the Canadian league, and we had one director of player personnel, that's all you had in the entire department. He asked our owner, and our owner said, yes, he could hire three guys he knew part-time down in the states to scout NFL training camps, and we'd try to pick up late cuts. One of the three he hired, and I didn't meet him, was Bill Polian. When I read any of those reports, I said to our director, 'Who is this guy? Man, he's sharp.' I got to meet Bill and when I went to Kansas City, I interceded on his behalf and he became a scout for us there. Later he went up to Winnipeg as the director of player personnel for the Winnipeg Blue Bombers. Then when I went to the Blitz, I recommended him to Ron Potocnik, and we hired him. Among the scouting staff that preceded me with the Blitz was a scout who did not want to move to Arizona. He was an Illinois guy and asked if he could stay on. George Allen told me he was outstanding, so we kept him on and made him our director of player personnel. His name was John Butler, who later became quite an executive in the NFL."

Levy's efforts kept the team surprisingly competitive in its five losses that opened the year. Late field goals had twice doomed their efforts, and they dropped another game in overtime. They nipped Washington to end their skid and made it two in a row in overtime over San Antonio. Following a loss to Philadelphia, they conquered L.A. in a shootout, before a pair of losses halted their momentum. After that, they managed to top Denver, but could win only more game, that over faltering Oklahoma.

"Marv was different than George [Allen)," Kojich said of the Blitz's two coaches. "George liked the spotlight. That was part of it with him, he enjoyed it. He always talked about not letting it take away from football, but he understood it. Marv wasn't as comfortable in the spotlight. Marv was very cerebral, a very intelligent man."

"The same things won there that won in the NFL," said Levy. "If you run, throw, block, tackle, catch and kick better than your opponent, you're going to win. You realized that they were getting a paycheck, yes, but most of these guys were playing for the love of the game. They weren't going to blow you away with their salaries like they do now in the NFL. They were hard-working and were happy to be playing football. We had a few former Bears stars such as Vince Evans and Doug Plank. They played real hard, and they were a good group."

The team had played its last and would officially fold on July 1, with the Chicago market taken over by new ownership. Levy had done a remarkable job assembling a squad that was at least competitive for much of the year even though he had less time, and certainly less money, to do so than even the expansion teams. The franchise received little if any cash to replace injured players down the stretch, partly accounting for their poor finish. Vince Evans completed 200 of 411 throws for 2,624 yards with 14 touchdowns and 22 interceptions, while Larry Canada gained 915 yards on the ground for the surprisingly decent rushing attack. Marcus Anderson, the team's most consistent offensive threat, topped the squad with 50 catches for 940 yards. The defense was terrible most of the time, surrendering 466 points, second most in the league. They ended the season as the worst unit in the USFL against the run and third from the bottom versus the pass. The Blitz finished minus 15 in turnover differential thanks to a league-low 30 take-aways. Jeff Gossett at least made it slightly more difficult on opposing offenses by leading the USFL in punting with a 42.5-yard average.

Chicago's 1984 attendance was simply pathetic. The offseason roster changes, front office problems and media indifference, not to mention almost complete lack of a marketing staff resulted in an average crowd of just 7,455 with a high of only 11,713 in April for the game against Steve Young and Los Angeles. Not even 6,000 turned out for any of the final three home dates with a low of 4,307 in May for the New Jersey contest. What just a year earlier had looked like the league's strongest franchise had spent its second season under the wing of the league office and would not play another game.

"Crowds were very sparse," Levy concurred. "The team wasn't strong, the better team from the year before left and the 1984 Blitz was just hanging on. The league wanted to maintain it so that all the scheduling and everything else that they had in place didn't fall apart. I used to joke that if you came to the game, you'd have a seat at the 50-yard line. Everybody could have one.

"You never knew if the league would blossom the way the old AFL did. We hoped that there would be a buyer at the end of the year. There were people who looked at it, even the White Sox owners were expressing a lot of interest in buying the team at one time, and that would have been good. We were just hopeful that things would get better, and it wasn't anything I was going to run away from."

San Antonio Gunslingers

The San Antonio Gunslingers looked from the beginning to be one of the league's weakest organizations. The coaching staff was a question mark and the strange machinations of the front office throughout training camp did little to inspire confidence. The only draftee the team signed was quarterback Rick Neuheisel, a rookie out of UCLA who had spent less than one season as a starter in college before leading the Bruins to an improbable Rose Bowl victory, earning him MVP honors in the process. Wide receiver Danny Buggs who had played well with the Bandits in 1983 was the only other offensive player of note. The inexperience extended to the front office, which irascible owner Clinton Manges had assembled.

"Here was a good ol' boy who was given the opportunity to have a professional football team in San Antonio," remembered league PR man Jim Byrne. "He did not have a front office that understood what they were doing. They were in trailers in a parking lot, which were their offices."

"Our general manager, a guy by the name of Roger Gill, who was a great guy, but hadn't had a lot of experience doing this, walked in one time and said, 'What are you guys watching?'" Neuheisel recalled. "And we were watching practice film. He goes, 'Y'all watch practice, y'all film practice?' And we looked around, 'Yeah, we film practice.' 'Boy I bet you could learn a lot from that.' There's a guy who's got it figured out.

"Another time our lead executives came in and said, 'What color should be the visitor helmets?' He thought we had to supply equipment to the visiting team. 'They bring their own gear.' 'Really? Well that will save us some money.' It was an interesting group of guys that just decided football might be a fun little adventure."

"Our president, Bud Haun, turned to our equipment manager before the first season and asked, 'Now how many helmets and what color do we have to buy for the visiting teams?'" laughed assistant coach Tim Marcum. "He was a banker, and he and Manges had a bank together, Groos National Bank. They had already got a bunch of people's money in San Antonio with a bad banking thing. He sued everybody, Manges did."

Like Arizona the year before, the Gunslingers got a late start in assembling their team. They found their coach early enough but had to fight the local school board to gain access to Alamo Stadium, expending considerable time and effort in the process. The rough beginning manifested itself in four straight losses in which they scored just 36 points over the stretch but were blown out only once. From there, though, San Antonio played respectable, tough football, compiling a 7–7 record the rest of the way with a win over Arizona and narrow losses to Philadelphia and Houston in the mix.

Even with their credible play, the franchise displayed a penchant for making itself look foolish at times. Manges quickly developed a dislike/hate relationship with the local media, causing his public relations staff numerous headaches. Following their slow start, they fired their offensive coordinator and nearly lost their defensive coordinator in protest over the move. In the most public slip-up, the lights went out at Alamo Stadium during an ESPN game, causing a lengthy delay.

"I went out to cover Clinton's second home game, San Antonio playing Houston," remembered Camera. "It was held at a stinking high school field. The locker rooms were minuscule. You had these enormous guys, no air conditioning, and people were sweating like animals. You had guys out on the field with guns, real guns, dressed as the San Antonio Gunslingers, and they're shooting the guns in the air. I thought, 'What the hell is going on?' I'd traveled with him for a bit after we signed him, and Jimmy Kelly looks at me and said, 'Dom, these guys are crazy.' I told him, 'Jimmy, I don't know what's going on, but we're in trouble.' I went over to Mouse Davis, and he said, 'I'm not going on the field. These guys are nuts!' There were gunshots, cannons and high school cheerleaders. Clinton got a good deal on the field.

"So we started to play. They got temporary lights, and we're playing the ESPN game of the week. Everybody wanted to see Kelly play. And the lights go out. All power goes down. It's now pitch black, and the fans are all tanked up. You can't move. So I took the teams off the field. I was the league representative, so I said, 'Get them off the field.' About 45 minutes later they got up temporary power, and we finished the game. I don't know how television looked, but it was still kind of dark out."

"First of all, we had a hell of a time getting back into the locker room, so we had to screw around outside for a little while," remembered Houston offensive coordinator Mouse Davis. "Finally about the time we got in, it was time to go back out again. I said, 'Here's what we're going to do, we're going to go right back out there and score.' And we did."

"I was in the press box, and we came down when the teams went back into the locker rooms," added Marcum. "We were playing Houston on national TV. It was quite embarrassing, but it was kind of typical of our time in San Antonio."

"Monday night football in San Antone," chuckled Neuheisel. "I later found out what actually happened. Clinton Manges had all kinds of business dealings around town and some were above board and some I guess were not. And in some way, shape or form he had crossed the guy in charge of the power in San Antonio, and so the guy, to get even, shut it down while they were on national television in his first game. It was just supposed to be some power outage and an accident, but later I found out this was a comeuppance to our owner, to just make sure that he wasn't going to treat this guy like that again."

A punchless air game hampered the team all year, as they ended the season second from the bottom in team passing. Neuheisel completed 211 of 383 throws for 2,542 yards with 14 touchdowns and 15 interceptions. Although Scott Stamper led the team with just 500 yards on the ground, they still finished in the middle of the pack with 2,213 rushing yards thanks to strong contributions from Marcus Bonner, Mike Hagen and George Works. The "Bounty Hunter" defense gave up a few passing yards but topped the USFL with 31 interceptions, five each by Peter Raeford, Maurice Tyler and Rodney "Rock" Richmond. End Mike St. Clair led the unit with eight and a half sacks. The Gunslingers lined up in a unique 4–2–5 defensive alignment which handed a lot of responsibility to linebackers Putt Choate and Rich D'Amico. The defense which finished third in stopping the run even had its own song, "The Ballad of the Bounty Hunters," that was played at Alamo Stadium. Mike Ulmer ended the year second in the league with a punt return average of 11.2 yards, while former NFL kicker Nick Mike-Mayer connected on 21 of 27 field goal attempts.

The team averaged just 15,444 fans for the home schedule, but had drawn three of their top five crowds in their final three games with a high of 21,625 for the year-ender against Oklahoma. Their low came in their week four matchup with Los Angeles when just 9,821 showed up.

"Clinton Manges was the owner, the infamous Clinton Manges," Neuheisel recalled. "He has an interesting reputation there in South Texas. You know our stadium was Alamo stadium, which was really a high school stadium. And the league had a rule that you had to have 32,000 seats to be a stadium in this league. Well Alamo Stadium really held 18,000. So they put seven thousand folding chairs in each end zone. Fortunately, Clinton did splurge and make them team colors so we had green and blue folding chairs in each endzone."

"I remember that every time it rained, the water would pour down in our meeting room," recalled Marcum. "They had gone in and added some offices under the stadium. To say the least, it was very spartan."

"We fly down in this charter that looked like it flew in World War II," recalled LA Express quarterback Steve Young. "So we get down to San Antonio in May. It's gotta be 100 degrees; never been hotter in my whole life playing football. And it was this kind of a high school field with these stone stands that you kinda climb up and sit on. In the ends they created all these extras places to sit, because I guess the USFL had a minimum-seating requirement. So they had to put out all these folding chairs, like 10,000 folding chairs out there that were never going to be sat in, but you had to have them or else you couldn't hold the game. So we get down there and we start warming up and it is just brutally hot. I mean it's like scary. And so we get playing, and I remember the old Nike turf shoes back then with the big black sole. We came off the field and one of our receivers, all of a sudden his shoe, the glue between the black and the shoe essentially came off, and he says, 'My shoe just melted.' I mean stuff like that, you just can't believe: a shoe that literally melted off it was so hot."

From the start, the franchise had faced an uphill credibility battle, mostly due to Manges' less than stellar reputation. The team had a difficult time generating positive press and had instead established a combative relationship with local reporters. Their press releases frequently arrived days after the game they were promoting because the club was trying to save postage costs by sending them out in bulk rather than first class. Operating out of a trailer and mobile home as their offices, the Gunslingers hardly looked like a professional organization and made an easy target for those looking for a reason to criticize the USFL.

"He was kind of a brash guy," Marcum said of Manges. "You had to do it his way. He was a big, tough-talking guy. He got into it with some newspaper guys. He locked them out and wouldn't give them press credentials, so they bought tickets and sat in the stands."

Other strange events surrounded the team. Dodge gave away a car at each USFL game, and when the Gunslingers public address announcer divulged the winner during the Houston game, he stunned the crowd by saying, "Tonight's winner of the 1984 Dodge Charger is … oh, my God, it's me!" The fans chanted "fix," but he had indeed bought the winning ticket.

Arizona Wranglers

The Arizona Wranglers ceased being patsies the moment Dr. Ted Diethrich bought the franchise and transferred coach George Allen and the talent-laden Chicago Blitz roster to the Valley of the Sun. The club had finished 12–6 the year before with only a heartbreaking overtime loss standing between them and the championship game. Allen expected more success in Arizona, stating in local radio ads, "We aren't going to lose. I won't allow it."

"I along with Jeff Kiewel, an offensive tackle that played at U of A, were the only two people of the original Wranglers who were kept behind when they switched the franchises," said quarterback Alan Risher. "I think they cut him in training camp there, so I was the only one left during the year. I had made an impression on Coach Allen the year before, so he wasn't going to let me go to Chicago. I backed up Greg Landry and actually started three games. I had my moments in some spot duty, but never hit the field full time."

Allen's squad struggled to find their way for much of the season. They walloped Oakland, Washington and Oklahoma in the early going but fell to Tampa Bay, Michigan, Denver and Philadelphia along the way. Arizona displayed an alarming penchant to look like world beaters one game and patsies the next. They stumbled to the halfway mark at 4–5 by taking out New Jersey and then falling at Houston.

Few of Allen's fellow USFL coaches were shedding any tears for him. He had been handed a big budget and used it to assemble a team many of them would love to have had. Oklahoma's Woody Widenhofer and Denver's Craig Morton were two of his most vocal detractors. Morton even refused to do an interview with an Arizona radio station because he did not want to do anything that could help Allen.

Another loss, a head-scratcher to San Antonio, dropped them three games off the Pacific Division pace. The Wranglers responded by dropping just one more game that season to record a 10–8 record, good enough for a wild card slot in the postseason, just as they had done as the Blitz a year prior. Down the stretch, they won meetings with fellow playoff teams Birmingham and Los Angeles.

"He was a very unique individual," Risher said of Allen. "He came to us toward the end of his coaching career. He was very eccentric. I thought he was a defensive genius, however, he was a little paranoid in a lot of cases, relative to coaching staffs working long hours, making sure nobody was spying and all kind of crazy stuff. It was really a wild experience. George was a defensive genius. He had his own little idiosyncrasies about a lot of things.

"We'd have a team meeting at 10:00, and he'd always show up at 10:20, 10:25, like the grand entrance of a king coming into the room. He'd always name drop. He'd say he just got off the phone with President Reagan or Chet Simmons or whoever. It was funny because we always knew it was coming. But he treated you like men, treated you like pros. He worked you long hours. Our practices were close to three hours long; we were out there a long time. I remember one night during the summer time when it got hot out there we were practicing in the evening so we could beat the heat. Somehow, we had an electrical outage one night at East High School in Phoenix where we had our facility. He made us all get in our cars and drive around the track that surrounded the practice field and shine our headlights on the field so we could finish practice. Balls were banging off people's heads and stuff. It was comical. He was nuts like that."

A 10–8 record was far below the expectations of league observers and certainly those of George Allen. It was even more mystifying when one considers that Arizona allowed the second fewest points at 284 and scored the third most with 502. A look at their injury list helped to clear up some of the confusion. The secondary in particular was hit hard as only Luther Bradley started every game during the year. Corner back Frank Minnifield missed four games with ankle and groin injuries, fellow corner Carl Allen sat out the first seven with a separated shoulder and strong safety Bruce Laird failed to take the field for five contests due to a knee injury. In addition, dangerous wideout Wamon Buggs played only five games and missed the rest of the season after an injury. The Wranglers also frequently hurt themselves. They were far and away the league's most penalized team.

Tim Spencer and Kevin Long again joined the dual 1,000-yard club with 1,212 yards and 17 touchdowns and 1,010 yards and 15 scores, respectively. Ageless wonder Greg Landry completed 283 of 449 throws for 3,534 yards with 26 touchdowns and 15 interceptions. Trumaine Johnson topped the receiving corps with 90 catches for 1,268 yards and 13 scores, while Lenny Willis caught 48 for 814 yards. The passing offense benefited from the addition of quarterback coach Roman Gabriel who had worked with the Breakers the year before. The defense, ranked tops in the league overall, continued its solid play with the exception of a few fourth-quarter collapses. In particular, they finished as the USFL's stingiest group against the pass. They recorded a league-high 73 sacks for 558 yards in losses thanks to their terrific front known as the Rushmen. John Lee led the USFL with 20 sacks, and Karl Lorch contributed 13.

The franchise drew an average of 25,568 fans per game to Sun Devil Stadium, nearly the same as the year before, despite their improvement. Just 12,259 turned out for an April game against San Antonio, but they drew a season-high 35,258 for the finale against Los Angeles. Diethrich needed much better turnouts to cover the bulging contracts on his team, particularly since Dr. James Hoffman who bought the Blitz from him, still owed $6.7 million of the $7.2 million purchase price, money the doctor likely would never see.

Gifted wide receiver Trumaine Johnson became a USFL All-Star with the Chicago Blitz and Arizona Wranglers, topping 1,000 yards receiving in both his seasons in the league. Photograph by Jim Turner, from author's collection.

"One of the highlights of that season was the Houston victory because a lot of people didn't think we were going to win that game," Diethrich recalled. "That was a very exciting game. Then when we had the game here and won, that was great. We ended up really pumped up. Everybody was excited, but behind the scenes things weren't so good because the economics weren't what we hoped they were going to be. We weren't sure what we were going to have in terms of contracts and support. While everybody was excited about the end of the playing season, I personally became more concerned about whether we could really make this a viable product."

Denver Gold

The Denver Gold, on the other hand, was not a team stocked with superstars. The frugality of owner Ron Blanding assured that the franchise would not be able to compete on raw talent alone in the face of his free-spending peers. Coach Craig Morton instead planned to unveil a revamped passing attack dubbed "Airborne '84" to inject some life into what had been a dull offense.

"I'll always remember when we left Arizona before the start of the second season prior to our first game in Los Angeles," remembered Blanding. "We were so together. It was obvious we had a good team and at a low payroll. It was done through real good management. We had Craig Morton at the time and he was our kind of guy. He'd sit down in the meetings and discuss the way things should be done. He was just a good employee."

True to Blanding's suspicions, Denver started out as one of the hottest teams in the league at 7–1, scoring victories over higher-priced clubs such as Los Angeles and Arizona in the process. Like any good team, they were winning the close ones, including one in overtime and another in the final minutes. Somehow, though, they lost their next five games in succession, most in listless fashion, to fall back to the rest of the Pacific pack. Desperately trying to hang in the playoff race, they managed wins over San Antonio and Oakland but lost their other three to finish out of the postseason picture when arch-rival Arizona won its finale. Denver's losing ways coincided with the sale of the franchise from original owner Blanding to Colorado automobile dealer Doug Spedding at midseason.

"He got in for a song and then sold the team the next year for $8 million because he couldn't deal with the other owners," Camera recalled of Blanding. "He was a hard-working guy. He got his hands dirty and did everything, a lot like John Bassett, but the frustration of winning and losing was eating him up. Blanding was a terrific guy, fun to be with. He would disagree with you, and then once you got him to a point, he would say, 'If it's good for the league, I'll do it.' So Blanding jumped out because he was smart. He sold it to Doug Spedding. You now went from having a very family-run kind of a team now being run by a car guy. He was gonna run it like he would be selling cars."

"We were in Commerce City, Colorado, at this little school, and the next thing you know when you called the Denver Gold you got a car place at the same time," recalled running back Harry Sydney. "'Doug Spedding Used Cars, can I help you? Denver Gold, which one do you want?'

"Doug was a good guy. I think it was 1984, and I went to the USFL bowl game in Tampa, Florida. I went representing the Denver Gold, and we were in the elevator with Doug Spedding and my wife. All of a sudden Donald Trump comes in. Donald Trump said, 'Hi,' almost like, 'Okay, little guy, if you need something, give me a call.' I thought that was cool.

"Doug Spedding got the knock because he was a used car salesman, and every time he said something, you were worried about what he was saying. But he always treated me fairly."

The late season collapse resulted in a disappointing 9–9 record after a terrific 7–1 start. Second-year man Sydney led the weak running game with 961 yards and ten touchdowns and topped all Denver receivers with 44 catches for 354 yards, while Craig Penrose led a bevy of passers by throwing for 1,984 yards with 12 touchdowns and 14 interceptions. Leonard Harris finished the year with 657 receiving yards. David Martin topped the league in punt returns with a 13.6-yard average, and Harris added 1,084 yards in kickoff returns. Defensive end Dave Stalls collected 12 ½ sacks, and Calvin Turner contributed ten for the nameless defense.

"Craig Morton was an ex-player and I think he loved the game of football," said Sydney who later went on to a coaching position with the Green Bay Packers. "But he had to deal with the business aspect instead of being a player. It was different for him because it was his first coaching job. He had the right ideas and right philosophies. I've found being a coach now, you can give the players latitude in a lot of things if they can handle it. But if they can't handle it, you've got to do some other things. I think he thought that everyone could handle it the way he did when he was player. We had a lot of young guys who couldn't handle it."

The average attendance at Denver fell by nearly 8,000 from the year before to 33,953 per game which still was not at all bad for the USFL. But two games early in the season drew fewer than 20,000 spectators. The franchise had not seen a crowd under 30,000 the year before. Worse yet, the Gold had won just two of nine home games in two seasons in which they had drawn over 40,000 fans. It seemed the bigger the crowd, the worse the team performed.

"I don't want to be one to criticize Spedding, but I think it all starts at the top," said Blanding. "Every company does. You get what you create. If you don't create it, it's your fault. When Spedding took over, he made some changes. I mean he opened the players' mail and he did some things that hastened the slide a little bit. I think that's the kind of thing that destroys camaraderie. I don't think the operation was as together. You don't have to have the best players, but you've got to have the best operation."

Memphis Showboats

Memphis, Tennessee, had long sought an NFL team and had sat without pro football since the failure of the WFL and John Bassett's Memphis Southmen in 1975. For a while it looked like the new Showboats might never get off the ground as original owner Logan Young, Jr., became overwhelmed by the expenses of running a USFL franchise. Fortunately, cotton magnate William Dunavant stepped in and took control of the fledgling club. Less was known about the team they would field. The defense appeared solid with blue chip rookie Reggie White, but the offense had failed to put the ball into the end zone in two preseason games. Coach Pepper Rodgers, however, vowed to keep things entertaining.

"I've always wanted to coach a pro football team because I wanted to see if I had to play by their rules," said the coach. "I don't intend to play somebody else at their game when I know they're better than I am. I ask you, how do you beat Philadelphia when you do what they're doing? You don't. You don't have a chance."

He used some unconventional methods to convince players to join his team rather than the NFL. "When I bring in a player, I take him out for a big spare ribs dinner, show him Memphis and take him to my big ol' house overlooking the beautiful Mississippi," he told *Sport* magazine. "Then I ask him, 'Boy, do you *really* want to play in *Buffalo*?'"

"The laid-back style of the 'Boats reflected the personality of Coach Pepper Rodgers," wrote Reggie White in *In the Trenches*. "Everything about Coach Rodgers was laid-back— his wildly mismatched clothes, his unruly hair, and his shoes worn without socks. He had a laid-back way of talking, a laid-back style of coaching, and friendly, inspiring style of motivating his players, which contrasted with the loud, raucous, and even abusive style of many other coaches. As a football strategist, he was rambunctious, unpredictable, and daring—sometimes pulling a running or passing play out of a hat in punt situations. The other teams never knew what to expect from Pepper and his Showboats."

After playing Philadelphia tough, they posted their first victory over Chicago in week two but then lost six of their next seven to fall well out of the race in the Southern

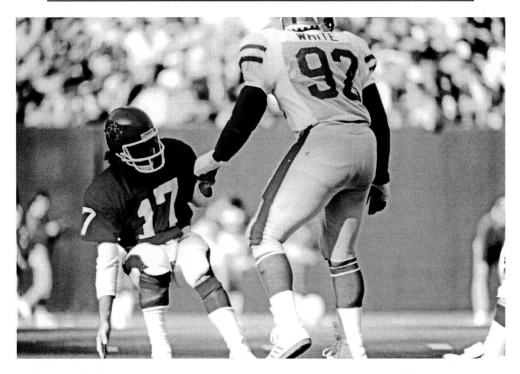

Rookie Memphis Showboats defensive lineman Reggie White helps veteran New Jersey Generals quarterback Brian Sipe off the ground in this Sunday, April 8, 1984, matchup. Photograph by Jim Turner, from author's collection.

Division. Limping along at 2–7, they played much better ball the second half of the year, rolling up a three-game winning streak against Pittsburgh, Washington and San Antonio and adding victories over Tampa Bay and New Orleans to finish with a 7–11 mark.

Memphis lost one game when running back Alan Reid was tackled in the end zone for a safety in a 12–10 decision against Jacksonville. "It was a draw," remembered Reid. "I was handed the ball at the 15 and was hit right at the handoff. I broke the tackle and spun to my right at the 10. I broke two more tackles, spun around to the left and found I was in the end zone. By this time I had broken about six tackles. I looked back and saw the linebacker there, but I anticipated Walter Lewis making the block. I knew if he made that block I could get the sideline. I had the sideline, but he didn't make the block.

"I asked Walter, 'Why didn't you make the block?' and he said, 'I was afraid I was going to clip the guy. I was like, 'Thanks a lot, Walter!'

"The worst part was the next day I had to appear on the Pepper Rodgers show and listen to coach call me 'Wrong-way Reid' the whole time. It was a very humbling experience."

Rodgers would not let him forget it, either. Later in the week, the two were to be interviewed on a local radio show. After they showed up late, the coach quipped, "I would have been here earlier, but Alan got lost on the way."

The 'Boats hosted Birmingham in their final home game of the year, the USFL's second sellout, which the local media and the Showboats dubbed the "Revenge Bowl" because they had been beaten so soundly in Birmingham earlier in the year. The mayors of the two cities placed a bet on the outcome. The Memphis mayor offered a weekend vacation for two in his city if the Stallions won. The Stallions proved too much for Memphis again, but the raucous crowd provided plenty of hope for the Showboats' future.

Rookie signal caller Walter Lewis completed 161 of 276 passes for 1,862 yards, 15 touchdowns and ten interceptions before being shelved with a finger injury. Former Bandits backup Mike Kelley filled in admirably, clicking on 82 of 120 throws for 1,014 yards with eight scores and six interceptions. Reid topped the running game with 723 yards, while Lewis added 552 yards. Dangerous Derrick Crawford caught 61 balls for 703 yards and a dozen touchdowns, while tight end Gary Shirk, who had also played for Memphis in the WFL, made 57 catches for 604 yards. Crawford topped the league in kickoff returns with 1,237 yards and a 26.3-yard average. The defense struggled with only 15 interceptions on the year, second worst in the league. Reggie White led the club with 12 sacks despite missing three games with an ankle injury.

"One time Reggie went to a store and bought a ton of socks," remembered Rodgers. "He thought it was like it was when he was back in college, and somebody was going to give them to him. He bought 50 pair. I don't think he thought he was buying them. He thought they were giving them to him, and he got a bill for 50 pair of socks. All the DJs were making fun of him and saying, 'We got Reggie. Bring some socks to the game so he'll have more socks.' Reggie was so upset, his mother was so upset.

"I bought a bunch of socks and told him before the game, 'Here's what I'm going to do, Reggie. I'm going to give one sock to everybody on the defensive team, which we'll introduce tonight, and you'll be introduced last. And you'll run out with about 20 socks in your hands. You run around the stadium throwing those socks up in the stands, and they will love you. We'll call our defense the Sock Exchange.'

"I told him that people can't make fun of you if you make fun of yourself. He was always a good-time guy. It was just something where they were poking fun at him and he was embarrassed. It came out fine."

"Reggie White was a great player for the Memphis Showboats," Philadelphia Stars Coach Jim Mora recalled. "I mean we didn't have hardly anyone who could block him one on one. We had to prepare to really zero in on Reggie White."

The USFL had found a receptive market in Memphis. After drawing two crowds under 20,000 in their first four games at home, the franchise averaged 34,349 over the final five home dates. All told, the club drew an average of 27,599, highlighted by a sellout in their last home appearance.

"The fans were great," Reid remembered. "We had great support for the team from the fans. It was a very positive experience living in Memphis."

Tampa Bay Bandits

The Tampa Bay Bandits entered the 1984 campaign with few changes but with high hopes of eclipsing their 11–7 mark of the year before. The addition of Gary Anderson midway through their inaugural season had added even more offensive firepower to one of the league's most exciting teams, and only injuries to their top two quarterbacks stood between them and a 1983 player berth. Now, the Bandits wanted to march to the second USFL title game, which was to be held in Tampa Stadium.

Steve Spurrier's club opened its second year with wins over Houston, Arizona and Jacksonville, all by a field goal. Three consecutive losses, due in large part to a running game that could not get on track, dropped them back to .500. They rebounded quickly by whipping Oakland, New Orleans, Michigan, Washington, Jacksonville, Oklahoma and New Orleans again. They dominated the competition over the seven-game stretch, winning by more than 21 points per contest. Their 48–21 dismantling of the Oklahoma Outlaws was particularly pleasing to Tampa Bay fans because former Buccaneers quarterback Doug Williams saw the worst of the action.

A loss to Memphis only temporarily interrupted their impressive string before the Bandits pasted New Jersey, 40–14, and then gained revenge on Memphis with a 42–24 blowout. Upset that Memphis coach Pepper Rodgers had surprised him with an onside kick in the loss to the Showboats, Spurrier bested Rodgers with a pair of successful onside attempts in the winning rematch. Although the Bandits offense slowed down a bit, they closed out the year with wins over Pittsburgh and Birmingham to clinch a wild card spot behind Birmingham in the Southern Division. Tampa Bay entered the playoffs as one of the hottest and most explosive clubs in the USFL.

Not surprisingly, the offense led the way. Fullback Greg Boone beat out Gary Anderson for the team rushing lead, 1,009 yards to 1,008, but Anderson also ran in 19 scores compared to Boone's eight. John Reaves overcame some early turnover troubles to headline the circuit's second deadliest passing game with 313 completions in 544 attempts for 4,092 yards with 28 touchdowns and 16 interceptions. Eric "E.T." Truvillion topped the receivers with 70 catches for 1,044 yards and nine touchdowns, Marvin Harvey also caught 70 balls for 938 yards and nine scores and Anderson contributed 66 catches for 682 yards and a pair of six-pointers. End Mike Butler, who had jumped from the Green Bay Packers, topped the defense with 11 sacks while Mike Clark added eight and a half.

"They always had a good offense," recalled Panthers quarterback Bobby Hebert. "They had a guy who was unbelievable, Gary Anderson. They called him "Freaky GA." He had a Jheri curl; he was like the old school Darren Sproles with all the yards after the catch. I remember how good he was."

The fans of the Tampa Bay area continued to be some of the most loyal in the USFL, turning out to an average of 46,158 per game, just behind cross-state rival Jacksonville for the best figures in the league and more than the Buccaneers averaged that year. They were also consistent rain or shine, hitting a low of 37,899 for the March game against the Stallions and peaking at 58,777 in April for the blanking of Oakland. Florida was clearly very receptive to the idea of spring football.

Bassett threw his full weight behind his team. He treated nine of the Bandits offensive linemen to dinner, rolling up a bill of $1,400. Guard Fred Dean handled two whole lobsters and an 18-ounce steak all by himself. The maverick owner, the loudest opponent of Donald Trump's plan to move the league to the fall, challenged the New England Patriots to a game after Dick Steinberg, player development director for the NFL club, insulted Bassett's team. The Patriots declined the invitation, despite Bassett's offer of a $1 million prize for the winner. Like Trump, Bassett knew how to generate positive press, but Bassett's way didn't cost anything.

Birmingham Stallions

The Birmingham Stallions entered their second campaign optimistic of bettering their .500 record of the year before. They had taken on a distinctive Pittsburgh flavor with head coach Rollie Dotsch, new quarterback Cliff Stoudt and receiver Jim Smith all ex–Steelers. They were expected to be strong contenders in the Southern Division. Former Buffalo Bills Pro Bowl runner Joe Cribbs would spearhead the offense.

They split their first two games before trouncing Pittsburgh, 30–18, in front of the league's first sellout crowd in Three Rivers Stadium. The fans pelted ex–Steeler Stoudt with everything from snowballs to beer bottles throughout the game. The players had to keep their helmets on the entire game, and a couple of people on the sidelines were hit with flying objects. Stoudt suggested that he, Smith and Dotsch keep their distance from each other so "one grenade wouldn't get them all."

Dotsch admitted that he considered removing his team from the field for their own safety even if it would have meant forfeiting the game.

"We just kind of held together," added Cribbs in the *Pittsburgh Post-Gazette*. He took the pressure off Stoudt with 191 yards rushing and two scores. "You could feel it when we were back near our own goal line in the third quarter and all the ice balls were flying down at us. We felt like we had to move the ball, had to get it out of there. Some of the linemen got a little excited."

The object of the fans' missiles agreed that his team used the fans' behavior as a motivator. "The louder it got, the more it fired the team up," Stoudt told the *Post-Gazette*. "One thing I had forgotten, though, was when it snows up North, how large and hard the snowflakes get."

Embarking on an important four-game stretch with Southern Division opponents, the Stallions made the most of the opportunity by pelting Memphis, Tampa Bay, New Orleans and Jacksonville to grab the division lead.

Once they had it, they hung onto it for the remainder of the season. They won their next three to make it nine consecutive victories following their opening day loss, before Philadelphia roughed them up. Birmingham responded with two of its most impressive decisions of the year: a 42–10 drubbing of Jacksonville and a 41–7 beating of Chicago. Even a two-game contract dispute by Cribbs could not get in their way. They made it five out of six by defeating New Orleans, Washington and Memphis, cementing the division title in the process. The Stallions closed out the 14–4 campaign with a close loss to Tampa Bay.

Birmingham led the league in rushing for the second year in a row with 3,313 yards on the ground behind their excellent offensive line, dubbed the "Mule Team." Despite missing a pair of games during his holdout, Cribbs topped the USFL with 1,467 yards and added eight touchdowns. He also caught 39 passes for 500 yards and five scores.

Fullback Leon Perry chipped in with 774 yards and found the end zone 13 times. After a slow start, Stoudt provided the desired boost to the passing game with 212 completions in 366 attempts for 3,121 yards, 26 touchdowns and just seven interceptions. He not only finished as the league's second-leading passer but also ran for 440 yards and nine more scores. Former Steeler teammate Jim Smith became the chief recipient of the new quarterback's aerials, making 89 catches for a league-best 1,481 yards and eight touchdowns. On the defensive side, Chuck Clanton placed third in the USFL with ten interceptions for 249 yards and returned three of them for touchdowns. His thefts helped the Stallions finish tied with Philadelphia for league honors in turnover differential at plus 19. Dave Pureifory sacked opposing passers ten times, while Mike Perko added 8 ½ sacks. They ended the regular season allowing the second-fewest rushing yards in the league.

Birmingham fans appreciated the improvements the team had made and turned out

The Birmingham Stallions signed quarterback Cliff Stoudt away from the Pittsburgh Steelers in 1984, teaming him in the backfield with three-time NFL Pro Bowl running back Joe Cribbs. Photograph by Jim Turner, from author's collection.

an average of 36,850 per game, nearly 15,000 more per contest than the year before, the largest improvement in the league. Their season ticket base jumped above 18,000, an improvement of nearly 4,000 from year one. They reached their high with 62,300 in week one against New Jersey and broke the 40,000 barrier three more times over the next four home games. Somewhat troubling was a drop at the end of the season in which 22,100 came out for the Washington game and 24,500 attended the finale against Tampa Bay.

Postseason

After 18 weeks, the USFL's second playoff field was set. With the expansion from 12 to 18 teams, the league added an additional playoff round. The East featured two intriguing matchups with the Stars hosting the Generals who had handed Philadelphia its only two regular season losses and Birmingham battling Tampa Bay in a rematch of their season finale. In the West, Michigan would have to take the wild card route to defend its title, starting with a game against surging Los Angeles and rookie QB Steve Young. In Houston, George Allen's tried and true Arizona veterans would have to contend with Jim Kelly and the explosive Gamblers.

The Generals and Stars met at Philadelphia's Franklin Field on Saturday, June 30 in the first quarterfinal playoff game of the weekend. New Jersey had beaten the Stars in both meetings between the two clubs during the season largely because they had forced seven Philadelphia turnovers in those two games. The contest had to be moved from

Veterans Stadium because the Phillies had a game scheduled. The dressing rooms at Franklin were too small so the teams had to dress for the game a block away, walk to the stadium and enter through gates in the back. After a solid year at the Philly box office, a crowd of 19,038 attended the contest.

The two squads battled to a scoreless first quarter in a period much like their first two games, a defensive struggle. Stars linebacker John Bunting recovered a Brian Sipe fumble at midfield and three plays later Bryant broke the deadlock with a 10-yard run three minutes into the second quarter. The Philly defense held again and forced a New Jersey punt from the 15-yard line. Bob Grupp boomed a 55-yarder that settled into Garcia Lane's arms at the 30. The punt returner burst through a hole in the New Jersey coverage and outraced the Generals on a 70-yard touchdown that put the Stars up by a 14–0 margin. Philadelphia made it 21–0 with just a minute left in the half on a Fusina to Bryant 11-yard toss.

"We're in the huddle and Chuck starts talking about a dream he had the night before where he was getting ready to throw a touchdown pass to Kelvin," David Riley told *The Philadelphia Daily News.* "We're supposed to be calling the play and he's sharing this dream with us. We all start laughing and we break the huddle and what does he do? He goes and throws a touchdown to KB."

The Philadelphia defense continued to steal the show in the second half as the two teams played a scoreless third quarter. Bryant capped a demoralizing 20-play, 75-yard drive and extended his team's advantage to 28–0 with a one yard burst with 10:41 to play, effectively slamming the door on Donald Trump's team. Clarence Collins caught a 14-yard throw from Brian Sipe with just over five minutes left to spoil the shutout, but the Generals were never in any danger of getting back in the game.

Bryant ran 23 times for 117 yards, while Fusina completed an efficient nine of 14 passes for 121 yards. Sipe, meanwhile, threw 40 times, nearly twice what he averaged in the regular season, completing 24 for 259 yards with an interception. Walker managed just 15 yards on 15 carries as New Jersey had to abandon its running game for much of the second half. Considering that the Generals roughed up the Stars twice in the regular season, it was a surprisingly easy win for Philadelphia.

"In 1984 we only lost twice and that was to the New Jersey Generals," Riley said. "We weren't going to lose any more. We were always banged up to the point where we got ready to play them, we didn't have everybody together. When we went into the playoff, everybody played so they saw a whole different team"

Philadelphia's defensive effort also turned some heads. "Their corner backs laid back and took any long stuff we had away, and they blitzed like mad," explained Sipe to *The Sporting News.* "They played us better today than anybody else this season."

The Los Angeles Express played host to their first playoff game against the Michigan Panthers later that afternoon. Just 7,964 showed up to watch the home team's attempt to knock off the defending champs. The Panthers originally expected Anthony Carter to return for the game, but he re-broke his arm in an off-the-field accident.

Los Angeles tallied the only points of the opening quarter on a five-yard burst by Kevin Nelson just 4:34 into the game. It took until the middle of the second period for the scoreboard to move again when the Express extended their advantage to 10–0 on a 32-yard Tony Zendejas kick. A fumble recovery led to Michigan's first successful drive, and, with less than two minutes remaining in the half, Cleo Miller finally cracked the end zone for the Panthers with a three-yard run. Michigan then picked off an errant

Steve Young throw and Bobby Hebert took advantage by connecting with Ken Lacy on a 22-yard scoring pass with 1:19 remaining before intermission to put the visitors on top by a 14–10 margin when the halftime gun sounded. The two quick scores had erased the defending champs' 10-point deficit and let some of the air out of the young Express.

Zendejas brought his team back to within a point of even with a 34-yard field goal late in the third, but Hebert gave the Panthers their largest lead of the day with a two-yard scoring pass to Mike Cobb 5:57 into the fourth quarter to make it 21–13. Los Angeles used the rest of the period to battle back. With 8:57 remaining, the Express took over at its own 20-yard line. Young would have to drive the team 80 yards for them to have a chance, and that's exactly what he did. On the first play of the drive, the quarterback took a hard hit that nearly knocked him out after a seven-yard scramble.

"[Coach John] Hadl told him to come out," left tackle Gary Zimmerman told *Sports Illustrated*. "Steve said, 'No way,' and came back to the huddle. After that, there was no doubt. There was just … an electricity."

Using 14 plays with a pair of fourth-down conversions, they crawled within 21–19 on Nelson's one-yard run on fourth down with 52 seconds left in regulation. On the crucial drive, Young scrambled for four yards on fourth and one and later scampered for 11 more to move the ball to the one. The quarterback ran around left end for the two-point conversion to knot the game at 21–21, forcing overtime after the Express defense stifled Michigan's last drive.

The Panthers had the better of it in overtime and appeared poised to win it on a short field goal. Novo Bojovic, playing without his customary garlic in his socks, barely missed a 37-yard kick as the teams battled to a standstill for the remainder of the period. Hebert went down with a knee injury before backup Whit Taylor got Bojovic close enough to try again, but this time he blew a 36-yard field goal attempt wide left in the second overtime session. The game then entered its third overtime period, and the Express finally were able to move the ball. Young needed four plays to drive Los Angeles down to the Panthers' 24-yard line. On the team's one-hundredth offensive play of the game, the rookie quarterback handed the ball to Mel Gray who dodged and juked his way down to the one-yard line before barreling into the end zone for the winning score at 3:33 of the third overtime. He landed on his left arm as he crossed the goal line, breaking his humerus.

"At some point, I was like, 'Please, somebody just win,'" remembered Panthers receiver Derek Holloway. "I was obviously going to do my best to make it my team, but it came to a point where everyone was tired, it was warm, and after playing a game and three-quarters, we were exhausted. It was a long, hot day out there."

"We were just trying to set up for a field goal," Young explained to the Associated Press. "It was a simple slant off tackle that turned into a Mel Gray special."

The incredible run ended the longest game in professional football history after 93 minutes and 33 seconds of game time. The Miami Dolphins and Kansas City Chiefs previously held the record in a 1971 playoff game that lasted 82 minutes and 40 seconds.

Young led the winners with 295 yards in the air on 23 of 44 passing with a pair of interceptions. He also added 44 yards rushing on seven attempts and the critical two-point conversion at the end of regulation. Gray paced the club with 124 yards on the ground on 31 tries, while JoJo Townsell caught five balls for 96 yards.

The defending champs had been dethroned, but it was not because of a lack of opportunities. Hebert completed 13 of 27 throws for 201 yards with a pair of interceptions, while John Williams led the runners with 113 yards on 23 carries. Holloway caught four balls for 67 yards to pace the team's receivers. Four turnovers and three missed field goals ruined an otherwise solid offensive day.

"That was one of the great games, one of the real memorable games in all of college and pro football history," said Ehrhart. "That was probably the high point of the franchise. That was the Don Klosterman assembled team. NFL people were salivating over the talent that Klosterman had collected. Steve Young had matured into one of the great quarterbacks of all time. But I was concerned because as great a game as it was, there was not the kind of crowd that you wanted.

"In my mind, that game was the epitome of the conundrum that the league faced. We had an absolutely wonderful product on the field with some of the great young stars in professional football, yet it was in the heat of the middle of summer in Los Angeles, and the crowd was quite frankly disappointing. Nobody to this day disputes that wasn't one of the best games in professional football with great stars. The people said, 'You're playing at the wrong time of the year. If this would have been November 30 in the middle of the traditional football season, it would have been so much better.'

"This is why when people ask who was right in the spring-fall debate, you look at that game and see why there are two sides to the discussion. You had Trump contending, 'We've got a great product with terrific players, not top to bottom, but as many bright stars as the NFL has. You take this product and put it into the fall, you're right there. It's a winning combination.' On the other hand, you had people saying, 'You can't go and compete against the NFL during their season.' That's why that game was such a prime example of the huge, difficult decisions we had to tackle over the next 12 months. That's why it was so debated. Great game. We got way beyond expectations with the terrific coaches and players, but was the fan base in cities like Los Angeles and Chicago saying, 'We appreciate great football, but we only appreciate it during the traditional time of the year?'"

The action continued on Sunday, beginning in Birmingham where the Stallions battled the Tampa Bay Bandits. The teams had split their two regular-season meetings with the Bandits edging Birmingham, 17–16, the week before in the teams' final regular season contest. A crowd of 32,000 came out to Legion Field to cheer on their Southern Division champions.

The home team scored first on a one-yard scramble by Cliff Stoudt five and a half minutes into the game. Tampa Bay's Zenon Andrusyshyn answered with a 50-yard field goal late in the period to make it 7–3 at the end of the first 15 minutes. Stoudt added his second touchdown run, this one from two yards out, to make it 14–3 with 10:50 left in the half. John Reaves countered by guiding his team into the end zone on a seven-yard scoring toss to Willie Gillespie midway through the period. With 32 seconds remaining before halftime, Danny Miller knocked one through the uprights to stake the Stallions to a 17–11 advantage at the intermission.

In the third period, Miller hit a 49-yard kick before Joe Cribbs barreled in from three yards out to put Birmingham up by a 27–11 count. Reaves hit Wilford Morgan with a 20-yard scoring pass, but they failed on the two-point conversion to make it 27–17 at the end of three. Miller then ended any hopes of a Tampa Bay comeback with field goals from 35, 42 and 32 yards out in the final quarter.

"Birmingham was always such a tough defense for us," said Spurrier. "We could move the ball against the Stars. They were so disciplined, we felt like we knew where

After four standout campaigns with the Buffalo Bills and three Pro Bowl appearances, running back Joe Cribbs jumped to the USFL's Birmingham Stallions in 1984 and instantly became one of the new league's best backs. Photograph by Jim Turner, from author's collection.

they would be, but Birmingham had such a good pass rush. They knocked us out of the playoffs one year. We played them back-to-back. We beat them in the regular season game, and then they beat us in the playoffs."

The Stallions forced five turnovers, including three interceptions of Reaves and ran for 209 yards compared to 73 for the Bandits. They held Gary Anderson to a paltry 21 yards on eight attempts. On the other side, Cribbs led the Birmingham charge with 112 yards, while Stoudt completed 13 of 26 throws for 147 yards and avoided the turnovers that hurt his counterpart. Reaves hit on just 15 of 34 passes for 213 yards and was picked off twice by Chuck Clanton and once by Dennis Woodberry. Danny Miller, who had taken over kicking duties from the injured Scott Norwood, hit all five of his field goal attempts.

"The way Birmingham played, it would have been very difficult to beat them if we had played a lot better," Bandits coach Steve Spurrier told *The Evening Independent*. "But the way we played, we just about gave ourselves no chance to win."

The quarterfinal round came to a close with the matchup between the Gamblers and Wranglers at the Astrodome. The game pitted the league's top scoring offense in Houston's run and shoot against Arizona's tough veteran defense in a marked contrast of styles. In their only meeting of the regular season, Houston scored a 37–24 victory.

The Gamblers moved the ball early on and tallied the first points of the ballgame when Jim Kelly found the corner of the end zone with a 14-yard scramble in the first period. The run capped an impressive nine-play, 74-yard drive. Toni Fritsch added a 38-yard field goal midway through the second quarter to extend Houston to a 10–0 advantage. Frank Corral finally got the Wranglers on the board with a 32-yard kick 34 seconds before halftime. Houston's defense dominated the first 30 minutes of play, holding George Allen's crew to negative yardage for most of the half.

Fritsch connected on his second kick of the day, a 22-yard effort, for the only points of the third period before he opened a wild fourth quarter with another field goal, this one from 25 yards away, to make it 16–3 Gamblers. Houston punter Dale Walters cracked the door for Arizona with a weak 15-yard punt that gave the Wranglers the ball at midfield. It took Greg Landry two plays to get them to the 20-yard line where Tim Spencer finished off the drive with a touchdown scamper with 6:11 left. Houston's offense sputtered and Walters uncorked a lousy 13-yard punt to set Arizona up at the Gamblers 47-yard line with four minutes remaining. Landry completed the eight-play scoring drive with an 11-yard touchdown toss to halfback Doug Dennison. Corral's extra point put the visitors up 17–16. After leading the entire ballgame, the Gamblers found themselves fighting for their post-season lives. Houston drove to the Arizona 38 with 48 seconds left but fell short of the comeback as Kelly's fourth-down effort was intercepted.

Offensively for the winners, Landry connected on 11 of 22 throws for 130 yards with an interception. The Arizona defense proved to be the real heroes, collecting six sacks, two and a half by Karl Lorch, and holding the Gamblers to a season-low 16 points. Houston piled up 415 yards, 301 from Kelly's arm, but he failed to throw a touchdown pass for the first time on the season. He completed 23 of 34 throws with two interceptions. Receiver Scott McGhee caught seven of those balls for 122 yards, while Todd Fowler ran for 84 yards.

"Patience was the reason we were able to win," a relieved Allen told *USA Today*. "Our game plan was to come in here and be patient on offense and defense and not give them anything. We felt we had to keep our poise and be physical. They had many chances to put us away and couldn't do it."

The results in the quarterfinal round set up a pair of interesting match-ups to determine who would participate in the league's second championship game at Tampa. The surging Stallions would travel to Philadelphia to meet the dominating Stars on Sunday, July 8, while the Wranglers would host the Express the day before. Because they were the Pacific Division champs, Los Angeles was supposed to host the game, but preparations for the 1984 Summer Olympics made the Los Angeles Coliseum unavailable.

In fact, the location was not the only aspect of the game to change. League officials had to move the playoff contest's starting time from 12:30 in the afternoon to 8:30 that night because of the extreme heat in the Phoenix area. Even with the time change, it was still more than 100 degrees at game time. The weather seemed to favor the visiting Express, a much younger ball club than the Wranglers, but their triple overtime contest of the week before had certainly taken a lot out of the youthful bunch. Many wondered how the Arizona defenders would be able to chase Young for four quarters even after they clamped down on Jim Kelly and the Gamblers.

"A 110-degree temperature at game time during the day here would really be a bad thing," explained Arizona owner Dr. Ted Diethrich. "There was a lot of discussion back and forth about what should be done. At the end, that was not my decision. It had to be a league decision, but I agreed with it."

"We had the same issue the NFL faced when the temperatures were below zero, only at the opposite extreme," recalled Ehrhart. "We contacted medical professionals about whether it was too hot to play. We were concerned about the health of the players and decided to move the game time."

The Pacific Division rivals had split their two regular season meetings, with Los Angeles taking a 24–17 win at home in week 14 and Arizona scoring a 35–10 beating to close out the regular season in a game that Young sat out.

Indeed, the Express lit the scoreboard first on a Zendejas field goal from 25 yards out. Arizona bounced right back to take a 7–3 advantage thanks to a Luther Bradley interception at the L.A. 36 that eventually resulted in a four-yard scoring gallop by Spencer. They held the lead for just over five minutes before Kevin Nelson ran in a touchdown from 11 yards out early in the second quarter. Nelson made it a 17–7 game midway through the second period when he found the end zone on a one-yard effort. But Los Angeles got greedy and Arizona batted away L.A. punter Jeff Partridge's attempted fourth-down pass to defensive back Troy West. Arizona took over on the L.A. 35 and Spencer bolted in from the six with 1:21 remaining in the first half to cut the Wranglers' deficit to 17–14 at halftime.

Both offenses ground to a halt in the third period with Steve Young in particular struggling throughout the quarter. He found the going even tougher when Nelson sprained his neck, forcing him from the game. The Wranglers finally took advantage of the tiring Express with a 10-play, 80-yard drive that ended 40 seconds into the fourth period. Kevin Long put the home team ahead for the first time on a one-yard burst to end their best march of the night. Spencer extended the advantage to 28–17 when he scored his third touchdown of the evening on a six-yard pass from Landry five minutes later. Following an interception by linebacker Jim Fahnhorst, Mack Boatner then put it out of reach with a five-yard run with less than three minutes left in the game to make it 35–17. Young, who completed just seven passes in 23 attempts for 126 yards, closed out the scoring with a 20-yard throw to running back David Hersey to make the final score 35–23 before 33,188 very warm people at Sun Devil Stadium.

"In the first quarter, we were physical and controlled the line of scrimmage and moved the ball on them," L.A. coach Hadl told the AP. "But you've got to play 60 minutes and not 30. We played only 30 minutes tonight."

Spencer carried the offensive load for the winners with 94 yards on 18 carries with three touchdowns, and Long added 60 yards on the ground. While not playing a great game, Landry was again effective when he had to be, completing ten of 21 throws for 158 yards with an interception. With Young struggling, Kevin Mack rolled up 88 yards in 14 tries and Nelson contributed 72 yards in 18 attempts in just over a half.

"Steve Young is a fine quarterback, but we out-toughed them," Allen explained to *The Sporting News*, "We were tough tonight, and I thought we were in better shape than they were. L.A. talked all week about how hot it would have been here if we played in the afternoon instead of at night. But if this game had been played at the time it was originally scheduled to be played, it wouldn't have been a contest. We still would have won."

The Wranglers defense, at first keying on the rookie quarterback, finally began to play the run in the second half, lifting Arizona to the USFL's second title game. They held Los Angeles to just 79 yards after the intermission and sacked Young four times on the night. Fahnhorst came up with ten unassisted tackles, most of them in the final two quarters.

"We just beat the $40 Million Man with a defense that's too old to play," added Allen to *The Sporting News*. "And we did it with a coach who everybody says is too old … whose concepts are old-fashioned … who won't change.

Cagy veteran quarterback Greg Landry guided the Arizona Wranglers to the USFL's championship game in 1984, a year after guiding the Chicago Blitz offense. The 14-year NFL veteran added a fifteenth season in the NFL when he joined the Chicago Bears following the 1984 USFL campaign. Photograph by Jim Turner, from author's collection.

"But we're going to the championship game, and no team has worked harder or deserves it more."

"What a great stretch we had," remembered Risher. "We were 6–8, looking like we were going nowhere, and won the last four games to get to 10–8 and sneak into the playoffs. We wound up beating Houston in Houston when they had Jim Kelly and were scoring like 50 points a game. George Allen put together a great defensive plan that game because they had beat the shit out of us once before that. We then had the chance to play L.A. and Steve Young and had to move the game to like 10:00 at night because it was so hot. We ended up beating Young and them to get to the USFL championship game. It was a helluva ride there, a six-game stretch where we got hot."

In the East, Birmingham traveled to Philadelphia Sunday to take on the Stars. The final playoff contest of the weekend would decide who would battle Allen's Wranglers for the league's second title. Once again, the Phillies had Veterans Stadium tied up so the teams battled at Franklin Field where a crowd of 26,616 turned out to see the Eastern Conference championship game.

Much to their delight, Bryant put Philadelphia on top, 7–0, on a two-yard run with 6:22 left in the first quarter following a fumbled punt return by Birmingham's Ron Frederick. The Stars also controlled the second quarter with a Bryant one-yard touchdown run sandwiched between a pair of David Trout field goals, the last one coming with just two seconds left before halftime. Birmingham found itself down 20–0 at the break and thoroughly dominated in every phase of the game much as they had been in their week 11 match-up. The Stars out-gained them 272 yards to 72 in the opening 30 minutes.

With Philadelphia playing more conservatively on offense but just as impressively on defense, the two squads battled through a scoreless third period. At last, Danny Miller gave the Stallions some points with a 39-yard kick nearly four minutes into the fourth period. They clawed within 20–10 with 6:45 remaining in the game on a seven-yard Cliff Stoudt to Jim Smith throw, but that was as close as they could get, and Philadelphia's "Doghouse Defense" wrapped up their second straight trip to the USFL title game.

Bryant stole the spotlight as the lone offensive star of the ballgame with 152 yards on the ground on 28 carries. He collected 141 of those yards in the first two periods alone.

Fusina completed 15 of 27 throws for 135 yards. The Stars defense was the difference in the game. It forced five turnovers including three interceptions, two of them in the decisive second quarter. They also sacked Stoudt six times on the day and knocked him out of the game twice. Sam Mills recorded 12 tackles with two assists while fellow linebacker George Cooper contributed five tackles, six assists, one sack, a forced fumble and a fumble recovery.

"Their defense robbed us crazy," admitted Stallions coach Rollie Dotsch to *The Sporting News*. "[The Stars] are so strong and force you into so many things. They got us into their game and took us out of ours real early. By far, they're the most solid defense we've faced all year."

Stoudt, playing with a sore shoulder, connected on just ten of 26 throws for 109 yards and frequently found himself running for his life against the Philly onslaught. "I threw seven damn interceptions the whole year and I threw three today," he said to *TSN*. "Their defense is a lot more sound than any other in this league. They get into their zones well and double-cover as well as anybody I've seen."

Cribbs failed to take much of the pressure off of his quarterback with just 72 yards in the game. Birmingham ran for 141 yards in the contest, but it was not enough to extend their season.

"I wouldn't want to run the ball against those guys," Philadelphia tackle Irv Eatman told *The Sporting News* about his defensive teammates. "I wouldn't want to have to run into a guy like Sam Mills too often. Since I've been with the Stars, I've run into Sam about six times. I think I might've—might've—come out on the right end of that once.

"All I've got to say to anybody who has to run against them is good luck. Those guys are phenomenal. They bend sometimes, but they don't break very often. There isn't a team in this league that can run against them well enough to beat us. They just can't do it. [The defense] is just too good."

The second United States Football League championship game featured two of the best defenses in the league. The Wranglers entered on a roll, winners of their last six games while the Stars continued their two-year dominance in which they had won 34 of their 40 games. In their only previous meeting of the year, Philadelphia nipped Arizona 22–21 on April 8 on the strength of a late comeback.

On July 15, 1984, the United States Football League staged its second championship game. A steady rain fell in Tampa on championship day but finally stopped about 90 minutes before the game started. Philadelphia took the opening kickoff and drove 66 yards in ten plays, the last four yards on a Bryan Thomas touchdown run right up the middle of a confused, overpowered Wranglers defense. The march consumed six minutes and 41 seconds against the league's top-rated defensive unit. Fusina kept the Stars moving with a 10-yard jaunt on third and four, the only time on the drive they were in real danger of being stopped. It was time for Philly's defense to take the field and they were just as good as the offense, holding Landry and company to three downs before forcing a punt. It took Fusina nine plays and 4:30 to drive 54 yards, the last one on a one-yard sneak to extend the advantage to 13–0 after Trout missed the point after. The first quarter ended with the Wranglers showing just nine total yards gained to Philadelphia's 120 yards.

In the second period, dazzled Arizona received a break when safety Luther Bradley knocked the ball out of Philadelphia tight end Ken Dunek's hands and recovered the fumble on the Wranglers 43-yard line. That set up a drive that ended with Frank Corral's

37-yard kick to trim the score to a 13–3 margin. Philadelphia set out on another long drive only to be thwarted by a rare Bryant fumble at the goal line that resulted in a touch-back for Arizona. Another Stars possession stalled on the 11 and the usually reliable Trout missed a 27-yard field goal attempt. That left the badly outplayed Wranglers down by just ten at the break. The halftime statistics told of Philly's complete dominance over the first two quarters. They piled up 249 yards compared to just 49 for the Western Confer-ence champs. They also led in time of possession, 22:37 to just 7:23, and the Wranglers had yet to convert a third down.

Trailing 13–3, Landry got the ball first and drove his team 40 yards to the Philadelphia 39-yard line where they faced a third down-and-three situation. On the crucial play, the officials may have missed a pass interference penalty on Mike Johnson's defense of a throw aimed for Tim Spencer, and the Wranglers had to punt again. Again, Fusina marched his squad steadily toward another score. This time, though, his third down pass from the 16 was tipped by defensive tackle Kit Lathrop and intercepted by linebacker Ed Smith who returned his prize into Stars' territory at the 46. That insurgence ended when Corral missed a 40-yard kick. Arizona had come out fired up in the third quarter and had nothing to show for it.

Early in the fourth, Philly's Don Fielder sacked Landry, stripping him of the ball which Buddy Moor recovered at the 11 to put the Stars back in business. It took them seven plays to move those 11 yards, but Bryant hung onto the ball this time as he hurtled in from the one. With the Stars championship all but secure, many of the 52,622 fans in attendance began to shout "Bandit" and "Ball" back and forth across Tampa Stadium. A 39-yard Trout kick midway through the period provided the final points in a convincing 23–3 victory. The new champs carried Coach Mora on their shoulders.

"It was personally exciting to play the championship in Tampa," said Fusina, a former Tampa Bay Buccaneers quarterback. "It was fun to go back to where I worked and played for four years. We got a lead and knew with our defense we could be a little comfortable. It was a very good feeling to win. It felt as if two years of work culminated in something we deserved. It was icing on the cake."

"I knew after the first drive we'd dominate," a jubilant Eatman told *Sports Illustrated*. "We stuffed it down their throats." When asked to describe his team's game plan, the hulking tackle summed it up in two words, "Kick ass."

The media named Fusina the Most Valuable Player of the game, against the quar-terback's wishes. He connected on 12 of 17 throws for 158 yards with an interception. Bryant, the quarterback's choice for MVP, carried 29 times for 115 yards.

All told, the offense rolled up 414 yards, 256 of those on the ground. Thomas added 69 yards on 11 tries, while fullback David Riley gained 43 yards on nine attempts. The defense limited Landry to only six completions in 20 throws for a minuscule 54 yards. Arizona managed just 119 yards and, after falling behind early, never threatened with the running game. Spencer led the way with 33 yards while Long added 29. After winning six games in a row, George Allen's team ran out of gas.

"It was not that you tried any harder or prepared any better or anything like that," Mora said of facing Allen. "I always had a lot of respect for George Allen. I grew up in LA, and he was coaching the Rams, I remember. He was an outstanding coach, a Hall of Fame coach, and our players knew they were going up against a guy like George Allen, too. It might have been a little more incentive, but I don't know if I sat down and said, 'Hey, this is an extra special game because we're going against George Allen.' I never felt

Kelvin Bryant of the Philadelphia Stars rips off yardage against the Arizona Wranglers in the second USFL championship game on July 15, 1984. Photograph by Jim Turner, from author's collection.

that way. We knew his teams would be tough and well prepared, and they were. But we never lost to them."

"We were on a mission," said Dunek "We felt like we should have been the champions the year before. The resolve on that team is something that I'll always remember. Other than those two losses to New Jersey, we really ran the table and beat a very good George Allen–coached Arizona Wrangler team in that championship game."

"We were better the second year," added Mora. "We lost the championship game after we had a really good regular season the first year. I think losing the championship game to Michigan really spurred us on for the next season because our guys felt like we were still the best team, and it was kind of in the back of our minds, 'Hey, man, we're going to win it this year.' We had a couple losses during that second year, but once we got into the playoffs, there was no stopping us. We just dominated the playoffs, the two playoff games and the championship game. We were really good. We were better the second year because we added some players but kept our core guys and had another year of experience with our coaching staff."

5

After a Big Season,
a New Course

The day after the Stars' championship victory, an estimated crowd of 250,000 people lined Philadelphia streets to honor their newest champion. "When we came back from Tampa, we were welcomed with a victory parade," said Myles Tanenbaum. "It was a great turnout in the center city. The best part of it to me was the number of young people who were there. We had that kind of a following, teenagers and people in their early 20s."

"They had a parade in Philadelphia, a nice parade," added Mora. "The city supported us pretty darn well. It's a great sports town, and they liked our team."

"The championship was played in Tampa, Florida, and we stayed at George Steinbrenner's hotel and threw a huge party after the game," laughed tight end Ken Dunek. "We flew home a day later to a victory parade in Philadelphia that rivaled the Phillies and 76ers parades that I had been part of as a spectator. It was a great time to be in Philly."

In addition to its growth in the U.S., the USFL took an international step. During the season, Tampa Bay owner John Bassett became the driving force behind scheduling an overseas exhibition game. Philadelphia owner Myles Tanenbaum agreed to join him, working through the season to arrange a game in London between the Bandits and the Stars. Growing ESPN, which would televise the contest, also saw a chance to increase its international profile.

One day after the parade, the Stars players and coaches flew to London for the game at historic soccer venue Wembley Stadium. While NFL contests in Europe became commonplace decades later, the meeting was only the second U.S. pro football game held in Europe, a year after an NFL exhibition between the Minnesota Vikings and St. Louis Cardinals. The game brought out 21,000 curious spectators, about 16,000 fewer than the NFL contest had attracted.

"We got on a plane a couple of days later and flew to London to play at Wembley Stadium against the Tampa Bay Bandits," recalled Mora. "That was kind of fun, too. After having won the championship, that was kind of a vacation and a reward for us."

"Hard to believe we jumped on a plane to play in London," laughed Dunek. "I think half of us were still hung over on the plane. We thought we were going to go over there and just fool around and have a vacation. Jim Mora being the professional and disciplinarian he was, made us practice and hit. We practiced at Hyde Park every day.

"We were guests of Parliament that was in session and toured Windsor Castle and got to know London and the people who were so friendly to us. I remember the taxi cabs were so clean and the drivers were so polite. Caught a couple of plays in London and got to bring our wives, of course. A great memory."

"We practiced in their central park in the days before the game, and I remember the people stopping to watch us and looking at us as if we were crazy," laughed Fusina. "Even during the game there was a good crowd, but I'm not sure how many of them understood the game."

Spurrier, for one, took the opportunity to win over some new fans for the Bandits, even if they were across the Atlantic Ocean.

"It was extraordinary," said Peterson. "We were the 'home team,' even though we were Philadelphia colonials to the British. On the introduction of both teams, Steve had conjured this up and we didn't know it, but his team ran out and each player had a union jack flag sticking out of their helmets. And Steve came out dressed in knickers and the vest and everything else. And immediately the home team was no longer the Stars; it was the Bandits. He was a great showman and he understood that very much. And he was very, very keen on the USFL."

With starters for both teams playing sparingly, the newly-crowned champs took a hard-fought 24–21 victory. They bounced back from a 14–0 deficit on a pair of Tim Riordan to Victor Harrison touchdown passes. Another Riordan scoring throw, this one to Dunek in the fourth quarter followed a David Trout field goal and provided the winning margin. John Reaves, Wayne Peace and Jimmy Jordan each threw touchdown passes for the Bandits. John Bassett, Jr., son of the Tampa Bay owner, played his first and only game on special teams for the Bandits as did the team's assistant equipment manager, Bull Norman.

"I was probably 21, 22, and I was the assistant equipment manager, which entitled me to dig holes for the fence, stripe off the practice field, wash clothes and things like that," said Norman. "I was always out during practice catching punts and kickoffs. We were going to London, England to play an exhibition game after the season. The Philadelphia Stars had played the Arizona Wranglers in the championship game, and the next week we went to London and played at Wembley Stadium and played against the Philadelphia Stars. Charlie Bailey was our defensive coordinator, and he came up to me while we were in Tampa and said, 'Hey, Coach Spurrier is going to let you play.' I said, 'Nah, he isn't.' He said, 'Yeah, he's going to let you cover on a kickoff.' I didn't think much about it. So we got to the airport in Orlando, and he said, 'I tell you, Steve's going to let you cover on a kickoff. He's going to let you play.'

"When we got to England, I asked Coach Spurrier if he was going to let me play. He said, 'Yeah, as long as it's okay with Timmy Sain, the head equipment guy. As long as you do your other duties, I'm going to let you play.' I'd never played football in my life. Well, the second half rolls around and Coach Spurrier's not real happy. He looks at me, and I've got this uniform on, and he asked, 'Have you played yet?' I go, 'No, sir.' He said, 'You go in on the next kickoff.' Okay. 'You go down there and see Coach Rauch.' So I went down by our special teams coach John Rauch, and I said, 'Coach, Coach Spurrier says I'm going in on the next kickoff.' We scored three or four plays later, and he said, 'You're third man in on the opposite side. We're kicking the ball. You run down the field about 10, 15 yards and curl towards the middle.' I said okay.

"When I went out there, all the players told me, 'Whatever you do, don't hang around the pile because that's when you're going to get knocked out. Just be heads up.' Anyway, we kicked off, and I started running down the field. I thought, 'Man, I must be running pretty slow because everybody else is blowing me away.' The guy from the Stars returned the ball, and he was coming right at me. The pursuit pushed him toward the sideline, and I got pushed in the back a little bit, but I ended up making the tackle. I come off the field and Coach Spurrier and all the players were giving me high fives. He said, 'At least you showed effort.'

"What made it so funny was that Carl Franks was up in the press box. He was a running back for us who was hurt. He was a spotter for Jim Simpson and Paul Maguire for ESPN, and he told them who I was. I didn't know it at the time, but they came off one of those John Madden commercials, and Jim Simpson said, 'You think that man's a football player? You're out of our mind. That's Bull Norman, the assistant equipment manager.' They showed the play again and did an isolation on me, and Maguire's just cracking on me the whole time. It was really, really funny."

Following its second season, USFL executives beamed at the quality of football the league had put on the field. The infusion of veteran National Football League players and another sterling rookie crop upgraded talent around the league.

"I think year two was the acknowledgement by the nation of the quality of play," Ehrhart said. "Even though we'd had the great success in the first year, 1984 was the advent of the quarterback: Steve Young, Jim Kelly, Doug Williams and Brian Sipe all came in. The second year was the year of the quarterback and recognition of the talent by the country. After the first year there were still NFL-style people asking whether it was really first-class, major football. As some of the younger players matured, people recognized there was some high quality football being played.

"I personally gave credit to Al Davis. We flat out borrowed a page out of his book that said quarterback was the most visible position, so we borrowed his game plan of signing both the best young quarterbacks coming out of college as well as bringing over from the NFL top-ranked passers such as Brian Sipe and Doug Williams. We had a combination of great young quarterbacks and accomplished veteran quarterbacks. It sent a message to the country that this is high quality football, and nobody could take away from that.

"Detractors would say the depth was not as strong, but I think there was a good shift in the country that we were no longer considered an upstart new league that was a notch below the NFL. We were being compared at every turn to the NFL, and that was both a blessing and a curse. Now the sleeping giant was no longer damning us with faint praise. It was outright battle. We had threatened them by taking the best young players, and we had taken away their established veteran stars. Players were pounding on our door, and their agents were calling. We were too good, too fast. By the middle of that second year, at the height of franchise sales, people were asking how the league had built that quickly and were comparing it to the AFL. We were happy when somebody would compare the young quarterbacks in our league to Joe Namath 20 years earlier. Everybody kept writing about that. Is Steve Young, Jim Kelly or Bobby Hebert going to be to the USFL what Namath was to the AFL? Certainly in L.A., Don Klosterman who was a highly respected NFL executive was touting Steve Young as the new Joe Namath of the USFL. The good news is how well we were doing, and the bad news was how well we were doing."

"We could survive in the NFL," said Mora of his Stars in *Sports Illustrated*. "I look back to the four years I spent with the Seahawks, and by the third year we were 9–7 and competitive.

"I would have to compare this team favorably with that team. It's a young football team and it takes time. We still don't have the talent of the great teams. We have a lot of players the NFL would love to have, and I also see a lot of NFL players come into this league and play well, but they don't dominate.

"The good teams in this league could go into the [NFL] and survive. I'm not saying we'd be a playoff team, because we wouldn't. But we wouldn't get crunched."

The USFL's second All-League Team showcased the quality of its players. Houston's Jim Kelly edged Philadelphia's Chuck Fusina for the first-team quarterback spot. Teammate Richard Johnson's record 110 catches enabled him to join Arizona's Trumaine Johnson as the honored receivers, and Joe Cribbs of Birmingham and Kelvin Bryant of Philadelphia grabbed the running back spots. Both Bryant and Johnson had accomplished the feat the year before. The media chose New Orleans' Dan Ross as the top tight end, while tackles Irv Eatman (Philadelphia) and Pat Phenix (Birmingham), guards Chuck Commiskey (Philadelphia) and Buddy Aydelette (Birmingham) and center Bart Oates (Philadelphia) made up the all-Stallions/Stars offensive line. Eatman and Aydelette were also repeat performers.

Ends John Lee of Arizona and Pete Catan of Houston joined tackles Kit Lathrop of Arizona and Pete Kugler of Philadelphia to form the defensive line. Linebackers Kiki DeAyala (Houston), Sam Mills (Philadelphia), Jim LeClair (New Jersey) and Ed Smith (Arizona) made the cut as did San Antonio's Peter Raeford and Philadelphia's Garcia Lane at the corner back spots. At safety, Oakland's Marcus Quinn and Philadelphia's Mike Lush rounded out the defense. The media chose 12 players because of the mixed use of 3–4 and 4–3 alignments. Gamblers kicker Toni Fritsch, Oakland punter Stan Talley, Memphis kick returner Derrick Crawford and Denver punt returner David Martin captured the specialist spots. Lathrop, Mills, Talley and Martin had all been voted as all-league selections the season before. All told, 11 players in their first year in the league made the team, including five rookies.

Jim Kelly's spectacular rookie campaign earned him the Most Valuable Player award even as Chuck Fusina won Outstanding Quarterback honors. Fellow Star Irv Eatman was tabbed as Man of the Year, and Philadelphia's Jim Mora picked up Coach of the Year kudos. The league chose newcomer Joe Cribbs of Birmingham as the Outstanding Running Back. Houston's Toni Fritsch and Richard Johnson won at Leading Scorer and Leading Receiver, respectively, while Oakland's Marcus Quinn picked off Defensive Player of the Year honors. Arizona's Kit Lathrop captured Outstanding Lineman, while Tampa Bay's Zenon Andrusyshyn earned Special Teams Player of the Year.

Unionization

Relishing their success, the players voted to unionize and after an intense battle aligned themselves with the Federation of Professional Athletes, a collection of unions that also included the National Football League Players Association. The NFLPA gave the United States Football League Players Association $25,000 to get started. Some of the items they desired to discuss with league management were injury protection, preseason pay, minimum salaries and the developmental squad. The players had voted down attempts at unionization in 1983, partially because of the damage done by the 1982 NFL strike.

In addition to battling the NFL for players, the USFL also found itself at odds with its new players' union.

"There were some arguments when the two unions were fighting with each other," Ehrhart recalled. "Was there going to be a new independent union, the USFL Players Association, or was the NFL Players' Association going to run the union in our league? It ended up being the same leadership for both league unions, which ultimately turned out to be a bad situation. There was not any help coming from the union when it should have been there.

"We hired some collective bargaining consultants about how to go about the process. I can remember in '82 when I was running back and forth to meet with the player's reps when they were out on strike, there was much encouragement and understanding. 'Hey, we need you to get started.' 'It would be the best thing ever.' 'It would give us some leverage because we're trying to get wages up.' 'It will be an alternative so more players can play,' and all those kinds of things. Then it certainly changed. The jealousies with the top player contracts hurt most of all. The Players Association couldn't reconcile that a Steve Young could make a whole bunch of money, but that there would not be enough money to pay everybody the same way including all the same benefits.

"Once the NFL Players' Association became the labor representative for the players, they pushed for many more benefits, and they created additional demands on the teams to pay for player salaries, benefits, working conditions, per diems, all those kinds of things that really increase your costs of doing business. Instead of continuing to nurture the growth of the competitive league to make sure that there were two, it was the impression of a lot of our people that the union could not understand that they should make sure they don't kill the golden goose. Some of the owners felt that the union was squeezing so damn hard that instead of understanding that this is not the established, long time league, they should have been more thoughtful and should have nurtured the competitor because it's created so many new jobs. They were not cooperative.

"When we told them we had a lot of challenges, they didn't believe it. They were like a typical union. All these USFL players, and great games and star players, big contracts and Steve Young is making huge money, but I don't think they ever appreciated the difficulty of keeping 18 franchises funded and going when we had the crisis in Chicago and the crisis in Los Angeles. We had teams moving, so even though there was great success, there was also high risk in a new business venture. It was still only in its second year of full operation, and we were still fragile. Instead of recognizing that fragility from the union side, they said they were the NFLPA and they were trying to get similar kinds of benefits for our players and restrictions and rules."

Doug Allen, the executive director of the USFL Players Association, threatened a strike during the preseason in February. Despite not having an agreement finalized by the start of the season, players did not walk out.

"We had a very good working group," said McSherry. "We were trying to get a union contract. Our committee that was charged with doing that was me, Vince Lombardi, Jr. of Michigan and Paul Martha. Martha represented the Pittsburgh owner, who operated out of Youngstown. We tried like hell to get a salary cap into our union contract, and we probably could have done it, but the owners ran out of steam. We had some people who would have come into the league as owners if we had a salary cap. The guy who at the time owned the San Antonio Spurs, which had been an ABA team, was a guy I knew pretty well, and he would have bought a team. He would have even taken the Gunslingers from Manges if we would have had a salary cap. But without a salary cap, he wasn't going anywhere near the league. We eventually didn't do a salary cap. We had drafted agreements with salary caps in them and there were all sorts of novel things like wild cards, one or two players who wouldn't count toward the cap.

"But in the end, we needed to get a union contract in place, and Paul Martha and Doug Allen walked around the block and negotiated an NFL-like contract in less than an hour. Paul just said, 'We got to get a deal, and the salary cap was where we had all the problems.' I don't remember any owner pushing against the cap, except that they didn't want it to apply to them. They didn't mind if the other owners had caps. There was an irresistible impulse to spend money on players, even if you didn't have any money."

"Some owners wanted to fight the union and not be unionized," said Ehrhart. "Others in our ownership group felt that it was better to have a union. Remember we had just come out of the players strike in '82, and here we are getting ready to kick off our first season in '83, and a lot of people were very scared. Some of the people like Paul Martha, I remember talking to him a lot, were of the opinion that a union would be supportive of what we're trying to do because we offer more jobs. Others would argue that unions just don't work that way. Once they get entrenched, their demands would be too difficult for a young league to handle.

"I had represented a number of the player reps. It just worked out that a number of the player reps in '82 had been clients of mine in my sports law practice, so I had good communication with them based on years of work. I had admired their tenacity in fighting a system that was holding down their ability to move. Cullen Bryant of the L.A. Rams had been a client of mine, and we had been able to get a court ruling to knock out the 'Rozelle Rule' in 1975. Commissioner Rozelle unilaterally tried to force Cullen to the Lions as compensation when the Rams signed a Detroit player. It was a way to suppress free agency. It was the old days of chattel. I had a high admiration of the players' mission in '82, and they were right. The NFL player reps were very appreciative of the efforts of the USFL to get established, and it was very sad that within two years it became an adversarial situation.

"Once the union was in place, it pushed so hard against the USFL. Instead of helping nurture the league to become a true competitor, they were putting financial and economic pressure on it by making so many demands. The ownership split. I can remember Alfred Taubman suggesting we bring in labor experts to see if we could battle against the vote on the union. Others felt that the union understood that this would be the smartest thing for players overall and would be helpful to have new good employers. The player's association soon forgot from whence they came."

Television Challenges

The USFL had fulfilled one of its top priorities with the improved play but fell well short in its bid for an unqualified success. Several other areas caused the owners some concern. Television ratings were still strong but had dropped to a 5.5 on ABC, a figure that still remained 10 percent above initial projections. In its first season, 98 percent of ABC's markets carried USFL games. Surprisingly, that number fell to 94 percent in 1984 despite the addition of six more teams. The league and ABC could do little about that since several local affiliates had chosen to air alternate programming.

"We had that initial burst of interest, especially spurred on by the Herschel Walker signing, so I think it was maybe somewhat natural that we fell off a bit," said ABC's

Spence. "Were we concerned? Yes, we were. It was spring football. We were trying to establish professional football in the spring, which was a challenge."

The first round of the playoffs drew a 5.7 on Saturday, June 30, and a 6.0 on Sunday, and were the top-rated sports programs of the weekend. The championship game drew a 9.7 in prime time, placing it 41st among primetime programs that week. All told, ABC made a $14 million profit televising the USFL, up at least 16 percent from the year before due to higher commercial rates. The league again ranked as the second most profitable sports property on the network, right after the 1984 Olympics. Meanwhile, ABC had lost money on Monday Night Football both years.

"We did very well," confirmed Spence. "We made, as I recall, a $12 million profit that first year and a $14 million profit the second year."

"The problem we had, and it's what I started to push really hard, was that ABC made one mistake with us. They should have given us more promotions," said Camera. "They made a mistake: they didn't promote us. There should have been a promo that fit into every nightly news. There should have been promos every other day on prime time saying 'Stay tuned for USFL on Sundays,' a clip of it; they didn't give us the promotion we wanted. Why? Because I don't think they ever really wanted to piss off the NFL. I believe that they felt that they were in a very difficult circumstance and that maybe if they started to really die-hard promote the heck out of us, the NFL would be upset. What they would have done, I don't know. It was always my feeling. That was the thing we missed the most; I always felt like the weak sister."

"By that time we were getting into the demand for more revenues," recalled Ehrhart. "As the beast became bigger, we needed to feed the beast by trying to find more revenues to pay the cost of this higher level. Of course our television contracts were signed before the league started play. They were both two-year deals with ABC and ESPN, and the ABC deal was two years with a two-year option. Those were based on projections that had us being a young startup spring league that nobody ever said would even approach a comparison to the NFL. The revenue streams from television were based on pre-founding projections of a nice, little spring league. By the middle of the second year, the comparisons and the impression of the league was so high, but our costs were going up higher. Our revenues were still stuck on a much smaller, cute little spring league. That began the huge debate of if we're going to challenge the NFL for players, respect, perception and television, then we have to get increased revenues from television. That led into Marvin Warner saying ABC and ESPN should be ponying up more money."

The network was happy enough with the ratings to exercise its $15 million option for 1985 midway through the 1984 season. What would have been considered great news less than 18 months earlier was treated with disdain by some USFL owners. Some in the league had hoped to break free of the ABC contract to pursue other options with a network that might pay more, do more to promote the league and increase prime time exposure. Chicago White Sox co-owner Eddie Einhorn, who had helped fund the Blitz through its season, began to look for alternatives.

"We had a contract that allowed us to exercise separate options for '85 and '86," explained Spence. "In other words, we didn't have to pick up '85 and '86 at the same time. The reason we did that was that we wanted to take a look at the first two years and decide if we wanted to go for year three or not, then after year three decide if we wanted to go for year four. As I recall, the USFL asked us to exercise the option for '85 early, rather than wait for the end of the '84 season. The reason they asked for that was to give them credibility. Here ABC Sports thought enough of them to exercise its option earlier than ABC had to. It gave them more credibility in the marketplace, so we agreed to do that."

"Look, the NFL is a going organization," Taubman explained to *Sports Illustrated*. "We're just a babe in the woods. It doesn't take a mathematical genius to tell they can afford a lot more than we can. In our league there are lots of owners with very deep pockets. But nobody can sustain losses year after year. The difference is TV revenue. What our entire league receives from TV is less than any one NFL team gets by itself."

"It's not a good idea when you're dealing with a broadcast rights fee that's a fraction of what your competitor is getting," furthered McVay. "We're competing with the NFL for players with a smaller gate and a fraction of their television contract. You can't compete with those guys and you shouldn't."

"It was a two-edged sword," Ehrhart said. "On one hand, we were glad we had the television contract, but it wasn't enough revenue. They exercised it based on the terms in the original contract before we ever kicked off the ball. I can remember some of the ABC people pushing back, saying, 'You're just like a player. You have a couple of good years, and now you want to renegotiate your deal.' I think everybody said, 'Absolutely, you have great ratings and an almost NFL-quality product.' ABC was in a squeeze because they said they really didn't want an NFL-quality product because now the NFL was mad at them. The NFL was pushing them, saying, 'You cannot feed these guys with more revenue. They're stealing our players. You have ABC Monday Night Football sitting over here, and that's the franchise.' We argued hours and days and weeks about how we could get out of the deal. By that time we had the advent of Eddie Einhorn who was introducing the idea of CBS, saying we needed to have a different network, some competition. ABC had exclusive over the air rights. Had we received an increase in revenue from ABC, we might still be playing today."

Several team owners felt the USFL needed regionalized coverage and local blackouts to help increase attendance at televised games. Most importantly, though, the league required a lot more money to keep up the pace it had set with player signings. ABC offered none of those things. Chet Simmons talked frequently with ABC's Spence, but despite their long-standing friendly relationship, could make no progress.

"Jimmy had worked for me, for a company called Sports Programs, Incorporated, that had started a number of years before and had become the sports department at ABC as it moved through the years," explained the commissioner. "I had known Jim since he was a young man just getting into the profession. That had little to do with it. I mean, he answered my phone calls quickly and we'd be able to make meetings quickly, but he was still representing ABC, a company that was looking to make a profit on an investment, and we were trying to get more money to help us grow. We were not at odds and we never had a bitter word between us, but we were at loggerheads as to who wanted what and who was willing to give what. I had not much to give. We could have added years to the contract, which we didn't want to do because it would have hindered our opportunity to grow financially in the long run if we had already given our rights away for less money in a shorter period of time.

"I spent a lot of time with Jim. His responsibility was the league. We talked to each other on the phone weekly and saw each other quite often. I tried to move the deal around to make it more attractive to them to either add additional years or put additional money up or do whatever, but nothing seemed to work. They were probably a lot smarter than

I was in knowing that they put this amount of money up and that was as far as they were going until they proved they could do better than that. There was no budging. It was something new and it had to be proved.

"Every day I had to go walk over to ABC and ask for more money. That was my job, get more money, 'Jim can we have more money?' No, that was not fun.

"At least once a week I would take the walk over there. I knew what it would be, and I tried every which way to try and convince them that if this league was successful then it would be something that they could slap their chest about, but if it failed, it would be their nickel because they didn't put enough money in.

"I was hired for one reason: money for television. They didn't care if I didn't show up, as long as I was in Jim Spence's office getting turned down."

"In my opinion, Chet agreed with ABC," said Camera. "We made a deal. David Dixon, the founder, he believed in the commitment. I think John Bassett believed in the commitment. I think Walter Duncan, the original New Jersey owner, believed in the commitment. Those were the ones I recall. I think that's what occurred and I think Chet believed totally that we had a contract, and we have to live by it, and I don't think he ever really had the fire to go in and push it."

The relationship between the league and network had grown increasingly rocky. ABC refused to consider blacking out games in the home team's market, citing a likely drop in the ratings. They also decreased the number of Sundays that they covered multiple games, mentioning production costs of $250,000 per game as the main reason. The network moved the week 11 showdown between Philadelphia and Birmingham from Friday night to Sunday afternoon, a move which the already perturbed Warner said cost the Stallions an estimated $200,000 on 20,000 lost ticket sales. Blue laws prevented beer sales for Sunday games at Legion Field which always hurt the franchise's attendance on those dates. The move also placed the game in direct competition with a NASCAR Grand National race. The change made Warner, already a vocal opponent of the network, livid at the network's treatment of the league. Simmons and a dwindling minority of team owners continued stressing the importance of the ratings over game attendance, but their voices were drowned out.

"You couldn't tell them that. They didn't understand that," Simmons exclaimed. "Every person coming through the turnstile was another buck in their pocket to help them run the team. They just didn't understand how important exposure was. This was a long time ago now. Things have changed quite a bit since the days of the USFL. It was a different time, a different day."

Much to Simmons' chagrin, Trump conducted his own television negotiations as well, creating some awkward situations for the commissioner. Simmons found he was powerless to control the strong-minded owner.

"Donald would make phone calls where he shouldn't make phone calls representing the league," explained Simmons. "He would call Leonard Goldenson who was the chairman of ABC directly. Leonard Goldenson wanted as much to do with the United States Football League as you wanted to do with a pain in your stomach. It was a very tough time for me, trying to, forget the word 'run,' you didn't run those guys. You tried to get them on a path, push them in the right direction and hope they do the right thing. He just wanted to take over and do things on his own. He would make phone calls where I told him he couldn't. He would constantly be bothering the ABC, NBC and CBS guys, and they would call me and tell me to get him off their backs. Hey, this is Donald Trump.

He owned Trump Tower. This is Chet Simmons. He had a house in Connecticut. Let's be honest with what we were dealing with here."

Stuart Evey, chairman of ESPN at the time, wrote in his book *Creating an Empire* that Trump became a "real headache" to ESPN programmers and was continually "nagging" ESPN President Bill Grimes, Simmons' successor, to get more Generals games aired. Evey wrote that Trump eventually contacted him, saying, "Goddamn it, it's my money that's keeping this league alive. I should get more games." Evey refused to budge from the terms of the league's contract. Trump turned his attention back to Goldenson, but found he had no more success in getting the contracts changed than Simmons did.

"Donald with the strength that he has for whatever he did convinced him to have a meeting," Simmons added. "Leonard convened the meeting with myself, Bassett and I think Steve. He had Roone [Arledge], Spence, and the man that was head of finance for the network, and we're all sitting in his office and he said 'Why are we here?' Somebody piped up and said, 'The USFL has requested more money from us and to rewrite the contract, and we're at a standstill.' He turns to Roone and looks at me, 'The two of you will settle this. The meeting is over.' I thought Donald was going to have a heart attack, because he didn't get to get anything out of it. But he never stopped, he made life miserable. He'd make phone calls to people who shouldn't have had calls made to them. I asked him not to, and he would do things all on his own. He was disturbing, he was irascible; he was the worst thing in the room."

"I had a phone call one day with Trump that was over 90 minutes in duration," laughed Spence. "Trump told me at the time that it was the longest business phone call he'd ever had in his life. The substance of that call was fall vs. spring. He reiterated his firm preference for fall, and I said, 'Donald, we're just not going with you to the fall. We're not.' I tried to espouse the virtues of staying in the spring, and I believe during that call I talked about ultimately moving the league to primetime in the spring, too. He reiterated his feelings that Roone Arledge was being influenced by Pete Rozelle and the NFL, saying 'That's why you guys don't want us to go to the fall.'

"My point during that 90-minute plus phone call with Trump was that I really thought that his primary objective for moving the USFL to the fall was to create a merger situation with the NFL whereby the NFL would absorb certain teams from the USFL, one of those being the Generals. I really think Trump's ultimate objective, which he denied to me, was to get an NFL team. He wanted to be an NFL owner in New York. That was his ultimate goal, in my opinion. Was he going to be able to get an NFL team through normal means, the usual path, with the Giants and Jets already in existence? No way. The only way he thought he could do it was to force himself in, move the USFL to the fall, create a competitive force against the NFL, leading to an AFL-NFL type merger. He knew a lot of the USFL teams were just not strong enough for the NFL, but a few teams would be absorbed into the NFL, one of which would be the Generals. I really think that was his ultimate objective. He denied it. My question was, 'Do you want the league to survive as its own entity or do you really want to become part of the NFL?' He said, 'No, I want it to be its own entity.' He mentioned something called the 'Galaxy Bowl.' He said, 'I see the Super Bowl champion playing the USFL champion in a Galaxy Bowl.'"

"There's no question that Donald wanted to have a large voice and was basically irrepressible," added Ehrhart. "He believed so much in wanting to make the league successful, it was just how he was going about it. There was a lot of anguish amongst the owners, but it was still manageable though it was starting to drive serious divisions throughout the league as Donald started staking out the fall scenario."

Ratings pleased ESPN which televised 36 USFL contests, drawing an average 2.9 mark, still far and away their most popular offering. The numbers had not escaped the attention of Ted Turner whose Superstation WTBS in Atlanta needed additional sports programming. With the USFL's cable contract up, he entered his network in the bidding for their rights. Not about to lose its top-rated property, ESPN ended up bettering Turner's $62 million offer with an incredible $70 million bid for three years. The cable station had paid $11 for the first two seasons. At least on cable, the USFL had made progress in its television deals. Interestingly, the deal did not specify that the league had to play its games in the spring.

"I remember Ted Turner being in the office several times," Ehrhart said. "Ted had an amazing presence about him. Once we were sitting over by a side table in my office, and pretty soon Ted was sitting behind my desk with his feet up on it, opening my drawers. I was hoping he wasn't going to find anything embarrassing. He had a way of capturing a room. He had gone through funding the replacement players' games the year before during the strike. He said, 'We need to shake up the establishment.' He ended up putting an increased offer on the table for the cable portion. ESPN had the right of first refusal, and they matched that offer. We did get increased revenue for year three from ESPN. Ted was a key factor in that. It worked out and supported the league. It's so ironic now that ESPN ended up gobbling up even ABC. At the time, ESPN was the small child, and ABC was the big power that had all the money."

"We had a lot of negotiations with ABC and even more with ESPN," added McSherry. "We started the '85 season without a signed agreement with ESPN. We were negotiating the written agreement with them for most of that season. I think even when I left they still hadn't signed it. It was like a $70 million contract, so it was the biggest asset the league had. Of course by that time ESPN was like 80 percent owned by ABC."

"Chet and I would brainstorm every day, asking, 'Where can we get revenue?'" recalled Ehrhart. "We went to the well with Turner to try and get him to bid, and we did. We got the ESPN contract to increase several fold. When we jumped from being a young upstart spring league to being on the same level as the NFL, trying to sign the best young players and the best coaches and playing in the best stadiums, we had to have a supply of revenue."

ABC increased the potential payout for spring football by offering $175 million for four years, including the ESPN rights, but only if the league remained in its current season with the first three years guaranteed. The contract would run from the 1985 season through the 1988 campaign, effectively replacing the two option years remaining on the original ABC pact for 1985 and 1986. That figure amounted to an annual share of $2.43 million for each of the USFL's 18 franchises, a substantial increase over the $700,000 and $900,000 each team received in broadcast revenue in 1983 and 1984, respectively. Spence, who believed that ESPN had vastly overpaid for the rights, started at $150 million with two years guaranteed in negotiations with Simmons, Bassett and Einhorn before sweetening the pot with an extra $25 million and another year guaranteed. The new deal would have gone a long way toward covering the losses for most of the USFL's franchises, but wouldn't be of much help to the bigger spenders. In addition, the league would be locked in with ABC through 1988, though ABC could hold the spring rights through 1986 on the original pact. The network was well aware of the ongoing discussion about moving to a fall schedule and had no desire to lose what had become a valuable spring and summer advertising property. The increased payments would have also helped move several USFL teams toward the black. The league declined the proposal.

"I was flabbergasted that they would not take our deal, take a sure thing in the spring," Spence exclaimed. "Why not remain in the spring for another few years and see how things evolve? Say they accepted our deal and played in the spring in '86 and '87, and say things had remained relatively the same or even if '86 and '87 had been negative. Then maybe you say, 'We stayed in the spring for five years, and it's not working as well as we hoped. We have to go to the fall, let's do it.' But to go to the fall in '86 with no television agreement didn't make sense."

"Although the $175 million offer sounded like a lot, the committee never deemed it appropriate to communicate to the ownership as a whole," said Ehrhart. "Chet and I had already secured the increased fees from ESPN. When you broke it down, ABC itself was only giving us a marginal increase for their rights."

League officials later explained that they had already reached agreement with ESPN on a three-year, $70 million pact that would provide the USFL with $23.33 million for each of the next three years for cable rights alone. Under the ABC proposal, the league would get $43.75 million per season for the bundled cable and broadcast rights, meaning that ABC would add just under $20.5 million per year to the deal, less than the league was getting for the cable rights alone, and less than a 50 percent increase over the $14 million ABC would pay for exercising its 1985 option for broadcast rights.

"John Bassett was a strong advocate of staying in the spring," Spence added. "He strongly wanted to accept our deal. He resigned from the television committee out of frustration. He wrote me a wonderful letter saying, 'Sorry, ABC Sports tried so hard to make things work for the USFL and yet we're not taking the deal.'"

Part of ABC's rationale for offering more for USFL rights was to keep the league in the spring in order to eventually fulfill Spence's goal of televising it regularly in primetime, plans that were dashed by the league's rejection of his offer.

"It wasn't going to happen in '85 or '86, but say we went to the end of that deal," said Spence. "If we had done reasonably well, turned the ratings around and the league continued to grow, then I think there was a good chance we would have proposed moving it to primetime starting in 1989 or 1990, but maybe even earlier, as part of a new agreement. If we had turned things around in '86 or '87, it's very conceivable we could have gone to primetime before the end of the $175 million contract."

Simmons had been unable to gain any further traction in renegotiating the USFL's television contract with ABC. The network had made nice profits from televising league games but wasn't about to pay any more than their agreement called for unless the league extended the deal and bundled the cable rights. League officials felt there was an additional reason ABC took a hard line in the negotiations.

"They were having reverse pressure coming down from the NFL," said Ehrhart. "The NFL would say, 'These guys are our arch-enemies. They're stealing our players.' Cleveland went nuts when Brian Sipe left to join the USFL. In 1984 some very harsh rules came out of the NFL about no talking, no communications from NFL teams to USFL teams. People were rattling their sabers on the litigation side at that time. The armed camps had developed by that third year. The first year, they'd damn you with faint praise. The second year competition developed and by the third year there were armed camps."

Financial Fallout

Losses continued to mount for league teams. Los Angeles, with its huge payroll and dwindling attendance, led the way with a $15 million shortfall on the year, thanks to a staggering $13.1 million in player compensation, nearly nine times David Dixon's original projection for league teams. Pittsburgh came in with the next largest deficit at $10 million, while Chicago dropped $6 million. Houston, Arizona, Memphis, Michigan and New Jersey each lost about $5 million, while Washington and New Orleans both came up about $4 million short. Oakland, Oklahoma, Birmingham and Jacksonville all missed the black by $3 million, and San Antonio, Philadelphia and Denver ended up $2 million short. Tampa Bay, meanwhile, wound up on the positive side by $900,000, the only franchise to turn a profit. All told, USFL teams lost approximately $80 million during the season, mostly due to player expenses that had grown way beyond the original projections. Even ABC's $175 million offer wouldn't have been enough to stop the hemorrhaging.

"In one sense the league far exceeded our expectations of performance on the field and public recognition and awareness," said Ehrhart. "In a number of owners' minds, it also far exceeded the amount of investment that they had originally anticipated. The Michigan owner certainly poured more money into his team, and since Taubman had the financial resources, he had the ability to do that, as opposed to some of the more modest ownership groups such as the Washington Federals consortium or the partnership in Oakland."

"We were fighting like hell to make every nickel we could within the league office from the sale of our products and marketing," added Simmons. "We had a pretty good little organization going, but I think we were constantly the target of the owners as to what were we doing next for them. It was not an easy gig."

Many continued to decry the increased spending, including some of the more successful teams.

"Myles and I were strict constructionists," said Oakland owner Taube of Philadelphia owner Myles Tanenbaum. "We felt the league had a very viable plan for its survival and growth, and we felt that plan needed an opportunity to work its way out. By the time we got into the second year, we had ownership groups that weren't really party to the original agreements, people like Argovitz in Houston and a couple of other franchises, which were more aggressively-oriented than the original owners were. I would say by the time we got into the second year that the agreements relative to player compensation had basically broken down."

The mounting losses also intensified debate about whether the league should have expanded as quickly as it did. Several of the new teams were among the USFL's loss leaders. "I was against it from the very beginning," added Peterson. "I felt that from the personnel standpoint, we had a tremendous beginning. We acquired a number of fine, young players in the 1983 draft. Those people, coupled with a lot of guys who didn't make it in the NFL because they weren't in the right place at the right time, gave us a solid nucleus of players.

"For a number of reasons, including player identification and stability, I was never an advocate of expanding, even by one team. I felt 12 was the right number. The American Football League had only eight teams and they did just fine. We got carried away with the idea of expansion. The expansion fees were nice. But it was too much too fast. There was a great dichotomy last year between the good teams and the bad ones."

The Push for the Fall

The financial crunch experienced by so many of the owners accelerated the Trump-led debate about the proper playing season for the league. With talk of moving to the fall becoming louder all the time, Simmons publicly backed off from his preseason advocacy of the spring as the USFL's best time to play. "What hurts most is that we've built something far beyond anything even we ourselves expected," he told *Sports Illustrated*. "Yet TV ratings are down and there's no sign that sufficient revenue is going to be available as things exist now. Frankly, I can't find a financial upside in our continuing to play in the spring."

"Certainly the debate had heightened about spring-fall," said Ehrhart. "There had not been a decision made, but the pressure was coming from Donald and folks who said, 'We've arrived. We're being compared to the NFL so we have to go play in the fall.' That led to the issues of television, locations and all those kinds of things that were on the minds of Taubman, Myles and Carl. What do we do with our franchises if we end up moving to the fall? Can we end up playing head-to-head against the NFL in places like Detroit and Philadelphia? Then there were the movement issues, and the issues of Chicago and Los Angeles."

Trump had put the wheels in motion, and Oldenburg and several of the other owners had helped push them beyond the point of no return. The spring simply could not provide them with the revenue they needed to survive at the current level of spending.

The league's front office suffered a loss when Ehrhart left to become the president, general manager and part owner of the Memphis Showboats. He had been an invaluable sounding board and confidant of Simmons, and his ability to work adeptly in both football and business circles would be missed.

"I had mixed feelings leaving, but I had so much respect for Billy Dunavant," Ehrhart said. "He was just seen as such a dynamic owner. He was the world's largest cotton merchant, and he had founded the National Indoor Tennis Tournament in Memphis and used to play Bobby Riggs in tennis. In the spring of '84 John Bassett who had known Billy Dunavant from the days of the Grizzlies ten years earlier, had recommended Billy ought to talk to me about coming down and being president and general manager of the Showboats. Billy had been recruiting me since February of 1984, and I had told him no, that I had made a commitment to Chet Simmons that I would stay for two years in New York, August of '82 to August of '84. When I first turned Billy down, I said, 'I'm sorry, but I gave my word to Chet that I would stay through August of '84.'

"But the opportunity to be a president, part-owner and general manager of a team, along with Billy being a great guy, it just seemed like a wonderful opportunity where I could continue to help with league matters. After consultation with Chet and after Dunavant came back to me and said, 'Well, if I wait for you until the end of your two years, will you come down and do it then?' I did come down and started in Memphis in August of '84. There was no animosity whatsoever. In fact, some of the owners kind of wanted me stay up there, but I thought I could help from the point of view of a franchise and take a role coming from an ownership point of view rather than a league employee point of view. I started working on league politics and stayed on league committees and eventually ended up on the Executive Committee. I hated to leave, but it was a great opportunity. I was from Colorado, and I certainly enjoyed my time in New York, it was a great learning experience, but ever since I was a dumb and young football coach years before, I wanted to be able to put together a team."

Throughout the season, Trump had continued his drumbeat to switch the league to a fall schedule. He now did so as a member of the league's Executive Committee. He had also continued to work on his stadium project and was more convinced than ever that he could force his team into the NFL. He publicly denied that he sought a merger with the other league and maintained that the two rivals could participate in a common draft in much the same way as baseball's American and National Leagues. But football did not enjoy the same antitrust protection that baseball did, nor did the NFL have any interest in such an arrangement.

"Chet probably had to be dragged kicking and screaming at the idea of putting Trump on the Executive Committee with the philosophy that it's better to have somebody in the tent with you, pissing out of it, than somebody outside pissing in," said Jim Byrne who had joined the USFL's communications department. "When you come right down to it, Donald Trump was everyone's mother-in-law rolled into one and all of the problems you could associate with that."

"Donald would capture the room," Simmons recalled. "He would interrupt you, and you would stop. Now why stop? You're talking, but he would interrupt and he would try to bully you because the strength of his voice, the strength of what he was saying, he was just a very difficult guy to move around. Interrupt you, don't even think about it, you're in the middle of making a presentation, he'll just start talking about waxing his car, and everybody will be like, 'Wow, that sounds like a good thing to do today.' Very convincing man."

With the Blitz an utter failure, the league announced in May of 1984 that Chicago White Sox co-owner Eddie Einhorn had acquired a "new" Chicago franchise but was uncertain about fielding a team in 1985. Einhorn, whose TVS network had televised the WFL in 1974, would instead concentrate on television negotiations with ABC. He had become one of Trump's biggest supporters regarding the switch to the fall and busily worked to obtain a new television contract for that season, even though many owners still preferred to stay in the spring. Just a year earlier Einhorn had helped negotiate baseball's blockbuster six-year, $1.125 billion deal, so there was little doubt he knew his way around TV circles. Still, several owners distrusted him and his motives because of his baseball ties and his alliance with Trump.

"He was absolutely serious," countered Ehrhart. "In fact, he had several millions of dollars into the thing. I can't remember when he started putting money into it, but he would have been terrific. He then became the alliance with Trump saying we needed to move to the fall. Some people suspected him of being there from baseball to get us out of the spring. There were a lot of accusations thrown around there. He just believed that in Chicago you had to go head-to-head and be in the time of the year when football was played. He was much like Trump, and he was going to be a television maven as well and he certainly knew the television business.

"During the competition of the '84 season when we were kind of nursing the franchise along, Eddie was going to be the guy to step in. Anybody that would say that he wasn't sincere and didn't put any money into it is wrong. Now he didn't lose as much as some of the others who were in it since day one, but he was legitimate. He was a pioneer in his way with television having started TVS. He was inducted into the College Basketball Hall of Fame. He produced the famous college game of Alvin Hayes vs. Lew Alcindor, the first primetime college basketball game. He understood the television business as well, and he was very well thought of. People were glad to bring in a credible sports figure who had an established position in the Chicago market.

"We worked hard to try to figure out what our end solution was in Chicago, and that was to find good, quality local ownership. That's when Eddie Einhorn surfaced. Eddie was secret throughout the spring season because he had indicated that as a White Sox owner, he had to get through that season and figure out how many other White Sox owners were going to participate in the Blitz. That was one way in which we were moving down the field, and that would have been the solution: to have famed sports executive Eddie Einhorn, chairman of the White Sox, step in. That would solve that situation, so that was the endgame there."

"Eddie is the co-owner, majority owner of the Chicago White Sox, and he had been in the television business," remembered McSherry. "He was an old friend of Chet Simmons. Eddie was appointed as the head of the USFL television negotiating committee, a committee that consisted of him.

"We got a huge contract, for the time, out of ESPN that Eddie took the credit for, but Chet actually did. I was just beginning to get involved with the league when that happened. Chet had gone to Turner to try to get them to make an offer so that ESPN would think they had competition and up the price, and that's exactly what happened."

"There was one other individual who was very supportive of [the move to the fall]," remembered Peterson. "His name was Eddie Einhorn. And he was the owner of the Chicago Blitz but the Blitz had gone dark that year. And he was involved with major league baseball as a part owner, with Jerry Reinsdorf in the Chicago White Sox. And Eddie who is a bright guy from Pennsylvania, was on the broadcast committee of Major League Baseball. He along with Donald felt that if we did move to the fall, that we would be very quickly in line to either get television network contracts in the fall, or there would be a violation of the antitrust laws by the NFL and they would shut us out. Then we would be successful in litigation."

Despite all their efforts, Einhorn and Trump failed to unearth any network interest in televising the USFL in the fall.

"In addition to the fact that we already had two packages, there were already three other football packages in the market: the CBS and NBC NFL packages and CBS's college football package," explained Spence of ABC's disinterest in the USFL as a fall product. "If we had agreed to go to the fall in '86, that would have meant six football packages in the marketplace—four professional and two college. In addition to ABC having to move three of our own packages, there was so much football in the marketplace per se, that it was difficult.

"We were not interested in any way, shape or form in moving to the fall."

An Illness

Unbeknownst to his fellow owners, Tampa Bay owner John Bassett had been suffering from headaches, which he thought were the result of stress. Recalling a bout he had with skin cancer in the late '70s, Bassett decided to have himself checked out.

"I thought it was all caused by the frustrations I was having with the USFL," Bassett recalled in *Sports Illustrated*. "I went home for a full physical. They gave me the works. No problem, said I could play for my team. Then, the doc said he'd also give me a CAT scan."

The scan revealed the worst case scenario: a pair of brain tumors. Treatments had sapped much of his strength and drew his attention away from the USFL. Bassett soon learned the tumors were inoperable.

"John had been ill years before that," recalled McVay. "He held off melanoma, but it came back. We were aware he was battling that last year. We knew what was going on with John and his family. It was very painful for all of us. John had a lot of good friends, and a lot of people believed in John. A lot of people respected John. He wasn't perfect, nobody is. There were things I'm sure the league had issue with John or John had issues with the league. We tried some things that didn't work. We signed some players that didn't work sometimes, and we tried marketing ideas that didn't work, but overall when you grade the effort and the creativity and the success we had in a difficult circumstance, John was a real prince."

"By the time I was fulltime, in house, he was pretty sick," recalled McSherry. "I didn't know what was wrong with him. I thought it was some kind of cancer, but I didn't know at the time. He came up with this whacked out idea, where he was going to make the league into some kind of giant entertainment factory and play multiple sports and offer other types of entertainment. It was a grandiose project that he had written this gigantic tome about, and he was trying to give to people at an owners' meeting, and nobody would take it from him because he was so clearly sick. Nobody thought that what he had to say would make any sense.

"Bassett was a genius, though. The Tampa Bay team, I wouldn't be surprised if they actually made money that first year. The official version of the facts was that only the Denver Gold ever made money in the USFL. I think that Tampa Bay also made money. It didn't have any owners with real money. I mean, John Bassett didn't have real money. Steve Arky was just a lawyer, but they had innovative marketing things that they did. They had mortgage burning ceremonies. They'd pick a seat at halftime, and if you were sitting in the right seat, they'd burn your mortgage, car payment book or whatever.

"There was just something about John. If he had stayed well and actively involved, I think the league would have gone in a different direction. It wouldn't have bet its entire existence on a lawsuit. It would have come up with a business strategy. He would have been able to deflect some of the influences that Trump brought to the table and given people alternatives. He might even have been able to talk Trump out of some of the bad ideas. I don't think Trump listened to anybody in the presence of anybody else, but you had to listen to John because he clearly understood how to market the game."

"I can tell you one thing, he made a mark on my life," Gould said of Bassett. "He was a good friend, loyal. He had great instincts and was honest. He was totally committed to his view and his opinion, and you couldn't shake him if your life depended on it. He wanted spring football and that was it. He didn't want to hear about anything else."

With Bassett weakened, Trump took on a larger role with the league.

"John could always keep Donald at bay, because he was smarter when it came to sports," recalled Camera. "He understood it; he understood all of the aspects. Donald was a marketing genius. He is a smart man, he can build buildings; he puts his name on the buildings. You've got to be pretty good if you are going to build a building and put your name on it 'cause everyone is going to see it. So he could control everyone else, but he couldn't control Bassett, and the only one he would listen to was Bassett. When John started to lose his physical strength, Donald took over. He was like a shark and ate up everything around him. It was now his game plan, and he wasn't worried about it because he was going to come out a winner."

"Donald was very outspoken," concurred Taube. "That might not surprise anybody. He was abusive to anybody that didn't agree with him, particularly John Bassett, who at that point became kind of a sad figure because he had had like a stage three or four brain tumor and he was not going to make it. And Donald Trump gets his way, and I don't say this in a critical sense because it works for him, but he gets his way through intimidation. And he did try to intimidate the owners. Some of the owners were quite caught in Donald's spell. I mean most of us were real estate people. Donald was the epitome of the real estate player in the broadest possible sense, and some people among our ownership group idolized him and really hung on every word."

"Unfortunately, the real heart and soul of the league, John Bassett, was ill the last year, and John did not have the ability as he became more ill to take on the challenges of some new philosophies with the league," McVay stated. "And it was very unfortunate because John was one of the guys that conceptualized what the league would be and where it would go, a tremendous visionary in sports marketing, and how things should have been done, but his health did not help him as he tried to take on some of the challenges of the new owners."

The long-range planning committee commissioned by Simmons in New Orleans had conducted its own investigation of the proposed move to the fall. At the committee's behest, the league spent more than $500,000 on a McKinsey and Company study to find out how the public would take to the change. After three months of work, Sharon Patrick presented the study which revealed widespread knowledge of the league, as 98 percent of the respondents had heard of it, and also surprising acceptance of the USFL in the spring. A majority of those polled wanted to see the USFL remain with its current playing schedule. Additionally, 75 percent of the season ticket holders surveyed preferred that the league stay in the warm weather. Less than half the respondents stated that they would watch the USFL on television if it switched to the fall.

"Donald Trump wanted to fight the NFL, so he convinced the ownership to do so," remembered Breakers coach Dick Coury. "I remember the meeting. Our owner, Joe Canizaro, was selected by the league to hire a consultant and find out if we should stay in the spring or move to the fall. He came back to the ownership and said, 'There is no way we should go to the fall and play against the NFL. We should just stay where we are.'"

"We had commissioned a study to get a recommendation about what the league should do," Diethrich recalled. "The results of the study came out that we should stay in the spring. We had the ABC contact and the ESPN contract, and we were getting good commercial support. The audiences were climbing and our ratings were getting better. At that point, we were economically solvent and had we held the course, there could have actually been a profit."

"Right around when that season ended, the league went into an extended period of study," McSherry explained. "They hired McKinsey to study the question of where they would be best positioned to play their games, the spring or the fall. Most of the report was a business analysis that Sharon did. Sharon had done the original business plan for ESPN. I don't remember the exact words, but the essence of it was, 'You're nuts if you do anything other than play in the spring. Going head-to-head with the NFL would be a disaster.' Some of the people were persuaded, including me, but not Donald Trump."

"We hired McKinsey to take a look at the league, and I've done that with a couple of companies," stated Simmons. "I find them very good for particular things. I hired them to give us a look at the league as it was, successful and not successful. What should we do? Should we go forward to the fall? When they finished, the gal who was in charge of the group, Sharon Patrick, who later became president of Martha Stewart's company, a very bright, smart woman, to me bright and smart are different, she said her recommendation was that the worst thing we could do at that point was try to move to the fall.

"Everyone was all mumbly because they didn't get the answer that they wanted, but we had a press conference after their meeting with us. A pretty good size group of writers came, and I was told to say that the move to the fall is very important and we're going to look into it and go eventually. I said, 'I don't want to say that.' They said, 'Well, that's what it's going to say.' That's what I faced. It was not all of them, but a bunch of them. Donald was in the group that told me, 'To hell with what McKinsey said; we know better and we're going to move to the fall.' My instinct at that point was to say the owners have said this is what I should say. That was my instinct, but I knew if I did that, it would not be fun and I didn't want to do that at that point, but I did it privately with every writer in the room. After we finished with the press conference, I'd go to the corner with one of those really good TV/radio writers or a sports writer, and I'd tell them, 'That's bologna what I said.'"

The study brought to light some logistical problems the USFL faced if it planned to change seasons.

"The NFL stadium leases, several of them had these exclusive provisions in them, including the one in Washington, DC, so that was a problem," added McSherry. "We had stadium issues of our own, and we had constant fights among the owners as to where the other owners should be playing their games. They shouldn't be in the L.A. Coliseum because it was too big. The TV cameras would show all the empty seats, so they should play in a high school stadium somewhere, that kind of nonsense. There were some analyses of leases that McKinsey did to determine whether or not each team could actually play in the fall, and whether the right teams could play in the right cities in either the fall or the spring. That was a pretty lengthy part of their report."

Trump downplayed the study, saying in his book *Trump: The Art of the Deal*, "When it comes to making a smart decision, the most distinguished planning committee doesn't hold a candle to a group of guys with a reasonable amount of common sense and their own money on the line." He and Einhorn claimed that two networks had shown considerable interest in the USFL as a fall product. In fact, there had been no interest, and Trump later admitted as much under oath.

"I believe that he thought he could change the mentality of the networks toward another football league in either the spring or the fall that they might be interested in it, and that we could hook our fortunes to that tail, and it would lead to the accommodation," Simmons explained of Trump's motivations. "I think he believed all these things, but I don't think any of them had any sense to them. I think he became a Pied Piper. He spun a web of stories to the rest of the owners that all this could be accomplished, and it could be accomplished if you followed what he believed in and the people that he knew and his ability to get to people who we couldn't get to in order to raise the level of income from the networks, to get the interest of Pete Rozelle and the rest of the National Football League at a higher level, that they would think about the United States Football League in terms of the accommodation of a few teams. And away he'd go being the savior of what was the United States Football League. He was wrong on all counts. ABC wanted no part of him. Neither did NBC or CBS."

"We went into it as a small, modest programming venture," ABC News and Sports

President Roone Arledge told *USA Today* of the network's contract with the USFL. "Then, they started with the $40 million contracts and changed the concept. Now they want to go to the fall where there is already an oversaturated market. The last thing you need is more football in the fall."

"We made our position clear," ABC's Irv Brodsky told *USA Today*. "Jim Spence told the league we are really not interested in the fall of '86."

At an owners' meeting, Trump went so far as to deliver a thinly veiled threat that if the league stayed in the spring, he and his money might drop out of the picture for good. With the owners licking their wounds over the tremendous losses of the first two seasons, he felt he had an audience receptive to change. He and his backers, including Oldenburg and Birmingham's Marvin Warner, wanted a vote to move to the fall and they wanted it right away.

"We had a lot of fights amongst our own owners," recalled Argovitz. "I think that there were even some threats that if it was going to continue in the spring that Donald was going to disband the Generals. He wasn't going to play in the spring. If there is no team in New York in the USFL, then what kind of league do you have?"

"There was a lot of opposition to the idea," said Taube. "It was being essentially ram-rodded by Donald Trump with strong support from Argovitz and a couple of the other newer owners. The original group believed in the original plan which was to build stars and play in the spring. It was mostly the expansion owners who came in when we expanded the league to 18 who were among the large drumbeat for moving the league's playing schedule to the fall."

"Donald didn't have any more patience," Camera said. "He now knew he could control the league. It was easy, who was going to take him on? Fred Bullard out of Jacksonville? Delightful guy, home builder, yeah, yeah, but he wasn't Donald Trump. Donald would have them all come in, wine 'em, dine 'em, show them all around, talk to them about what could be. That's what Donald did, he was smart."

"We had a big-mouth who never shut up, and he had his own purpose," Tanenbaum said of Trump. "At that time, the NFL did not have a team playing in New York, and I think that Donald looked at that, and he's a *brilliant* man. You ask him, and he'll guarantee you that. His thought was that we could condense and ultimately merge ourselves with the NFL. No one knew how many teams could possibly even move over that way, but there certainly would be a New York team. And who better, who more desirable than big-mouth to have a team in New York? Of course, he didn't and he still doesn't know that the NFL hated him, *hated him*. They did not want him in the league at all, but he'll tell you a different story. He kept pushing it and kept telling everyone how football is really a fall sport, etc., etc., etc., and it came to a point where we had a vote."

On August 22, 1984, Donald Trump finally won the battle when the owners voted to switch to a fall schedule beginning in 1986. Trump and Einhorn pushed to make the switch in time for the upcoming 1985 season but fell short of an immediate move. Not everyone who voted for the change believed it was set in stone. Several owners wanted to see if a fall television contract developed and believed they could reverse course if it did not. Rumors of the decision surfaced in the *New York Times* a week earlier, probably provided by Trump. Berl Bernhard, still negotiating a sale of the Federals to Miami interests, was not allowed to cast a ballot, nor was owner-less Los Angeles. The first official vote on the change of playing seasons yielded a 14–2 margin for fall play with Philadelphia's Myles Tanenbaum and Michigan's Robert Taubman both opting for the spring.

The league announced a unanimous decision on the final ballot, but Taubman had already walked out of the meeting. Amazingly, Tampa Bay's John Bassett voted for the switch, though he maintained that his Bandits were a spring team.

"The vote was eventually called unanimous, but it really wasn't," McSherry recalled. "I think on the final vote, everybody voted yes, but there was a lot of discussion. Trump voted yes, but a whole lot of things had to happen to make it work. We had too many teams playing in cities where the NFL had a team, so strange and unproductive things occurred."

"I thought we should play in the spring," said Billy Tatham. "I was this young goofball, and I was learning. I'm still not sure about going to the fall, but on the other hand, what choice did we have? The NFL was going to put us out of business, so the only thing we could do was take 'em on."

"There was the big fight between spring and fall, and we finally thought we had the vote blocked," recalled Tanenbaum. "They needed I think 75 percent or maybe two-thirds of the owners, and of all people, John Bassett was the crucial vote. He voted to move to the fall, and he was one of the leaders of staying in the spring! We couldn't understand it. He said, 'It'll never work in the fall. All we have to do is prove that we'll never get a TV contact in the fall, and we'll stay in the spring.' I said, 'John, you're forcing me to move to Baltimore. Other people, like the Michigan franchise, are making arrangements to move.' It was a mistake. That, more than any other element, is what cooked the league in my estimation."

That was just one example of the confusion that, more than anything else, seems to have spurred the all-important decision. According to a report in the *Boston Globe*, one owner came out of the meeting and asked another why they had just decided to switch seasons. The other owner replied, "I don't know. You tell me." Reports persisted that many of them voted to make the move in order to appease Trump and still felt that it would never happen if a TV contract failed to materialize. Others had been persuaded by the possibility of a merger with the National Football League. Whatever the reasons for the decision, the USFL had drastically switched its course.

"They decided that the goal was always to force a merger with the National Football League," said Keller. "I don't think anyone really wanted that at the start. I'm sure if they came and offered one we would have taken it, but we never thought it would happen. We were always content that we were going to be a standalone league playing in the spring and carve out our niche. We thought ultimately we could be a representative, first quality, top notch football league, playing in the spring. "

While Trump's influence cannot be denied, the severe problems in the league's other two largest markets contributed to the decision. Los Angeles had virtually no ownership by the time the vote was taken, and Einhorn had taken over Chicago but had no intention of fielding a team in the spring. Faced with the possibility of also losing Trump if the league remained in the spring, some of the owners wondered if they could even have a league without teams in New York, Los Angeles and Chicago.

"Donald had put so much into these guys heads that that's all they talked about for the most part," said Simmons of the move to the fall. "That's why I call him the Pied Piper. He convinced owners that were there from the beginning that the only way they could be successful was to make a move to the fall, or merge, whatever the words were, and it was too bad."

"The ultimate vote was unanimous because Bassett agreed to it at the end, but I would say it was always split 50–50," Camera said. "It was never overwhelming to go to the fall, but there were some back-room deals."

"John was in favor of the spring, but the record will reveal that he voted to move to the fall," acknowledged McSherry. "He was going to lose the vote, so all the people who were voting 'no' decided to make it look like it was unanimous, that the league had a united front."

"It was not unanimous, but there were plenty of votes," a victorious Trump told *Football Digest*. "Certain teams will have difficulty with stadiums, but that won't stop us."

"He is very convincing and very domineering," Diethrich stated. "Overall, I don't think that most people felt that was the right thing to do. I know that he was a dominant influence in that decision."

"I was against it," said Oakland's Tad Taube. "A lot of it was orchestrated by Donald Trump. Donald sold himself and sold some of the other owners on the idea that we would always be a second class league as long as we were playing in the spring, that nobody would ever really take us seriously, that we would never be able to compete successfully for a television contract, etc. And that argument caught on with a majority of the owners. Not a big majority. We may have ultimately called it a unanimous decision for PR purposes, but it was a very hotly debated subject. The alignment was strong against it. There were very strong opinions on both sides, but we finally capitulated and moved forward with that decision. Besides myself, others who were against it included Myles Tanenbaum, Al Taubman, Marvin Warner in Birmingham, and certainly John Bassett. At the end of the day, the decision to move to the fall was carried by Trump, Argovitz, Oldenburg, although at that point he was very shaky himself, and some of the new franchises."

"He's always been an overpowering young man," recalled Taubman. "He convinced them that they should take the NFL on head-to-head, which was sort of ridiculous. They had the stadiums, they had the history. I mean I didn't go into this on the basis that I wanted to be an NFL owner. If I wanted to be, I'm sure I could have worked it out, with expansion teams and so forth. But I didn't want to go elsewhere."

"We were disappointed and we were also angered by that decision," recalled ABC's Spence. "It meant that in essence the league was a lame duck in '85 in terms of ABC Sports, dealing with our affiliates and advertisers. The advertising community would ask, 'Well, are you guys going to move with them to the fall?' and we'd tell them no, so it was a lame duck situation we were in. It hurt our sales department in terms of their negotiations for '85 because they couldn't talk about '86. I'm not a sales guy, but I know enough about how they deal, and they would negotiate with advertisers, 'Give us x dollars in '85 and we'll make it attractive for you in '86.' But we couldn't do that. We couldn't talk '86."

The logistics of the long layoff between the last spring season and the first fall campaign were not discussed at length. Later, the owners gave some thought to a split season with half the games in the spring and the other half in the fall. The owners announced that they based their decision on the McKinsey study, a contention that upset consultant Sharon Patrick so badly that she threatened to tell the truth to anyone who called her. Trump did not care. He would gladly take credit for the move that he had called for since his first day in the league.

"He has, in his mind, set up a challenge," Tanenbaum told *The Sporting News*. "What he wants to do is take on the Jets and the Giants for supremacy in the New York area. Donald wants to beat them so badly that he already envisions how it's going to happen. It's basically a case of 'me versus them.' That's all very well and good for him, but what about the good of the league as a whole? The thing that worries me is that some may be looking at a move to the fall as a means of gaining entry into the NFL."

Tanenbaum, one of just four original owners still in the same city in which he started, lambasted the decision at every turn, commenting to *TSN*, "It was wrong. It was wrong because no one cared about the teams, no one cared about the players, no one cared about the cities. I was so ashamed. There are no sportsmen. No one cares about the sport, not just our league, all the leagues. Suddenly, I saw the truth. This is the worst of all worlds. Good luck to us."

"He couldn't care less about these other guys," Simmons said of Trump. "If it came down to it, he'd kill them all, leave them in blood on the street if he got his franchise. So that's Donald."

But Trump and his allies correctly pointed out that the league would never be able to generate the necessary revenue in the spring to cover their burgeoning expenses. With player salaries growing and expected to continue in that direction, they would need a much better television contract and greatly increased attendance to stay on the pace they themselves had set. They reasoned that those goals could only be achieved in the fall. Of course, Trump had helped spur the rapid salary escalation, and others, some unwittingly, had followed. Many were beginning to realize that Trump and company wanted not a financially secure USFL but to force a merger with the NFL.

"I think some owners felt they could get to the NFL faster by doing this to accelerate the process," Peterson said of the vote. "There were some owners who were struggling financially and felt let's bring this thing to a head right away and this is one way to do it, that's for sure. But we all knew it would certainly be a collision course with the NFL and the USFL."

"What we have here is a car that got too big for the road so we've got to change the road," Bassett told *Sports Illustrated*. "Personally, I would've gotten into a smaller car."

"I tell people, when asked I would say that Donald Trump was the greatest owner his first year, along with Bassett because Bassett controlled him," recalled Camera. "Bassett would say, 'Donald, stop it. You may know how to build buildings, but I know how to do sports.' And they had that love-hate relationship which was terrific. Donald got us on the back page of the *New York Post*, got us on television every day. He signed Brian Sipe; he's got Herschel, brought in every good player, did everything that was necessary. That team was good, and we were getting good crowds, too, of 35, 38, 40,000 at the Meadowlands. Trump was doing a helluva job. But as soon as Bassett got sick, which started at the end of the second year, Donald took over because John didn't have the energy to keep up. Donald pushed and pushed to go to the fall. It was really a difficult time."

"The league should never have gone to the fall," said Breakers coach Dick Coury. "As a matter of fact, the New Orleans owner was the head of a committee that chose the marketing research firm to determine when the USFL should be playing. They spent like $800,000 on this marketing study, and they came back and said definitely stay in the spring. At the owners' meeting, it was determined that we would move to the fall and buck the NFL anyway, which was crazy to do. But that's what happened."

Many players were also upset by the move. The *Denver Post*, for instance, polled members of the Gold on the matter, and they strongly supported the spring. "I can't argue with the guys," said team general manager Rich Nathan. "I side with the players. I think the players are right. I think it's a valid concept. If you keep playing spring football, you get more and more integrity and develop a greater fan base."

"I was bummed out," said Jim Kelly. "I was an outdoors-man, and I loved to hunt; I loved to fish and do all those things. I loved to go back and watch my college, the University of Miami, play. I got to watch my high school team play, and now all of a sudden, they're changing the season. I was not for it because I thought we had a good thing going. Even though there were some teams struggling, I thought in due time we could get this thing going and have a good run. I thought it would be something that people would grow to love. I was a little bummed out, there's no doubt."

The Fallout

Aside from the players, the league's announced move had severe repercussions for several franchises, especially those in NFL cities. Several USFL franchises shared stadiums with NFL teams which had first choice of playing dates in the fall. Some Major League Baseball teams would also tie up venues into October. The first franchise to throw in the towel was a huge loss for the USFL.

As soon as the league decided on the season switch, Alfred Taubman announced that the Michigan Panthers would fold. He had no intention of competing with William Clay Ford's Detroit Lions or his beloved Michigan Wolverines in the fall. The Panthers would seek a merger with another team, eventually settling on Oakland. To his credit, Taubman took over primary ownership of the team even though it was thousands of miles from his home in Michigan, and he had already dropped several million dollars. Before its third year, the USFL had lost its first champion and one of its most popular teams.

"So the whole process began that we were going to play in the fall, not in the spring," sighed Michigan's Keller. "Not right away; our last season in the spring would be 1985, then we'd begin the transition of moving to the fall. Two things happened. Number one, we had TV contracts. The TV guys liked us in the spring; they didn't need us in the fall. Second, we were playing in stadiums that were used in the fall. We couldn't get stadium leases.

"They were creating a problem. The universities didn't want us playing at their stadiums, so we would have had to play on Wednesday or Thursday nights. It was an impossibility. We couldn't get Saturday or Sunday games. It was a tidal wave of things we had to overcome to play in the fall. What ultimately did us in was all this stuff was going to be impossible."

"The Taubmans decided they weren't going to play in Detroit because the Lions were already there," McSherry said. "But they still wanted to be in the league. They knew that Tad Taube who owned the Oakland team was running out of money, or at least said he was. They decided to partner up with him, so they gave up the Michigan Panthers and became partners in the Oakland Invaders."

"He was young and impetuous, like all of us when we're young," Taubman said of Trump. "We want to make everything happen today, won't wait for tomorrow. He proposed that we go to the fall instead of playing in the spring. Of course, we didn't have a stadium in the fall. We lost our stadium because we had the same stadium that the Lions were using.

"I wasn't there when they voted to move to the fall. My son Bobby was there. I know when he came back and reported to me that the teams voted to move the league to the

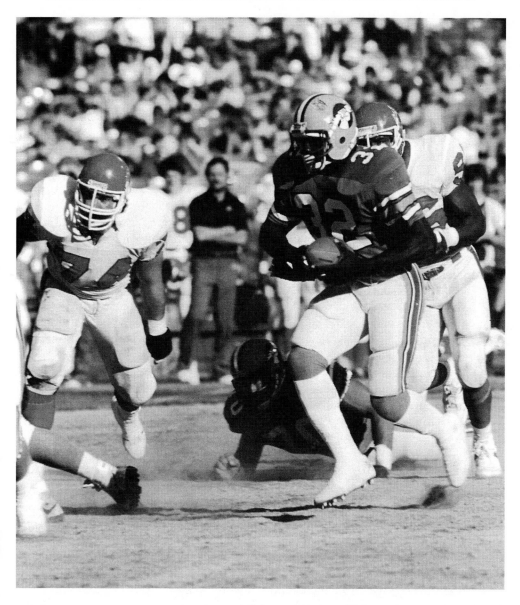

Running back Albert Bentley, one of the former Michigan Panthers who joined the Oakland Invaders roster, picks up yardage on the dirt infield of the Oakland-Alameda County Coliseum in 1985. Bentley went on to play in the NFL for seven seasons with the Indianapolis Colts and one with the Pittsburgh Steelers. Photograph by Jim Turner, from author's collection.

fall, my remark to him was, 'Well, we're out of business. We can't take the NFL on head-to-head. It doesn't make any sense. It's an ego trip. Our owners aren't wealthy enough to take them on.' Generally our owners were very nice guys but not necessarily that rich or willing to spend the money."

The Stars, fresh off their first championship and a year in which their attendance had shot up, realized that Philadelphia would not support them and the Eagles in the same season. Plus, they faced a battle with the Eagles and Phillies for the use of Veterans

Stadium. They, too, would have to find a new home. Above the protests of Trump, they settled on Baltimore, recently vacated by the Colts. Trump claimed that Tanenbaum's franchise was invading his territory, but the league allowed the move anyway. Unfortunately, Memorial Stadium, the home of the Orioles, was not made available to the team until 1986 so the Stars would have to play the next season at College Park in the University of Maryland's 41,000-seat Byrd Stadium, a field without lights.

"For us to stay in Philadelphia and for us to play in the fall, albeit two years from now, there's no room at the Vet," said Peterson. "The Phillies and the Eagles were there and we were there, but we were able to work it out during the baseball season for dates in the spring whereas in the fall, they were still playing baseball and obviously playing football, so we figured we'd have to go the first six or eight weeks of the season on the road. It made no sense, so Myles said, 'Let's start looking around for a move.' The obvious choice was one that had just lost an NFL team, the Baltimore Colts. Myles and I went down there and we met a guy named William Donald Schaefer, who was the mayor at that time, later became governor. He was very instrumental in building the inner harbor. He was very angry and bitter over how the Colts left town. He wanted a professional football team in a big way.

"We opened a ticket office down there, and then the only thing we couldn't get done was getting into the stadium. Not surprisingly, the owner of the Baltimore Orioles forbade us from playing in Memorial Stadium with the Orioles for the spring of 1985, so we played at College Park at the University of Maryland."

"We lost a heck of a lot of money," said Tanenbaum. "It was a terrible disappointment when we voted to move to the fall which meant that we could not play in Philadelphia anymore. We could not work a schedule in between the Eagles and the Phillies, especially if the Phillies went to the World Series. If that happened, we could not play a home game until November. It just was not feasible, so we had to head out of town. It was personally heartbreaking to me, because we were winning some fan loyalty in Philadelphia. To pull up stakes was disgusting.

"Fortunately, the people of Baltimore were great. They were very lovely people, warm and nice. They reminded me a lot of the people of Philadelphia. Don Schaefer, the mayor of Baltimore who subsequently became governor, was incredibly good and supportive. There were four teams that wanted to go there, and mayor Schaefer decided the team that he wanted was the Stars because of our record and character of the team and organization. He welcomed us.

"I went to see Edward Bennett Williams who owned the Baltimore Orioles at the time, and he told me that his general manager or manager just did not want us to play in Memorial Stadium in the spring because he was afraid that we would rip it up with the early spring rains. They had a good team, and he said, 'Why don't you just wait another year?' so we did. We didn't do it just because he asked, of course. He would have created a big problem, and his concerns were understandable. It was a grass field. Then it became a matter of playing at the University of Maryland or Annapolis, which is farther away. We liked the facility at the university better."

"It was unfortunate that we couldn't get back to Philly in 1985," lamented tight end Ken Dunek. "I believe our average attendance in 1984 was about 28,000, and we would have drawn 40,000 or 50,000 easily had we been able to come back as the champions."

"It was a shame that we couldn't have made it to a third year in Philadelphia," added Peterson. "The Eagles at that time were struggling. They were not a very good football team. Philadelphia fans, like all fans, want you to win, and the Stars were exciting. We had a unique thing in the territorial draft, and I know the NFL has looked at it. Each team had five local schools, or fairly local. We had Temple, Pitt University and Penn State as three of ours, and we got some terrific players from there. Chuck Fusina was our quarterback, Tommy Donovan, Scott Fitzkee and Pete Kugler were some of them. These guys were important to our team, and there was also a sort of hometown love for these guys as well as the other players we had. Philadelphia supported us very well for the two years we were able to play there."

After finally having found a home in New Orleans, the Breakers now faced the unenviable task of taking on the Saints. Rather than confront another battle to secure playing dates, Joe Canizaro decided to move his club. He considered Sacramento, California and Columbus, Ohio and a merger with Birmingham before Portland, Oregon, stepped forward. The Rose City, which hosted NFL exhibitions in the 1950s and 1960s, made an impression on Canizaro, and he tabbed it as the next home of the Breakers. Coach Coury and his intrepid squad would have their third different home in as many years. This was one city that Coury was familiar with, though, having coached the WFL's Portland Thunder in 1974. The community rolled out the welcome mat for the club and within 12 hours had sold its 6,000 highest-priced tickets. Two days after the move, the franchise had sold all 3,800 season tickets available in the $19 price range. The team received an even better break on the rental of 32,500-seat Civic Stadium. They had to pay just $1 per year and received a share of stadium concessions. As good as it was, it was still a great step down from the Superdome.

"It probably would have succeeded in New Orleans over the long haul, but it was kind of the same situation with Woody Weiser in Miami," Ehrhart said. "Woody and Schnellenberger would have been good owners, but this over-riding issue that no matter how good and solid you were, let's not go head to head with the NFL, just what Taubman said in Michigan. That's why the Breakers looked to Portland that third year—they were getting positioned just like Philadelphia moved to Baltimore. It was kind of a Catch-22. Taubman was terrific in Detroit: good local ownership, staying power, politically and corporately connected. Joe had the same thing in New Orleans. If New Orleans would have been like Memphis with no NFL franchise, they would have been very successful."

"We moved three times in three years, which is unheard of," said Coury. "Usually, you get fired and the team stays where it is, but we took our team and moved. We decided to move to the fall, and playing in an NFL city against an NFL team, we thought that was ridiculous, so we moved to Portland."

The Pittsburgh Maulers disappeared from the USFL landscape just as quickly as they had arrived. Although their attendance was solid for having such a poor record, they had no desire to face the Steelers head to head. Playing in the fall further meant scarce playing dates as they would have to compete with the NFL team and baseball's Pirates for playing dates early in the fall at Three Rivers Stadium, similar to the situation in Philadelphia. Even the tough Edward DeBartolo Sr., wanted no part of that battle. Hank Bullough, named as the team's next head coach during the 1984 season, found himself without a job before he even stepped on the field. The club announced that it would seek a merger with another team and folded its tent without ceremony. The first expansion team in league history became the first to call it quits.

"The irony is that at the same time the Pittsburgh Maulers, owned by Eddie DeBartolo, Sr., had to move also for the same reason," recalled the Stars' Peterson. "They were playing at Three Rivers Stadium with both the Steelers and Pirates, and there wouldn't be room for them in the fall. They had made a foray to William Donald Schaefer. He said, 'We'd love to have you both.' Myles and his partners certainly knew Eddie DeBartolo because they were in the same business. He and Eddie Sr. started talking, and they put together a deal. For six months, the Pittsburgh Maulers and the Philadelphia Stars were merged and working toward that. Three or four months into it, Eddie Sr. called Myles and said, 'My wife Marie has said that I need to get out of the USFL. She said we've got a team in the NFL called the San Francisco 49ers that Eddie, Jr. has. We've got a team in the NHL that my daughter Denise has and horse tracks.' Of course, his business was still building shopping malls, so he pulled out."

Washington also hit the road, but it wasn't out of any fear of the Redskins. To be sure, the successful NFL club would have clobbered the Feds at the gate, but owner Berl Bernhard decided long before the vote to switch seasons that they were playing their last year in the nation's capital. The team's inept play and the apathy of the Washington fans convinced him it was time to get out. Bernhard had worked out a deal with hotel developer Sherwood Weiser to move the franchise to Miami where it would be coached by Howard Schnellenberger, the former head man at the University of Miami. Once the move to the fall became official, though, Weiser pulled out because he didn't want to fight the Dolphins.

"It was like the Federals had a black cloud over them their entire time in the league," recalled Ehrhart. "From day one the high hopes were dashed, but they were wonderful people. Berl Bernhard was a high-profile attorney. In fact, one of the limited partners went on to become CEO of Northwest Airlines, Doug Steenland. He was a young lawyer in Berl's firm, one of the limited partners. That's the kind of quality people who were involved in the ownership.

"Woody was very aggressive and felt that in Miami they could really make a go of it. I was still in the league office when that was going on. Schnellenberger was just coming off a national championship and Orange Bowl victory with Miami. During our '84 season, even though the Federals hadn't finished the season yet, negotiations were already going on. I remember meeting with Schnellenberger and visiting with him about the role he would have and about the league. Then we went to a Blitz game in Chicago during our regular season of '84.

"The Federals were struggling, but here we had one of college football's iconic coaches and a guy who had been in the NFL, quitting the job at the top of the game to come join the USFL. Even though we were having certain challenges there, so many positives were happening. It was a great coup for the guys in Washington and Woody to land Coach Howard Schnellenberger. They were getting geared up to have the team relocate to Miami. So it was all seen as very positive to have a team that had been struggling without much fan support in Washington and not doing well, to have them emerge in Miami under the fabled Howard Schnellenberger. It was only after the big vote to move to the fall that the deal fell apart. Woody did not want to be in a competitive position with the Dolphins. Woody pulled out because he didn't want to go head-to-head with the NFL."

In stepped Don Dizney who bought the club and shifted it to Orlando. Dizney, a member of the Tampa Bay Bandits ownership group who had joined Weiser's Miami bid, owned United Medical Corporation in Orlando, an operator of a string of hospitals in the South. The $5 million deal for the Federals nearly fell through in September when

Schnellenberger pulled out, but the Orlando Renegades announced in early October that they would be the third USFL team to settle in Florida.

Bernhard breathed a deep sigh of relief after parting with the franchise. "I'm sad it didn't work, but I'd be lying if I claimed not to be relieved it's over," he told *USA Today*. "Washington won't tolerate football losers any more than a political loser. Lose too often at anything here and you're in danger of becoming a non-person. Fans in Washington are so spoiled because of the Redskins' success that we never had a chance when we stumbled so early. If you intend to compete in this city, you come out firing or you fold."

The Chicago Blitz was dead in the water the moment that it traded rosters with the Wranglers following the 1983 season. The move alienated the small fan base the Blitz had built in its first season, and even Marv Levy's excellent coaching job and the front office work of future NFL gurus Bill Polian and John Butler could not bring the club enough wins to capture the city's attention. Although Eddie Einhorn acquired a "new" Chicago franchise, he claimed he would field a team in 1985 only if another team would merge with his and they could draft as if they were an expansion franchise, stipulations he was reasonably sure the league would not accept. He did not want to waste any money on a lame duck season, knowing that the league's future belonged to the fall. He later decided to wait until 1986 to field a team. The league would lose the Blitz and the third-largest market in the country in the process which would further hurt the television ratings. The USFL was so glad to find ownership for the team that he had only to post a $1.5 million letter of credit to gain control of a new franchise minus its debts. At least Marv Levy was not unemployed for too long. He moved from the field back to the announcing booth, taking a job as a commentator on ESPN's coverage of the league.

"The league said, 'Hang in there, there are some people who are thinking of buying in,' but no one did," recalled Levy. "Bill didn't see much happening in the future there, and he was offered a scouting job with the Bills, and he took it. Finally, the thing just sort of petered out. It just sort of slowly fizzled out, no one said anything and pretty soon no paychecks were coming. I went back to my home in California and reconnected with the television networks."

"The Chicago team had been sold to Eddie Einhorn, who didn't like the idea of playing football in the spring at all, so he asked for permission to 'go dark,' as he put it," remembered McSherry. "We entered into kind of a strange agreement with him that he'd still have a vote and he was still owner of a team, but he didn't have to play in 1985."

The Tathams had quickly learned that they simply could not make it in Tulsa's Skelly Stadium. Poor weather early in the season and an even worse parking situation had kept crowds down to an unacceptable level. Without building a bigger and better facility, the city could not provide them with the revenue they needed to run a team in the new, more expensive USFL. The Outlaws worked out a deal to play in a planned new stadium in Oklahoma City, but they needed to use the University of Oklahoma's field in Norman in the interim. Once the USFL announced its move to the fall, Norman fell through. The elder Tatham then nixed a deal that his son had worked out with Honolulu.

The Tathams wanted to retain control of the franchise but sought a partner. The team nearly merged with the Oakland Invaders, prompting some members of the press to refer to them as the "Inlaws," but that deal fell apart as well.

The father-son Tatham duo soon found a willing party in Phoenix. Ted Diethrich had taken a financial beating for two years and never saw $6.7 million of the Blitz's $7.2 million sale price thanks to Dr. Hoffman's troubles. The Wranglers played well before losing the championship game, but Valley fans had been cautious. Now they would see basically their third team in as many years when the Arizona Outlaws began play in 1985. The new ownership announced that 20 Wranglers and 13 Outlaws would make up the 33-man offseason roster, with everyone else available in a dispersal draft. Initially, the plan called for the Tathams to own 75 percent of the club while Diethrich retained a 25 percent interest. But Diethrich soon wanted out all together, and the Wranglers technically folded with the Outlaws taking their place. The Tathams considered Phoenix an excellent candidate to join the NFL if the two leagues were ever to merge. In the end, George Allen and his son Bruce, the team's GM, left the USFL altogether.

"Now dad and I are thinking, 'It looks like we're going to a fall schedule and the way this thing's moving, we're either going to crash and burn or we're going to force a merger,'" Billy Tatham, explained. "That's the only two ways it could go. Otherwise, everybody was just going to spend themselves out of business.

"We kept running into guys who were either broke or didn't want to lose any more money, so they saw us as not really a 50/50 partner but rather as someone who could come in and fix their problems. We were there talking to Ted, and George Allen was still there. They had spent a small fortune and lost their rear ends. We're just about to do the deal in a downtown boardroom in Phoenix, and Dr. Diethrich's attorney said, 'I should probably tell you, part of the plan is as soon as we do this merger, we may have to file Chapter 11, and you're going to get stuck with everything.' That went over like a lead balloon. It had already leaked out in the media that there was going to be a merger. Dr. Diethrich still owed about $1 million in the community to vendors and others. He also sold like 15 or 17,000 season tickets for the upcoming season, and that money was already gone.

"Now it wasn't going to be a merger at all. Dr. Diethrich still owed all this money in the community, the community already thought it was going to be a merger and there was no way we could change that, so the guys he owed money to thought we now owed them the money. And how do we sell season tickets ... again? There was zero revenue. The league wanted us in Phoenix for television. My dad did the honorable thing. We stayed in Phoenix and had no season ticket revenue that first year. That's my dad. He's a league guy. Already we're losing money anyway. It was a nightmare.

"Having said that, we had a tre-

Arizona Outlaws quarterback Doug Williams scowls on the sidelines of San Antonio's Alamo Stadium during a March 3, 1985, 16–14 loss to the Gunslingers. Photograph by Tim McGrath.

mendous market. In the long range, it was a pretty smart move by dad, but in the short range it cost probably an extra $5 or $10 million. I was spending dad's money, but it felt like it was coming right out of my stomach lining."

"I had the prediction this thing was going to go south," recalled Diethrich of his reaction after Trump won the battle to move the league to the fall. "He was insistent the league should go to the fall. That was in spite of the recommendation we were getting that we were doing pretty well and we should stay where we were. All that made me say that it was time for me to get back to my profession.

"The folks from Oklahoma, the Tathams, were very interested in the Wranglers. I kind of took a leadership role when I had the team. I was very much involved, and I made the decision that I'd be glad to turn this over to somebody else. Psychologically, I was ready to leave so it wasn't an earth-shaking mental exercise for me. I'd made my mind up."

"Ted lost a lot of money in both places and it was understandable since he was not enormously wealthy," said David Dixon. "He was a wealthy and brilliant heart surgeon with a very fine operation in Phoenix with his institute, but he did not have unlimited capital. I don't blame him for pulling out in the least. A couple of other owners were in the same situation."

"Diethrich was so desperate to get out of Chicago in the end that he got the league office to overlook some things," said Jim Foster of the doctor's deal the year before with fellow surgeon Jim Hoffman. "When the deal went south, Diethrich not only was on the hook for almost the entire sale price of the Chicago Blitz, but he was also on the hook for the purchase of the Arizona Wranglers. There were stories of him doing eight, ten heart operations a day months later just trying to pay the bills."

Not everyone was sorry to see Diethrich go. "We were very upset with what happened in Chicago last year," said Philadelphia owner Myles Tanenbaum to *The Sporting News* referring to the Blitz-Wranglers swap. "If Diethrich wants to take a trip to Arizona, fine. He should have a good trip. But you've got to have more compassion for fans in Chicago. They were starting to support that team. I think the whole league was hurt by what happened in Chicago, not just Chicago."

Once all was said and done, the league had dropped four franchises down to 14 teams or two more than it had the first year. Coincidentally, that is the same number that Trump wanted to see entering the previous season. Gone from the USFL's ranks were several of the larger markets including Chicago, Detroit, Washington, Pittsburgh and Philadelphia, causing some concern about the league's ongoing television appeal. The first offseason saw the swapping of the Arizona and Chicago rosters and the transfer of the Breakers from Boston to New Orleans plus the addition of six expansion teams. With the exception of the Wranglers/Blitz trade, the moves were seen as positive, or at least the league could put a good spin on them. This time, the USFL had retreated from major markets and lost some of its most popular teams. Speculation mounted that the USFL would try to force a merger with the older league.

"There were just signs that the whole league was beginning to suffer from overspending and from the very bad press that we got," remembered Taube. "There was a very hostile environment in the media toward the USFL. We were constantly being disparaged as a second class league and our players were constantly being maligned. A lot of this I'm sure was being orchestrated by the relationship that these writers had with the NFL, on whom they depend for their livelihood. The unity that existed in year one, which, had it been maintained could have caused this league to eventually succeed, virtually fell apart by the end of the second season."

"I was a football guy learning the business part of marketing and selling professional football in the spring and the importance of sports marketing," recalled Carl Peterson. "The thing that I was fearful of was that we expanded too fast. It's like any business. You have to crawl before you walk and walk before you run. We started with 12 franchises and then went right to 18, one and a half times as many, in the second year. Then we had to cut back to 14 in our third year. That put a tremendous strain on the viability of the ownership."

Other franchises faced an uncertain future after the final spring season. New Jersey, in particular would have to fight the Giants and Jets just to get playing dates at Giants Stadium if they could not work out a deal with Shea Stadium by that time. The Gamblers were betting that Houston, in the midst of an economic downturn, would support both them and the Oilers in the fall. Already battling for its life without an owner, the Express had to worry about the Rams and Raiders as well, not to mention college programs at USC and UCLA. The popular Broncos would certainly take a bite out of the Gold's fan base in Denver. Unless Bassett made good on a promise to keep the Bandits in the spring, they were going to see just how much of a dent they had made in the Buccaneers' Tampa Bay standing.

Collateral Damage

Regardless of the switch to the fall, some franchises faced a life and death struggle. The USFL pledged its support for the Los Angeles Express through the upcoming season even if another owner could not be found. For his part, J. William Oldenburg refused to give up the ship easily in Los Angeles. He had sold off his jet and one of his mansions and trimmed his IMI staff from 200 to just 40 employees. He publicly blamed the press for many of his problems and wondered aloud whether the NFL had conspired against him. The USFL had seen the last of Oldenburg's support. The league would be calling the shots and paying the bills until a new owner could be found.

"They go to play the Arizona Wranglers in Tempe and they lose the game, which is a good thing because an equipment company had confiscated the equipment after the game," Dufresne recalled of the Express playoff loss. "So if they had won that game they weren't going to get their equipment back for the next round because they owed $33,000 that hadn't been paid."

"Nobody knew what the resources of Oldenburg were because that was a myth," Taube said. "We didn't really come to terms with what that myth was until the various actions against him by various regulatory agencies and so forth that unmasked what he was doing."

"Oldenburg was involved in federal investigations," recalled Dufresne of the Express owner's collapse. "The off season between '84 and '85 was literally just chaotic. Oldenburg eventually lost reign of the team, and then it was just a circus after that. The league took over ownership of the team. All the other owners had to chip in $500,000 to keep the team afloat. All this did was it paid the players' salaries, and they had the biggest payroll in the league. Their parking lot was Mercedes, Rolls Royces."

"I went out to see him the first time at his building, and wow, was it impressive," remembered Camera. "You had to go through the secretary to even get in the building. Before security was in, it was secure. One time Trump told me, 'He hasn't got a pot to piss in.' I said, 'What are you talking about? I saw his building.' Donald said, 'You want to see buildings? Come on.' It surprised me, but Oldenburg as it turns out had something like a Ponzi scheme going, I guess. He was moving money around, billing people, and in the end he didn't last all that long."

Though he was cleared of fraud charges years later, Oldenburg drifted out of the picture entirely due to his mounting legal and financial problems, and the Express fell into the league's hands.

"So Oldenburg skips town, literally walks out of town," said McSherry. "A scandal erupted that suggested he had defrauded some people. There was a transaction that he did with a small bank that he owned where he sold some real estate to the bank for an enormous amount of money, and the property wasn't worth one-tenth the price that the bank paid. That was the money he used to make believe he owned a football team. He just skipped town without paying his bills."

"He was another big mouth that probably did more to destroy the league than anybody else by virtue of the fact that he went after big-profile names with big-profile compensation packages, and at the end of the day the league had to bail out his franchise because they were unable to make their payroll," said Taube. "Certainly during the last year of the league, the league operated or tried to operate the Los Angeles Express."

"You had a disaster in Los Angeles because of an owner who called himself 'Mr. Dynamite,'" said league PR man Jim Byrne. "He almost blew up the team and the league both, single-handedly."

Houston Gamblers' part-owner Jay Roulier had acted as the Express owner since October, helping to meet the team's payroll, but he was unable to sell his stake in the Gamblers and had to back out of the Los Angeles deal. To cut costs, the league fired 13 front office employees in L.A., mostly in the marketing department, after the 1984 season concluded. The possibility of losing both Chicago, the country's third largest market, and Los Angeles, the second biggest, could have severely crippled the USFL's chances for another television deal. The owners hated the idea of supporting another team the way they propped up the Blitz in 1984 but had little choice in the matter if they were to fulfill their contract with ABC. They also decided to support the Houston Gamblers if that franchise's situation worsened.

"Roulier was from Denver, and he was very interested in the USFL," remembered Ehrhart. "He became a minority owner of the Houston team and then expressed to the league that he wanted to take over in L.A. Being in the league, he knew that Oldenburg had imploded, so he made a proposal to take over the Los Angeles team. In fact, they spent weeks and months doing the paperwork for Roulier to own the team, but quite frankly Roulier did not have sufficient resources to close the deal."

Even with the team's instability, general manager Don Klosterman refused to call the Express a failure. "People didn't give us a chance in the AFL either," he told *Sport* magazine. "The press was as bad as this, or worse. When I managed the Houston Oilers I had to play in a high school stadium. So I know how this goes. The first two years you have novelty and momentum on your side. These are the critical years, the third and fourth. If we survive these two seasons, we'll do all right. But we've got to win." At least one person still believed in the Los Angeles Express.

The circus behind the scenes in Los Angeles took attention away from one of pro football's best young teams. "Some of the owners were very solid people, and then there was this guy who bought the Los Angeles Express, Oldenburg," said Myles Tanenbaum. "He offered some comic relief, while at the same time his general manager, Klosterman, went out and put together probably the greatest draft of football talent that anybody's ever had."

Uncertain not only about the league's future, but its immediate present as well, new investors shied away from the league.

"There were no longer reasonable prospects for finding more owners," summarized McSherry. "The accommodation of the expansion they did after the first season; that kind of brought out of the woodwork all the potential expansion owners so there really weren't any more people to go to. Certainly there wasn't a line outside of our office looking to make an investment in the USFL."

"At one of our meetings, before the thing even started, each owner was asked to write down what he thought his team's season-ticket base would be," Bassett recalled in *Sports Illustrated*. "I wrote 20,000. And that's what I had the first year. Almost everybody else wrote 30,000, 40,000. They were living in a dream world. They thought just because they had a football team, everybody would run out and support it.

"They spent too much on every conceivable budget item. People didn't act in a professional, businesslike manner, except our team. The original concept worked; it was the people who screwed it up. Now, instead of making money, we're losing our asses. Our payroll is 2½ times what it's supposed to be. We never budgeted $800,000 this year to help save the L.A. franchise."

A New Commissioner

The USFL's tumultuous offseason had only just begun. Rumors sprung up that Commissioner Simmons was on his way out. Though some owners denied that there was any movement to oust the commissioner, it became apparent that some of them were looking elsewhere for leadership.

"The owners, none of them had any football experience, sports experience and television experience so it was a brand new thing for all of them," said Simmons. "You had to teach them and that was very difficult because realize that they're all millionaires, multi-millionaires. They had never been told 'no' in their lives, and here is me. I come along and I got to tell them what to do. They didn't like that much, you know. We tried, we tried hard."

"Chet was between a rock and a hard place," Spence explained. "Even though he was the commissioner, it was hard to control Trump. It's hard for anyone to control Trump. On the one hand, Chet knew that the USFL, given the way they were acting, was not doing right by ABC Sports. But on the other hand, he really didn't have the power to control what was going on, specifically to control Trump. A lot of the smaller market owners went along for the ride saying, 'Well, Trump's super successful, and we have to follow his lead.' Maybe Bassett was the only guy who might have been able to put the brakes on, but then he became ill. John was the only one with enough strength to slow Trump down."

"Chet is a very sweet man, very knowledgeable about television and knowledgeable about sports," McSherry said. "He was very reliant on Steve, and he was somewhat afraid of some of the owners like Taubman, Tanenbaum, Trump, all of the T's, all very powerful people. Chet fell out of favor with the owners, probably by the end of the season in '84. It wasn't so much about issues as it was about style. Trump wanted the USFL commissioner to be in the NFL's face every day. That's not Chet's style."

"I don't think Chet ever wanted to be a commissioner," explained Camera. "I think Chet wanted to give birth to the league, and it would've been better had he left after the championship game because he'd done a hell of a job. Step aside and said, 'Guys, it ain't for me. It's terrific, I've done a good job, but I really don't like this commissioner stuff. I don't like you guys calling me every week.' He'd get six owners complaining, and six owners saying, 'Hey, Chet, how'd you like my game? You see that throw? But every week he couldn't deal with it. Pete Rozelle dealt with it. Chet couldn't deal with it. It would affect him. He didn't recover until Wednesday. That's when they stopped calling him."

"I think there are owners who feel that the leadership that is being produced out of the league office hasn't been sufficient," Tampa Bay's John Bassett said in *The Sporting News.* "I think it's a bad rap, and the owners should look at themselves before they look at the league office. There aren't five owners that spend the amount of time on league affairs and on their teams' affairs that they should."

"I could spend two or three hours just talking about owners' meetings," said Tad Taube. "You'd have intelligent people who had the capacity to build huge financial empires, but once they entered that room, they'd act and talk like blithering idiots. Because of my involvement with the USFL, I've had the chance to talk to owners in other sports, and that happens in other leagues as well. We might be in the middle of a discussion about an issue that dealt with the life or death of the league in the near term, like Bill Oldenburg folding in the middle of the season, and another owner might start talking about the two-point conversion. Then we'd get sidetracked on that for an hour. I'm not exaggerating. That's exactly the way it happened. Other discussions were equally idiotic. Sometimes you could tell people were thinking about what they had to do after the meeting and the last motion presented, no matter what it was, would be the last one passed, just so they could get out of there."

Simmons was not around to see much more of anything happen with the league. Pressure had been mounting for him to step down from his post with one anonymous league source labeling him "useless." Many wondered if that source had a New York accent. Some of the owners complained that he had not acted assertively enough in league matters, but most of the frustration with the commissioner resulted from the lack of progress in renegotiating the ABC contract, something that he was powerless to correct. ABC had a deal that had proven extremely profitable over two years and was not about to give any more back to the league than it absolutely had to. Simmons understood the network's position and in explaining it to the owners, frequently came off as an apologist for ABC. He had also been beset by a stiff neck that had become so bad at one point that he had to be hospitalized. The malady had sapped much of his strength when he needed it most. He resigned his post under pressure on January 14.

"Chet had a problem with I think a disc in his neck," remembered McSherry. "He was physically uncomfortable, wearing a neck brace for the last two or three months that he was with the USFL. He had his agent negotiating a buyout. While he was doing that, he preferred not to be in the office, but he had to be nearby. My office was two blocks away from the league office. Chet used to come and sit in my office all day. All of a sudden one day Chet says, 'I think we have a deal.' He was there for two months. We called it 'USFL North.'"

"It was kind of mutual, I didn't want any more of them, they didn't want any more of me and that's lovely," said Simmons. "I had a man that worked for me, an agent, whatever the word is, and we discussed my leaving. The league got Alfred Taubman to represent them, and we went to dinner to have a meeting with Alfred. It was on 5th Avenue or Park Avenue, and it was outrageously beautiful. It was big like Alfred. Taubman, he's a big man, and first we had a waiter and a waitress serve us dinner, the three of us, and then they go into the conversation. While it should've bothered me that I'm sitting there listening to my life being discussed, it didn't. It was like a big, heavy boulder coming off my back. I really wanted out of there. I wanted away from the owners, I wanted away from their stupidity. I wanted away from Donald Trump. I didn't want to get away from my staff which was very good. I mean, let's cut the cord, you know, let's do it right now."

"We were losing control," said Camera. "Chet now had no one defending him. He was taking abuse from everybody. It was really running into a problem. His health was failing. He got a pinched nerve and was in constant pain. These guys were running around, and at the meetings were shouting, 'I invested a lot of money!'"

"He had a neck collar for a while," recalled Ehrhart. "I remember he came to one meeting and he was wearing a neck brace. That caused some people to worry about Chet. Other than that one period of time when he was hospitalized for the neck problem, I think his health was pretty good. It was probably one of the most challenging jobs ever, keeping this vast and different group of people together."

"The owners would come, and he would get very tense," added Camera. "He would have difficulty. He liked the job. You have to respect that he was able to walk away. Don't forget there was a difference in age. Chet was ten years older than I was, and it was a good job. I think they sensed in Chet he was too much of a gentleman, which is a compliment. Everyone will tell you that Chet was a gentleman, and he was and is."

"I think there was a sense we needed somebody who could handle some of us a bit better," agreed Diethrich. "He was a gentleman who tried very hard, and I think he was always giving his best effort."

"I liked Chet," said Ron Blanding. "I thought he got overwhelmed by the strength of some of the owners to where they dominated him. He didn't have enough control over them. In other words, he wasn't allowed to be the commissioner and that was a weakness in our league. Several owners just overpowered him."

"As a person, I really liked Chet." added Billy Tatham. "He got it going. When it became apparent that this was a war, and I don't mean a war just selling tickets—it was an absolute business battle—we needed a guy right out of Korea or Vietnam, because there were absolutely no rules. It was cutthroat with the NFL."

"Chet was a good person, but Chet was not the strong type of personality that was needed to lead men who were very strong themselves," agreed David Dixon. "What's really not known is that [Chicago Bears GM] Jim Finks was within a breath of becoming the commissioner of the league. Had Jim come aboard, then we would have been in great shape.

"Some of the owners felt, erroneously, that Chet Simmons could help them with television. I don't think that Chet really had anything to do with the television contract. We were playing football and we were playing it at a time of the year when there was no other football. I'm not saying that disparagingly of Chet, I'm just saying that as a matter of fact. I think that you and I could have gotten television."

"Chet was one of the smartest guys I've met," countered Ehrhart. "He knew the television business inside and out. He had been president of NBC, an ABC executive, was an Olympic pioneer and to this day people don't recognize what an unbelievable job he did getting ESPN off the ground. He had done such a marvelous job at every one of his television stops. He was saddled with a contract that had been done before he was ever hired, and with an ownership group that had a voracious appetite for revenues because the spending demands were so high, he was in a no-win situation. Our only source of national media revenue was boxed in by our competitor, the NFL. He was in an almost impossible situation.

"I have great admiration for Chet. In a lot of ways, I think people expected miracles. He did a terrific job, but the circumstances were beyond anyone's control. All of a sudden, bam, here's a product where nobody could have ever projected we'd have some of the best stars in the game. It's unheard of. People say, 'It's different today.' It wasn't different. The NFL was the power player then, too; they were on all the networks. People just could not believe how quickly we had become a true competitor. Quite honestly, we out-hustled them and were guerrilla warriors. We put together an outstanding product, but we got ahead of our supply line. We advanced so far that the supply train that was bringing in the dollars couldn't catch up to us."

"There are so many instances in business or anything else where, when things aren't going the way you like, there are a lot of people pointing fingers at everybody else as to what they might have done and should have done," said Myles Tanenbaum. "Chet took a lot of heat, and some people thought that we could and should do better. We also had some ownership changes that started after the first year, and for the second year, we brought in several additional franchises. There was a lot of instability that was generated there. The upshot was that we got a new commissioner. There were a lot of things happening during the 1984 season because the real issue that was underway was Donald Trump leading the charge that we should be playing in the fall."

"I left, and I left under good circumstances," Simmons concluded. "I'm sure I wasn't loved by the owners. I rarely heard from any of them. I'm sure they felt that I was not able to bring them a better television contract because I was the television guy they hired, but Trager had done a good job. They had locked themselves into an agreement you couldn't change."

Harry Usher, a 45-year-old California attorney, took Simmons' place as commissioner of the USFL the very next day with a three-year agreement. The owners had obviously been prepared for Simmons' departure.

Usher graduated from Brown University and was an honor student at Stanford Law School. While there, he served as editor of the *Stanford Law Review*. He formed Litz and Usher in 1974 where he specialized in entertainment law. As vice president and general manager of the Los Angeles Olympic Organizing Committee since February of 1980, Usher had been instrumental in making the 1984 summer games a success as Peter Ueberroth's right hand man. The duo received much of the credit for making the games profitable despite universal dire predictions.

The Olympics had been beset with problems prior to the 1980 Games and had a history of losing money. Israeli athletes were murdered by terrorists at the 1972 Games in Munich, the 1976 edition in Montreal ran up a $1 billion deficit, and the United States had boycotted the 1980 effort in Moscow. The Soviet Union would boycott the 1984 games in L.A. to return the favor. Usher and Ueberroth talked the United States Olympic Committee into being a co-guarantor of the L.A. Games, the first Olympics which would be privately funded. Usher watched the purse strings like a hawk, requiring his signature on any expense of $1,000 or more. The Los Angeles Olympic Games earned an unheard of profit of more than $225 million.

"I am not here to rearrange the deck chairs on the Titanic, but I'm here to take this ship forward," Usher told the Associated Press when he accepted the USFL post.

"The great Harry Usher ... Harry was a piece of work," said McSherry. "He had been the number two guy on the L.A. Olympic Committee under Ueberroth. The L.A. Olympics were a financial success, notwithstanding the fact that Moscow didn't show up. Harry got a lot of the credit along with Ueberroth. Ueberroth went to Major League Baseball, and Harry wanted a similar position. The only one that was around was the USFL, so he took that job."

"He was a very proud guy, kind of distinguished," remembered Dufresne. "But to me it was a sham when he took over. Almost everything he said was a lie, and I knew it. It was like, 'Don't believe that man behind the curtain.'

"Harry Usher was telling everybody, 'Don't worry, don't mind this fire over there. We'll put it out.'"

"I basically hired him," said Tad Taube. "The thing that made Harry appear to be an attractive candidate was that the world had just gotten through an extraordinarily successful Olympiad and it was commonly known that while Peter Uebberoth was a good promoter and a good leader, that the behind the scenes success and efforts of the organization were being handled by Harry Usher. At that point, he had left his business as a sports attorney to go to work for Uebberoth. I met with Harry on more than one occasion, and he was intrigued with being the commissioner of a new league and we eventually hired him.

"The state of affairs by the time we hit the 1985 season was so disjointed as far as the owners and their various independent agendas are concerned, that I'm not sure that Jesus Christ Himself could have done anything about it. Decisions were being made that proved to be catastrophic."

"This is a tremendous challenge and one that I look forward to with great anticipation," Usher said to the AP. "A challenge as stimulating as the 1984 Olympic Games is difficult to match. However, there is no question that the USFL will be equally demanding and exciting."

Unbeknownst to those outside of the league hierarchy, his contract contained a clause that would pay him $400,000 if any USFL team merged into the NFL.

"Harry Usher, the commissioner, I thought did a pretty good job," Argovitz argued. "Harry gave a lot of thought to the things he did. He was bombarded, and Donald Trump was always there. You know every team was trying to get their own competitive edges if possible, of putting their own two bits in. Harry had to deal with all these high profile owners. And I give Harry credit; he dealt with them, he listened and he was strong enough to stand up to how he felt. And he kept people in check, kept the owners in check."

"I mean this with no disrespect to Chet, because I like and respect him, but had Harry Usher come in right after the first year, the league would still be going," said Camera. "Harry Usher would smile at the owners and just tell them, 'We're going to do it this way. Thank you for your input.' That was Harry; he was a no bullshit guy. Even Trump, he'd start fighting with Harry, and Harry was a brilliant guy, a lawyer. He'd say, 'Donald, you've got a good idea, but you're going to have to do it this way. Otherwise, you can put the team up for sale or the league will take over the team.' He didn't have a pot to piss in, but that was Harry."

"The day that he took the job he called me on the phone and introduced himself," recalled McSherry, who would develop an entirely different opinion of the new commissioner. "He asked me if I wouldn't mind going out to L.A. and having a couple of meetings with him. Harry had to finish up some business with the Olympics, had some money he needed to give out to some people. He wanted to introduce me to some people he wanted to hire to help the league. So I flew out to L.A., and met him at David Murdock's club at the top of a building in downtown L.A. for breakfast which became lunch. He had a parade of people from LAOOC come into see him, and he gave them their bonus checks. Some of them stayed and chatted for a while. There was a PR woman; a lawyer who he eventually married, her name was Jane Ellison; and a financial guy.

"Harry dropped this bomb on me. Harry said, 'I don't know anything about running a football league, and I don't want to move to New York. Your firm is making $200,000 a month representing the USFL. I'd rather use that on an L.A. firm that I'm more familiar with. I think I can get them to do it for less money. Here's the deal: if you'll come into the league office as a full-time person, I'll continue to use your law firm. I'll continue to pay you whatever they're paying you, you can have whatever title you want, and you're going to run the league office on a day-to-day basis, and I'm going to be in California. Frankly, I may try to run for the Senate in California, and if I do that I'm not going to have any time for the USFL.'

"I said, 'No way, I like being a lawyer.' I went back to New York, went to see my managing partner and tell him about this proposal. He said, 'You have to accept it.' So I backed into a position with the USFL because my law firm wanted the money.

"I talked to Steve [Ehrhart], who had been the executive director of the league, which was a title I was somewhat unfamiliar with. I knew people who were executive directors for not-for-profits and things like that, but in sports you have presidents of the National and American Leagues and commissioners. Steve persuaded me that executive director was the correct title for essentially a chief operating officer position, and I went to work at 52 Vanderbilt.

"I still did some little things at the law firm that were not USFL related; I had some clients, but to the outside world I was fulltime. I used to go to the USFL office at eight in the morning and then go to my law firm office at 6:30 at night.

"I was doing 100 percent of the day-to-day stuff. Very quickly the owners figured out Usher wasn't in the office, and they let their feelings be known that they didn't like that. In fact, what was really happening was that the owners were talking to me all the time. They didn't really know what was going on unless I told them. I tried to keep them informed, but I'm sure I didn't remember everything that happened all the time."

With Simmons gone and Ehrhart in Memphis, the top two men in charge were Commissioner Harry Usher and Executive Director Bill McSherry. Where Simmons and Ehrhart became friends, Usher and McSherry did not see eye-to-eye. Usher's desire to remain in California, even though the league offices were in New York, rankled some of the owners as well.

"I didn't always get along with Harry very well," said McSherry. "I thought he was delusional. I thought he was deceptive, a dishonest guy. Eventually Trump got mad at

Harry for being in California, so Usher had to come to New York. He came to New York, but he brought his girlfriend with him. At the time he was married and so was she. He made her the general counsel of the USFL, which meant that not only did he go home with her at night but she sat in his office all day.

"Harry was kind of neurotic over closing his door. You have some people who wash their hands all the time; Harry closed doors. Whatever room he was in, the door had to be closed. So they came into my office, and they closed the door. There were meetings orchestrated in my office, and my office was like a closet. He had a nice big office. He would herd five or six people into my office and close the door. Everybody had to stand up because there was no place to sit down. It was ridiculous. There wasn't anything that we were discussing that was really confidential."

"Was he really dedicated to the league?" asked Ehrhart about Usher. "Of course, he had a big contract but it took him a long time to move to New York, where the league offices were. He didn't have that same kind of investment of self, blood, sweat and money that a lot of other people had put into the USFL."

Suing the NFL

Trump further ensured that the USFL implemented the second part of his strategy to force an accommodation with the NFL: legal pressure. The USFL and McSherry researched the merits of suing the NFL on antitrust grounds.

Chet Simmons had previously sent a series of letters to the NFL, one of which, sent on September 13, 1984, stated: "The position of the USFL as a new sports enterprise, and the market position of the NFL, make it essential to the survival of the USFL that the NFL and the NFL owners operate within the bounds of the laws and regulations which govern the conduct of a business having a dominant market position."

Two months after they announced their decision to compete head-to-head with the NFL, the USFL filed an antitrust suit against the older league on October 17, 1984.

"It was discussed in the summer of '84," recalled McSherry. "We were hired late in the summer of '84 to see if there were any grounds for bringing a suit. So simultaneously while the McKinsey study was studying the business, we were studying the NFL's leases at various facilities. They were contracts and we could get them. We were reading congressional history because Rozelle had testified several times in Congress, and some of the ways in which the television contracts arose were because of the Sports Broadcasting Act, which allowed the teams to pool their rights. Otherwise, that would be an antitrust violation. It restricted the NFL to two networks and precluded them from playing on Friday nights or Saturdays to protect high school and college football. We finished our investigation and filed the lawsuit in early October."

Soon, infamous New York attorney Roy Cohn, who had gained his fame as Senator Joe McCarthy's right-hand man during the Army-McCarthy hearings on communism, began work on the case. While some in the USFL saw the suit simply as a way to get the NFL to stop interfering in their business, Trump, a Cohn client, had pushed for the lawsuit, believing it was yet another way to apply merger pressure on the National Football League, an organization with a poor track record in court. Trump and Cohn took it upon themselves to announce the suit at a press conference in New York without any other league officials present. They also quickly increased the stakes, though the notorious lawyer would soon be forced to sit out the case due to his deteriorating health.

"Trump made our firm join as co-counsel a man named Roy Cohn. It wasn't the best situation to be in, to be co-counsel with Roy Cohn," added McSherry. "At the federal courthouse the judge that we drew in the lottery was a former assistant US attorney.

"Cohn was ill; he was dying. He didn't talk about it, but you just took a look at him and you knew he was sick. He claims to have had liver cancer, but many people believe he had AIDS. He was a friend of Trump's. They never could convict him. They tried Cohn three times and he always got acquitted; mostly dealing with taxes, I think. Roy did nothing on the case except go on television with Trump. The day we filed the complaint, they were on *The Today Show*, which of course pissed the judge off."

The suit alleged that the NFL conspired to force the USFL out of business or at least make it more difficult for it to operate. The main thrust of the motion was that the NFL's contracts with all three networks made it impossible for a competitor to succeed in the fall. The NFL was a monopoly which could blackmail the networks into keeping the USFL off the airwaves by threatening not to renew their NFL pacts, Cohn claimed. The USFL sought $440,000,000 in damages, which when trebled under antitrust law, would amount to $1.32 billion or more than $46 million per NFL team.

"The National Football League wanted no part of him," recalled Simmons about Trump. "The only thing that he used to scream was, 'Lawsuit, lawsuit!' and I'm sure it frightened the National Football League to a degree because they didn't want another lawsuit. They had plenty of them. Donald with his brazen way of doing things could frighten somebody in that way, and I think he did to a degree. Hence came the lawsuit with the big names and all the hoopla and glory of Cohn and this guy and that guy."

"Once the owners starting to talk about moving to the fall, that was to force a lawsuit with the NFL," explained Argovitz. "Donald Trump was behind this, Eddie Einhorn was behind this, but a lot of the other owners weren't for this. A lot of the owners were losing a lot of money and they were finally convinced once they brought the lawyers in telling them about the antitrust violations against the NFL. They felt this was a short cut to getting into the NFL and consolidating the league with maybe six teams with the NFL and the other owners would have an opportunity, either being a partner in 'em or getting paid off. But to me it was a drastic mistake."

Los Angeles Raiders owner Al Davis, himself a recent winner of an antitrust suit against his fellow owners in the NFL over their attempts to block his move from Oakland, had a different opinion: "I think several [USFL] owners could sue other owners for destroying their league, or at least what that league was in its original concept," he told Knight-Ridder Newspapers. "Take the Philadelphia franchise. Do you really think the guy who owns that team wanted to do what they're forcing him to do? He could have said, 'Hey, this isn't the way it was supposed to be,' and then he could have gone to court to protect his rights. But when they start talking up this 'unity' stuff, your rights get forgotten pretty quick." Nevertheless, Davis decided to testify against his NFL compatriots and would be excluded from the USFL's complaints.

"The USFL felt that we had, not one, but maybe ten smoking guns to demonstrate in a trial court, demonstrate to a jury, that there were oppressive efforts to restrict the USFL from access to stadiums, from access to television networks, from access to players," countered Taube. "I mean, it wasn't just the Oakland conspiracy, which was very visible because Al Davis became a star witness for the USFL. There were many instances in the formation of the league, where the league was precluded from using certain stadiums that were city property. We were precluded from considering San Francisco. And those occurrences of flagrant antitrust violations were heavily documented, and we had a really outstanding case."

Trump replaced the ailing Cohn with Harvey Myerson, an attorney known for his courtroom theatrics and unquenchable enthusiasm. He lit into preparation for the case with marked enthusiasm and left no stone unturned in his search for proof against the other league. Like Cohn, Myerson had few fans.

Larry Felser of *The Sporting News* described Myerson as "Danny DeVito with hair." The hair came from a collection of toupees of varying lengths the lawyer cycled through to give the illusion of growing hair. "I don't hate the guy, but I've called him a 'pathological liar' and I absolutely believe he's one," fellow attorney Leon Marcus later told the *New York Times*. "He'll tell you a different story about the same thing today, tomorrow, Sunday and Monday, as if he's never told any of them before."

"A man who was later convicted of various crimes named Harvey Myerson wrote a letter to Donald Trump, basically telling Trump that he was the lawyer for the case and that the lawyers who were handling the case were basically fucking it all up and they didn't have the publicity machine that his law firm had," McSherry recalled. "If they would hire him, they would have Trump and the USFL's lawsuit on TV every day and every night, which is of course exactly what Trump wanted to hear. Trump sent the letter to Usher, and I saw the letter. It's a disgraceful and unethical letter, but nonetheless it existed.

"Sure enough, Usher, who would be loath to fail to do something Trump told him to do, hired Myerson to be co-counsel. By this time, I wasn't really running the lawsuit anymore; I was running the league, so it meant that some of my partners would have to work with this guy Myerson. The significance of that was manifold. First of all, Myerson's law firm represented ABC, and he never told anybody, so it was unethical for him to ask for the work in the first place and doubly unethical for him to ask for it in the face of that kind of undisclosed conflict. Later, I had the unfortunate task of bringing the fact that they had represented ABC to the attention of some of the owners. I did that, and incurred the eternal wrath of Mr. Myerson and of Usher.

"Meanwhile, I think the USFL was the only client that Myerson didn't overbill. Eventually he was convicted of double billing his clients and served two years in jail for it. The reason he didn't overbill the USFL was that he knew that all of the people who were running the USFL including Usher and Usher's wife who became the general counsel, they were all lawyers and knew how to read a legal bill. Eventually, we quit. We couldn't work with Myerson, and Myerson handled the case all by himself and did whatever Trump wanted him to do."

"My indirect role was joining with Myles Tanenbaum in opposition to the counsel that Donald Trump wanted to hire to conduct the trial," recalled Taube. "The guy that Trump fell in love with was a bombastic, cigar-chewing litigator by the name of Harvey Myerson. He had zero antitrust experience. He was a good litigator in civil and criminal cases because those trials generally were shorter and Myerson was able to dazzle the jury with his fancy footwork and his oratory skill."

The USFL was not the only league shifting through different attorneys. With potentially more than $1 billion at stake, the NFL made sure it put its best foot forward. After litigating unsuccessfully against the Raiders' Davis about the team's move to Los Angeles, it also was in no hurry to see the inside of another courtroom.

"After we filed the case, Paul Tagliabue, who eventually became the NFL commissioner called me up and told me he needed an extension of time for the NFL to find counsel," remembered McSherry. "He had just been involved in the Oakland Raiders case. He was the lawyer for the NFL who lost that case to Al Davis, so there was no way the NFL was going to hire him to do another one. It was in New York, anyway, and Tagliabue was a Washington lawyer. So he asked me for three months … to find a lawyer. I said, 'Paul, I'm a gentleman, and I would normally accommodate any reasonable request, but that's not a reasonable request. You don't need three months to find somebody to represent the NFL in this case. You'll have to go see the judge and see if he gives it to you, but I can't voluntarily give it to you.'

"So I grabbed my lawyers' directory, which is a very insightful thing for me to do. It's this big, big Bible-sized red book that contains a list of all the lawyers in New York City, and I shoved it into my briefcase and went down to the court, because Paul said he was calling me from a place near there. Judge [Peter K.] Leisure was there, and we walked into the court room. He said, 'Tell me what's your problem.' I'm the plaintiff, so I get to speak first. I told him exactly what happened with Tagliabue's request and that I'm sorry to be a burden on the court's time, but it just was not a reasonable request. I had my red book in my hand. Judge Leisure, who was a brand new judge on his first case, said, 'Is that the New York Red Book? Can I borrow it for a minute?' I handed it up to him, and he turned to Tagliabue and said, 'I know you're from Washington. You're probably not familiar with this book, but I'm sure he'll let you borrow it. It contains a listing of all the lawyers in New York City, and I guarantee you all of them would take this case representing the NFL. All you have to do is make a phone call, and you'll get a lawyer.' He gave him like an extra two weeks.

"Then another bad thing happened before the season started. A man named Arthur Liman called me and said that Tagliabue had asked him to represent the NFL in the case. I didn't want that to happen because I had tried a case with him when we were both younger. He was a fabulous trial lawyer. So I said, "Arthur, I have a problem. Your law firm represented the USFL until I came around. For over a year, your law firm was the USFL's counsel. You can't sue the USFL unless the USFL consents, and I doubt very much that it is going to consent.' He said, 'You don't know what you're talking about.' I said, 'I'll do some homework and prove it to you.'

"I went over to the league office, asked around and found some old files, found all the old bills. Sure enough, Liman's law firm, Paul, Weis, Rifkind, Wharton & Garrison, had received $175,000 in fees. They had 16 different people bill time for USFL representation. They had written opinions that various NFL leases violated antitrust laws because the leases restricted the facility from leasing it to any other football league. There was a person from Liman's firm in every USFL owners' meeting I could find the minutes on. In fact, when Steve first called me about representing the league, one of his reasons was that at the last owners' meeting they had six lawyers from Paul, Weis there and three of them slept during parts of the meeting, which irritated him and some of the others.

"Liman refused to accept my representation as to what the bills said. He did no investigation of his own which forced me to file a motion to disqualify him. Eventually that motion prevailed, but unfortunately about four months went by while nothing was happening in the lawsuit."

Other Developments

The NFL faced other problems as well. Television ratings for the older league had fallen roughly 10 percent in the last year, continuing a decline started in 1982. The older league attributed some of the decline to oversaturation caused by year-round football. Escalating player salaries spurred by the USFL had taken a bite out of the increased revenue the NFL had attained in its last TV deals. The NFL Players' Association, rebuffed in its attempt to get 55 percent of team gross revenues for its members in 1982, observed that because of the USFL's emergence and the ensuing bidding war, they now earned more than that figure. The younger league had helped to raise NFL salaries by more than 54 percent in just two years.

"History has shown that no team sport can survive for any period of time with competing leagues," Dallas Cowboys President Tex Schramm said in *Forbes*. "At some point the situation will be resolved. Meantime, people are going to fight to survive."

Einhorn gave up his work to get the league a new television deal early in 1985, admitting the courts would have to force the NFL off at least one network, presumably making it available to the USFL. The networks had shown no interest in the USFL as a fall entity and Einhorn did not want to waste anymore of his time. The promise of a fall contract had helped convince the owners to switch seasons, but Einhorn found no interest despite a variety of proposals. "I'm sure a lot of guys are disappointed that I didn't come back with a deal, but I never promised them a rose garden," he told *Sports Illustrated*. Usher took over the negotiations to no avail.

"Einhorn was going to work this and work that," remembered Camera. "Now I'm head-to-head because he's trying to build his own syndication network, saying, 'We can build our own television with syndication. I did it before, and I can do it again.' And I said, 'You want to use Ku Band, direct feed satellite into people's homes? What are we talking about?' He wanted more money from the networks. Being a television guy I said, 'They're our partners, we have to stay with them.' Long story short, it was a disaster. Eddie Einhorn, I'm not a big fan. Einhorn was a front guy, and it was a joke. Eddie Einhorn is a very shrewd, great salesman. It was like being at the Borscht Belt with everybody. He would sit there and talk about these far out scenarios, and it didn't make sense. Chet was hanging his hat on Eddie because he knew him from his television days. But Eddie wasn't a fan of Chet. I think he buried Chet more than anybody else in hindsight. That was my feeling because I could see him do it. Trump worked Eddie Einhorn like a fiddle. He knew exactly what he wanted out of him, and he worked him."

"It's very difficult to keep your enthusiasm up in the face of horrible decisions," Bassett said in *Sports Illustrated*. "And some of them I've made, I'll admit that. We never should have given Eddie Einhorn the chance to negotiate with television for a fall league. But at the time, we were at the end of our second year, and we had lost $100 million. We were forced to go to the fall. When he couldn't negotiate a TV contract within 60 or 90 days, we should have either gone out of business or voted to go back to the spring."

"John was going through treatment, and the league was really starting to come apart at the seams," recalled McVay. "It was a tough battle for John. He was taking on the league battles, taking on his health battles. It was really a very sad time."

One More Fling in the Spring

The league had one more spring season to play. The off-season maneuverings saw the USFL get smaller but stronger on the field as 14 teams would make up the United States Football League in its third and final spring campaign. Gone were the Michigan Panthers, Chicago Blitz, Arizona Wranglers, Pittsburgh Maulers, Oklahoma Outlaws and Washington Federals. New on the scene were the Orlando Renegades and Arizona Outlaws.

All the changes left the appearance of instability. While the USFL had expanded from 12 to 18 teams after its first season, it shrunk to 14 just a year later. The league announced the switch to a fall schedule in 1986, but some owners openly questioned whether that switch would actually occur, and John Bassett continued to decry the move. Chet Simmons had been on the job as commissioner for just over two years before being replaced by Harry Usher. Financial problems stole headlines as the Los Angeles Express remained without an owner. The league's billion-dollar antitrust suit against the NFL stole some attention from the on-field product. The USFL only finalized its 1985 schedule ten weeks before the start of the season.

The franchise reshuffling meant that once again the USFL would see its share of coaching changes. New Denver owner Doug Spedding released Craig Morton from the Gold's top spot and entertained the notion of hiring several big-name coaches such as Dick Vermeil, Bud Grant, John Madden and Hank Stram before tabbing Houston Gamblers offensive coordinator Darrel "Mouse" Davis to run the show. The hiring touched off a war of words between Davis's new employer and Houston owner Jerry Argovitz who had tried to keep the coach. Davis took top assistant June Jones with him as his offensive coordinator. Argovitz, who publicly blamed the coach for his team's playoff loss to Arizona, claiming that his mind was not on the game, filed a letter with the league office that charged the Denver owner and his team with tampering. Said Spedding of the letter, "They've misspelled my name and the word 'initiate.' That's awful." The Gamblers fired Davis's daughter Debbie who worked in the team's personnel department. The league eventually awarded Argovitz Denver's first-round choice in the upcoming draft and levied a $50,000 fine against the Gold. The fine was later rescinded, but the bad blood remained. At least the affair would add extra significance to the teams' two regular season games.

Jim Bates moved up from his defensive coordinator position and took over as head coach of the San Antonio Gunslingers after Gil Steinke, the team's first head man, became the franchise's director of football operations. Bates had never held a head coaching position before and, prior to his first season in San Antonio, had never coached with a professional team in any capacity, having served as an assistant at Texas Tech, West Virginia, Kansas State, Villanova and Southern Mississippi. Assistant Tim Marcum took Bates' former position as defensive coordinator.

They were not the only personnel moves for the franchise as the club's financial picture darkened. The team fired all its secretaries, and resignations left it without a public relations department. A film man was answering the team's phones. With little help from management and less money from owner Clinton Manges, whoever coached the Gunslingers would need a lot of patience.

"In 1980 oil was an unheard of $40 a barrel," explained Marcum about Manges' sudden financial troubles. "It dropped down to $11 or $12. There were people in Houston in '86 and '87 who bought houses on their credit cards."

"I never thought he was intentionally trying to hurt anybody," added Greg Singleton, a member of the team's front office. "He wanted to do it right, but the economy in Texas at the time ate him alive. All his money was on paper, and he was always struggling to get cash."

With Schnellenberger out of the picture, Lee Corso became the head coach of the new Orlando Renegades. He had just completed his first year as a head man at Northern Illinois University where he compiled a 4–4–1 mark. Previously, he held the top job at Louisville from 1969–1972 and Indiana from 1973–1982. His 1979 Indiana Hoosiers went 8–4 and took a thrilling 38–37 Holiday Bowl decision over Brigham Young. Corso had become familiar with the USFL as part of ABC's 'B' team which broadcast secondary games not covered by Keith Jackson and Lynn Swann. In fact, he presided over the Federals debut in 1983, the first USFL telecast. As a player at Florida State University, Corso had been the roommate of none other than future actor and Tampa Bay Bandits part owner Burt Reynolds. Lewis "Bugsy" Engelberg, the man who had assembled the Bandits a couple of years earlier, joined the franchise as vice president and general manager.

"The Washington Federals, which happens to be the worst team in the history of football, so the guy buys it and they go to Miami, and they become the Miami Federals," Corso explained. "A guy named Howard Schnellenberger, head football coach of the National Champion Miami Hurricanes, resigns and takes the job. He's the head football coach of the now Miami Federals. Before the season, Miami Federals is sold to a guy named Dizney, who is in the medical business here; really good guy from Louisville, Kentucky, who happened to belong to the same country club that I did when I was a coach at the University of Louisville. So I get a call. I'm up in DeKalb, Illinois, freezing my ass off. It's like 400 degrees below zero, and Don calls me and says 'How would you like to be the coach of the Orlando Renegades?' I say, 'What's the temperature?' He says, '80.' I said, 'I'll take the job!'"

"We were the worst football team in the history of football," said ex–Federals running back Craig James, who later ended up working with Corso at ESPN. "They went to Lee Corso. Are you kidding me? You go get Lee Corso to coach your team, you know you're bad. Lee says, 'Goddamn it, I get the job and my best player, you, quit.' I didn't quit, Lee, I got traded. No, we were pretty bad, but we had a lot of fun. We might have been terrible on the scoreboard, but we were darn good in the locker room."

"I go from the television booth of doing the game, to the coach of the Washington Federals who were the Miami Federals, who became the Orlando Renegades, and that's how I got involved in the United States Football League," laughed Corso. "I think I must be the only guy in history to televise the first game and then coach the same team a couple of years later. I thought it was a great idea! It was exciting, there was a nice crowd there, it was a niche for football in the spring time, and for professional football there were some pretty good athletes, stars. I really thought it was a great idea."

Frank Kush left the Indianapolis Colts with one game remaining in their 1984 schedule to take the top job of the Arizona Outlaws. It was a homecoming of sorts for the coach who was a local legend after guiding Arizona State to a 176–54–1 record from 1958 to 1979 with a 6–1 record in bowl games. He had been fired after allegedly punching a player in 1978 and asking his assistants and some players to cover up for him the following year. A phony grade scandal also emerged the year after he left, which resulted in the Sun Devils being placed on probation by the NCAA. From there, he went on to coach Hamilton in the CFL before taking control of the Baltimore Colts in 1982.

Unfortunately, the Wranglers had also promised the job to someone else, Paul Lanham, George Allen's offensive coordinator. According to Lanham, Bill Tatham had agreed to honor that deal after the merger, but the job went to Kush, and Lanham sued the Outlaws for breach of contract.

Although already named to the position during the 1984 season, Charlie Sumner had to wait until 1985 to take over the reins of the Oakland Invaders. After playing in the NFL for six years with the Bears and Vikings, he left to become an assistant coach with the AFL's Oakland Raiders from 1963–1968 before moving over to the Pittsburgh Steelers for the following four seasons. He served at New England from 1970–1978 and then headed back to Oakland from 1979–1983. Sumner received an unexpected talent infusion when the Michigan Panthers merged with the Invaders.

Following a year spent battling a nagging ankle injury with the Pittsburgh Maulers, 1983 Heisman Trophy–winning running back Mike Rozier came into his own with the Jacksonville Bulls in 1984. Photograph by Jim Turner, from author's collection.

Coaches were not the only ones playing musical chairs. In player transactions, Mike Rozier found himself without a home after the Pittsburgh Maulers closed up shop. He bought his way out of his contract and, after flirting with the NFL's Houston Oilers, the runner stayed with the younger league, inking a pact with the Jacksonville Bulls.

The Bulls improved further by outbidding the Minnesota Vikings for the services of Washington State defensive end Keith Millard, the Vikes' top draft pick. He became the third Minnesota draft choice to opt for the USFL and the sixth in three years.

Corner back Leonard Coleman spurned an offer from the Indianapolis Colts and signed instead with the Showboats. Joining him in Memphis was fellow corner Mossy Cade who could not reach an agreement with the Chargers. Both signed four-year, $2 million contracts, making them one of the highest paid corner back tandems in all of football. Memphis also acquired offensive lineman David Huffman from Arizona and linebacker John Corker from Michigan. They further moved to shore up their running game with the addition of Arizona's Tim Spencer, although his status was uncertain because of an off-season ankle injury. They later traded for Denver's Harry Sydney on draft day for insurance.

The USFL also lost some players prior to the 1985 campaign. In addition to Ken Lacy's defection from Michigan to Kansas City, Jim Fahnhorst decided to leave Arizona behind and join San Francisco, while Wrangler teammate Frank Minnifield latched on with the Cleveland Browns. The financially strapped Express waived Kevin Mack who immediately signed with the Browns, resulting in a much-needed $200,000 payment from the NFL club to the USFL franchise. Arizona's Greg Landry went back to Chicago to join the Bears, and Stan White retired. Washington's Mike Hohensee never waited around to see how things turned out in Orlando, instead jumping to the CFL's Toronto Argonauts. Arizona received another blow when top receiver Trumaine Johnson left the Outlaws' camp in a contract dispute. The USFL found itself on the other side of a futures contract when Houston Gamblers running back Todd Fowler signed a pact with the Dallas Cowboys to take effect after the 1985 season.

Despite continued claims that the USFL's players were vastly inferior to its own, the NFL held a three-round supplemental draft on June 5 for USFL and CFL players who would have been eligible for their 1984 draft. An amazing 20 of the 84 players chosen resided on the roster of the Los Angeles Express, topped by Steve Young who was tabbed by the Tampa Bay Buccaneers with the first choice. The Houston Oilers grabbed Mike Rozier and the New York Giants chose Young's teammate tackle Gary Zimmerman. All told, 78 of the 84 players chosen had homes on USFL rosters.

"It was a competitive thing," Peterson said of the league's relationship with the NFL. "Without question, we did open the eyes of the National Football League because initially, and I guess if I was on their side of the street I would have said the same thing, Tex Schramm came out immediately when the USFL was announced and said, 'That league will be made up of players, coaches, administrators and scouts we will have no interest in, and that league won't last a year.' How wrong he was. We did get the attention of the league to the point they had a supplemental draft, a totally illegal violation of antitrust laws while we were still in business."

In the USFL's 1985 draft held on January 3, 351 players were chosen in the territorial phase and 221 in the open portion. Birmingham picked first and tabbed Mississippi Valley State wide receiver Jerry Rice as the number one choice. The Houston Gamblers chose Hawaii quarterback Raphel Cherry for the sole purpose of keeping him away from the Denver Gold. There were still some hard feelings over Mouse Davis's departure.

Unlike the wholesale signings that had occurred the previous two seasons, very few USFL teams actively pursued their high draft choices this time around. There was a feeling that the teams were already overpaying their players and there was no way they could recoup additional expenses with current revenue.

Donald Trump could still afford a few more players, and always one to make a splash, he set his sights on college football's best player. In one of the few major rookie signings for the new season, the New Jersey Generals wooed Boston College quarterback and 1984 Heisman Trophy winner Doug Flutie to the USFL. Flutie inked a six-year, $8.3 million contract after ten days of highly publicized negotiations which required the services of no less than ten lawyers. The document they finally hashed out was a legalistic marvel, containing clauses that provided for the star quarterback if he was injured, if the USFL went out of business or if the league merged with the NFL. The USFL's instability had found its way into the contract of its newest star. Furthermore, Trump guaranteed half of the contract if the league folded and the entire deal if the Generals closed up shop and the league lived on.

"The day I signed, the press conference at Trump Tower was ridiculous," Flutie recalled. "We were in the lobby in the atrium with the waterfall behind us and seven floors of media hanging over balconies all in front of you and over balconies. Cameras everywhere, only as Donald could pull it off, and that was a shock. I had just gone through the whole Heisman thing and all that attention, and that was over the top to begin with, and this just took it to a whole other level."

"Behind the scenes so much had happened that the public and the media never knew," recalled Flutie in his book *Flutie*. "Somewhere along the line Donald Trump got real pissed off and took the deal right off the table; just pulled it and said, 'The hell with this. I'm not going to do it.' The problem involved a breakdown in communication. It was pretty obvious to me the most secure thing to do was to take this deal. Now all of a sudden Trump had pulled it off the table. The guy who got Trump and Bob Woolf back to the table was Howard Cosell. He was a mutual friend of theirs and kind of calmed Donald down. A few days later they got back to the table and we got back to the same deal we originally had, and I decided to go with it."

Flutie's agent recalled another interesting aspect of the negotiating process when he, Flutie, Doug's father and college roommate Gerald Phelan visited the owner at Trump Tower for the first time. Trump immediately took them into a mini theater in the building to show them his own highlight film. "The lights went down and the curtains parted and for the next 20 minutes, we were shown a slickly produced, visually attractive, highly impressive presentation detailing the triumphs and achievements of Donald Trump," remembered Woolf in his book *Friendly Persuasion*. "It was impressive. It was his commercial. Maybe he wanted to make sure we knew the extent of his accomplishments. It was his

Nineteen eighty-four Heisman Trophy winning quarterback Doug Flutie warms up before a game under the watchful eye of New Jersey Generals head coach Walt Michaels. Flutie went on to a long career in the CFL and NFL. Photograph by Jim Turner, from author's collection.

attempt to earn our respect and create the right atmosphere before our negotiations took place. Only after we had seen the film in its entirety were we shown into Mr. Trump's office."

Flutie's signing on February 4 gave the league its third consecutive Heisman winner. He gained fame in college when his 64-yard "Hail Mary" pass on the last play of the game floated into the hands of Phelan for the winning touchdown in a crucial game against the University of Miami. Besides leading his team to that important 47–45 win, he also set an NCAA record with 10,579 passing yards in his career. Many compared the Flutie magic to the drawing power of Joe Namath and wondered if the USFL expected its newest star to accomplish the same feats as the former New York Jets passer did for the AFL nearly two decades earlier. Flutie was so popular in his hometown of Natick, Massachusetts, that the city even named a street after him and threw him a parade after he signed with the Generals. Within two weeks of the quarterback's agreement with the team, the Generals sold an additional 7,000 season tickets. His new coach, Walt Michaels, was an assistant coach with the Jets when Namath began there but shied away from the comparison, preferring to let the rookie sit on the bench for a while and learn from Brian Sipe.

Coach Michaels intended to bring Flutie on slowly under the guidance of starting quarterback Brian Sipe, eventually working him into a starting role. But Trump had other ideas. Against Michaels' wishes, the owner oversaw the trade of Sipe and his $550,000 salary to Jacksonville just two days after Flutie signed. That left the young passer as the Generals starting quarterback by default. Trump was determined to see an immediate return on his newest investment.

The league held a dispersal draft to allocate players from the Maulers and the Blitz rosters. At the time it appeared as if Pittsburgh would merge with the Stars, so the champs had the option of protecting 33 players from among the two rosters or keeping one team intact. They did not see too much on the 3–15 Maulers that they wanted so they kept their championship team together. The league allowed the Oakland Invaders, who merged with the Michigan Panthers, and the Arizona Outlaws, the combination of the Arizona Wranglers and Oklahoma Outlaws, to also protect 33 players with the rest available in the draft. Those two teams had to sit out the first three rounds of the dispersal draft before they could join in for the final ten.

All the changes had an effect on ticket sales. The Stars sold 16,000 season tickets, 782 to fans who would make the trek from Philadelphia. Portland had sold over 13,500 season passes, and Orlando totaled nearly 20,000 before the season began, many more than Washington would have provided. Despite the infusion of Michigan Panthers talent and Taubman's money, Oakland stood at just 15,000, down 10,000 from their total just two years before. New Jersey, with two Heisman winners on the roster and coming off a playoff year, came in at around 44,000 season passes, while Tampa Bay showed up in the 38,000 range. Not surprisingly, Los Angeles came in as the bottom-dweller with only about 6,000.

After Further Review

In one addition to its rules, the league announced that it would utilize a limited television instant replay system to review disputed officials calls. With widespread television coverage and the use of slow-motion instant replays, fans of both college and professional football had been able to view controversial plays in slow motion, and often from different angles. USFL brass reasoned that utilizing television replays would give them a chance to correct game-changing calls. Under the USFL's plan, each team could challenge one play per half. If their challenge was unsuccessful, the team would be charged a timeout. The official would throw a red flag to indicate the challenge.

"Chet Simmons and I talked about it," remembered Ehrhart. "Is that going to look goofy throwing a red flag out on the field? Here it is more than 30 years later, and they're still throwing a red flag out. That all started right in the USFL."

"The USFL did several things for football," explained Argovitz. "One is we created the instant replay. Our competition committee consisted of Larry Csonka, Carl Peterson, Steve Spurrier, Vince Lombardi, Jr. and myself. We were the ones who initiated and got approved the instant replay for the USFL. And several years later the NFL adopted that and so have many other sports today."

"There are many football fans who were not even born when the red flag was first dropped in the USFL," said Steiner. "Or the revolutionary two-point conversion: 'Oh you're cheapening the product,' is what the NFL said at the time. Well, it worked out alright."

"These officials are good, and they do a good job but things happen quickly out there," Mora said. "Did that guy touch the line or not? It can cost you a game, and it's hard to win in professional football; it's hard to win. You don't wanna lose a game by an incorrect call on an official, so if a replay can correct that, I'm all for that. It started in the USFL, and I liked it."

"I enjoyed it because it was doing everything trying to make the game perfect," Orlando Coach Corso added. "Yeah, that was on the cutting edge, because, they would never think of that [in the NFL] because this was almost like against the officials, as if you don't trust them. No, it wasn't that. It was that we had an idea that we could get this thing right and why wouldn't we get it right? That was another really good thing that they did."

"We had more conversation about instant replay than we did about any other subject," said McSherry. "You were tinkering with the rules. You were distracting the fans from the field. Most of the people who ran the league came out of the NFL. The director of operations for the USFL had worked for Rozelle. Usher was in favor of it. Hadhazy was against it. Cal Lepore, who was the head of officials, was against it. The owners didn't understand it, so they had ignorant opinions on the subject. ABC and ESPN were willing to do it. Most of the arguments came down to what was the penalty if you challenged something and you were wrong, what price did you have to pay? Eventually we came up with the timeout.

"The NFL took 15 years to get where we got in 1984, and that's just because they never wanted to do anything that we did."

On the eve of its third season, "change" had become the new buzzword in the USFL. The league would begin a spring season for the final time. It had lost four franchises but now clung to the promise of a huge payout from its antitrust lawsuit. The league faced an extended break before shifting into the fall and direct competition with the NFL. Owners, coaches and players had come and gone. It remained to be seen whether many of the changes were for the better.

6

Strong Play
but Mounting Problems

The USFL displayed some of its best football in its last spring campaign. The mergers and consolidation of league talent meant that virtually every team became stronger on the field. They also took a swipe at the NFL's recently instituted "hot dog" rule that curtailed on-field celebrations with a marketing campaign that proclaimed, "The USFL: Where Football is Still a Game." It featured several players celebrating after big plays, displays that would have been penalized in the other league.

"When the USFL came around not only were we new, we didn't have all these rules like no celebrations in the end zone," said Breakers running back Buford Jordan. "But in the USFL we could do all that stuff, especially as running backs. They promoted it as a league that was still fun because it gave opportunities to guys who would never have been playing ball if it wasn't for the USFL."

"We had a wide receiver from Penn State, one of our territorial schools, Tommy Donovan, a really fine flanker back," recalled Peterson. "And he always wanted to do a flip, but he was never allowed to do it. He did it one time at practice at Penn State and Joe Paterno said, 'Don't ever do that again.' But after he scored a TD he would always do a forward flip in the end zone. And that became his signature. The only thing is we would hold our breath that hopefully he made the flip successfully. But he loved the opportunity to do that, and those types of things that were kind of an example of this fun league and playing football, the game we all love, and playing it at I think an exceedingly high level."

"You could throw the ball in the stands, you could do flips, you know, the more the merrier," agreed Tampa Bay's Nate Newton. "The NFL has this thing where it's looking out for itself. If the right fans say, 'Oh, that's not classy,' or 'Why did they do that?' then the NFL will comply with it."

"I was starting at center and we drove down the field and scored in a preseason game down in Fort Lauderdale," remembered Newton's teammate Chuck Pitcock. "So I ran over and I grabbed the ball out of the guy's hand, and I spiked it and I ran off the field. My old line coach grabbed me and said 'Coach Spurrier don't like nobody hot doggin' it, we don't like people doing that,' and I was thinking, 'Oh man, I'm screwed, you know.' 'Don't be hot playing out there and bullshitting like that,' he said.

"Alright so then we got back on the field and we drove down again, and we scored, and I didn't go get the ball and slam it. I come off the field and Spurrier grabs me, 'Why didn't you spike the ball?' I said, 'Well, okay I gotcha, bro,' and from then on it was a race to the football. After about two or three games, the whole offensive line got into it, so now you had to outrun somebody to get to the football to spike it. It was a lot of fun."

"They always talk about the NFL being the No Fun League," added Generals radio man Charley Steiner. "The USFL was *the* Fun League. We all had a good time."

The franchise reshuffling caused the league to abandon the divisional lineup it had used the previous couple of years. Instead, teams were simply divided into two conferences. Joining the Eastern Conference were the Baltimore Stars, Birmingham Stallions, Jacksonville Bulls, Memphis Showboats, New Jersey Generals, Orlando Renegades and Tampa Bay Bandits. The Arizona Outlaws, Denver Gold, Houston Gamblers, Los Angeles Express, Oakland Invaders, Portland Breakers and San Antonio Gunslingers comprised the Western Conference.

Tampa Bay Bandits

Bandits owner John Bassett continued to decry the move to the fall. "I wish I could say nicer things, and maybe we can," he told *The Sporting News*. "I can't lie. I just hope there is a change of heart and we stay in the spring ... but I am tired of saying that. I lost. I couldn't sell it."

Bassett made news by announcing that his team would play in the spring of 1986 regardless of whether or not the United States Football League switched to a fall schedule. While he still hoped to persuade his fellow owners of the folly of taking on the NFL, he claimed to be ready to start a new spring league with his Bandits as the cornerstone if the other owners did not follow his advice. He made the announcement against the strenuous objections of Commissioner Usher and the threat of a $50,000 fine. He also revealed the reason for his vote to move to the fall at an earlier owner's meeting. He explained that he felt it would be virtually impossible to swing enough votes his way, so in order to appease Donald Trump and provide Eddie Einhorn with the necessary go-ahead to approach the networks about a fall television contract, he voted for the fall. Once it became obvious that no television contract was forthcoming, just as he had long suspected, Bassett was trying to convince them to reverse course. He began plans for a new spring circuit in case he was unsuccessful. He used a public announcement of those plans on April 29 to try to force the other owners' hands.

"The commissioner is upset," he told the media. "I don't speak for the league—this press conference is for the Tampa Bay Bandits. Mr. Usher thinks we're not helping him with his negotiations, but for four years I've done nothing but act in the best interest of the league. Now, I'm acting in the best interests of the Tampa Bay Bandits."

Bassett had also made his cancer diagnosis public. After several weeks of rumors, he admitted in April that he had been diagnosed with two brain tumors and was undergoing radiation treatment on them. Bassett would continue to receive treatment from his doctors in Toronto, but the tumors were reported to be inoperable. As a younger man he had faced a battle with skin cancer that had required two operations. The illness had caused the driven entrepreneur to retreat from his business activities. He maintained a cool exterior throughout his latest malady, but few doubted that it scared him, much as his earlier bout had.

"[Business Operations Director] Ralph Campbell came in and kind of let us know that Mr. Bassett wasn't doing well," remembered Pitcock. "We kind of had a speech before that he was diagnosed with the cancer, tumors in his head, from Zenon at a hotel meeting one night."

"I was coming up there to do a film and I was hoping that we could spend some time together and do some things," recalled Reynolds. "He said, 'I might not be around, pal,' and I said 'What? Where are you going?' He said, 'Oh, probably down,' and I said, 'What?' He said, 'I got a brain tumor, a couple of them, and I think they're inoperable.' There was just this silence, and he said, 'Come on, you're quicker than that, come up with something,' and I said 'I'm sorry, John.' He said, 'No, never, never; I never want to hear that. I had a great life, and I love you, and don't ever say that to me again.'"

Though Bassett's future was uncertain, he made sure his players enjoyed being Tampa Bay Bandits.

"Every year Mr. Bassett would take the offense and defensive lines out," recalled Nate Newton. "He was a great owner, man. I'm gonna tell you what Mr. Bassett did, and this amazed me. I've never seen anybody do this. We were out and I want to say the name of the place was Veranda or something, and Mr. Bassett just was serious. He said, "You know I got all the money in the world. You all know I'm rich.' He said he was dying, he said, 'I'd give it all. I'd give all that money to anybody just to live longer.' It just, it took the wind out of us. And then behind that he said, 'In a couple of months I'm gonna put my money in a trust. And all my unfinished business is going to get held up for a long time.' And we were just looking at him. We didn't know where he was going with this. He said, 'So if I owe any of you bonuses or any of you all money, I want you to get it now 'cause I don't know what it's going to be like in another six months.' Man, he didn't have to do that. He didn't have to do that, and we were just like, 'All right, Mr. Bassett.' I'm like, 'Whoa,' and Rufus [Brown] said, 'What you gonna do?" I said, 'I'm going over there tomorrow and get my money.' I know that ain't funny."

"We went and had that fabulous dinner, a remarkable moment that none of us ever forgot, because there was 20-something football players on the offensive and defensive lines that won a chance to go do this dinner with Mr. Bassett," Pitcock said. "We had to win this one game for the offensive line to go, and the next game we had to win for the defensive line to go, and we did it, so he chalked up and we had limos and we went and did the big party. There wasn't one of us that didn't gain 15 pounds that night, I promise you. I've seen four-pound lobsters and steak and shrimp that were three pounds. It was marvelous; the Veranda was unbelievable that night."

"John Bassett took all the offensive and defensive linemen to dinner at an exclusive restaurant in Tampa," added Nordgren. "We were transported in limos and when we arrived, we were seated in a big circle. Kicker Zenon Andrusyshyn showed up—dressed as a chef. After stuffing ourselves, Mr. Bassett suggested we play the game 'Bumble Bee.' The idea was to flip coins with John and each player would call odd or even. If the player got it right, he would receive a bonus equal to the cost of the meal. About half of us won about $2,500, including the 'Big Zee.'"

Versatile running back Gary Anderson starred in the Bandits' opening win over Orlando, but Jim Kelly exploited their defense the following week to even their record at 1–1. With John Reaves throwing better, they rebounded with victories over San Antonio and Arizona before New Jersey knocked them off. The Bandits chalked up wins over Memphis, Jacksonville and Denver thanks to Reaves' strong play. Birmingham blew them out to halt their string, but Tampa Bay took out Baltimore, L.A. and Jacksonville to stake the club to a 9–3 record, one game better than both Birmingham and New Jersey in the Eastern Conference. Just as quickly, they slipped off the pace due to a four-game losing

Tampa Bay Bandits quarterback John Reaves reclaimed his career in the USFL and helped make the Bandits one of the league's most exciting and unpredictable teams. Photograph by Tim McGrath.

skid that threatened their playoff hopes. The Bandits topped Birmingham to make the postseason but faltered at Baltimore to end the regular season.

With all that they had been through, the team tried to ignore the worsening attitude of one of its best players. Eric Truvillion's injuries had lingered on throughout the season, causing some of his teammates to wonder if the initials E.T. stood for "Extra Tender." Reports speculated that the receiver had been working out with NFL clubs and no longer wanted to play for the Bandits. He was deactivated after an argument with John Reaves during a practice session, and the team eventually cut the talented player loose.

"I wanted to run some plays, and he's standing back behind the huddle," said Reaves in *The Sporting News*. "We were waiting 20 seconds for him to stroll up there. About the fourth time, I said, 'How about joining the huddle to begin with?' And he snapped back, 'You do your job and I'll do mine.' I said to him, 'Part of your job is practicing.'" Reaves added that the receiver was making faces while Spurrier talked with the team after one practice.

"John Bassett was sick at that point in time," explained Truvillion. "The league was also in disarray because they were going to possibly suspend play for a lawsuit. They were doing everything, and at that point in time being injured wasn't in my best interest or anybody's because that put me directly on the bubble of not knowing and trying to get well based on a league that might not be there. So that could end my career going forward in this league or in the NFL. So there was a lot of things happening, and then internally we were having somewhat of a breakdown just because management was changing. We had some other guys stepping in for John that were thinking things differently, more from the corporate side of things versus the sport end and the football side of things so there were a lot of different things going on with myself, with teammates, with coaches, with everything. Everybody was learning I guess day to day a new scenario, so roles were being changed and there was a lot of uncertainty."

Tampa Bay also lost the services of receiver Chris Collinsworth before he ever played a game with them when Lloyds of London refused to issue an insurance policy on him, a necessary part of his futures deal he had signed a year earlier. He then re-signed with the Cincinnati Bengals.

It seemed as if the Tampa Bay Bandits constantly were recovering from one major blow after another throughout the 1985 season. First, the question of when and in which league they would play failed to disappear. Then came the announcement of John Bassett's illness and his deteriorating health throughout the season. Truvillion's tantrum and suspension provided a lengthy distraction and numerous injuries took their toll. Despite all the difficulties, they recovered in time to earn a playoff spot and a date in Oakland for the quarterfinals.

"We were a group of individuals who were brought together this season under a lot of pressure," Andrusyshyn told *Sports Illustrated*. "There was a lot of turmoil for a moment; then we banded together like a chain, and we became very strong.

"We look at this moment and realize it will never repeat itself. This could be it. There may never be another Bandits. So we're going to make sure we're the best we can be."

Team co-owner Burt Reynolds ensured a road game at Los Angeles would be extra special when he threw a party for the team at his Beverly Hills home.

"The guys who had been in the league for three years with the Bandits were invited to go to Burt's house," recalled nose tackle Fred Nordgren. "We didn't find out until we got off the plane. It was pretty exciting; a lot of fun for us. We were picked up and spent a few hours with him. Dom DeLuise, Ricardo Montalban and other actors sang and told jokes. DeLuise was hilarious.

"Loni Anderson was serving appetizers. She brought them out and set them down on the bar, and Dom just shoved his way between us and said, 'Oh man, these are my weakness.' So we competed with him over food that evening. He loved to eat, so we fit in with him well."

The Bandits kept the team competitive, ranking second in the entire USFL despite a whopping 59 turnovers that left them a league-worst minus 15 in turnover differential. Gary Anderson proved to be one of the most consistent offensive threats in the USFL, running for 1,207 yards and 16 touchdowns and topping the team with 72 catches for an additional 678 yards and four scores. He also completed two out of three throws for three yards and a touchdown. He finished second in the league in scoring among non-kickers with 120 points, trailing only Herschel Walker. Reaves completed 314 of 561 throws for 4,193 yards with 25 touchdowns but was haunted by 29 interceptions. The surprising Larry Brodsky wound up with 69 receptions for 1,071 yards, and Marvin Harvey made 59 grabs for 723 yards. Safety Marcus Quinn, acquired from the Invaders, led the team with seven interceptions even though he did not join the Bandits until the third week, and nose tackle Fred Nordgren totaled seven sacks.

The Tampa area fans continued to support the team even though its future looked uncertain at best. They averaged 45,220 fans per home game or about 1,000 less per contest than the year before. Those numbers were good enough for the top spot in the league for the year and easily beat out Buccaneers' crowds.

Portland Breakers

The Portland Breakers, in their third different home city in as many years, figured to battle San Antonio to stay out of last place in the Western Conference. Robert Pennywell and Jearld Baylis moved in at linebacker, while former Jacksonville Bull Matt Robinson and 1984 backup Doug Woodward would battle for the right to replace the retired Johnnie Walton behind center. Walton joined the staff as an assistant coach. Former Invaders boss John Ralston lent stability to the franchise as its new president. The move to Portland was a homecoming of sorts for Dick Coury who coached the WFL Storm in the Rose City more than a decade earlier.

The Breakers opened the season in Arizona and received two blows that day. First they dropped a 9–7 ballgame, but even worse they lost star running back Marcus Dupree for the rest of the season with a knee injury. Although Buford Jordan filled in admirably, very few backs enjoyed the abilities of Dupree. Portland never recovered from the loss and settling into their third home in as many years did not help their cause any. Over the course of the year, Portland managed victories over L.A., Orlando, Oakland, Memphis, Tampa Bay and Denver, four of the six being playoff teams. A six-game losing streak and a sputtering offense kept them from doing any better than a 6–12 record, their worst mark in three seasons. The news off the field was just as discouraging as $500,000 in player salary remained unpaid at the conclusion of the season.

Both the offense and defense ranked near the bottom of the league. In truth, Coury probably received the maximum from the squad. Jordan paced Portland with 817 yards on the ground and a 5.0-yard per carry average, but the passing game struggled to find its bearings the entire season. Robinson led the way with 156 completions in 310 attempts with 15 touchdowns and 20 interceptions. Dan Ross's 41 catches for 522 yards and five touchdowns topped the team's suddenly weak receiving corps. On defense, Bruce Miller collected six interceptions and Jearld Baylis added 6.5 sacks.

"It was all centered around Marcus Dupree," recalled team president John Ralston of the 1985 season. "First game out he got hurt and it just ruined us. You're not talking about an average football player. You're talking about an exceptional football player. He might be in the ten best backs of all time. When he went down it just destroyed us. He got tackled on the sideline right in front of our bench. What a loss! Oh, could he run with the football. If we'd have had him in the lineup the whole year, we would have sold a lot more tickets. We probably would have doubled our attendance."

"It was our worst season," added Coury. "We were replacing Johnnie Walton at quarterback. He was going to be a player-coach, so we had to find a different quarterback. We had a tough time getting back to our normal type of play.

"We really received good support. I had been there in the World Football League, and my son had been an All-American at Oregon State, so we had some credibility going in there. The stadium in Portland is not real conducive to drawing fans. It's right downtown with little parking. It's not a situation where you can develop a real big fan base. We drew well for a stadium like that and being in our third city, which is not easy to do."

The Portland fans showed their support of the vagabond Breakers with an average attendance of 19,919 per game. Although a drop from the number in New Orleans, not much more could be expected considering the franchise's unstable history and state of the league itself. The numbers were nowhere close to providing enough income for Canizaro to break even, and he began talks about merging the franchise with other teams in the league. Whatever the outcome, by the day of the third championship game, everyone in the organization knew that the franchise had played its last.

"Poor Canizaro, he bought that team when it was in Boston then he moved it to New Orleans and then to Portland, always calling it the Breakers," said McSherry. "Canizaro's a very nice man, but he had no business owning a football team. He wasn't strong. Everybody took advantage of him."

"The following move to Portland was kind of a letdown," said Mazzetti. "That's when I realized it. Unlike some of the other players who probably rarely read a newspaper outside of the sports section or the funnies, given the fact of my background and I was working in the offseason and doing television, I was much more involved in what was going on in the league. At one point I considered not going to Portland and just working fulltime for Joe, but Joe said, 'Look, you've got nothing to lose. Go to Portland, and you'll have your job when you get back here. I need your marquee name there. Go do it.' So I did a lot of publicity there. I view it from a perspective of people I met, and I still have some friends up in Portland I talk with today. All good from that perspective. That was kind of going back to Boston with a smaller stadium and smaller-type market and smaller environment, although I still had a lot of fun."

Arizona Outlaws

The Arizona Outlaws looked to be an interesting if not downright perplexing bunch. Of the 33 players the franchise protected before the dispersal draft, 20 came from the

Wranglers and 13 from the Oklahoma roster. They later signed 13 former Outlaws and only four from the 1984 Arizona squad after the draft, giving them 26 from the 6–12 Oklahoma team and 24 from the Wranglers squad that had appeared in the championship game.

Doug Williams took over the quarterbacking duties when Greg Landry departed, but trouble appeared to be brewing with his receivers and the secondary. Trumaine Johnson held out the entire year, and his agent demanded that he be paid as an injured player. The team failed to hold on to corner back Frank Minnifield who jumped to the NFL as well as safety Luther Bradley, who landed with the Gamblers. New coach Frank Kush had the responsibility of solving those problems. He also had to deal with infighting that resulted from melding the two rosters.

"We were in the midst of changing our coaching staff when we left Oklahoma because the team sucked at the end of the year," said Billy Tatham. "We had a new head coach in Frank Kush. We all thought George Allen had a great defensive team, so we kept his defensive staff. Frank brought his offensive guys with him. Most of our offensive guys were our players from Oklahoma, and most of the defensive players were Wranglers. You can imagine some of the inter-team feuds going on because some of George's guys were like 'F' it. Our guys were younger, working hard. His guys were older, kind of savvy professionals—the coaching staff and the players. Frank had to deal with all that, and it made life really difficult for him. The offense and the defense hated each other. I had to go in a meeting and say, 'Listen, if you don't knock this shit off, I'm going to fire the whole defensive staff.'"

The Outlaws opened with a squeaker against the Breakers, followed by a narrow loss to San Antonio. They walloped Jacksonville and then fell to Tampa Bay. Arizona took its record to 4–2 by stopping Los Angeles and then surprising New Jersey, bringing them within a game of the conference's top spot. Just as quickly, they dropped their next six in succession to drop out of the playoff chase two-thirds of the way through the year.

With the departure of Tim Spencer to Memphis before the season and the trade of Kevin Long in the middle of the year, the running game struggled, although newcomer Reggie Brown proved to be a pleasant surprise by topping the team with 1,031 yards and 12 touchdowns. Doug Williams hit on 271 of 509 passes for 3,673 yards with 21 touchdowns and 17 interceptions. Trumaine Johnson held out the entire year, so Al Williams stepped in and caught 55 balls for 1,020 yards and eight scores, while Greg Anderson made 51 grabs for 915 yards. The defense managed just 17 interceptions with four players tied with three apiece. Dave Tipton, obtained from Michigan, topped the squad with 14 sacks, Karl Lorch added 9.5 and Kit Lathrop contributed eight despite having his year cut short by knee surgery. The defense ranked second against the pass but just tenth against the run. Injuries, trades and the loss of key personnel in the allocation draft took their toll.

Tension on the team finally boiled over in the most unlikely of places.

"It was costing us like $35,000 for round trip flights," recalled Tatham. "I found we could save like $20,000 and fly commercial. Brilliant idea. We went to Houston and lost. It was really depressing. Just my luck we had a four-hour delay, and some of the guys were getting wasted. By the time we get on the plane, they're looped. John Teerlinck was our defensive line coach, and he was insane. A lot of George Allen's guys were kind of old school; they really didn't respect our authority that much. We had an offensive tackle named Donnie Hickman, who is black. Now they're sitting in the back of the plane; this is a commercial flight at 35,000 feet. Teerlinck said something like, 'Listen, boy,' and puts his finger in Hickman's chest, and Hickman, who's a black belt, just cold-cocked him. The players forgot they were on an airliner and thought they were in a locker room. Guys are jumping up and bodies are flying all over the place. The stewardesses ran back to the galley and were on the floor sobbing. You can imagine the passengers. These 200-plus pound guys are bouncing into the exit doors and falling on top of passengers. We finally get it cooled off, and the pilot actually flies on to Phoenix! When we land, the FBI is waiting for us. I said, 'This is really the airline's responsibility once we're in the air, so I don't think we're going to get sued, but we might have a bit of a PR problem.' Kush asked, 'What are you going to do?' I'm going to fire Teerlinck the minute the sun comes up. 'What about Hickman? You gotta be fair,' he replied. You're right: $50 fine. I had to work with Continental Airlines the next two months appeasing passengers."

No other market had seen as much off-season turmoil as Phoenix, and the bottom fell out of Arizona's attendance. After averaging over 25,000 fans per game over the first two seasons, they fell to 17,881 per contest. Four times, they dropped below 14,000, including the final three home dates over which they averaged less than 10,000 fans. Seeing basically their third group of players in three years, not to mention their third coach, the Valley fans did not take to the new bunch.

Baltimore Stars

Perhaps no other team showed the strains of the league's troubles as much as the Baltimore Stars. In just a few short months, the franchise had gone from celebrating a championship in Philadelphia with a growing fan base to a college field without lights 40 miles from Baltimore. With Memorial Stadium unavailable until 1986 due to the objections of the Baltimore Orioles, the defending champ Stars would continue to practice in Philadelphia while playing in College Park, Maryland, on the University of Maryland campus.

"We began what is maybe the oddest season in the history of sports in that we lived and practiced in Philadelphia and played our games in College Park, Maryland," recalled Ken Dunek. "We referred to ourselves as the I-95 Stars. Home games were a three-and-a-half-hour drive. It was easier to play an away game because the airport was only 20 minutes away. It took its toll."

"Every week it was a road game," Peterson remembered. "We'd pile the coaches and players into buses on Saturday afternoon in Philadelphia, bus down and spend the night in a hotel. Then we'd get up, go over to College Park to play the game and bus back. We were literally playing 18 regular season games and 18 road games."

"We didn't have a practice field down there," added Myles Tanenbaum. "It was a nice playing field, but the parking was limited and a lot of people didn't know how to get there. The first game we had down there, most people didn't get there until halftime. The traffic was very difficult, and they didn't know exactly how to get into the campus."

"We decided that if there was some kind of a merger or something, then we'd have a better chance in Baltimore where there was no team than we would in Philadelphia, so we decided to become the Baltimore Stars, although we worked out of Veterans Stadium in Philadelphia until about halfway through the season when they kicked us out," recalled Mora. "That was tough. The move to Baltimore was tough. We had established

In an on-field celebration, Baltimore Stars owner Myles Tanenbaum lifts the USFL championship trophy won in 1984 when the team played in Philadelphia. Photograph by Jim Turner, from author's collection.

something in Philadelphia. The fans liked us; we had won a championship, played in two championship games and had good teams. A lot of players had homes around there, and I did too in South Jersey. All of a sudden, now we're moving to Baltimore and having to commute every weekend to play a game at the University of Maryland."

In contrast to their first two seasons, the Stars struggled in the early going. They opened the campaign with a shocking loss to Jacksonville and followed with a tie at Oakland in a game they had led by 17 points. Another loss, at Memphis, sunk their record to 0–2–1, before they finally got off the schneid by drubbing New Jersey in their inaugural game in Maryland. Birmingham handed them another loss, but they took care of Houston and Los Angeles to make it three out of four. The Stars sandwiched a victory over Portland between two more losses, pushing their record to 4–5–1, the second worst in the Eastern Conference.

The Stars faced additional challenges off the field as well. They lost their practice location in Philadelphia, sending them scrambling to find another several weeks into the season.

"The city council decided that we could no longer practice and have offices inside Veterans Stadium since we weren't playing there any longer," said Peterson. "I think we literally got an eviction notice. Much credit to Myles and his contacts on the athletic board at the University of Pennsylvania, we were able to move over there and use their facilities. It worked out terrific. They were great to us. It was much different because it obviously wasn't a pro football atmosphere, but I learned to love the University of Pennsylvania, and I'm always cheering for the Quakers."

"They kicked us out of the stadium about halfway through the season, so we had to move up to the University of Pennsylvania in their ROTC building, which was a totally different situation, tougher on the coaches and the players," added Mora. "It made it difficult, and we had a bad start as a team. I'm sure the Baltimore fans weren't real happy with us initially because we weren't winning."

"We had to move our practice facility over to the University of Pennsylvania in an ROTC building," added Dunek. "We all met in the same room and had our meetings in different corners of the room. I remember hanging our shoulder pads on a nail. It was not a great atmosphere. But as a testimony to the character of that team, the players got together and said, 'Listen, we've had a lot of things go against us this year, but we're still a good football team. It's time to get ourselves together.'"

With just eight games remaining, the Stars had to make their move for a playoff berth. They triumphed in four of their next five, losing only to New Jersey over that stretch, to get back into the race. They finished by blasting Orlando and Tampa Bay to finish at 10–7–1, good enough for a wild card berth. The "Doghouse Defense" stepped up during the second half of the season, halting opponents and grabbing turnovers as they had the first two years.

Bryant again proved to be the key to Baltimore's offensive success with 1,207 yards and 16 touchdowns. While slipping from the year before, Fusina remained solid with 303 completions in 496 attempts for 3,496 yards, 20 touchdowns and 14 interceptions. Fitzkee topped the receivers with 73 catches for 882 yards.

"I don't know what sparked it," admitted Mora of the Stars' turnaround. "I think it was just guys believing that hey, we can get it done. There isn't any one incident I can think of; it was just keep plugging, keep plugging. We went most of the season without being above .500. We didn't get above .500 until toward the end of the season. We'd win, we'd lose, we'd lose, we'd win, and we were really struggling because we pretty much won almost every game we played the previous two years during the regular season. I remember there was one game, I think we were playing Jacksonville, and we had to beat them to even have a chance to make the playoffs. Once we beat them, we knew we had a chance to get to the playoffs, and we started playing better for some reason. It was a struggle. That third year was a struggle with all the things that happened, the move and all that."

"We had a lapse with our play in the middle of the season, but somewhere in there we said, 'Hey, why can't we get back in it?'" remembered Fusina. "The situation was hard, but rallying to get into the playoffs was maybe even a bigger feat than what we accomplished the year before."

The defense remained the true strength of the Stars. They held opponents to 260 points, 39 fewer than anyone else in the circuit thanks to their third-ranked pass defense. Mike Lush contributed ten interceptions with four of them in a five-game stretch to end the year. John Walker recorded ten sacks, Don Fielder nine and William Fuller eight and a half for the crew that dumped opposing quarterbacks 60 times, most in the USFL. The team caused 11 more turnovers than it gave up, second only to Birmingham. The Stars would face their arch-rival, the New Jersey Generals, in the opening round of postseason play.

The defending champions' shift from Philadelphia to a college campus in Maryland crippled the Stars' bottom line. They averaged just 14,275 patrons per home game, about half of what they had the year before. They started strong with 31,027 in the home opener against the Generals but dropped steadily until hitting a low of 6,988 against Orlando. Even the USFL's strongest team was not immune to the instability that gripped the league.

"Rather than uprooting everybody immediately, we gave them that additional period to get acclimated," said Stars owner Myles Tanenbaum. "We opted to practice in Philadelphia and move down to Baltimore for our games during the 1985 season. It turned out that the team that didn't know how to lose found it difficult to win. Some of it was coming off the championship win and some of it was the travel. Every game was like an away game for the players. There were a lot of distractions because of that."

Oakland Invaders

On the other hand, Oakland's fortunes appeared to be on the upswing thanks to the influx of talent from the disbanded Michigan Panthers. Of the 33 players protected in the merger, 13 were from the 10–8 Panthers and 20 from the 7–11 Invaders. The franchise added six more Michigan players and seven from the Oakland roster during and after the draft. Once the season began, 23 Invaders and 14 former Panthers remained on the Oakland payroll. New coach Charlie Sumner bore the task of blending the rosters but didn't have the same problems as Frank Kush in Arizona.

"What I can remember that year was that he would smoke on the sidelines," Hebert said of Sumner. "You think about the political correctness and all now, it wouldn't fly. When the cigarette was going down, he would light up another one during the game. I'd go over to talk with him on the sidelines, and there would be all this smoke coming in my face."

Sumner boasted one of the top quarterbacks in the league in Bobby Hebert with former two-year starter Fred Besana backing up. They boasted three great receivers at their disposal in Anthony Carter, Derek Holloway and Gordon Banks. Although running back Eric Jordan, who had ignited the Invaders offense in the second half of the 1984 season, held out in training camp, Michigan imports John Williams and Albert Bentley looked to be capable of bearing the load behind a solid offensive line. Only the resignation of offensive coordinator Joe Pendry, formerly head coach of the Maulers, one week before the season began hurt the offense's development. Defensively, David Shaw and Ray Bentley anchored a strong linebacking corps.

The Invaders showed their improvement from 1984 right away. They started the year by blasting Denver and then rallying from a 17-point deficit to tie Baltimore in week two. Hebert hit Carter with the tying touchdown throw on the last play of regulation in the moral victory which would go down as the only tie in USFL history. Following an embarrassing loss to Houston, Oakland ran off three victories in a row before tripping at Portland, dropping them to 4–3–1.

With so much talent at his disposal, Coach Sumner's biggest problem in the first half of the year appeared to be getting everyone to work together as a team. With eight weeks under their belts, though, they began to click, much to the chagrin of the rest of the USFL. They reeled off seven consecutive wins to take control of the Western Conference and become the first team to clinch a playoff spot. Twice Fred Besana replaced Hebert and led the club into the victory column. Following a defeat at Arizona, they closed with decisive wins over fellow playoff teams New Jersey and Houston to cap the 1985 regular season at a league best 13–4–1.

"We were a helluva team," recalled personnel man Mike Keller who had come over from Michigan. "We were strong on the offensive line, at receiver, quarterback and defensively. All of our young guys, the Ray Bentleys who were now in their third year, made us into a juggernaut. We didn't lose many during the regular season. It was fun to go and watch because we were such a dominant team. We knew every week that it would be hard for other teams to physically stand up against us."

Their offense, which featured three receivers and two running backs on most plays, became one of the most dangerous in the USFL. Bentley and Williams turned into a powerful one-two punch on the ground, ending the year with 1,020 and 857 yards, respectively. Hebert solidified the passing game with 244 completions in 456 attempts for 3,811 yards, 30 touchdowns and 19 interceptions, while Besana provided valuable insurance in relief. They benefited from one of the best receiving corps in the league. Carter led the way with 70 catches for 1,323 yards and 14 touchdowns, while Banks hauled in 62 passes for 1,115 yards, and Holloway made 47 grabs for 824 yards. Banks became the only player to catch a pass in each of the USFL's 54 regular season weeks over three years. Thanks to Michigan imports, the Invaders finally fielded a stable offensive line.

Stan Talley topped all punters with a 44.3-yard average and 23 kicks inside the 20, and Novo Bojovic finished with 111 points. Vito McKeever and Derrick Martin collected six interceptions apiece, and Angelo Snipes topped the squad with 11.5 sacks. The Invaders defense sacked opposing quarterbacks 56 times and completed the year as the league's second-best unit against the rush, although they sometimes had a tough time against passing teams.

Despite the success, Bay Area fans ignored one of the best clubs in the USFL. They averaged just 17,509 per game, a little over half of what they had drawn in their inaugural season. They topped 20,000 fans only three times and failed to draw even 13,000 for three of their final four home games despite playing excellent football. Their offseason instability and the league's continued well-publicized problems had a lot to do with the sudden disinterest. Team management had also criticized city officials for failing to support the team. They claimed that community leaders

The speedy Gordon Banks played three seasons in the USFL with the Oakland Invaders, becoming the one of the league's most dangerous and consistent players. Photograph by Jim Turner, from author's collection.

were more interested in a fruitless effort to bring the Raiders back from Los Angeles rather than supporting a USFL franchise that desired to play in Oakland.

San Antonio Gunslingers

Even with a season under its belt, the Gunslingers were every bit as much of a mess as they had been the year before. Tackle Jeff Gaylord who came over from the Breakers was San Antonio's lone big addition after a 7–11 campaign. It was easy to find other evidence of the team's financial struggles. Team management decided against setting up the 9,000 temporary bleacher seats they had used in their inaugural season, content to leave Alamo Stadium's capacity at a cozy 23,000. In other cost-cutting moves, the franchise operated without scouts and a developmental squad and had even gone so far as to use outdated stationary, which listed Ray Evans as the publicity director when he had not been with the team in nearly a year. Late paychecks became the norm. The budgetary constraints forced the coaching staff to grab whatever talent it could find.

"We had Greg Fields, the guy who nearly knocked Hadl out when he cut him," recalled defensive coordinator Tim Marcum. "San Antonio was like the Green Bay of the '50s. Other teams told guys, 'If you don't straighten up, we're going to trade you to San Antonio,' because they knew we played at a high school stadium, our owner didn't pay us, etc."

"I picked up Clinton Manges at the airport and Bud Haun was with him. Bud said, 'We can't pay the players,'" remembered photographer Tim McGrath. "Clinton replied, 'Pay 'em what you want. Players are like cattle. You can herd one group out and herd another bunch right in.'"

The hunt for off the field talent proved equally interesting. "One of the things we did was try out pre-game and halftime entertainment," recalled team media relations director Greg Singleton. "It was actually kind of like American Idol. Fall football had marching bands, but schools had already hung up their uniforms for the year by the spring, so we couldn't rely on that.

"One day this guy dressed up as a cowboy came into the office with this huge whip and said he wanted to try out. I followed him out to his truck where he had a bunch of cans and candles set up on the back. He started twirling this whip around and then whipping at the candles and cans. Instead of hitting them, he was chipping the heck out of his truck's paint. I was trying not to laugh, so I told him to hang on, and I ran to get the coaches. He started up again, still hitting his truck and not the candles, and then he whipped his ear, giving himself a nice gash. By this time, the coaches are all laughing and snickering, and I told the guy, 'That's a very interesting act, but I don't think the act and the venue match. It will be hard for people to see you whipping stuff while they're sitting in the stands.' I was trying to let him down easy. He just looked so disappointed, like I was crushing his dream. Then he looked up and said, 'Well, I also do a gun trick with live ammunition.' The coaches just lost it, and I had to explain that might not be the best idea in a stadium with people in it."

After dropping their opener, the Gunslingers rallied to down Arizona for their first win of the season. With the offense grinding to a halt amid reports of the franchise's impending collapse, San Antonio lost its next three, costing offensive coordinator Tom Rossley his job. Quarterback Rick Neuheisel was replaced first by Fred Mortenson and then by Whit Taylor before winning the job back. The Gunslingers thumped Portland 33–0 to end the skid and then stunned powerful Birmingham 15–14 in one of the year's biggest surprises.

The *San Antonio Light* broke the news that the Internal Revenue Service had filed two liens against the franchise for $404,763.63 in back federal payroll withholding taxes, all of which was due in 1984. The club was three hours late in meeting its payroll in March. Owner Clinton Manges, reeling due to rapidly falling oil prices, attempted to trade Neuheisel in order to dump his $120,000 salary. When they were paid, players and team employees often raced each other to the bank to cash their checks.

"The checks bounced; then they didn't pay us the next week, so we were down two checks," said Marcum. "The third week they paid us, through a little country bank about 30–40 miles away from the stadium. It was like the Indianapolis 500 to get to that bank. About the first 20–25 guys who got there, got their money, then there was no more. It was crazy."

"He came to practice," Neuheisel said of Manges. "It had been a couple weeks now since we'd received a check, or one of the checks had bounced, so now it had gone on two and three weeks, this was in year two, and he said, 'We got it all solved guys. I've got a deal with the bank. You're all going to get your checks, and you need to go to Lavernia, Texas.' Now for those of us who know Texas, there's a name. You could name any word in the dictionary and there's a town in Texas, so none of us really knew where Lavernia was. It turned out it was at least an hour, probably more like an hour and a half away and we literally had a gumball rally because guys knew by experience that the first half of those checks were going to clear and the second half were sketchy at best. And guys were flying down this freeway, waving at each other, trying to cut each other off to make sure that they got their checks to that window first and it was a scene of all scenes."

"Tom Aiken who was the director of marketing had an office in the trailer," explained Singleton. "He would call us at our offices down by the coaches and say, 'The eagle is landing,' or 'The birds are flying,' or some other code he'd make up, and then he'd hang up. We knew that meant they were printing our checks. We'd go grab our checks and we'd run right away to whatever bank they were drawn at, usually one that was out of town. The players were usually stuck at practice at the time so we'd get a head start on them."

Former UCLA passer Rick Neuheisel took the reins of the San Antonio Gunslingers offense and also helped keep the team together off the field. He later became a well-known college football coach for Colorado, Washington and UCLA. Photograph by Tim McGrath.

From that point, the franchise fell apart as Clinton Manges missed two more payrolls. Several checks from the second one bounced because of the IRS liens and the third arrived three days late. Corner back Peter Raeford stated that he was just happy to be able to buy groceries after finally receiving his paycheck. The owner issued an order that no employees could discuss the franchise's financial situation and even went so far as to send men into the team's locker room to get rid of reporters.

"When the money got a little bit questionable, this was literally true, we would vote to see if we were going to practice because checks had not been forthcoming," explained Neuheisel. "I figured out the most important position in that deal was the guy who counted the votes 'cause then I could swing it."

"The first year everything was pretty good," added Marcum. "We won seven games, and we all got paid. We were looking forward to getting a few more weapons. He did a pretty good job of paying his bills the first year. The second year is when all hell broke loose. That's when Seattle SeaFirst went down, checks bounced. We just came off a few real good games, won two out of three including a shutout of Portland, and our checks bounced. Well, if you're a pro football players and your checks are no good, that's not very good for the morale of the team. Right before the Jacksonville game, we had two guys who were best friends, Jim Bob Morris, our union rep, and his best buddy Rich D'Amico, right after our pregame meal, they're in their room beating the hell out of each other. Needless to say, we didn't play very well that night, got beat. We were trying to keep the thing together."

With the players on the verge of a walkout, the team dropped its next eight games. If possible, things had grown even worse between the players and Manges. They all walked out of a morning practice on May 29 after not being paid on time and only returned when team president Bud Haun threatened to fold the team if they did not come back in the afternoon.

"The team president, Bud Haun, entered the locker room one day to assure all the players they would be paid," recalled McGrath. "It was all a front, of course; they were out of money. The players knew it, and they totally lost it. They were throwing their helmets and everything. It descended into chaos."

"He had to cover up a lot of shit, no doubt about it, because he was there," Marcum said of Haun. "One time after the checks bounced, the guys were in front of the trailer and Haun crawled out the back window and ran down the hill."

"There was a time in Orlando when the plane wasn't going home 'cause the check had bounced," Neuheisel recalled. "Now we're sitting in the locker room trying to figure out how we're getting home. And then, great news, the Lieutenant Governor of Texas has okayed the check! Four hours later you get to get on the plane."

Coach Jim Bates, who had nearly resigned earlier in the year when management failed to meet payroll, had seen enough. This time, he quit after paychecks bounced once again, just hours before a game against Oakland. Gil Steinke, the director of football operations and head coach of the team in 1984, assumed the reins again. Late season wins over L.A. and Portland soothed some of the pain, and considering the state of the front office, their 5–13 mark could be considered a minor miracle.

"After the twelfth game of the year, Jim resigned," explained Marcum. "He said, 'If you're not going to pay our kids, I'm going to resign.' He was gone. Steinke came back, and I love him to death, but by that time Steinke just didn't get it or he didn't care, he just wasn't all there.

"Jim Bates was kind of the leader both years. Everybody looked to Jim instead of Steinke. When Jim left, we had six games left to play. They paid us for the next two games, through game 14. Fifteen, 16, 17 and 18—no payment. They were not paying anything for four games, and we won two of them.

"Here's what I told them: 'Guys, I'm not getting paid. You're not getting paid. Whatever you guys want to do, I don't give a shit; I don't care. But here's the deal. If you decide to play, I'm going to coach you. I'm not going to coach you to lose. I'm going to coach you to win, and we're going to win because we're going to show these MFers that we're going to win because we have pride and we're playing for the love of the game.' We went out there and won two of the final four, and that's something I'm pretty proud of."

The ground game struggled all year as George Works topped the club with just 452 yards. Neuheisel completed 239 of 421 throws for 3,068 yards with 18 touchdowns and 25 interceptions despite a lack of receiving help. Receiver Danny Buggs tore thumb ligaments early in the season, knocking him out for the rest of the year and costing the Gunslingers a much-needed weapon. Don Roberts caught 53 balls for 653 yards, while Jerry Gordon added 44 catches for 693 yards. The addition of former Breaker Frank Lockett helped later in the year. Defensively, Vic Minor hauled in eight interceptions for the Bounty Hunters who proved to be particularly tough against the run. On the down side, the unit's 29 sacks ranked second lowest in the circuit. Jim Bob Morris, Ken Gillen and Brad Anae led the way with four apiece. The team finished at minus 12 in turnover differential, placing them second to last in the league.

Still, the hardships seemed to forge a bond among the players and staff.

"We were all forced to go see Clinton's daughter participate in a play," laughed Singleton. "He just popped into the office one day and said, 'You're all going.' She was out of college and it was a dinner theater type of deal. Tim Marcum put on Bill Bradley's giant cowboy hat, went backstage and kept sticking his head through all the doors and windows of the set. We found ways to keep ourselves entertained."

"We were so close to those guys," said Marcum. "After practice, we'd run over and drink beer at this little ice house in San Antonio. Wednesday after practice we'd all head over to a park and have hamburgers and drink beer over there together. It was a great time."

The team's average attendance dropped to 11,721, far below what it needed to continue operations. Crowds dipped under 10,000 four times and cracked the 20,000 mark just once. The Gunslingers had little luck with the press, especially after banning two reporters from the *San Antonio Express-News* from the press box and locker rooms. The irascible Manges claimed the club would return in 1986 but many wondered how it made it through the 1985 season. He still owed players money for the last four games. *The Sporting News* reported that after Harry Usher refused to release the balance from Manges' own letter of credit, more than $400,000, to pay his players that Manges "went after" the commissioner at a July meeting before being held back by Jacksonville owner Fred Bullard. Instead, $61,500 from each owner's letter of credit went to funding Usher's salary for the next three years.

"We had a guy like Greg Fields, after the season was over, they got him paid," laughed Marcum. "Fields sat out in his car in front of their offices in the trailer. He leaned down in his chair with the window down and when Bud Haun came out he'd growl, 'I want my money, now. You better pay me my money.' So they paid that crazy bastard. Fields was the guy who hit Hadl when Hadl cut him, so they weren't going to take any chances."

"I knew it was over when I went out to get the mail and my car was gone," added McGrath. "It had been repossessed because I hadn't made the payments. When you go months without being paid, something's gonna give."

Denver Gold

New coach Mouse Davis brought his exciting run and shoot offense to the Denver Gold, a team notably lacking in offensive firepower and overall excitement over its first two seasons. The team did not hire defensive coordinator Joe Haering until midway through training camp, again proving that the emphasis was on the other side of the ball. Four NFL coaches visited Davis's training camp to get a look at his innovative scheme. With the departure of Harry Sydney, Denver's leading rusher the first two seasons, they would rely on second-year man Bill Johnson to carry much of the load. The squad picked up quarterback Vince Evans from the defunct Blitz to pull the trigger.

"He's got the loudest voice for a little guy," recalled kicker Jim Asmus of Davis. "I still remember, we were playing in San Antonio, and the snapper hiked the ball over my head. I one-handed it and had to run for my life just as I got a grip on it. I'm running away from Mouse Davis to the other side, and he yelled so loud behind me, I could hear him over the crowd, 'What the hell are you doing!?' I could hear him yelling from the back side, and I think he yelled at me afterwards. It's amazing that while I was running the other way I could still hear him. That's pretty darn loud.

"Mouse is really emotional. If he was on the sideline and things didn't go well, you would know it, yet you'd respect him. You wanted to play pretty hard for him because he was a really good guy."

Denver shot out to a 5–2 mark with wins over Birmingham, Portland, San Antonio, Orlando and Arizona. The offense, which had started slowly behind Evans, began to click toward the middle of the season. They dropped two of their next three, though their lone win during the stretch was a 51–0 demolition of Los Angeles before completing season sweeps over San Antonio and Arizona and a narrow win over New Jersey. Denver finished the year by winning just two of its last five, still good enough to make the playoffs with an 11–7 mark, the best in the club's three-year history.

The vagaries of Denver's weather provided a light moment during practice. "I had never seen snow fall in my life, and we were practicing some pretty long field goals," recalled Hawaii native Asmus. "Mouse spends a lot of time on special teams. It started snowing and the ball was snapped. There was this big snowflake that came down, and I just stopped because I had never seen snow before. Everyone's all piled up trying to block the kick and everything, and Mouse shouts out, 'What the hell's going on? What'd you stop for?' I go, 'Coach, I've never seen snow before.' He goes, 'Damn Hawaiian kid,' just joking around. Just the way he said it cracked everyone up."

As promised, Davis delivered a much more potent offense as Denver scored 433 points, third best in the league. Despite stumbling late, Bill Johnson ended the year as the third best runner in the league with 1,261 yards and 15 touchdowns. Instability at the all-important quarterback position hampered the club all year though their offensive scheme helped minimize the damage. Bob Gagliano, who filled in for the injured and sometimes ineffective Evans, completed 205 of 358 throws for 2,695 yards with 13 touchdowns and 17 interceptions, while Evans hit on 157 of 325 passes for 2,259 yards with 12 scores and 16 interceptions. Leonard Harris blossomed in the run and shoot with 101 catches, second most in the league, for 1,432 yards and eight scores, while Marc Lewis caught 75 balls for 1,207 yards and six touchdowns.

"We took the offense to Denver the following year with a bunch of nobodies and did the same thing: took them to the playoffs," said assistant coach June Jones who had also moved over from the Gamblers. "I remember one game we played against the L.A. Express, and when the league folded I think they ended up having like five or six guys on the All Pro NFL team the next year, and we beat them 51–0."

"I've never played against anything like that offense," Arizona Outlaws' defensive back Bruce Laird told *The Sporting News*. "You very seldom see teams line up with four wide receivers except in extreme circumstances. But these guys line up with four receivers and one back for the whole game. You've got these midgets running around in the defensive backfield and you don't know what to do. You have to throw in some zone, some nickel, some man-to-man. But most of all, you have to make sure they don't know what kind of defense you're in. If they know, you're dead."

Bruce Thornton topped the Gold defense with 12.5 sacks and Calvin Turner hauled down opposing quarterbacks 11 times. Inconsistency haunted the weak secondary which also had to contend with the injury and then trade of former all-USFL performer David Martin.

The Gold put together their best showing in three years, making the playoffs, but the denizens of Denver showed little interest. Once a USFL attendance leader and site of the first championship game, turnout at Mile High Stadium dropped to an average of 14,446, less than half that of the previous season and about a third of their inaugural year. They drew more than 20,000 just once and fell below 13,000 five times. The franchise's continuing gyrations off the field and promise of going head to head with the city's beloved Broncos in the fall proved too much for Mouse Davis and his players to overcome. Owner Doug Spedding also speculated that his reputation as a used car dealer may have hurt. It did not help that he had allegedly worked out a deal to move the franchise to Hawaii at one point and had further dealt with representatives from Sacramento and Mexico City. A vendor inside Mile High Stadium was even seen selling "Go Hawaii" Gold T-shirts during the last home game.

"Doug Spedding was looking into going to Honolulu," confirmed Asmus. "He was talking to me and some others about how we were going to do some of the marketing stuff. I told the general manager that I'd be happy to help with some of the PR and everything else. I didn't know how that was going to look, but if it was going to go that way, I was getting everyone on the team pumped up about what we'd be doing. Still, I wondered if the Gold was going to make it. The team did so well, it was the best Denver team they had, but the attendance wasn't there."

Los Angeles Express

Perhaps the Los Angeles Express best displayed the dichotomy between the USFL's on-the-field product and its off-field problems. Examining the roster, it was hard not to view the 1985 season with optimism. It featured one of the top offensive lines in all of football, one of the game's best young quarterbacks, a solid fleet of receivers and the elusive Mel Gray returning at running back. The squad that had won the Western Division in 1984 with the most talented young roster in all of football seemed to be in solid shape on the field.

On the other hand, the financial state of the franchise was a nightmare. The government was pursuing former owner Bill Oldenburg, who would lose his fortune, leaving the league to pay for the talented club and its monstrous payroll. Cost cutting became evident everywhere. The *Los Angeles Times* reported that the franchise fired its cheerleaders to save just over $800 per game. Management claimed that they were fired for poor performances, and they planned on replacing them.

"I was talking to Harry Usher during the dark times of '85, and he assured me the L.A. Express was going to be fine," remembered *Times* reporter Chris Dufresne. "It wasn't fine; it was all going to blow up. You're looking at your watch; the only thing we didn't know was the exact hour when it was going to fail."

"Right when the season was beginning, this would have been in February of 1985, a whole lot of bad things started to happen in rapid succession," recalled McSherry. "First, they found out that one of the owners, Jay Roulier, who had been a minority owner in Houston, and had agreed to take over the L.A. franchise because the L.A. owner Oldenburg was running from the police, had no money. There was some amount of money that was left in the L.A. Express checking account when Roulier took over the team, like $600,000. He had a woman lawyer who represented him, who was not the brightest lawyer in the world. She was in my office one day, and I got the distinct impression from her that she was uncomfortable talking about Roulier's finances, where he was getting the money he was spending on the team's training camp. It turned out that he was using the money that was in the account already, which belonged to the league.

"I told Usher what I suspected, and Usher said, 'You better tell the Executive Committee.' The Executive Committee was Trump, Ehrhart, Tad Taube and Myles Tanenbaum, the owner of the Baltimore team. I remember having dinner with Einhorn at a restaurant in Manhattan and telling him about my suspicion, and he was very upset. The guy had just lied to everybody. We ended up kicking him out of the league. Now we had a contract with ABC which said that we had to have a team in L.A. We had a contract with ESPN that said the same thing. We had a team; we had players; we had uniforms; we had a lease at the Coliseum, but we had no money, no owner. So Usher then called an owners' meeting which we had in New York shortly thereafter, and the owners voted to put up the money to fund the L.A. Express. We had Don Klosterman out there who was the general manager and obviously qualified to run a team. I became the president of the L.A. Express. We set up an entity to run the team, and I became its president so I could sign checks. The remaining teams had to fund it, which they did, usually late and with a lot of complaints."

The owners agreed to pay players' and coaches' salaries and little else. No money was made available to replace injured players, pay office bills or even buy tape for the trainers. Rumors quickly surfaced that the franchise might not make it through the year.

"They expect only 7,000 fans a game," said Commissioner Harry Usher in *Sports Illustrated*. "We had that many ushers in the Coliseum stands during the Olympics! We're going to saturate the L.A. area with hype." To that end, he hired Richard Stevens who worked with him on the 1984 Olympics to run the team and look for someone to buy the franchise. It soon became clear to Stevens that the league would not pay for hype so he had to make do with numerous special promotions and contests. *Sport* magazine went so far as to declare his "The Worst Job in Sports."

Director of marketing Chuck DeKeado recalled the turbulent off-season. "It was six months of shake and bake," he told *Sport*. "Sometimes we had no postage. We didn't even have renewal applications for season tickets until December. When we did get them I had to talk a benevolent local company into letting us run them through their postage meter. Sometimes the lights got turned off. You couldn't be sure the phones would work. By August and September I was getting phone calls at home at night from creditors demanding to know when they would be paid.

"We held a Booster Club barbecue in the fall, just to let people know that we were alive. What we didn't let them know was that many of the people that they met had been laid off months before, and that we didn't have a dime to pay for the barbecue. We fed 239 people using no money at all, just the donations of food and beverages from sponsors who were willing to help us out."

"By the '85 season the league had taken over," recalled *LA Times* writer Chris Dufresne. "They were just meeting payroll for the players. Meanwhile the light bill wasn't getting paid; the cheerleaders uniforms weren't getting cleaned, bills were coming due. They shut the water off at Express camp because they owed $136. Now they're paying Steve Young $40 million, or whatever the percentage of that was, and they couldn't afford to have the grass mowed. The grass would just grow on the field and you had all these high-priced players running around."

Obligated to keep a team in Los Angeles in order to continue receiving television money, USFL officials found themselves warding off the ghost of Bill Oldenburg.

"There was a bank that had loaned him some money, the San Fernando Valley National Bank," furthered McSherry. "They brought a lawsuit in L.A. and brought an order of attachment, attaching the player contracts and the franchise. I got on an airplane and called up the president of the bank and asked him to come to my hotel and meet me. He showed up with the chief financial officer of the bank and about five lawyers, and I was there with one lawyer for the league in my hotel room. They arrived, and I said, 'Boy, am I glad to see you guys. The USFL never needed a bank as a partner before any more than they do right now.' They said, 'What!?' I said, 'Well, you glommed onto the assets of the team so presumably that means you'll continue to play and pay the payroll. In fact, we have a payroll due this Friday. It's a million three or something like that.' That never occurred to any of them. They thought they had just attached assets. They didn't think there were liabilities attached to those assets. Within a day, the bank had given up the lawsuit and vacated the order of attachment. I think they actually wrote a letter of apology to Usher, and we ended up with the team."

Keeping control of the team was one matter; holding onto its star player proved to be yet another.

"After we took over the Express, Steve Young was owed an installment of his long-term deal," McSherry continued. "It was a million and a half dollars. It took me awhile to get that money together from the owners, but I did eventually get it together. I had a cashier's check for $1.5 million. I didn't want to mail it anywhere, so I called Leigh Steinberg who represented Young and said, 'Leigh, I'm going to be in L.A. at the end of the week. Can I drop the check off?' He said, 'Sure. When are you coming?' I told him I'd be there Friday. So Friday I drive up to his office building, go up to his office and it's locked. There's nobody there. So I slipped the check under the door, $1.5 million. I think I went right to the airport and flew back to New York. I got to the office the next morning, and the check is on my desk, sent back by Federal Express. The reason he didn't want the check is that if he didn't get paid, he could sign with the Tampa Bay Bucs, who owned his rights in the NFL. I finally got his father's law office in Connecticut to accept the check. I think the lawyers were a little afraid to be ducking messengers and checks. So we had secured Steve Young for the rest of the season.

"Probably in May, the L.A. Express came to New Jersey to play the Generals, and I was at the game. Somebody from the BBC came up to my box. I had the commissioner's box because he never went to the games. I don't think he liked football. They came up to the box and said, 'We're looking for somebody to talk with us at halftime. Can you talk to us?' I asked, 'What do you want to talk about?' They said, 'The state of the league and things like that.' I thought to myself, 'Oh my God, if I have to tell the truth, I'm going to be in a lot of trouble. If I can get away with a little moving my feet, I'll be alright.' So I go, 'Okay.' They said they'd send somebody to get me just before halftime. Later somebody comes to get me, we get on the elevator and we're going down. The elevator stops at another stop, and a woman gets on and says to me, 'Hi, my name is so-and-so Young.' I said, 'I'm Bill McSherry.' She asked, 'Are you the guy with the check?' I said, 'Yes, the million-and-a-half-dollar check, that was me.' She punched me. She hit me in the shoulder. It was a real punch, not just a love-tap or something. 'I don't like you,' she said. Fortunately, I was able to dance my way through the interview. They interviewed her, too, and she didn't say anything bad about the USFL."

At points it seemed the Express had inherited the Washington Federals' bad luck.

"We're on the plane and we're waiting for everyone to get ready to go, and boom, the plane gets rocked," recalled Young of a team flight. "And we're like, 'What was that?' So everyone's kinda mumbling, 'What the heck was that?' Then Don Klosterman comes on, and he's got this little microphone, and he goes, 'Uh, fellas, the equipment truck has just backed in to the plane. And it hit the engine, so I'd like the pilot here to tell you what the situation is.' He hands the mic over to the pilot and the pilot goes 'Okay, fellas, I flew in World War II and I have seen a lot of things on planes and there is a gaping hole in the engine. I have flown a lot of planes and that's just cosmetic. It means nothing about its flight safety, everything's fine. We should be taking off momentarily.' No joke, 50 guys go, 'Over my dead body!' and all take off, get down the plane and get off. We all look at this thing, and there is a huge, gaping hole in the engine. The truck had just hit it and split it, and so we look at it and we're like, 'We love you, Don, and it looks like you have flown for a long time in your military history, but, NO! We're not going.'"

BYU quarterback Steve Young had been projected as the top pick in the 1984 NFL draft. Instead, he joined the high-priced lineup of the USFL's Los Angeles Express. Photograph by Wilf Thorne.

Even after repairs, Mel Gray and David Howard opted to take commercial flights back to L.A.

The 1985 season for the Los Angeles Express turned out to be a nightmare to all concerned, including the players. Despite their obvious talent, the Express never got rolling. A 20-point fourth-quarter lead evaporated in a loss to Houston on opening day, the first of three consecutive losses to start the year. After beating San Antonio, they lost three more before gaining revenge on Houston. Following a walloping by Denver, they made it two out of three when they downed Portland for their third win of season. Rumors had persisted that the Express would fold after the Portland game, but the league instead reaffirmed its financial support for the franchise. Injuries, including the loss of Young for several weeks, took their toll, and L.A. did not manage another win.

"The last game at Orlando they were so depleted that they ran out of running backs during the game," recalled Dufresne. "Steve Young was standing on the sideline and said, 'I'll go in and play,' and he actually ran out on the field. He never carried the ball. I think he was in the game for two plays, but the idea of Steve Young having to go into that game and volunteer to play running back just kind of summed up what happened in the league."

"I'm sitting at the office on a Monday and the owner comes in and says, 'We're not going to have the game against the Los Angeles Express,'" recalled Orlando Coach Lee Corso. "I said, 'Why?' He said, 'They don't have any money to fly over here.' I said, 'What are you going to do?' He said, 'I'm going to pay for them because we have to have a game.' I said, 'You're going to pay them to come over and beat my butt with Steve Young and all these guys?' So we get into the game, and it's a hell of a game and at halftime they move Steve Young to fullback. He didn't even play quarterback the second half. We were fortunate to beat them, but that was one of the few games in the world that would pay for a team to come over and play you, and then they were going to beat your butt."

"We traveled so few guys we didn't have 11 guys that could play the position, so I had to play running back," confirmed Young. "And my memory of it was just pure fun. I lined up at running back."

With the league refusing to free up any money to help Coach John Hadl's squad sign replacements for the injured players, the team hired a 39-year-old truck driver for the grand salary of $100 a game to play tackle. It got so bad that during one game Young reportedly told the center to snap the ball over his head and, "Let's see what happens."

"They couldn't pay their bills, they couldn't buy tape, and they couldn't replace injured players," explained Dufresne. "They had 11 players I think in '85 that had season-ending surgeries, and they couldn't replace them. They hired a guy out of trucking school, this big guy. I don't know what kind of experience he had, but the next week he was like starting offensive tackle. And Steve Young, I remember him telling me the story, he said, 'We told the guy just get out of the way, just get out of the way, and I'll run around you.'"

Several owners, including Orlando's Don Dizney, blamed the league assessments to support the Express for their inability to sign star players before the season began.

"The league had to take over the team," furthered Dufresne "The other owners all agreed to pitch in $500,000 to meet the payroll. These were real, legitimate contracts that had to be paid or one of your flagship franchises was going to go under so the league had to begrudgingly step in. That's when it went wheels up because they were paying the players, but they weren't paying anybody else. The scene at the headquarters in Manhattan Beach became almost comical and sad. I was there many times and there would be Mercedes and Porsches in the parking lot from the players, but they couldn't mow the grass on the practice field because they didn't pay the landscapers. The grass was overgrown, the lights would go out, the water would be shut off. Carpenters would come in and threaten the receptionists' lives until they got what they were owed.

"All the infrastructure was falling apart, yet the players were walking around with Gucci bags because they were getting paid. It became absurdist almost, watching this juxtaposition."

"Very quickly, things got unraveled financially, but we still played and it was just kind of funny," recalled Young. "At one point in the Coliseum, because no one came, they would hand out big stacks of tickets to you just to pass them to people that would come because the USFL needed to look like people would come to the game. I'd be out at the stadium handing them to kids, and the kids would go out and try to sell them, and no one would buy them. In the Coliseum we would have 10,000 people but it looked like it was two people. Because the money was tight, there wasn't the intercom, there was no announcer, I mean there was no hoopla. There were no cheerleaders; there wasn't a lot of stuff going on in my second year. And so it got so quiet that we had to move the huddle back. The defense would be like, 'Oh, you know, off tackle, I heard tackle!' The linemen were talking; they heard the call in the huddle. So we moved the huddle back, and I tried to whisper some more 'cause there was no noise."

In one of the more bizarre chapters in league history, the Express closed out its home schedule against Arizona at tiny Shepard Stadium at Pierce College in the San Fernando Valley. The league moved the home game from the Coliseum, figuring the transfer could not hurt the franchise's attendance. A preseason scrimmage against the Breakers drew 6,400 to the 5,500 seat facility. A few thousand curious fans showed up for the regular season finale, a 21–10 defeat. It cost the junior college $50,000 to put up 10,000 portable seats to boost the stadium's capacity to 15,500. The team sold 1,000 advance tickets for the contest, up from a high of 50 for any game in L.A. that year. Arizona had to bring clocks and goal posts for the stadium, resulting in a rental dispute that nearly canceled the whole deal.

"They decided to take the team out to showcase them out in the valley at Pierce College," said Dufresne. "I remember going out there for the game and they had to setup folding chairs on the field because I think they had to comply with a minimum attendance requirement so they had to put out chairs that no one would sit in to comply with the attendance requirement. It was a surreal game."

"They decided that the crowd was too small at the Coliseum, and we had to go somewhere else to make it look like there was a big crowd," added Young. "And so there was a big game with Doug Williams from Arizona who was going to come in and play us. They went to Pierce College. Who, what? Pierce College is a high school field with the silver metal stands, maybe eight rows of it, between the 40's. What are you going to show, a little shot of the crowd all packed in there? Oh, wow, there's a lot of people today.

"So we bussed up there. So the bus shows up and we get on, and the guy says, 'I can't, my boss says you've got to pay me before I go.' You know because there is no credit with the USFL or with the Express. Hadl says, 'I'll write you a check.' He said, 'No, cash only.' Well, I don't have 400 or 500 bucks to give you a ride to Pierce College, what are you going to do? Guys on the bus were like, 'Hey, I don't want to pay this guy money. Maybe we'll just go home.' I came up with the money. I go get the money and hand it to him and we drive off and play at this field.

"This was an old, crappy field, where they painted the dirt green and the holes, they put sand in them, and the scoreboard was one of those old high school scoreboards in the middle of the day you can't see it. So there is no time on it: 20 seconds, 40 seconds, 30 second clock, so the referee is behind me going, 'Okay, you got five seconds, four, three … to snap the ball. And after the game there's no place to change or anything.'"

"It was the Arizona Outlaws and the L.A. Express, and the two quarterbacks were Steve Young and Doug Williams, two future Super Bowl MVPs basically playing a playground game at a junior college," Dufresne recalled. "I remember interviewing Steve Young, and it was like being at a high school game interviewing the quarterback before he got on the team bus to go back to the high school. The motor was running. I remember Doug Williams being very pissed off to have been there."

Los Angeles scored only 266 points over the course of the season, the worst total in the league, while allowing 456, second-worst in the circuit. Injuries played their part in the team's demise. Almost the entire offensive line, Young, tight end Gordon Hudson and running back Kevin Nelson missed time with injuries, resulting in the second-worst passing offense in the circuit. At one point, JoJo Townsell was the only offensive player to have played every game. Gray led a very weak rushing attack with 526 yards. Young hit on 137 of 250 throws for 1,741 yards with six touchdowns and 13 interceptions, and Frank Seurer completed 120 of 242 passes for 1,479 yards with seven scores and 18 interceptions. Even with the instability behind center, Townsell may have been the most consistent offensive threat with 47 catches for 777 yards and six touchdowns. Defensively, Darrell Pattillo picked off six passes, and Ben Rudolph led the way with eight sacks. They were the worst team in the USFL against the pass. Tony Zendejas connected on 26 of 34 field goals to finish with 101 points.

"I do remember a time when the coaches said that they didn't get paid," continued Young. "And so the players got paid, but the coaches didn't. So the coaches kinda said, 'Forget it, we're not gonna work if we're not getting paid.' That was when we started making our own playbooks and offensive game plans and so forth. There was a lot of frustration. It did devolve into something that was comical, embarrassing and crazy."

The attendance in 1985 was no laughing matter. Los Angeles opened with a season-high crowd of allegedly 18,828 against Houston and dipped to 3,059 for the Denver game. They wound up averaging just 8,415 per game, nearly half of the previous year's number. Even those figures were widely acknowledged to be inflated. For their Easter Sunday matchup with Baltimore, they offered $11 tickets for $5 or tickets for a family of five for $10 and still drew just 5,637 against the defending champions. For another contest, they gave away 30,000 tickets at nearby military bases. Just 5,000 people took advantage of their generosity. In most other circumstances, moving the final game to a junior college stadium in the L.A. suburbs would have hurt a team's credibility. By that time, though, the Express had precious little of it left.

"Every picture you see of the L.A. Express shows a lot of empty seats," explained Dufresne. "I saw a lot of great games that nobody saw. Incredible individual performances by Steve Young in front of nobody. It was almost like glorified scrimmages, but he did some things that reminded me of the best of Fran Tarkenton in the '60s and '70s in the NFL. Only Tarkenton did it in front of 70 or 80,000 people, and Steve was doing it in front of 3,000 in the 90,000-seat Coliseum."

"It was brutal, and I think that's why the league was so embarrassed," Young said. "You have this LA team with all these big money guys and it just looks awful. In LA, the city never really knew there were games going on. That's a tough city to get people's attention."

Memphis Showboats

An entirely different atmosphere permeated the Memphis Showboats. Memphis bulked up its roster by signing rookie corner backs Leonard Coleman of Vanderbilt and Mossy Cade of Texas, both projected NFL first round draft choices, to help against the pass and veteran linebacker John Corker from the Michigan Panthers and defensive end Sam Clancy from the Pittsburgh Maulers. Clancy in particular would help relieve some of the pressure put on fellow defensive end Reggie White. On offense, Pepper Rodgers remained undecided on his quarterback with Walter Lewis and Mike Kelley vying for the job. They would be helped by an improved running game thanks to the acquisition of Tim Spencer from Arizona and Harry Sydney from Denver. Spencer, though, was coming off a broken ankle suffered during the off-season and would not be available for the first few weeks. League executive Steve Ehrhart joined the team as its new general manager and vowed to show everyone that Memphis would improve in its sophomore season.

"I remember when I came to Memphis we signed two NFL number one draft choices, Leonard Coleman and Mossy Cade," he said. "They were coming right out of college. I was a big believer in Al Davis's man-to-man coverage strategy with outstanding defensive backs. We already had Reggie White down here and then we got Tim Spencer who had been a number one pick. Then we signed Luis Sharpe away from the Cardinals, essentially giving us five NFL first round draft choices. So the war was on. The NFL wanted to crush the USFL in everything from the media to striking back with player signings, and that just got worse and worse."

"By the third year, the competition was great," recalled Sydney. "It was excellent. Our offense had Derrick Crawford who played at San Francisco for a time, Greg Moser who was a heck of a college receiver, Walter Lewis and Mike Kelley at quarterback, Tim Spencer and myself were running backs. Tim Spencer played for years in the NFL. On defense we had Reggie White, Mossy Cade, Leonard Coleman and Don Bessillieu who had played in the NFL. We were a pretty good team."

The 'Boats showed their improvement right away with victories over San Antonio, Jacksonville and defending champion Baltimore. Somehow, they managed to follow that perfect start with four consecutive losses, even becoming Orlando's first ever victim. They managed to right the ship with another win over Baltimore, but dropped to 4–5 with a loss to New Jersey, their fifth defeat in six tries. From there, though, they became one of the better teams in the league with four straight decisions, among them a pasting of hated Birmingham, which kept them in the heart of the Eastern Conference race. Two losses dropped them to 8–7 before they closed out with three blowouts by a combined margin of victory of 65 points. Their 11–7 showing was a four-game improvement over 1984 and good enough for a wild card playoff berth.

After missing the first three games and playing at less than 100 percent for the next several, Spencer topped the USFL's second best rushing offense with 789 yards. Mike Kelley completed 165 of his 260 passes for 2,186 yards with nine touchdowns and 14 interceptions, while Lewis hit on 97 of 184 attempts for 16 scores and just five interceptions and also ran for 591 yards. Crawford led the way on the receiving end with 70 catches for 1,057 yards and nine touchdowns, and Moser added 57 catches for 1,145 yards and six scores. The defense, helped further by the addition of Don Bessillieu early in the season, allowed 118 points less than the year before and fared much better against the run. Reggie White paced the squad with 11.5 sacks.

"Reggie White is the best nose tackle in any league," Showboats defensive line coach Chuck Dickerson told *The Sporting News*. "He's an awesome force. Nobody handles him. Nobody will. He can destroy your offensive line from tackle to tackle."

"What I remember about Reggie White is that you'd hear about this big guy, a teddy bear who was incredibly strong, and he didn't know how to play, he just played," said Sydney. "When we were playing, they weren't calling him 'Sack man,' they were calling him 'Sock man,' and I wondered what was going on. In Memphis, they would start throwing socks. And I went, 'What the heck is this?' I realized that when he got his contract he went down to one of the clothing stores and bought an unbelievable amount of different pairs of socks, so they were calling him the 'Sock Man.'"

White also helped to keep the team loose by doing impressions of famous people for his teammates.

"He was incredible: Rodney Dangerfield, Don Meredith, Howard Cosell, you name it," said Sydney. "He was a clown. We used to tease him that we were glad that he didn't drink."

White had assistance keeping Memphis a fun team in unconventional coach Pepper Rodgers.

"Pepper Rodgers is one of the most unique individuals ever known to mankind," Sydney laughed. "He was off the wall. We played against the New Jersey Generals one day, and he came out to practice in a tuxedo and a top hat, representing Doug Flutie. When I first got there, not knowing who he was, I saw him running down the street in Memphis shit-faced.

"It was unconventional, anything goes. He had great assistant coaches, but as far as Pepper goes, he was a great motivator, speaker, story teller."

Head coach Pepper Rodgers kept things interesting for the Memphis Showboats, leading the talent-rich squad to an 11–7 record in its second season. Photograph by Jim Turner, from author's collection.

The people of Memphis responded to the franchise's four-game improvement by turning out at the rate of 30,948 per game, an increase of more than 3,000 per contest over the previous year. More than 44,000 attended the New Jersey game and the club drew more than 23,000 for each date on its home schedule. One particularly rowdy group of Memphis fans known as the "Boat People" occupied the seating behind one of the end zones and regularly made things difficult on the opposition when they ventured to that end of the field.

Jacksonville Bulls

Like Memphis, the Jacksonville Bulls, coming off a season which was much more successful at the turnstiles than on the field, made a number of changes to its roster entering the 1985 campaign. First and foremost, they brought in New Jersey castoff Brian Sipe to carry the load at quarterback and Mike Rozier, formerly with the defunct Maulers, to take over at running back. Two-time Heisman Trophy winner Archie Griffin, who had last played with the Cincinnati Bengals, joined them in the backfield. Former NFL guards Roy Simmons and J.T. Turner looked to bolster the offensive line, and rookie Keith Millard of Washington State brought his formidable presence to the defensive line.

The Bulls opened their second season with a surprising and costly win over Baltimore. Sipe separated his shoulder and would miss several weeks with the injury. With their starting signal caller out of action, they dropped five of their next six, only tipping winless Orlando in overtime. Fortunately, Jacksonville ran off a four-game winning string in which they topped both Birmingham and New Jersey. After losing to Tampa Bay for the second time, the Bulls welcomed Sipe back to the lineup with a 20–17 win at Houston and 21–7 decision versus Los Angeles. The victory moved them to 8–6, just two games behind Eastern Conference leader Birmingham. Their playoff hopes unraveled, though, when Sipe separated his shoulder again, effectively ending his career, and Jacksonville lost three of its last four.

"Brian Sipe was a fun guy to work with, and unfortunately we lost him in the very first game of the year," remembered Bulls coach Lindy Infante, who had coached against the passer in the NFL when he had been on Cincinnati's coaching staff while Sipe quarterbacked Cleveland. "We acquired him in the offseason, and we ended up having to let Matt Robinson go who was our number one quarterback the year before, due to financial reasons. I had a great deal of respect for Sipe after watching him play in the NFL, and he proved every bit of it when he came down and started working with us. Brian in the very first series of the first game that second year, he took us right down the field to about the 12-yard-line in about five plays, just looking like a million dollars. He went back to pass and got blind-sided, and blew his shoulder out. They had to operate and replenish a ligament that had been torn beyond repair. Bottom line was that we lost our premier starting quarterback in our first game.

"He came to me afterward and said, 'I will be back before the year is over.' Of course, the surgeons said that would be a miracle. It turned out that he did, and it was against the Stars, against whom he had been hurt the first time, and he ended up getting hurt again. We had him on the field for a very short time. A guy named Robbie Mahfouz stepped in and played admirably for us throughout the year, but Brian was a special guy. I really enjoyed the time I got to work with him. Unfortunately, it was very short."

One day before their final game, Bulls management showed that even they needed to pinch pennies. They released Mahfouz to avoid paying him a $10,000 bonus due him if he was still on the active roster at the end of the season. Players were so upset by the move that Infante had to cancel practice that day.

Mike Rozier finished second in the league rushing race with 1,361 yards and added 12 touchdowns. Though he tallied just two 100-yard games, both against Orlando, he proved to be the Bulls most consistent player and also gave them a go-to guy when they broke into scoring range. After a horrendous start, Ed Luther completed 240 of 400 throws for 2,792 yards with 15 touchdowns and 21 interceptions, while Sipe hit on 55 of 89 passes for 685 yards with four scores and a pair of interceptions. Gary Clark, the team's leading receiver from the year before, managed just ten receptions as he struggled with two pulled hamstrings before being waived. Alton Alexis filled in nicely in his stead with 83 catches for 1,118 yards, and Perry Kemp added 59 grabs for 915 yards. Keith Millard proved to be just what the defense needed as he topped the Bulls with 12 sacks.

"I didn't do too well in Pittsburgh," said Rozier of his 1984 rookie campaign. "I was still coming off an injury from college in the Orange Bowl, a high ankle sprain. It took me a year to come back from that. When I went to Jacksonville, I was back up to 100 percent. I had more fun. I was the second leading rusher that year behind Herschel. The general manager down there was Larry Csonka. They brought Archie Griffin out of retirement, and he was on the squad. He was teaching the offense. Archie came down from Cleveland, and he told me that if I could learn this offense, I could learn any offense in the NFL. Archie was there to teach me how it worked."

Jacksonville continued to be one of the USFL's most receptive markets. The Bulls averaged 44,325 per game, a drop of about 2,000 from the year before but good enough for second highest in the league after in-state rival Tampa Bay. The team drew 60,100 against New Jersey and topped 50,000 three other times without falling below 31,000 the entire home schedule.

"It was nice in Jacksonville," added Rozier. "I had a good time playing in the Gator Bowl. We had great fan support that reminded me of the University of Nebraska. Fans come out, and it doesn't matter if it's raining, cold or whatever, the stadium is sold out."

Despite the team's popularity in the Northern Florida city, Fred Bullard was unable to sell many of the 124,950 shares of stock (49 percent of the team) he put up for public sale. Priced at $100 per share, it was still too much for most fans, especially after Bullard revealed that the team had lost $7 million in 1984 and expected to lose an additional $4 million in 1985.

"A person would not invest here to receive a dividend check once a month," the owner explained in *The Sporting News*. "You would invest for a number of reasons, including pride in Jacksonville." When asked what would happen if the team went out of business, he replied, "If you buy enough, you can wallpaper your bathroom."

He eventually withdrew the offering when less than 1,000 of the shares sold. He had lost nearly $12 million in two years and sought other investors.

New Jersey Generals

After a busy offseason signing veterans the year before, New Jersey shored up its few remaining holes with former Maulers Don Maggs at tackle and Jerry Holmes at corner back. But in 1985, their biggest signing was rookie Heisman Trophy winning quarterback Doug Flutie. The main question for the team that had gone 14–4 the previous year was how long it would take their rookie QB to adjust to the pros. There was little time for him to learn since Donald Trump had traded Brian Sipe away to Jacksonville. Just hours after his contract had been announced in New York, the passer found himself on a plane bound for the team's training camp in Orlando. From the moment the plane landed, Flutie found himself under a spotlight. Any ideas Coach Walt Michaels had of protecting him from the media and immersing him in football vanished as soon as the diminutive passer arrived in Florida.

"Well, best laid plans didn't happen that way," said former New Jersey assistant media relations director Gary Croke in *Flutie*. "As soon as we came out it was just a mob scene. They just basically leapt on Doug and stuck cameras in his face and asked him a barrage of questions. It was like a rock star type of atmosphere. We had the security guards trying to hustle Doug through. Through all the madness we lost our head coach, Walt Michaels. Somehow he got caught up in the back of the group and was cornered by more media people. We had to send someone back to get him, rescuing him from the media, then we finally got out to the curb and threw Doug into a Cadillac. We had three Cadillacs and threw Walt and our front office staff into the others and took off toward training camp. From the time he got off the plane until we got him into the car it was bedlam."

"I signed and I figured Brian Sipe was the starting quarterback," Flutie explained. "I'd learn under Brian; he'll take me under his wing, I'll get an opportunity somewhere and I'll start to play. No, with the amount of money Trump spent on me, next day Brian Sipe was traded and, boom, into the fire. At that time if you went to the NFL you sat for four years. That's what you did: you sat, learned, waited for your opportunity. I had the opportunity to play right away."

"I came in after holding out during training camp, signed this stupid contract with ridiculous numbers where a lot of guys are making 60 grand and the starting QB, an NFL veteran, an MVP, a guy who did great the year before, he's gone day one," Flutie added about his first days with New Jersey. "Day two Walt announces we're going through an extra week of doubles because Doug just got here, and he's gonna be our starting QB, so now we have to go through doubles again. The guys were done with doubles, the most torturous, worst part of football, and here comes this rookie holdout, big money guy and you're all gonna go through an extra week for him. So I wasn't real popular right away."

The hype over Flutie would take some of the spotlight off his backfield mate and fellow Heisman winner Herschel Walker who was coming off a shoulder operation to fix an injury that had afflicted him since he was a freshman at Georgia and shelved him for a few games the season before. The shoulder problem had been more severe than the running back had let anyone know. He had dislocated the weakened shoulder several times in college and during the 1984 preseason. The injury became worse throughout the year until Walker finally opted for surgery.

After a shaky start in their opening day loss to Birmingham, Flutie rebounded with a four-touchdown performance in a victory over Orlando. After considerable prodding by Trump, Michaels grudgingly opened up the offense to take advantage of his quarterback's abilities.

"We started the game against Orlando in a no huddle offense," wrote the quarterback in *Flutie*. "I was in the shotgun, calling my own plays, and we were off and running. I threw four touchdown passes, three in the first half, and it was like night and day from the previous game. We blew them out in the first half, and in the second half, we went back to the old offense and didn't do squat."

The Flutie magic continued with a 10-point comeback against L.A. in the Generals home opener, but New Jersey dropped two of its next three as he struggled. While Flutie continued to adjust to his new surroundings, Herschel Walker provided much of the punch in the Generals arsenal. He powered New Jersey to four straight victories and ran up a league-record 233 yards in an Easter Sunday triumph over Houston.

With the Generals at 7–4, Walker was just getting started. He ran for more than 100 yards for the sixth straight game in a 10–3 win over Baltimore, the third time in the last four regular season meetings that the Generals had beaten the mighty Stars. Following a loss to Denver, Walker continued to dominate in decisions over Tampa Bay and Memphis. Not all the news in the Showboats game was good, though, as Doug Flutie broke his collarbone, ending his rookie year prematurely.

"Reggie White ran me down on a bootleg," recalled Flutie. "I didn't see him coming, and he wrapped me up and body slammed me into the turf. I knew right away my left shoulder was messed up. I just got up, walked to the bench, and sat down. At halftime ABC announced I had broken my collarbone and was out for the season, which only had three games left in it."

Walker's incredible rushing numbers had continued to pile up to the point where he was just 138 yards shy of Eric Dickerson's single-season rushing mark of 2,105 yards set in 1984. He'd have his chance to break the record in a week 16 Monday evening tussle with visiting Jacksonville. With much of the damage done in the first half, Walker needed 51 yards to break Dickerson's mark. In the third period, the runner stunned the Bulls and electrified the crowd at the Meadowlands when he took a handoff at the New Jersey 45 and sprinted 55 yards into the end zone, vaulting him into the record books as the most prolific pro runner in a season and helping the Generals to a 31–24 victory.

Two losses to Oakland and Birmingham ended the season on a down note, but not before Walker had run for 100-plus yards in 11 straight games. Herschel Walker proved to be the story of the 1985 United States Football League season. He finished as the circuit's leading scorer with 132 points with a league-high 21 rushing touchdowns. He ended the year with a pro-football record 2,411 yards on the ground and was also the team's leading

New Jersey Generals running back Herschel Walker became the story of the 1985 regular season when he ran for a professional football record 2,411 yards. Photograph by Jim Turner, from Richie Franklin's collection.

receiver with 37 catches for 467 yards. The Generals finished with the USFL's best running offense and worst passing game.

Despite his slow start and a weak receiving corps, Flutie finished his rookie campaign with 134 completions in 281 attempts for 2,109 yards with 13 touchdowns and 14 interceptions in 13 games before going down with the broken collarbone. Kerry Justin intercepted eight passes and James Lockette tallied 13 sacks to spearhead the defense.

Thanks to the addition of Flutie and the year-long headlines generated by Walker's record season, the Generals became one of the few USFL teams to see an increase in attendance over the 1984 season. They averaged 41,413 per home date, up about 3,500 per game from the year before. They peaked at 58,741 for the Los Angeles victory that opened the home slate and did not fall below 34,000 the entire season.

Houston Gamblers

The Houston Gamblers players greeted the 1985 season with enthusiasm, a sentiment unfortunately not shared by the Houston fans. The team had racked up incredible offensive numbers in its inaugural season and looked for more of the same with a few key improvements on both sides of the ball, particularly on the offensive line, a weak point the year before.

In their opener at Los Angeles, the Gamblers fell into a 33–13 fourth-quarter deficit before Kelly went to work. He started with a 52-yard scoring throw to Richard Johnson, added a 40-yard touchdown strike to Vince Courville and completed the 34–33 comeback with a 39-yard aerial to Ricky Sanders, all in eight minutes of game time. The quarterback ended the day with incredible stats. He completed 35 of 54 passes for 574 yards, the highest total in American football history. He broke the 34-year-old record professional record of 554 yards set by Norm Van Brocklin of the Los Angeles Rams. He also tossed five touchdowns for the second time in his brief career and led the Gamblers back from a 20-point deficit in only 12 offensive plays.

"It was an exciting football game," Argovitz recalled. "I'll never forget one of the last plays coming down at the end of the game. We were at one time down like three touchdowns, and at the end of the game, I think with less than two minutes to go, we were on our own 20-yard line, and Kelly got the team in a huddle. He said, 'We got them right where we want 'em. Let's go get' em.' So at my 20-yard line, I'm thinkin' three plays, we'll score a touchdown and the game was over for us."

"I remember that game, seriously because it's talked about all the time in all my interviews, as one of the most exciting games." Kelly explained. "It was myself against Steve Young, the Houston Gamblers vs. the LA Express. It was a game where we were pretty much getting blown out. In the fourth quarter, eight minutes something left in the game, playing against Steve Young, one of the best athletes as far as QB's I've seen in a long time, and I remember how our offense was. We could be struggling for two or three series in a row and all of a sudden, boom, we would click on four or five. I remember being down by three touchdowns with just a little time left, and wind up coming back and winning that game. I remember reading the article recently within the last five years, but it said it was 'the greatest game that no one saw,' or something like that in *Sports Illustrated*. It was announced that there was something like 8,000 people or something like that, but in the LA Coliseum, 7,000 fans looked like it was about 50 fans. We knew what

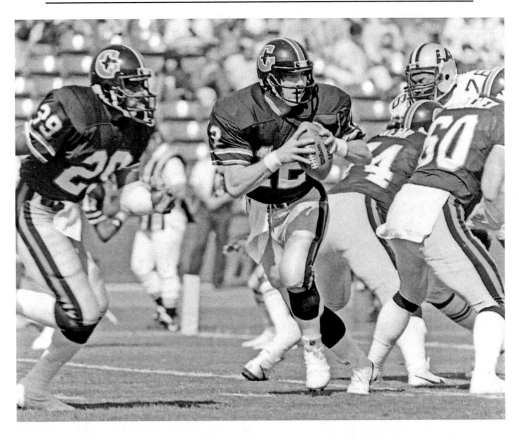

In the "Greatest Game That No One Saw," Houston Gamblers quarterback Jim Kelly drops back on one of his 54 pass attempts against the Los Angeles Express on February 24, 1985. Kelly threw for a pro football record 574 yards and three late touchdowns in a 34–33 victory. Photograph by Wilf Thorne.

we had to do and we were out there to play the game of football, and our style of offense and our team, it was like playing a pick-up game in the backyard. We would just go and throw it all over the place. Ricky Sanders, touchdown. Richard Johnson, touchdown. Gerald McNeil, touchdown. I remember throwing three touchdown passes with just seven or eight minutes to go in the game, and we came back and beat them. And I still mess with Steve about that too when I see him sometimes. That was one of the most memorable games because 574 yards passing, that's a lot of yardage, and I never threw for that many yards ever again. It was a game that I will definitely remember for the rest of my life."

"When we see each other, that's the first thing we talk about, and we have played in a lot of Super Bowls and championship games," added Young. "I don't know why, maybe it was because it was so high-flying and pure. We both think of it the same way. As a memory that was just seared into our minds and it wasn't just that game. There was a game in Houston, and there was another game in LA that were just like that. From a quarterback's perspective, they were just a pure, absolute shootout. It was like 'Oh yeah?' 'Oh yeah!' 'Oh yeah?' 'Oh yeah!' It was this crescendo of 'Oh really, you think you can?' It's just wonderful memories. It's funny because we just talk all those years later and think about it that way."

The Houston offense continued to riddle the opposition, scoring 50 points at Tampa Bay, 42 at Oakland and 36 against Denver, all wins. After struggling to a win over Portland, they suffered their first losses of the year to Baltimore, New Jersey and Los Angeles.

The Gamblers got back on track by downing Arizona, San Antonio and Portland, but close defeats to Memphis and Jacksonville dropped them to 9–4, one-half game behind Oakland for the Western Conference lead. A 41–20 win against Arizona kept them in the race but also cost them the services of Kelly for the rest of the year. He tore a ligament in his knee and would be lucky to be ready by the postseason. With Todd Dillon taking over behind center, Houston lost three of its final four, still good enough for a playoff berth.

For the season, Kelly completed 360 out of 567 passes for 4,623 yards with 39 touchdowns and 19 interceptions, despite missing more than four games with injuries. Dillon connected on 121 of 225 throws for 1,495 yards with nine scores and nine interceptions in relief. Richard Johnson again led all USFL receivers with 103 catches for 1,384 yards and 14 touchdowns, while Clarence Verdin placed fourth with 84 grabs for 1,004 yards. Gerald McNeil joined the 1,000-yard club with 1,017 yards on 58 catches. Ricky Sanders started only three games and missed eight others entirely due to a week-three knee injury that required surgery. One problem for the Gamblers all year was the lack of a running game. Injuries to backs and the offensive line hurt as Todd Fowler led the way on the ground with just 402 yards. In fact, the Gamblers led the USFL in passing and placed dead last on the ground, a mirror image of New Jersey's offense. Pete Catan topped the defensive charge with 11 sacks. Luther Bradley provided the secondary help Houston was looking for by picking off 12 passes, the second most in the league, and Durwood Roquemore added seven thefts. The special teams also shone as McNeil finished tops in punt returns with a 13-yard average and two scores and Verdin paced the league with a 26.6-yard average and three touchdowns on kickoff returns. Toni Fritsch led all kickers with 122 points, including a 21 out of 24 showing on field goal attempts.

Although the franchise was one of the most exciting teams in the USFL, Houston fans turned their backs on them in 1985. They averaged just 19,120 fans per game, a drop of 9,000 from the year before, and failed to draw even 18,000 over the final five home dates. They hit a low of 11,780 against San Antonio late in the season. Despite fielding one of the most exciting teams in all of football, the announced move to the fall hurt them, alienating Oilers fans who knew they would have to choose one team over the other beginning in 1986. The ongoing ownership and financial problems did little to inspire confidence among Houston sports fans. The league loaned the franchise $3 million early in the year and returned their $1.5 million letter of credit to help Jerry Argovitz and company pay the mounting bills. The team missed its final payroll, and rumors swirled throughout the final weeks of the season that the Gamblers would either fold or move. The league appointed McSherry, already caretaker of the Los Angeles Express, to keep Houston afloat late in the season.

"I was also running Houston because they eventually ran out of money," he said. "I was the president of two teams at the same time, which was probably a violation of some rule somewhere. Argovitz and Alvin Lubetkin were left there. I don't think they had any money at the beginning of the year. We just didn't find out about it for a while."

One of the league's most exciting teams could not overcome the problems facing the league as a whole. The brash Argovitz received little sympathy from some of his fellow owners.

"Some of the players wanted to grab Jerry Argovitz by his throat, throw him down and beat on him," recalled Kelly. "A lot of players wanted to do that to all the owners. I in my own mind, yeah, you're mad, but you have a job to do, you have some focus. Interceptions, forget about it, move on. Super Bowls, you lose you move on. It's being able to make sure to focus on the right things, and that things will happen over time. You as one individual, you're not going to be the reason it folds or you get paid. You do what you have to do and you continue to do it and let everything fall in its place."

"Argovitz was one of these guys who had a mouth that was a lot bigger than his wallet," said Oakland's Tad Taube. "That was unfortunate because he verbalized support to sign players to large compensation packages, but in the long run he didn't have the financial wherewithal to follow through and survive as an owner in the league. I think he was one of the first people to have some financial difficulties playing at the salary level that he himself had advocated."

Orlando Renegades

The USFL welcomed the Orlando Renegades as a replacement for the Washington Federals. Don Dizney and Jim English, both previously involved in the ownership of the Bandits, did a superb job of marketing the franchise in a city best known for its many tourist attractions. They worked to make sure that locals and visitors alike would, "Catch the Renegade Rage," as their marketing suggested. Unfortunately, the schedule maker had not been kind to the team. The team's first three games would be against squads that had finished 14–4 the year before and the next three would be on the road. It would be a challenge to Coach Lee Corso and his band of former Federals.

"They were really, I mean really, bad," Corso said. "I had a practice here, the first practice, and I'll never forget it. A big offensive tackle walked in to me and said, 'Coach, can I talk to you?' I says, 'Sure thing, yeah, come on in,' and he said, 'I wanna renegotiate my contract.' I said, 'We had one practice.' He said, 'With this team here, I wanna renegotiate my contract.' I said, 'Close the door.' I said to him, 'Do you realize where you are? You're with the Orlando Renegades which is the Washington Federals, which is the worst team in the history of pro football, which makes you the worst right tackle in the history of pro football, and it makes me the worst coach in the history of pro football. You got any questions?' He said, 'No,' and I never had another guy say a word about negotiating, so this is it! This was *the* bottom of the barrel of pro football, so I never had any more problems with the guys."

Orlando struggled in the early going and failed to win any of the first six games, although the last three losses, to Portland, Jacksonville and Denver, came down to the final minutes or overtime. The Renegades eventually chalked up their first win, 28–17 over Memphis, thanks to a Reggie Collier scoring run late in the game. After making it two in a row with their first and only road win at Arizona, they dropped their next three prior to pulling out a squeaker over San Antonio. A surprising 37–7 whipping of Tampa Bay followed a couple more visits to the loss column, and a season-ending win over Los Angeles lifted the club to a 5–13 mark, last in the Eastern Conference but not bad by the standards of the dearly departed Federals.

"It's embarrassing, but I lost the first six games," added Corso. "And it was bad. It was so bad, I never covered the spread, not once, and people were not only losing the game, but they were losing their money like crazy. Well, I needed somebody to do my radio show so I hired this young guy named Chris Russo to do my radio show, live from the steakhouse. So he and I get together and they were waiting for us, and they were throwing stones at us and butter and everything. They were so mad because not only didn't we win, we didn't cover the spread. It's bad stuff. So I survived that and after that, we got the team going pretty good, and we won some ball games at the end of the year. We got to be very, very good, but, boy, was that shaky. I still talk to Russo about that, the first assignment we ever had, doing a live radio show in a bar, with people losing money. Believe me, not a good gig."

Russo would later gain fame when he teamed with Mike Francesa for the popular "Mike and the Mad Dog" radio show.

Curtis Bledsoe led the team in rushing with 781 yards, and Collier finished close behind with 606 yards and 12 touchdowns on the ground. He also completed 229 out of 427 throws for 2,578 yards with 13 scores and 16 interceptions. The dependable Joey Walters topped the squad with 58 receptions for 784 yards. Defensively, Victor Jackson and former Bandit Jeff George each intercepted eight balls, tying them for fourth in the league. Jackson also recovered six fumbles, best in the league. He and Jerry Parrish highlighted one of the USFL's best return games. On the defensive side, they reminded many of their predecessors, managing a paltry 24 sacks, the worst total among the 14 teams, while finishing dead last in rushing defense. They fared a little better against the pass, mostly because teams could slice through them with their running attacks and did not bother to throw the ball much.

"We go to New Jersey to play, and we're at the hotel," remembered Corso. "We get up for breakfast, and the owner comes and he says, 'I got a good feeling about this game.' I says, 'You do?' 'I think you guys can upset this New Jersey team.' I said, 'Did you read the *Times* this morning? Did you see where Flutie and Walker make more money than my entire team? Those two guys are worth more than my entire team. Oh yeah, we're gonna beat these guys. That's for sure!' So the talent was pretty good alright, and they have a lot of it and pretty good players. The talent around it was pretty good at different places, too, but not with the Renegades. We had a low budget show, but we had a lot of fun doing the games, and we had some really exciting ball games."

A five-win season was nothing to crow about for most teams, but considering Orlando's humble beginnings as the Washington Federals and the aborted move to Miami, it was quite an accomplishment for Corso and his staff. After an 0–6 start, the Renegades played competitively over the final two-thirds of the season, compiling a 5–7 mark. They also did much better than the Feds at the gate, averaging 24,136 fans per game with a high of 32,748 for the home opener against New Jersey. The franchise dipped below 20,000 just once when an estimated 15,000 showed up for the San Antonio game. The figures were a vast improvement over Washington's 1984 average of 7,694 per game.

Birmingham Stallions

Coming off a 14–4 season, the Birmingham Stallions did little to alter their roster. Joe Cribbs and Cliff Stoudt had helped to turn the offense around and looked to be even better with a year under their belts. The defense had also established a reputation as a hard-hitting, ball-hawking bunch, not surprising considering coach Rollie Dotsch's connection to the Pittsburgh Steelers Steel Curtain defense.

Following an opening game victory over Doug Flutie and the New Jersey Generals, the franchise received a pair of jolts. First came a blowout loss to Denver, but the news off the field was even worse for Birmingham. Home State Savings Bank in Ohio, of which Stallions' owner Marvin Warner owned 96 percent, closed amid mounting financial problems. The Securities and Exchange Commission also shut down ESM Group, a company to which many of Warner's businesses had ties. Days before its closure, he withdrew $37 million and his son-in-law Stephen Arky, a minority owner of the Tampa Bay Bandits, withdrew $2 million. The developments cast considerable doubt over Warner's ability to fund the Stallions. One of the USFL's strongest and best-supported franchises suddenly found itself in tenuous financial shape.

"The next bad thing that happened that I remember was that Marvin Warner, the former ambassador to Switzerland, very well-known politically and as a banker from Ohio, showed up at the office in New York, and he looked like a homeless person," McSherry remembered. "He owned the Birmingham Stallions, and he showed up at the office and said that he didn't have any more money and he wanted to give the team back to the league. The problem he had was that he was associated with a savings bank in Columbus called Home State Savings Bank, and Home State had gone under very publicly, and its crash had brought Marvin Warner to his knees. The problem we had became apparent that afternoon when I went to the safe deposit box to look for his letter of credit. I discovered it had been written by Home State Savings, so we had a worthless letter of credit. The letter of credit was just a worthless piece of paper."

Publicly, franchise president Jerry Sklar confirmed that Warner wanted to sell his stake in the team and had withdrawn all of his financial support. Charlotte businessman George Shinn, who would later buy the NBA's Charlotte Hornets, expressed interest in purchasing the team and moving it to North Carolina if a local buyer could not be found. He had staged a couple of USFL exhibition games in his hometown but did not have an adequate stadium in Charlotte. To keep the team from moving, Birmingham Mayor Richard Arrington hired a bond attorney to investigate whether the city could buy a limited partnership in the franchise for $1 million.

The players, though, proved adept at ignoring the turmoil. They took out any frustrations on Orlando, Memphis, Baltimore and Jacksonville in quick succession. Following an upset loss at San Antonio, they foiled Oakland and crushed Tampa Bay to run out to an Eastern Conference leading 7–2 mark.

Meanwhile, the Birmingham city council revealed that the franchise had not paid the city for the rental of Legion Field for the past five games, including a preseason contest. While the city had the right to impound the Stallions' equipment, mayor Arrington continued his efforts to keep the team. He ultimately persuaded the council to lend $1 million to the Alabama State Fair Authority so it could purchase a stake in the franchise. Not all involved were convinced that it was a good move.

"It's awfully easy to let our heartstrings rule our pocketbooks," councilman Russell Yarbrough told *The Sporting News*. "We're dealing with taxpayers' money here. I think if we invest any money at all in the Stallions, we're going to lose it."

Two consecutive losses dropped Birmingham a game out of first place, but they quickly dispatched Portland, Los Angeles and Orlando to wrest back the top spot in the East. Birmingham nipped Houston and Baltimore to make it five in a row before Tampa

Bay ended their victory string. The loss made little difference when they took out New Jersey in the final week to capture the conference crown at 13–5.

Offensively, Cribbs fell to 1,047 yards and seven touchdowns with his longest run of the year just 28 yards, even though their running game continued to be one of the circuit's strongest. Stoudt made up for it by hitting 266 of 444 passes for 3,358 yards with 34 touchdowns and 19 interceptions, numbers which ranked him second in the league behind only Jim Kelly of Houston. The quarterback also ran for 437 yards and five scores. Jim Smith remained in his role as Stoudt's favorite receiver with 87 catches for 1,322 yards and 20 touchdowns, more scores than any other receiver in the USFL. On the defensive side of the ball, Chuck Clanton led the way with a league-high 16 of the team's 38 interceptions, also the best mark in the league. Bill Roe totaled 8.5 sacks and Herb Spencer added 6.5 of the team's total of 50. They ended the year ranked number one against both the run and the pass and finished a USFL-best plus 17 in turnover differential.

Birmingham had proven the year before that it was fertile ground for the USFL, and the city's unflagging support in the face of the ongoing ownership problems only confirmed that notion. Although their average attendance fell by nearly 5,000 to 32,065 per game, their support placed among the top teams in the league. Considering the problems of 1985, the drop could have been much greater in other cities. They hit a high of 44,500 in the middle of the season for an April game against Oakland but settled for 24,300 for the final home contest against Baltimore.

Postseason

The top eight teams in the league advanced to the postseason, with five coming from the East and three out of the West. On Saturday, June 29, Birmingham's solid defense would host Houston's run and shoot in the 1985 playoff opener. On Sunday, Oakland hoped to defend the league's top record of 13–4–1 against Tampa Bay, while Memphis would play host to Denver, the league's other run and shoot team. The Baltimore Stars looked to start its title defense at New Jersey in a game bumped to Monday night.

The postseason lid-lifter at Birmingham marked the return of Houston's Jim Kelly who had missed the final four games of the season with a knee injury. A season-low 18,500 Stallions fans turned out to see the contest at Legion Field.

The hosts opened the day with a four-minute drive that resulted in the first points of the ballgame on a 39-yard Danny Miller field goal. On the ensuing kickoff, Ted Walton created the first big play by stripping Houston's Clarence Verdin of the ball which Dennis Woodberry recovered at the Gamblers 34-yard line. It took Cliff Stoudt just four plays to find Jim Smith for an eight-yard score that made it 10–0 Birmingham six minutes into the first period. The Gamblers fought back to tie it on a 23-yard Kelly to Gerald McNeil throw and a 20-yard Toni Fritsch kick. Miller then connected on a boot from 26 yards out to make it Stallions 13, Gamblers 10 at the half.

The Birmingham kicker made it three-for-three by splitting the uprights on a 41-yard effort in the third before Kelly responded with a 21-yard touchdown throw to Richard Johnson to give Houston its first advantage at 17–16. Johnson made a spectacular catch in the end zone, spinning completely around in the air to make the grab. Their lead did not hold up for long, though, as Miller boomed a 57-yard field goal, the longest ever in the USFL, late in the third period to make it 19–17. Fritsch countered with a 46-yarder of his own before Miller connected on his fifth attempt in the same number of tries from 35 yards away with under two minutes left. Houston started its last ditch effort on its own ten and drove all the way to the Stallions 32 with time left for one more play as Fritsch lined up to try the 49-yard field goal. The kick was long enough but hooked to the left by about a foot as time expired sending the Stallions on their way to the semifinals with a 22–20 victory.

With Miller providing most of the offense, Stoudt hit on 13 of 26 throws for 156 yards and a score, and Cribbs gained 70 yards on 16 tries. Dennis Woodberry collected the only interception of the game, and he and his defensive mates held Houston to 76 yards on the ground and collected a fumble. On the losing side, Kelly performed admirably especially considering his long layoff. He completed 23 of 40 passes for 319 yards and a pair of scores, with Johnson making seven of those receptions for 120 yards and a score.

The following day Denver squared off against Memphis at the Liberty Bowl in front of 34,528 Showboats supporters who turned out despite a major Professional Golfers' Association event in the city. The Gold had dropped their final two games of the season while the Showboats rode a four-game winning streak. Though Denver owned the fourth seed and Memphis placed fifth, the league controversially moved the game to Memphis due to the Gold's poor attendance.

"Now you know that they really are trying to get you when you earn the playoff at your place, and they move it to another venue!" laughed Gold coach Mouse Davis. "That's a struggling league. Obviously, they're trying to do it to get more people in the stands, but it's still kind of a ridiculous thing when you've already set up standards to do it one way, and they end up doing it another. But hey, in new leagues, you sometimes do that. That's how it works."

Memphis started on the right foot, picking off Vince Evans' opening pass attempt of the game. It was the Gold quarterback's first start since April 15, and he looked rusty throughout. Denver's defense held up well early but soon tired. It took the Showboats 12:38 before they finally lit the scoreboard on a Mike Kelley to Greg Moser 12-yard scoring throw. Alan Duncan added a field goal early in the second quarter and another one minutes later to put Memphis up, 13–0. They had a chance to pull away even further, but Kelley's throw into the end zone from the Denver one fell incomplete on the final play of the first half. The Gold looked awful in the first two quarters. Of their eight drives, six ended in disaster: three lost fumbles, an interception, a partially blocked punt and another play on which Jim Asmus could not even get off the punt.

Memphis was not about to toy with Denver any longer, and they put the game out of reach on their opening two drives of the second half. First, they marched 67 yards, ending with Ricky Porter's one-yard burst, and then the team traveled 76 yards, the last 35 on Leonard Williams' scoring run. After the defense held Denver yet again, Derrick Crawford took Asmus' punt on his own 37 and raced 63 yards for a touchdown to make it 34–0 at the end of three quarters. Porter added another short scoring burst before Bob Gagliano, on relief of Evans, finally put the Gold on the board with a 22-yard pass to Leonard Harris. Walter Lewis came in for mop up duty and connected with Mark Raugh on a 25-yard scoring play to make the final score 48–7, the biggest blowout in USFL playoff history and Memphis's most impressive win of the season.

The Showboats running game churned out 296 yards on the day, allowing them to control the tempo and the clock against Denver's sputtering run and shoot. Tim Spencer piled up 113 yards on 16 tries in his best outing of the year. The defense collected five sacks, two by linebacker Steve Hammond, and collected three interceptions and three fumble recoveries. Playing with the lead for nearly the entire game, they also held the Gold and dangerous runner Bill Johnson to a measly 30 yards on the ground. Harris stood out on the other side with six catches for 91 yards and his team's lone score.

"We put it together in the second half," said Showboats coach Pepper Rodgers. "It was a game where we did a lot of things right."

Meanwhile on the left coast, the Oakland Invaders, sporting the league's best record at 13–4–1, hosted 10–8 Tampa Bay in front of 19,346 fans at the Oakland-Alameda Coliseum. Novo Bojovic began the scoring when he hit a 37-yard kick midway through the first period. The Bandits struggled until early in the second quarter when John Reaves led a drive that ended with his five-yard scoring toss to Spencer Jackson. The Tampa Bay defense held Bobby Hebert and company on their next series and forced a punt. Reaves made short work of the next drive, hitting Gary Anderson with a 73-yard touchdown pass. Hebert brought the Invaders back and connected with Derek Holloway on a 25-yard scoring pass to make it 14–10 at the half. Tampa Bay's Zenon Andrusyshyn missed a 28-yard field goal attempt in the second quarter that could have given them a seven-point bulge at the break.

Instead, Oakland jumped back into the lead on its first drive of the second half as Hebert connected with Anthony Carter on a 40-yard touchdown and Bojovic booted a 52-yard field goal to make it 20–14. Reaves made sure the Invaders' lead was short-lived by sneaking into the end zone from five yards out with 2:28 left in the third. Tom Newton struck back for Oakland with a one-yard jaunt across the goal line two minutes into the final period to make it 27–21 Invaders. Reaves again led the Bandits downfield, ending their next drive with a 15-yard toss over the goal line to Willie Gillespie. On the extra point, though, consecutive penalties pushed the ball back and Andrusyshyn missed the 35-yard effort, leaving the game knotted at 27–27 with 9:42 remaining. Oakland came right back, but Bojovic, making his first appearance in the playoffs since blowing a pair of short field goals in Michigan's triple-overtime loss to Los Angles exactly a year earlier, failed on a 31-yard attempt. Andrusyshyn was also struggling and he uncorked a short 34-yard punt late in the game to give the Invaders good field position. Hebert took his team deep into Tampa Bay territory in the waning moments, setting up Bojovic from 23 yards out. This time, he atoned for his past mistakes by knocking the ball through the uprights on the final play for a 30–27 victory for the Western Conference champs.

With the running game below par, Hebert completed 15 of 27 passes for 271 yards with two scores and a pair of interceptions. The defense picked off three passes, two of them by Oliver Davis. Anderson led the way for the Bandits, catching five passes for 111 yards and running 13 times for an additional 90 yards, while Reaves hit on 18 of 30 throws for 315 yards.

The last quarterfinal game between the 11–7 Generals and the 10–7–1 Stars at New Jersey had to wait until Monday night because Giants Stadium was being used over the weekend. The game, attended by 26,982, was not televised because ABC had committed to Monday Night Baseball and they would not allow ESPN to show it, fearing a smaller audience for their baseball game. New Jersey and Baltimore had split their two regular season meetings, both defensive struggles.

The hosts would again have to play without Doug Flutie who Walt Michaels continued to hold on the sideline while the quarterback's collarbone healed. The Generals team doctor had cleared the passer to play, but Michaels thought that Trump had pressured him to make a favorable diagnosis. The coach delivered Flutie's x-rays to a friend of his who was also a doctor. He confirmed Michaels' suspicions that Flutie's collarbone had not yet completely healed.

"I had Richard Todd with a broken collarbone when he was with the Jets," said Michaels in *Flutie*. "It took Richard six weeks before he could even practice, so we didn't play him until the seventh week and mostly in the eighth week. And Richard was a much bigger guy. I was definitely afraid. I didn't want anything like that possibly on my mind no matter what anyone said that Doug Flutie went into a game and I let him in there and I could have kept him out as the head coach. I didn't care who said anything because I had checked it with another doctor who had more experience with sports injuries and, in particular, collarbones.

"I'm sure Doug realizes it now, and I said, 'Doug, you'll thank me for this years from now. You may never play again if that thing were to shatter and break downward however it may happen.' I'd still do it again whether it would be Doug Flutie or Joe Blow. Whatever the reasoning was behind Donald Trump saying he was fine, well, Donald Trump was not an orthopedic doctor who should have recommended anything on that. And the strangest way it happened was that the team orthopedic said, 'Walt, I don't think there's any way he could be ready.' And he came to me two days later and said, 'Walt, I've reevaluated the X rays and I think you should play him.' That's when I went and checked again. Donald Trump didn't particularly like that I did that, and I'm not sure he really realized even today that I did that, but I would do it again."

With Flutie dressed for the game, the opening minutes provided a familiar sight. Baltimore's Garcia Lane caught New Jersey's first punt at his own nine and raced 91 yards for the first points of the night with 6:30 elapsed. Lane had burned the Generals in the 1984 playoffs as well with a 70-yard punt return touchdown. Playing with the lead, the Stars defense again held New Jersey and forced another punt. This time, Lane took it back 35 yards before punter Rick Partridge yanked him down. Chuck Fusina finished off that drive four plays later with a four-yard scamper into the end zone to make it 13–0 after David Trout missed the point after.

Ron Reeves brought the Generals back, completing five straight passes on their next possession to set up a one-yard touchdown dive for Herschel Walker with 2:26 remaining in the first half. The running back lay on the ground for several minutes after landing awkwardly on his head but was able to return to action. New Jersey had stopped Baltimore's next drive, but Frank Mattiace jumped offsides and the penalty gave the defending champions a first down. Fusina made them pay for the error with a 33-yard throw to David Riley that set up a five-yard scoring toss to Scott Fitzkee. They needed just two plays after the critical error to extend their lead after seemingly being stopped. Walker continued the string of New Jersey errors when he fumbled after the ensuing kickoff, but New Jersey finally caught a break when Trout's 42-yard field goal attempt went awry.

Trailing 20–7, the Generals defense helped them get back into the game in the second half. Kerry Justin picked off a Fusina aerial which set up a 40-yard kick by Roger Ruzek. Kyle Borland then intercepted the Baltimore passer again, setting up a 37-yard kick attempt by Ruzek. He missed it, but the Stars had jumped offsides, giving New Jersey a first down. Maurice Carthon then tore through the defense on a three-yard scoring burst to make it 20–17. Though the defense continued to hold Fusina and company, Reeves, Walker and the rest of the New Jersey offense struggled throughout. A fourth-down sack and an interception on their final two drives closed their small window of opportunity and ensured their second-straight loss to the Stars in the opening round of the postseason.

Key special teams plays and New Jersey mistakes made up for a lack of offensive production. The normally-efficient Fusina hit on ten of 20 throws for only 98 yards with three interceptions, two by Kerry Justin. The running game finished with 85 yards, just 54 by Bryant.

The defenses controlled the day on both sides of the ball. Walker ran 25 times for only 66 yards and fumbled twice. Reeves, who completed 16 of 32 passes for 172 yards, tossed a pair of interceptions, and the Stars partially blocked a first-quarter field goal attempt as they eliminated Trump's Generals for the second straight year.

"Donald is a dear friend, and I see him fairly often. He used to grab me and say, 'Carl, I have the highest payroll, and I think I've got the best players, yet you guys always find a way to beat us. How do you do that?'" laughed Stars GM Carl Peterson. "I said, 'Donald, it's a very simple answer. Football is a team sport; it's not an individual sport.' He's never let me forget that.

"It was always fun to beat Donald because he was such a high profile guy, and Donald was Donald. He bought the New Jersey Generals after the first year and did all those things with Herschel and Doug Flutie and so forth because he was promoting Donald Trump first and the USFL maybe second. He's an interesting guy; I've always enjoyed him. He's a master marketing guy; he's proven that maybe more than anyone else in this country. It was fun beating him and very satisfying."

"The only thing was they got all the attention," Mora said of the Generals. "They were the team that everybody thought was going to be the best team in the league, the New Jersey Generals, probably every year. They were right up the road from us, and it made those games a little more, I don't want to say important, but we knew we were playing a team from New York, the Generals with Herschel Walker and all the name players they had. It was probably a little more incentive for our players, but it wasn't because of Donald Trump. It wasn't for me."

The semifinal round began on Saturday, July 6, in Memphis where the streaking Showboats hosted the Invaders. Oakland, owner of the league's best regular season record at 13–4–1, had to make the trip because baseball's A's had the Oakland-Alameda Coliseum tied up over the weekend. It marked the second playoff contest that had to be moved or rescheduled due to a stadium conflict after the L.A.-Arizona tilt the year before. Fortunately, Memphis would almost certainly prove a more enthusiastic host for the game than the Bay Area. A rowdy gathering of 37,796 came out to the Liberty Bowl to watch their 'Boats fight for a title game berth.

The Invaders launched the first scoring drive late in the first quarter. Starting on their own nine, Bobby Hebert moved them the length of the field before John Williams took a pitchout and ran the final seven yards over the goal line on the first play of the second period. It took Memphis until midway through the stanza to light the scoreboard when Alan Duncan kicked a 34-yard field goal to make it 7–3. Late in the first half, they claimed the lead by driving 73 yards to score a touchdown. Anthony Parker's burst up the middle for the final 23 yards on a draw play made it 10–7 with 1:43 left in the half.

The Showboats continued to move the ball after the intermission, using their first drive of the third quarter to extend to a 13–7 advantage on Duncan's 47-yard boot. Hebert, who threw a pair of interceptions in the first half, brought Oakland right back in six plays that covered 66 yards. He hit Anthony Carter with a 16-yard toss to the Showboats eight, and the speedy receiver broke a pair of tackles and ran it in from there to give Oakland a 14–13 advantage. The Hebert to Carter connection clicked again later in the period when they combined on a 19-yard touchdown to cap an 11-play, 61-yard drive and make it 21–13 heading into the final quarter. Memphis, meanwhile, struggled offensively. After Carter grabbed a critical third-down pass to extend an Oakland drive, Hebert appeared to put the game out of reach with a one-yard sneak with 5:55 remaining. Trailing by 15, Mike Kelley finally got Memphis moving. They traveled 66 yards in four plays, the last 27 yards on Parker's second scoring run to make it 28–19 with 4:19 to go. They went for two, and Walter Lewis looked to hit Derrick Crawford for a two-point conversion. Unfortunately for Memphis, the officials called Greg Moser for an illegal pick, a penalty which wiped out the important conversion. Their on-side kick was recovered by the Invaders who shut them down for the rest of the game to take the 28–19 decision and advance to the title game.

Hebert's second-half resurgence lifted the Invaders to the team's first, and Hebert's second, appearance in the championship tilt. He completed 18 of 33 throws for 287 yards

despite his early struggles. Carter seemed to always be in the right place at the right time as the dangerous speedster collected nine receptions for 154 yards and two big second-half touchdowns. While much of the pregame attention focused on the Showboats pass rush headlined by Reggie White, it was Oakland that collected six sacks while holding Memphis to just one.

"We knew Hebert and Carter were two of the best and they proved it again," Reggie White told *The Sporting News*. "But as good as Hebert and Carter are, you've got to give credit to Oakland's offensive line. They kept us away from him most of the day."

On the losing side, Kelley hit on 13 of 25 throws for 202 yards with one interception. Moser topped the squad with five catches for 103 yards.

"I will say this about Oakland," said Memphis coach Pepper Rodgers in *TSN*. "They've got one of the most impressive passing games I've seen. Hebert is a tremendous passer and he did what he had to do in the clutch."

Elusive wide receiver Anthony Carter helped lift the Oakland Invaders to the 1985 USFL championship game. Carter spent two years with the Michigan Panthers before joining Oakland in the merger of the two teams. He later played 11 seasons in the NFL. Photograph by Jim Turner, from author's collection.

"This was a hostile atmosphere, going to the Liberty Bowl in Memphis and playing the Showboats," recalled Hebert. "It was packed. At the end, there were some crazy Memphis fans, and Coach

Sumner said, 'Keep your helmets on,' because they were throwing whiskey bottles at our bench. That was a hostile atmosphere. My dad, my grandpa and some others got in a motor home, and probably 15–20 people came from Louisiana to Memphis, Tennessee for that game. Both of their corner backs were high draft picks, great prospects for the NFL, and me and Anthony Carter hooked up and burned 'em pretty good. To me, that atmosphere was what I experienced later playing in the NFL; you really felt like you were in a hostile environment."

The next day the resurgent Stars battled the Stallions in Birmingham in a matchup of the league's two best defenses. As was typical of most of Baltimore's games, they had staged a pair of defensive struggles in losing to the Stallions by 7–3 and 14–7 scores in the regular season. Both franchises had battled adversity the entire season, Baltimore stumbled on the field early in the year and Birmingham played through its ownership problems. A crowd of 23,250 fans attended the Eastern Conference championship game at Legion Field on Sunday, July 7.

The Stallions received the ball first, something that turned out to be a big break for Baltimore when corner back Jonathan Sutton picked off Cliff Stoudt's first throw and returned it 36 yards for a touchdown just 1:46 into the game. The Stars defense held on Birmingham's next possession, and Chuck Fusina quickly led the defending champs downfield. He hit Victor Harrison from 30 yards out over the fallen David Evans minutes later to make it 14–0. Already, they had scored more points in six minutes than they had in the two previous games with Birmingham. And again, they had struck quickly as they had the week before against the Generals. While Stoudt's team failed to get anything going, the Stars also slowed down until midway through the second period when Fusina found Kelvin Bryant covered by a linebacker. That turned out to be a major error after the runner caught Fusina's throw and ran the rest of the way for a 70-yard score. The Stallions had their chances, but a missed field goal and two unsuccessful fourth-down attempts near the Baltimore goal line ended crucial drives. The Stars had turned in all the big plays in the first 30 minutes.

With a 21–0 advantage in the second half, Baltimore concentrated on its potent running attack. Neither team could score in the third quarter, but Bryant lit the scoreboard early in the fourth. He broke free for a 76-yard touchdown run and broke the Stallions backs in the process while making it 28–0. Stoudt hit Joey Jones with a 14-yard scoring pass and Cribbs ran in from the one with 55 seconds remaining to make the final 28–14 in favor of the Stars.

With the exception of his early costly interception, Stoudt moved Birmingham well, connecting on 29 of 50 throws for 327 yards. Jim Smith caught ten of those balls for 110 yards, and Jones made five grabs for 87 yards. Joe Cribbs, though, managed a paltry 13 yards and the team only totaled 46 on the ground.

"The early interception was a mistake on my part," Stoudt told *The Sporting News.* "He got a good jump on the ball, read the route and made a great defensive play. There were times today when I wish I could have crawled into a hole."

For the game, Bryant paved the way for the winners with 13 carries for 116 yards and four receptions for an additional 101 yards. Fusina completed ten of 16 passes for 210 yards, while the defense kept the Birmingham running game in check. The Stars relied chiefly on the four big plays to earn their third trip to the title game in as many years.

"I can't begin to give the full story of how this team has had to battle back," Jim Mora said in *TSN.* "There were many times when this team was counted out—including

Kelvin Bryant of the Philadelphia Stars secures the handoff from quarterback Chuck Fusina. Photograph by Jim Turner, from Richie Franklin's collection.

by me, too. Everybody knows about the move, our eviction from practice facilities in Philadelphia and playing three hours from where we practice.

"But there are a lot of things that happened that nobody realizes. I'm proud of all our teams for getting to the championship game, but I'm probably prouder of this one. It had to overcome a lot just to get into the playoffs."

Commissioner Harry Usher did not attend either semifinal game, opting instead for a family function in California. The move did not endear him to several owners who already questioned how committed he really was to the USFL.

Originally, the league picked the Pontiac Silverdome to host the third championship game, but after the Panthers moved they switched the location to Giants Stadium, home of the Generals, after some extensive lobbying by Donald Trump. The championship tilt would be the league's last game for 14 months, leading into the long offseason ahead. For the third consecutive year, rain was a large part of championship day and threatened to hurt attendance.

On July 14, 1985, the USFL staged its final summer football game. After a subpar 10–7–1 regular season, the resurgent Stars remained alive to defend their title, although they now called Baltimore home. On the other sideline, the revamped Oakland Invaders, featuring nine members who had played on the Michigan Panthers squad that had knocked off the Stars for the inaugural league championship, sported the league's best record at 13–4–1. Their previous meeting early in the season resulted in the only tie in USFL history.

Continuing their postseason habit of playing well early, Baltimore struck first on its opening drive when Chuck Fusina finished it off with a 16-yard scoring toss to Scott Fitz-kee. The two teams were fired up for the tilt and several early skirmishes resulted. With their offense struggling, Oakland's defense provided the big play later in the first quarter when safety David Greenwood intercepted Fusina's toss and raced 44 yards into the end zone to tie it at 7–7. But Baltimore's defense was not one to take a back seat to anybody. Their safety, Scott Woerner, intercepted Bobby Hebert on the Invaders' next possession, and that led to Kelvin Bryant's seven-yard jaunt across the goal line less than a minute into the second period. Periodic fighting had continued with the officials having little luck in stopping the fisticuffs. They called offsetting penalties twice in the span of a couple of minutes.

Oakland bounced right back from Bryant's score when John Williams ended their drive with a one-yard touchdown burst to tie it up again at 14–14 early in the second. Their effort was aided by a personal foul on the kickoff by Stars kicker David Trout of all people and a roughing the passer call on linebacker Mike Johnson. Later in the quarter, Oakland linebacker Gary Plummer drew a personal foul penalty to help even out the calls. The Baltimore offense continued to pound away, though, and they retook the lead on a 17-yard effort by Bryant with 1:41 remaining in the half. All things considered, Oakland had to be happy to still be in the game with only 19 yards of offense to their credit. The very physical first half ended with Baltimore dominating the statistics but ahead just 21–14 on the scoreboard.

The Invaders' offense emerged from the locker room ready to prove that its halting first half play was an aberration. They began with the ball at their own 16 and used big plays to work their way toward Baltimore's goal line. Hebert hit Anthony Carter for gains of 18 and 17 yards and scrambled for a 19-yard pickup as they moved to the Stars' two-yard line. They had to settle for a 19-yard Novo Bojovic field goal, though, as the Stars defense stood its ground. The Oakland defense also seemed to be inspired, bottling up the defending champions for most of the period. The Invaders then took their first lead in the closing seconds of the third on a seven-yard Hebert to Carter aerial. Baltimore left the third quarter behind with only eight yards of offense and trailing 24–21. The Stars franchise had played eight playoff games and failed to score in the third period of all eight.

With their backs against the wall once again, Baltimore responded the same way it had all season. They drove 49 yards in nine plays, the last seven on a run by Bryant to make it 28–24 with 8:15 to go. Shawn Faulkner mishandled Trout's kickoff, and Oakland found itself pinned at its own four, 96 yards away from the goal line.

"I turned to a guy on the sidelines" Stars coach Jim Mora recalled in *Sports Illustrated*, "and told him, 'If they can drive the length of the field on us and score, they deserve the game.'"

Hebert and Williams were up to the challenge. The quarterback hit Gordon Banks for nine yards and Williams ran twice for 23 yards to move the ball out to their 36. A pass to Albert Bentley netted six yards, and Williams continued his strong running with a 17-yard gain into Baltimore territory. A throw to Carter covered 28 yards and brought them to the Stars' 13. Williams lost two yards on a run, but Hebert made up the ground with a 10-yard toss to Derek Holloway, setting up a third-and-two situation from the five. On that play, Williams attempted to turn the right corner, but Sam Mills blasted him at the line of scrimmage. With a big fourth and two play apparently looming, the complexion of the drive and the game suddenly changed. Side judge Grover Klemmer called Oakland running back Tom Newton for a personal foul against Stars' corner back Jonathan Sutton in the corner of the end zone, well away from the play. Now needing 17 yards for a first down, Hebert uncorked a pair of incompletions and Baltimore held on for the narrow 28–24 win and their second consecutive championship.

"I was just too aggressive," admitted Newton in *Sports Illustrated*. "We were both kind of fighting back and forth in the end zone, but I got caught. Hey, he had me, too. I think the refs were looking for something…. I'm getting the first flight out of here. This'll haunt me for a long, long time."

The late foul overshadowed several fine performances for the Invaders. Williams ended the night with 96 yards on the ground with a score, and Carter led the way on the receiving end with five catches for 74 yards and a touchdown. Hebert completed 14 of 30 throws for 187 yards and a pair of interceptions.

"It's a shame the outcome of the game came down to a call that had nothing to do with the play," Oakland coach Charlie Sumner told *The Sporting News*. "I'm not taking anything away from Baltimore, but the game should have been decided by the players."

"The whole game there had been more confrontations than I like to see," said the Stars Jim Mora in *TSN*. "I just don't like that. I told my team to control it. We kept our cool a little better in the second half, and I guess it paid off."

On the winning side, Bryant deservedly earned Most Valuable Player honors. He ran for a game-high 103 yards on 23 carries with 31 of those yards coming on his three scoring runs. Fusina spread the ball around, hitting 15 of 26 throws for 155 yards with only the one mistake to Greenwood.

"We just hung on to win the championship," Fusina recalled. "They had an excellent team, again with Bobby at quarterback. It rained that day and it was kind of an ugly game. We played terrific, scoring early, and then there were a lot of ups and downs."

"It was the strangest thing that we lived and practiced in Philadelphia, and basically we had 18 away games," laughed Landeta. "Our home games were a three-hour drive. Some teams would fly and get home quicker than we did. It was amazing that we ended up winning the championship under those circumstances, where we lived and played in one city, and the only time we were in the town and where we played wasn't even the name of the town we played for. We played at College Park, right outside of Washington D.C. at the University of Maryland, which was 40 miles away from Baltimore. You know initially the thought was to play right in Baltimore, but we're the Baltimore Stars, living and practicing in Philly and playing outside of Washington."

"We came through a lot together," remembered Jim Mora in *Sports Illustrated*. "I guess the low point came when they threw us out of our offices in Veterans Stadium in June. There was a problem with the contract between the club and the city, and one Tuesday they told us to prepare to be evicted. We were trying to get ready for our second Birmingham game. We were drawing plays on the way because the chalkboard was in the moving truck. The coaches were sitting on the floor because all our furniture was gone. Yeah, we lost that Birmingham game, but then we won five straight."

The triumvirate of Mora, GM Carl Peterson and owner Myles Tanenbaum had provided stability to a team in the midst of the USFL's chaos. One of just two USFL owner-GM-coach trios to last all three years in the spring, they had shown a knack for not only finding and developing talent, but getting it to work together as a team.

"Myles was a great owner because he loved football. He had a real interest in the team," Mora recalled. "He didn't get involved in the coaching aspect of it or the personnel aspect of it, from my standpoint. Basically, he let Carl do his deal and let me do my deal. He was very supportive, win or lose. He was an outstanding owner. Some of those teams didn't necessarily do things in a first class way, but our team always did. There was never a time where we were unable to do what we wanted to do or have the facilities we wanted. You never felt as though you were with a second class organization when you were with the Stars, whether we were in Philadelphia or Baltimore, and I think that was a lot because our owner Myles believed in doing things first class, getting the right good players and paying them what we needed to pay them.

"Of course, a lot of that has to do with Carl, too. Carl's outstanding. I've known Carl since 1974. We're good friends. The thing about Carl is that he was always going to give you every opportunity to be successful if you were his coach. He'd get you the players, the facilities, the coaching staff, all those kinds of things. 'Whatever you need, we're going to get it for you, Jim. Now go win.'"

Peterson credited Mora's leadership for the turnaround: "I'll never forget that Jim got the team together and said, 'Okay, we need to talk about this. It's time for us to stop feeling sorry for ourselves. Yes, we do have to commute every home game to Baltimore and play there, but I know who's on this football team and the character of it and the talent on it. We can, and we should, and we will win the championship. And we won out. We won our last three of four games and then swept the playoffs. We were not the number one seeded team, but it was a great job by Jim, our coaching staff and the players. They stopped feeling sorry for themselves and played football and enjoyed it."

"After our first title in Philadelphia, they gave us a fabulous parade, 250,000 people," remembered Landeta. "It was magnificent. I remember after that third championship game thinking, 'Wow, probably not going to play with these guys again, what a great league,' and everything good. Everything was up in the air."

"We had a party at the team hotel, but it certainly wasn't the joyous atmosphere of the party we had in 1984 because there were some real question marks about the league at that time," added Dunek.

7

A Long Wait for the Fall

The USFL completed its final spring football season on July 14, 1985, and began preparations for its first fall campaign 14 months later. While it had played perhaps its best football in year three, the USFL spent much of the season fighting fires after several well-publicized fiascos that dogged several of its teams. The final spring campaign further eroded television ratings, and discussions of the USFL's present were drowned out by doubts over its future.

The problems overshadowed the progress the league had made in some markets. Jacksonville continued to be a bright spot with some eye-popping crowds, and surprisingly, Orlando joined them. The Renegades still lost, although not with the regularity of its predecessor, the Washington Federals, but the team had developed a nice following in the central Florida tourist mecca. Memphis continued to receive great community support, and Trump and his millions could hold out forever in New Jersey. As usual, Arizona was unsettled, but the Tathams infused more money and remained committed to the Outlaws. In Birmingham, the fans as well as the city government showed their loyalty to the Stallions, while Tampa Bay rivaled the NFL's Buccaneers in popularity, though both faced unresolved ownership questions.

The play around the league had greatly improved over three seasons. The consolidations and mergers had an upside, concentrating talent on fewer teams, leading to better overall football. The maturation of many of the USFL's younger players further helped the quality of play. There was no question that on the field the USFL was more entertaining in year three than it was in year one.

The league named Herschel Walker its Most Valuable Player after his record-breaking season, while Reggie White took Man of the Year honors and Birmingham's Rollie Dotsch captured Coach of the Year accolades.

Jim Kelly earned first team honors at quarterback with Walker and Tampa Bay's Gary Anderson sharing space in the top backfield. Birmingham's Jim Smith and Richard Johnson were named the circuit's top receivers, and the Bandits Marvin Harvey captured honors at tight end. New Jersey center Kent Hull, tackles Irv Eatman of Baltimore and Ray Pinney of Oakland joined Birmingham guards Buddy Aydelette and Pat Saindon on the all-league offensive line.

On defense, ends James Lockette of New Jersey and Bruce Thornton of Denver joined tackles Memphis' White and Dave Tipton of Arizona on the line. Baltimore's Sam Mills, Houston's Kiki DeAyala and Oakland's Angelo Snipes made up the linebacker corps, while Generals corner back Kerry Justin joined Arizona's David Martin. Birmingham's Chuck Clanton and Baltimore's Mike Lush earned honors at safety.

"Later I got a chance to go play in the NFL," said Gunslingers quarterback Rick

Neuheisel. "The USFL was not quite the NFL in terms of the numbers and the depth and so forth, but the quality of play was pretty darn good. There were a number of great players that went from the USFL back to the NFL or joined the NFL and became very, very good players at the professional level regardless of which league they were in. Across the board as I said the depth not being quite the same, but certainly enough guys out there to make for great football on Saturdays and Sundays."

"It was very comparable, very parallel to the NFL experience as far as pure talent," Flutie said. "The one difference is depth. When you had injuries, when receivers went down, the back-ups weren't quite that caliber and that was the difference. I know that defensively we had our linebacker corps and all our secondary went in the NFL right away."

"The main difference between the USFL and the NFL, and I know ourselves even versus the Detroit Lions being in the Michigan area, was the depth," agreed Bobby Hebert. "Once you had somebody hurt on the first string, it was a big drop off who you're actually putting in the game when you're having to deal with injuries."

"You had a handful of stars in the USFL on each team that could play in the NFL as well, but the depth, you didn't have that," recalled Craig James. "It was hit and miss. That doesn't mean that the other 11 couldn't play, but you had those two or three mixed in to support the eight that weren't great but they were okay, but in the NFL all 11 are good."

"This is the way I would characterize it," said Memphis and former Denver running back Harry Sydney. "The first year of the league, of the 11 starters on offense, I'd say five or six were pretty good and the others were filling up space. Now you go to the second year, I think it was more like eight and three. And the last year when I was in Memphis, you had 11 starters who could play in the NFL."

1985 Fallout

A report in *The Sporting News* stated Houston, Portland, San Antonio and Tampa Bay had not met their final payrolls. The Gamblers faced debts of just over $1 million and the Bandits $300,000, which the league assessed the other members to cover. Portland owed the league more than $500,000 by season's end, while the USFL needed half a million dollars to keep the Los Angeles Express operational.

The ownerless Express had been a weight around the league's neck all season. Old-enburg's collapse and the league's limited ability to properly fund the star-studded team left it the butt of jokes in the country's second largest market. The Express had little trouble providing ammunition to its detractors. Finishing with a USFL-worst 3–15 record, being forced to play its final home game at a local college after drawing minuscule crowds at the Los Angeles Coliseum, using ballyhooed quarterback Steve Young at running back for part of a game, firing its cheerleaders during the season, not to mention staggering financial losses borne by the rest of the league, left USFL owners eager to leave L.A. far behind. It was a testament to their will and pocketbooks that the team had made it through the season, but it certainly would not see another under league ownership.

"I grew up in LA, and my dad was a founding season ticket holder of the LA Rams when they came from Cleveland," said Stars GM Carl Peterson. "There are a lot of things to do in LA. It is a fair weather city and every weekend there are lots of other alternatives.

Perhaps that wasn't the right place for us to place a USFL team, but we needed some major cities, obviously for the television and the markets."

An excellent team likewise failed to bring out the fans to the North in Oakland. The merger with the Michigan Panthers had brought the Invaders to within a penalty of capturing the USFL title, but Bay Area fans turned their backs on the team, cutting attendance drastically from the team's inaugural year.

Financial problems in Houston and Birmingham plagued two of the circuit's better squads, while Portland and San Antonio stumbled on the field and still owed their players money for part of the season. A near player revolt and coaching resignation in San Antonio highlighted the problems some teams had just paying the bills.

As if that wasn't enough, Tampa Bay, once the gem of the USFL, was reeling after John Bassett announced his fight against cancer. His determination to keep the Bandits playing in the spring hadn't been enough to rally the rest of the league around his cause, and Tampa Bay was going to have to withdraw from the USFL if it intended to play again in the spring. It soon became clear that was a war Bassett no longer had the strength or time to fight.

"John had another plan that if this thing wasn't going to work, he had a concept for another league," said Jim McVay. "That's true. I don't know what he was going to call it, but we talked about it several times. I think he was creating an alternative, something he believed in. I don't think John was playing a leverage game. He believed in the concept, and it was a comparable concept that could work. Let's do it this way, but with some restrictions taking into account some of the lessons we've learned. It was going to be league controlled with regards to how payroll was going to be handled. I think that maybe it was going to be a landing spot for people who believed in his concept."

"He expressed his anger about what was going on in the league," added Bandits player Fred Nordgren. "He was considering starting a new league with some people in the entertainment business, and they were talking about starting out as a worldwide league. He was talking about having teams in Europe, Asia and Australia. It was a pretty neat idea, and it was all going to be financed by actors and investors. He was pretty serious about it. I think he probably would have done that if he would have stayed healthy."

"At that time we were getting checks that were slow coming, maybe a week late sometimes," recalled Bandits offensive lineman Chuck Pitcock. "We'd run to the bank sometimes as everyone makes jokes of it, but it was a race to the bank to make sure that we could cash our checks. It was true, you know, and those things happened."

Even support in Denver, once a league stronghold, had collapsed. In spite of fielding easily it's most competitive and entertaining team in three years, average attendance had tumbled from over 41,000 in 1983 to just over 14,000 per game after the move to the fall had been announced. Fans in the Mile High City clearly had no intention of supporting a squad that would compete directly with their beloved Broncos.

The Philadelphia Stars had anticipated similar problems and vacated the Pennsylvania city before the season. With Baltimore's Memorial Stadium undergoing renovations, Myles Tanenbaum's team had to set up shop a half-hour away at the University of Maryland in College Park. The remote location killed attendance but the club was still kicking.

When David Dixon formed the USFL, each owner had to submit a $1.5 million letter of credit to guarantee the operation of his franchise. Each expansion owner also put up a letter of credit. That money had been the financial backbone of the USFL and had helped insure it against the rapid failure experienced by the World Football League. It had proven its worth when the league used Chicago's to help the Chicago Blitz make it through the 1984 season without an owner. Owners had also voted for special assessments to support faltering franchises such as the Los Angeles Express, Portland Breakers and Houston Gamblers.

"We took a whole bunch of them," McSherry said of the letters of credit. "I remember we took Houston's; took Canizaro's; we couldn't use Marvin Warner's because it was from a bad bank. Houston only had two-thirds of it because Roulier had withdrawn his share."

Television ratings tumbled from a 5.5 in 1984 to a 4.1 on ABC and from a 2.9 to a 2.0 on ESPN. Playoff ratings for the first round fell to a 2.9 on Saturday and a 3.1 on Sunday. The championship drew a 7.6, down from 9.7 the year before and 11.9 in 1983. The league had vacated several large markets including Chicago, Philadelphia and Detroit prior to the season, and its presence in Los Angeles may have hurt ratings more than it helped. More than twice as many ABC affiliates as the year before opted for local programming over USFL coverage, further eroding the league's national presence and ratings potential. ABC again made it clear they had no interest in the USFL as a fall property, and CBS and NBC echoed the sentiment.

"We thought going to the fall with the USFL didn't make any sense primarily from a sales standpoint, and we also had some ratings concerns going against the NFL on CBS and NBC on Sunday afternoons," said Spence. "Our USFL decision was primarily driven by our sales concerns especially since our ratings went down in '84 and '85."

Many teams found themselves on shaky ground, and still more observers expected fewer teams in 1986 if the USFL was able make it to its first fall outing.

"It distresses me to read about owners who can't financially keep up anymore," former Michigan Panthers co-owner Judge Peter Spivak told the Associated Press. "This out-of-hand escalation of costs was never part of the plan. The plan was no bidding wars. The plan was good, exciting football on a manageable budget."

"An offensive tackle, obviously not considered one of the skill positions that were very visible, but offensive tackles that in the first season might have been making $30,000 a year, were now pulling down compensation levels of $150,000 to $200,000," explained Oakland's Taube. "We were comparable to the NFL. I think in the third season the payroll for the Oakland Invaders was approaching something like $7 million, and that compared to a player payroll for the San Francisco 49ers of around $8 million. The big difference was we were still struggling with our share of the TV contract. It was maybe a million dollars at that point. And the various franchises in the NFL were enjoying TV revenues of $15 to $20 million dollars. So we just didn't have it at the gate, or in television receipts, or radio receipts to finance the kind of expenditures we were making for football operations."

"We could have and should have been telling some guys it's time to get out if you can't put in another x million apiece, this is what we're going to have to do," said Camera. "And Harry tried to do that. He realized it, too.

"We'll reduce our numbers or do what we have to do. And Harry started to do that, move us down in size. We started to strengthen the ownership, but a lot of these guys gave you nothing but lip service."

Usher's efforts to winnow the ownership group further exacerbated the tensions between him and the owners, several of whom were not only paying their own bills but those for faltering teams as well. "There was high tension at that period of time," recalled Ehrhart.

"Trump used me to get information on what was going on," McSherry recalled. "It got to the point where Donald used to come to my house. He had a house in Greenwich in addition to living in Trump Tower. He would have his driver take him up to his golf course in Greenwich, and he'd play a round of golf in the morning. Then his driver would take him to my house where we'd give him something that looked a little bit like lunch. If it was in the season, we'd watch a game on TV; if it wasn't the season we'd just talk. It was because he needed me to give him information about what was really going on because none of the other owners would talk to him. It was kind of a tough position because I was always giving him bad news."

More Questions

Instability ruled the day, and commissioner Harry Usher could not avoid the plague. Many owners were livid when they discovered Usher was spending much of his time in California instead of the league office in New York. They forced him to move, but he had skipped both conference championship games. Just days after the title game, rumors swirled that he would be replaced by former Major Indoor Soccer League commissioner Earl Foreman. Once again, the rumors had emanated from New York and a disgruntled Donald Trump.

"Let's say the jury is still out on Harry," Trump threatened in *USA Today*. "It's a simple thing to pull this off in court and make us a winner. I really feel strongly about that. And if he doesn't pull it off, somebody else will."

Several franchises faced a tough time fighting off bill collectors and needed immediate help. Stephen Ross, a real estate magnate, appeared ready to buy the Houston Gamblers after New Yorker Larry Fisher dropped out of the bidding. Fisher had planned to buy the Gamblers and move them to Shea Stadium in New York City before that deal fell apart. The league announced the Ross agreement in August, and he went so far as to pay the players their final checks to keep them all from becoming free agents, much as Jay Roulier had done with the Los Angeles Express a year earlier. Losing Jim Kelly alone would have been a terrible blow. Shortly thereafter, the new Gamblers owner announced that he was merging his franchise with the New Jersey Generals and would become an equal partner in the team with Donald Trump. The merger set up the Generals as possibly the best team in the USFL and potentially one of the most talented in all of pro football. The "Dream Team" as Trump dubbed it would feature Jim Kelly at quarterback, the Mouseketeers catching his passes and Herschel Walker in the backfield. New Jersey would be tough to stop. Presumably, this left Doug Flutie warming the bench. Not even Trump needed two multi-million dollar quarterbacks, though, leading to speculation that Flutie would be traded.

"We think Jim Kelly is the best quarterback in pro football," Trump told *Sports Illustrated*. "He's the quarterback and right now Doug is on the team. I've talked to Herschel about the merger and he's thrilled. I've also talked to Doug. Let's just say that Herschel's more thrilled than Doug. We're going to be very loyal to Doug and Doug's going to be loyal to us."

"I figure it'll be like my rookie year," said Flutie to *The Sporting News*. "Like Brian

Sipe, I'll be traded within the USFL. But I can't plan. I don't know what the heck is going on. I'm skeptical because there's a lot of uncertainty."

"I remember very vividly, after the New Jersey Generals and the Houston Gamblers merged I had two great quarterbacks," stated former Gamblers owner Argovitz, who joined the Generals as team president. "I had Jim Kelly from the Gamblers and Doug Flutie from the Generals. After about three weeks of working out, Doug Flutie comes to my office one day. Doug says, 'I need to talk to ya.' And I said, 'Let's talk, Doug.' He said, 'I have some real concerns. I know Jim is your guy for the Gamblers. I just wanna know if I have a chance at being the star for this football team.' I said, 'Doug, both of you guys are my players now. You have the chance to be the number one quarterback just like Jim has the chance to be the number one guy, but whoever is the second team quarterback, will be the highest paid quarterback in all of football.'"

Five months later, however, the merger hadn't been completed. Houston's staff and coaches had not been paid since June, something that head coach Jack Pardee had experienced in his days with the WFL's Florida Blazers. It took until January for the employees to win a $500,000 out of court settlement for their back wages. Upon looking over the Gamblers books, Ross had run into larger debts than he was prepared to handle and called off the consolidation. Finally, Trump reimbursed Ross for his interest in the Gamblers and became the sole owner of the merged team.

"When they merged with the Gamblers, it had all the makings of being one of the best teams in the USFL and if it goes the way of the ABA-NBA, they're going to pick off the three best teams, and we'd be maybe the best team," said MacConnell. "With Kelly and the wideouts he had with Houston, and with Herschel and Maurice Carthon, they could have scored 70 points."

"Herschel Walker was going to be my running back," recalled Kelly. "Kent Hull was going to be my center. I remember the talk about it being the dream team of football, having the greatest running back that there was playing in an offense that loved to throw the football but also had 1,000-yard rushers from Houston. I was looking forward to it, having Donald Trump as your owner. Everything you would want in a team, we had it all right there."

Ross, meanwhile, took his money to Baltimore and purchased a controlling interest in the Stars from Trump nemesis Myles Tanenbaum. He left no doubt about why he was so interested in what appeared to be a very shaky investment. He openly stated that his motivation for purchasing the franchise was that he considered it prime NFL expansion territory. Meanwhile, Tanenbaum became the last of the original owners to give up majority ownership of his team.

"Once we moved out of Philadelphia, as much as I became fond of Don Schaefer, the mayor of Baltimore at the time, it wasn't the same," said Tanenbaum. "For instance, I couldn't pick up the paper and read about what was happening, so I would get the Baltimore papers sent up to me. I'd read it, and it would be a couple of days old. The Baltimore papers also weren't following the team the way the Philadelphia papers had, and it just wasn't the same. While I could go down and see the team practice, each game for me was an away game. Fortunately, it was only 100 miles away, but it was still an away game. It really lacked the kind of enjoyment I was getting out of the team being in Philadelphia, plus we were still running in the deep red.

"My two funding partners and I were footing a very substantial bill. The two of them had come to me during the early part of the 1985 season, saying that they really

With the USFL v. NFL trial taking place in New York, New Jersey Generals owner Donald Trump showcased new acquisition Jim Kelly to the media, including *Sports Illustrated* which used him on that week's cover. Photograph by Jim Turner, from Richie Franklin's collection.

wanted out. They wanted to close down the team. I said, 'I'm not closing down the team. If you want out, I'll pick up your shares, but I can't possibly terminate this franchise. It would be the wrong thing to do for the coaches, players and other people who believed we were going to honor our commitments.' With that they decided that if I was staying in, they were staying in. I also told them that I thought they would lose more money if we closed it down than if we continued, and subsequently that proved to be the case."

Not all situations worked out so well. San Antonio failed to pay its players and wound up waiving its entire roster. Not surprisingly, none of the members of the 5–13 club were immediately picked up by other teams. The Breakers also found themselves without anyone to put on the field when it failed to meet its final payroll even after the league gave them a one-day extension to do so.

"None of us got our full salaries," Coury said. "We had signed agreements, and I don't think anyone came away with nothing, but as far as the percentage of the contract, I don't know how that worked out legality-wise with the team folding. I know I had to fight to get our coaches some money before the team folded. I can't remember the percentage, but it wasn't everybody being paid what their contracts called for."

With Bassett fading out of the picture due to his rapidly deteriorating health, new investors in Tampa Bay provided $300,000 just minutes before a deadline so they could make their final payments to players. Lee Scarfone, a real estate magnate, assumed control of the franchise.

On November 1, the league announced that nine teams would compete during the first fall season, down five franchises from the 1985 lineup. Still kicking were the Arizona Outlaws, Baltimore Stars, Birmingham Stallions, Jacksonville Bulls, Memphis Showboats, New Jersey Generals, Orlando Renegades, Tampa Bay Bandits and Denver Gold. Denver owner Doug Spedding announced that his franchise would move to Portland and take the place of the recently departed Breakers. The Gold eventually gave up the idea and merged with the Bulls on February 19, 1986, to complete the 1986 version of the USFL at eight teams. Gone were the Houston Gamblers, Los Angeles Express, Oakland Invaders, San Antonio Gunslingers and the Breakers, the entire Western Conference with the exception of Arizona. Once again, Eddie Einhorn chose not to field his Chicago entry and said that he would instead concentrate his energies on securing a league television contract.

The USFL tried its best to put a positive spin on the situation, refusing to say that most of the franchises were folding. Technically, the USFL counted eight active members as being able to field teams in 1986 and five inactive teams in Chicago, Los Angeles, Oakland, Portland and San Antonio. Inactive teams could not or would not field a squad for the coming year but hoped to take part in the 1987 season.

Consolidation or Implosion?

Even on the solvent franchises, players began to feel insecure about the league and its future. In preparation for the long off-season before the first fall campaign, most teams trimmed their rosters to 35 players, although Denver, Los Angeles and Oakland kept just 15 because they were thought to be close to merger agreements. All told, USFL teams kept 330 players while releasing 243 others. Some of the protected players such as Steve Young, Joe Cribbs and Reggie White remained on rosters for a time until their teams secured buyouts of their contracts from NFL clubs. The USFL managed to sell off several players to NFL teams to bring in much-needed cash. With a long off-season ahead, the league had to utilize any source of revenue it could find. All protected players remaining on USFL rosters would receive $10,000 per month from March to July to help secure their services for the later 1986 start. It was a unique move as typically contracts called for players to be paid their entire salaries during the regular season, the same as in the NFL.

"In the negotiated deal with the players' association when we went into hiatus all of us paid 30 percent of the salaries to ten designated players," recalled Ehrhart. "For the fall season in '86, each team had already pre-paid 30 percent of the salaries for ten players, so there certainly was good will and good faith that we were going to play in the fall of '86. We had full staffs on duty, and we pre-paid these players."

Nevertheless, the player exodus that had begun in earnest the previous season reached a fever pitch immediately after the 1985 campaign came to its conclusion. Herschel Walker's talented blocking back Maurice Carthon stayed in the Meadowlands but switched his allegiances to the NFL's New York Giants, and Stars punter Sean Landeta skipped Baltimore to join Carthon with the Giants. Mike Rozier became the first of the Heisman winners to leave the USFL when he inked a long-rumored deal with the Houston Oilers. Keith Millard bolted Jacksonville for the Minnesota Vikings, while Bobby Hebert went from Oakland to the New Orleans Saints. His favorite target, Anthony Carter, joined the Minnesota Vikings, and Reggie White bid adieu to the Showboats for the Philadelphia Eagles.

"My contract was up, and I took the approach, selfishly, that whether the USFL was there or not, I was going to use the USFL as leverage to go to the NFL," admitted Hebert. "I knew where I was at in my career that I had options. During the season Coach Sumner and Vince Lombardi, Jr., who was our GM, tried to get me to sign a long-term deal with the Invaders, and I wouldn't do it. There was a rumor that the USFL was not going to be around."

"At that time, most of the USFL didn't know what was going to happen," recalled Sydney. "There were a lot of guys who had played in the NFL, hoping that if the USFL folded they were going to get back to the NFL. By the third year, you were positioning yourself to hopefully get back to the NFL or just have expansion in the league itself."

Those who left to join NFL teams for the 1985 season would play football for more than ten straight months. "When these guys talk about walking into an NFL training camp after going through an 18 game season here, actually 21 games for us, I don't think they realize what they're getting into" Philadelphia's Pete Kugler told *Sports Illustrated.* He had jumped from the 49ers to the Stars in 1984 without a break. "A defensive lineman who does it would be looking for real trouble.

"Noseguards aren't built for 40 game seasons. It killed me for two years, '84 and '85, not just one. My body still hasn't caught up. I started getting injured, the kind of injuries I never got before. I missed one week with a groin pull, another with a hamstring pull. I never got those before. I got a kidney injury, and I was passing blood for a week. I tore a ligament in my knee and missed six weeks. Right now I'm a wreck."

With the short career span of a football player, not many were going to let such considerations stand in their way. Plus, the USFL started encouraging some of the defections. "The current position is that, if they want to go, we won't hold them," admitted one league official to *Sports Illustrated.* "We'll save the money on their contracts and use it to invest in future draft choices. With some players, though, the price will be higher. If Steve Young wants to get out of the last two years of his contract, for instance, it'll cost him $2 million." Young eventually escaped from the crumbling Express for a $1.1 million buyout. He signed a six-year, $5.5 million pact with the Tampa Bay Buccaneers.

Season-long holdout Trumaine Johnson finally received his wish and left the Arizona Outlaws for the San Diego Chargers. The Chargers later also lured Tim Spencer away from Memphis, and San Diego continued its haul of USFL talent by inking Tampa Bay's Gary Anderson. New Chargers owner Alex Spanos, once a minority investor who had purchased a controlling interest from Gene Klein, paid a total of $1,000,000 to buy out the contracts of Johnson and Anderson much to the delight of USFL front offices. Spanos had originally been interested in a USFL franchise in 1982 but pulled out prior to the league's first press conference when he bought a piece of the Chargers.

"If there ever is a USFL Hall of Fame, Alex Spanos should be in it," Outlaws assistant general manager Bruce Kebric told *The Sporting News.* "Tampa Bay would have folded without him, and we wouldn't have been able to pay all our bills. Spanos has done as much as anyone in the United States to keep the USFL going."

After granting most of the Express players their release, Usher and the owners simply allowed Los Angeles to evaporate. A few players, among them Steve Young, bought out their contracts, giving the league a much-needed infusion of capital. The team had been an incredible drain on league finances for more than a year, and not too many people in the USFL hierarchy shed any tears when the team folded.

On Saturday, April 5, the Portland Breakers auctioned off their football equipment and office furniture to pay back taxes of nearly $47,000, most of it owed to the state of Oregon. Items sold at the auction included jerseys, helmets, posters, programs, media guides, weight machines, whirlpools and a pair of goal posts. The auction brought in $54,627, leaving little for the unpaid Breakers players.

San Antonio and Oakland had both failed to make the $500,000 payment the league required by the first of November to maintain active membership, but both claimed they would be back. Very few believed the Gunslingers would ever play another game. Clinton Manges still had not paid his players or staff for the final four weeks of the 1985 season.

The players at least ate a few dollars' worth of food at a postseason barbecue hosted by the owner at his mansion. The team office was later emptied by court order to pay off some of the organization's debts. Items taken included jerseys, helmets, two buses and a pickup truck. The Bexar County sheriff's office assumed ownership of the team on March 26, 1986, and ordered all the franchise's assets be sold at auction to pay off the $664,000 still owed to the players. A large portrait of Manges was one of the few items not taken for sale.

"No one got paid there at the end," furthered McGrath. "The sheriff came to Alamo Stadium and said, 'We're going to haul everything away.' I started grabbing the photos to make sure they didn't get taken."

"He has a sixth-grade education," Gunslingers assistant coach Tim Marcum said of Manges. "It is amazing what this guy has done. He came up through the politics of Texas. To say it was shady was an understatement. Illinois and Louisiana had nothing on Texas in those days. He came through Duvall County, which was run by a guy named George Parr. He ran it out of his back pocket. That's where Lyndon Johnson, 'Landslide Lyndon,' had all those dead voters vote for him in the 1948 senatorial race. So here comes Clinton Manges who has a 150,000-acre ranch. The details on how he got it are suspect, but he had it and got it refinanced for $40 million by Seattle SeaFirst. He and the state of Texas sued Mobil Oil because they had not drilled at the times they were supposed to in their lease. Manges went back and found this out and sued Mobil Oil for $150 million. Mobil Oil backed off and gave him some wells. Oil was at $40 a barrel, then went down to $16, and that's when all hell broke loose. He owed Seattle SeaFirst, he owed the Gunslingers; he owed everyone. It was a mess."

Meanwhile, the withdrawal of Alfred Taubman finished off the Oakland Invaders. He had lost an estimated $30 million over three seasons and had seen his Panthers fold despite bringing his beloved Detroit a championship. His money had kept the Invaders afloat in 1985, but his heart remained in Michigan. His net worth stood in excess of $600 million at the time, but he had no intention of wasting any more of it 2,000 miles from home. Tad Taube stepped back to the helm and had gone to the meetings in Memphis reportedly armed with a $500,000 check but claimed that he had differences with the rest of the owners concerning the lawsuit. The Oakland Invaders had played their last game.

The franchise mergers and failures resulted in either unemployment or relocation for several coaches. Trump, never thrilled with the Generals' conservative philosophy, now had Jim Kelly at his disposal, so he brought in Kelly's coach from Houston, Jack Pardee, to replace Walt Michaels. The former New Jersey coach became the defensive coordinator of the Memphis Showboats. With the Gold throwing its lot in with Jacksonville, Fred Bullard similarly brought in Mouse Davis and released Lindy Infante, who became the offensive coordinator for the Cleveland Browns. Dick Coury, late of the Breakers, became the quarterback coach of the Los Angeles Rams.

The league office also got smaller as McSherry left to return to practicing law full-time.

"I quit in the summer of '85," he said. "I got through the season; the season was over, and I went to see Usher and said, 'Look, we're not going to play in the fall. The league is going to go dark for basically a year and half. You don't really need me, and you don't need my expense. Let me go back to practicing law. You can call me if you need me.' So I left. I went to a couple more owners' meetings at the invitation of specific owners, but I wasn't in the loop. Usher and his wife ran whatever was to be run, mostly the lawsuit.

"The third season of the USFL, I really didn't want to go to the office every day because I knew something bad was going to happen. I was a prisoner. When Usher finally decided to come east and he got an apartment in Manhattan, my life was over. He was a miserable guy to work for. His wife was a miserable person, and she thought that she was actually going to function as the general counsel of this football league, so she was out there doing things, almost all of which had to be undone. And she was a snoop. She'd open the drawers of my secretary's desk. God knows what she was looking for. How can you work with somebody like that?"

Merger Talk

Spring football became a memory after the 1985 championship game. Several owners looked to a merger with the National Football League as their best hope. Knowing that not every USFL team could join the NFL, they dreamed of a deal much like the one the American Basketball Association negotiated in 1976 when four of its teams joined the National Basketball Association. The quartet paid a reduced but substantial fee to join the older league and then paid off the remaining ABA teams which were not admitted to the NBA.

Professional hockey had also utilized a partial merger in the recent past. In 1979, the established National Hockey League accepted four franchises from the World Hockey Association, a competing league which began play in 1971. The WHA's remaining two teams each received a payment to agree to the deal.

In addition to completing a merger with the American Football League in 1970, the NFL had previously used a partial merger to dispatch with competition. In 1949, the league admitted three members of the four-year-old All-America Football Conference and made accommodations with two other AAFC team owners to end that league's existence.

"There is a fund that's set up that if there is a merger with the NFL, that the USFL teams that don't merge will get an automatic $14 million," Orlando Renegades limited partner Charles Givens told National Public Radio. He realized that Orlando would not be an NFL expansion candidate. "Well, if you have got $5 million to $8 million invested, you have just doubled your money, walked away with a big profit anyway. So that's just one of those no-lose situations. Wherever you are, you are going to win."

"The NBA-ABA merger was precipitated by two lawsuits: by the Oscar Robertson case where the players of the NBA sued the NBA and the ABA, and a separate lawsuit that the ABA brought against the NBA," explained McSherry, who represented the ABA's Indiana Pacers in merger negotiations. "I think if you look at the history of the NFL, they took in those teams from the All-American Conference back in the late '40s, and they added the Dallas team to keep the AFL from being able to move forward in Dallas. Everyone assumed that at some point the NFL would want to stop player salaries from going up and their lawsuit expenses from going up, and buy real peace by making peace with the USFL. That's what they thought. They were wrong, but that's what they thought."

"They must have a game plan, but I can't figure it out," Spivak said of USFL owners in an AP interview. "If the plan isn't for a merger, I don't know what it is."

At an NFL owners' meeting on December 10, the older league tried to quell rumors that it would merge with the USFL. At attorney Paul Tagliabue's urging, they passed a tersely-worded resolution that stated, "The NFL member clubs have no interest in merger with the United States Football League or settlement of the United States Football League's suit against the National Football League." Al Davis, who was pushing for a merger to avoid large losses in the courts, was not a part of the announcement since he had been excluded as a defendant in the suit.

Commissioner Harry Usher remained unfazed by the pronouncement. "We won't comment on the motivation and timing for this resolution passed by the NFL owners," he told the Associated Press. "Actually, I am somewhat amused by it. Remember, these are the same owners who agreed unanimously to litigate against Al Davis and lost multi-millions of dollars for antitrust violations."

Rumors next came to light that USFL attorney Harvey Myerson proposed that New Jersey, Memphis, Baltimore and one other team be allowed to merge into the NFL in exchange for the league dropping its court action. Tampa Bay Buccaneers owner Hugh Culverhouse, smarting from being outdrawn in his own market by a USFL team, stood vehemently against any merger. Tagliabue echoed Culverhouse's sentiments. Acting as an intermediary, Al Davis presented the plan to Art Modell, owner of the Cleveland Browns. A group of NFL bigwigs that included Rozelle, New York Giants owner Wellington Mara and the league's antitrust lawyers rejected Myerson's deal out of hand. With Rozelle branding the suit, "blackmail litigation," in *Sports Illustrated*, Modell stated "We're going to court with these people and there will not be any settlement."

The NFL's determination in the matter shook the faith of some USFL executives in the plan to force their way into the older league. Support for the move had never been universal despite any announcement that the league had made. Nevertheless, they pressed on.

"I believe this league belongs in the fall, ultimately," said Usher in *The Sporting News* before the 1985 season began. "If, however, conditions aren't right, the decision to move to the fall may be reconsidered. A sense of realism has to prevail in terms of a network contract."

Doug Spedding, who had joined John Bassett as a champion for remaining in the spring, opined in *TSN* that Usher "must be drinking his own bath water."

"I only care about what makes the most sense and what is financially sound," added the Gold's owner who would merge his team with Jacksonville.

The owners, frustrated and desperate for some good news, were drained by the USFL's mounting financial problems.

"You're sitting in a meeting midway through the season, getting your ass kicked everywhere, and then you find out the Los Angeles Express guy is getting indicted, and the league says they need another $500,000 from each guy," recalled Billy Tatham. "That's when you find out who's really in. The guys like Billy Dunavant, my dad, Bassett, Donald Trump, Taubman; it was a lot easier for some of these guys, and my dad was kind of like at the mid-level. But it didn't make any difference; you were still writing the check under tremendous adversity. You really find out what guys are like when they're losing $3 million and getting ripped in the media for either being cheap, minor league guys who aren't spending the money or for being a bunch of millionaires spending themselves out of business, sometimes on the same page."

The Small Screen Becomes a Big Headache

With the league in disarray, the owners continued to watch the bad news pour in. ABC withheld $7 million of its $14 million rights fee because of the loss of major markets precipitated by the announced move to the fall. After arbitration failed to resolve the disagreement, the league sued the network. Several franchises desperately needed that money and having it tied up in a lengthy court battle further hindered operations. The dispute became public, giving the USFL another black eye. The two parties eventually settled out of court.

"The ABC contract required that the league have a certain number of teams and they had to play in a number of key large metropolitan areas," McSherry explained. "The move out of Philadelphia to Baltimore and not playing in Chicago were enough to trigger a clause that would have allowed ABC to terminate its coverage. You have to remember that when the league started it had teams in Chicago, New York, Los Angeles, Boston, Tampa, but now it was like Jacksonville, Memphis and Baltimore. The total population of the cities in which the USFL played was a lot smaller now than when it had started, so that was the legal reason ABC put the squeeze on. We always suspected the real reason was that ABC as a partner of the NFL wanted to do whatever they could to help the NFL to take away our money supply since we were suing the NFL. A big part of the antitrust case was that the NFL was on all three networks."

"We respected the right of the USFL to play their games whenever they wanted to play them," countered Spence. "Throughout my career I've felt that there should be a separation of church and state, if you will, a separation between a sports organizing group and the television network. It's the television network's job to cover the games, but it's the responsibility of the organizing group, in this case the USFL, to determine when they want to play their games. My point is that if they chose to play their games in the fall, fine, but don't paint us as bad guys because we didn't want to go with them."

While angry about the loss of revenue, other owners blamed themselves. "Our guys have made ABC the bad guys," Bassett told the Associated Press. "We were happy as hell with the contract. It was only when the management of our teams got out of whack that ABC became the bad guys."

"There were four milestone moments in ABC Sports' relationship with the USFL," said Spence. "One is the initial agreement for 1983–84, firm, and the NFL didn't say a word about that to my knowledge, and I was handling negotiations. Nobody said to me, 'We can't do this.' The second milestone involved our exercising our option for 1985 for year three. Again the NFL exerted no influence on that decision at all. The third milestone was our offer to the USFL of $175 million to extend our agreement in the spring. That included cable rights. Again, the NFL did not weigh in on that. There was no pressure put on us not to make that offer. That offer was rejected by the USFL. The fourth and final milestone was our decision not to move to the fall in 1986. Again, there was no influence, no pressure from the NFL on that decision. Those were the four key decisions, and all those major decisions were made by ABC Sports, to my knowledge without any pressure or influence on the part of the NFL.

"The only thing done involving the NFL was that I made two phone calls. Val Pinchbeck was the head of broadcasting for the NFL at the time, and since we were partners of the NFL for Monday Night Football, as a courtesy, I called Val before I first met with the owners and said, 'I just want to let you know, FYI, I'm going to be meeting with a number of United States Football League owners. I don't know what's going to come of it, but I just didn't want you to read about it in the press.' Secondly, I called him after we concluded the arrangement for '83 and '84, and said, 'We've concluded an arrangement with the USFL, and we're going to be announcing the deal at a press conference.' Again, that was an FYI. Other than those two phone calls, Pete Rozelle never called, we never got any writings from the NFL, Roone Arledge never said, 'Don't do this,' or 'Do that.' Did we discuss internally the fact that the NFL probably wasn't jumping up and down with glee that we were making the deal with the United States Football League? Of course we knew they were not enamored with that. But the key point was the move to the fall. Instantly we at ABC Sports were opposed to the fall move for the reasons I mentioned earlier."

By March, the eight surviving franchises employed just 82 non-players including coaches while publicly preparing for its first fall season. With only eight franchises remaining, the USFL realigned its teams into two divisions. Baltimore, Birmingham, Memphis and New Jersey would battle for the top spot in the Liberty Division, while Arizona, Jacksonville, Orlando and Tampa Bay would make up the Independence Division. The division champs and three wild-card teams would make the playoffs with the second and third wild card teams squaring off in the first playoff game. The regular season would remain at 18 games beginning on September 13 with the championship contest slated for February 1 in Jacksonville.

Many observers wondered who would be able to see the games. ESPN, while growing rapidly due in part to its USFL coverage, was still not available in more than 50 percent of American homes with televisions. The league's amended contract with ESPN called for the cable network to televise 22 games on Thursday and Sunday evenings. Friday night and Saturday telecasts were out because the sports broadcasting legislation passed in 1961 and the NFL-AFL merger agreement of 1966 had nixed the idea of professional games on days when college and high school games were played. Instead of receiving $23.3 million for the season, ESPN would pay the USFL a much lower amount, reportedly between $7.1 and $9.5 million. League brass continued their efforts to put together a syndication deal but were only able to line up enough stations to cover 30 percent of the country. They needed 60 percent coverage to make it work.

"ABC would only cover us in the spring," Camera said. "ESPN would take us either way and would have bumped up their money. In the fall, it would have only been ESPN and then we were devising a way to deliver product through our own television network via satellite. It's funny because everybody has that now."

Preparing for the Fall

Despite the gloomy outlook, the remaining eight teams set about preparing for training camps.

"This long without football is weird," Herschel Walker told *Sport* magazine. "Ever since high school, I've had athletics nonstop. Now this. It's hard to keep the right frame of mind."

If they were able to get the season off the ground, Trump's Dream Team looked to be the odds-on favorites to win the league title or at the very least the Liberty Division. With Jim Kelly throwing to his favorite receivers from Houston and Walker coming out of the backfield, their offense would be nearly impossible to stop. A strong secondary would help make up for a weak defensive line and linebackers. The franchise had staged several practices at the Meadowlands with the trial as a backdrop in nearby New York.

"You had Houston moving over to New York because Trump was convinced that he was going to build the new Shea Stadium," recalled Camera. "It was genius. Had he been able to build there, it would have been perfect. He would have delivered 60,000 fans at whatever rate he wanted. He originally came up with the personal seat tax. Trump knew what he was doing. It was a great team, and at that time they probably would have beaten the Giants and the Jets. They had Jimmy Kelly, and the backup was Flutie. They had running backs, wide receivers and an offensive line that was enormous. They had a great team on paper. They were going to be a real force had Trump been able to build in Queens."

Kelly had been rumored to be headed to Los Angeles to play for Al Davis and the Raiders, but the league was not about to let one of its strongest drawing cards go, especially now that he would be playing in the media capital of the country. "I'd like to play for the Raiders," said Kelly who was featured on the cover of the July 21, 1986, issue of *Sports Illustrated* in a Generals uniform. "I'd like to live in California. But what I'd *really* like to do is play for the New Jersey Generals and Donald Trump and merge with the NFL and take the run and shoot with Herschel Walker in the backfield and *just kick ass.*"

The acquisition of Kelly put Flutie's status with the team in limbo. "During the trial, we had a couple of minicamps in New Jersey," he wrote in *Flutie*. "We had four quarterbacks: Jim Kelly and myself, Todd Dillon, and Danny Barrett. Both Todd and Danny later played in the CFL. Danny, in fact, was traded to British Columbia by Calgary a month after I signed with the Stampeders. When I left Calgary to join Toronto, Danny signed with the Stampeders after leaving Ottawa. Danny and I always had some interesting games.

"There was all this talk about the battle between Jim Kelly and myself for the starter's job.

"Jim was an excellent quarterback. Todd Dillon was his backup, and Jim considered him a very capable backup. *Sports Illustrated* did a cover story on Jim as the next great quarterback in pro football and indicated he dwarfed me physically and verbally. I said in the article that Jim treated me well; that I didn't think there was a problem between us, and that we could coexist.

"A few days later the *New York Daily News*' Paul Needell had a story headlined 'Kelly Warns Flutie,' in which he stated I would have to beat out Todd Dillon for the backup job. Jim said in the article I can 'win Heismans and everything and still wind up third string.' He was just reinforcing that Dillon was a good quarterback. However, it came across that he thought Todd was better than me and I would be the third stringer. I think more than anything he was trying to boost up his buddy, Todd Dillon, at the time. Todd and I are good friends, and we get along great. Jim and I get along great. I run into him every now and then. There's never been any problems with me and Jim Kelly or Todd Dillon."

Memphis was one of the few teams in the USFL that had gone through the long off-season as if the league had no financial problems. Though they lost defensive stars Reggie White, Leonard Coleman, Mossy Cade and Sam Clancy to the NFL, they still had plenty of talent and were looking to bolster it with the addition of running back Stump Mitchell from the St. Louis Cardinals. As their marketing campaign declared, they believed that they would prosper in 1986.

"In Memphis everybody was driving around with bumper stickers that said, '86 Fall is Boats Ball' because everybody loved the 'Boats,'" recalled Ehrhart. "We had our May minicamps here in Memphis. There was high interest for that season. We kept a full coaching staff here recruiting and signing players. We still felt that we were going to play that '86 fall season."

Elsewhere, teams were considerably less settled.

"I had a house in south Jersey, and Myles had an office in downtown Philadelphia; Carl had an office there, and I'd go into work there," remembered Mora. "There wasn't much to do, and we weren't sure what was going to happen. The prospects were kind of dim as to whether we were going to survive, but I'd go into work every day, to the office. The other coaches were basically off."

In January, Mora left to join the New Orleans Saints. With other teams holding mini-camps, the Stars had no coaching staff after interviewing former USFL head men Lindy Infante and Joe Pendry and former Baltimore Colts head coach Ted Marchibroda. They also lost punter Sean Landeta, center Brad Oates and defensive back Garcia Lane but returned the nucleus of its championship ball club. They would be playing and practicing in Baltimore this time around, and the Doghouse Defense plus Chuck Fusina and Kelvin Bryant on offense were sure to keep them in the hunt. They added Orlando's Curtis Bledsoe to spell Bryant at running back.

Birmingham lost runner Joe Cribbs back to the older league but still had Cliff Stoudt calling the shots. With Joel Coles and Paul Ott Carruth remaining in the backfield, they were trying hard to land Heisman winner Bo Jackson of nearby Auburn University. Their strength, the defense, was still intact. After the Birmingham City Council loaned the team $1 million to keep it alive, local real estate developer and member of the team board Harold Ripps assumed control of the franchise. Former team owner Marvin Warner would later serve 28 months in an Ohio prison on state charges for his role in the collapse of Home State Savings Bank and its investments in ESM Government Securities, Inc., a firm guilty of $300 million of fraud. Warner was acquitted of federal charges.

In the Independence Division, the only non–Florida franchise appeared to be the strongest. The Arizona Outlaws, the lone Western Conference team to survive the off-season, brought in receiver Derek Holloway from Oakland and signed a slew of talent from the Invaders and Express plus brought back much of their 1985 squad. Experienced offensive and defensive lines and the return of quarterback Doug Williams made them the favorites to win the division. Former Gunslinger Rick Neuheisel would back up Williams, giving the Outlaws depth at the crucial position.

"There were teams that were going to go forward, and one of them was the Arizona Outlaws owned by the Tathams," said assistant coach Tim Marcum who moved over from San Antonio with Jim Bates. "Coach Kush was there, and their GM, Bruce Kebric, liked Jim. We had done a pretty good job defensively. We won games on defense, seven one year, five the next. I was the defensive coordinator the second year. It was February or March and they hired Jim as the defensive coordinator. Jim, David Knaus and I went out there to coach. They had Doug Williams and Kit Lathrop, the leading sack guy, so we had a pretty good football team. We had two mini-camps out there. The first one was in March, I moved out there in May, and we had our last one July 4. We were getting ready to rock and roll.

"They were selling tickets based on the possibility of getting an NFL team. That was the whole purpose coming back. That's why the Tathams loaded up, moved the team from Tulsa, Oklahoma and bought the Wranglers. They brought Doug's contract down there. They thought when this thing all went down and the NFL had to absorb four teams that Arizona would be one of them, and it probably would have been. There were two million people in the Valley."

In Jacksonville, new coach Mouse Davis, late of the Denver Gold, had to choose between quarterbacks Ed Luther and Bob Gagliano to operate his run and shoot offense. The merger with Denver made the Bulls much stronger particularly on the offensive line and the defensive side. With Davis in charge, one thing was certain: the Bulls would put the ball in the air.

Orlando captured quarterback John Reaves away from the Bandits and could always bring in Reggie Collier when they wanted to throw a scare into opposing defenses. Unfortunately, Coach Lee Corso could not do much to help the weak defense. Running back Curtis Bledsoe, the team's leading runner in 1985, signed with Baltimore, but receiver Joey Walters remained with the Renegades and would give Reaves a dangerous target.

Tampa Bay took some big hits, losing Reaves to Orlando and running back Gary Anderson to the San Diego Chargers. Reaves' backup Jimmy Jordan would run the offense, and coach Steve Spurrier would have to find even more creative ways of keeping defenses off balance with his brand of Banditball.

In addition, the Bandits found themselves under new ownership. Bassett had given up the team and remained in Canada nursing his health. Former partner Steve Arky, son-in-law of former Birmingham Stallions owner Marvin Warner, had tragically committed suicide in July of 1985. Arky, a lawyer and former investigator for the Securities and Exchange Commission, had vouched for a client's securities firm, ESM Government Securities, Inc., during an SEC investigation only to find out later that ESM was guilty of massive fraud amid losses of approximately $300 million. According to Paul M. Clikeman, author of *Called to Account*, Arky appeared unconnected with the fraud but despondent over the damage to his reputation, he took his life. Warner's bank had invested $144 million in ESM, largely causing the collapse of Warner's financial empire. In his suicide note, Arky claimed that neither he nor Warner were aware of the fraud. Tampa architect and developer Lee Scarfone bought a controlling interest in the Bandits.

"Lee was an owner who showed up and infused some dollars to try to get it from a very troubling point to wherever he thought it was going to go after that," added McVay. "We really didn't have a functional operations system in place where we were trying to accomplish anything except keep certain key employees in position as we got through the lawsuit. We really didn't have that much of a chance to interact with Lee Scarfone. He did step in and paid the bills and kept a handful of us around—Steve Spurrier, Tim Ruskell and myself—keeping us in a position to do something in the event that we were all going to keep going forward."

"A guy by the name of Lee Scarfone bought the Bandits, put up a million bucks, I think," said Spurrier. "Mr. Scarfone said, 'We want you to stay on as head coach through the offseason. The assistants have to find something else to do for now, but we want you here.' I think we had one minicamp the whole offseason. I played a lot of golf that year up until the trial finished."

"There were a lot of questions about everything at that point," McVay explained. "There was no absolute course mapped out that anybody could say was one-hundred percent. We didn't know. We knew generally what the thought was, but you'd have to go around and poll every team to see what they were thinking. Were they all ready to go forward in the fall? If not, how many were? If the lawsuit worked out and there were additional dollars, what was going to happen?"

It was much the same around the rest of the league.

"All I did was just make speeches and sell tickets for a whole year, because of the fact that there was no football and there was no team," said Orlando's Corso. "There was nothing, so my job became a public relations director for the Renegades while waiting for the trial."

The cutdown to eight teams had left the USFL quite a bit stronger on the field, just as the reduction from 18 to 14 franchises had the year before. Within three years, all the original majority owners had abandoned the league and only Tanenbaum stayed on as a minority owner.

Usher left little doubt about the importance of the league's case against the NFL, Telling the Associated Press, "The long-term future of the USFL is dependent on this trial."

"The future of professional sports in this country is going to be decided in the courtroom," Argovitz stated in *Football Digest*. "A judge and jury are going to decide which league will survive and which won't."

8

A Trial and Tribulations

On April 11, 1986, the courtroom battle between the United States Football League and the National Football League began. USFL lead attorney Harvey Myerson appeared in New York before U.S. District Judge Peter K. Leisure to ask for a summary judgment in the $444 million case. As expected, Leisure declined and ruled that the case would be heard by a jury to resolve questions of fact. Of particular importance in his ruling, he negated Myerson's contention that the NFL's broadcast contracts with all three networks were a violation of law in and of themselves. Because the contracts were nonexclusive and did not preclude any of the networks from televising USFL games, the younger league would have to prove that the NFL had used the threat of not renewing the contracts to keep the networks from televising the USFL in the fall.

"It is the Court's determination that the fact of the three NFL network contracts does not by itself constitute a violation of the antitrust laws," Leisure wrote. "Whether the intent or effect of such arrangements are to exclude a competing league, such as the USFL, from selling any of its television rights presents material questions of fact … [that] will be addressed, presumably, in the upcoming trial in this case."

"The NFL had contracts with NBC, CBS and ABC," recalled Trager. "What were they going to do? Drop the NFL? For us? Why do they need another football league to pay rights fees to? I never bought the argument. The only legitimate argument might have been with ABC who wasn't televising NFL games on the weekend, but then USFL games would have been up against NFL games. The cable guys might have done it, but not for the money Trump and those guys wanted."

In a key ruling, Leisure further forbade the USFL from introducing evidence concerning the NFL's reactions to other rival leagues such as the All-America Football Conference and the American Football League and also barred the USFL counsel from discussing the 18 other antitrust cases brought against the NFL over the years. In addition, Myerson could not bring up the NFL's efforts to obtain antitrust exemptions in the 1960s. Leisure encouraged both parties to reach a settlement out of court.

Representing the NFL was attorney Frank Rothman, who had replaced Bob Fiske as the NFL's lead counsel in the case, though Fiske would remain part of Rothman's team. In stark contrast to Myerson, Rothman specialized in antitrust law, and he had represented NBA player Spencer Haywood in the landmark case that struck down the NBA's college eligibility requirement. Rothman had just returned to practicing law after leaving for almost four years to run MGM movie studio for billionaire client Kirk Kerkorian.

Jury selection began on May 12 and ended the following day, concluding with a final pool of five women and one man, all self-professed football non-fans. Three of the jurors, Miriam Sanchez, Bernez Stephens and Margaret Lilienfeld, were born outside

Left to right: **Jurors Patricia S. McCabe, Stephen Ziegler, Margaret Lilienfeld, Bernez R. Stephens, Patricia Sibilia and Miriam F. Sanchez listen to arguments. CC BY Image courtesy The Courtroom Sketches of Ida Libby Dengrove, University of Virginia Law Library.**

of the United States. Lilienfeld replaced Wendell James who dropped out in the early going.

Early on NFL lawyers identified Lilienfeld, whom they nicknamed "The Dutchess," as being friendly to their case. Sanchez, on the other hand, seemed more inclined to the USFL's arguments.

"Each side had their own experts advising them on the sidelines of what type of jury they should have, and it seemed obvious to me that Myerson was trying to get a jury of lay people who did not like sports, weren't interested in Sunday television, and also if possible, were anti-establishment type people," recalled Leisure. "He did a good job. He got on that jury as many of those types as he could."

The Trial Begins

After months of waiting, the trial which would determine the future of professional football finally started on May 14 with opening statements from both sides. Ominously, former Tampa Bay Bandits owner John Bassett, one of the league's founding members and its biggest pro-spring advocate would not live to see the outcome of the trial. He succumbed to cancer the same day that arguments were finally heard in the league's antitrust suit against the NFL.

Myerson kicked off the proceedings in the New York courtroom with a bang, charging the NFL and the New York Jets with a conspiracy to keep the Generals out of New

York City. The lawyer claimed the older league and the Jets misled city and state officials into believing that the NFL team was ready to return to Shea Stadium. With Trump looking on, Myerson dutifully promised to detail how the Generals had been hurt by NFL interference. He further stated that none other than Al Davis, an NFL owner, would "blow the cap off the conspiracy." Davis' Raiders were the only NFL team not being sued.

Myerson also introduced the "Porter Presentation," a study which Harvard Business School Professor Michael Porter presented to the NFL in February of 1984. The lawyer described the study as the first of three "smoking guns" that would remove any doubt about the NFL's anti-competitive practices.

The "Porter Presentation," a 47-page study actually entitled, "How to Conquer the USFL," had been delivered to the NFL's Management Council and 65 NFL representatives, including team owners and league and team officials, attended the meeting. Professor Porter and colleague Michael Bell outlined strategies to hurt the USFL. They suggested the league pressure ABC to remove the USFL from its schedule, persuade the USFL players to unionize to drive up player costs, and to offer the wealthiest USFL owners NFL franchises in exchange for them leaving the young league behind.

The NFL acknowledged the meeting but denied that it had implemented any parts of the plan. Since its revelation, Pete Rozelle portrayed the presentation as an unfortunate but undeniable event and quickly attempted to distance the league from it. In his deposition, Bell claimed that much of the information used in the report came directly from the NFL Management Council. Chicago Bears President Mike McCaskey asked Porter to make the presentation again at an NFL owners' meeting, but Rozelle nixed the idea. The NFL paid Porter's consulting company $3,000 for his work.

"What the NFL was accused of was willfully acquiring and maintaining a monopoly power in the professional football market in the United States," explained Judge Leisure. "The USFL grounded their complaint, and the NFL played into their hands by having at Harvard Business School, a presentation of a strategy to conquer the USFL, and that was presented by Professor Porter and 65 representatives from the NFL attended this Harvard Business School presentation, not a very smart thing to be doing if they had a lawyer advising them of the consequences of the possible antitrust violations in trying to put the USFL out of business. Also the National Football League went into a supplemental draft of USFL players, which was an attempt to weaken the USFL's ability to compete."

The USFL called Rozelle as its first witness. During his 13 and a half hours on the stand over three days, Myerson asked him about a memo written by Jack Donlan, executive director of the NFL Management Council, in February of 1984, just one month after Rozelle admitted the USFL had become his league's chief concern. "There is going to be a 'closet' meeting of all the owners before the league meeting at a place and time yet to be decided," wrote Donlan. "My function is to scare all of them about the USFL, e.g. economics, draft, undergraduates…." Donlan further encouraged NFL owners to target lower-salaried USFL players in an effort to inflate their salaries and thereby tie up the league's financial resources, hindering its ability to sign rookies. Rozelle claimed to be unaware of the memo and said that the meeting never took place, a contention that another NFL official later supported.

Myerson further questioned Rozelle about the NFL's television deals and the pressure tactics the league allegedly used to get the networks to increase their bids. When asked about the "Porter Presentation," Rozelle said that he had no interest in it when it was shown to him and did not attend the meeting. He further stated, "When I read that presentation I almost got physically ill." Apparently feeling quite a bit better, he admitted to meeting with Porter nearly 18 months later at the request of a friend.

Myerson also revealed that Rozelle had called CBS executives in 1974 after he heard that they were considering televising World Football League games. Rozelle acknowledged the call but denied that he had tried to pressure the network into keeping the WFL off of CBS. The USFL then introduced a 1981 memo from one CBS executive to another in which it was claimed that sending a network representative to a USFL meeting "would be considered an unfriendly act by Pete."

Myerson wound up his questioning of the commissioner by grilling him about promises of expansion teams allegedly made to the cities of Oakland and New York in exchange for their cooperation in keeping the USFL teams out of their stadiums. Rozelle said that no such promises were made and that he only told the cities that he would consider them. Myerson strongly suggested that Rozelle had dangled a franchise in front of New York officials in an attempt to keep the Generals out of the city.

"If anyone said that, they are lying, because I never said that to anyone," said an emotional Rozelle, angrily pointing in Myerson's direction.

Rozelle appeared on the stand longer than anyone else, during which time Myerson laid out most of the USFL's case. The league amended its damage request to $500 million, an increase of nearly $60 million.

"The lawyer who represented the NFL early on was Bob Fiske, who was eventually fired in favor of Rothman, but Fiske handled most of the case," said McSherry. "He was a former United States attorney for the Southern District of New York, a partner in Davis Polk & Wardwell. Bob knew me, and said, 'You're going to be a witness for the USFL.' I said, 'I doubt that Myerson would think I knew anything worth talking about.' So he said, 'I know you do, but I really don't want to take your deposition. I'm going to have to take your deposition if you're going to show up as a trial witness for the USFL. You'll have to promise me if it ever comes about that you're going to be a witness.'

"Myerson didn't like me, and he didn't want to talk to me, so obviously I wasn't going to be a witness. I never was deposed; I never was a witness at the trial. I was in the courthouse once during the trial, and I decided to go down to the courtroom to see what was going on. I had a client with me, and we went to this big courtroom where they had the trial. They had these 40-foot high oak doors that make a lot of noise when you open them. I opened the door and Leisure looks at me while Myerson is cross-examining Bill Grimes, who was the president of ESPN. As I opened the door, and I'm not making this up, Myerson says to Grimes, 'And then what did McSherry say to you?' Judge Leisure said, 'Very fortuitous time for you to arrive, Mr. McSherry.' I felt like leaving or crawling under a table."

During her time on the stand, economist Nina Cornell estimated that the USFL needed a minimum of $301 million and possibly up to $565 million ($100.3 to $188.3 million before trebling) to continue operations thanks to the NFL's actions. NFL attorney Robert Fiske claimed the estimates were excessive.

The USFL concluded its case with testimony from Donald Trump, Al Davis and sportscaster Howard Cosell. Trump, the only USFL owner to testify, claimed that NFL commissioner Pete Rozelle advised him not to invest in the new league during its formative stages in 1981 and 1982. He further told the jury that Rozelle promised him an expansion franchise if he could help convince the USFL to remain in the spring during a secret meeting in March of 1984.

NFL lawyer Frank Rothman (far right) cross examines New Jersey Generals owner Donald Trump while Judge Peter K. Leisure (far left) and NFL attorney Robert Fiske (center foreground) listen. CC BY Image courtesy The Courtroom Sketches of Ida Libby Dengrove, University of Virginia Law Library.

He admitted on the stand that ABC never showed any interest in the USFL as a fall league, an apparent contradiction of what he had told his fellow owners prior to their vote to switch seasons. Trump blamed the network's lack of enthusiasm on pressure from the NFL. New York state officials and U.S. Senator Alfonse D'Amato testified that the NFL had strung them along, claiming that the Jets might return to New York City when they just wanted to keep Trump out of it. At the time, though, they were also trying to salvage Trump's stadium project, partially in hopes of bringing the Jets back.

Trump left no doubt that as far as he was concerned the USFL's future was dependent upon the trial. "If we do not show victory, my feeling is that the league should not play," Trump stated flatly. "We will not be able to compete against the horror that is the NFL. Jobs and millions of dollars hinge on this trial. My feeling is there can't be a USFL and there will never be another football league to compete against the NFL if the USFL loses its case."

Davis, who had successfully sued his fellow owners in 1982 over their attempts to block the Raiders' move to Los Angeles, testified that he thought that the NFL and Oakland city officials worked against the Invaders and attempted to kill community support for the team. He claimed the NFL tried to "destroy" the Invaders and that Rozelle made "an enticement" to Oakland owner Alfred Taubman for the purpose of luring his support away from the USFL franchise. He also said an understanding was reached in October of 1983 to not place another team in the New York area.

"Al Davis gave great testimony for the USFL," Argovitz said. "Al was a maverick, you know, he had his problems with his own partners in the NFL. I had a great deal of respect for Al Davis. He got in the NFL because he was with the AFL. And he knew what it was all about and he knew we put together a good league and good players and I think he respected what we had done."

"I'm not going to let them take me down again," said Davis of the NFL after completing his testimony, "when I've been told they're indiscriminately breaking the laws. It's their power structure they're protecting."

During Cosell's time on the stand, NFL attorney Frank Rothman told Cosell to interrupt him if he asked a question that the broadcaster did not understand. "If you ask a question I don't understand, we will have the biggest story of the century," replied the notoriously pompous Cosell, also a former lawyer. He and Rothman sparred throughout Cosell's nearly three-hour testimony.

Cosell claimed that ABC Sports President Roone Arledge told him, "You gotta understand. Pete [Rozelle] is all over me because I`m sustaining the United States Football League for the spring contract," a statement that Arledge denied. ABC's Jim Spence sided with Arledge, saying the NFL never applied any pressure although he added that he did not imagine they were all that happy with the network's deal with the young league. Spence then revealed that he had offered $175 million for four years of broadcast and cable rights if the USFL stayed in the spring.

"I might just say that Howard Cosell would've been a more effective witness and been somebody that would've concerned greatly the National Football League, had not Frank Rothman neutered his testimony," Leisure stated. "It was again a very impressive way of handling the situation with a difficult witness. A good trial lawyer is somewhat theatrical, and in the summation, Frank Rothman commented on every witness that testified that was a major witness, and when he came to Howard Cosell in talking about him to the jury in his summation he walked back and forth in front of the jury panel as if he was in thought, having mentioned Howard Cosell's name, and then he, after walking several times back and forth, he stopped and said, 'Poor Howard, no one listens to him anymore.' Masterful handling of it, because the jury never asked for any re-read of Howard Cosell's very damaging testimony as an expert and as a witness, so that it's about as masterful way of neutralizing a difficult witness as I've ever seen."

"Howard Cosell actually hurt us in the lawsuit," admitted Trump. "He was totally a fan of the USFL, but he went there in the morning he was a great witness. Then he went out to lunch, he had a serious problem with something and he came back and he was a disastrous witness. I loved Howard, he was a friend of mine, but he was so bad and so arrogant and so crazy that it turned out to be very much of a disaster."

"Both Cosell and Trump felt without any evidence that the NFL was putting pressure on ABC Sports in regard to the USFL," said Spence. "That was just flat out untrue. Never did I see any evidence of any pressure put upon ABC Sports by the NFL. In theory, could Pete Rozelle have spoken to Roone Arledge about the USFL? Sure, in theory, but was there any evidence of NFL pressure on ABC Sports? Not that I ever saw, and I was the lead negotiator representing ABC Sports in dealings with the United States Football League."

The National Football League began its defense on June 26. Rothman immediately set the course of their arguments in his opening remarks when he said, "The USFL is controlled and dominated by Donald Trump, who can buy and sell many of the owners in the NFL." Rothman painted Trump as not only the face of the USFL but also its puppet

Sportscaster Howard Cosell (center) is cross-examined by NFL lawyer Frank Rothman (far right) while Judge Peter K. Leisure (top left) looks on. CC BY Image courtesy The Courtroom Sketches of Ida Libby Dengrove, University of Virginia Law Library.

master. He introduced a letter from Stars owner Myles Tanenbaum sent to Oakland owner Tad Taube in which Tanenbaum expressed concerns over Trump's machinations.

"My purpose in writing is to share with you a concern that surfaced in New Orleans," wrote Tanenbaum. "That concern has to do with Donald Trump's grand plan for the USFL. Donald wants to move the league into the fall so that a merger with the NFL could be forced—he told me that in so many words on two occasions, and I believe that his comments at the league meeting included that statement as well." He went on to write that there were, "three ways to make money in professional football: tickets, TV and treble damages."

Rothman called former USFL commissioner Chet Simmons as his first witness. Rothman summoned a parade of witnesses to contradict earlier testimony given on the USFL's behalf, particularly that of Davis and Trump. For instance, Dallas Cowboys President Tex Schramm testified that his league never acted on the "Porter Presentation," and Jets owner Leon Hess disputed Al Davis's claim that NFL owners reached an understanding to not put another team in New York. He also defended himself against accusations that he participated in any conspiracy to keep the Generals out of New York or that there was any conspiracy at all.

One moment considered as a turning point in the trial occurred when Usher admitted that one of the reasons for the franchise shuffling after the 1984 season was to position the teams for a merger with the NFL. The NFL made note of the clause in Usher's contract that provided a $400,000 payment for each USFL franchise that joined the NFL. That the USFL had been hurt was undeniable. Whether they had done the damage to themselves was now the question.

Rothman also presented a taped ABC interview with the late John Bassett from March of 1985. In the interview, the ailing Tampa Bay owner acknowledged his league's mismanagement and placed most of the blame for the USFL's troubles on the announced move to the fall. A USFL owner, and a deceased one who could not revoke or clarify his comment, was perhaps the best witness the NFL presented.

ABC's Spence damaged the USFL's vital television claims when he testified to the network's $175 million offer for four more years of spring football, an offer the league rejected.

"Harvey was screaming at me on the stand trying to break me down. At one point the judge turned to me and asked, 'Mr. Spence, are you okay?' I said, 'I'm fine, your honor. Thank you.' Following one of Harvey's rants while I was on the stand, I remember saying, 'Mr. Myerson, you can scream and yell at me as long as you want, but the simple truth is that ABC Sports made an offer of $175 million to your client, and it was rejected.'"

Rozelle, the first witness called in the case, also became the last when he wrapped up the NFL's defense. He claimed that he never advised Trump against buying a USFL franchise and at no point offered him an expansion franchise. Rozelle also said that he never even met Trump until March 12, 1984, making it impossible for him to advise against joining the USFL in 1981 and 1982. He claimed that at that meeting Trump begged for an NFL franchise and said he would "find some stiff" to buy his USFL franchise. According to the commissioner, Trump threatened him with a lawsuit if Rozelle failed to accept his demands. Rozelle admitted that he did not reject the proposal immediately and promised to get back to Trump about a possible one or two team merger, an idea he rejected in April of 1984.

"He was going to buy a cheap USFL franchise and force his way through litigation and merge with the NFL," Rothman stated. "And Mr. Trump used some poor, unfortunate people."

"There was a meeting which Trump went to with Rozelle at the Plaza Hotel," recalled McSherry. "Two people testified in their depositions to completely opposite recollections of what was discussed. Rozelle said that Trump begged him to take him into the NFL, and that if he did, he would make sure that the lawsuit went away. Trump said that Rozelle begged him to drop the lawsuit, and if he dropped the lawsuit, Rozelle would put him in the NFL. There was no way anybody would put Donald Trump in the NFL. The NFL owners would never have allowed it, so the whole premise of Trump's version of the truth is perverted. In the end, the question of which one of the two was lying was resolved at the trial when the lawyer for the NFL asked Rozelle who paid for the room. Rozelle said, 'Trump.' Trump's wife owned the frickin' hotel, the Plaza Hotel."

Rothman contended throughout his defense that the NFL's position of dominance had come about naturally through solid business practices, the same practices that the USFL had abandoned. Leisure's earlier rulings prevented the USFL from pointing out how the NFL had dealt with competing leagues in the past or from mentioning the NFL's checkered record in other antitrust cases.

Rothman introduced evidence showing the USFL's instability through franchise shuffling and numerous ownership changes. He maintained that not only had the NFL not harmed the USFL, it had no reason to do so. The USFL had done that all by itself. Myerson had instructed other USFL team owners not to attend the trial, and Rothman took full advantage of their absence. He pointed out that the other USFL owners did not attend his summation because, "they didn't want to talk about Trump taking them down the road of despair." He portrayed the USFL's founding owners as men who were overwhelmed by the new owners who proclaimed, in Rothman's words, "I'm going to have it my way because I have to have an NFL franchise and then I get a free stadium," a direct shot at Trump. He also introduced Tad Taube's letter in which the Oakland owner complained about the excessive spending of some of his colleagues, exclaiming, "We have sighted the enemy and they are us!"

"A number of the other USFL owners and executives wanted to testify, but Myerson's strategy was to focus on Trump," explained Ehrhart who had been deposed by NFL lawyers for two days prior to the trial. "Myerson instructed us to stay away so we wouldn't be subpoenaed, but this was a strategic mistake by Myerson because so many of us could have added details about what happened in other markets besides New York City. A few years after the trial an NFL executive told me that they had read my deposition and were worried that I would testify because I had knowledge of so many details."

Rothman pointed out the NFL obtained its third network television contract 12 years before the USFL's birth and only with the approval of Congress. "My question to you is: What was the NFL supposed to do at that point?" Rothman asked the jury. "Are we supposed to call in the three networks and sit them in a room and say: 'Gentlemen, here is a new league that wants to start. They can't wait until 1987 when our contract is up, so I think we have to cancel one of our contracts with you.' What were we to do?"

The attorneys offered their summations in the case on July 24. Rothman contended that the NFL had secured its dominant position through hard work over more than six decades, while Myerson stressed that the very essence of competition in America was at stake.

"The World Football League died, the American Football League was absorbed, and now if the USFL is allowed to go down the pipe, that's it for professional football in this country, in our lifetime," Myerson said, reiterating Trump's position that the USFL was dead without a court victory.

"This is not a case of the little guy versus the big guy, of David versus Goliath," Rothman countered in closing arguments. "It's more like Donald versus Goliath." He went on to state, "You don't have to be a football expert to understand that integrity of management, integrity of ownership is critical. The USFL owners have priced themselves out of playing football. You have to walk before you run and run before you fly."

Trump was the only USFL owner called to testify in the trial, though he had not suffered as much as many of his fellow owners, and he was one of the few who could shrug off a loss of several million dollars without much of a problem. This hardly showed the damage suffered by some of his compatriots. While Myerson talked of his "itty-bitty" league, Trump hardly looked part of any such organization. "In retrospect," wrote Trump in *Trump: The Art of the Deal*, "we might have been better off to put on the witness stand several of the smaller owners who'd lost their shirts and had genuinely sad stories to tell."

After 44 days of testimony, the jury began deliberations July 24. Judge Leisure delivered his charge to the group that morning, outlining the USFL's case in the context of the Sherman Antitrust Act. He gave them 155 pages of instructions with 61 questions of fact for them to determine. The questions condensed the six antitrust claims and three common law charges to their most elemental issues.

"The NFL was established and operating before the USFL was formed," wrote Leisure to the jury. "Often the first person to start a business will acquire things like locations, the services of people or supplies or other things under contracts. A person who later starts a business may desire later what the first competitor already has. But the first competitor is not required to give any or all of the things it acquired to the newcomer to enable the newcomer to compete with it.

"The mere fact that the NFL has arrangements with all three networks is not necessarily unlawful. Thus you should infer no anticompetitive intent or effect from the mere existence of these contracts. The contracts did not prevent the networks from televising games of another league." Instead, the jury would have to decide if the NFL had used the agreements to pressure the networks. With that, the jury left to discuss the case.

"Antitrust cases are very complicated," said Leisure. "Charging the jury of lay people on an antitrust case is a challenging task for the judge at the end of the trial. It's really like a first year law school presentation of what antitrust laws are. So that's part of the challenge for the judges: to be sure that the jurors understand the case."

The entire matter was now out of the hands of the lawyers. All either side could do was wait for the verdict. With USFL training camps less than a month away, Myerson called the damages more important to his clients than in any other case he had argued. "Without minimum damages, this league is dead," he admitted.

"We knew we had proven they were a monopoly," remembered Camera. "We knew we had them and it was all a matter of how much we were going to get, and whether we got enough to cut a deal. Rozelle didn't go down to hear the answer because he was convinced they had lost."

The Verdict

On July 29, Rozelle and NFL broadcasting director Val Pinchbeck hopped into a cab to head to the courthouse when they heard that the verdict would be announced shortly. Neither man could believe his ears when the news came over the radio: the USFL had won the case.

"I remember, I was afraid maybe he was gonna have a heart attack," Pinchbeck said of Rozelle in Michael MacCambridge's book *America's Game*. Pinchbeck ordered the cab to head back to the NFL offices.

"It seemed like we kept riding for another 30 minutes, but, of course, it was only five or six minutes," Pinchbeck told *USA Today*. "We were thinking of quotes about why we lost."

Rozelle and Pinchbeck had indeed heard correctly. In the trial that would determine the future of professional football, the National Football League had been found guilty of monopolizing the sport. With more than $1 billion at stake, their minds raced with the possible ramifications. Before they returned to the NFL offices, though, their moods had brightened considerably as more details came over the radio. The NFL had been found guilty of possessing and maintaining a monopoly of professional football, but the USFL had lost its other claims, including the important charges based on television damages.

"With that, Rozelle and Pinchbeck launched off of the back seat in an excited celebration, slapping the seat backs and door frames with joy, while Rozelle gave the new directive, 'Let's go down to the courthouse!'" described MacCambridge.

"I remember driving the day that the jury was deliberating, and it came on the radio," Argovitz recalled. "It said that the jury has just finished their deliberations and to our understanding the USFL won the antitrust lawsuit with the NFL. That's what I remember hearing. And we were rushing back to the courthouse to hear the final verdict. So we walked in, sat down, then the jury came out and delivered to the judge the verdict. The NFL was guilty of antitrust violations and we award the USFL one dollar. My heart sank. I mean it was like giving birth to your child, and I'm sure all the other owners' hearts dropped because we felt that we had something that was viable. We all spent a lot of time and effort and energy and love to give people jobs, to give people opportunities, to build a fan base that we developed, and to see it go up like it did was just heart wrenching."

While the jury had concluded that the NFL had "willfully acquired or maintained monopoly power" in the market of professional football and that the NFL's monopoly power had caused injury to the USFL, they decided that the older league's contracts with the three networks were not an unreasonable restraint of trade and were not used as such by the NFL. The jury also concluded that Rozelle and company did not have the power to deny the USFL access to a national television network. Those were the cornerstones of the USFL's damage claims, and they were the arguments the jury rejected. In addition, Rozelle had been personally exonerated of all the charges, something the USFL would not contest. The jury appeared to believe Rozelle above Donald Trump.

To add insult to injury, they found that the USFL had hurt itself through poor business practices. In particular, the league had quickly abandoned its original plan of low-budget spring football, expanded too quickly causing franchise instability and had tried in the end to force a merger with the NFL, wounding itself irreparably in the process. The jury saw many of the moves as acts of desperation caused by the owners' impatience. The jurors pinned much of the blame for the USFL's troubles squarely on the shoulders of the younger league. Mismanagement and not the other league were to blame for the bulk of the USFL's problems in the eyes of the jury.

"The USFL shot itself in the foot," exulted Rozelle in *Time* magazine. "Now we can go back to playing football." Dallas Cowboys president Tex Schramm agreed. "I'm totally elated," he said. "We said all along that there was no basis for this lawsuit and this has justified it."

"This was the biggest threat we'd ever faced," Cincinnati Bengals owner Paul Brown echoed in *Sports Illustrated*. "While I felt all along that we were in the right, I didn't have that much faith in what the jury might decide."

For their part, USFL officials were stunned by the verdict. Two and a half months in court and more than 40 witnesses had resulted in a payoff of just $1 which would be trebled to a paltry $3, even after they won the case. That was small consolation when the league needed approximately $250 million just to cover money already spent.

"It defies logic and common sense," a dejected Myerson told *Time*, his trademark enthusiasm a distant memory. "What we have on our hands is $1. That is absolutely bizarre."

"This doesn't make sense unless there was a misunderstanding among the jurors," furthered Showboats president and general manager Steve Ehrhart in *USA Today*. "I can see why it was confusing. The instructions were 155 pages and there was a 30-page list of questions. As a lawyer, I read it and was confused. They were the most complicated instructions I've ever seen."

"I was on vacation when the jury came in with the verdict and only realized what was happening when I saw myself on television," McSherry remembered. "NBC had for years used the same footage whenever they did a story about the USFL, which wasn't very often, and it was a picture of Trump and me standing in front of a USFL banner at an owners' meeting. I saw this come up on the screen when I was in the Catskills. They said they won, but not so fast, they won a dollar. I was pissed off. I was pissed off at Myerson and Usher. Usher testified at the trial. The general counsel, his wife, sent an email to all the owners telling everybody how fantastic Harry's testimony was and how it made the case."

"Was that a jury or a bleeping circus?" former Breaker Nolan Franz asked in *Sports Illustrated*, who had signed with the Green Bay Packers. Joe Canizaro still owed him money for the 1985 campaign and now the receiver saw no way he would ever get it. "My 35,000 bucks just went down the tubes."

"I was playing in the NFL at the time, and you hate to use the word 'comical,' but it was comical and almost ridiculous that one group was proven to have won, and proven in the situation that they have been harmed, and then to see what the outcome was," said Landeta. "You almost couldn't believe that this could happen in a legitimate court of law. You know something was proven, this and that with all the damages and everything, why would you even go through all that? Well, you won, but here is what you won."

"We were in the Tampa Bay Bandits office on Himes," recalled McVay. "We were all anxious to hear what happened. They came back and said the USFL won the lawsuit. We said, 'Terrific, maybe we have a chance to keep this moving forward.' Then they said the damages were $1, but they were trebled damages, so $3. Everybody went, 'Oh, that's probably not good news.' It was very disheartening."

"My heart still pounds from that day," Ehrhart added. "We had our entire staff and players huddled around this very office waiting for word when were heard the jury was coming back on this phone right behind me here. We got the call: we win. People are screaming and running up and down. We have a job! And remember this was their life, their career. We're gonna be able to play; all that hard work. And then 14 minutes later, I still remember the time period, another call comes in. Wait a minute, the initial USFL wins is now the USFL wins one dollar, and I said, 'Wait a minute.' I'm trying to quiet everybody down so I can hear what the hell's going on. And I was just stunned for two days. We couldn't figure out what was going on. We were trying to get through to New York to say, 'What does this mean? Did we win injunctive relief? Are we going to be able to play? Does this mean because the NFL had violated the antitrust law that we would have the opportunity to be able to play?'"

Comments by the jurors outside the courthouse only added to the confusion surrounding the verdict. It became immediately clear that deep dissension and bitter arguing had played a major part in the jury's discussions. In fact, the deliberations frequently became extremely heated and even featured several shouting matches. Foreman Patricia McCabe nearly passed out on the way home after one particularly brutal session. She was taken to a hospital where she was told that her problem was the result of stress.

"We were closed inside this room and there was a certain amount of dissension," Lilienfeld told *USA Today*. "It was very taxing."

"A hung jury is what we were afraid of, especially after the emotional outbursts we were going through," added Miriam Sanchez. "Some people were actually getting sick."

All the jurors agreed that the NFL had created and sustained a monopoly, and two of them, Sanchez and Bernez Stephens, were ready to award some damages, while Patricia Sibilia generally favored their view. Lilienfeld, McCabe and Steven Ziegler argued vehemently against any award, believing the USFL had inflicted harm on itself when it positioned itself for a merger by abandoning large markets and increasing their player spending too far ahead of available revenue. "We were a unanimous jury on liability, but we were a hung jury on damages," summarized Sanchez in *USA Today*.

Confusion about the law and the powers of the court also played a role in the compromise for at least one juror. Sanchez wanted to award the USFL up to $300 million but agreed to the $1 amount because she thought that the judge could increase the award. "We would leave it up to the court to decide how much damage would be coming to the USFL," she said in *USA Today*. "We'll give them a chance that way to go one way or the other." Unbeknownst to her, Leisure could only lower any amount, not increase it.

Lilienfeld admitted that at the beginning of their deliberations "there was some confusion," but denied in *The Sporting News* that anyone else was befuddled in the end. "Six people took a vote and it was unanimous." She said that she was surprised by Sanchez's statements of confusion among the jurors. "I was absolutely shocked when I read that," she said. "I, for one, knew exactly what I was doing. I'm not a woman who is easily confused. And don't forget, to any of the basic questions before any of the jurors, there had to be a complete understanding of the English language, written or oral. I frankly can't see how any juror can consent to a verdict, then go in front of the court and have the verdict read to which they assented."

"There were antitrust Sherman Act monopolization by the NFL of professional football in the United States, and unfair competition," stated Leisure. "The jury did find a monopoly on the part of the NFL, and the problem for the USFL as it ended up was, they found that the USFL had shot themselves in the foot as far as damages were concerned."

"The NFL put us out of business," argued Billy Tatham. "It's easy to criticize the USFL guys. We were losing our asses. It's like watching a house fire and making fun of people who are bumping into each other trying to find their way out. Meanwhile the NFL's outside tossing in the matches. Were there mistakes? Of course there were mistakes, but we didn't start the fire."

"I really do think, I thought it then and I believe it today, that the key point in the entire litigation was the rejection of the $175 million proposal by the USFL," said ABC's Spence. "I stated that there was no pressure from the NFL. How much pressure could there have been if we offered the USFL $175 million?

"I'm still not sure to this day why the jury found the NFL was a monopoly. That aside, I think the main reason the NFL was only to be charged $1, trebled to $3, was because of the $175 million proposal. I testified in federal court to that deal. To me, that was a key point in the NFL-USFL suit. Here the USFL's crying foul, saying the NFL's a monopoly, etc., yet they have a $175 million deal that they rejected. First, it made no sense from an antitrust litigation point of view, but also from a practical point of view it made no sense. Why not accept it, play in the spring for a few more years and table your desire to go to the fall? Tell Trump, 'Back off, Donald. We're going to take this money for x number of years and let us grow and see if at some point in time we really want to move to the fall or not.'"

The Wrong Counsel

Others felt the case had already been lost before it landed in the hands of the jury. Though he maintained the USFL was justified in pressing the suit, Taube questioned its handling.

"It was the right decision with probably the worst execution that one could ever imagine given the stakes that were on the table," he said "This is where Donald Trump probably had the most negative influence on the league. Donald took the lead in terms of either proclaiming himself, or by default becoming, the leader of the group executing the antitrust litigation. In doing that, Donald selected counsel. First, he selected Roy Cohn, who was one of the more unsavory attorneys in all of law at that point. He had a very questionable moral background and had made his reputation during the McCarthy hearings. That was followed by the decision to hire Harvey Myerson, who was a bombastic, cigar-chewing egomaniac who had enamored himself to Donald Trump. He convinced Donald that he was really going to go out and get 'em. Unfortunately, he knew little if anything about antitrust law.

"The verdict came in two parts. The first part was the part about culpability, and the jury came down with a positive verdict for the USFL, affirming that the NFL had in fact participated in predatory antitrust activities which were meant to harm the USFL. We won that phase of the trial. The second phase of the trial was the damages phase. The jury never did understand the damages aspect because Myerson essentially had totally theoretical arguments of damages based on stadiums being full five years out, television revenues being five times what they were then, etc., etc., etc. The entire framework of the loss the USFL suffered was based on theoretical future arguments, and the jury didn't understand those arguments.

"What he should have done, and what any first-year law student would have done, is they would have simply gone to the jury and said, 'Look, these guys had $300 million invested in this venture, and because of these predatory actions by the NFL, they were caused to lose their investment because they couldn't continue with the league. The league became essentially impossible to operate because of the failure of the league to secure a new television agreement, which there was evidence that the NFL had interfered in that, the fact that certain stadium arrangements couldn't be made, etc. We were able to establish that the NFL had interfered in those, and so forth and so forth. And as a result therefore *ipso facto* these owners collectively lost $300 million of their investment.' That was an argument that everybody would have understood, case closed. Verdict for the USFL for $300 million, trebled $900 million, and we now own a significant part of the NFL. The way the trial was conducted was really the *coup de grâce* of the USFL. That was essentially the knife by which we died, and that was by listening and being influenced by Donald Trump in picking an attorney who was not equipped to get us the kind of verdict we needed."

"It was all showmanship," said Camera. "It was well-prepared showmanship, but Harvey didn't stick to the script. The script was hit and run, get the story out and let it go. Harvey got caught up with it, and it came down to who the jury was going to believe. Harvey attacked Rozelle masterfully, but who were they going to believe? They wound up believing Tex Schramm over Donald Trump. Pete got beat up a lot. He was hurting during the trial because he knew a lot of the things that took place were on his watch as commissioner so everybody could slam him in their own way.

"We thought we had it because the only problem was, and Harry called it early on, was that Myerson wanted to get Cosell on because Cosell was a performer. The problem was that Cosell was great in the morning, and then we all went for lunch and Howard pounded down a couple. He went on in the afternoon and started telling stories, and he just lost the jury."

"When we got into the antitrust litigation, Harvey Myerson became a showman instead of a lawyer," sighed Taube. "Meanwhile, the NFL had hired a very journeyman, New Englander type who was highly respected among the judges. I think that if the trial had lasted for three weeks, Myerson's antics might have carried the day. As it turned out, the jury got tired of the bullshit and the failure of Myerson to deal with factual issues rather than rhetoric.

"The choice of witnesses was terrible. Of all the people you want to put on the stand to demonstrate how we had been mistreated by the NFL, the last guy you want to put on the stand was Donald Trump. The world had to feel sorry for Donald. In fact, notwithstanding the pathetic legal performance of Myerson, it became clear that the NFL was guilty of predatory antitrust practices. We had the smoking gun! They overtly tried to preclude us from getting television contracts, from having the ability to utilize stadiums for our games and a whole host of guerrilla-type dirty tricks and activities to discredit the league.

"In an antitrust case, you have to first of all establish culpability and then you have to prove damages. Look at the evidence that was brought in for establishing damages. The league had basically been driven out of business. The owners collectively had lost about $250 million. All Myerson had to do was say that, just let the jury know that through a very meticulous and well-executed plot to drive us out of business, we had lost our investment. That's the measure of damages. He didn't do that. He had charts and graphs and witnesses, projecting out to ten or 15 years what revenues might be at $85 ticket prices and it was all pie in the sky. He completely lost the jury.

"In many conversations about this case with many accomplished antitrust lawyers, many of whom had been active on behalf of Al Davis in his suit against the NFL, collectively and individually they said that a first-year law student who knew nothing about antitrust could have won this case. With all the things that the league did that were wrong, the thing that was most wrong of all were the criminal antitrust violations that were committed by the NFL. The jury agreed that there were antitrust violations. I think that the argument that those things caused the loss of our investment was one that the jury would have understood. At the end of the day, instead of getting $3, we might have ended up with $750 million."

"I think Harvey Myerson was a great disappointment," added Argovitz. "In fact, he was a major reason, in my opinion, why we lost the lawsuit because he wouldn't listen to reason. He was parked on his ego and he took us down a dark alley."

"Flat out, wrong lawyers," Ehrhart concurred. "I would not normally say that, but we had lawyers who had a different agenda, a different mission. They saw it as an opportunity not only for fame and fortune but to hit this home run. This had just been a way to stop the NFL from their inappropriate, illegal interferences with our right to do business, and it was not seen as the end all just to make money. It was just to get the NFL off our back, quit interfering with our contracts so we could keep playing and building. Then the lawsuit ended up taking on a life of its own, as if this was the only thing that the USFL was. So unfortunately I have to say that, but the truth is that we did not have good counsel."

"They should have put me up as a witness because I could have talked about the influence the NFL had against getting deals with sponsors," Camera added. "It was told to them straight up: 'If you give them a better deal, an improved deal over what you're doing with us, we'll drop you out of the NFL sponsorship list.' And that was true, especially with the clothing manufacturers. There were a lot of things that I had documented. But they didn't want to go that direction; they wanted to focus on the high-level, big-name people. They didn't put me or Hadhazy on. They took our depositions for two days, but they didn't put us on."

"The funny part is that we had the chance to succeed even after the league failed and made the stupid decision to move to the fall," stated Taube. "We could have recouped everything by managing one lawsuit, and we even fucked that up."

Even Trump second-guessed Myerson, the man he handpicked to handle the case. "He took a case in which no one gave us a prayer going in, and he managed to win on antitrust grounds, even though we were awarded only token damages," wrote Trump in 1989's *Trump: The Art of the Deal*. "Even so, I've wondered, since the trial, whether perhaps Harvey was just a little too sharp for some of the jurors. Every day he'd show up in one of his beautiful pinstripe suits, and a little handkerchief in his pocket, and I'm just not sure how well that went over.

"Overall, I think he did as good a job as anyone could, and I still believe he's our best hope on the appeal. One thing I like about Harvey is his enthusiasm. He's still absolutely convinced he's going to win the appeal."

"He and Trump designed a high-profile designer lawsuit, not a lawsuit about a small football league struggling to survive with a monopolist trying to drive it out of business," countered McSherry. "He had Senator D'Amato as witness. He had Howard Cosell as a witness. For a player, he chose Herschel Walker, who had a personal services contract with Trump, which the NFL knew about.

"Myerson was a terrible choice. He was hated by the judge. He eventually was hated by the jury. He tried his own case just to make himself famous; then became infamous because of the combination of the $3 jury award and the fact that he got indicted shortly thereafter. He was the poster child for a bad choice to handle a major case."

"Myerson was so full of bull," agreed Ehrhart. "There were a couple young lawyers with his firm who did some good work on the case, but every time Myerson touched it, it was from a public relations standpoint, not a legal one. It was a PR campaign, not what made sense from a legal standpoint. Myerson was a bombastic, unprincipled guy whose true colors came out later. It was so unfortunate because the bulk of ownership was very ethical and principled and was trying to do good things such as providing jobs. It was such an anomaly that we had the exact opposite representing us."

McSherry credited Rothman with taking attention away from the NFL's misdeeds and casting Trump as the face of the USFL.

"I've heard from several people that the NFL supposedly did two mock trials before they went to trial in the USFL case," he said. "They did them in Boston. In each case the USFL got a verdict in excess of $2 billion, so they fired Bob Fiske as their lawyer, one of the best lawyers in the country and a former US attorney in New York, and they hired Frank Rothman who had been the president of a movie company and worked for a big firm named Skadden, Arps. They had to figure out what they were doing wrong. The jury consultants told them they had to have a villain within the USFL, someone for the jury to dislike. So they chose Trump as the person to dislike.

"I think that what happened is the NFL did a very smart thing the way they tried the case. They basically presented the USFL as if it were Donald Trump. That's one of the reasons why Myerson trying the case the way he tried it was not very smart for the USFL. Instead of having Trump, Senator D'Amato, Howard Cosell and Herschel Walker as witnesses, he should have had the mayor of Birmingham, Alabama talk about how prideful he was that they had a professional football team in Birmingham. Maybe he could have chosen a general manager who used to be in the NFL who couldn't get a job in the NFL any longer and had found work in the USFL. If he wanted a player, he could have picked a player who had been forced to retire from the NFL who got a job in the USFL, not Herschel Walker, a Heisman Trophy winner. There was no sympathy. They convinced the jury that it made no sense to give Trump more money. He really wasn't doing it for the money, anyway. All he was really trying to do was push his way into the NFL."

"We've always said if they would have got guys like my dad on the witness stand, you'd have seen that these are just regular guys doing their best, trying to have an opportunity," added Billy Tatham. "I think that would have really changed the dynamics. The decision came down in his hometown, New York, so Donald became the mouthpiece because he lived there. The NFL used that against us by framing it as billionaires vs. billionaires. It was nonsense."

"It should have been brought in Memphis or some other place where the USFL was the only football team in town," said lawyer Jeffrey Kessler to "The AM Law Daily." He would work on the appeal of the suit. "[The case] was about destroying football for those teams, not about Donald Trump's desire to be an NFL owner, which is what the New York jury thought. But Trump wanted all the attention and publicity that comes from being in New York."

"I've never had a case where I won but I didn't win money," Trump stated. "You can win cases and you can lose cases, but we literally won one dollar. I think honestly the NFL did a very good job in that they did lose a big antitrust case, but they convinced everybody that Trump is very rich he doesn't need the money, so the jury sort of said, 'We're going to give the victory to Trump, but he doesn't need the money.'"

Unwilling to take all the blame for the USFL's failure to win large damages upon his own strategy, Trump went so far as to blame Bassett.

"I like John Bassett; he was a really nice guy," Trump explained. "He got very sick at the end. It affected John very strongly, very greatly, even during the trial, and I think, you know unfortunately, some of John's statements were the reason we didn't get the kind of damages that we would've been able to get."

"It was a disappointing thing to me, of course," David Dixon said about the outcome. "I took a great deal of pride in the USFL and I rooted for them always. I was sorry to see that the league was not making it. There were a number of things that the NFL did that made it tough on us. I don't think that there was any question that the NFL was guilty of antitrust violations as the jury found, but to say that there were no damages was ridiculous. I think that it was the judge's instructions to the jury that confused everyone and an appeal really should have been heard."

"I just remember being with Scott McGhee. The Generals and the Houston Gamblers had merged so Jim Kelly was on this team with all those wide receivers, Scott McGhee being one of those wide receivers," recalled Flutie. "We were all down in Houston working out, throwing every day and all of that. The lawsuit was finalized and was coming down to a verdict, and we won the verdict and I could remember all of us sitting in Scott's living room, 'We won the verdict!' Damages: one dollar, and the best the judge could do was triple it. The phone rings a little while later and Scott answers, 'Job search.'"

Aftermath

The decision left the United States Football League in turmoil. They had technically won the case, but that was not going to pay any of their mounting debts. With training camps set to open, the league had to decide if it was going to move forward.

The owners spent a tumultuous weekend sorting out their situation. They had waged one of the most famous and expensive court battles in sports history and had won a hollow victory. They had heard the guilty verdict read only to be followed by the insulting judgment. They had spent an estimated $200 million in three seasons and had already allocated $6 to $7 million on player salaries for 1986, not to mention their legal bills from the antitrust suit. Another season, this one without a network television contract, certainly meant tens of millions in additional losses. The league had scheduled its first fall season to begin on September 13, but several members of the ownership ranks questioned the plausibility of going on after the verdict. The owners met on Monday, August 4, for seven hours to determine what to do next. They realized that they stood to lose an additional $40–$50 million by playing without a network television contract. Following an emotional meeting, they decided they were in no shape to play in just a matter of weeks and voted to suspend the season. Before playing again, they would appeal the damages and try to force the NFL off one of the networks. The league announced its decision at a press conference later that day. Donald Trump did not attend the press conference that followed the meeting, reportedly because he had to attend a real estate closing.

"Because of the unbelievable impossibility of effectively playing pro football without a television agreement with a network, we are postponing play until the injunctive relief is granted or until the eradication of the confusion created by the $1 damage award," Usher stated at the press conference.

The Arizona Outlaws, Jacksonville Bulls and Memphis Showboats strongly wanted to proceed with the 1986 season. Though Arizona's Tatham tried until the end to convince his fellow owners to play, he understood the others' refusal. The Birmingham Stallions, Orlando Renegades and Tampa Bay Bandits also leaned toward going ahead with the season, but Trump and new Baltimore majority owner Stephen Ross stood firmly against playing. Since the ESPN contract stipulated that the league must have a New York franchise, Trump's refusal was enough to kill the season all by itself. Though he certainly could have funded his franchise through the entire campaign, doing so no longer served his purposes. He decided the Generals' best chance of survival was in the courts. When Trump and Ross refused to budge, the other owners realized they had no other options and the league announced the vote unanimous. The owners also agreed that they needed to activate the Chicago and Oakland franchises before playing again to increase their chances of garnering a television deal.

"I was talking with Steve Ehrhart and some of the guys, and I said, 'Look this next season is the season. Screw them. Let's play football. We're already down a ton of money, let's play the season,'" recalled Billy Tatham. "We knew the NFL was going to strike. Plus, they were now deemed to be an illegal monopoly as a matter of law. We got on the phone and we needed eight teams, and of course we needed New York. After many phone calls, we got seven guys to commit to another season, seven guys who actually had the money to do it. I remember Stephen Ross was to my left, he was the new guy in Baltimore, and Donald's sitting across the room. We're down to New York, and I said, 'Donald, let's just do it. Just one more year.' We argued back and forth and it got kind of heated. He said,

'Bill, I just can't do it.' I remember looking at him and thinking, 'You know what, I understand.' And that was it. That was the end of it. He had personally put himself out there so much. When it didn't work he took the personal, not financial, brunt, and he was just tired. He could have written the check to continue, but he was done."

"That was the most tragic decision that was made," Ehrhart explained. "This was even after the verdict, and there was debate about it. Myerson carried the day by promising that the appeals court would reverse the verdict or issue injunctive relief. Myerson led us down the wrong road. We just needed to keep playing. We had already pre-paid for a good portion of it, we got into the fall, and we were ESPN's only pro football.

"I think that was one of the worst decisions we made, when Myerson convinced us that we could go into hiatus instead of continuing to play through. He was going to win the appeal because he was so full of bullshit. The single biggest mistake was not the lawsuit and everything; it was the suspension of the play.

"Let's assume the fall decision was the right decision. We would have been positioned in all those wonderful markets such as Arizona, Baltimore, Memphis, Orlando and Trump in New York: all very strong organizations. We would have been in a very strong position in the fall. We positioned ourselves to do it, but then we didn't do it. It was sad."

"Where we fell apart was that Trump decided to not keep playing," agreed Gould. "I think it was through impatience because he may have had the proper vision, but he needed to keep playing. Instead, he filed a lawsuit against the NFL because of the antitrust relationship with the networks, which he was correct about at the time, but by not continuing to play, I think he hurt himself dramatically because when the jurors ruled and gave him a dollar, three for trebled damages, it was because one, we had spent a tremendous amount of our own money signing high visibility ballplayers, and two, we weren't playing anymore. Therefore, we were out of sight, out of mind, whereas if we had been in the front, signing players and playing, I think we would have been more viable and had a greater value."

"I remember being on the plane, flying back from New York after we shut it down, and I was sitting up there with dad," said Billy Tatham. "We had just ordered dinner, and I was a basket case. I'm thinking about what we were going to do in the morning. Let's figure out another way to kick the NFL's ass. The league had voted to go dark and launch an appeal, but I was still thinking it was a dumb ass decision to go dark. I was ballistic. I knew how much money my dad lost, and I'm getting more and more worked up. I stood up and walked around, all pissed off. My dad said, 'Listen, let me tell you the way you have to look at this. When I get off the plane in Fresno, I'll know that, yeah, we lost a lot of money, but we went for it and have a lot of good friends and memories. It's not going to change my lifestyle one bit. We're going to survive and move on.' I admired it and will never forget it. He was right."

With over 400 players still under contract to the league, the decision to suspend play for a year left them all in limbo. Coming off a 14-month vacation, the last thing that football players wanted to do was take another year off, particularly with NFL training camps opening up across the country. The owners were also understandably averse to paying them for an additional year.

"That's like their decision was to make no decision, and to just put everything on hold, which we've been on hold for over a year and a half," Doug Flutie complained to the Associated Press.

His mood brightened considerably on August 7 when, after 12 hours of negotiations, the league reached an agreement with the players' association to release nearly all players so they could seek jobs in the NFL and CFL. The clubs would maintain 10-player skeleton rosters and each franchise would retain USFL rights to all other players it released. Players with guaranteed or personal services contracts would have to get permission to talk with NFL teams, but would not be impeded from joining other leagues. While the USFL hung on to some stars in the interim in the hopes of obtaining payment from the NFL to buy out their contracts, others, including Doug Flutie and Herschel Walker were allowed to leave. "While I have a legal right to their services, I don't think I have a moral right to stand in the way of their careers," said Donald Trump in *Time*. When the USFL switched to the fall, players were given a choice of one-third of their salary or a $10,000 payment. The players could keep these payments as part of the agreement. Management at first wanted them to return the portion of their 1986 salaries already paid, but the players adamantly refused before management relented.

"How quickly I can get into training camp is the key to the rest of my career," Baltimore's Irv Eatman told *Sports Illustrated*. "I need to compete for a roster spot. The only thing I'm competing against now is insanity."

While many players made their way onto NFL and CFL rosters, several others were hurt by the timing of the court decision. The NFL was already midway through its training camps and the Canadian league nearly halfway through its season. Some would be able to fill in for injured players in the two leagues, but for many their dream came to an end. Having already sat out of action for more than a year, sitting out another seemed an impossibility. "I've got to start looking for another job," said Stars defensive back Jonathan Sutton to the Associated Press. "That's what it boils down to."

"If I miss this year, I'll be done," Baltimore nose tackle Pete Kugler told *Sports Illustrated*. "You've got to have a certain mind set for football. You get too soft if you don't play. It's hard to get aggressive again. If you're out in the real world too long, you start acting normal."

"I certainly wanted to help out as many of the Stars players as possible, help them get relocated and continue their careers since a career in professional football is generally pretty short," said Peterson. "So I set about doing that as quickly as possible. We had a lot of good players, players in demand by a lot of NFL teams and I was very happy about that."

"Since I made some good money, I don't have a vested interest in this comment, but I just really rued the fact that we lost all those jobs," Steve Young said. "They were guys that really loved to play. My memory of the USFL was that if you liked to play football that was your spot. The USFL seemed like guys who were really good players, maybe never really had that chance. You had the stars when they came out of college and so forth, but league-wide, the underpinnings of the league, were made by guys who had a passion for football."

With the season scrapped, franchises had to refund season tickets already purchased for the canceled campaign. New Jersey had not sent out renewal notices to its season ticket holders or printed tickets for that matter. Birmingham also did not sell any, but Baltimore had to refund payments for 9,500 season passes, Memphis had to do the same for more than 12,000 people and Orlando had to give back money for more than 4,000 tickets. The Bandits offered full refunds for their 5,000 ticket-holders plus 10 percent interest. Jacksonville and Arizona also offered refunds.

Falling on Deaf Ears

Judge Leisure denied the league's request for a new trial on October 2. Determined to exhaust its legal options, the league asked Leisure and the court for injunctive relief. The USFL wanted him to split the NFL into two distinct entities as in the 1960s when the NFL and AFL fought head to head, limit the older league to contracts with no more than two of the networks, or order the NFL to expand into ten USFL cities, including the surviving eight, Chicago and Oakland. Leisure declined the request later that year.

"We were retained by the league over Donald Trump's objection as additional counsel apart from Myerson, who was Trump's guy," lawyer Jeffrey Kessler of Dewey & LeBoeuf told "The AM Law Daily." "We tried to [get an injunction on the grounds that] the NFL had contracts with all three TV networks and use that as leverage to pull a victory out of a loss. But the judge said the record wasn't properly developed by Myerson at trial, so while we got an injunction, it wasn't the one we wanted."

In the October decision, Leisure attempted to clarify the jury's verdict. He stated that the jurors awarded nominal damages because they could not determine the amount the NFL had injured the USFL apart from the injuries that the younger league had caused itself through its own mismanagement. He stated the USFL had not shown the jury how much the NFL had hurt it in a concrete dollar amount and did not separate those damages from the injuries caused by other sources including itself. Thus, they had nothing to work with and were entitled to award any amount they deemed proper, even one dollar.

Leisure wrote in his decision on the appeal, "When a firm has committed a myriad of blunders in the marketplace and seeks to gain benefits through treble damages that it could not acquire through fair competition, neither juries nor courts should be condemned for obstructing such an effort."

With the league's legal appeals falling on deaf ears, the USFL's surviving teams completed their death throes. As the owners voted to suspend the 1986 campaign, the Hillsborough County Sheriff's office confiscated all the Tampa Bay Bandits' equipment, souvenirs and weights. Former Bandits safety Bret Clark had been awarded $150,000 in an arbitration case and the seized items would be used to satisfy that judgment. Spurrier and other Bandits employees maintained that Clark's contract should have been negated because Bassett had been very sick and not of sound mind when he signed the deal.

Even those who had displayed a positive facade throughout the legal process knew that they were seeing the league's final days. "We're very disappointed, but we realized this was a possibility," Steve Spurrier explained to the Associated Press. "It's sort of like having a friend with a serious illness and he finally passed away."

By March 17, 1987, Tatham admitted that his Outlaws would never play again and pulled out from any further appeals. He planned to continue work on acquiring an NFL team for Phoenix, but Bill Bidwell beat him to the punch when he moved the St. Louis Cardinals following the 1987 NFL season. In short order, the other USFL owners also threw in the towel.

The Second Circuit Court of Appeals in New York upheld Leisure's decision on March 10, 1988, ending the legal battle for all intents and purposes. The three-judge panel focused on Trump for leading the USFL to failure.

"The league, over the objection of some owners, expanded from 12 teams to 18 teams," they wrote in their decision. "Five of the original owners left the league. Some of the new owners, notably Donald Trump, believed the USFL ought to play in the fall.

Thereafter, the issue of when to play became divisive and several owners came to believe Trump was trying to bring about a merger that would include only some USFL teams.

"The NFL introduced extensive evidence designed to prove Trump's USFL merger strategy and that strategy ultimately caused the USFL's downfall."

"There was ample evidence that the USFL failed because it did not make the painstaking investment and patient efforts that bring credibility, stability and public recognition to a sports league," summarized Judge Ralph K. Winter in the 91-page opinion.

"I guess we died today," admitted Usher to *The Washington Post*.

Former Miami Dolphin star and Jacksonville Bull administrator Larry Csonka tried to revive the league with a plan to merge it with the Canadian Football League, and Usher floated the idea of a reincarnated USFL in 1987 when the NFL ran into labor trouble. Both plans amounted to nothing. Several dozen former USFL players saw action during the three weeks of 1987 NFL strike games, but that would be as close as the USFL would get to taking the field again.

Trump's Side

"Frankly, I would've been better off if I had just went in and bought an NFL team," Trump said. "It would've been a lot easier and it fits more with what I do, because I wasn't a big believer, as you know, in spring football. It had a little place but it could never be great."

In a subsequent book, *Think Big: Make It Happen in Business and Life*, he wrote of the USFL: "I thought it might be an inexpensive way into the NFL. I did not spend a great deal of money, and I gave it a shot. In the end I would have been better off paying up, going first class, and buying an NFL team. It is like buying Fifth Avenue real estate. It is the way to go. I learned something from that whole USFL experience—go first class!"

"If there was a single key miscalculation I made with the USFL, it was evaluating the strength of my fellow owners," he declared in his 1987 autobiography *Trump: The Art of the Deal*. "In any partnership, you're only as strong as your weakest link. Several of my fellow USFL owners were strong as hell financially and psychologically. Among them were Michigan Panthers owner Al Taubman and Philadelphia Stars owner Myles Tanenbaum, both of whom, coincidentally, had made their personal fortunes building shopping centers, as well as Memphis Showboats owner Billy Dunavant and Jacksonville Bulls owner Fred Bullard.

"Unfortunately, I quickly discovered that a number of USFL owners lacked the financial resources and the competitive vision to build the sort of top-quality league necessary to defeat the NFL. They shuddered at the prospect of any direct confrontation with the NFL, they were quite content to play in obscurity in the spring, and they spent much more time thinking about ways to keep their costs down than about how to build the league up."

"I knew the league couldn't compete with the NFL because of its monopoly," Trump maintained in *USA Today*. "I knew the USFL could not survive in the spring. I felt the lawsuit would be a winner. Had we stayed in the spring, we would have slowly bled to death."

"A lot of guys blame Trump, and I think that's nonsense," stated Billy Tatham. "The

NFL was putting us out of business. First, it's a brand new league anyway, which is really hard. The NFL went to Harvard, got their game plan, and they were executing it. They ran up the salaries of the lower end players to keep us from spending money on the big guys. They kept the networks from giving us a contract by threatening to pull off Monday Night Football, for example. They were executing these things perfectly, and it was killing us, which is why we won the lawsuit; we just didn't get the damages. We weren't sitting in a room with a billion-dollar television contract making bad decisions. We were dying at the local level and the national level and getting ridiculed because the flippin' NFL controlled the media, too! We were apologizing for losing $5 million."

Other owners shared the blame. "I don't think we can blame Donald," Jacksonville Bulls owner Fred Bullard told *USA Today*. "He was very vociferous from the start when it came to going to the fall, but we agreed."

"It's hard to tell what these guys really wanted out of this," Simmons said. "They wanted to make money? Well, they should have gone into a different business. They wanted the glorification of winning? Some of them won. They wanted their picture in the newspaper sports page? They could have gotten that anytime. They wanted to pal around with big-time players? They could have gotten that. That's easy for them. I don't know what came out of it. They looked across the street, and they saw the NFL with its huge success with big stadiums starting to be built and all this adulation to the best professional league in sports. Maybe that's what they were caught up in. I haven't the faintest idea. I wouldn't put a nickel against owning a professional football team unless I had all the money I ever wanted."

"If you were going to be an owner, you had to be prepared to keep reinvesting in the quality of your team and you had to be prepared to keep investing in the league," agreed Camera. "That started out as the biggest strength: good ownership playing in big-time stadiums with big-time coaches that would build the league. As it turned out, the owners were the ones that broke down."

Trump claimed he lost $22 million on the USFL and suffered a black eye from the well-publicized trial. He also saw his stadium project go up in smoke. He insisted that the jury felt sorry for Pete Rozelle and NFL attorney Frank Rothman, both of whom he saw as clearly overmatched by USFL lawyer Harvey Myerson, and that was the reason for the paltry $1 award. He surmised that the jury even went so far as to blame Myerson for what he saw the pair's pathetic performance. The very public defeat and a messy divorce preceded a financial downfall from which Trump would not recover for nearly a decade.

Others remained unconvinced by Trump's strategy. "The league really was pretty successful," countered David Dixon. "Our TV ratings were good, and our attendance was okay. We made two mistakes—expanding by as many teams as we did and the move to the fall."

"I would not say that Donald set out to intentionally subvert our program," said Taube. "I think Donald Trump believed in his heart of hearts that we were playing in the wrong season, that we would have a lot more leverage if we could move to the fall. I think his mistake in essentially selling that perspective was that he was dealing with people that didn't have his financial wherewithal to back up that kind of financial decision. And Donald Trump never really views anything with empathy in terms of how it might look through other people's eyes. He's just a guy that's programmed to go for it with his ideas. He's been very successful doing that in every endeavor. I mean he has done things in terms of getting permits to do things, in terms of zoning and gambling and other things that most people would have said he could never succeed in doing. So his personal view on that was devastating.

"You can say a lot of things about Donald, the Donald, but he wasn't suicidal, you know. The Donald did not intentionally pursue actions and decisions with respect to the USFL that he knew in advance would bring the league down. Rather he pursued things that he thought were in the best interests of the league, but he was wrong."

"His dream was to be in the NFL, and they didn't want him, so he got in another league and he was going to get in there with that league," Burt Reynolds added. "But he was taking a lot of people with him that were building their own house, and it wasn't an empire but it was a house and it was doing pretty damn good. I never got over the fact that I still feel and will always feel that his ambitions, his personal ambitions, were what sunk the league."

"I don't think there's any doubt that once the decision was made to move to the fall, it was the beginning of the end," Byrne agreed. "Basically it was over, because Philadelphia didn't want to wait, and they moved to Baltimore. The Michigan franchise folded, wound up merging with Oakland in California. And so you lost two of the top ten television markets at that time."

"Somebody like Trump doesn't care about family or happiness, as long as he's happy," furthered Simmons. "I don't believe he cares. There was only one thing that he wanted: he wanted to have a team in the NFL no matter how he got it, and he worked toward that end and it just fizzled. The league fizzled and it brought him along, and the only thing that he had to look forward to was suing them. 'I want to go play for them, but let's sue the bastards.' Now go figure that one out, because he didn't get his own way so now he's going to sue them."

"Donald Trump seemed to me that he may have been the reason why the USFL deteriorated and why they didn't win this case," judge Leisure concurred. "When I say that the USFL shot themselves in the foot, it's because they were moving to direct attack on the NFL for the fall season where they were established, and it also irritated the networks. The television networks were so important, and the USFL had contracts for their spring season. The networks themselves tried to accommodate the USFL when they wanted to compete, but I think it's the most important reason why the USFL failed was wanting to have a fall competition and therefore either merge with the NFL so that it'd became an issue of either getting damages from this huge case—over a billion dollars was being sought—or merging into the National Football League; and these things all came out during the trial discussions between Pete Rozelle and Donald Trump and others."

The Check

On January 19, 1989, Leisure awarded the USFL nearly $5.7 million in attorney's fees and other costs that the USFL owners had already paid Myerson's firm. Because the NFL had been found guilty in the case, they were liable for the USFL's court costs. The lawyer's joy would prove short-lived, though, as he was found guilty of double-billing other clients in 1992 and would spend five years in prison.

On March 15, 1990, with all its court options exhausted, the NFL finally ponied up and sent the USFL a check for $3.76, $1 trebled with interest. The NFL also had to pay the USFL more than $5.5 million in attorney fees and over $62,000 in court costs. The older league fought all the way to the Supreme Court which ruled that as the prevailing party, the USFL was entitled to have all its costs covered. As the last man standing, Steve Ehrhart collected the checks.

"After Harry Usher had moved back to California and there really was no league office, I got elected to be the chairman of the owners' committee which was charged with following up the business of the league and collecting the attorneys' fees and sending those out according to the formulas that we had all signed on to," he recalled. "That's how I wound up with the last bit of the business side of the league. When we had the hearing in New York, after the trial and after the appeals, this was a year later after the NFL had appealed the case all the way to the Supreme Court, I still had the documentation of what share Bill Tatham should get, for example, and who had put in what money as their share of the attorneys' fees. I received the check from the NFL through the courts and divided it up according to a formula. It wasn't an even split. We had agreed on a formula that took into account how many years you owned the team and how many years contributed to the league. It was on a unit basis and that was going to be our formula. If there was a settlement reached, it was going to be like the old ABA-NBA merger, we tried to pattern it after that, so we knew who got what rights. We hammered that out while we were still an active business because at the time some people said, 'I'm not going to support the lawsuit,' or, 'I'm not going to pay my share.' That's how I ended up with the final business."

While he distributed the attorneys' fees, Ehrhart did not cash the $3.76 check from the NFL. He remains its custodian and says that someday he will consider donating it to the Pro Football Hall of Fame.

9

The Last of Its Kind

The United States Football League saw more than ten million fans attend its 413 games over three seasons, played to national audiences on ABC and helped launch ESPN into its role as a heavy hitter in the world of sports television. Hall of Fame players such as Jim Kelly, Steve Young, Reggie White and Gary Zimmerman all played in the league along with three consecutive Heisman Trophy winners. Famous coaches with lengthy NFL resumes guided USFL teams, including a pair of Hall of Famers, and the league captured headlines from coast to coast in an incredibly short time.

USFL owners spent in excess of $200 million after playing three seasons, and in the end could not find a lasting foothold on the American sports landscape. After three seasons in the spring, the league had given up playing during football's traditional offseason. Its antitrust suit against the NFL, which had the potential to change professional football's future, had instead resulted in a slap-in-the-face $1 judgment.

"They just didn't give it enough time," said Infante. "You never know what could have been or what might have been. Had the league stayed in its form and performed for another two or three years, who knows? There might have been another AFL-NFL merger simply because of economics. You had enough guys like Steve Young who went on to have great careers in the National Football League."

"We had very good owners, but unfortunately we did not have the type of ownership discipline that would be necessary to operate profitably and to do the things that needed to be done," said David Dixon. "I don't want this to be misunderstood because we really had very good owners who I respected a great deal, but owner ego is the greatest enemy that any sports league has, particularly any new sports league because it means that people will not operate financially in a prudent manner. They will attempt to win the league championship because it bolsters their own purposes. That inevitably leads to paying too much for players, and that's what happened with the USFL."

"I supported Dave Dixon's idea when we started the league that if we have a premier player like a Herschel Walker, we could add a lot of attention and build our own stars," concurred John Ralston. "After all, the players that are on television and become household names are a product of what we had on the field. That would bring enough attention and create a lot of interest to where we could build attendance without having to raid the NFL players."

"We had some terrific ownership, guys like Eddie DeBartolo Sr., Alfred Taubman, Donald Trump, these are some guys of means," recalled Carl Peterson. "I think we made two strategic mistakes. One was expanding too fast. Secondly, in that ownership group, although there were some very well-heeled guys, there also were some weaker ones who really struggled.

"We had a gentleman's agreement, saying that we would all try to adhere to some type of reasonable compensation for players and each year we'll go out and get one or two marquee players who we think will be good for the league and your franchise. There were a few owners who exceeded that, and that put a lot of pressure on other owners. We see it here in the National Football League. That part never changes.

"The last aspect that really hurt us was deciding that we should move from the spring to the fall after only three years of building professional spring football. To declare that and then go to court head-to-head with the NFL, obviously the legal experts were correct in that we did prove that the NFL is a monopoly and were in violation of the Sherman Antitrust Act. They underestimated for the damages, though. The damages were practically nil, and that really sunk the league.

"I think we would have been better off to go with our original game plan to at least give it five years in the spring. Then we could see where we were at that time, see what franchises were thriving and successful, and then see what would happen from there. Lamar Hunt would tell you that some of the analogies of the United States Football League were very similar to the American Football League. They started from the onset to take the NFL on directly, and they had ownerships go under and some franchises had to move."

"I just thought it was unfortunate that we didn't have staying power," added Dick Coury. "Financially, some of the owners lost a lot of money, and I really felt bad for them. Had we stayed with the original concept to limit the amount of money we were paying players and keep the costs down, I think we would have made it. They all went into the league with the opportunity to make something out of it. It could have been very big. The caliber of football got better as we went along, and I think the owners would have gotten some of that money back had we been able to latch onto a better network TV contract."

"I don't know the master plan from all the bigwigs in the league," said Infante. "I don't know what their timetable was or how soon they wanted to put pressure on the NFL to play head-to-head with them. I thought it was a mistake and if we had given ourselves enough time in the slot we were in, with the way we were acquiring players and with the overall organization of the USFL, they had a great game plan. Money has a way of being hard to compete with, and some of the teams that had a lot more money to work with than others were driving some of the teams that didn't toward folding, and then you lose your credibility. It turned out to be a bad move. I honestly felt like the USFL was the best product outside the NFL that had come about in quite a while. The USFL had enough good players and enough name players, coaches and front office people to be around forever."

"The fact is we should have continued to play in the spring for a number of years and then maybe at some point in time, we should have had a plan to alter that strategy," said former Trump employee Jim Gould. "We probably altered too quickly. I think certain people got burnt out on it. I think Trump had a higher regard for people who don't mind taking on a higher level of competition. He wanted into the NFL clearly. Not that Bassett didn't, it was just that Bassett was prepared to get there through hard work and perspiration. I don't think that was something that Trump was ever going to buy into. It just wasn't going to happen."

Memories

The disappointment over the league's demise doesn't stop former USFL owners, administrators and players from looking back with almost universally fond memories. Even the men who lost a lot of money do not regret their involvement with the USFL.

"I'm very glad I did it," said Tad Taube. "I can look back and think of discrete moments when I could have, through the force of my personality, maybe forced some decisions that could have caused the whole thing to have a different result. I also learned a lot about being a public person and the visibility associated with owning a sports team, even a USFL team. It's unreal and scary at times. I still have people today when I take out my credit card to charge something at a store, who'll ask me if I was the owner of the Oakland Invaders. The amount of publicity and the amount of ink that this enterprise was able to generate in a very short period of time I think is unparalleled in any other experience that I've had. I don't think it can be replicated in the American business scene. I can't think of any endeavor where a startup became virtually a household word almost overnight. This attracted a level of attention that I don't think that any of us who were involved in it could have anticipated."

"The fun was in the challenge," Michigan co-owner Spivak told the Associated Press. "People, friends told me universally it wouldn't work. I loved that. We got the contract with ABC when everyone said the networks wouldn't deal with us. We got stadium leases, well-regarded coaches—we were making it work."

"It was really good," agreed Myles Tanenbaum. "A new restaurant opened in Philadelphia in late 1997, and I was there a week or two after it opened having dinner with my younger son. After we ended our dinner, the guy who waited on us said to me, 'Listen, I just wanted to tell you how much I enjoyed the Stars.' We had that kind of recognition.

"I remember one time being stopped by a police car for speeding a little bit in an area where the limit was something like 25, and I was going 35. The guy stopped me and told me what speed I was doing and so forth. I said, 'I was speeding. I'm sorry, I was going too fast.' Then he said, 'Okay, Mr. Tanenbaum, just don't do it again. I said, 'Gee, that was great officer.' He replied, 'Let's just say that I was a fan of the Stars.' That was four or five years after we played our last game."

"When my family and I talk about it, collectively and definitely from my standpoint, I look upon it as an experience that in a lifetime, very few people get," furthered Diethrich. "If I had the chance to repeat it, I'd do the very same things I did then. I don't look upon it at all negatively. For me, it was a wonderful experience in so many aspects. First of all, in dealing with professional football players, dealing with their agents, something I didn't do a lot of, but of course I was involved with some of those things. Being involved with the sports media was very interesting for me. Overall, it was a wonderful experience that I would repeat in a second."

"I think spring football proved it worked," said Taubman. "We had an audience; we had interest; we had the media interested. I think if the owners had been stronger and had they kept the original direction, the theme of how it should work, it would have been successful. It wouldn't be the NFL probably ever. But I think if they had kept to the budget, it would have succeeded."

"There's no question in my mind, none, that the concept of the USFL, which was really quite simple, was eminently viable," said Taube. "If I was 20 years younger, I'd go out there and do the same thing today."

"Overall, it was such a positive experience prior to the '83 season when we made the deal and through the '83 season," said ABC's Spence "Then things started to go south rather quickly from there. Our ratings started to go down in '84 and then again in '85. And there was Trump coming on board.

"It's just a shame looking back because I really do think that if the league had remained in the spring and we moved it to primetime, who knows, it might still be around today."

"They signed exactly the players that the fans wanted to see, exactly the players that TV would want, and they were on exactly the right track to either make it as a league because football has become the complete cultural dominant force in America, a bonanza," said player agent Leigh Steinberg. "Had that league simply stayed the course and continued playing in the spring and continued signing away top players it would not have taken them very many years to have either forced a merger, where the NFL would have tried to pluck off the top four or five teams, or simply made it as an independent league.

"The sadness of the approach they later took was that they in essence committed business suicide. They were growing a following, they had a television contract, they were way ahead in their first year or two of where the AFL had been. All the trends in terms of the components necessary to have a successful league were about to explode. They were sitting on top of a goldmine. The popularity of football was exploding. The need for product was exploding. The revenue sources, brand new stadia, fantasy football: everything was in their future. "

"We had a franchise here in Memphis that we operated just like an NFL team, first class in every way," said Ehrhart. "Billy Dunavant, the primary owner, ran this like it was an NFL team. We had signed five number one draft choices. We brought in Luis Sharpe who was the best offensive lineman at the time that I believe the St. Louis Cardinals had, to play with us. We signed rookies such as Walter Lewis and Reggie White. It was first class in every way. So we were ready to be an NFL team in Memphis for many, many years. Memphis had aspired to have a NFL team. On the other hand, we were very successful in the spring in Memphis. We had sellout crowds. People came to the playoff games. I still remember the sadness at the Liberty Bowl when Oakland Invaders receiver Anthony Carter caught the fade route to knock us out of the playoffs. There's a great feeling about what should have been and could have been, would have been, and that human element is so important that even today everybody talks about it. You can even see with me that the great, treasured time in my life was as part of the Memphis Showboats."

More Spring Flings

The NFL became intrigued enough with the possibilities of spring football that it launched the World League of American Football in 1991 with games airing on ABC and cable's USA Network. Apparently, oversaturation was no longer a concern when the NFL was running the show. Pushed largely by Cowboys president Tex Schramm, one of the USFL's biggest detractors, the hurriedly-assembled WLAF featured six American teams, one Canadian squad and three European outposts. The WLAF functioned as a fully sanctioned minor league with NFL team owners providing much of the financial support.

The American WLAF teams averaged just over 20,000 fans per game with their

European counterparts pulling closer to 30,000 average attendance. With only one major U.S. market represented in the league, ABC struggled with ratings which averaged a minuscule 1.7 over two years, while cable's USA Network averaged a 1.1 for league games, far less than half its initial projections.

Following year two, the NFL suspended the World League for the next two seasons following $23 million in losses since startup. The NFL owners folded the North American teams before re-launching the World League in 1995 with six European squads. In 1998, they changed the circuit's name to NFL Europe. After rechristening the league "NFL Europa" in 2007, new NFL commission Roger Goodell shut down the circuit following that season, citing losses that had grown to $30 million annually as the reason.

"Here's the irony, and it's not surprising," laughed Stars GM Carl Peterson, who went on to lead the Kansas City Chiefs front office. "We made this decision to leave the spring and go to court and of course never get to the fall. What does the National Football League do? In 1989 I come back into the league [the NFL] and they start something called the World League of American Football, which was a combination of domestic and international pro football *in the spring*. We went dark for a couple years and then restarted it 'NFL Europe,' the perfect place to develop young players or players who just needed some more time: Kurt Warner, Jake Delhomme, Dante Hall and Brian Waters, all Pro Bowl guys. They needed some place to develop, and we had that in the spring. It was a very good idea. It was just unfortunate that we had no patience and owners who wanted to move too rapidly."

"On a long range basis, if we [the USFL] would have maintained our existence in the spring, became very competitive, very visible, I think the NFL would have stepped in and made us an offer to be a minor league for them much like the World League," said former USFL coach John Ralston. "If the NFL would have been smart, they would have encouraged us and they wouldn't have gone to Europe and spent a heck of a lot of money fooling around over there. They could have cultivated our league, and if we're playing in the spring, it's at a different time and they could watch our players and sign some of them, bringing in a lot more football."

"One of the problems with spring football is that the public perceives, correctly, that the USFL failed," stated USFL founder David Dixon. "They don't see the reasons that it failed, but they perceive that it failed. Secondly, the NFL's World League, which was started to head off any other possible replacement spring leagues, was so poorly put together and so hurriedly put together that it was a dismal failure. So the public sees these two examples of the World League and the USFL, and I don't think that a spring league can ever be seen as a true major league and that is of course what we were seeking—a true major league, not a class B league or a class AAA league or anything of that nature."

With the departure of the World League from America, the ailing Canadian Football League placed new franchises in the United States. The CFL had struggled mightily in the 1970s and 1980s and had a particularly tough time keeping a franchise in Montreal, losing both the Alouettes and expansion Concordes. It had seen attendance erode throughout the league for more than two decades, and Commissioner Larry Smith felt that it had to expand into richer American markets to ensure the CFL's future.

The CFL's incursion into the U.S. in the 1990s proved to be a disaster. Between 1993 and 1995, the league based American teams in Sacramento; Baltimore; Las Vegas; Birmingham; Memphis; Shreveport, Louisiana; and San Antonio. Of the group, only Baltimore showed any long-term promise, but once the NFL announced expansion into Baltimore in 1996, the CFL's Stallions moved to Montreal and the CFL quickly retreated back north. The league's fortunes improved in the ensuing years thanks to television money.

Jim Foster, who had worked in marketing with the Arizona Wranglers and Chicago Blitz, launched a football league of his own. It had a unique twist in that it played its games inside basketball and hockey arenas on a playing surface one-quarter the size of a regulation field with nets strung to either side of the goal posts to keep the ball in play. He brought in Ray Jauch, former coach of the Federals, and Mouse Davis, formerly of the Gamblers and Gold, to help him with the project. His Arena Football League played for 22 seasons before falling to bankruptcy in 2009. After a year off, the league re-launched in 2010.

"I invented Arena Football in 1981 while I was promotion manager with the National Football League," he remembered. "I did that in Madison Square Garden while watching my first indoor soccer game on February 11 of 1981. I put that on the backburner when the USFL was announced because I didn't feel I could compete with that. I was still a young Turk, working my way up the ladder, and I wasn't prepared for the challenge of building my own football league. The idea of building a team was challenging enough. So when the USFL came along, I thought that it was a pretty good opportunity. While I was with Arizona, I made a lot of observations about the costs of outdoor football, of starting a new league and competition with the NFL."

He credited the USFL with allowing him the freedom to try several new marketing ideas. "We created some special VIP club sections and things like that which the NFL really hadn't done much of," he said. "We were kind of innovative in that area as far as football goes. Now I look back at some of the stuff we did and everybody does it. We were really left to our own innovations at the team level, and that was the exciting part of it for me—getting to do a lot of different things. There were a lot of things that we were able to do to try to drive the grass-roots marketing interest. Quite honestly, when I started the Arena Football League, we did the same exact thing, and we're continuing to do it."

Several other groups have attempted to launch new outdoor leagues with very little success. None of them competed with the NFL for players, making them *de facto* minor leagues. The Professional Spring Football League, for instance, came within ten days of its opening weekend in 1992 before folding under the weight of its bills and lack of television contract.

One league that didn't have difficulty landing a network television contract was the XFL, partly owned by NBC in a joint venture with Vince McMahon's World Wrestling Entertainment. The eight-team loop launched in 2001 with Saturday night games airing on NBC and other contests broadcast on the fledgling UPN Network and cable's TNN. Though full of bluster fueled by WWE's marketing machine, ratings tumbled on NBC after the first week, and an overtime game delayed an episode of network staple *Saturday Night Live*, shaking NBC's commitment to the venture. The brash McMahon used scantily-clad cheerleaders and several of his wrestlers to promote the league, including Dwayne "The Rock" Johnson, who delivered an anti–NFL rant prior to a game, but all ultimately to no avail. When a late season broadcast drew the worst ever rating for any primetime sports event on network television, the XFL's fate was sealed. After averaging a 3.3 rating over the course of the season, NBC declined to renew their deal, and the XFL died after just one year.

The United Football League, owned by former Oakland Invaders investor Bill Hambrecht, eschewed the spring when it debuted in October of 2009 with four teams. Like the XFL, it did not compete with the NFL for players, but fielded many with NFL experience. It illustrated the difficulties of playing in the fall by scheduling most of its games on Wednesday and Thursday nights, when pro and college contests are rare. Meager ratings on cable nets Versus and HDNet, complemented with equally abysmal attendance of well under 10,000 per game, created a $30 million loss after one year. After three more seasons, the last two of which it failed to complete, the UFL quietly died.

The NFL Surges

Meanwhile, the National Football League has continued to grow and reinforce its claim as perhaps the strongest professional sports league on the planet. That's not to say that everything has gone smoothly for the old league. Franchise shifts, both real and threatened, characterized the NFL during the latter part of the 20th century. After the Raiders moved from Oakland to Los Angeles and the Colts from Baltimore to Indianapolis in the 1980s, the Cardinals left St. Louis for Phoenix in 1988 and eventually became known as the Arizona Cardinals. Los Angeles was completely vacated in 1995 after the Raiders decided that Oakland wasn't so bad after all and the Rams jumped to a brand new domed stadium in St. Louis. The Houston Oilers left Texas in 1997 and completed a move to Nashville, Tennessee after a season in Memphis.

Finally fulfilling years of promises, the NFL expanded again in 1995 with Charlotte, North Carolina, and former USFL market Jacksonville, Florida, the lucky recipients. Snubbed by the expansion committee, Baltimore lured the Cleveland Browns, renamed the Ravens, to fill the vacancy created by the Colts. In order to complete the maneuver without tremendous legal obstacles, the NFL promised that the Cleveland Browns would return by 1999 through another expansion. The Houston Texans joined in 2002 to bring the NFL to 32 teams. The St. Louis Rams moved back to Los Angeles in 2016. In the end, St. Louis, Baltimore, Oakland, Cleveland, Houston and Los Angeles all lost teams only to regain them later. In each case, the NFL came back to either a new stadium or saw vast improvements to the old one.

Labor troubles became an increasing problem for the league. Another strike in 1987 caused the cancellation of one week of games before the NFL owners brought in replacement players. The so-called "scab" games counted in the standings, despite the strenuous and sometimes violent objections of some regular players and a few coaches. Though the quality of play fell predictably below NFL standards, the replacements, with many former USFLers in the mix, began to win over the fans during their three weeks of play. With the USFL gone, the union had no leverage to negotiate and a trickle of players returning to work turned into a flood. NFL owners forced the NFLPA to knuckle under and abandon the strike. Several players, including former USFLer Reggie White, decided to take matters into their own hands and sued the league for free agency in the early 1990s. The players finally won a limited free agency plan for the entire league.

The NFL has also steered its way through changes in its leadership following the USFL's demise. In 1989 Pete Rozelle ended his 29-year stewardship of the league. Under Rozelle, the league had grown from 12 to 28 teams and withstood challenges from the AFL, WFL and USFL. Franchise values had climbed from $2 million to between $150 million and $250 million, while its television pacts ballooned from under $5 million a year to more than $1 billion per season. Jim Finks, once a frontrunner for the USFL job, nearly succeeded Rozelle, but in the end the owners tabbed NFL lawyer Paul Tagliabue for the position. Tagliabue had been instrumental in convincing NFL owners not to settle with the USFL before the antitrust trial. He held the position until 2006 when he was succeeded by Roger Goodell.

NFL television revenues continued to skyrocket. The next round of contract negotiations won the NFL $4.35 billion over the life of the deals. The league brought games to cable television by featuring Sunday night battles on cable networks ESPN and TNT. Monday nighters continued on ABC, while NBC and newcomer Fox Network, which outbid CBS for the rights to NFC games, ruled Sundays. In early 1998, the grand old league further demonstrated its mastery over the networks by more than doubling its income from television in spite of falling ratings. Not content to be left out in the cold again, CBS outbid NBC for the rights to AFC games, while ESPN snatched the entire Sunday night lineup away from TNT. Fox and ABC quickly re-upped their contracts. Beginning with the 2006 season, ESPN began airing Monday Night Football, and Sunday night games moved to NBC, leaving only ABC without the NFL, as sister network ESPN took on a bigger role. In addition, the league formed its own cable channel, the NFL Network, which began broadcasting a slate of games in 2006.

The USFL did not succeed in its attempt to carve out a place for itself in the American sports scene, but the bitter recollection of the league's shortcomings is overshadowed by the memories it gave to its fans, players and administrators. The USFL provided quality football for three years; the first time a secondary football league had lasted that long in nearly a quarter of a century. It brought a new twist on rival leagues by playing in the spring, a time of the year previously untouched by professional football. The league placed its franchises in several communities that were either disdained, deserted or ignored by the NFL, and gave front office personnel, coaches and players alike an alternative to a monopoly.

Though the league had its share of detractors, even its most vocal critics could not accuse the USFL of being dull off the field. Numerous ownership changes, quick expansion, an almost equally fast consolidation, the wrenching decision over when to play its games and a billion-dollar legal challenge to the NFL kept the USFL in the headlines like no other rival league in any sport since the fourth incarnation of the American Football League in the '60s.

In truth, the league also had its share of excitement on the gridiron. At a time when many fans and sportswriters accused the NFL of providing dull football by teams all running the same plays, the USFL brought the professional game widely divergent teams in both their images and their styles of play. The Houston Gamblers and Denver Gold unveiled run and shoot offenses that made mincemeat out of secondaries throughout the league, while the Tampa Bay Bandits preferred to pull out all the stops and surprise the opposition with halfback passes and double reverses. On the other end of the spectrum, the Philadelphia/Baltimore Stars and the Birmingham Stallions opted to win not with finesse, but to dominate with power on both sides of the ball.

The USFL played some undeniably entertaining football, pushing the envelope where the NFL feared to tread. To keep things interesting, the Breakers welcomed play suggestions from their fans. "I prefer the crazy ones," Coach Dick Coury told *Sports Illustrated*. "I just figure, what the hell, I've called enough dumb plays—I can let somebody else call one." One fan's suggestion, dubbed "Crazy Spread Right," actually went for a long touchdown before being called back due to a penalty. New Jersey's Walt Michaels also used plays sent in by fans. "Trump Tower" used six linemen and a running back lined up 15 yards to the left of the center, two receivers out to the right and just the center and Doug Flutie in the middle of the field to take advantage of the quarterback's running ability.

"The NFL did such a powerful job of demeaning the efforts of all these people by putting the tag on it, 'It's a one-dollar league,' and that infuriated all of those people who had worked so hard," commented Ehrhart. "They put down the great efforts of people trying to create new jobs and to create entertainment and activity for people. It was wrong of the NFL to dismiss those efforts so cavalierly. And that was when the memory of the league really started going downhill because of the label. If the award had been, say, a thousand dollars, it wouldn't have changed anything dramatically except they would have taken that propaganda ability away from the NFL to parade their so to speak victory, although it wasn't really a victory. The NFL was found to have violated the law, so they had to pay all the attorney's fees, which was $6 million. I would have rather had the verdict come out as $6 million because then people would have said, 'Wow, USFL wins,' even though it wouldn't have changed anything from a practical standpoint. But the USFL only won one dollar. It didn't come out until months later that we had won $6 million in attorney's fees. So the infamous one-dollar verdict had so much negative perception, and perception becomes reality. Then the NFL could say, 'It's a $1 league, and it ain't worth a darn,' when it really was a wonderful endeavor."

"That's sad," agreed McVay. "It really is sad when you think of the money, the commitment, coaches, players, front offices, ownership groups: it was a lot that went into that. And the USFL had a real chance. The USFL could be alive and functioning at a really high level today. Unfortunately, we just couldn't quite push the ball over the goal line, so to speak, at the end. We were really close. We were getting models in place in cities, we were getting the marketing plans. Everything was starting to move in a little bit better direction. We just couldn't be patient enough and couldn't show enough restraint to make the decisions that needed to be made to give us a chance for long-term survival and success. But it was close. A lot of talented people came out of the USFL. Those were fun days, they really were."

Perhaps more than anything else, though, the contributions of its alumni are what sets the USFL apart from other rival leagues. Walt Michaels, who coached in the AFL, NFL and USFL said that the USFL was leagues ahead of the AFL in its formative stages.

"What I want people to take from the USFL is to kind of get rid of the notion that it was bad football or that it was subpar football," said Steve Young. "I can tell you, I went from the USFL to the NFL in about three weeks, 'cause I played that spring and then that fall I played in Tampa Bay, so it wasn't like I took a year and wasn't sure. I could compare and contrast very quickly. And the football I played in the spring was better than the football I saw in the fall on that team. Now I'm not talking about league wide, but I went to the Tampa Bay Bucs which was probably the worst team in the league. I could just tell you that the organization and just the football we played were better [in the USFL]."

"The quality of the play was always better than it was given credit for," said Stars coach Jim Mora. "It wasn't as good as the NFL, of course, but that takes time to develop."

The Proof Is in the Players

With the demise of the USFL, the NFL began its 67th season with a tremendous infusion of talent, perhaps the most it had ever seen in a single year. While some teams such as Dallas and Buffalo salivated to get a crack at the USFL's top players, such as Herschel Walker and Jim Kelly, other franchises continued to downplay the league's talent. "We're not looking for much help from over there," Cincinnati Bengals assistant general manager Mike Brown said in *Sports Illustrated*. "There are a half-dozen USFL players who will be stars. And a dozen or maybe a score who will be backup players. That's about what the impact will be. Not much." Brown, whose Bengals had been decimated by USFL defectors, had seriously underestimated the talent of United States Football League players.

"It really bothered me when I'd read an NFL coach, scout or general manager say something like, 'Well, the guys that signed with them obviously don't have the guts or the stamina for the NFL and we don't want them anyway.'" said former Washington Federals running back Craig James. "It didn't show much class on their part and I lost a lot of respect for a few of those people that said that." USFL players were eager to prove their detractors wrong.

"When you play, you improve," added Bill Kuharich who moved from the Stars front office to the New Orleans Saints. "Guys who came to the USFL got the chance to play."

Herschel Walker signed with the Dallas Cowboys, joining the great Tony Dorsett in the backfield. Even as he headed to the NFL, Walker continued to be one of the USFL's staunchest supporters. "Everybody looked down on us," he told *Sports Illustrated*. "That made us play *so* hard. The USFL was fun. It was what the NFL used to be. I'm not much for dancing, but I loved to watch the shimmies in the end zone, the high fives, the sack dances. The league where I'm going to now, you can't do that stuff."

Though injuries and splitting time with Dorsett hampered him in his first couple of years with the Cowboys, he broke out in 1987 with a league-leading 1,606 yards from scrimmage. The following season he topped the National Football Conference with 1,514 yards rushing, a total which landed him a spot on the league's All-Pro squad. The Minnesota Vikings made Dallas an offer they could not refuse the following year, and the Cowboys traded him for a pile of draft choices that they used to rebuild the franchise into a perennial Super Bowl contender. The Vikings, however, never used the runner effectively in his three seasons there and let him go to Philadelphia in 1992. In Philly he broke through for his second 1,000-yard season in the NFL. The Eagles also allowed him to showcase his talents as a dangerous pass receiver more than ever before and named him their offensive MVP in both 1993 and 1994. With his playing time decreasing with age, he volunteered to play on special teams where he also became a force. After a year back at the Meadowlands with the Giants, he returned to the Cowboys in 1996 where he continued to shine on special teams and as the team's fullback. He compiled over 13,000 yards from scrimmage and 18,000 total yards in his NFL career.

Three years after letting him slip through their fingers, the Buffalo Bills finally inked Jim Kelly. After back-to-back 2–14 seasons, the franchise needed all the help it could get. The quarterback had long held doubts about the Bills, even admitting that he cried on the day the NFL team drafted him. Kelly settled for an $8 million contract that covered five years. The citizens of Buffalo quickly forgave his negative comments about their city and team and embraced their new star. Average attendance at Rich Stadium soared to 66,476 in his rookie season, an increase of nearly 30,000 from the year before.

"The following year after the Blitz went out of business, Bill Polian was hired as a scout with the Buffalo Bills," recalled former Blitz coach Marv Levy, who later became the head coach at Buffalo. "I went back to work and broadcast USFL games. One day, I broadcast a game the Gamblers were playing down in Houston, and Bill Polian and Ralph Wilson came to that game and were seeking to woo him, so they asked me what I thought about him. I gave him one of the most sterling recommendations ever, not realizing that someday I would join him in Buffalo. I was very aware of Jim Kelly at that time."

Later with Polian as general manager and Levy as head coach, the pair would take Buffalo to four straight Super Bowls with Kelly at the helm.

Even without a full training camp, the quarterback immediately infused some much-needed excitement back into the Bills, impressing his teammates and opponents with his toughness and competitiveness. Although Buffalo finished the year at 4–12, he completed nearly 60 percent of his passes for 3,593 yards and 22 touchdowns with 17 interceptions without much of a supporting cast.

Kelly soon showed that Buffalo's faith in him had not been misplaced. He made the first of his five Pro Bowl appearances following the 1987 season and spearheaded the Bills' steady improvement over the next few seasons. By 1988, the club had improved to 12–4 and in 1990, they made the first of four consecutive Super Bowl appearances. In the course of redirecting the Bills' fortunes, he rewrote the team record book, breaking nearly every franchise passing mark along the way. He completed over 60 percent of his throws and compiled 35,467 yards with 237 touchdowns in 11 seasons. In addition to the quartet of Super Bowls, he led Buffalo to a 101–59 record as a starter with a 9–8 mark in the postseason. The gutty passer retired at the end of the 1996 season, much to the chagrin of Buffalo's fans and offense. In 2002, he became the first USFL player enshrined in Pro Football's Hall of Fame.

"I just enjoyed it because I knew the USFL made me what I was when I played in the NFL because we threw the ball 40 or 50 times," Kelly explained of his time with the Gamblers. "I understood that that was the platform that I took to get to where I was at and eventually the Pro Football Hall of Fame and to lead my team to four consecutive Super Bowl appearances. I knew that one of the major reasons I got to that point, was because of the USFL."

Injured for much of his senior season with the University of Miami, Jim Kelly took the USFL by storm, quarterbacking the Houston Gamblers to eye-popping numbers at the head of the team's run and shoot offense. Photograph by Jim Turner, from Anthony Nunez's collection.

Outlaws quarterback Doug Williams agreed to a contract with the Washington Redskins, settling for a spot on the bench behind Jay Schroeder. When Schroeder struggled with injuries and inconsistency, Williams filled in and kept the team afloat. The former Outlaw took over the starting spot in the 1987 regular season finale and guided the squad to playoff wins over the Bears and Vikings and into Super Bowl XXII. He suffered a knee injury early in the game but scraped himself off the ground in time to lead the Redskins to a record 35 points in the second quarter and a convincing 42–10 victory over the favored Denver Broncos. His then-record 340 yards passing and four touchdowns earned him Most Valuable Player honors for the game. Two of those touchdowns throws went to former Houston Gambler Ricky Sanders, who caught nine balls for a then-record 193 yards, and another went to former Jacksonville Bull Gary Clark. Williams went on to coach Morehouse College and then took over the reins at his alma mater Grambling following the retirement of the legendary Eddie Robinson.

Clark enjoyed a lengthy career, totaling 699 receptions for 10,856 yards and 65 touchdowns, most of them with the Redskins. Sanders, his teammate for many of those seasons in the nation's capital, ended his NFL career with 483 catches for 6,453 yards and 37 touchdowns. Former Star Kelvin Bryant also became a Redskin, but nagging injuries shortened his NFL career. Still, he enjoyed several seasons as a dangerous third-down back.

Former Michigan and Oakland signal caller Bobby Hebert competed for 11 NFL seasons, compiling 21,683 yards and 135 touchdown passes in seven years with the Saints and four with the Atlanta Falcons. Tampa Bay's Gary Anderson became a 1,000-yard rusher with the Chargers and eventually made his way back to Tampa in the Buccaneers' backfield. Former Federal Craig James improved New England's running game, and his 1,227 yards helped the Patriots gain a berth in Super Bowl XX following the 1985 season. Los Angeles' Kevin Mack became a mainstay with the Cleveland Browns, supplanting Earnest Byner, while Mike Rozier played for seven years with the Oilers and Falcons. Tackle Irv Eatman of the Stars went on to a long NFL career filled with Pro Bowls, while former Bandit Nate Newton proved peerless at the guard spot in Dallas. Centers Bart Oates (Stars) and Kent Hull (Generals) did the same with the New York Giants and Buffalo Bills, respectively.

Steve Young bought his way out of his mammoth Express contract for nearly $1 million. The "$40 Million Man" ended up making much less in two seasons with Los Angeles. Young struggled with the Tampa Bay Buccaneers. He did not start for them until the final five games of 1985 and had a tough campaign the following year before leaving for San Francisco. There he assumed a backup role behind Joe Montana. Beginning in 1989, he began to see more action as Montana's age caught up with him, and Young finally assumed the starting mantle in 1991.

Taking over for a legend, he flourished in the glaring spotlight. Young became the NFL's Most Valuable Player in 1992 and repeated the honor in 1994, the same season in which he led the 49ers to a 49–26 Super Bowl XXIX trouncing of the San Diego Chargers with a record six touchdown passes. He also captured MVP honors for his performance in the title game. He led the league in quarterback rating a record five times, including four times with a rating better than 100, another record, and continued to be a dangerous scrambler as well. All told, he finished eight seasons with a 100-plus rating, and reigned as the NFL's passing leader a record-tying six times. He retired in 1999 after being voted to seven Pro Bowls and being chosen first team All-NFL three different years. In 2005 he joined Jim Kelly in the Hall of Fame.

"I thrived under the challenges as you can tell," stated Young "I followed Jim McMahon, arguably the greatest college quarterback ever. In the future, I didn't see it coming, but I was going to replace Joe Montana. There's something about me that kind of thrives when something gets hairy. So I think the USFL towards the end got a little hairier, in some weirdly way, exciting, too. Like I said, 'Snap one over my head, and let's see what we can do.'"

Anthony Carter, the former Panther and Invader receiver, settled into a starring role with the Minnesota Vikings for nine years. The dangerous wideout finished his career with the Detroit Lions in 1995 after amassing 486 receptions for 7,732 yards and 55 touchdowns in the National Football League. He became the first Vikings receiver to gain more than 1,000 yards in three straight seasons. He is best remembered for his playoff-record 227 yards receiving in a 36–24 upset win over the 13–2 San Francisco 49ers in 1987.

Doug Flutie traveled a longer road to NFL stardom. The diminutive passer played in the NFL for four unspectacular years with the Bears and Patriots before joining the CFL's British Columbia Lions in 1990. In his second year in BC, he established league records for completions (466) and yards passing (6,619) in a season. Flutie then headed to the Calgary Stampeders where he won a Grey Cup championship in 1992. He signed with the Toronto Argonauts in 1996, and led the franchise to consecutive Grey Cup victories. Along the way, he captured an unprecedented six Most Outstanding Player awards, including four in a row, and was widely heralded as the greatest player in the long history of the Canadian league. His dominating performance up North earned him another shot at the NFL with the Buffalo Bills in 1998. He made the most of the opportunity, unseating the Bills starting quarterback and leading Buffalo into the playoffs in what was supposed to be a rebuilding year. His terrific play earned him NFL Comeback Player of the Year honors and a Pro Bowl berth. After three years in Buffalo, he played four seasons for San Diego before finishing his 13-season NFL career in 2005 with New England.

On defense, no one dominated the NFL in the late 1980s and '90s more than former Memphis Showboat Reggie White. Playing with the Eagles, Packers and Panthers, he blew past Lawrence Taylor to become the NFL's all-time sack leader and won a championship in Super Bowl XXXI with Green Bay. He collected 21 sacks in just 12 games during the strike-shortened 1987 season on his way to capturing league Defensive Player of the Year honors. He set a Pro Bowl record with four sacks in the 1986 game and then set a Super Bowl record when he dropped Drew Bledsoe three times in the Packers' Super Bowl victory. His addition to the Green Bay roster in 1993 helped their defensive unit improve from twenty-third in the league to second and finally to the best in 1996. Forsaking retirement, White topped the Packers with 16 sacks in 1998, his last season with the team. The performance earned him his second Defensive Player of the Year award. He returned after a year out of football for one season with the Carolina Panthers, bringing to a close his 15-year NFL career with 198 sacks. As the ultimate testament to his performance, the National Football League named him to their 75th Anniversary All-Time Team, the only USFL player so honored. White passed away suddenly in 2004, two years before becoming the third USFL player enshrined in the Hall of Fame.

Former Jacksonville Bulls tackle Keith Millard also captured a Defensive Player of the Year nod when he recorded 18 sacks in 1989 with the Minnesota Vikings. Pete Kugler returned to San Francisco to play five more seasons, while another member of the Stars, William Fuller, led a strong Houston Oilers defense for years before moving to Philadelphia and then San Diego. The Stars' Sam Mills and Jacksonville's Vaughan Johnson solidified the New Orleans linebacker corps into one of the best in the league. Mills went on to the Carolina Panthers, while Johnson played out his career in Philadelphia. Frank Minnifield, late of the Chicago Blitz and Arizona Wranglers, became one of the NFL's top corner backs with the Cleveland Browns.

Offensive tackle Gary Zimmerman, one of Steve Young's teammates in Los Angeles, joined the Minnesota Vikings where he played from 1986 to 1992 before moving on to the Denver Broncos from 1993 to 1997. He was named to both the 1980s and 1990s NFL All-Decade Team, rolling up 169 consecutive starts, eight first- or second-team All-Pro selections and seven Pro Bowl nods. In 2008 he became the fourth former USFLer, and second member of the Express, to be elected to the Pro Football Hall of Fame.

Several special teams players also signed their names into the NFL register. Roger Ruzek kicked for seven seasons for Dallas and Philadelphia, and Scott Norwood did the same for the Bills. Tony became one of four Zendejas's to kick in the NFL and lasted the longest, 11 years. Jeff Gossett and Sean Landeta were two USFL punters who went on to long NFL careers. Los Angeles' Mel Gray became the league's deadliest kick returner for New Orleans, Detroit and the Oilers, taking back six kickoffs and three punts for touchdowns in his career. Though not used as much as a receiver as he was with the Gamblers, Clarence Verdin also contributed on special teams, returning five punts and a kickoff for touchdowns in his nine-year NFL stint.

A pair of future Pro Football Hall of Famers took the field for the Los Angeles Express as lineman Gary Zimmerman protected quarterback Steve Young. Photograph by Wilf Thorne.

While some of the players seemed destined for stardom with or without the USFL, many of the league's players may never have received a shot if it had not been for the United States Football League. Generals center Kent Hull had played in a wishbone offense in college, so he used his time in the USFL to learn the art of pass blocking. Linebackers Gary Plummer and Sam Mills were two others who benefited greatly from playing experience.

Plummer played for two years at a junior college before transferring to the University of California. The anonymous Plummer was not selected in the 1983 NFL draft and instead signed on with the Oakland Invaders for their inaugural season. After three years of steady improvement in the Bay Area, he joined the Chargers in 1986 and played with them until 1993, starting 106 of 119 games over that stretch. He played four more years with the San Francisco 49ers with whom he collected a Super Bowl ring with Steve Young.

"We had severe trepidation about Gary because we thought he was too small,"

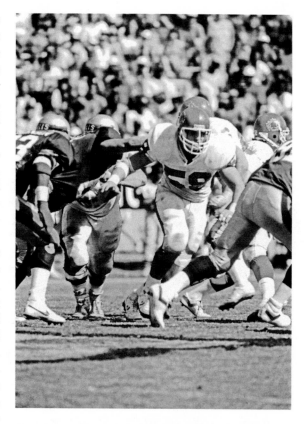

New Jersey Generals center Kent Hull proved to be a vital piece of the offensive line which cleared holes for Herschel Walker. He went on to play 11 NFL seasons with the Buffalo Bills, earning three Pro Bowl nods. Photograph by Jim Turner, from author's collection.

remembered Oakland Invaders owner Tad Taube. "He came out of Berkeley, very bright player, competed very well at the college level, but was completely passed over in the draft. I think when he came to us he weighed maybe a hair over 200 pounds. He gradually developed into a great linebacker, went over to the 49ers and became an even greater player. He put on maybe 50 pounds or more and became among the ranks of the top NFL players. He's a typical story of a player who had not matured sufficiently to qualify for the NFL when it was time for him to be drafted, and there are literally hundreds of those."

"We had so many players who signed into the NFL," said John Ralston, Plummer's first coach in Oakland. "Gary Plummer was one we changed from a nose guard to a standup linebacker. Every time I see Gary, he thanks me. I have a lot of pleasant memories. When you see the Gary Plummers and Steve Youngs of the world, you tend to feel good."

At 5'9", Mills, a linebacker out of Division III Montclair State College, had to constantly fight for respect at his position. One of the toughest fights was with the man who would coach him in the USFL and the NFL.

"I coached Sam for three years in the USFL, and then I had him for nine years with the Saints," said Mora. "I've said this many times, he's the best player I've ever coached, and I've been around a lot of good ones. Sam was short in stature, like 5'9" and a quarter, weighed 225. I remember we'd come in each night during our first camp, and Vince Tobin who was our defensive coordinator and linebackers coach, when I'd have him rank our linebackers, he would have Sam Mills at the top of the list. I remember looking at the guy, 5'9" and a quarter; he'd been cut by the Cleveland Browns a couple of years before and been cut by the Canadian team the year before that. I'm thinking, 'Well, now can we win with a 5'9" and a quarter linebacker?' I had some doubts, I had some questions. But once I started watching him in practice and saw what kind of a player he was, I was convinced that he could at least make our football team, the Stars. He ended up being perhaps our best overall player with the Stars, certainly our best defensive player, and we had the best defense in the league. Then I signed him with the Saints, and he ended up going to five Pro Bowls.

"He's the best player I've ever coached. All the things you look for as a coach in a player, all the assets, he had them all. He was something special, a very special person, a very special player. Yeah, I had some doubts. That's why he got cut by the Cleveland Browns; he was too short. He got cut by the Canadian team probably because he was too short. People always said he was too small. Well, he wasn't too small. He was a little short, but his lack of height in a lot of ways helped him."

"Sam Mills was a nemesis to a guy named Herschel Walker," added Peterson. "I remember a great goal line stand at Giants Stadium in a game between the Stars and the Generals. Sam Mills on three consecutive plays hit Herschel Walker trying to get in from like the two-yard line, and it was as if Herschel hit a fireplug, and he couldn't go an inch farther. I know that Herschel, the last time Sam hit him, didn't ask, 'How tall are you or what college are you from?' He said, 'That's one hell of a football player, and I just got my ass handed to me.'"

"His nickname was 'Field Mouse,'" recalled Hebert who played with Mills at New Orleans after facing him in two USFL championship games. "We went to Bible study every week, and he was a great man. One week we had played the Rams, and Eric Dickerson stayed over and came to our practice. He wanted to see who was this little guy who had knocked the crap out of him. He said it was the hardest he ever got hit. Sam was hiding behind the linemen, Dickerson thought he saw a hole, and Sam drilled him right in the jaw. Dickerson said he'd never been stung like that before.

"Pound for pound, Sam was unbelievably strong in his legs. He was Coach Mora's favorite. Coach Mora gave him a chance after he was cut by Cleveland, the CFL, and he did a terrific job for the Stars in Philadelphia and Baltimore and then with the Saints before he finished with Carolina."

Mills' career spanned 12 NFL seasons for the New Orleans Saints and Carolina Panthers. After playing under Mora in New Orleans, he joined former Stars defensive coordinator Dom Capers in Charlotte. Mills made five Pro Bowls, was an All-NFL selection three times in his career and became the first member of the Panthers Hall of Honor. After retiring as a player, he coached linebackers with Carolina for six seasons before succumbing to cancer at the age of 45. The Panthers erected a statue of him in front of their stadium.

Others players spent only a brief time in the NFL. San Francisco signed Showboats receiver Derrick Crawford after the 49ers had tried to buy out Crawford's contract for nearly two years. With the USFL gone, the team inked the receiver as a supplemental

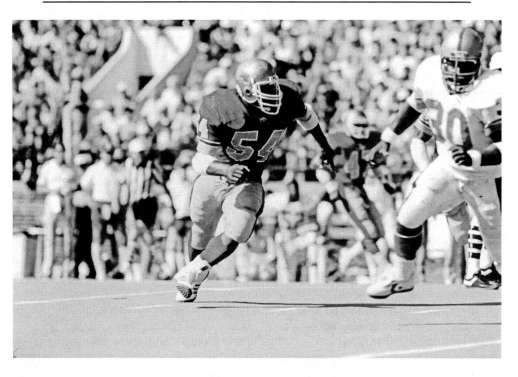

Jettisoned by NFL and CFL teams, diminutive Stars linebacker Sam Mills became a force in the USFL. Mills would later play 12 NFL seasons with the New Orleans Saints and Carolina Panthers, earning five Pro Bowl berths and four All-Pro nods. Photograph by Jim Turner, from author's collection.

draft choice without giving the Memphis owners any money. Injuries shortened his NFL career after a single season but he caught on in the CFL. Dallas similarly brought in former Birmingham, Washington and Orlando quarterback Reggie Collier for a short time. He stayed on as a backup quarterback for Dallas for a year and with the Steelers during the strike games of 1987. Many others such as the Stars' Chuck Fusina, Dan Ross of the Breakers, Kit Lathrop of Arizona, Birmingham's Jim Smith, Memphis' John Corker and Oakland's Novo Bojovic played sparingly as reserves for a short time. More than 150 others including Mike Hohensee, Rick Neuheisel, Stan Talley, John Reaves, David Trout, Marcus Quinn and Joey Walters saw action during the 1987 NFL players' strike.

About half of the 1,569 men who played in the USFL also played in the NFL at some point in their careers. All told, 211 USFL players, about a third of the season-ending 1985 rosters, went on to play in the NFL in non-strike seasons after they played in the USFL. An additional 163 players joined NFL rosters during the 1987 strike season. In 1986, 132 former USFL players finished the year on NFL rosters despite the late start most of them had in joining NFL training camps. By 1992, 55 former USFLers remained active in the NFL, not bad in a profession in which the average career lasts about four years. During the 1997 season, 13 years after the league played its last game, 11 former USFL players were still active in the National Football League.

"The USFL woke a lot of NFL people up to the fact that there were a lot of guys out there who could play football," Herschel Walker told *Street & Smith's Pro Football*. "When the USFL went under, you noticed that all the NFL teams ran out and signed USFL players. It wasn't like they didn't want us or didn't feel we were good enough. They knew these guys could play."

USFL alumni went on to make 60 Pro Bowl appearances, captured two NFL MVP awards, three Defensive Player of the Year nods and two Super Bowl MVP honors. Four players who began their careers in the USFL have been inducted into the Pro Football Hall of Fame.

"The USFL gave me an opportunity to stay hungry. Not only stay hungry, but it gave me a place to eat," said Harry Sydney who would go on to play six seasons in the NFL with San Francisco and Green Bay. "If it hadn't been for the USFL, I never would have made it to the NFL because I couldn't stay sharp. I had to constantly work out, constantly chase the dream. If it wasn't for the USFL, what would I have been chasing? That's what it did for a lot of people. It gave guys the opportunity to keep their dreams alive."

"Having been in pro football for most of my life, I know you have to have a quality product," added Peterson. "You can't fool the public; they know what they're seeing. What they saw with the USFL was damn exciting, quality football. Every team was starting 11 guys on defense, 11 on offense and 11 on special teams that had been starters at their respective schools, and many if not most of them at Division 1 or 1A schools. It was quality. Sprinkled in were guys who were either finishing their careers or just needed more time and the right opportunity, and you saw some really good football."

"Seven years after the Express folded there were still 12 players from that team playing in the NFL," added *Los Angeles Times* reporter Chris Dufresne. "And they weren't chumps, either. Two of them, Steve Young and Gary Zimmerman, the offensive lineman, are in the Hall of Fame right now. You had Mel Gray and Kevin Mack who made a couple Pro Bowls with Cleveland."

"We had Kent Hull at center, a perennial Pro Bowler for the Buffalo Bills, Herschel at tailback, a Pro Bowler, Maurice Carthon at fullback, a Pro Bowler, guys at linebacker, defensive backs all that jumped to the NFL right away," recalled Flutie.

Like Flutie, Henry Williams earned his fame north of the border in the Canadian Football League. There he became one of the most dangerous punt returners and receivers in the CFL. Known as "Gizmo," a nickname given to him by Reggie White during their days with the Showboats, he played a season with the Philadelphia Eagles before moving on to a starring role with the Edmonton Eskimos. In just over a decade with the Eskimos, he broke the league record for all-purpose yardage gained in a career.

Many others never received another shot after the USFL folded. NFL clubs remained cautious, and CFL teams were hindered by their league's limit on the number of non–Canadians who could be on their rosters. Oakland's Fred Besana returned to his beer distributorship, while Jacksonville's Brian Sipe took the advice of his doctors and retired from football altogether. Tim Mazzetti learned the real estate game from Breakers owner Joe Canizaro. Luther Bradley, Walter Lewis and many others were not able to crack an NFL roster after the USFL's demise.

For some players the USFL was a place to cut their teeth, to learn the pro game from Hall of Fame coaches such as Sid Gillman and George Allen. For others such as Brian Sipe and Cliff Stoudt, it was a chance to prove that they could still play the game. And for still others such as Joe Cribbs, it was an opportunity to earn more money and play closer to home. For everyone, it was a much different place to play than the NFL.

"I'll miss what the USFL gave to me—what it gave everybody who played in it—so much confidence, excitement, freshness," Birmingham's Cliff Stoudt, who caught on with the Cardinals, Dolphins and then Cowboys, told *Sports Illustrated*. "For seven years I was a backup in Pittsburgh. I wasn't sure I could be a starter. Now, I know I can."

"Playing in the USFL was great," Reggie White wrote in *In the Trenches*. "I've never experienced anything like it in the NFL (though playing for the Packers comes close in many ways). It was a much less strict and structured place to play football. One reason the USFL was such a fun league to play in was that it was run by football people, not by accountants and lawyers like today's NFL. It was a warm, congenial, *family* atmosphere. Our entire team, players and coaches alike, were a family. In fact, we included our families in many of our team activities. As a team, we ate together, practiced together, and even spent leisure time together."

"I was cut by Seattle," said Harry Sydney, who later played with the 49ers and coached at Green Bay. "At the time, I was the leading rusher in the preseason, and I think I was the leading scorer and playing on special teams. But the numbers got me. I went to Cincinnati and got cut again. I was the backup fullback, and they only wanted to keep one fullback. Then I went to the USFL. The USFL gave me a chance to put film together and face competition. By the time I was a 27-year-old rookie at San Francisco, I had played for three years. I wasn't making the rookie mistakes. I had already had the chance to go through training camps and all those things.

"I have great memories. I got a chance to play football and do some things that I knew I could do and show some people. It's amazing how God works things out. I could have played in the USFL for three years or not played in the USFL and gone to another team. After I played in the USFL, I went to San Francisco and won a couple of rings as a player and then another as a coach at Green Bay."

"The USFL never got the credit that it deserved," Mora said. "The NFL didn't want to recognize it. The media didn't give it the credit that it deserved. There were a lot of good football players in that league, and that was proven by the number that went on to have very, very successful careers in the NFL. There were really good coaches, good administrators, and it was a lot better league, a lot better quality of competition, quality of players and quality of football than it got the credit for during its three years, by far."

"The quality of the players that we were able to attract didn't really surprise me," added Stars GM Carl Peterson. "One of the things that we had going for us was that we were professional football but playing in the spring. For young players drafted after finishing their college careers in December or January, it was an opportunity to take the first bite out of the apple in the USFL because we started in the spring. We had our draft in January.

"I think Ara Parseghian said it best when he talked to Myles. He felt, and I felt the same way, that there's an awful lot of football talent out there every year. We only draft 210–250 picks, of whom about 50 percent make it. There's almost 5,000 college seniors that play college football at all levels—NCAA division I, II, III, IA, NAIA division I and II. Talent is where you find it. Then you have to have the ability and the coaches to develop it. We made a concerted effort in our league to try to attract the top college talent each year we were in existence, and we were able to do that with a lot of talented players.

"Our first couple picks were Irv Eatman and Bart Oates. They played all three years for us and were outstanding and then went on to long careers in the National Football League. Lots of talented guys like Gary Zimmerman whom we've seen every year at Denver played for the Los Angeles Express. You can go on and on. There's a lot of talented players, coaches, scouts and administrators who started in the USFL. I wasn't that surprised. It was a lot of fun and excitement. We had a lot of fine players in the league, that I thought made the game exciting."

"I always thought we were better than the media made us out to be," Mora told *Street and Smith's Pro Football*. "But I didn't think we had as many good players as it turns out we did. I didn't appreciate how many good players we had until they came to the NFL and played so well."

Though he had last appeared on an NFL roster more than a year earlier, former Philadelphia and Baltimore Stars punter Sean Landeta announced his retirement from the NFL on March 6, 2008, exactly 25 years after he made his professional debut for the Stars. He became the final USFL player to say goodbye to his playing days.

The Coaches

The coaches of the USFL also found their share of success. When Jim Mora took the head coaching job at New Orleans in 1986, the team had never experienced a winning season and had not been to the post-season. He led the Saints to five winning seasons and their first four playoff berths. He used several USFL players to accomplish the feat, including quarterback Bobby Hebert, tackle Chuck Commiskey and linebackers Vaughan Johnson and Sam Mills. He assumed the top spot of the Indianapolis Colts in 1998, replacing Lindy Infante, and led the team to the playoffs in his second season with the franchise.

"The USFL was just a special time because it was my first time as a head coach in professional football, and the opportunity to be with the people we had was great," he said. "Just what we went through: getting the job late, hiring coaches I'd never even met before, hopping on a plane and flying down to Deland for our first staff meeting the night before our first practice, it was fun, the whole experience. And then the last year with the move and getting kicked out of Veterans Stadium halfway through the season, struggling through the season and then ending up winning it, that was great.

"We had some success in New Orleans when I was there. I took my whole staff to New Orleans with me. New Orleans had never had a winning season until our second year there. They had gone 20 years without a winning season, and our second year there we won 12 games and went to the playoffs. That was fun, too, because we went into a situation in New Orleans where the fans were very hungry. You can imagine, they're an emotional people anyway, and we had success there, so that was a big part of my career. Same thing in Indianapolis. The first year we go 3–13 with a rookie quarterback in Peyton Manning, and the next year we win the division and win 13 games. But the USFL was just a special time. It ranks right up there toward the top."

Not only did Mora right the ship in New Orleans and Indianapolis, but two members of his Stars staff also landed head coaching jobs in the NFL. Defensive backs coach Dom Capers headed up the expansion Carolina Panthers beginning in 1995 and led them all the way to the NFC championship game in only their second year of play. He went on to become a highly-respected defensive coordinator and the architect of a Packers defense which won Super Bowl XLV. Stars defensive coordinator Vince Tobin took over the head job with the Arizona Cardinals the following season and coached them to the playoffs in 1998, their first such berth in a non-strike year since 1975. Their general manager with the Stars, Carl Peterson, went on to direct the fortunes of the Kansas City Chiefs for 20 years, turning the franchise into a perennial league power throughout the 1990s and early 2000s.

"For myself, the greatest thing I learned was the importance of sports entertainment marketing," said Peterson. "I'm a football guy. I came into the NFL as an assistant coach with the Eagles. I coached at UCLA and as a head coach at California State University before that. In the USFL, I had to learn the importance of our game as entertainment. I admire what the NBA has done behind David Stern. I remember when the NBA franchises were literally on their heels, and now I look at where they are today. We can't ever forget that we're in the sports entertainment business, and that there's only so many discretionary sports entertainment dollars. What are you going to do with your product to make it such an exciting, entertaining experience that your fans want to come back over and over? And that can't be based solely on the old, archaic idea that if you win, they'll come, and if you don't, they won't. That's a very foolish thing.

"Frankly an awful lot of things that I learned in the USFL, I applied when I came to the Chiefs in 1989. They had been down for 17 years, and I used a lot of the things I had done in the USFL, and they helped us resurrect this franchise from 25,000 season tickets to a self-imposed 72,000 cutoff. We had an average of probably 35,000 paid in a 78,000-seat facility to 60 sellouts and leading the league in attendance the last four years. I brought a lot of people with me from the USFL, and they understood what it took. For myself, I only look upon my time in the USFL with fond memories, as a lot of fun, and a terrific learning experience."

Former Gamblers boss Jack Pardee became the head man of the Oilers in 1990 and kept the run and shoot operating in Houston. With quarterback Warren Moon pacing the offense, he led the team to four straight playoff appearances and later became the only head coach in the short history of the CFL's Birmingham Barracudas. Former Gamblers and Gold assistant June Jones later became the leader of the Atlanta Falcons and San Diego Chargers.

New Orleans Breakers offensive coordinator Jim Fassell assumed the reins of the New York Giants in 1997 and guided them into the playoffs in his first year. Even the Orlando Renegades made a contribution to the NFL head coaching ranks when former Orlando receivers coach Steve Mariucci took over for George Seifert at the helm of the San Francisco 49ers in 1997 and led them to four playoff berths. He later coached the Detroit Lions.

Jacksonville's Lindy Infante was named head coach of the Green Bay Packers in 1988. The following year he captured Coach of the Year honors by guiding the club to a 10–6 finish after a 4–12 record the year before. He later coached the Indianapolis Colts.

"I was quite lucky actually," laughed Infante of his post–USFL career. "Marty Schottenheimer came calling and offered me the coordinator job with Cleveland. That year we ended up going like 12–4, and the year after that 12–4 and went to the AFC championship game twice, and some people felt I knew what I was doing a little bit. From there I got hired by the Green Bay Packers.

"I don't know if I'd ever have been offered the head job in Green Bay if I had not been a head coach before that. I think that had a bearing on me being able to compete for and land that job. I was lucky enough that when I left Jacksonville I had head coaching experience that I could tack onto my resume. Then I had the chance to work with Mary Schottenheimer and his people, and that gave me some more credibility. It was a step for me to get to the head coaching positions that everybody strives for in the business. To me, it was a good decision. Not that leaving Cincinnati was good because at that time we had gone to the Super Bowl and been to the playoffs once. It was hard for me to leave there because I really enjoyed the guys I worked with there as much as if not more than any other group of players since. Kenny Anderson, Chris Collinsworth, guys like that, I had a great experience there. But it was the right step for me to take at that time.

"It was a good, healthy experience. I think it was a legitimate challenge, and I've said that over and over whenever the subject comes up. It was a bold step in a good direction. It's amazing how often somebody comes up and say, 'Oh, yeah, you were the head coach of the Jacksonville Bulls,' and then start talking about the Bulls."

Former Blitz head man Marv Levy replaced Hank Bullough (who would have been coach of the Pittsburgh Maulers in 1985) in Buffalo during the 1986 campaign. With Jim Kelly at the helm, he led the Bills to four consecutive Super Bowl appearances and compiled an 11–8 mark in the post-season. The NFL named him AFC Coach of the Year three times and NFL Coach of the Year in 1988. He retired from coaching in 1997, and later served a two-year stint as the Bills general manager. Levy was inducted into the Pro Football Hall of Fame in 2001, joining fellow Chicago Blitz coach George Allen in the Hall.

"The USFL really resurrected Marv Levy, because I think he was doing color commentary for the Montreal Alouettes at the time," Blitz PR man Don Kojich said. "He went from being, I don't want to say on the scrapheap, but he was on the fringe. He came to the USFL and coached a year. Bill Polian went to the Buffalo Bills and when they made a change, Marv went in and they built a dynasty."

"Chicago is where I really got close with Bill Polian and John Butler," added Levy. "I was back in my hometown which I did enjoy very much. It kept me coaching and meant that I was only out of coaching for one year when I came back to Buffalo, not three which is when people begin to say, 'He's been out of it too long.' I think it did make a difference. I look back at it with mostly fond thoughts."

Tampa Bay's Steve Spurrier eschewed the pro ranks at first, opting instead for a college job. He went back to Duke University for three years starting in 1987 and captured Atlantic Coast Conference Coach of the Year honors his last two seasons there. He took the head coaching job at the University of Florida in 1990, the same school for which he had played when he won his Heisman Trophy. In 1996, he led the Gators to the pinnacle of college football and the national championship with a 52–20 win over arch-rival Florida State. His explosive teams at Florida won six Southeastern Conference titles and never finished a season ranked worse than thirteenth in the nation. He went on to coach the Washington Redskins for two years before becoming the head man at the University of South Carolina.

"The USFL helped give me an opportunity to be a head coach and experiment with the offense a little more," he said. "I didn't have a lot of people telling me you can't do this or you can't do that. College coaching jobs weren't lined up waiting for me when the Bandits shut down. The SEC was still a run-first, pass-second conference, and it was that way until about 1990. Fortunately, the Duke job opened up, and I still had friends there. Again, I took the job without knowing what I'd make. I asked, and they said, 'The last guy made $74,500, but we're going to bump you all the way up to $75,000.'"

Many other USFL coaches found work as top NFL assistants. Arizona's Doug Shively became a defensive coordinator with the Tampa Bay Bucs and Atlanta Falcons, and San Antonio's Jim Bates became one of the NFL's top defensive coordinators and served as the interim head coach of the Miami Dolphins in 2004. The Invaders' Charlie Sumner returned to Oakland as the Raiders defensive coordinator in the late '80s, and Oklahoma's Woody Widenhofer also rose to become a defensive coordinator with the Detroit Lions. The Breakers' Dick Coury coached in the NFL until 1999, including a stint as the offensive coordinator with the New England Patriots. Pittsburgh's Joe Pendry served as offensive coordinator of four NFL clubs, while Michigan's Jim Stanley served as an assistant with Tampa Bay and Houston before moving into Arizona's personnel department where he helped turn the fortunes of the ailing Cardinals.

USFL front offices also had their impact on the football world. Former Blitz personnel man Bill Polian became one of the NFL's legendary general managers with the Bills, Panthers and Colts, with whom he won a Super Bowl title. Stars GM Carl Peterson directed the fortunes of the Kansas City Chiefs for 20 years. Memphis' Steve Ehrhart and Tampa Bay's Jim McVay went on to lead the fortunes of college football bowl games. Jay Wright, a member of the Philadelphia Stars marketing staff in 1984, carried the team's championship pedigree over to an entirely different sport when he coached the Villanova Wildcats to college basketball's championship in 2016.

Stephen Ross, who bought the Baltimore Stars from Myles Tanenbaum after the move to the fall, became the first USFL owner to buy an NFL franchise when he took control of the Miami Dolphins in 2008. Donald Trump was outbid in 2015 when he attempted to buy the Buffalo Bills and instead turned his attention to politics.

Looking Back

"I just look at it as a pioneer," said Hebert. "If you ever talk to the old AFL guys from the early '60s, it's just like a pioneer who enabled professional football to grow for players and coaches and fans, promoting the game of football.

"What I'm most proud of is I know the USFL was legit. It wasn't NFL Europe; it wasn't a developmental league; it wasn't AAA baseball. If you look at the rosters of all the teams, at every position there was a USFL player who became a top player."

"The best way I can describe it was a bunch of talented, class people who just loved the game," said Breakers kicker Mazzetti. "Quite frankly, I don't believe enough credit is given to the USFL, but I truly believe in my view, and I'm not saying this because I played in the USFL, I think they were a large contributor to the true free agency market that exists in the NFL today because they were the first league that really gave the NFL a run for its money and did a good job of taking away some really high caliber players. 1985 was the last year, and the NFL had a strike in '87 and by '90, '91 basic salaries just went through the roof. The USFL really established the groundwork that gave people the feeling that the NFL could not continue to run indentured servitude forever. When I was traded from Atlanta to Cleveland and went up there and said I really don't want to play there, they told me that if I didn't play there, I didn't play anywhere. It was like, what country do we live in? They really believed that they owned you. I always had a problem with that. That was always the issue with the NFL, where I did not get that feeling with the USFL because it was a lot more casual. Whenever I look back, the memories are just good, they're just fun."

"I think all of us are proud of that short-lived league; the enthusiasm and the excitement," Peterson said. "When practice would end, Jim Mora would say, 'Gentlemen, I need your attention.' Everyone was riveted. In the National Football League I've had some great football coaches that I've hired—Marty Schottenheimer, Dick Vermeil, Herm Edwards and so forth. I've seen the coach a thousand times bring the guys together and say, 'I want your undivided attention' or 'I want to talk with you,' and there's always some guys in the back pulling the tape off or can't wait to get to the locker room and hit the shower. In the USFL, at least with the Stars, that wasn't the case. They were riveted on what we were doing and committed and focused. That's what really stands out to me."

"I enjoyed coaching and working with some young men who knew they had an opportunity," agreed Infante. "They weren't being paid like many of the NFL players or even some other players in the USFL, but they were fun to go to work with and be around because they were interested in learning. They were having fun. It was a fun time for a couple of years to coach young men who were very interested in what you were teaching. We all knew they were trying to get good enough to move on, but at the same time they were working hard and learning and being good people, and they were fun to be around. I really enjoyed that about that time frame in my coaching career. They were hungry. A guy would come to work, and he wanted to know how he could get better. He wasn't coming in to see if he could make an extra buck or something like that. I thought that was fun to be around."

"To this day you can still see the owners and the players and the coaches in this league, I mean, we all have a certain camaraderie," Argovitz explained. "We came; we fought; we did everything we could do to establish opportunity in a great sport, football, which we all loved. And I think we provided the fans with a great deal of entertainment and cities which didn't have football at that time. Everybody at the time came out better for it except the owners."

"Reggie White and I talked for years until he passed away, talking about the USFL days," Steve Young recalled. "I never remember talking to someone in the USFL who played then and wasn't proud of it. I never sensed it was like, 'Oh yeah, I don't really like to talk about that.' Everyone was very proud of the fact that they played in the league. So I think that says something."

"It was three of the best years of my life," added Dunek. "Myles Tanenbaum said, 'I lost $6 million on the Stars, and it was the best three years of my life.' If you talk to any of the people who went on to great success in the NFL whether it was Vince Tobin or Terry Bradway, who went on to become the general manager of the New York Jets after he was a scout with the Stars, to Carl Peterson, so many of the players who played in both leagues, they almost to a person all say their best three years in football were those three years with the Stars."

"I had a blast," added Jim Kelly. "When you talk about going out and having fun, I don't think I ever had that much fun. Yes, I did have a lot of fun in Buffalo because we became a family, but I don't think there's any doubt I had fun in that offensive scheme with Mouse Davis, June Jones and John Jenkins. We had a bunch of minds who knew the game and knew that style of offense. I loved it, too. I bought in, and I had a blast."

"I'm glad I did it; I'm glad I was a part of the USFL, great memories," concurred Craig James. "It's a small fraternity. Every time I see someone around the country who was a part of it, from front office to players, you all feel like you were part of the same fraternity, so I'm glad that I did it."

"What we went through, it just doesn't happen often," said Gould. "I'd say it was remarkable in its creation. It was particularly unique in that it was ever able to play a game. The fact that it lasted more than a couple years was unbelievable.

"I think that to a degree, nobody for a while at least knew whether it would sustain itself. So while we were up and running, it was one of the most exciting things I've ever done. It was like watching the final seconds of the Kentucky Derby over and over again. You had to pinch yourself, 'Whoa, we're actually there?'"

"Great players, good people and everlasting friendships," said Stars running back David Riley. "It was a blessing."

The End of the Competitors

The United States Football League proved to be the last legitimate attempt to establish a true major league in one of America's big four sports of football, hockey, basketball and baseball. Though competing circuits had been a part of the professional sports landscape virtually since players began drawing paychecks, the USFL became the last of its kind.

In baseball, the National League fought off a challenge by the American Association, ending in 1891 with four AA teams joining the NL. The rival Players' League, formed to gain greater rights for players, folded after just one season in 1890. The American League began major league play in 1901, reaching an agreement with the NL two years later to form Major League Baseball. Partially because of baseball's antitrust exemption, the Federal League of 1914–15 was the last alternative major baseball league to take the field. MLB headed off the start of the Continental League in 1960 by expanding into several of its proposed markets.

The death of the Continental League, however, proved to be the dawn of an era of competing leagues in other sports. In 1967, the National Hockey League added six-teams to its long-time six-team lineup to fend off a potential challenge from a western league. From 1972 to 1979, the World Hockey Association stood as another major league before four of its teams agreed to join the NHL and the league ceased operations.

The National Basketball Association grew in 1949 from the Basketball Association of America when it took on teams from the National Basketball League. The accommodation helped it outlast the first American Basketball League, and the NBA withstood a challenge from a second ABL in the early 1960s. The American Basketball Association proved more problematic, playing eight seasons from 1967–1968 to 1974–75 before the NBA absorbed four of its teams.

In football alone, the NFL had seen six major challenges to its supremacy in just over six decades before the USFL's formation. But the landscape changed dramatically as the established leagues and their television partners moved to quench America's seemingly insatiable thirst for professional sports, leaving little room for anyone else. NFL team revenues from television rights increased more than 650-fold in just over five decades since the league's first pooled rights agreement in 1962, reaching more than $218 million per team per season.

In the time since the USFL's demise, no league in football, hockey, basketball or baseball has competed for players with the NFL, NBA, NHL or Major League Baseball. The USFL was the last of the barbarians at the gate, a gate which has now been fortified with additional teams, multi-million dollar salaries and billions of dollars of television money.

The USFL supplied memories to last a lifetime not only to those who participated in it as players, coaches and administrators but also to the ten million fans who walked through its turnstiles and many millions more who watched the games on television. Football fans did not have to wait six months after the Super Bowl for training camps to open. With the USFL in the spring, they were able to jump right into a fresh new season, full of its own stars and storylines. The league offered an opportunity for cities such as Memphis, Birmingham and Jacksonville to compete on the same stage as New York, Los Angeles and Chicago and gave fans in midsize markets the chance to enjoy professional sports at a major league level.

The USFL provided countless opportunities for players, coaches and staff alike to show they could contribute to professional football teams. It gave players the ability to control where and for whom they played, and forced the NFL to increase salaries and benefits. USFL alumni flooded into the older league and proved their worth, not only as men who could compete for roster spots but for some as those who would dominate the game and end up immortalized in Pro Football's Hall of Fame. After three seasons in the sun, they made a lasting impact on the professional football world. The USFL was the final major league competitor America has seen. Its story also serves as one of the most unique and star-crossed chapters in professional football history.

Bibliography

Books

Balzer, Howard, ed. *The Sporting News Official USFL Guide and Register*. St. Louis: The Sporting News, 1985.

Clikeman, Paul M. *Called to Account: Financial Frauds that Shaped the Accounting Profession*. London: Taylor & Francis, 2009.

Evey, Stuart. *Creating an Empire*. Chicago: Triumph, 2004.

Flutie, Doug. *Flutie*. Champaign, IL: Sports Publishing, 1999.

Libby, Bill. *The Coaches*. New Orleans: Garrett County Press, 1972.

MacCambridge, Michael. *America's Game*. New York: Random House, 2008.

Richards, David. *Once Upon at Time in Texas*. Austin: University of Texas Press, 2002.

Trump, Donald. *The Art of the Deal*. New York: Ballantine, 2004.

Trump, Donald. *Think Big: Make It Happen in Business and Life*. New York: HarperCollins, 2008.

White, Reggie. *In the Trenches*. Nashville: Thomas Nelson, 1997.

Woolf, Bob. *Friendly Persuasion*. New York: Berkley Trade, 1991.

Periodical Articles

Ballard, Sarah. "Portrait of a Hero in Limbo." *Sports Illustrated* (December 2, 1985): 53–61.

Balzer, Howard. "Pro Football Focus." *The Sporting News* (December 20, 1982): 22.

Balzer, Howard. "Pro Football Focus." *The Sporting News* (February 21, 1983): 26.

Balzer, Howard. "Pro Football Focus." *The Sporting News* (February 24, 1983): 36.

Balzer, Howard. "Pro Football Focus." *The Sporting News* (February 28, 1983): 48.

Balzer, Howard. "Pro Football Focus." *The Sporting News* (June 27, 1983): 40.

Balzer, Howard. "Pro Football Focus." *The Sporting News* (October 17, 1983): 34.

Balzer, Howard. "Pro Football Focus." *The Sporting News* (December 19, 1983): 28.

Balzer, Howard. "Pro Football Focus." *The Sporting News* (January 16, 1984): 23.

Balzer, Howard. "Pro Football Focus." *The Sporting News* (February 20, 1984): 33.

Balzer, Howard. "Pro Football Focus." *The Sporting News* (March 12, 1984): 32.

Balzer, Howard. "Pro Football Focus." *The Sporting News* (April 2, 1984): 59.

Balzer, Howard. "Pro Football Focus." *The Sporting News* (April 30, 1984): 46.

Balzer, Howard. "Pro Football Focus." *The Sporting News* (June 11, 1984): 48.

Balzer, Howard. "Pro Football Focus." *The Sporting News* (July 16, 1984): 16.

Balzer, Howard. "Pro Football Focus." *The Sporting News* (September 3, 1984): 27.

Balzer, Howard. "Pro Football Focus." *The Sporting News* (September 10, 1984): 51.

Balzer, Howard. "Pro Football Focus." *The Sporting News* (November 26, 1984): 30.

Balzer, Howard. "Pro Football Focus." *The Sporting News* (February 25, 1985): 30.

Balzer, Howard. "Pro Football Focus." *The Sporting News* (March 4, 1985): 49.

Balzer, Howard. "Pro Football Focus." *The Sporting News* (April 8, 1985): 48

Balzer, Howard. "Pro Football Focus." *The Sporting News* (May 6, 1985): 45.

Balzer, Howard. "Pro Football Focus." *The Sporting News* (July 1, 1985): 47.

Balzer, Howard. "Pro Football Focus." *The Sporting News* (July 15, 1985): 51.

Balzer, Howard. "Stars Stay Cool, Claim 2nd USFL Crown." *The Sporting News* (July 22, 1985): 49.

Balzer, Howard. "Pro Football Focus." *The Sporting News* (December 23, 1985): 12.

Bowen, Ezra. "Sacked!" *Time* (August 11, 1986): 12–13.

Bryan, Jimmy. "Big Plays Move Stars into USFL Final." *The Sporting News* (July 15, 1985): 53.

Chester, Gary. "Last Line of Defense." *The Sporting News* (August 11, 1986): 4–5.

Craig, Jack. "Is Lagging TV Deal a Sign of USFL's Intentions?" *The Sporting News* (June 9, 1986): 6.

Dooley, Pat. "Jacksonville Stock Far from Bullish." *The Sporting News* (April 29, 1985): 42.

Domowitch, Paul. "Dupree Finds a Job Way Down Yonder." *The Sporting News* (March 12, 1984): 27.

Domowitch, Paul. "5–9 Mills Standing Tall." *The Sporting News* (April 11, 1983): 33.

Domowitch, Paul. "Fusina Was in Elite Company in USFL." *Philadelphia Daily News* (July 18, 2014).

Domowitch, Paul. "Mazzetti Positive about USFL." *The Sporting News* (May 2, 1983): 57.

Domowitch, Paul. "The USFL-NFL War That May Never End!" *Lou Sahadi's Pro Football*, Vol. 7 (Summer 1983): 42–46.

Felser, Larry. "'Battle of Philadelphia' Might be Close." *The Sporting News* (July 30, 1984): 30.

Felser, Larry. "'Smoking Guns' Could Shoot Down USFL." *The Sporting News* (June 23, 1985): 45.

Felser, Larry. "$3 Court Case Produced Both Winners, Losers." *The Sporting News* (August 18, 1986): 41.

Fiffer, Steve. "Puttin' on the Blitz—Without Cash." *Inside Sports* (July 1984): 70–75.

Fleming, Mike. "Hebert-to-Carter Pays Off for Invaders." *The Sporting News* (July 15, 1985): 53.

Flower, Joe. "The Worst Job in Sports." *Sport* (June 1985): 93–96.

Gosselin, Rick. "The Legacy of the USFL." *Street and Smith's Pro Football* (1993), 20–24.

Henderson, Joe. "Tampa Bay Bandits: A Hollywood Touch." *Lou Sahadi's Pro Football*, Vol. 7 (Summer, 1983): 29–31

Johnson, William Oscar. "Can The USFL Cut The Mustard?" *Sports Illustrated* (January 16, 1984): 76–81.

Johnson, William Oscar. "Football: A Rite or Wrong of Spring?" *Sports Illustrated* (May 23, 1983): 39–46.

Johnson, William Oscar. "For Spring Football, The Future Is No Go." *Sports Illustrated* (July 23, 1984): 24.

Johnson, William Oscar. "It Was Up, Up And No Way." *Sports Illustrated* (May 14, 1984): 78–81.

Johnson, William Oscar. "Whole New League, Whole New Season." *Sports Illustrated* (May 24, 1982).

Lieber, Jill. "Just a Pause? Or Is It Sayonara?" *Sports Illustrated* (August 18, 1986), 34.

Lieber, Jill. "Rebels with a Good Cause." *Sports Illustrated* (June 3, 1985): 55–60.

Lieber, Jill. "So Long, USFL-Now What?" *Sports Illustrated* (August 18, 1986), 30–35.

Looney, Douglas S. "He Has Seen The Light." *Sports Illustrated* (April 18, 1983): 48–54.

Looney, Douglas S. "The Odd Man Out Is In." *Sports Illustrated* (March 7, 1983): 47–50.

Madden, Michael. "Tales of Two Coaches." *Boston Globe* (June 4, 1983).

McDonough, Will. "Caught In A Draft." *Sport* (April 1983): 47–51.

Miller, J. David. "USFL Preview: Before the Fall." *Sport* (March 1985): 55–57.

McCallum, Jack. "The Man with the Golden Arm." *Sports Illustrated* (March 12, 1984): 29–31.

Morwin, John. "Who's Getting Clipped?" *Forbes* (November 5, 1984): 38–39.

Neff, Craig. "The Award Was Only Token." *Sports Illustrated* (August 11, 1986), 18–19.

"Notebook." *The Sporting News* (March 24, 1986): 26.

Panaccio, Tim. "Gagliano Escapes Obscurity with Gold." *The Sporting News* (May 6, 1985): 43

Panaccio, Tim. "Gamblers-Gold Feud Ends in Rainstorm." *The Sporting News* (June 24, 1985): 49.

Schlein, Alan M. "United States Football League." *Oui* (March 1983): 87–90.

Spander, Art. "Football Is Not the Spring Game." *The Sporting News* (February 21, 1983): 11.

Stanton, Barry. "A 'Dream Team' Keeps the Dream Alive." *Football Digest 1986 Yearbook* (1986): 58–61.

Stanton, Barry. "Ties That Are Binding." *The Sporting News* (March 10, 1986): 24.

Sullivan, Robert. "Scorecard." *Sports Illustrated* (May 26, 1986), 13.

Sullivan, Robert. "The USFL Chooses a Bigger Road Over a Smaller Car." *Sports Illustrated* (September 3, 1984): 9.

Taaffe, William. "The Networks' Cupboards Were Bare." *Sports Illustrated* (February 25, 1985): 28.

Tyers, Tim. "L.A. Express Rookies Are Learning Together." *The Sporting News* (June 4, 1984): 46.

"USFL Roundup." *The Sporting News* (July 9, 1984): 56.

Wiley, Ralph. "Invaders of the Raiders' Space." *Sports Illustrated* (March 21, 1983).

Wiley, Ralph. "A Pocketful of Dreams." *Sports Illustrated* (February 25, 1985): 25–30.

Wiley, Ralph. "This One Was a Game And a Half." *Sports Illustrated* (July 9, 1984): 22–24.

Wiley, Ralph. "When It Got Dark, the Stars Came Out." *Sports Illustrated* (July 18, 1983): 24–27.

Wiley, Ralph. "The Wranglers Were Star Struck." *Sports Illustrated* (July 23, 1984): 22–27.

Zimmerman, Paul. "The Choice Is Leftovers." *Sports Illustrated* (April 30, 1984): 32–36.

Zimmerman, Paul. "A New Round of Star Wars?" *Sports Illustrated* (March 7, 1983)

Zimmerman, Paul. "A Heavenly Night for the Stars." *Sports Illustrated* (July 22, 1985): 22–27.

Newspaper Articles

"ABC's 'Live Aid' Seen by 40 Million." *New York Times*, July 17, 1985.

Attner, Paul. "USFL Deja Vu: Is Allen Up to Old Tricks?" *Washington Post*, August 13, 1982.

Berry, Walter. "Allen: Wranglers' Victory over Express No Fluke." *Schenectady Gazette*, July 9, 1984, 30.

Cafardo, Nick. "Generals Ready to Relax After Long Season." *Lewiston Daily Sun*, July 5, 1983, 17.

"Court Denies Appeal, Signaling Death of USFL." *Schenectady Gazette*, March 11, 1988, 25.

Denise, Tom. "USFL Needs Great Spring for Growth." *USA Today*, January 22, 1985.

Fernandez, Bernard. "Davis: Someone Will Replace USFL in Spring." *The Day*, October 25, 1984, 31.

Finney, Peter Jr. "Super Stars Give USFL Credibility Boost." *The Times-Picayune*, July 10, 1984.

Flanagan, Mike. "Elimination Leaves Bandits Looking Forward to London—And Maybe a Fast Gorilla." *The Evening Independent*, July 3, 1984, 4C.

"Flutie: 'On Vacation'" *Lewiston Daily Sun*, August 5, 1986, 15.

"For the Panthers, It Was the Best of Years." *Observer-Reporter*, July 19, 1983, B-9.

Forbes, Gordon. "Chargers' Klein No Laughing Matter to USFL." *USA Today*.

Forbes, Gordon. "Tampa Bay Wins 27–22, Stays Unbeaten." *USA Today*, March 28, 1983, 3C.

Forbes, Gordon. "Trump Looks at Foreman for the Job." *USA Today*.

Forbes, Gordon. "USFL Wins a Point But Loses the Fight." *USA Today*, July 30, 1986, 3C.

Fox, Larry. "USFL Taking to Air with ABC Pact." *New York Daily News*, May 27, 1982.

"George Allen, Coach, Dead at 72; Led Redskins to Super Bowl VII." *New York Times*, January 1, 1991.

Goldberg, Dave. "USFL Finally Gets Suit into Court." *The Times-News*, May 13, 1986, 15.

"Harry Usher Named as Commissioner of USFL." *The Daily Reporter*, January 14, 1985, 3B.

Janofsky, Michael. "Rozelle Acts to Study U.S.F.L. Effects." *New York Times*, March 23, 1984.

Janofsky, Michael. "U.S.F.L. Cautions Rival on Fall Shift." *New York Times*, September 14, 1984.

Janofsky, Michael. "U.S.F.L. Owners' Merger Strategy in '84 Revealed." *New York Times*, June 8, 1986.

Keidan, Bruce. "Attacks Against Stoudt Leave City with Black Eye." *Pittsburgh Post-Gazette*, March 12, 1984, 11.

King, Larry L. "Where Winners Take All." *San Bernardino County Sun*, September 9, 1984, 101.

Margolick, David. "Can A Tarnished Star Regain His Luster?" *New York Times*, February 25, 1990.

Mihoces, Gary. "USFL Wins in Principle, Not Principal." *USA Today*, July 30, 1986.

"Most USFL Teams Will Oppose Fall Games, Tampa Owner Says." *Eugene Register-Guard*, April 26, 1985, 5C.

"NFL Salaries Up 25%, Average $162,000." *Los Angeles Times*, January 14, 1985.

"Pioneer Claims USFL Has Become Monster." *Bangor Daily News*, July 15, 1985, 25.

"Pro Football's Longest Day." *Eugene Register-Guard*, July 1, 1984, 7B.

"Rising Salaries Major Concern for Both Leagues." *The Milwaukee Journal*, January 21, 1984, 9.

Schmitz, Brian. "Facing Big Financial Losses, USFL Scraps 1986 Season." *Orlando Sentinel*, August 5, 1986.

Seltzer, Robert. "USFL's Owners Decide to Scrap the 1986 Season." *Inquirer*, August 5, 1986.

"Spurrier to Lead USFL Bandits." *Boca Raton News*, November 23, 1982, 2B.

"USFL Adds to Visibility with Cable-TV Deal." *New York Daily News*, June 18, 1982.

"USFL Commissioner Unsure About When to Move to the Fall." *Sarasota Herald-Tribune*, February 26, 1985, 4C.

"USFL Union Official Says If There Is No Agreement, There Will Be No Games." *Los Angeles Times*, February 11, 1985.

Vecsey, George. "USFL: Born to Litigate." *The Times-News*, May 13, 1986, 15.

"Walker's Tentative Running Has Surprised Fairbanks." *Herald-Journal*, March 31, 1983, D1

"Washington Is Not a City for Losers." *USA Today*, February 7, 1984.

Weisman, Larry. "Trump Dealing All the Aces." *USA Today*, February 22, 1985.

West, Bob. "Dennison's Catch Gives Arizona 17–16 USFL Playoff Win." *USA Today*, July 2, 1984.

"What They Said about the Verdict." *USA Today*, July 30, 1986, 3C.

"You Can't Trust All You Hear in a Taxi." *USA Today*, July 31, 1986.

Interviews

Argovitz, Jerry. Video interview for *Small Potatoes: Who Killed the USFL?*

Asmus, Jim. Personal interview, June 25, 2009.

Blanding, Ron. Personal interview, July 21, 2009.

Camera, Dom. Personal interview, June 2, 2009; Video interview for *Small Potatoes: Who Killed the USFL?*

Coury, Dick. Personal interviews, May 19, 1998 and October 19, 2009.

Davis, Mouse. Personal interview, July 28, 2009.

Diethrich, Dr. Ted. Personal interview, February 3, 2009.

Dixon, David. Personal interviews, March 5, 1998 and June 3, 2009; Video interview for *Small Potatoes: Who Killed the USFL?*

Dufresne, Chris. Personal interview, March 8, 2016; Video interview for *Small Potatoes: Who Killed the USFL?*

Dunek, Ken. Personal interview, March 11, 2016.

Ehrhart, Steve. Personal interviews.

Foster, Jim. Personal interview, August 18, 2009.

Fusina, Chuck. Personal interview, February 17, 2016.

Gould, James. Personal interview, November 19, 2009; Video interview for *Small Potatoes: Who Killed the USFL?*

Hebert, Bobby. Personal interview, February 26, 2016; Video interview for *Small Potatoes: Who Killed the USFL?*

Holloway, Derek. Personal interview, February 19, 2016.

Infante, Lindy. Personal interview, June 10, 2009.

James, Craig. Video interview for *Small Potatoes: Who Killed the USFL?*

Jauch, Ray. Personal interview, June 9, 2009.

Jones, Joey. Personal interview, May 5, 2009.

Jones, June. Personal interview, February 29, 2016.

Keller, Mike. Personal interview, February 25, 2016.

Kelly, Jim. Personal interview, February 25, 2016; Video interview for *Small Potatoes: Who Killed the USFL?*

Kojich, Don. Personal interview, June 23, 2009.

Landeta, Sean. Video interview for *Small Potatoes: Who Killed the USFL?*

Levy, Marv. Personal interview, February 4, 2010.

MacConnell, Kevin. Personal interview, July 1, 2009; Video interview for *Small Potatoes: Who Killed the USFL?*

Marcum, Tim. Personal interview, June 9, 2009.

Mazzetti, Tim. Personal interview, June 19, 2009.

McGrath, Tim. Personal interview, February 22, 2016.

McSherry, Bill. Personal interview, October 6, 2009.

McVay, Jim. Personal interview, February 1, 2010; Video interview for *Small Potatoes: Who Killed the USFL?*

Mora, Jim. Personal interview, July 29, 2009.

Newton, Nate. Video interview for *Small Potatoes: Who Killed the USFL?*

Nordgren, Fred. Personal interview, March 11, 2016.

Norman, Bull. Personal interview, June 29, 2009.

Peterson, Carl. Personal interviews, May 18, 1998 and August 15, 2009; Video interview for *Small Potatoes: Who Killed the USFL?*

Ralston, John. Personal interview, May 27, 2009.

Reynolds, Burt. Video interview for *Small Potatoes: Who Killed the USFL?*

Riley, David. Personal interview, March 10, 2016.

Risher, Alan. Personal interview, June 24, 2009.

Rodgers, Pepper. Personal interview, June 10, 2009.

Rozier, Mike. Personal interview, June 11, 2009.

Simmons, Chet. Personal interview, July 27, 2009; Video interview for *Small Potatoes: Who Killed the USFL?*

Singleton, Greg. Personal interview, May 5, 2009.

Spence, Jim. Personal interview, February 3, 2010.

Spurrier, Steve. Personal interview, May 5, 2009.

Steinberg, Lee. Personal interview, March 24, 2016.

Steiner, Charley. Video interview for *Small Potatoes: Who Killed the USFL?*

Sydney, Harry. Personal interview, June 25, 2009.

Tanenbaum, Myles. Personal interview, May 28, 2009.

Tatham, Bill. Personal interview, July 8, 2010.

Taube, Tad. Personal interviews, April 5, 1998 and May 6, 2009.

Taubman, Alfred. Personal interview, July 22, 2009.

Trager, Mike. Personal interview, May 11, 2009.

Truvillion, Eric. Video interview for *Small Potatoes: Who Killed the USFL?*

Websites

Baxter, Brian. "The Sports Litigation Archives: USFL v. NFL." The AM Law Daily. http://amlawdaily.typepad.com/amlawdaily/2009/11/a-trip-down-sports-litigation-memory-lane.html (accessed April 21, 2016).

Tinsman, Brian. "Missing Tapes: Bruce Allen on '30 For 30.'" Redskins.com. http://www.redskins.com/news-and-events/article-1/Missing-Tapes-Bruce-Allen-on-30-For-30/e75c7420-8d7c-4631-be94-ddf7bd868ae7 (accessed March 24, 2016).

Legal Actions

North American Soccer v. National Football League, 670 F.2d 1249 (1982).

U.S. Football League v. National Football League, 644 F.Supp. 1040 (1986).

U.S. Football League v. National Football League, 842 F.2d 1335 (1988).

Index

Page numbers in **bold italics** indicate pages with illustrations.